Children's Media Market Place

Fourth Edition

Barbara Stein
Consulting Editor

Lucia Hansen
Assistant Editor

Neal-Schuman Publishers, Inc.
New York   London

Published by Neal-Schuman Publishers, Inc.
100 Varick Street
New York, New York 10013

International Standard Book Number 1-55570-190-6
International Standard Serial Number 0734-8169

Printed and bound in the United States of America

CONTENTS

PREFACE

Children's Media Market Place (CMMP) is a directory of sources for locating multimedia materials and services designed for children; for people who work with children, including teachers, parents, librarians, and media specialists; and for creators, distributors, and others whose work is geared to children. Although the primary focus of the entries in CMMP are pre-K through middle school, information appropriate to upper levels is also included.

CMMP is designed to be a ready reference for names, addresses and phone numbers of those organizations, companies and others who provide services of interest to those who work with children or children's materials. Inclusion of an entry does not constitute a recommendation or judgment of value but does indicate a significant connection to children related interests.

Children's Media Market Place, fourth edition, has been revised and reorganized. The directory is divided into two parts: Directory of Children's Media Sources and Names & Numbers Index to Children's Media Sources. The directory is arranged in 21 areas of interest.

Publishers (1) includes hundreds of the most active houses, large and small, in the children's field. Special attention has been given to imprints, one of the more confusing results of an industry characterized by mergers and acquisitions.

Software Producers & Distributors (2) has been updated in part from the data maintained by evaluation and review organizations. At the end of the section, an index classifies companies by subject areas for additional access.

Audiovisual Producers & Distributors (3) covers active companies selling to the library and education fields. An index to areas of special interest — as reported by the producers themselves — completes this section.

The next sections include major Wholesalers (4) of children's books, Children's Booksellers (5), established Antiquarian Booksellers (6), the largest Children's Book Clubs (7), and Agents for Children's Properties (8).

Periodicals are divided into three sections: Periodicals for Children (9), Periodicals for Professionals & Parents (10); and Review Journals, Services & Indexes (11).

Two new areas of interest follow: K-12 Computer Networking Resource List (12) reflects the growing technological shift toward communication via the Internet. Cultural Diversity Resources (13) lists organizations representing different cultures and providing children's and youth programs, information services and resources, bibliographies, and general assistance to teachers and students.

Final sections include Museums (14), which highlights noteworthy permanent exhibits, Associations (15) that are concerned with children's media and services, State Library & Media Associations (16), State School Media Offices (17), a list of Federal Grants For Children's Programs (18), both national & state Literary Awards (19), a Calendar of Events & Conferences (20), and a Bibliography of Selection Tools (21).

Each source in the directory contains the address, telephone number, and names of personnel who may be contacted for information. An introduction at the beginning of each section provides further information concerning the methods of selection and sources of additional information.

At the end of CMMP the user will find the Names and Numbers Index which contains the name, address, and telephone number for each organization listed in the directory. Each name is followed by the code number that corresponds to the section(s) of the book in which the name appears.

We have made our best efforts to include material submitted; we take no legal responsibility for accidental omissions or errors in listings. Wherever information is not given, it may be assumed that information was not supplied and that our editorial research staff was unable to complete it. Because information supplied in catalogs and brochures is not uniform, data in annotations may vary. Readers are urged to contact companies for updated information on materials, staff, titles, hours, etc.

Many people generously gave their time, skill, and resources to prepare this manuscript. Karl Suhr and Sid Viswakumar provided data entry with the assistance of Nadja Gardner, Kerry Tehan, LeAnne Coffey, and Paula King. A special thanks goes to Raymond von Dran for his support of this project and to Elizabeth Findley who provided proofreading. It was John Vincent Neal's determination that made this a reality. The editor is indebted to his considerable personal contribution.

Barbara Stein *Consulting Editor*

Contributing editors:

Chapter 1	Publishers: Karl Suhr
Chapter 2	Software Producers: Sharon Johnson, Catherine Murphy, Charles Crisman
Chapter 5 & 6	Children's Booksellers & Antiquarian Booksellers: Marjorie Rosenthal
Chapter 12	K-12 Computer Networking Resource List: Sandy Sharps
Chapter 13	Cultural Diversity Resources: Barbara Blake
Chapter 14	Museums: Yvonne Chandler
Chapter 18	Federal Grants For Children's Programs: Chris Schafer
Chapter 19	Awards: Ginny Taylor
Chapter 20	Calendar of Events & Conferences: Jeanette Pfalzgraf
Chapter 21	Bibliography Of Selection Tools: Betty Morris, Isabel Feldman, Jane Allen

DIRECTORY OF CHILDREN'S MEDIA SOURCES

The following companies and associations publish materials for or about children. These materials include books, other print formats, and, in some cases, nonprint formats, which may either accompany the books or be purchased separately. Publishing companies with separate software or audiovisual divisions are listed in Sections 2 and 3, respectively.

Since the last edition of this directory, the children's book industry has continued to expand, but to consolidate as well. New and acquired imprints are cross-referenced to the parent company.

Each company was asked to list subjects and any special interests. The vast range of subjects submitted, as well as the wide variation in terminology, limited and finally rendered useless attempts to provide classified indexes to the program specifics of these companies. Instead, users are urged to consult the new section on *Cultural Diversity Resources (13)* and publications listed in the last section, *Bibliography of Selection Tools (21)*, for help in identifying publishers of special interest materials.

AIMS INTERNATIONAL BOOKS, INC.
7709 Hamilton Ave., Cincinnati, OH 45231
513-521-5590, 800-733-2067;
  Fax: 513-521-5592
Mktg Dir: Elizabeth Koffel

Publications: Trade books
Audience: K-12, adult
Subjects: Foreign languages
Special Interest: Imported books in Spanish
Discount: 25% on orders of over $100
Services: Catalog. Exhibit at ALA, ABA

ABBEVILLE PRESS
488 Madison Ave., New York, NY 10022
212-888-1969, 800-227-7210;
  Fax: 212-644-5085
Pres: Robert E. Abrams
Ed-in-Chief: Alan Axelrod
Children's Ed & Lib/Sch Prom Dir: Jane Lahr
Mktg Dir: Steven Pinkus

Publications: Library editions, paperback originals & reprints
Audience: Preschool-8
Subjects: Foreign countries & languages, art, hobbies, biographies, picture books, crafts, fine art illustrated books & photography, dance
Discount: Inquire
Services: Catalog. Exhibit at ALA, ABA

ABINGDON PRESS
Div. of the United Methodist Publishing House
Box 801, Nashville, TN 37202-0801
615-749-6290, 800-251-3320;
  Fax: 615-749-6512

Pres: Robert K. Fenster
Ed Dir: Neil M. Alexander
Children's Ed: Patricia Augustine
Product Mgr: Patty Erwin

Publications: Trade books, library editions, paperback originals & reprints, church school literature, teacher's materials. Cassettes, filmstrips, videotapes, multimedia kits
Imprints: Cokesbury
Audience: Preschool-12, adult Subjects: Family Life, animals, fiction, biographies, picture books, crafts, religion, drama, reference, Bible study
Special interest: Handicapped, African-Americans, Hispanics, Asian Americans
Discount: 25%
Services: Catalog, author brochures, posters. Exhibit at ALA, AASL, ABA, CBA, Tennessee Library Association conferences

HARRY N. ABRAMS
Div. of Times Mirror Co.
100 Fifth Ave., New York, NY 10011
212-206-7715, 800-345-1359
Pres & Ed-in-Chief: Paul Gottlieb
Dir of Sales & Mktg: Don Guerra

Publications: Trade books, paperback originals & reprints
Audience: Preschool-12, adult
Subjects: Crafts, environment & energy, hobbies, sports, animals, dance, family life, art, music, biographies, drama, foreign countries, picture books, health, sciences
Discount: Inquire
Services: Catalog, brochures. Exhibit at ALA & ABA

ACADEMIC THERAPY PUBLICATIONS
20 Commercial Blvd., Novato, CA 94949-6191
415-883-3314, 800-422-7249 (orders outside CA); Fax: 415-883-3720
Pres: Anne M. Arena
VP: James A. Arena
Mktg Dir & Lib/Sch Prom Dir: Arleta Quesada

Publications: Textbooks, workbooks, paperback originals, programmed learning systems, tests, professional books for teachers, school administrators, school psychologists, optometrists, remedial therapists. Audiorecords/cassettes
Imprints: High Noon Books
Audience: Preschool-12, adult
Subjects: Auditory & visual, vocational training, learning disabilities, special education
Special interest: Reading disabled, motor impaired, sensory-motor dysfunctional
Discount: Assorted titles, 20%; 26 or more, 40%
Services: Catalog

ACADEMY CHICAGO PUBLISHERS
363 W. Erie St., Chicago, IL 60610-3125
312-751-7300, 800-248-7323 (orders outside IL only); Fax: 312-751-7306
Pres & Ed: Anita Miller
Mktg Dir: Paul Bennett

Publications: Trade books, paperback originals & reprints
Audience: 9-12 (limited), adult
Subjects: Art, biographies, fiction, memoirs, history
Special interest: Nonsexist education
Discount: Stores, 40-45%

Services: Exhibit at NCTE, ABA, MLA, MMLA

ACCENT PUBLICATIONS
12100 W. Sixth Ave., Denver, CO
  80215
303-988-5300; Fax: 303-989-7737
Ed-in-Chief & Children's Ed: Mary
  Nelson
Mktg Dir & Lib/Sch Prom Dir: Don
  Wagner

Publications: Church resources, professional books for teachers, librarians
  & school administrators in Christian
  education, Sunday school curriculum
Audience: Preschool-12, adult
Subjects: Church resources, Christian
  education, curriculum for churches
Special interest: Christian education
  resources
Discount: Inquire
Services: Catalog

Ace Science Fiction & Fantasy, see
BERKELEY PUBLISHING GROUP

**ADDISON-WESLEY PUBLISHING
  COMPANY, INC.**
Children's Book Department
One Jacob Way, Reading, MA
  01867-3999
617-944-3700, 800-447-2226; Fax:
  617-944-9338
Cust Serv: Pat Casey

Audience: K-8
Subjects: Sciences, math, hobbies, lan-
  guage, arts
Discount: 20-46%
Services: Exhibit at ALA, ABA, Boston
  Globe Book Festival

Aerial, see **FARRAR, STRAUS &
  GIROUX**

Aerie Books, see **TOR BOOKS**

AFRICA WORLD PRESS
Box 1892, Trenton, NJ 08607
609-771-2666; Fax: 609-771-1616
Pres: Kassahun Checole

Publications: Trade books
Audience: Juvenile, adult
Subjects: Afrocentric children's books

**AFRICAN AMERICAN IMAGES/
  AFRO-AM**
1909 W. 95th St., Chicago, IL 60643
312-445-0322; Fax: 312-445-9844
Pres: Jawanza Kunjufu
Mktg Dir: Adrian Williams

Publications: Workbooks, trade books,
  library editions, paperback originals,
  multimedia kits, posters, prints. Audi-
  orecords/cassettes, filmstrips, video-
  tapes/cassettes

Audience: Preschool-12
Subjects: Picture books, biographies,
  socials studies, fiction, sports, for-
  eign languages, music
Special interest: Black Americans, mul-
  ticultural understanding
Discount: Libraries, RIF chapters, 15%
Services: Catalog

Afro-Bets, see **JUST US BOOKS**

AKIBA PRESS
Box 13086, Oakland, CA 94661
Pres: Murray Narell
Ed-in-Chief: Sheila Baker

Publications: Paperback originals
Audience: 8-12
Subjects: Biographies, history

ALFRED PUBLISHING COMPANY
16380 Roscoe Blvd., Ste. 200, Box
  10003, Van Nuys, CA 91410-0003
818-891-5999, 800-292-6122; Fax:
  818-891-2182
Pres: Morty Manus
Sr Ed: John O'Reilly
Mktg Dir: Andrew Surmani

Publications: Textbooks, workbooks,
  professional books for teachers.
  Audiorecords/cassettes, computer
  software, videotapes/cassettes
Audience: Preschool-12, adult
Special interest: Performance music
  for all instruments
Discount: Wholesale dealers, 40%
Services: Catalog. Flyers. Exhibit at
  music educators' national conventions & music trade shows

Aladdin Paperbacks, see **SIMON &
  SCHUSTER**

ALYSON PUBLICATIONS
40 Plympton St., Boston, MA 02118
617-542-5679
Ed-in-Chief: Sasha Alyson
Assoc Pub: Karen Barber

Publications: Trade paperbacks
Imprints: Alyson Wonderland
  (children's)
Audience: 5-10 young adult, adult
Subjects: Gay & Lesbian fiction & non-
  fiction

AMERICAN BIBLE SOCIETY
1865 Broadway, New York, NY
  10023-9980
212-408-1200, 800-543-8000; Fax:
  212-408-1512
Bd Chmn: James Wood
Pres & CEO: Dr. Eugene Habecker
National Program Area: Maria Martinez

Publications: Paperback originals &
  reprints. Audiorecords/cassettes,
  filmstrips, videotapes/cassettes

Audience: Children, youth, adult
Subjects: Bibles and scripture
  resources in many languages
Special interest: Hearing & visually impaired, heritage groups, special education
Services: Catalog

**AMERICAN FOUNDATION FOR THE
  BLIND**
AFB Press
15 W. 16th St., New York, NY 10011
212-620-2000, 800-232-5463; Fax:
  212-620-2105
Ex Dir/Pres: Carl R. Augusto
Dir Pub: Mary Ellen Mulholland
Sales/Marketing Manager: Karen
  McVeigh
Managing Ed/Books: Natalie Hilzen

Publications: Textbooks, training manuals, resource guides, videos, assessment tools, research and practice
  reports, public education brochures
  & pamphlets
Audience: Preschool-12, adult
Subjects: Early childhood, mobility,
  literacy, independent living, rehabilitation, employment, aging, education, career development
Special interest: Blindness & visual impairment
Discount: Libraries & library distributors; bookstores & bookstore distributors; public schools & state
  agencies
Services: Catalog

**AMERICAN LIBRARY ASSOCIATION/
  ALA EDITIONS**
50 E. Huron St., Chicago, IL
  60611-2790
312-944-6780, 800-545-2433; Fax:
  312-944-8741
Dir: Don Chatham
Assoc Pub: Art Plotnik
Mktg Dir: Evelyn Shaevel

Publications: Directories, bibliogra-
  phies, manuals, periodicals.
  Videocassettes, CD databases
Imprints: Booklist Publications
Audience: Librarians & teachers
Subjects: Professional materials for
  librarians & teachers, bibliographies,
  library media skills, children's litera-
  ture, educational media
Special interest: Native Americans,
  Spanish-speaking, nonsexist educa-
  tion, mentally disabled
Discount: Up to 25%
Services: Catalog, Exhibit at ALA

**AMERICAN LIBRARY PUBLISHING CO.,
  INC.**
Box 4272, Sedona, AZ
  86340-4272

602-282-4922
Pres: Marietta Chicorel

Publications: Professional books for teachers, librarians & school administrators
Audience: 9-12, adult
Subjects: Biographies, environment & energy, film, mental health, theater, video
Special Interest: Learning disabilities, reading disabilities, bilingual education
Discount: Inquire
Services: Catalog

Amphoto, see **WATSON-GUPTILL PUBLICATIONS**

AMSCO SCHOOL PUBLICATIONS
315 Hudson St., New York, NY 10013
212-675-7000; Fax: 212-675-7010
Pres: Albert Beller
Mktg Dir & Lib/Sch Prom Dir: Jack Willig

Publications: Textbooks, workbooks, paperback originals & reprints. Videocassettes
Audience: 6-12
Subjects: Foreign languages, social studies, auditory & visual, language arts, business, mathematics, environment & energy, poetry, fiction, sciences
Discount: Schools, inquire
Services: Catalog. Exhibit at NCTE

ANCHORAGE PRESS, INC.
Box 8067, New Orleans, LA 70182
504-283-8868; Fax: 504-866-0502
Pres & Ed-in-Chief: Orlin Corey
Mktg Dir: Ann Loggins

Publications: Textbooks, professional books for teachers, plays for children & youth
Subjects: Drama, language arts
Services: Catalog. Exhibit at theater conferences, speech communication & private school assns, gifted conferences

ANDREWS & McMEEL
A Univeral Press Syndicate Co.
4900 Main St., Kansas City, MO 64112
816-932-6700, 800-286-4216; Fax: 816-932-6706

Publications: Trade books, paperback originals
Audience: K-12, adult
Subjects: Cartoons, children's humor, family life, fiction, hobbies, nonfiction consumer reference & gift books
Services: Catalog

ANNICK PRESS
15 Patricia Ave., Willowdale, ON M2M 1H9, Canada
416-221-4802; Fax: 416-221-8400
Orders: Firefly Books Ltd, 250 Sparks Ave., Willowdale, ON M2H 2S4, Canada
Eds: Anne Millyard, Rick Wilks
Publicity Dir: Maral Bablanian

Publications: Trade children's books in English & French
Subjects: Picture books

APPLE ISLAND BOOKS
(formerly Orchard Press)
Box 276, Shapleigh, ME 04076
207-324-9453
Pres & Ed-in-Chief: Bruce McMillan
Mktg Dir: Benner McGee

Publications: Children's trade books
Audience: Preschool-6
Subjects: Picture books
Discount: Inquire

ARCADE PUBLISHING INC.
141 Fifth Ave., New York, NY 10010
212-475-2633; Fax: 212-353-8148
Orders: Little, Brown & Co., 200 West St., Waltham, MA 02254, 800-759-0190
Pres: Richard Seaver
Mktg Dir: Allison Davis

Publications: Trade fiction & nonfiction
Audience: Children, adult

Archway Paperbacks, see **POCKET BOOKS**

ARO PUBLISHING CO.
Box 193, Provo, UT 84603
801-377-8218, 800-338-7317
Pres: Robert Reese

Publications: School books, high interest/low vocabulary
Audience: K-4
Subjects: Poetry, animals, safety, fiction, sports, health, picture books
Special interest: Native Americans, bilingual students, reading disabled
Discount: Inquire
Services: Catalog. Exhibit at ALA, IRA

ARTE PUBLICO PRESS
University of Houston
4800 Calhoun #429 AH, Houston, TX 77004
713-749-4768, 800-633-ARTE; Fax: 713-743-2847
Pres & Children's Ed: Nicolas Kanellos
Ed-in-Chief: Julian Olivares
Mktg Dir: Marina Tristan
Lib/Sch Prom Dir: Cynthia Juarez

Publications: Trade books, paperback originals & reprints

Audience: Preschool-12, adult
Subjects: Art, fiction, poetry
Special interest: Bilingual students, American Hispanic authors
Services: Catalog. Exhibit at ALA, ABA

Artists & Writers Guild Books, see **WESTERN PUBLISHING CO., INC.**

A.R.T.S.
32 Market St., New York, NY 10002
212-962-8231

Special interest: Multicultural literature

ASIA RESOURCE CENTER
Box 15375, Washington, DC 20003
202-547-1114
Dir: Roger Rumpf

Publications: Textbooks, library editions, paperback originals, professional books for teachers
Audience: K-4, 10-12, adult
Subjects: Asia
Special interest: Bilingual students, nonsexist education

ASSOCIATED PUBLISHERS' GROUP
1501 County Hospital Rd., Nashville, TN 37218
615-254-2450; Fax: 615-254-2456
Sales Dir: Donetta Duncan
Mktg Dir: Sandra Hall

Publications: Trade books
Audience: Preschool-12
Subjects: Picture books, early readers, Ideals children's books, inspirational, gift books
Discount: Inquire
Services: Distributor for Ideals Children's Books; Ideals Publications, Inc.; Pockets Press; Impressions INK; WorldCom Press; East West Publications

ASSOCIATION FOR CHILDHOOD EDUCATION INTERNATIONAL
11501 Georgia Ave., Ste. 35, Wheaton, MD 20902
301-942-2443
Pres: Carol Vukelich
Ed: Anne Watson Bauer

Publications: Library editions, paperback reprints, professional books for teachers & librarians
Audience: Preschool-8, adult
Subjects: Picture books, business, sex education, dance, family life, home economics, animals, poetry, career development, social studies, dictionaries, fiction, language arts, art, religion, computer software, sports, drama, foreign countries & languages, mathematics, auditory & visual, safety, consumer education, vocational training, encyclopedias,

health, music, biographies, sciences, crafts, environment & energy, hobbies, physical education
Special interest: Spanish-speaking, nonsexist education, mainstreaming
Discount: Schools & libraries, 10-24 copies, 10%; 25-99, 20%; 100-500, 25%
Services: Promotional newsletter. Exhibit at ACEI Exchange

Atheneum, *see* **SIMON & SCHUSTER**

AUGSBURG FORTRESS PUBLISHERS
Publishing House of the Evangelical Lutheran Church in America
426 S. Fifth St., Box 1209, Minneapolis, MN 55440-1209
612-330-3300, 800-328-4648; Fax: 612-330-3455
CEO: Gary Aamodt
VP, Cust Res & Rel: Rev. Marvin Roloff
Dir Mkgt/Product Dev: Luther Dale
Dir/Sales: Bill Korte

Publications: Textbooks, trade books, paperback originals & reprints, professional books for teachers, picture books. Audiovisual & audiotape cassettes & compact discs.
Audience: Preschool-12, adults
Subject: Religion
Services: Catalog

AUGUST HOUSE PUBLISHERS INC.
Box 3223, Little Rock, AR 72203
501-372-5450, 800-284-8784; Fax: 501-372-5579
Pres: Ted Parkhurst
Publicity: Anne Holcomb

Publications: Trade paperbacks
Audience: Children, adult
Subject: American folklore and storytelling; fiction
Services: Distributor for National Storytelling Press

AVON BOOKS
Div of the Hearst Corporation
1350 Ave. of the Americas, New York, NY 10019
212-261-6800, 800-238-0658; Fax: 212-261-6895
Dir Educ/Mktg: Dorothy Millhofer

Publications: Trade books, library editions, paperback originals & reprints, computer books
Imprints: Avon Paperbacks, Camelot, Flare
Audience: 3-12, adult
Subjects: Fiction, animals, hobbies, biographies, sex education, computer software, family life
Discount: Schools, quantity orders, RIF, inquire Dir of Special Mkts
Services: Catalog, brochures, tip sheets. Exhibit at ALA, IRA, NCTE, ABA, MLA, NACS

THE B & R SAMIZDAT EXPRESS
Box 161, West Roxbury, MA 02132
617-469-2269
Pub: Richard Seltzer
VP: Barbara Hartly Seltzer
Eds: Robert R. Seltzer, Heather K. Seltzer, Michael R. Seltzer, Timothy Seltzer

Publications: Trade books, paperback originals, books on computer disk
Audience: 3-12, adult
Subjects: Fiction
Discount: 10-99 copies, 40%; 100 or more, 50%
Services: Catalog

BACKYARD SCIENTIST
Box 16966, Irvine, CA 92713
714-552-5351; Fax: 714-552-5351
Pres: Jane Hoffman
Mktg PR: Arnold Hoffman

Publications: Paperback originals
Audience: Preschool-8
Subjects: Hands-on science experiments in chemistry, physics, biology
Special Interest: Inservice instruction for teachers
Discount: Inquire
Services: Catalog. Promo video available. Exhibit at ALA, ABA, Educational Dealers Suppliers Assn

BAHA'I PUBLISHING TRUST
Subs of the National Spiritual Assembly of the Bahai'is of the United States
415 Linden Ave. Wilmette, IL 60091
708-251-1854, 800-999-9019; Fax: 708-251-3652
Mgr: Larry Bucknell
Children's Ed: Betty J. Fisher
Mktg Dir: Patrick Falso

Publications: Textbooks, workbooks, trade books, library editions, paperback originals & reprints, professional books for teachers. Audiorecords/cassettes
Imprints: Bellwood Press
Audience: K-12, adult
Subjects: Biographies, fiction, picture books, religion
Special interest: Nonsexist education, blind, reading disabled
Discount: Schools & libraries, 30%
Services: Exhibit at ALA, CBE

BAKER BOOK HOUSE
Box 6287, Grand Rapids, MI 49516-6287
616-676-9185, 800-877-2665; Fax: 616-676-9573
Pres: Richard L. Baker
Children's Ed: Betty De Vries
Mktg Dir & Lib/Sch Prom Dir: John Topliff

Publications: Trade books, paperback

originals, professional books for teachers, programmed learning systems
Audience: Preschool-12, adult
Discount: Schools, libraries, 20%; trade, 40%
Services: Catalog. Exhibit at CBA, ABA

BALA BOOKS
12520 Kirkham Ct, #7, Poway, CA 92064
619-679-9080
Dir: Philip Gallelli

Publications: Trade books, library editions, paperback original
Audience: K-7, adult
Subjects: Health, language arts, religion, East Indian philosophy & stories, folktales, fairy tales
Discount: Inquire
Services: Catalog. Exhibit occasionally

BALL-STICK-BIRD PUBLICATIONS, INC.
Box 592, Stony Brook, NY 11790
516-331-9164
Ed-in-Chief: Renee Fuller

Publications: Textbooks, library editions, professional books for teachers, programmed learning systems
Audience: Preschool-12
Subjects: Fiction, language arts, poetry, children's reading series
Special interest: Bilingual students, reading disabled, mentally disabled
Services: Catalog

BALLANTINE PUBLISHING GROUP
Div. of Random House, Inc.
201 E. 50 St., New York, NY 10022
212-751-2600, 800-726-0600; Fax: 212-572-870
Pres: Linda Grey
Ed-in-Chief: Clare Ferraro (Ballantine)
Children's Ed: Leona Nevler
Lib/Sch Prom Dir: Tamu Aljuwani

Publications: Trade books, paperback originals & reprints, computer books. Posters
Imprints: Ballantine, Del Rey, Fawcett, Ivy
Audience: 6-12, adult
Subjects: Fiction, sports, biographies, health, science fiction, fantasy, paranormal/occult, movie/TV tie-ins, humor, business, home economics, career development, religion, dictionaries, social studies
Discount: Orders over $50, 25%
Services: Catalog, promotional newsletter. Teacher's guides. Exhibit at ALA, IRA, NCTE, NACS, California Reading

BANTAM DOUBLEDAY DELL BOOKS FOR YOUNG READERS
Div of Bantam Doubleday Dell Publishing Group
1540 Broadway, New York, NY 10036

212-354-6500, 800-223-6834; Fax:
212-302-7985
Contact: Theresa M. Borzumato,
Beverly Horowitz, Andrew Smith,
Craig Virden, Lisa Alpert, Marjorie
Jones

Publications: Trade books, paperbacks
Imprints: Rooster, Skylark, Young Skylark, Starfire, Delacorte, Doubleday,
Laurel Leaf, Picture Yearling,
Yearling, Young Yearling
Audience: K-12, adult
Subjects: Picture books, business, sex
education, dance, family life, home
economics, animals, poetry, career
development, social studies, dictionaries, fiction, language arts, art,
religion, computer software, sports,
drama, foreign countries & languages, mathematics, auditory &
visual, safety, consumer education,
vocational training, encyclopedias,
health, music, biographies, sciences,
crafts, environment & energy, hobbies, physical education
Discount: Schools & libraries, hardcover trade editions only, 20%
Services: Catalog. Promotional newsletter. Exhibit at ALA, IRA, NCTE,
NCSS

BARRON'S EDUCATIONAL SERIES
250 Wireless Blvd., Hauppauge, NY
11788
516-434-3311, 800-645-3476; Fax:
516-434-3723
Pres: Manuel Barron
Mang Ed: Grace Freedson
Mktg Mgr: Maria Kissanis
Lib/Sch Prom Dir: Andrew Dunning

Publications: Textbooks, workbooks,
trade books, library editions, computer books. Audiorecords/cassettes,
computer software
Audience: Preschool-12, adult
Subjects: Computer software, encyclopedias, language arts, sex education, animals, consumer education,
foreign languages, mathematics, social studies, art, crafts, health, picture books, sports, business, dance,
hobbies, safety, career development,
dictionaries, home economics,
sciences, fiction & nonfiction for
children & YA, parenting, gardening,
pet care
Special interest: Spanish-speaking,
bilingual students, test preparation
materials
Discount: Libraries, 10%; schools,
20%. Orders under $25 require
prepayment
Services: Catalog. Exhibit at ABA

WILLIAM L. BAUHAN, PUBLISHER
Box 443, Old County Rd., Dublin, NH
03444
603-563-8020
Pub & Mktg Dir: William L. Bauhan

Publications: Trade books, paperback
originals & reprints
Subjects: New England
Discount: Schools & libraries, 10%
Services: Exhibit at ALA, NCTE

BEARS for BOOKS
Box 1158, Carpinteria, CA 93014
805-569-2398; Fax: 805-969-4278
Contact: Neil Bryson, Penny Paine

Publications: Workbooks
Audience: Children
Subjects: Webster & Winona's Wonderful World of Words, storytelling activities

PETER BEDRICK BOOKS, INC.
2112 Broadway, Ste. 318, New York,
NY 10023
212-496-0751, 800-788-3123; Fax:
212-496-1158
Orders: Publisher's Group West, 4005
Hollis St., Emeryville, CA 94608
510-658-3453, 800-788-3123
Pres, Ed-in-Chief & Children's Ed: Peter
Bedrick
Lib/Sch Prom Dir: Muriel Bedrick

Publications: Trade books, library edi-
tions, paperback reprints
Imprints: Bedrick/Blackie
Audience: Preschool-12, adult
Subjects: Encyclopedias, animals,
health, art, picture books, biogra-
phies, sciences, dictionaries,
mythology
Discount: Inquire
Services: Catalog, Exhibit at ALA, IRA,
NCTE, ABA

Beech Tree Books, see **MORROW
JUNIOR BOOKS**

BEHRMAN HOUSE, INC.
235 Wachtung Ave., West Orange, NJ
07052
201-669-0447, 800-221-2755; Fax:
201-669-9769
Pres & Ed-in-Chief: Jacob Behrman
Children's Ed: Ruby G. Straus
Mktg Dir: Adam Bengal

Publications:Textbooks, workbooks,
trade books. Audiorecords/cassettes,
filmstrips
Audience: K-12, adult
Subjects: Religion
Special interest: Jewish education
Services: Catalog

**ALEXANDER GRAHAM BELL
ASSOCIATION FOR THE DEAF, INC.**
3417 Volta Place NW, Washington, DC
20007
202-337-5220; TTY same
Dir Pubns: Lucy Cuzon Du Rest
Mktg Dir: Elizabeth Quigley

Publications: K-12 storybooks & tapes,

textbooks, workbooks, paperback
originals & reprints, professional
books for teachers & school administrators, flashcards, captioned
(open or closed) videotapes
Audience: K-12, adult
Subjects: Hearing-impairment, language arts, lipreading, special education
Special interest: Deaf, emotionally disturbed, mentally retarded
Services: Catalog

Bell Books, see **BOYDS MILLS PRESS**

BELLEROPHON BOOKS
36 Anacapa St, Santa Barbara, CA
93101
805-965-7034, 800-253-9943; Fax:
805-965-8286
Pres: Ellen Knill
Ed-in-Chief: Lawrence Knill

Publications: Art/History activity books,
trade books
Audience: K-12, adult
Subjects: Picture books, animals, histo-
ry, art, dance, music
Services: Catalog

Bellwood Press, see **BAH'I
PUBLISHING TRUST**

ROBERT BENTLEY, INC.
1000 Massachusetts Ave., Cambridge,
MA 02138
617-547-4170, 800-423-4595; Fax:
617-876-9235
Pres: Michael Bentley
Mktg Dir: David Bou

Publications: Textbooks, library editions, professional books for
teachers & school administrators
Audience: 9-12, adult
Subjects: Fiction, automobile maintenance, children's education, Montessori Method
Discount: Textbooks, 20%

BERKELEY PUBLISHING GROUP
Div. of The Putnam Berkeley Group,
Inc.
200 Madison Ave., New York, NY
10016
212-951-8800, 800-223-0510
Pres: David Shanks

Publications: Fiction, nonfiction, mass
market paperbacks
Imprints: Ace Science Fiction & Fanta-
sy, Berkeley Books
Audience: Young adult, adult
Subjects: General interest, science fic-
tion, fantasy
Discount: Inquire

BESS PRESS
Box 37095, Honolulu, HI 96837
808-845-8949; Fax: 808-847-6637

Pres, Mktg Dir & Lib/Sch Prom Dir:
    Benjamin E. Bess
Ed-in-Chief & Children's Ed: Reve
    Shapard

Publications: Textbooks, workbooks,
    trade books, library editions, paper-
    back originals
Audience: Pre-K to adult
Subjects: Asian & Pacific languages,
    social studies, Hawaii, the Pacific,
    Asia
Discount: None
Services: Catalog. Exhibit at ALA

BETHANY HOUSE PUBLISHERS
11300 Hampshire Ave. S.,
    Minneapolis, MN 55438
612-829-2500, 800-328-6109; Fax:
    612-829-2768
Pres: Gary L. Johnson
Ed-in-Chief: Carol A. Johnson
Youth Ed: Barb Lilland
Lib/Sch Prom Dir: Steve Oates

Publications: Textbooks, workbooks,
    trade books, library editions, paper-
    back originals & reprints
Audience: K-12, adult
Subjects: Family life, fiction, religion,
    sex education
Special interest: Christian materials
Discount: Inquire
Services: Catalog. Exhibit at ABA, CBA,
    ALA

Betterway Books, see **WRITER'S
DIGEST BOOKS**

BILINGUAL EDUCATIONAL SERVICES
2514 S. Grand Ave., Los Angeles, CA
    90007
213-749-6213, 800-448-6032; Fax:
    213-749-1820
Publications: Library editions,
    textbooks
Audience: K-12, adults
Subjects: ESL materials, books in
    Spanish
Services: Catalog. Exhibit at ALA,
    NABE, CABE

Black Butterfly Children's Books, see
**WRITERS & READERS PUBLISHING
INC.**

BLACKBIRCH PRESS INC.
One Bradley Rd., Ste. 205, Wood-
    bridge, CT 06525
203-387-7525, 800-831-9183; Fax:
    203-389-1596
Pres: Richard S. Glassman
Mktg Dir: Teresa Rogers

Audience: Children, young adult
Subjects: Nonfiction, biography, biolo-
    gy, geography, sports, women

BOB JONES UNIVERSITY PRESS
1700 Wade Hampton Blvd., Greenville,
    SC 29614-0060
803-242-5100, 800-845-5731
Ed-in-Chief: George R. Collins
Children's Ed: Jim Davis
Mktg Dir: John L. Cross

Publications: Textbooks, workbooks,
    trade books, paperback originals &
    reprints, computer books, profes-
    sional books for teachers & school
    administrators. Audiorecords/
    cassettes, filmstrips, computer soft-
    ware, transparencies, video-
    tapes/cassettes
Audience: Preschool-12, adult
Subjects: Dictionaries, mathematics,
    social studies, art, drama, music,
    biographies, family life, poetry, com-
    puter software, fiction, religion, con-
    sumer education, language arts,
    sciences
Discount: Inquire
Services: Catalog. Promotional news-
    letter. Exhibit at Christian school
    conventions, AACS, ACSI

Booklist Publications, see **AMERICAN
LIBRARY ASSOCIATION**

R.R. BOWKER COMPANY
(a division of Reed Reference
    Publishing)
121 Chanlon Rd., New Providence, NJ
    07974
908-464-6800, 800-521-8110
Pres: Ira Siegel
Children's Ed: Yvonne Rose

Publications: Professional books for
    teachers, librarians & school ad-
    ministrators. Videodisc, CD-ROM
Audience: Adult
Subjects: Computer software, music,
    art, consumer education sciences,
    auditory & visual, encyclopedias,
    library science, bibliographies, cata-
    logs, directories, handbooks, biogra-
    phies, fiction, business, health
Special interest: Reading disabled,
    mentally disabled, handicapped
Discount: First year, 10%; following
    years, 5%
Services: Catalog. Promotional news-
    letter. Exhibit at ALA, ABA, SLA,
    Canadian Library Assn, ASIS, Michi-
    gan Library Assn, Online, NY Library
    Assn, CLA, MFL

BOY SCOUTS OF AMERICA
Supply Division
1325 W. Walnut Lane, Irving, TX
    75015-2079

Publications: Library editions, paper-
    back originals. Filmstrips, video-
    tapes/cassettes

Audience: 1-12, adult
Subjects: Computer software, family
    life, religion, animals, consumer edu-
    cation, health, sciences, art, crafts,
    hobbies, social studies, business,
    drama, music, sports, career de-
    velopment, environment & energy,
    physical education, scouting, camp-
    ing directories, family camping
Special interest: Reading disabled, Na-
    tive Americans, mentally disabled,
    Spanish-speaking, Cambodian &
    Vietnamese-speaking, blind, deaf
Services: Catalog

BOYDS MILLS PRESS
Subs. of Highlights for Children Inc.
910 Church St., Honesdale, PA 18431
717-253-1164; Fax: 717-253-0179
Pres: Clay Winters

Publications: Trade books
Imprints: Bell Books, Caroline House,
    Wordsong
Audience: K-12

BRAILLE INSTITUTE PRESS
741 N. Vermont Ave., Los Angeles, CA
    90029
213-663-1111
Children's Ed: Douglas Menville

Publications: Anthology of children's
    literature in braille
Audience: 7-12
Subjects: Picture books, poetry
Special interest: Blind

BridgeWater Books, see **TROLL
ASSOCIATES**

BROADMAN & HOLMAN PUBLISHERS
Div. of Southern Baptist Convention,
    Sunday School Board
127 Ninth Ave. N., Nashville, TN
    37234
615-251-2553, 800-251-3225 Fax:
    615-251-3870
Pres: James Draper, Jr.
Children's Ed: Janis Whipple

Publications: Textbooks, workbooks,
    trade books, library editions, paper-
    back originals and reprints, com-
    puter books, professional books for
    teachers, librarians & school ad-
    ministrators. Audiorecords/cassettes,
    films, filmstrips, computer software,
    transparencies, videotapes/cassettes,
    multimedia kits
Subjects: Safety, career development,
    encyclopedias, health, music,
    animals, sciences, consumer educa-
    tion, environment & energy, hobbies,
    physical education, art, sex educa-
    tion, crafts, family life, home eco-
    nomics, picture books, auditory &
    visual, social studies, dictionaries,
    fiction, language arts, poetry, biogra-

phies, sports, drama, foreign countries & languages, mathematics, religion
Discount: Inquire
Services: Catalog. Promotional newsletter

Browndeer Press, see **HARCOURT BRACE & COMPANY**

BRUNNER/MAZEL INC.
19 Union Sq. W., New York, NY 10003-3382
212-924-3344, 800-825-3089; Fax: 212-242-6339
Pres: Mark Tracten
Children's Ed: Susan Cakars
Mktg Dir: Matt Laddin

Publications: Textbooks, professional books for teachers, psychologists, psychiatrists, & other medical personnel. Audiocassettes, videocassettes
Imprints: Magination Press
Audience: 3-teen, adult
Subjects: Family life, child development & education, hypnotherapy, child psychology & psychiatry, health, medicine, special education
Special interest: Children's drawings, child abuse, family therapy, child illness, hyperactivity, coping
Discount: Inquire
Services: Catalog

Bullseye Books, see **RANDOM HOUSE**

CAMBRIDGE BOOK COMPANY
Sylvan Rd., Rte. 9W, Englewood Cliffs, NJ 07632
201-592-2000, 800-221-4764
Pres: Bill Moore
Mktg Dir: Karen Jczynski

Publications: Textbooks, workbooks, paperback originals, professional books for teachers & school administrators, programmed learning systems. Computer software (GED only), videotapes/cassettes (ESL & preGED)
Audience: Adult
Subjects: Health, auditory & visual, language arts, consumer education, mathematics, family life, sciences, fiction, social studies
Special interest: Spanish-speaking, bilingual students, High School Equivalency (GED), ESL materials for any national origin
Discount:Schools, 1-199 copies, 40%; 200 or more, 41-50%
Services: Catalog. Free workshops. Free sampling of books & videos. Exhibit at ALA, IRA, AECT, NCTE, AAACE

Camelot, see **AVON BOOKS**

CANDLEWICK PRESS
2067 Massachussets Ave., Cambridge, MA 02140
617-661-3330; Fax: 617-661-0565
Contact: Rick Richter, Susan Halperin

Publications: Trade books
Audience: Children, young adult
Subjects: Fiction and nonfiction

CAPSTONE PRESS INC.
2440 Fernbrook Lane, Minneapolis, MN 55447
612-551-0513; Fax: 612-551-0511
Contact: John Coughlan, John Martin, Robert Coughlan

Publications: Trade books
Audience: Upper elementary & junior high
Subjects: Easy-reading, high-interest nonfiction books
Discount: Inquire
Services: Exhibit at ALA

Caroline House, see **BOYD MILLS PRESS**

CAROLRHODA BOOKS
241 First Ave. N., Minneapolis, MN 55401
612-332-3345
Orders: Lucent Books, Box 289011, San Diego, CA 92198-9011; 619-485-7424, 800-231-5163; Fax: 619-485-9549
Ed: Emily Kelly
Lib/Sch Prom Dir: Jeff E. Reynolds

Publications: Trade books, library editions
Audience: Preschool-6
Subjects: Animals, fiction, picture books
Services: Catalog. Exhibit at ALA, IRA, CBC, ABA

CAY-BEL PUBLISHING CO.
272 Center St., Bangor, ME 04401
207-941-2367
Pres, Children's Ed & Pub: Viki G. Baudean
Ed-in-Chief & Lib/Sch Prom Dir: John E. Cayford
Mktg Dir: D. D. Baudean

Publications: Textbooks, trade books, library editions, paperback originals & reprints
Audience: 4-12, adult
Subjects: Biographies, sea stories, regional history & genealogy
Special interest: Native Americans, bilingual students, French-speaking
Discount: 20%: schools, quantity
Services: Catalog. Promotional newsletter

CHARILL PUBLISHERS
4468 San Francisco Ave., Box 150124, St. Louis, MO 10012
212-491-3869
President: Fred Hill

Publications: Trade books
Audience: Primary
Subjects: Poetry, phonics, fiction
Special interest: Multicultural literature

CHARIOT FAMILY PUBLISHING
Div. of David C. Cook Publishing Co.
20 Lincoln Ave., Elgin, IL 60120
708-741-9558, 800-323-7543; Fax: 708-741-2444
Children's Ed: Catherine Davis
Mktg Dir: Randy Scott

Publications: Trade books, paperback orignals
Audience: Preschool-12, adult
Subjects: Picture books, religion, family life, fiction, activity books
Services: Catalog. Exhibit at CBA

CHARLESBRIDGE PUBLISHING
85 Main St., Watertown, MA 02172
617-926-0329, 800-225-3214; Fax: 617-926-5720
Pres: Brent Farmer
School Publishing: Donald W. Robb
Trade Publishing: Mary Ann Sabia
Editorial: Elena Dworkin Wright

Publications: Textbooks, workbooks, children's picture books, materials in Spanish
Audience: K-8
Subjects: Fiction, nonfiction, language arts, mathematics, thinking skills, learning strategies, team learning curricula
Discount: Inquire
Services: Catalog. Exhibit at ALA, IRA, NCTE, NCTM, ASCD

CHELSEA HOUSE
Div. of Main Line Book Co.
300 Park Ave., New York, NY 10016
212-677-4010; Fax: 212-683-4412
VP, Ed-in-Chief: Richard Rennert

Publications: Trade books, library editions
Imprints: Chelsea Juniors
Audience: K-12
Subjects: Nonfiction series
Discount: Inquire

CHILD WELFARE LEAGUE OF AMERICA
440 First St. NW, Ste. 310, Washington, DC 20001-2085
202-638-2952

Publications: Textbooks, paperback originals, professional books for teachers & school administrators, child welfare workers

Audience: Adult
Subjects: Infant & child welfare, education
Services: Exhibit at regional child welfare conferences

CHILD'S PLAY
310 W. 47 St., Ste. 3-D, New York, NY 10036
212-315-9623, 800-472-0099; Fax: 212-315-9613
Pub: Michael Twinn
VP: Joseph Gardner

Publications: Trade & Educational books, toys & games
Audience: Preschool-6

CHILDREN'S BOOK PRESS
6400 Hollis St., Ste. 4, Emeryville, CA 94608
510-655-3395; Fax: 510-655-1978
Pres & Pub: Harriet Rohmer
Mktg Coord: Susan McConnell

Publications: Trade books
Audience: Children
Subjects: Multicultural picture books

CHILDREN'S PRESS
Subs. of Grolier Inc.
5440 N. Cumberland Ave., Chicago, IL 60656-1494
312-693-0800, 800-821-1115; Fax: 312-693-0574
VP, Publ: Fran Dyra

Publications: Trade books, library editions. Audiorecords/cassettes, filmstrips, multimedia kits
Audience: Preschool-10
Subjects: Nonfiction series, career development, sports, animals, crafts, vocational training, art, dictionaries, auditory & visual, encyclopedias, biographies, environment & energy
Special interest: Reading disabled
Discount: 25%
Services: Catalog. Exhibit at ALA, IRA, NAEYC. Dist for: Child's World Books, ELK Grove Books, Golden Gate Junior Books

CHRISTIAN SCHOOLS INTERNATIONAL
Box 8709, 3350 E. Paris Ave. SE, Grand Rapids, MI 49518-8709
616-957-1070, 800-6358288; Fax: 616-957-5022
Ed-in-Chief: Gordon Bordewyk
Publications: Textbooks, workbooks, paperback originals, professional books for teachers & school administrators
Audience: Preschool-12, adult
Subjects: Language arts, sciences, art, mathematics, sex education, environment & energy, music, social studies, family life, physical education, sports, health, religion

Discount: W/membership, inquire
Services: Catalog. Promotional newsletter

THE CHRISTIAN SCIENCE PUBLISHING SOCIETY
One Norway St, Boston, MA 02115
617-450-2773, 800-288-7090; Fax: 617-450-2017
Pub Dir: Suzanna Penn

Publications: Trade books, paperback originals, pamphlets. Audiorecords/cassettes
Audience: Preschool-1, 4, 12
Subjects: Family life, music, picture books, religion
Services: Catalog. Promotional newsletter

CHRONICLE BOOKS
275 Fifth St., San Francisco, CA 94103
415-777-7240, 800-722-6657; Fax: 415-777-8887
Assoc Pub: Victoria Rock

Publications: Trade books
Audience: Preschool-6
Subjects: Picture books, board books, novelty & nonfiction, cookbooks
Special interest: Griffin & Sabine series, Phaidon art books (English)
Services: Catalog. Exhibit at ALA

CHRONICLE GUIDANCE PUBLICATIONS INC.
66 Aurora St., Box 1190, Moravia, NY 13118-1190
315-497-0330, 800-622-7284; Fax: 315-497-3359
Pres: Gary W. Fickeisen
Ed: Paul Downes
Mktg Dir & Lib/Sch Prom Dir: Raymond Spafford

Publications: Workbooks, professional books for teachers, programmed learning systems, career & guidance materials, charts, games, puzzles. Audiorecords/cassettes, computer software, multimedia kits
Audience: Preschool-12, adult
Subjects: Health, sports, art, home economics, vocational training, business, mathematics, career development, physical education, computer software, sciences
Special interest: Nonsexist education
Discount: Inquire
Services: Catalog. Counseletter. Exhibit at ALA, AACD, state ACD, AVA

CLARION BOOKS
Div. of Houghton Mifflin Co.
215 Park Ave. S., New York, NY 10003
212-420-5800, 800-225-3362; Fax: 212-420-5855

Publications: Trade books
Audience: Preschool-12
Subjects: Language arts, animals, picture books, biographies, poetry, family life, sciences, fiction, social studies
Discount: Inquire
Services: Catalog. Exhibit at ALA, IRA, ABA

CLASSIC WORKS
13502 Whittier, Ste. H276, Whittier, CA 90605
310-696-9331; Fax: 310-696-9331
Mtkg Man: Jan Sparks
Pub: Jenelle Macknight

Publicatons: Reinforced library editions, large print, books-on-tape, puppets, plush animals
Audience: K-6
Subjects: Folktales, storytelling kit
Discount: Inquire
Services: Brochure. Exhibit ALA, ABA

CLIFFS NOTES INC.
Box 80728, Lincoln, NE 68501-0728
402-477-6671, 800-228-4078; Fax: 402-423-9254
Pres: J. Richard Spellman
Ed: Michele Spence

Publications: Trade books, paperback originals, professional materials for teachers, software
Audience: 9-12, adult
Subjects: Teaching materials for literature (junior high & high school levels), study & review aids on literature & standardized tests
Discount: Inquire
Services: Exhibit at ABA, NACS, most major academic conventions

Cobblehill Books, *see* **DUTTON CHILDREN'S BOOKS**

Cokesbury, *see* **ABINGDON PRESS**

COLGIN PUBLISHING
7657 Farmington Rd., Manlius, NY 13104
315-682-6081
Also dist by Gryphon House Inc, 3706 Otis St, Mt. Rainier, MD 20712; Children's Small Press Collection, 719 N. Fourth, Ann Arbor, MI 48104
Pres, Ed-in-Chief & Children's Ed: Mary Louise N. Colgin
Mktg Dir & Lib/Sch Prom Dir: Barbara Gathman

Publications: Paperback originals, professional books for teachers & librarians
Audience: Preschool-6
Subjects: Language arts

Discount: 5 or more copies, 40%
Services: Mailers. Exhibit at ALA, ABA, school supply, NAEYC

COLLEGE ENTRANCE EXAMINATION BOARD
45 Columbus Ave., New York, NY 10023-6992
212-713-8000; Fax: 212-713-8143
Orders: College Board Publications, Box 886, New York, NY 10101
Pres: Donald Stewart
Mktg Mgr: Elly Weiss
Dir/Publications: Carolyn Trager

Publications: Workbooks, trade books, paperback originals, professional books for teachers & school administrators, programmed learning systems, software. Audiorecords/cassettes, films, filmstrips, computer software, transparencies, videotapes/cassettes, videodisc
Imprints: College Board
Audience: 7-12, adult
Subjects: Career development, language arts, vocational training, adult education, decision making, financial aid, guidance
Special interest: High school to college guidance
Discount: Inquire
Services: Catalog. Exhibit at AACROA, AACD, NACAC, ALA, ABA

COLONIAL WILLIAMSBURG
The Colonial Williamsburg Foundation
Box 1776, Williamsburg, VA 23187
804-220-7751; Fax: 804-220-7325
Dir/Pub: Marina Ashton

Publications: Trade books, paperback originals. Films, transparencies
Audience: K-12, adult
Subjects: Crafts, fiction, picture books, how-to, US colonial history
Discount: Inquire
Services: Catalog

COMMUNICATION & THERAPY SKILL BUILDERS, INC.
Box 42050, Tucson, AZ 85733
602-323-7500, 800-866-4446; Fax: 602-325-0306
Mang Ed: Patti Hartmann
Lib/Sch Prom Dir: Lanny Rosenbaum

Publications: Textbooks, workbooks, professional books for teachers. Filmstrips, videotapes/cassettes, multimedia kits, software
Audience: Preschool-12, adult
Subjects: Picture books, auditory & visual, dictionaries, language arts, mathematics
Special interest: Bilingual students, handicapped, speech disabled
Services: Catalog. Exhibit at IRA

COMPCARE PUBLICATIONS
Div. of Comprehensive Care Corp.
3850 Annapolis Lane, Ste. 100, Minneapolis, MN 55447-5443
612-559-4800, 800-328-3330; Fax: 612-559-2415
Pub: Michael Ballard
Ed-in-Chief: Margaret Marsh
Promotions: David Peterson

Publications: Trade books
Audience: K-12, adult
Subjects: Family life, health, alcoholism, drug abuse, eating disorders, child abuse, parenting, gift & humor
Services: Catalog. Exhibit at ALA, ABA

COMPREHENSIVE HEALTH EDUCATION FOUNDATION (CHEF)
22323 Pacific Hwy. S., Seattle, WA 98198
206-824-2907; Fax: 206-824-3072
Pres: Carl Nickerson
Book/Video Prom: Robynn Rockstad

Publications: Trade books, paperback originals & reprints, activity books. Videos, audiorecordings, transparencies, posters, teachers' materials, multimedia kits
Audience: K-12, adult
Subjects: Health, alcoholism, drug use, AIDS, sex education, self-esteem, media relations
Discount: Inquire

Computer Science, Inc. see W. H. FREEMAN AND CO.

CORINTHIAN PUBLICATIONS
Box 8279, Norfolk, VA 23503
804-587-2671
Ed: Paula Fitzgerald

Publications: Trade books
Audience: Preschool-12, adult
Subjects: Fiction, alphabet picture books
Services: Brochure

COUNCIL FOR INDIAN EDUCATION
Box 31215, Billings, MT 59107
406-252-7451
Pres & Pub: Dr. Hap Gilliland

Publications: Paperback originals
Audience: K-12, some adult
Subjects: Native American history & culture, fiction, picture books
Discount: Bookstores: 1-10, 30%; 11 & more, 40%
Services: Catalog

Coward-McCann, see THE PUTNAM BERKELEY GROUP, INC.

CRABTREE PUBLISHING CO.
350 Fifth Ave., Ste. 3308, New York, NY 10118

212-496-5040; 800-387-7650
Pres: Peter A Crabtree
Mktg Coord: Kathy Middleton

Publications: Trade hardcover and paperback
Audience: Children

CREATIVE EDUCATION INC.
Box 227, 123 S. Broad St., Mankato, MN 56001
507-388-6273, 800-445-6209; Fax: 507-388-2746
Pres: Tom Peterson

Publications: Trade books
Imprints: Creative Editions; Creative Education
Audience: Children

CREATIVE PRESS WORKS
Box 280556, Memphis, TN 38128
901-382-8246

Special interest: Multicultural literature

Crocodile Books, USA, see INTERLINK PUBLISHING GROUP INC.

CROSSWAY BOOKS
Div. of Good News Publishers
1300 Crescent St., Wheaton, IL 60187
708-682-4300, 800-323-3890; Fax: 708-682-4785
Pres: Lane T. Dennis
Ed-in-Chief: Leonard G. Goss
Children's Ed: Ted Griffin
Mktg Dir: Charles E. Phelps

Publications: Trade books, paperbacks originals
Audience: 4-12, adult
Subjects: Fiction, religion, social studies
Services: Catalog. Exhibit CBA

CROWN BOOKS FOR YOUNG READERS
Affiliate of Random House
201 E. 50th St., New York, NY 10022
212-572-2600; Fax: 212-572-8700

Publications: Trade books, library editions, paperback reprints. Audiorecords/cassettes
Audience: Preschool-12
Subjects: Family life, mathematics, social studies, animals, fiction, music, sports, biographies, foreign countries, picture books, drama, health, poetry, environment & energy, language arts, sciences
Discount: Inquire
Services: Catalog. Exhibit at ALA, IRA, ABA, NAEYC

DOK PUBLISHERS
Div. of United Educational Services Inc.

Box 1099, Buffalo, NY 14224
716-668-7691, 800-458-7900; Fax:
    716-668-7875
Pres: Richard O. Hopkins
VP, Mktg Dir & Lib/Sch Prom Dir: David
    L. Slosson

Publications: Workbooks, paperback
    originals, professional books for
    teachers & school administrators
Audience: Preschool-12, adult
Subjects: Science math, social studies,
    language arts/reading, whole lan-
    guage, study & thinking skills,
    creativity & gifts, parents/early learn-
    ing, assessment & professional de-
    velopment

DAWN PUBLICATIONS
14618 Tyler Foote Rd., Nevada City,
    CA 95959
916-292-3482, 800-545-7475; Fax:
    916-292-4258
Pres, Ed-in-Chief & Children's Ed: Bob
    Rinzler

Publications: Trade books, paperback
    originals. Audiorecords/cassettes
Audience: K-7, 10-12, adult
Subjects: Animals, environment &
    energy, family life, health & healing
Discount: Schools, libraries, 20%
Services: Catalog

DAYBREAK STAR PRESS
Box 99100, Seattle, WA 98199
206-285-4425
Pres: Sharon Patacsil

Publications: Trade books
Audience: Children
Special interest: Northwest coast
    Indians

Del Rey, see BALLANTINE PUBLISH-
    ING GROUP

Delacorte, see BANTAM DOUBLEDAY
    DELL BOOKS FOR YOUNG READERS

Dell Publishing Company, see
    **BANTAM DOUBLEDAY DELL BOOKS
    FOR YOUNG READERS**

DELMAR PUBLISHERS INC.
Subs. of International Thomson Pub-
    lishing Inc.
3 Columbia Circle, Albany, NY 12203
518-464-3500, 800-347-7707; Fax:
    518-464-0316
Pres: Joseph P. Reynolds
Mktg Mgr: Anne Lowenthal
Ed: Jay Whitmey
Mktg Dir: Joseph Keenan

Publications: Textbooks, professional
    books for teachers & school ad-
    ministrators
Audience: 10-12, adult
Subjects: Safety, health, vocational

training, language arts, mathematics,
    music, physical education, cur-
    riculum
Discount: Schools, 25%
Services: Catalog. Exhibit at AVA,
    NAEYC, ABA, Early Childhood Con-
    ventions

**DENOYER-GEPPERT SCIENCE
COMPANY**
5225 N. Ravenswood Ave., Chicago, IL
    60640
312-561-9200
Pres: Richard Gilbert

Publications: Chart skeletons, medical,
    anatomy teaching programs
Audience: K-12, adult
Subjects: Health, sciences
Special interest: Foreign languages,
    bilingual students, Black Americans,
    nonsexist education
Services: Catalog. Exhibit at NSTA

DHARMA PUBLISHING
2425 Hillside Ave., Berkeley, CA
    94704
510-548-5407, 800-873-4276; Fax:
    510-548-2230
Children's Ed: Elizabeth Cook
Mktg Dir: Rima Tamar

Publications: Library editions, paper-
    back originals & reprints
Audience: Preschool-12, adult
Subjects: Multicultural folktales (large
    format picture books), Tibetan epic
    tales
Discount: Inquire
Services: Catalog. Exhibit at NEA, Mon-
    tessori

**DIAL BOOKS FOR YOUNG
    READERS**
Div. of Penguin USA
375 Hudson St., New York, NY
    10014-3657
212-366-2000
Pres & Ed-in-Chief: Phyllis J. Fogelman
Children's Eds.: Janet Chenery, Paula
    Wiseman, Toby Sherry
Mktg Dir: Mimi Kayden
Lib/Sch Prom Dir: Donne Forrest

Publications: Trade books, library edi-
    tions, paperback reprints, board
    books, specialty books
Audience: Preschool-12, adult
Subjects: Drama, hobbies, religion,
    animals, environment & energy, lan-
    guage arts, sciences, art, family life,
    music, sex education, biographies,
    fiction, picture books, social studies,
    dance, foreign countries, poetry,
    sports
Discount: Inquire
Services: Catalog. Exhibit at ALA, IRA,
    NCTE, ABA, TLA

DISCOVERY ENTERPRISES
134 Middle St., Ste. 210, Lowell, MA
    01852-1815
508-459-1720, 800-729-1720; Fax:
    508-937-5779
Exec Dir: JoAnne Weisman

Publications: Nonfiction, curriculum
    materials
Audience: Juvenile, young adult
Services: Distributor for Childreach,
    Edutainment

DISNEY BOOK PUBLISHING INC.
Div. of The Walt Disney Co.
114 Fifth Ave., New York, NY 10011
212-633-4400; Fax: 212-633-4833
Orders: Little, Brown & Co., 200 West
    St., Waltham, MA 02254.
    800-759-0190
Dir: Thea Feldman
Mktg Dir: Lauren Wohl

Publications: Trade books, library
    editions
Audience: Preschool-8
Subjects: General fiction
Services: Catalog. Exhibit at ALA, ABA,
    IRA

DISPLAYS FOR SCHOOLS, INC.
1825 NW 22nd Ter., Gainesville, FL
    32605-3957
904-373-2030
Pres: Herbert C. DuPree
Lib/Sch Prom Dir: Sherry DuPree

Publications: Library editions, paper-
    back originals & reprints
Audience: Preschool-12, adult
Subjects: Religion, animals, foreign
    countries, picture books, poetry
Discount: Schools & libraries, 2-4,
    20%; 5-25, 40%; 26-49, 42%;
    50-99, 43%; 100 or more, 45%
Services: Catalog.

DON BOSCO MULTIMEDIA
Subs. of Salesian Society Inc.
475 North Ave., Box T, New Rochelle,
    NY 10802-0845
914-576-0122, 800-342-5850; Fax:
    914-654-0443
Pres: Rev. James J. Hurley
Edit Dir: Dr. James Morgan
Mktg Dir: John A. Thomas

Publications: Trade books, library edi-
    tions, paperback originals, profes-
    sional books for teachers. Films,
    slides, youth ministry, leadership
    books
Subjects: Biographies, family life,
    religion
Special interest: Spanish-speaking

DORLING KINDERSLEY INC.
232 Madison Ave., New York, NY
    10016

212-684-0404; Fax: 212-684-0111
Assoc Pub: Pamela Thomas
Prom Mgr: Beth Chang
Sr Ed: Alison Weir

Publications: Trade books, paper-backs
Audience: K-8
Subjects: Reference, fiction

DORRANCE PUBLISHING CO., INC.
643 Smithfield St., Pittsburgh, PA
   15222
412-288-4543, 800-788-7654 (orders
   only)
Pres: Elizabeth H. House
Mktg Dir & Lib/Sch Prom Dir: Cynthia
   Fliwa

Publications: Trade books, paperback
   originals, professional books for
   teachers
Audience: Preschool-12, adult
Subjects: Picture books, business, sex
   education, dance, family life, home
   economics, animals, poetry, career
   development, social studies, dictionaries, fiction, language arts, art,
   religion, computer software, sports,
   drama, foreign countries & languages, mathematics, auditory &
   visual, safety, consumer education,
   vocational training, encyclopedias,
   health, music, biographies, sciences,
   crafts, environment & energy, hobbies, physical education
Discount: Schools & libraries, 20%;
   trade, 5 or more copies, 40%
Services: Catalog

Doubleday, see **BANTAM DOUBLEDAY
DELL BOOKS FOR YOUNG READERS**

DOVER PUBLICATIONS
31 E. Second St., Mineola, NY 11501
516-294-7000, 800-223-3130; Fax:
   516-742-5049
Pres: Hayward Cirker
Exec VP: Clarence Strowbridge
VP Sales: Florence Leniston
Adv Mktg Dir: Paul Negri
Pub Mgr: Irene McCoy

Publications: Trade books, paperback
   originals & reprints
Audience: Preschool-12, adult
Subjects: Sports, consumer education,
   environment & energy, home economics, picture books, animals,
   coloring books, fairy tales, puzzles,
   folklore, crafts, fiction, language
   arts, poetry, art, dance, foreign
   countries & languages, mathematics,
   religion, biographies, dictionaries,
   health, music, sciences, business,
   drama, hobbies, physical education,
   social studies
Discount: 1 title, 25 copies, 10%
Services: Catalog. Exhibit at ABA,
   NACS, American Toy Fair

DOWN EAST BOOKS
Box 679, Camden, ME 04843
207-594-9544, 800-766-1670; Fax:
   207-594-7215
Gen Mgr: Thomas A. Fernald
Promotion: R. Timothy Moses

Publications: Trade books, calendars

DOWN THERE PRESS
938 Howard St., #101, San Francisco,
   CA 94103
415-974-8985; Fax: 415-974-8989
Pres, Ed-in-Chief & Lib/Sch Prom Dir:
   Joani Blank
Mgr Ed: Leigh Davidson

Publications: Workbooks, paperback
   originals
Audience: K-6
Subjects: Sex education

DRAMA BOOK PUBLISHERS
260 Fifth Ave., New York, NY 10001
212-725-5377; Fax: 212-725-8506
Pres: Ralph Pine
Sales Mgr: Judith Durant

Publications: Trade books. Audiocas-
   settes
Audience: 10-12, adult
Subjects: Drama
Services: Catalog. Exhibit at ABA,
   theater production conferences

DRAMATISTS PLAY SERVICE
440 Park Ave. S., New York, NY
   10016
212-683-8960
Pres: Stephen Sultan

Publications: Scripts
Audience: 5-12, adult
Subjects: Drama
Discount: Libraries, 10%
Services: Catalog. Promotional news-
   letter

DUFOUR EDITIONS
Chester Springs, PA 19425-0007
215-458-5005; Fax: 215-458-7103
Pres & Children's Ed: Kristin Dufour
Mktg Dir & Lib/Sch Prom Dir:
   Christopher May

Publications: Trade books, library
   editions, paperback originals &
   reprints
Audience: 6-12, adult
Subjects: Fiction, art, literature, literature in translation, social studies,
   biographies, music, history, dance,
   poetry, drama, religion
Discount: Libraries, 10%; 1-4 copies,
   20%; 5-14, 40%; 15-24, 41%;
   25-49, 42%; 50-99, 43%; 100 or
   more, 44%
Services: Catalog

DUTTON CHILDREN'S BOOKS
Div. of Penguin USA
375 Hudson St., New York, NY 10014
212-336-2000
Pres: Christopher Franceschelli

Publications: Trade books, paperbacks
Imprints: Cobblehill Books, Lodestar
   Books
Audience: K-12
Subjects: Drama, hobbies, religion,
   animals, environment & energy, lan-
   guage arts, sciences, art, family life,
   music, sex education, biographies,
   fiction, picture books, social studies,
   dance, foreign countries, poetry,
   sports
Discount: Inquire
Services: Catalog. Exhibit at ALA, IRA,
   NCTE, ABA, TLA

EAKIN PRESS
Div. of Sunbelt Media Inc.
Drawer 90159, Austin, TX
   78709-0159
512-288-1771; Fax: 512-288-1813
Pres, Mktg Dir & Lib/Sch Prom Dir: Ed-
   win M. Eakin
Ed-in-Chief: Melissa Roberts

Publications: Trade books, paperback
   originals
Audience: K-8, adult
Subjects: Biographies, history, Texana,
   cookbooks
Services: Catalog

EARLY EDUCATOR'S PRESS
70 Woodcrest Ave., Ithaca, NY 14850
607-272-6223
Dist. By Gryphon House Inc., Box 275,
   Mt. Rainier, MD 20712
Pres: Barbara Johnson Foote

Publications: Textbooks, professional
   books for teachers

ECONO-CLAD BOOKS
2101 N. Topeka Blvd., Topeka, KS
   66608
913-233-4252; Fax: 913-233-3129

Publications: Trade books, library technical services, CD-ROM
Audience: K-12
Subjects: Library collection development & curriculum resources

Edge Books, see **HENRY HOLT & CO.,
INC.**

EDUCATIONAL INSIGHTS
19560 S. Rancho Way, Dominguez
   Hills, CA 90220
310-637-2131, 800-933-3277; Fax:
   310-605-5048
Chair: Burton Cutler
Pres: Jay Cutler

Mktg Dir: Jim Whitney

Publications: Workbooks, programmed learning systems. Audiorecords/cassettes, multimedia kits
Audience: Preschool-12, adult
Subjects: Fiction, poetry, art, foreign countries, sciences, auditory & visual, language arts, crafts, mathematics, dance, music
Services: Catalog. Exhibit at NAVA, NSSEA

EDUCATIONAL SERVICES PRESS
99 Bank St., Ste. 2F, New York, NY 10014
212-924-7166
Pres: Dianne Weyers
Children's Ed: M. A. Hoyt

Publications: Textbooks, workbooks, trade books
Audience: K-8
Subjects: Sciences
Special interest: Nonsexist education, reading disabled
Discount: 25 copies or more, 10%
Services: Brochure

EDUCATORS PROGRESS SERVICE
214 Center St., Randolph, WI 53956
414-326-3126; Fax: 414-326-3127
Pres: Kathy Nehmer

Publications: Professional books for teachers, librarians & school administrators
Audience: Adult
Subjects: Home economics, vocational training, career development, physical education, computer software, sciences, consumer education, social studies, health, sports, elementary & secondary education
Special interest: Guides to free materials

EDUCATORS PUBLISHING SERVICE
75 Moulton St., Cambridge, MA 02138-1104
617-547-6706, 800-225-5750; Fax: 617-547-0412
Pres: Robert Hall
Ed Dir: John Hall

Publications: Workbooks, supplementary materials
Audience: K-12, adult
Subjects: Language arts
Special interest: Learning disabilities
Services: Catalog. Exhibit at IRA, NCTE, CEC, NAIS, CHADD, ALD

WILLIAM B. EERDMANS PUBLISHING CO.
255 Jefferson Ave. SE, Grand Rapids, MI 49503
616-459-4591, 800-253-7521; Fax: 616-459-6540

Pres: William Eerdmans
Children's Ed: Amy Eerdmans

Publications: Trade picture books
Audience: Juvenile
Subjects: Religion

EMC CORP
300 York Ave., St. Paul, MN 55101-4082
612-771-1555, 800-328-1452; Fax: 612-771-5629
Pres: Paul Winter
VP: Wolfgang Kraft
Children's Ed: Eileen Slater
Mktg Dir: Robert F. O'Reilly
Lib/Sch Prom Dir: Betty Waha

Publications: Textbooks, workbooks. Audiorecords/cassettes, filmstrips, computer software, transparencies, videotapes/cassettes, multimedia kits
Audience: 7-12, adult
Subjects: Home economics, social studies, career development, language arts, vocational training, consumer education, mathematics, fiction, music, foreign countries & languages, poetry
Services: Catalog

ENCYCLOPAEDIA BRITANNICA INC.
310 S. Michigan Ave., Chicago, IL 60604
312-347-7400, 800-554-9862; Fax: 312-294-2136
Pres: Joe Elliott
Mktg Dir: Leah Beaver
Lib/Sch Prom Dir: Michael Johnson

Publications: Children's library books. Audiorecords/cassettes, films, filmstrips, computer software, transparencies, videotapes/cassettes, multimedia kits.
Audience: Preschool-12, adult
Subjects: Picture books, business, sex education, dance, family life, home economics, animals, poetry, career development, social studies, dictionaries, fiction, language arts, art, religion, computer software, sports, drama, foreign countries & languages, mathematics, auditory & visual, safety, consumer education, vocational training, encyclopedias, health, music, biographies, sciences, crafts, environment & energy, hobbies, physical education
Special interest: Black Americans, French-speaking, Spanish-speaking, bilingual students, deaf, reading disabled
Discount: Inquire
Services: Catalog. Exhibit at ALA, IRA, NCTE, AECT

ENSLOW PUBLISHES, INC.
Bloy St. & Ramsey Ave., Box 777,

Hillside, NJ 07205
908-964-4116; Fax: 908-687-3829
Pres: Mark Enslow
VP & Ed: Brian Enslow

Publications: Trade books, paperback originals, professional books for librarians
Audience: 2-12
Subjects: Children's & young adult nonfiction, biographies, mathematics, business, sciences, career development, social studies, crafts, sports
Services: Catalog. Exhibit at ALA

EPM PUBLICATIONS INC.
1003 Turkey Run Rd., McLean, VA 22101
703-356-5111, 800-289-2339; Fax: 703-442-0599
Pres & Ed-in-Chief: Evelyn P. Metzger
Mktg Dir: Jon Metzger

Publications: Trade books, paperback originals. Videotapes/cassettes
Audience: K-9, adult
Subjects: Picture books, career development, quilting, needlework, crafts, health, home economics
Special interest: Native Americans
Discount: Inquire
Services: Catalog

M. EVANS AND COMPANY, INC.
216 E. 49th St., New York, NY 10017-1502
212-688-2810; Fax: 212-4486-4544
Orders: National Book Network, 4720 Boston Way, Lanham, MD 20706
Pres & Children's Ed: George C. deKay

Audience: 6-12, adult
Subjects: Crafts, home economics, animals, family life, sciences, art, selected fiction, sports, biographies, foreign countries, business, health
Discount: Inquire
Services: Catalog. Exhibit at ABA

FABER & FABER, INC.
50 Cross St., Winchester, MA 01890
617-721-1427, 800-666-2111; Fax: 617-729-2783
Dist by Cornell Univ. Press Services, 750 Cascadilla St., Ithaca, NY 14850
Pres: T. Kelleher
Senior Ed: Betsy Uhrig
Mktg Dir: Anna Lowi

Publications: Trade books, library editions, paperback originals & reprints
Audience: Preschool-12, adult
Subjects: Religion, animals, fiction, picture books, poetry
Discount: Libraries, 20%; retailers, 20-47%; schools, wholesalers, inquire
Services: Catalog

FACTS ON FILE
Subs. of Infobase Holdings Inc.
460 Park Ave. S., New York, NY
    10016
212-683-2244, 800-322-8755; Fax:
    212-213-4578
Pub: Martin Greenwald
Mktg Dir: Suzanne De Vito

Publications: Reference books Au-
    dience: K-12, adult

FAITH & LIFE PRESS
718 Main St., Box 347, Newton, KS
    67114-0347
316-283-5100
Pub: Norma J. Johnson
Ed Dir: Susan E. Janzen
Mktg Dir: Mark Regier
Children's Ed: Elizabeth Raid Pankratz

Publications: Trade books, paperback
    originals
Audience: Preschool-12, adult
Subjects: Religion, Bible
Services: Catalog. Exhibit at ALA

FARRAR, STRAUS & GIROUX
19 Union Square W., New York, NY
    10003
212-206-5366, 800-631-8571; Fax:
    212-633-9385
Mktg Dir: Michael Eisenberg

Publications: Trade books, paperback
    reprints
Imprints: Sunburst, Aerial, Mirasol
    Libros Juveniles
Audience: Preschool-12
Subjects: Foreign countries, art, pic-
    ture books, biographies, poetry, fam-
    ily life, sciences, fiction, social
    studies
Discount: 30-40%
Services: Catalog. Exhibit at ALA, IRA.
    Distributor for R & S Books

Fawcett, see **BALLANTINE PUBLISH-
    ING GROUP**

PHILLIPP FELDHEIM INC.
200 Airport Executive Park, Spring Val-
    ley, NY 10977
914-356-2282, 800-237-7149; Fax:
    914-425-1908
Pres: Phillipp Feldheim
Ed-in-Chief & Children's Ed: Marsi
    Tabak
Mktg Dir & Lib/Sch Prom Dir: Eli Hol-
    lander

Publications: Trade books, paperback
    originals
Imprints: Feldheim Publishers, Young
    Readers' Division
Audience: Preschool-12, adult
Subjects: Fiction, religion, historical fic-
    tion, Judaica
Discount: Schools & libraries, 10%
Services: Catalog. Exhibit at AJL

**THE FEMINIST PRESS AT THE CITY
UNIVERSITY OF NEW YORK**
311 E. 94 St., New York, NY 10128
212-360-5790; Fax: 212-348-1241
Pub: Florence Howe

Publications: Paperback originals &
    reprints, professional books for
    teachers, librarians & school ad-
    ministrators. Audiorecords/cassettes
Audience: K-12, adult
Subjects: Picture books, biographies,
    poetry, family life, sex education, fic-
    tion, women's history & literature,
    language arts
Special interest: Nonsexist education
Discount: Inquire
Services: Catalog. Exhibit at ALA,
    NCTE, ABA, NOW. Provide speakers

FIREFLY BOOKS LTD
250 Sparks Ave., Willowdale, ON M2H
    2S4, Canada
416-499-8412, 800-387-5080; Fax:
    416-499-8313
Pres: Lionel Koffler

Publications: Trade books
Audience: Juvenile
Services: Distributor for Annick Press,
    Camden House

First Avenue Editions, see **LERNER
PUBLICATIONS COMPANY**

Flare, see **AVON BOOKS**

FOREST HOUSE
Box 738, Lake Forest, IL 60045-0738
800-394-READ
Eds-in-Chief: Dianne Spahr, Roy Spahr

Publications: Library editions, trade
    books
Audience: Preschool-6
Subjects: Spanish titles, sign language,
    dictionaries, multicultural, easy-
    reading, arts, crafts, cooking
Services: Catalog. Exhibit at ALA

Forge Books, see **TOR BOOKS**

FOUR WALLS EIGHT WINDOWS
Box 548, Village Sta., New York, NY
    10014
212-206-8965; Fax: 212-206-8799
Orders: Publishers Group West, 4065
    Hollis Ave., Emeryville, CA 94608,
    800-788-3123
Pub: John G. H. Oakes, Dan Simon

Publications: Fiction, nonfiction

FRANKLIN WATTS
Subs. of Grolier, Inc.
5440 N. Cumberland Ave., Chicago, IL
    60656
800-672-6672; Fax: 800-374-4329
Contacts: Joseph Honn, John Sel-
    fridge,

Diane Pliens, Sharon Smalling

Publications: Trade books, library
    editions
Audience: K-12
Subjects: Fiction, nonfiction series
Services: Distributor for Gloucester
    Press, Bookwright. Exhibits at ALA

FREE SPIRIT PUBLISHING, INC.
400 First Ave. N., Ste. 616, Minneapo-
    lis, MN 55401
612-338-2068, 800-735-7323; Fax:
    612-337-5050
Contacts: Maurice Prater, Judy Gal-
    braith

Publications: Trade books
Audience: Children
Subjects: Nonfiction
Special interest: Self-help
Services: Catalog. Exhibit at ALA

W. H. FREEMAN AND CO.
41 Madison Ave., 35th fl., New York,
    NY 10010
212-576-9400; Fax: 212-481-1891
Pres: Robert Biewen
Ed-in-Chief: Burt Gabriel

Publications: Textbooks, computer
    books, professional books for
    teachers & school administrators.
    Computer software
Imprints: Computer Science Press,
    Scientific American Books for Young
    Readers
Audience: K-12, adult
Subjects: Computer software,
    mathematics, sciences
Services: Catalog. Exhibit at NCTM,
    NECC

FRIENDS UNITED PRESS
Subs. of Friends United Meeting
101 Quaker Hill Dr., Richmond, IN
    47374
317-962-7573, 800-537-8838; Fax:
    317-966-1293
Mgr: Ardith Talbot

Publications: Workbooks, trade books,
    paperback originals & reprints. Audi-
    orecords, cassettes
Audience: Preschool-12, adult
Subjects: Quaker history & faith ex-
    perience, Sunday School curriculum
Discount: Retailers, 40%
Services: Catalog. Quaker Book Club

FRIENDSHIP PRESS
Subs. of National Council of the
    Churches of Christ USA
475 Riverside Dr., New York, NY
    10115-0050
212-870-2586; Fax: 212-870-2550
Orders: Friendship Press Dist. Ctr., Box
    37844, Cincinnatti, OH 45222
Ed: Audrey Miller
Children's Ed: Margaret Larom

Publications: Paperback originals, teacher's guides, maps. Audiorecords/cassettes, filmstrips, videotapes/cassettes
Audience: Preschool-12, adult
Subjects: Family life, foreign countries, religion, social studies
Discount: Bookstores, 1-9 copies, 25%; 10 or more, 40%
Services: Catalog

FUN PUBLISHING CO.
Box 2049, Scottsdale, AZ 85252
602-946-2093
Pres: Howard Greenlee

Publications: Paperback originals
Audience: Preschool-6
Subjects: Social studies
Special interest: Native Americans
Discount: Educators/libraries, 20%
Services: Brochure

GALE RESEARCH
835 Penobscot Bldg., Detroit, MI 48226-4094
313-961-2242, 800-877-GALE; Fax: 313-961-6083
Mktg VP: Barb Eschner

Publications: Reference books, directories, library editions
Audience: Young adult, adult
Subjects: Biography, children's literature, multicultural
Discount: Inquire
Services: Catalog. Exhibits at ALA

GARETH STEVENS INC.
1555 N. River Center Dr., Ste. 201, Milwaukee, WI 53212
414-225-0333, 800-341-3569; Fax: 414-225-0377
Pres: Gareth Stevens
Ed Dir: Pat Lamtier-Sampon

Publications: Trade books, library editions
Audience: Juvenile
Subjects: Reference, nonfiction series

GARRETT EDUCATIONAL CORP.
Box 1588, 130 E. 13th St., Ada, OK 74820
405-332-6884, 800-654-9366; Fax: 405-332-1560
Contact: Lionel H. Garrett

Publications: Trade books, library editions
Audience: Juvenile
Subjects: Biographies, nonfiction, picture books

GEM PUBLICATIONS
502 Second St., Hudson, WI 54016
715-386-7113
Pub: Gary McCuen

Publications: Professional reading for librarians, teachers
Audience: Adult

Laura Geringer, see **HARPERCOLLINS CHILDREN'S BOOKS**

GESSLER PUBLISHING CO. INC.
55 W. 13th St., New York, NY 10011-7958
212-627-0099, 800-456-5825; Fax: 212-627-5948
Pres: Seth C. Levin
Ed-in-Chief: Warren Bratter
Mktg Dir: Nora Shwide

Publications: Textbooks, workbooks, trade books, paperback originals & reprints, professional books for teachers & librarians, programmed learning systems. Audiorecords/cassettes, computer software, transparencies, videotapes/cassettes, multimedia kits
Audience: Preschool-12, adult
Subjects: Computer software, foreign countries & languages, art, dance, language arts, auditory & visual, dictionaries, picture books, business, encyclopedias, poetry, career development, fiction, social studies
Special interest: Spanish-speaking, bilingual students
Discount: Inquire
Services: Catalog. Exhibit at ALA, ACTFL, ABA, National Catholic Assn., Northeast Foreign Language Assn., Assn. of Private Schools

GIBBS-SMITH, PUBLISHER
(formerly Peregrine Smith Books)
Box 667, Layton, UT 84041
801-544-9800
Pres & Ed-in-Chief: Gibbs M. Smith
Children's Ed: Lynda Sorenson
Mktg Dir: Sandra Dupont

Publications: Textbooks, workbooks, trade books, paperback originals & reprints
Audience: Preschool-12, adult
Subjects: Environment & energy, art, fiction, biographies, poetry, crafts, social studies, drama
Discount: Libraries, 10%; schools, 25% of textbooks
Services: Catalog. Exhibit at state social studies conventions

GIRL SCOUTS OF THE USA
420 Fifth Ave., New York, NY 10018-2702
212-940-7500, 800-221-4715; Fax: 212-852-6511
Ed: Bonnie McEwan

Publications: Textbooks, teacher's materials. Audiorecords/cassettes, films, filmstrips, video-

tapes/cassettes
Audience: 1-12, adult
Subjects: Family life, music, art, foreign languages, safety, career development, health, crafts, home economics, environment & energy, language arts
Discount: Libraries, 10%
Services: Catalog

GLENCOE PUBLISHING CO.
Div. of the Macmillan/McGraw-Hill School Publishing Co.
936 Eastwind Dr., Westerville, OH 43081
614-890-1111, 800-848-1567; Fax: 614-899-4379
Orders: Glencoe Order Department, Box 543, Blacklick, OH 43004-0543
800-334-7344 (telephone orders); Fax: 614-860-1877 (orders)
Pres: Jack Witmer
VP Secondary Mktg: David Whiting
VP Secondary Sales: Steve McClung

Publications: Textbooks, workbooks
Audience: 7-14 (grades)
Subjects: Crafts, home economics, safety, art, environment & energy, language arts, sciences, business, family life, mathematics, social studies, career development, foreign languages, music, vocational training, consumer education, health, religion
Special interest: Native Americans
Discount: Schools, 20-25%; libraries, 10%
Services: Exhibit at IRA, NCTE

DAVID R. GODINE PUBLISHER, INC.
300 Massachusetts Ave., Boston, MA 02115
617-536-0761; Fax: 617-421-0934
Pres: David R. Godine
Ed-in-Chief: Mark Polizzotti
Chidren's Ed: David R. Godine
Mktg Dir: Michael B. vanBeuren
Lib/Sch Prom Dir: Sally MacGillivray

Publications: Trade books, library editions, paperback reprints
Audience: 2-9
Subjects: Crafts, fiction, music, picture books
Discount: 1-5 books, 20%; 5-25, 40%; 25 & more, 45%
Services: Catalog. Exhibit at ALA

Golden Books, Golden Press, & Goldencraft, see **WESTERN PUBLISHING CO., INC.**

GOLDEN APPLE PRESS
Box 206, Mankato, MN 56002
507-388-2601; Fax: 507-388-2746

Publications: Trade books & paperbacks

Audience: Juvenile
Subjects: Fiction & nonfiction, nature, sports, books in Spanish

GREENHAVEN PRESS
Box 289009, San Diego, CA
92198-9009
619-485-7424, 800-231-5163; Fax:
619-485-9542
Pres: David Bender
Ed: Bruno Leone
Mktg Dir: Dan Leone

Publications: Library editions, paperback originals
Audience: 5-12, adult
Subjects: Social issues, global history
Discount: Net pricing
Services: Catalog

Greenwillow Books, see MORROW JUNIOR BOOKS

GROLIER EDUCATIONAL CORPORATION
Subs. of Grolier, Inc.
Sherman Tpke., Danbury, CT 06816
203-797-3500, 800-243-7256; Fax:
203-797-3285

Publications: Encyclopedias, educational reference

Grosset & Dunlap, see THE PUTNAM BERKELY GROUP, INC.

G. K. HALL & COMPANY
Box 159, Thorndike, ME 04986
207-948-2962, 800-223-6121; Fax:
207-948-2863
Children's Ed: Jamie Knoblock
Mktg Dir: Mary Kee

Publications: Large print library editions, professional books for librarians
Audience: K-9
Subjects: Fiction
Special interest: Reading disabled, large-print books
Discount: Inquire
Services: Catalog. Toll-free ordering. Exhibit at ALA

GERARD HAMON, INC.
Box 758, 525 Fenimore Rd., Mamaroneck, NY 10543
914-381-4649, 800-333-4971; Fax:
914-381-2607
Pres: Gerard Hamon

Audience: Preschool-12, adult
Subjects: Foreign languages
Special interest: Bilingual students, French-speaking
Discount: Schools & libraries, 10%
Services: Catalog. Exhibit at ALA, MLA, AATF. Dist for: all French publishers

GROSSET & DUNLAP
200 Madison Ave., New York, NY
10016
212-951-8700; Fax: 212-532-3693
Pres: Jane O'Connor
VP: Gary Gentel
Dir, Institutional Mktg: Nanette Knaster

Publications: Trade books, library editions, paperback originals
Audience: Preschool-12
Subjects: Picture books, general fiction
Discount: Inquire
Services: Catalog. Promotional materials. Exhibit at ALA

Gulliver Books & Gulliver Green Books, see HARCOURT BRACE & COMPANY

GUMBS & THOMAS
142 W. 72nd St., Ste. 9, New York, NY
10023
212-724-1110

Special interest: Multicultural

HARBINGER HOUSE
1051 N. Columbus Blvd., #100, Tucson, AZ 85711
Ordering: Box 42948, Tucson, AZ
85733-2948
602-326-9595, 800-759-9945; Fax:
602-326-8684
Pres: Charles Hutchinson
Mktg Dir: Connie Brown

Publications: Trade books, paperback originals
Audience: Preschool-8, adult
Subjects: Fine quality, literature-based books for children & adults
Special Interest: Unique activity books & multicultural books for children, self-help titles for adults
Discount: Inquire
Services: Catalog. Exhibit at regional & national library & educational conferences; national & international booksellers' conferences

HARCOURT BRACE & COMPANY
525 B St., Ste. 1900, San Diego, CA
92101-4495
619-669-6435, 800-543-1918 (orders); Fax: 619-699-6320
Director: Louise Howton
Inst Mktg Mgr: Jane Washburn

Publications: Trade books, paperback reprints
Imprints: Gulliver Books, Gulliver Green Books, Browndeer Press, Jane Yolen Books, Voyager Books/Libras Viajeros, Harcourt Brace Paperbacks
Audience: K-12
Subjects: Picture books, business, sex education, dance, family life, home economics, animals, poetry, career

development, social studies, dictionaries, fiction, language arts, art, religion, computer software, sports, drama, foreign countries & languages, mathematics, auditory & visual, safety, consumer education, vocational training, encyclopedias, health, music, biographies, sciences, crafts, environment & energy, hobbies, physical education
Discount: Inquire
Services: Catalog. Promotional author brochures. Posters. Exhibit at ALA, IRA, NCTE, local, state, regional school & library conferences

HARPERCOLLINS CHILDREN'S BOOKS
10 E. 53rd St., New York, NY 10022
212-207-7044, 800-242-7737; Fax:
212-207-7617
Pub: Marilyn Kriney
Children's Ed: Joanna Cotler
HarperTrophy Ed Dir: Jennifer M. Brown
Mktg Dir: Lisa Holton
Lib/Sch Prom Dir: William C.Morris

Publications: Trade books, library editions, professional books for teachers & librarians. Audiorecords/cassettes
Imprints: Laura Geringer, HarperCollins Interactive, HarperFestival, HarperTrophy Paperbacks
Audience: K-12, adult
Subjects: Family life, poetry, animals, fiction, sciences, art, hobbies, social studies, biographies, language arts, sports, crafts, picture books
Discount: Schools, libraries: library editions, 10%; trade editions, 10-40%
Services: Catalog. Exhibit at ALA, IRA, NCTE, NAEYC, NSTA, & through Publishers Book Exhibit

D. C. HEATH & COMPANY
School Division
125 Spring St., Lexington, MA 02173
617-860-1277, 800-235-3565; Fax:
617-860-1202
Pres: Albert Bursma, Jr
VP & Ed Dir: William Grace

Publications: Textbooks, workbooks, computer books, professional books for teachers. Audiorecords/cassettes, filmstrips, computer software, transparencies, videotapes/cassettes
Audience: K-12
Subjects: Sciences, dictionaries, social studies, foreign languages, spelling, modern language, language arts, mathematics
Discount: School, 25%
Services: Catalog. Exhibit at IRA, NCTE, NCTM, NSTA

HEIAN INTERNATIONAL INC.
Box 1013, Union City, CA 94587

510-471-8440; Fax: 510-471-5254
Ed: Liz Squellati

Publications: Trade books
Audience: Juvenile, adult
Subjects: Picture books, dictionaries, Oriental culture & customs, calendars

HEINEMANN EDUCATIONAL BOOKS, INC.
Div. of Reed Publishing
361 Hanover St., Portsmouth, NH 03801-3912
603-431-7894, 800-541-2086; Fax: 603-431-4971
Pres: John Watson
Ed: Toby Gordon
Lib/Sch Prom Dir: Lori Lampert
Sales Mgr: Michael Gibbons

Publications: Trade books, paperback originals, professional books for teachers & school administrators. Filmstrips, videotapes/cassettes
Audience: Adult
Subjects: Mathematics, biographies, poetry, drama, sciences, family life, social studies, foreign languages
Discount: Prepaid orders, 10%
Services: Catalog. Promotional newsletter. Exhibit at IRA, NCTE, AERA, NMS, TESOL

HEINLE & HEINLE PUBLISHERS INC.
20 Park Plaza, Boston, MA 02116-4507
617-451-1940, 800-237-0053; Fax: 617-426-4379
CEO: Charles Heinle

Publications: Textbooks, workbooks, professional books for teachers. Audiorecords/cassettes
Audience: 7-12, college, adult
Subjects: Foreign language, ESL
Special interest: Bilingual students
Services: Catalog. Promotional newsletter

HENDRICK-LONG PUBLISHING CO.
Box 25123, Dallas, TX 75225-1123
214-358-4677; Fax: 214-352-4768
Ed: Joann Long

Publications: Trade books
Audience: Juvenile, young adult
Subjects: Texas & Southwest

HERALD PRESS
Subs. of Mennonite Publishing House Inc.
616 Walnut Ave., Scottdale, PA 15683-1999
412-887-8500, 800-245-7894; Fax: 412-887-3111
Children's Ed: S. David Garber
Mktg Dir & Lib/Sch Prom Dir: Irene E. Lapp

Publications: Textbooks, trade books, paperback originals & reprints, professional books for teachers. Audiorecords/cassettes
Audience: K-12, adult
Subjects: Family life, social studies, biographies, fiction, social issues, cookbooks, hymnals, picture books, religion, environment & energy, sex education
Discount: Libraries, 20%
Services: Catalog. Exhibit at ALA, CBE

HIDDIGEIGEI BOOKS
120 E. Sunset, DeKalb, IL 60115
815-756-9908
Pres, Children's Ed & Mktg Dir: Nicholas J. Lahey
Ed: M. Cozad

Publications: Paperback originals & reprints
Audience: 2-12
Subjects: Fiction, foreign countries, adventure stories
Discount: 40%
Services: Catalog. Exhibit at ALA

High Noon Books, see **ACADEMIC THERAPY PUBLICATIONS**

HIGHLIGHTS FOR CHILDREN
2300 W. Fifth Ave., Columbus, OH 43216
614-486-0631
CEO: Garry Myers
Pres: Elmer Meider

Publications: Workbooks, paperback originals, magazines, continuities, textbooks
Audience: Preschool-6
Subjects: Crafts, hobbies, sports, animals, environment & energy, language arts, art, fiction, mathematics, auditory & visual, foreign countries, sciences, biographies, health, social studies
Discount: Inquire
Services: Catalog. Exhibit at ALA, IRA, ASCD, CEC

HILLSDALE EDUCATIONAL PUBLISHERS, INC.
39 North St., Box 245, Hillsdale, MI 49242
517-437-3179, 800-437-2268; Fax: 517-437-0190
Pres: David B. McConnell
Ed-in-Chief: Stella McElmurry

Publications: Textbooks, workbooks, paperback originals, professional books for teachers. Audiorecords/cassettes, computer software, videotapes/cassettes
Audience: 1-12, adult
Subjects: Michigan studies & history
Special interest: Regional materials

Services: Catalog. Exhibits at regional conferences

HISPANIC BOOKS DISTRIBUTORS, INC.
1665 W. Grant Rd., Tucson, AZ 85745
602-882-9484; Fax: 602-882-7696
Pres: Arnulfo D. Trejo
General Mgr: Bernardo Serrano

Publications: Spanish trade books & periodicals
Audience: K-12
Subjects: Fiction & nonfiction in Spanish
Discount: Inquire
Services: Catalog. Exhibit at ALA, ABA, others

HOLIDAY HOUSE INC.
425 Madison Ave., New York, NY 10017
212-688-0085; Fax: 212-421-6134
Pres: John H. Briggs Jr.
Ed-in-Chief: Margery S. Cuyler

Publications: Trade books
Audience: Juvenile, young adult
Subjects: Fiction, picture books

HENRY HOLT & CO., INC.
115 W. 18th St., New York, NY 10011
212-886-9200, 800-488-5233; Fax: 212-633-0748
Pres: Bruno Quinson
Ed-in-Chief: Jack Macrae
Children's Ed: Brenda Bowen
Lib/Sch Prom Dir: Heidi Gunlock

Publications: Trade books, paperback originals & reprints
Imprints: Bill Martin Books, Edge Books, Redfeather, Owlet Paperbacks
Audience: Preschool-12, adult
Subjects: Family life, animals, fiction, biographies, hobbies, consumer education, picture books, crafts, poetry
Discount: Schools & libraries, 20%
Services: Catalog. Exhibit at ALA, IRA, NCTE, ABA

HOUGHTON MIFFLIN COMPANY
Children's Book Division
222 Berkeley St., Boston, MA, 02116-3764
617-351-5000, 800-225-3362; Fax: 617-351-1111
VP: Walter Lorraine
Eds: Matilda Welter, Audrey Bryant, Laura Hornik, Margaret Raymo
Prom Dir: Jennifer Roberts

Publications: Trade books, paperback reprints. Audiocassettes
Audience: Preschool-12
Subjects: Family life, sciences, animals, fiction, social studies, foreign countries, sports, crafts, hobbies, environment, picture books

Discount: Inquire
Services: Catalog. Exhibit at ALA, IRA, NCTE, ABA

HUMANICS PUBLISHING GROUP
1482 Mecaslin St. NW, Box 7400, Atlanta, GA 30309
404-874-2176, 800-874-8844; Fax: 404-874-1976
Chmn: Gary Wilson
Mktg Dir: Jennifer Hall

Publications: Trade books, workbooks, paperback originals, programmed learning systems, professional books for teachers & school administrators
Imprints: Humanics Childrens House, Humanics Learning, Humanics Audio
Audience: Preschool-4, adult
Subjects: Music, family life, sciences, health, social studies, language arts, early childhood education, mathematics
Special interest: Native Americans, nonsexist education, Black Americans
Services: Catalog. Exhibit at CEC, NAEYC, National Head Start, NSSEA

HUNTER HOUSE INC., PUBLISHERS
Box 2914, Alameda, CA 94501-0914
510-865-5282; Fax: 510-865-4295
Pres & Ed-in-Chief: Kiran S. Rana
Children's Ed: Lisa Lee
Mktg Dir: Corrie Sahli

Publications: Trade books, paperback originals & reprints
Audience: 8-12, adult
Subjects: Family life, health, physical education, sex education
Special interest: Books for counselors & educators, crisis management, curriculum guides
Services: Catalog. Exhibit at ALA, IRA

HYPERION BOOKS FOR CHILDREN
Div. of the Walt Disney Co.
114 Fifth Ave., New York, NY 10011
212-633-4400; Fax: 212-633-4833
Orders: Little, Brown & Co., 200 West St., Waltham, MA 02254.
800-759-0190
Dir: Andrea Cascardi
Mktg Dir: Lauren Wohl

Publications: Trade books, library editions
Audience: Preschool-8
Subjects: General fiction
Services: Catalog. Exhibit at ALA, ABA, IRA

IDEALS PUBLISHING CORP.
Box 140300, 565 Marriott Dr., Ste. 890, Nashville, TN 37414-0300
615-885-8270, 800-558-4383; Fax: 615-885--9578
Ed Trade: Peggy Schaefer

Publications: Trade books
Audience: Juvenile, adult
Subjects: Cookbooks

IMPACT PUBLISHERS, INC.
Box 1094, San Luis Obispo, CA 93406
805-543-5911; Fax: 805-461-0554
Pres & Ed-in-Chief: R. E. Alberti
Mktg Dir & Lib/Sch Prom Dir: Melissa Froehner

Publications: Trade books, paperback originals. Videocassettes
Audience: Preschool-12, adult
Subjects: Self-esteem, sciences, family life, health, relationships
Special interest: Self-awareness, nonsexist, nonracist, nonageist
Discount: Libraries, 15%; 10-49 copies, 10%; 50-100 copies, 20%
Services: Catalog

INDEPENDENCE PRESS
Div. Herald Publishing House
3225 S. Noland Rd., Box 1770, Independence, MO 64055
816-252-5010
Ed-in-Chief: Roger Yarrington
Lib/Sch Prom Dir: Richard Fortman

Publications: Workbooks, trade books, paperback originals & reprints
Audience: 4-6, 10-12, adult
Subjects: Fiction, religion, US historical fiction
Special interest: Missouri, religion
Discount: Libraries, assorted titles, 1-4 copies, 30%; 5 or more 40%
Services: Catalog. Exhibit at ALA

INSIGHT BOOKS
Div. of Plenum Publishing Corp.
233 Spring St., New York, NY 10013-1578
212-620-8000, 800-221-9369; Fax: 212-463-0742
Ed: Frank Darmstadt

Publications: Trade books, paperback originals, computer books
Audience: Professional
Subjects: Career development, contemporary sexual issues, politics, social studies, health, environmental studies, alternative life styles
Discount: Inquire
Services: Catalog. Exhibit at ALA, NASW, ATA, ABA

INSTITUTE FOR THE ADVANCEMENT OF PHILOSOPHY FOR CHILDREN
Montclair State College, Upper Montclair, NJ 07043
201-893-4277
Dir: Matthew Lipman
Mktg Dir: Joanne Markowski

Publications: Textbooks, workbooks, paperback originals, professional books for teachers
Audience: 3-12
Subjects: Educational theory, philosophy for children

INTERLINK PUBLISHING GROUP INC.
99 Seventh Ave., Brooklyn, NY 11215
718-797-4292; Fax: 718-855-7329
Pub: Michel Moushabeck

Publications: Trade books
Imprints: Crocodile Books USA, Interlink Books
Audience: Children
Services: Distributor for Eyebright Publications, David Phillip, Quartet Books, Saqi Books, Scorpion Publishing, The Windrush Press, The Women's Press, Zed Books

ISLAND PRESS PUBLISHING
175 Bahia Via, Fort Myers Beach, FL 33931
813-463-9482
Ed: Rolfe F. Schell
Mktg Dir: L. W. Schell

Publications: Textbooks, trade books, paperback originals & reprints
Audience: K-12, adult
Subjects: Florida history, animals, foreign countries, physical education, poetry
Special interest: Spanish-speaking, bilingual students
Discount: 1, 20%; 2-11, 35%; 12 or more, 40%

Ivy, see BALLANTINE PUBLISHING GROUP

JALMAR PRESS
2675 Skypark Dr., Ste. 204, Torrance, CA 90505
310-784-0016, 800-662-9662; Fax: 310-784-1379
Pres: Bradley L. Winch
Mktg Dir: Bryan Bender, Brad Winch Jr.
Ed-in-Chief: Jeanne Iler

Publications: Trade books, library editions, paperback originals, professional books for teachers & school administrators.
Audiorecords/cassettes, filmstrips, videotapes/cassettes, multimedia kits
Audience: Preschool-12, adult
Subjects: Family life, picture books, affective education, positive self-esteem, right brain/whole brain learning, conflict resolution, transactional analysis series
Discount: Standard trade discount to 45%
Services: Catalog. Exhibit at ALA, IRA, ABA, NAEYC, ACLD, ASCD, CEC, AACD, NCEA, CBA, NEA, PTA, NASW, ICLD, CWLA, EDSA

JANUARY PRODUCTIONS
210 Sixth Ave., Box 66, Hawthorne, NJ 07507
201-423-4666, 800-451-7450; Fax: 201-423-5569
Pres: Allan W. Peller
Ed-in-Chief & Children's Ed: Barbara Peller
Mktg Dir & Lib/Sch Prom Dir: Carol Liess

Publications: Library editions, paperback originals. Audiorecords/cassettes
Audience: K-7
Subjects: Picture books, biographies, family life, fiction, language arts
Services: Catalog. Exhibit at ALA, IRA, SSLI, AASL

JEWISH BRAILLE INSTITUTE OF AMERICA, INC.
110 E. 30th St., New York, NY 10016
212-889-2525; Fax: 212-689-3692
Pres: Jane Evans
Lib Adm: Cantor Mindy J. Fliegelman

Publications: Textbooks, workbooks, trade books. Audiorecords/cassettes
Audience: K-12, adult
Subjects: Poetry, biographies, religion, drama, Jewish history, sociology, Israel & Zionism, holocaust, fiction, foreign languages
Special interest: Blind, reading disabled
Services: Catalog. Promotional newsletter. Brochure

JEWISH PUBLICATION SOCIETY
1930 Chestnut St., Philadelphia, PA 19103
215-564-5925, 800-234-3151; Fax: 215-561-6640
Ed-in-Chief: Ellen Frankel
Children's Ed: Bruce Black
Mktg, Lib/Sch Prom Dir: Jean Sue Libkind

Publications: Workbooks, trade books, paperback originals & reprints
Audience: K-12, adult
Subjects: Picture books, biographies, religion, family life, Judaica, fiction, language arts
Services: Catalog. Exhibit at ALA, ABA

JUDAICA PRESS
123 Ditmas Ave., Brooklyn, NY 11218
718-972-6200; Fax: 718-972-6204
Pres: Jack Goldman
Ed-in-Chief & Children's Ed: Bonnie Goldman
Mktg Dir & Lib/Sch Prom Dir: Norman Shapiro

Publications: Trade books, paperback originals
Audience: K-12, adult

Subjects: Picture books, religion, Jewish philosophy, Bible commentary
Discount: Schools, 10%
Services: Catalog. Promotional newsletter. Exhibit at ALA

JUDY/INSTRUCTO
Div. of Paramount Publishing, Elementary Division
4424 W. 78th St., Bloomington, MN 55435
800-525-9907; Fax: 612-832-9033
Contact: Marilyn Stanger, Julie Ober

Publications: Pattern books
Audience: Children
Subjects: Nursery rhyme & fairy tale activities

JUST US BOOKS
301 Main St., Ste. 22-24, Orange, NJ 07050
201-672-7701; Fax: 201-677-7570
Pres: Wade Hudson

Publications: Trade books
Imprints: Afro-Bets
Audience: Children
Subjects: Feeling good books
Special interest: African American

KALIMAT PRESS
1600 Sawtelle Blvd., Ste. 34, Los Angeles, CA 90025-3114
213-479-5668
Ed-in-Chief: Anthony A. Lee

Publications: Trade books, library editions, paperback originals
Audience: 3-12, adult
Subjects: Fiction, religion, books on the Baha'i faith
Services: Catalog

KALMBACH PUBLISHING COMPANY
21027 Crossroads Circle, Box 1612, Waukesha, WI 53187
414-796-8776, 800-558-1544; Fax: 414-796-0126
Pres: Walt Mundschau
VP Sales: Robert A. Maas

Publications: Paperback originals
Audience: 6-12, adult
Subjects: Railroads, model railroading, toy trains, astronomy, toys & collectibles, aviation, dollhouse miniatures, scale modeling, radio control
Discount: Libraries, 20%
Services: Catalog. Exhibit at ABA

KANE/MILLER BOOK PUBLISHERS
Box 529, Brooklyn, NY 11231-0005
718-624-5120; Fax: 718-858-5452
Co-Pubs: Sandy Miller (New York);
Madeline Kane (Box 8515,
La Jolla, CA 92038; 619-456-0540)

Publications: Trade books, paperback reprints
Audience: K-5
Subjects: Fiction & nonfiction, foreign countries, picture books
Special interest: Translations of foreign picture books
Discount: 1-9 copies, 10%; 10 or more, 25%
Services: Catalog. Exhibit at ALA, IRA, ABA

KAR-BEN COPIES INC.
6800 Tildenwood Lane, Rockville, MD 20852
301-984-8733, 800-452-7236 (800-4KARBEN); Fax: 301-881-9195
Pres: Judyth S. Groner
Ed-in-Chief: Madeline Wikler

Publications: Textbooks, workbooks, trade books, paperback originals & reprints. Videotapes/cassettes
Audience: Preschool-6
Subjects: Picture books, biographies, religion, crafts, fiction, foreign languages
Special interest: Jewish content only
Discount: 12-24 copies, 10%; 25 or more, 25%
Services: Catalog. Exhibit at ABA, Jewish educational conferences

KENDALL GREEN PUBLICATIONS
Div. of Gallaudet University Press
800 Florida Ave. NE, Washington, DC 20002
202-651-5488, 800-451-1073; Fax: 202-651-5489
Ed-in-Chief: Elaine Costello

Publications: Trade books
Audience: K-adult
Subjects: Deafness

KIDS CAN PRESS LTD.
29 Birch Ave, Toronto, Ontario, Canada M4V 1E2
416-534-6389, 800-265-0884; Fax: 416-960-5437
Orders: Univ. of Toronto Press, 5201 Dufferin St., Downsview, ON M3H 5T8 (for Canada); 340 Nagel Dr., Cheektowaga, NY 14255 (for USA)
Pres & Ed-in-Chief: Valerie Hussey
Children's Ed: V. Wyatt
Mktg Dir & Lib/Sch Prom Dir: Ricky Englander

Publications: Trade books, paperback originals & reprints
Audience: Preschool-12, adult
Subjects: Family life, sciences, animals, fiction, sex education, art, health, sports, crafts, hobbies, environment & energy, picture books
Services: Catalog

ALFRED A. KNOPF BOOKS FOR YOUNG READERS
Subs. of Random House, Inc.
210 E. 50th St., New York, NY 10022
212-572-2600, 800-638-6460; Fax:
  212-572-8700
Pub: Simon Boughton

Publications: Trade books, library editions, paperback originals. Audi-
  orecords/cassettes,
  videotapes/cassettes
Audience: Preschool-12
Subjects: Dance, hobbies, animals, environment & energy, picture books,
  art, family life, poetry, career development, fiction, crafts, health
Discount: Greenaway Plans
Services: Catalog. Promotional newsletter. Exhibit at ALA, IRA, NCTE

LANTERN PRESS
354 Hussey Rd., Mt. Vernon, NY
  10552
212-838-7821
Pres: Judith A. Furman
Children's Ed, Mktg Dir & Lib/Sch
  Prom Dir: J. R. Furman

Publications: Workbooks, library
  editions
Audience: K-10
Subjects: Picture books, animals,
  sports, crafts, fiction, hobbies
Discount: 1 copy, 25%; 2 or more
  33⅓%
Services: Catalog. Exhibit at ALA,
  NCTE

LAREDO PUBLISHING CO.
22930 Lockness Ave., Torrance, CA
  90501
310-517-1890; Fax: 310-517-1892
Contact: Clara Kohen, Sam Laredo,
  Rosana Infante

Publications: Trade books
Audience: K-12, adult
Subjects: Fiction, nonfiction, ency-
  clopedias, parenting
Special Interests: Spanish books

LARKSDALE
Box 70456, Houston, TX 77270-0456
713-461-7200; Fax: 713-973-0511
Orders: Box 801222, Houston, TX
  77280
800-666-2332
Ed-in-Chief: Frances Burke
  Goodman

Publications: Trade books, library edi-
  tions, paperback originals
Imprints: Post Oak Press
Audience: K-7, adult
Subjects: General nonfiction
Services: Brochures. Exhibit at ABA,
  TLA

Laurel-Leaf, see BANTAM DOUBLEDAY DELL BOOKS FOR YOUNG READERS

LEADERSHIP PUBLISHERS
Box 8358, Des Moines, IA
  50301-8358
515-278-4765; Fax: 515-270-8303
Dist by: Creative Learning Press, Man-
  field Center, CT; A. W. Peller, Haw-
  thorne, NJ; Dale Seymour
  Publicatons, Palo Alto, CA
Pres, Ed-in-Chief & Mktg Dir: Lois
  Roets

Publications: Textbooks, workbooks,
  professional books for teachers
Audience: 3-12, adult
Subjects: Biographies, drama, language arts, enrichment programs for
  gifted
Special interest: Nonsexist education
Services: Catalog. Promotional newsletter. Exhibit at NAGC

LECTORUM PUBLICATIONS, INC.
127 W. 14th St., New York, NY 10011
212-929-2833, 800-345-5946; Fax:
  212-727-3035
Contact: Teresa Mlawer, William
  Mlawer

Publications: Textbooks, workbooks,
  trade books, library editions, paperback originals & reprints, computer
  books, professional books for
  teachers, librarians & school administrators. Audiorecords/cassettes
Audience: Preschool-12, adult
Subjects: Children & YA titles, adult
  books, reference books
Special interest: Spanish-speaking,
  bilingual students
Discount: Schools & libraries, 20%
Services: Catalog. Exhibit at ALA,
  NCTE, Library Media Group, all state
  bilingual meetings

LEE & LOW BOOKS INC.
228 E. 45th St., New York, NY 10017
212-867-6155; Fax: 212-338-9059
Orders: Publishers Group West, 4065
  Hollis St., Emeryville, CA 94608,
  800-788-3123
Pres: Thomas Low
Pub: Philip Lee

Publications: Trade books
Audience: K-6
Subjects: Picture books
Special interests: Multiculturalism
Services: Exhibit at ALA

HAL LEONARD PUBLISHING CORP.
7777 W. Bluemound Rd., Box 13819,
  Milwaukee, WI 53213
414-774-3630, 800-524-4425; Fax:
  414-774-3259
Pres: Keith Mardak
VP Prod Dev: Herman Knoll

Ad Dir: Karen Waldkirch

Publications: Trade books,
  programmed learning systems. Audi-
  orecords/cassettes, video-
  tapes/cassettes
Audience: K-12, adult
Subjects: Music
Services: Catalog. Exhibit at ABA,
  NAEYC & other music & educational
  conferences

LERNER PUBLICATIONS COMPANY
241 First Ave. N., Minneapolis, MN
  55401
612-332-3344, 800-328-4929; Fax:
  612-332-7615
Pres: Harry J. Lerner
Children's Ed: Nancy M. Campbell,
  Mary M. Rodgers
Mktg Dir: James E. Kelly
Lib/Sch Prom Dir: Jeff E. Reynolds

Publications: Trade books, library editions, paperback reprints Imprints:
  First Avenue Editions
Audience: Preschool-12
Subjects: Wide variety of books for
  young readers, with an emphasis on
  multiculturalism. Featuring ''We are
  Still Here,'' ''Then and Now,'' biographies, cookbooks and natural
  science
Special interest: Native Americans,
  nonsexist education, nonracist
Services: Catalog. Promotional newsletter. Exhibit at ALA, IRA ABA

LIBRARIES UNLIMITED
Box 6633, Englewood, CO
  80155-6633
303-770-1220, 800-237-6124
Pres: Bohdan S. Wynar
Mktg Dir & Lib/Sch Prom Dir: Debby
  Mattil

Publications: Professional books for
  teachers, librarians & school administrators
Audience: Adult
Subjects: Current reference books,
  textbooks, & professional materials
  for librarians & media specialists
Special interest: Teachers resources &
  activity books
Discount: Libraries, standing order
  plans, 10-15%
Services: Catalog. Exhibit at ALA,
  AASL, some state & school media
  association conventions

LIBROS SIN FRONTERAS
Box 2085, Olympia, WA 98507-2085
206-357-4332
Dir: Michael Shapiro

Publications: Trade books, cassette
  tapes, audio CD's
Audience: K-12, adult

Subjects: Spanish language books, Latin American popular music, audio fiction
Discount: Libraries, inquire; approval plans
Services: Catalog. Exhibit at ALA, WA Library Assn, CA Library Assn. Professional binding reinforcement of paperback books

LIGUORI PUBLICATIONS
One Liguori Dr., Liguori, MO 63057-9999
314-464-2500, 800-325-9521; Fax: 314-464-8449
Ed: Rev R. Pagliari
Lib/Sch Prom Dir: K. Erker

Publications: Hardcover & paperback originals. Videotapes/cassettes
Imprints: Triumph Books
Audience: K-12, adult
Subjects: Bible study, Catholic education, meditations, Christian titles
Discount: Schools, 10-24 copies, 10%; 25-49, 12%; 50-99, 15%; 20%; 500 or more, one title, 30%
Services: Catalog

Linnet Books, see SHOE STRING PRESS

LINWORTH PUBLISHING INC.
480 E. Wilson Bridge Rd., Ste. L, Worthington, OH 43085-9918
800-786-5017; Fax: 614-436-490
Pres: Marlene Woo-Lun

Publications: Textbooks & professional journals
Audience: Adult
Subjects: Professional growth materials & books for school librarians
Discount: Inquire
Services: Exhibit at ALA, workshops

LION BOOKS
Div. of Sayre Publishing
210 Nelson Rd., Ste. B, Scarsdale, NY 10583
914-725-3572; Fax: 914-723-7012
Pres: Sayre Ross
Children's Ed: Harriet Ross
Mktg Dir & Lib/Sch Prom Dir: Bette Callet

Publications: Trade books, library editions, paperback reprints
Audience: 3-12, adult
Subjects: Language arts, animals, physical education, art, picture books, biographies, sports, crafts
Discount: Libraries, 5 or more copies, 10%
Services: Catalog. Exhibit at ALA, ABA

LITTLE, BROWN & COMPANY
34 Beacon St., Boston, MA 02108-1493

617-227-0730, 800-343-9204; Fax: 617-227-4633
Pres: Charlie Hayward
VP, Dir Mktg: Betsy Groban
VP, Pub: John Keller
VP, Ed-in-Chief: Maria Modugno
Publicity Manager: Linda Magram

Publications: Trade books, library editions, paperback originals & reprints
Audience: Preschool-12, adult
Subjects: Consumer education, health, safety, animals, drama, hobbies, sciences, art, environment & energy, picture books, sex education, biographies, family life, poetry, social studies, business, fiction, religion, sports
Discount: 20%
Services: Distributor for Disney Press, Hyperion Books, Arcade Publishing, Sports Illustrated for Kids. Catalog. Exhibit at ALA, IRA, NCTE, ABA

Little Rainbow, see TROLL ASSOCIATES

Little Simon, see SIMON & SCHUSTER BOOKS FOR YOUNG READERS

Lodestar Books, see DUTTON CHILDREN'S BOOKS

TEE LOFTIN PUBLISHER, INC.
685 Gonzales Rd., Santa Fe, NM 87501-6190
505-989-1931
Pres & Ed-in-Chief: Tee Loftin

Publications: Library editions, paperback originals, posters
Audience: K-12, adult
Special interest: Bilingual students (Greek-speaking)
Discount: Inquire
Other: Brochures

LOLLIPOP POWER BOOKS
Carolina Wren Press
120 Morris St., Durham, NC 27701
919-560-2738
Pres & Ed: Ruth A. Smullin
Mktg Dir & Lib/Sch Prom: Richard Morrison

Publications: Trade books, paperback originals
Audience: Preschool-3
Subjects: Picture books
Special interest: Nonsexist, nonracist stories; bilingual (English/Spanish)
Discount: Inquire
Services: Catalog

LOTHROP, LEE & SHEPARD BOOKS
Div. of William Morrow
1350 Ave. of the Americas, New York, NY 10019
212-261-6793, 800-843-9389; Fax: 212-261-6689

Publications: Trade books
Audience: K-12
Subjects: Picture books, business, sex education, dance, family life, home economics, animals, poetry, career development, social studies, dictionaries, fiction, language arts, art, religion, computer software, sports, drama, foreign countries & languages, mathematics, auditory & visual, safety, consumer education, vocational training, encyclopedias, health, music, biographies, sciences, crafts, environment & energy, hobbies, physical education
Services: Catalog. Exhibit at ALA, IRA, NCTE, ABA

LOYOLA UNIVERSITY PRESS
3441 N. Ashland Ave., Chicago, IL 60657
312-281-1818, 800-621-1008; Fax: 312-281-0555
Ed Dir: Rev. D. L. Flaherty

Publications: Textbooks, workbooks, trade books, programmed learning systems, professional books for teachers & school administrators. Filmstrips
Audience: K-12, adult
Subjects: Poetry, philosophy, auditory & visual, religion, biographies, sciences, foreign languages, social studies, language arts, vocational training
Discount: Inquire

LUCENT BOOKS
Affil. of Greenhaven Press, Inc.
Box 289009, San Diego, CA 92198-9009
619-485-7424, 800-231-5163; Fax: 619-485-9542
Pres: David Bender
Ed: Bruno Leone
Mktg Dir: Dan Leone

Publications: Library editions, paperback originals
Audience: 10-16
Subjects: Nonfiction, social issues, global history
Discount: Net pricing
Services: Catalog

Macmillan Children's Books, see SIMON & SCHUSTER

MAGE PUBLISHERS INC.
1032 29 St., NW, Washington, DC 20007
202-342-1642, 800-962-0922; Fax: 202-342-9269
Pub & Ed: Mohammad Batmanglij

Publications:: Trade books
Audience: Juvenile, adult
Subjects: Persian literature, bilingual

children's books, fiction, poetry, art, history

Magination Press, *see* **BRUNNER/MAZEL INC.**

Magpie Books, *see* **WINSTON-DEREK PUBLISHERS**

Margaret K. McElderry Books, *see* **SIMON & SCHUSTER**

MARSHALL CAVENDISH CORP.
Member of Times Mirror Group
2415 Jerusalem Ave., North Bellmore, NY 11710
516-826-4200; Fax: 516-785-8133
Gen Mgr: Albert F. Lee

Publications: Library editions
Audience: Juvenile
Subjects: Nonfiction series, reference books

Bill Martin Books, *see* **HENRY HOLT & CO., INC.**

MARYLAND HISTORICAL PRESS
9205 Tuckerman St., Lanham, MD 20706
301-577-5308
Pres, Children's Ed & Lib/Sch Prom Dir: Vera Foster Rollo

Publications: Textbooks, trade books, library editions, paperback originals, professional books for teachers
Audience: K-12
Subjects: Biographies, social studies, vocational training, Maryland history, geography, government
Special interest: Nonsexist, nonracial emphasis
Discount: Dealers, 30%
Services: Catalog

McDOUGAL, LITTEL & CO.
Box 1667, Evanston, IL 60204
708-869-2300; Fax: 708-869-0841
Chairman & CEO: Alfred L. McDougal
Pres & Ed-in-Chief: Julia A. McGee
VP & Natl Sales Mgr: Rita Schaefer

Publications: Textbooks, supplemental texts, multimedia products
Audience: K-12
Subjects: Language arts, mathematics, social studies, foreign language
Services: Catalog. Exhibit at NCTE, NCTM, NCSS, IRA, NABSE, ACTFL, ASCD

McFARLAND & CO., INC., PUBLISHERS
Box 611, Jefferson, NC 28640
910-246-4460; Fax: 910-246-5018
Pres & Ed-in-Chief: Robert Franklin

Publications: Professional & reference books for libraries
Services: Catalog. Exhibit at ALA, PLA

Medallion, *see* **TROLL ASSOCIATES**

MEDIA MATERIALS
111 Kane St., Baltimore, MD 21224
800-638-6470

Publications: Workbooks, cassette learning packages, manipulatives, games, teaching aids, flashcards
Audience: Preschool-8
Subjects: Social studies, auditory & visual, language arts, mathematics, reading, safety, health, sciences
Special interest: African-Americans, bilingual students
Services: Catalog. Exhibit at NAEYC, NHSA

MERIWETHER PUBLISHING INC.
885 Elkton Dr., Colorado Springs, CO 80907
719-594-4422, 800-93PLAYS; Fax: 719-594-9916
Pres: A. Mark Zapel
Ex. Ed: Arthur L. Zapel
Children's Ed: Rhonda Wray
Lib/Sch Prom Dir: Ted Zapel

Publications: Textbooks, workbooks, trade books, library editions, paperback originals & reprints, plays. Filmstrips, videotapes/cassettes
Audience: 6-12, adult
Subjects: Language arts, art, music, dance, religion, drama, theater, speech, communication arts, family life
Special interest: Plays for high schools & colleges
Services: Catalog. Exhibit at ABA, CBA

THE MIDDLE ATLANTIC PRESS INC.
848 Church St., Wilmington, DE 19899
302-654-4107; 302-455-9382
Pub: Norman Goldfind
Mktg Dir: George Stutman

Publications: Textbooks, trade books, paperback originals & reprints
Audience: 4-12, adult
Subjects: Fiction, social studiesDiscount: Schools & libraries, 20%, 30 days
Services: Catalog

MILKWEED EDITIONS
430 First Ave. N., Ste. 400, Minneapolis, MN 55401
612-332-3192; Fax: 612-332-6428
Pub: Emilie Buchwald
Prom Dir: Arlinda Keeley

Publications: Trade books
Audience: Juvenile, adult
Subjects: Fiction, poetry, essays, art

MILLBROOK PRESS
2 Old New Milford Rd., Brookfield, CT 06804

203-740-2220, 800-462-4703; Fax: 203-740-2526
Pres: Jean Reynolds

Publications: Trade books, library editions
Audience: Juvenile
Subjects: Nonfiction series, single titles
Services: Distributor for Newington Press

MILLER BOOKS
2908 W. Valley Blvd., Alhambra, CA 91803
818-284-7607
Pub: Joseph Miller

Publications: Textbooks, workbooks, library editions, professional books for teachers
Audience: K-12, adult
Subjects: Social studies, career development, language arts, music, poetry
Special interest: Reading disabled, mentally disabled
Services: Catalog. Exhibit at IRA, AECT

Minstrel Paperbacks, *see* **POCKET BOOKS**

Mirasol Libros Juveniles, *see* **FARRAR, STRAUS & GIROUX**

MODAN/ADAMA BOOKS
Box 1202, Bellmore, NY 11710-0485
516-679-1380
Pres: Oded Modan
Managing Ed: Bennett Shelkowitz

Publications: Trade books
Audience: Preschool-12, adult
Subjects: Encyclopedias, politics, animals, foreign countries & languages, art, picture books, biographies, religion, dictionaries, social studies
Special interest: Judaica, books from Israel
Discount: 1, 25%; 2-24,40%; 25-50, 43%; 50-99, 46%; 100 & more, 50%
Services: Catalog. Exhibit occasionally

MODERN CURRICULUM PRESS
Imprint of Paramount Publishing, Elementary Division
13900 Prospect Rd., Cleveland, OH 44136
216-238-2222
VP, Pub: Celia Argiriou
Dir, Product Mktg: Barbara Kittrick-Masterson
Sr Product Man: Christine McArtor

Publications: Original stories, big books, workbooks, activity sets, teacher's guides

Audience: K-6
Subjects: Language arts, mathematics, sciences, social studies, bilingual, ESL
Discount: Inquire
Services: Catalog. Exhibit at IRA, NABSE, NCEA, NCSS, NSTA, NABE

MONTANA COUNCIL FOR INDIAN EDUCATION
517 Rimrock Rd., Box 31215, Billings, MT 59107
Ed: Hap Gilliland
Lib/Sch Prom Dir: Liz Degel

Publications: Paperback originals, professional books for teachers, testing materials. Multimedia kits
Audience: K-12, adult
Subjects: Culture, history, animals, art, biographies, fiction
Special interest: Native Americans, bilingual students, reading disabled
Discount: 2-9 copies, 30%; 10 or more, 40%
Services: Catalog. Exhibit at IRA

MORNING GLORY PRESS
6595 San Haroldo Way, Buena Park, CA 90620-3748
714-828-1998; Fax: 714-828-2049
Pres: Jeanne Warren Lindsay
Mktg Dir & Lib/Sch Prom Dir: Carole L. Blum

Publications: Textbooks, library editions, paperback originals, professional books for teachers
Audience: 7-12, adult
Subjects: Family life, health, home economics, sex education, teen pregnancy & parenting
Discount: Quantity, inquire
Services: Catalog. Exhibit at ALA

MORROW JUNIOR BOOKS
Div. of William Morrow & Co.
1350 Ave. of the Americas, New York, NY 10019
212-261-6793, 800-843-9389; Fax: 212-261-6689
Contact: Lori Benton, Jazan Higgins

Publications: Trade books, library editions, paperback reprints
Imprints: Mulberry, Beech Tree, Tupelo
Audience: K-12, adult
Subjects: Dictionaries, encyclopedias
Discount: Inquire
Services: Catalog. Exhibit at ALA

Mouse Works, see PENGUIN USA

JOHN MUIR PUBLICATIONS
Box 613, Santa Fe, NM 87504
505-982-4078, 800-888-7504; Fax: 505-988-1680
Pres: Steven Cary
Mktg Mgr: Karen L. Moye

Publications: Trade books
Audience: Juvenile, adult
Subjects: Travel

Mulberry, see MORROW JUNIOR BOOKS

Mysterious Press, see WARNER BOOKS

NATIONAL BRAILLE PRESS INC.
88 St. Stephen St., Boston, MA 02115
617-266-6160; Fax: 617-437-0456
Mng Dir: William M. Raeder
Children's Ed & Mktg Dir: Diane L. Croft

Publications: Library editions, paperback originals & reprints, computer books, professional books for teachers
Audience: Preschool-5, 9-12, adult
Subjects: Family life, career development, fiction, computer software, home economics, consumer education, picture books, crafts
Special interest: Blind
Discount: Inquire
Services: Catalog. Promotional newsletter

NATIONAL COUNCIL OF TEACHERS OF ENGLISH
1111 W. Kenyon Rd., Urbana, IL 61801-1096
217-328-3870, 800-369-6283; Fax: 217-328-9645
Pres: Hanie Hydrick
Children's Ed: William Teale
Mktg Dir: Kent Williamson

Publications: Professional books for teachers & school administrators at the elementary, secondary & college levels
Audience: Adult
Subjects: Whole language/integrating the language arts, literature, reading, writing
Special interest: Multiculturalism, literacy, nonsexist education, bilingual students
Discount: Inquire
Services: Annual catalog. Exhibit at NCTE, IRA, ASCD

NATIONAL GEOGRAPHIC SOCIETY
1145 17th St. NW, Washington, DC 20036
202-857-7000, 800-638-4077; Fax: 202-775-6141
Ed: William Graves

Publications: Trade books, magazines
Audience: Juvenile, adult

NATIONAL TEXTBOOK COMPANY
4255 W. Touhy Ave., Lincolnwood, IL 60646

708-679-5500, 800-323-4900; Fax: 708-679-2494
VP Edit: Dick Smith

Publications: Trade books, reference books, foreign language materials for teachers
Imprints: Passport, VGM Career Horizons
Audience: Young adult, adult
Subjects: College guides, employment guides, general reference works

NEAL-SCHUMAN PUBLISHERS
100 Varick St., New York, NY 10013
212-925-8650; Fax: 212-219-8916
Pres: Patricia Glass Schuman
Dir, Acq & Devt: Charles Harmon
Cons Ed: Virginia H. Mathews

Publications: Professional books for educators & librarians
Audience: Adult
Subjects: Children's & young adult literature, curriculum support, annotated bibliographies, reference books, library science, multicultural resources
Discount: Inquire
Services: Catalog. Exhibit at ALA, PLA, AASL

NEW DAY PRESS
Karamu House, 2355 E. 89th St., Cleveland, OH 44106
216-795-7070

Special interest: African American literature

THE NEW ENGLAND PRESS, INC.
Box 575, Shelburne, VT 05482
802-863-2520; Fax: 802-863-1510
Pres: Alfred Rosa
Managing Ed: Mark Wanner
Mrkg: David Kissner

Publications: Trade books, paperback originals & reprints
Audience: 6-12, adult
Subjects: Animals, biographies, Vermontiana, New England, nonfiction
Discount: Libraries, 10%
Services: Catalog. Exhibit at NEBA, regional library conferences

NEW READERS PRESS
Div. of Laubach Literacy International
1320 Jamesville Ave., Box 131, Syracuse, NY 13210
315-422-9121, 800-448-8878; Fax: 315-422-6369
Exec Dir: Dennis Cook
Ed Dir: Marianne Ralbovsky
Mktg Dir: Christine Martire

Publications: Textbooks, workbooks, student supplements, paperback originals, audio, video, software,

teachers resources, weekly
newspaper, *News for You*
Audience: 7-12, adult
Subjects: Reading, writing, mathematics, spelling, workplace literacy, family literacy, life skills, ESL, staff
development
Special interest: Adult literacy, ESL
Services: Catalog. Exhibit at ALA, IRA

NEW SEED PRESS
Box 9488, Berkeley, CA 94709-0488
510-540-7576
Orders: Bookpeople or The Crossing
Press, Children's Small Press Col-
lection
Pres: Jan Faulkner
Children's Ed: Helen Chetin

Publications: Paperback originals
Audience: K-12, adult
Subjects: History, environment & ener-
gy, family life, fiction, foreign lan-
guages
Special interest: Nonracist, Chinese,
Native Americans, Spanish speaking,
Visit Turkish Family
Discount: Bookstores, 40%; distribu-
tors, 55%
Services: Catalog

THE NEW YORK PUBLIC LIBRARY
Office of Children's Services
454 Fifth Ave., New York, NY
10016-0122
212-340-0903; Fax: 212-340-3988
Coord of Children's Servs: Julie
Cummins

Publications: Bibliographies
Audience: Preschool-6
Subjects: Auditory & visual, bibli-
ographies on children's books
Special interest: Black Americans,
Japanese Americans, Spanish-
speaking, bilingual students, blind,
reading disabled

NORTH-SOUTH BOOKS
Affil. of Nord-Sud Verlag AG
1133 Broadway, Ste. 1016, New York,
NY 10010
212-463-9736, 800-282-8257; Fax:
212-633-1004
Mktg Dir: Kathleen Fogarty

Publications: Trade books
Audience: Juvenile
Subjects: Picture books
Services: Exhibit at ALA

NORTHLAND PUBLISHING CO.
Box 1389, Flagstaff, AZ 86002
602-774-5251, 800-346-3257; Fax:
602-774-0592
Ed: Erin Murphy

Publications: Trade books & gift items
Audience: Juvenile, adult

Subjects: Picture books, art & history
of the American west, Indian art &
culture

ODDO PUBLISHING
Storybook Acres, Box 68, Fayetteville,
GA 30214
404-461-7627
Pres: Genevieve Oddo
Children's Ed: Alvin M. Westcott
Mktg Dir & Lib/Sch Prom Dir: Charles
W. Oddo

Publications: Workbooks, trade books,
library editions, paperback originals.
Audiorecords/cassettes
Audience: Preschool-12, adult
Subjects: Language arts, animals,
mathematics, biographies, safety,
fiction, sciences, foreign languages,
social studies
Special interest: Reading disabled,
mentally disabled
Discount: Inquire
Services: Catalog

One Horn Press, *see* **WINSTON-DEREK
PUBLISHERS**

ORBIS BOOKS
Div. of Maryknoll Fathers & Brothers
Box 308 (Walsh Bldg), Maryknoll, NY
10545
914-941-7590, 800-258-5835; Fax:
914-941-7005
Exec Dir: Robert Gormley
Mktg Mgr: Bernadette Price

Publications: Trade books, paperback
originals. Audiorecords/cassettes,
films, videotapes/cassettes
Audience: Adult
Subjects: Religion
Special interest: Peace & justice
Discount: 25-46%
Services: Catalog.

ORCHARD BOOKS
Subs. of Grolier Inc.
95 Madison Ave., New York, NY 10016
212-951-2600, 800-433-3411; Fax:
212-213-6435
Contact: Neal Porter, Tom Sand,
Richard Jackson, Melanie Kroupa,
Anne Mao, Amy Parsons

Publications: Trade books, paperback
Audience: Preschool-12
Subjects: Quality picture books, board
books, pop-up books, fiction & non-
fiction, photo-essay & poetry
Services: Catalog. Exhibit at ALA

THE ORYX PRESS
4041 N. Central Ave., Ste. 700, Phoenix, AZ 85012-3397
602-265-2651, 800-279-6799; Fax:
800-279-4663
Pres: Phyllis B. Steckler

Mang Ed: Susan G. Slesinger
Mktg Dir: Natalie S. Lang
Sr Pub: Diane Wiesen-Todd

Publications: Professional books for
teachers & librarians. Computer
software
Audience: Adult
Subjects: Art, drama, reading,
literature-based education, storytelling, higher education series
(American Council on Education),
business, minorities, women's issues, health & nutrition, science &
technology
Special interest: Handicapped, scientific writing, grants & funding, multicultural subjects
Discount: Inquire
Services: Catalog. Exhibit at ALA, IRA,
NCTE, PLA

OUTDOOR EMPIRE PUBLISHING, INC.
511 Eastlake Ave., Seattle, WA
98109
206-624-3845; Fax: 206-340-9816
Pres: Bill Farden
Ed-in-Chief and Children's Ed: Fay Ain-
sworth
Mktg Dir: Terry McCormick

Publications: Workbooks, professional
books for teachers & school ad-
ministrators. Videotapes/cassettes
Audience: Preschool-12, adult
Subjects: Animals, environment &
energy, safety
Special interest: Bilingual students
Services: Promotional newsletter.
Flyers, price sheets. Exhibit at Safety
Council conventions

THE OVERLOOK PRESS
149 Wooster St., 4th fl., New York, NY
10012
212-477-7162; Fax: 212-477-7525
Dist. by Penguin USA, 375 Hudson St.,
New York, NY 10014-3657
212-366-2000, 800-526-0275
Edit Dir: Tracy Carns

Publications: Trade books
Audience: 4-12, adult
Subjects: Crafts, family life, picture
books, animals, dictionaries, fiction,
poetry, art, drama, hobbies, safety,
auditory & visual, encyclopedias,
music, sex education, business, environment & energy, physical education, sports
Discount: Inquire
Services: Catalog. Exhibit at ABA

RICHARD C. OWEN PUBLISHERS INC.
Box 585, Katonah, NY 10536
914-232-3903, 800-336-5588; Fax:
914-232-3977
Pub: Richard C. Owen
Mktg Dir: John Tugman

Publications: Professional reading for teachers
Audience: Adult
Subjects: Education, language arts

Owlet Paperbacks, see **HENRY HOLT & CO., INC.**

OXFORD UNIVERSITY PRESS
Children's Books Department
200 Madison Ave., New York, NY 10016
212-679-7300, ext. 7130, 800-451-7556; Fax: 212-725-2972
Pres: Edward Barry
Mktg Mgr: Annie Stafford

Publications: Workbooks, trade books, library editions, paperback originals & reprints, professional books for teachers & librarians, reference books for parents. Videocassettes
Audience: K-12, adult
Subjects: Hobbies, animals, music, art, picture books, drama, poetry, fiction, sciences
Discount: Libraries, 20%
Services: Catalog. Promotional newsletter. Brochures & pamphlets. Exhibit at ALA, ABA. Dist for: Methuen, UK

PACIFIC BOOKS PUBLISHERS
Box 558, Palo Alto, CA 94302-0558
415-965-1980; Fax: 415-965-0776
Pres & Ed-in-Chief: Henry Ponleithner

Publications: Textbooks, workbooks, trade books, paperback originals & reprints, professional books for teachers & school administrators
Audience: K-12, adult
Subjects: Language arts, social studies, biographies, mathematics, business, music, crafts, poetry, family life, sciences
Discount: Libraries, 10%; schools, text discounts
Services: Catalog. Exhibit at ALA

PARENT CHILD PRESS
Box 675, Hollidaysburg, PA 16648-0675
814-696-7512; Fax: 814-696-7510
Pres: Aline D. Wolf
Mktg Dir & Lib/Sch Prom Dir: Peggy Curran

Publications: Children's books & parent/teacher art manual
Audience: K-6
Subjects: Art, family life
Services: Catalog. Promotional newsletter

PARENTING PRESS, INC.
11065 Fifth Ave. NE, No F, Seattle, WA 98125
206-364-2900, 800-992-6657; Fax:

206-364-0702
Pres: Elizabeth Crary
Ed-in-Chief: Carolyn Threadgill
Mktg Dir: Jill Bell
Prom Dir: Ann Merrihew

Publications: Library editions, paperback originals
Audience: Preschool-5
Subjects: Social skills, parenting, biographies, family life, health, safety
Special interest: Nonsexist education
Discount: 2-4, 20%; 5-24, 40%; 25-99, 42%; 100-249, 44%; 250 & more, 45%
Services: Catalog. Exhibit at ABA. Dist for: Chas Franklin Press

PARKWEST PUBLICATIONS, INC.
452 Communipaw Ave., Jersey City, NJ 07304
201-432-3257; Fax: 201-432-3257
Mktg Dir: Brian Squire

Publications: Tarquin Educational Activity Books, Taplinger calligraphy
Audience: 4-12, adults
Subjects: Math, science, social studies, calligraphy
Discount: Schools, 20%
Services: Catalog. Exhibit at ALA. Importer for Taplinger (English)

PEACHTREE PUBLISHERS LTD.
494 Armour Circle NE, Atlanta, GA 30324-4088
404-876-8761, 800-241-0113; Fax: 404-875-2578
Pub: Margaret M. Quinlin

Publications: Trade books
Audience: Juvenile, adult
Subjects: Fiction, nonfiction, humor

PEBBLE BEACH PRESS, LTD.
Box 1171, Pebble Beach, CA 93953
408-372-5559; Fax: 408-375-4525
Contact: Chris Wojciechowska

Publicatons: Trade books, library editions, paperback originals
Audience: 4-12
Subjects: Fiction & nonfiction
Special interest: Newberry award winners (Dream series), sports, hobbies, self-awareness
Discount: Inquire
Services: Catalog. Exhibit at ALA, ABA, others

PELICAN PUBLISHING COMPANY
Box 3110, Gretna, LA 70054
504-368-1175, 800-843-1724; Fax: 504-368-1195
Pub: Milburn Calhoun
Ed: Nina Kooij
Mktg Dir: Kathleen Calhoun

Publications: Textbooks, workbooks, trade books
Audience: K-12, adult
Subjects: Picture books, poetry
Special interest: Spanish-speaking
Discount: Libraries, 20%
Services: Exhibit at ALA, NCTE, TLA, LLA, FLA, IRA

PENGUIN USA
375 Hudson St., New York, NY 10014-3657
212-366-2000, 800-331-4624
Pres: Marvin Brown
Mktg Dir: Dan Farley

Imprints: Dial, Mouse Works, Puffin, Frederick Warne
Audience: 9-12, adult
Subjects: Picture books, business, sex education, dance, family life, home economics, animals, poetry, career development, social studies, dictionaries, fiction, language arts, art, religion, computer software, sports, drama, foreign countries & languages, mathematics, auditory & visual, safety, consumer education, vocational training, encyclopedia, health, music, biographies, sciences, crafts, environment & energy, hobbies, physical education
Discount: Inquire
Services: Catalog. Exhibit at ALA, IRA, AECT, NCTE, state & regional library & educational conferences

PETER PAN INDUSTRIES
88 St. Francis St., Newark, NJ 07105
201-344-4214
Pres: Donald Kasen

Publications: Book & audiocassette packages. Videotapes/cassettes, CD's
Audience: K-12
Subjects: Read alongs, basic learning, social skills
Services: Catalog

PFEIFER-HAMILTON
Whole Person Associates Inc.
210 W. Michigan St., Duluth, MN 55802-1908
218-727-0500, 800-247-6789; Fax: 218-727-0505
Mktg Assoc: Patricia De Lano

Publications: Trade books
Audience: Juvenile, adult

S. G. PHILLIPS, INC.
Box 83, Chatham, NY 12037
518-392-3068
Ed: Sidney Phillips

Publications: Trade books
Audience: Children & young adult fiction & nonfiction

Subjects: Social studies, anthropology, science, arts
Services: Catalog. Promotional newsletters

Philomel Books, see **THE PUTNAM BERKELEY GROUP, INC.**

PICTURE BOOK STUDIO
10 Central St., Saxonville, MA 011701
508-788-0911; Fax: 508-788-0919
Ordering: 200 Old Tappan Rd., Old Tappan, NJ 07675, 800-223-2336

Publications: Trade books
Imprints: Pixie Books, Rabbit Ears Books
Audience: K-6
Subjects: Picture books, fiction
Discount: Inquire
Services: Catalog. Dist by Simon & Schuster Inc. Exhibit at ALA, ABA, NEBA, MSA, NSS

Picture Yearling, see **BANTAM DOUBLEDAY DELL BOOKS FOR YOUNG READERS**

PINEAPPLE PRESS, INC.
Drawer 16008, Southside Sta., Sarasota, FL 34239
813-952-1085
Pres: David Cussen
Ed-in-Chief: June Cussen

Publications: Trade books
Audience: 10-12, adult
Subjects: Fiction, nonfiction, science, nature, history, literature
Special interest: Florida
Services: Catalog. Exhibit at ABA, ALA

PJD LEARNING MATERIALS
5080 Timberway Trail, Clarkston, MI 48346
313-620-2736
Pres: Phyllis Childs

Publications: Workbooks, parents' manual
Audience: Preschool-K, adult
Subjects: Language arts
Special interest: Mentally disabled, developmentally delayed
Discount: Inquire
Services: Promotional newsletter

PLANETARY PUBLICATIONS
(formerly Univ. of the Trees Press)
Box 66, Boulder Creek, CA 95006
408-338-2161
Orders: The Borgo Press, Box 2845, San Bernardino, CA 92406-2845; 909-884-5813; Fax: 909-888-4942
VP Sales & Mktg: Kathy White
Mktg Dir: Euphrasia Carroll

Publications: Paperback originals, professional books for teachers

& parents. Audiorecords/cassettes
Audience: K-12, adult
Subjects: Family life, philosophy, conflict resolution, whole-brain learning, yoga, auditory & visual, health, biographies, music, business, sciences, environment & energy, social studies
Special interest: New Age materials
Discount: Inquire
Services: Catalog

Platt & Munk, see **THE PUTNAM BERKELEY GROUP, INC.**

PLAYERS PRESS, INC.
Box 1132, Studio City, CA 91604
818-789-4980
Pres: William-Alan Landes
Ed-in-Chief: Robert W. Gordon
Children's Ed: Marjorie E. Clapper
Mktg Dir: David Cole, Joseph W. Witt
Lib/Sch Prom Dir: Sharon Hoffman

Publications: Trade books, paperback originals, professional books for teachers. Audiorecords/cassettes, films, videotapes/cassettes
Audience: Adult
Subjects: Theater, musicals, film, entertainment industry, dance, drama, music, costumes, puppets
Discount: Inquire
Services: Catalog

PLAYMORE INC., PUBLISHERS
200 Fifth Ave., New York, NY 10010
212-924-7447; Fax: 212-463-7719
Pres: Jon Horwich

Publications: Workbooks, illustrated children's classics, trade books, paperback reprints, activity books
Audience: 4-8, adult
Subjects: Fiction, animals, mathematics, biographies, picture books, crafts, dictionaries
Special interest: Reading disabled
Discount: Inquire
Services: Catalog

PLAYS, INC.
120 Boylston St., Boston, MA 02116-4615
617-423-3157
Pres: Sylvia K. Burack
Mang Ed: Elizabeth Preston
Mktg Dir & Lib/Sch Prom Dir: Ann-Margaret Caljouw

Publications: Textbooks, paperback originals & reprints, professional books for teachers, collections of one-act plays for young people
Audience: 3-12, adult
Subjects: Language arts, crafts, dance, costumes, puppetry, drama, holiday programs

Special interest: Reading disabled, handicapped
Discount: Public libraries, 20%; bookstores, inquire
Services: Catalog. Exhibit at ALA, NCTE through Publishers Book Exhibit

PLEASANT COMPANY PUBLICATONS, INC.
8400 Fairway Pl., Middleton, WI 53562
608-836-4848, 800-233-0264; Fax: 608-836-1999
Orders: Box 620991, Middleton, WI 53562
Contact: Tamara England, Johanna Bierwirth

Special interest: American Girls Collection books & related products

POCKET BOOKS
Subs. of Simon & Schuster
1230 Ave. of the Americas, New York, NY 10020
212-698-7000
Orders: 200 Old Tappan Rd., Old Tappan, NJ 07675
800-223-2336
Lib/Sch Mktg Mgr: Ilese Levine

Publications: Trade paperbacks
Imprints: Archway, Minstrel
Audience: 6-12, adult
Subject: Fiction & nonfiction
Discount: Inquire
Services: Catalog. Exhibit at ALA, IRA, NCTE, ABA

PORTER SARGENT PUBLISHERS
11 Beacon St., Boston, MA 02108
617-523-1670; Fax: 617-523-1021
Pres: J. K. Sargent
VP: Jennie B. Fonzo
Mktg Dir: Heather Lane

Publications: Trade books, professional books for librarians & school administrators, counselors, educational reference for parents
Audience: Adult
Subjects: Directories of schools, camps, summer academic programs & facilities for disabled children
Discount: For retailers, inquire
Services: Catalog. Exhibit at ALA

Post Oak Press, see **LARKSDALE**

PRAKKEN PUBLICATIONS
Box 8623, Ann Arbor, MI 48107-8623
313-769-1211, 800-530-9673; Fax: 313-769-8383
Ed: George F. Kennedy
Mktg Dir: Deidree A. Devlin

Publications: Textbooks, professional books for teachers & school administrators

Audience: 9-12, adult
Subjects: Career development, language arts, vocational training
Discount: 20%
Services: Exhibit at AASA, AVA, ITEA

Price/Stern/Sloan Publishers, see **THE PUTNAM BERKELY GROUP INC.**

Puffin Books, see **PENGUIN USA**

PUSSYWILLOW PUBLISHING HOUSE
Box 1806, Gilbert, AZ 85234
602-892-1316
Dist. by Many Feathers, 5738 N. Central, Phoenix, AZ; Gem Guides, CA; Baker & Taylor
Pres & Ed-in-Chief: Ann Trombetta
Children's Ed: Mary Ellen Hawkins
Mktg Dir & Lib/Sch Prom Dir: Teresa Trombetta

Publications: Library editions, paperback originals
Audience: Preschool-4
Subjects: Picture books, self-help
Special interest: Nonsexist education
Discount: Inquire
Services: Promotional Newsletter. Exhibit at ALA, ABA

THE PUTNAM BERKELY GROUP INC.
200 Madison Ave., New York, NY 10016
212-951-8400, 800-631-8571; Fax: 212-532-3693
Pres: Margaret Frith
Dir, Institutional Mktg: Nanette Knaster

Publications: Trade books, library editions, paperback originals
Imprints: G. P. Putnam's Sons, Coward-McCann, Grosset & Dunlap, Philomel Books, Platt & Munk, Price/Stern/Sloan
Audience: Preschool-12
Subjects: Picture books, general fiction
Services: Catalog. Promotional materials. Exhibit at ALA

Questar, see **WARNER BOOKS**

Rainbow Bridge, see **TROLL ASSOCIATES**

Raintree, see **STECK-VAUGHN COMPANY**

RANDOM HOUSE
201 E. 50th St., New York, NY 10022
212-572-2600; Fax: 212-572-8700
Publ: Kate Klimo

Publications: Trade books, paperbacks, book/cassette packages, video cassettes

Imprints: Bullseye, Value, Derrydale
Audience: Preschool-12
Subjects: Fiction and nonfiction

REDBIRD PRESS INC.
Box 11441, Memphis, TN 38111
901-323-2233
Ed-in-Chief: Virginia McLean
Children's Ed: Susan Robinson
Mktg Dir & Lib/Sch Prom Dir: Lisa Snowden

Publications: Trade books, library editions
Audience: 6-12
Subjects: Foreign countries & languages, social studies
Special interest: Gifted
Discount: Schools, libraries, 20%; 25-49 copies, 25%; 50-99 copies, 30%; 100 or more, 33%
Services: Brochure. Exhibit at ALA, ABA

Redfeather, see **HENRY HOLT & CO., INC.**

NANCY RENFRO STUDIOS
Box 164226, Austin TX 78716
512-327-9588, 800-933-5512
Mgr: Lynn Irving

Publications: Paperback originals, professional books for teachers & librarians. Puppets
Audience: Preschool-8, adult
Subjects: Drama, language arts, art, crafts, dance, puppetry
Services: Catalog

REVIEW & HERALD PUBLISHING ASSOCIATION
55 W. Oak Ridge Dr., Hagerstown, MD 21740
301-791-7000, 800-234-7630; Fax: 301-791-7012
Pres: Robert Kinney
VP Ed: Raymond Woolsey
VP Mktg: Doug Sayles

Publications: Textbooks, trade books, paperback originals & reprints, professional books for ministers. Audiorecords/cassettes, filmstrips, computer software, videotapes/cassettes
Audience: K-12, adult
Subjects: Health, animals, music, biographies, picture books, family life, religion, foreign countries, social studies

RIZZOLI INTERNATIONAL PUBLICATIONS
300 Park Ave. S., New York, NY 10010
212-387-3400, 800-462-2387; Fax: 212-387-3535
Contact: Dan Tucker, Kim Harbour, Sherrie Murphy

Publications: Trade books
Audience: Children, adult
Subjects: Art, architecture, design

ROBERTS RINEHART
121 Second Ave., Niwot, CO 80544-0666
303-652-2921, 800-352-1985; Fax: 303-652-3923
Pub: Frederick Rinehart
Mktg: Shelley Daigh

Publications: Trade books. Audio books
Audience: Juvenile, adult
Subjects: Natural history

RODALE PRESS
Book Division
33 E. Minor St., Emmaus, PA 18098
215-967-5171, 800-441-7761; Fax: 215-967-3044

Publications: Textbooks, trade books, paperback originals, reference books
Audience: 3-12, adult
Subjects: Biographies, fiction, picture books, South Carolina history & culture
Discount: Libraries, schools, 10%
Services: Catalog. Promotional newsletter. Exhibit at South Carolina Association of School Librarians' conferences

Rooster, see **BANTAM DOUBLEDAY DELL BOOKS FOR YOUNG READERS**

THE ROSEN PUBLISHING GROUP
29 E. 21st St., New York, NY 10010
212-777-3017, 800-237-9932; Fax: 212-777-0277
Pres: Roger Rosen
Ed: Gina Strazzabosco

Publications: Textbooks, workbooks, library editions
Audience: 7-12
Subjects: Nonfiction books on self-help & guidance for young adults. Books for reluctant readers on self-esteem, values, & drug abuse prevention
Services: Catalog. Exhibit at ALA, AACD, PLA

ROURKE PUBLISHING GROUP
Box 3328, Vero Beach, FL 32964
407-465-4575: Fax: 407-465-3132
Contact: James Colandrea, Marilyn Brown

Publications: Trade books, library editions
Audience: Children, young adults
Subjects: Nonfiction series
Services: Exhibit at ALA

RUNNING PRESS BOOK PUBLISHERS
125 S. 22nd St., Philadelphia, PA 19103

215-567-5080, 800-345-5359; Fax:
    212-568-2919
Edit Dir: Nancy Steele

Publications: Trade hardcover & paper-
    back books
Audience: Juvenile, adult

RYMER BOOKS
22249 E. Tollhouse Rd., Clovis, CA
    93611-9761
209-298-8845
Pres, Children's Ed & Mktg Dir: Alta A.
    Rymer

Publications: Children's books/literature
Audience: 4-6
Subjects: Environmental science fiction
    for children
Special interests: Puppet patterns for
    teachers
Discount: Schools & libraries, 10%;
    dealers, 50%
Services: Catalog

ST. PAUL BOOKS & MEDIA
Div. of Daughters of St. Paul
50 St. Paul's Ave., Boston, MA 02130
617-522-8911, 800-876-4463; Fax:
    617-541-9805
Pres: Sr. Irene Mary Martineau, FSP
Ed-in-Chief: Sr. Mary Mark Wickenhiser,
    FSP
Children's Ed: Sr. Mary Anne
    Hefferman
Mktg Dir: Sr. Denise Cecilia, FSP

Publications: Paperback & hardback
    originals, religious textbooks, work-
    books, library editions. Monthly
    magazines: *My Friend* for children;
    The Family. Videos, audio & music
    cassettes, CD's, posters
Audience: Preschool-12, adult
Subjects: Value teachers, biographies,
    family life, music, spirituality, self-
    help, healing, religion

SANDLAPPER PUBLISHING, INC.
Box 730, Orangeburg, SC 29116
803-531-1658; Fax: 803-534-5223
General Mgr: Amanda Gallman

Publications: Textbooks, trade books,
    paperback originals
Audience: 3-12, adult
Subjects: Biographies, fiction, picture
    books, South Carolina history &
    culture
Discount: Libraries, schools, 10%
Services: Catalog. Promotional news-
    letter. Exhibit at South Carolina As-
    sociation of School Librarians'
    conferences

**SAN FRANCISCO STUDIES
    CENTER**
1095 Market St., Ste. 602, San
    Francisco, CA 94103

415-626-1650
Contact: Geoff Link

Publications: Trade books
Audience: K-12
Subjects: Fiction, nonfiction
Special interest: Multicultural

SANTILLANA PUBLISHING CO.
901 W. Walnut St., Compton, CA
    90220
310-763-0455, 800-245-8584; Fax:
    310-763-4440
Pres: Antonio DeMarco
Sr Ed: Mario Castro
Mktg Dir: Charles Meagher
Trade Dir: Marla Norman

Publications: Textbooks, workbooks,
    trade books, paperback originals,
    programmed learning systems.
    Audiorecords/cassettes
Audience: K-12
Subjects: Sciences, encyclopedias,
    literature in Spanish, fiction, foreign
    languages, language arts
Discount: Inquire
Services: Catalog. Exhibit at ALA, IRA,
    NABE, TESOL, CABE

SCARECROW PRESS
Sub. of Grolier
Box 4167, 52 Liberty St., Metuchen,
    NJ 08840
908-548-8600, 800-537-7107; Fax:
    908-548-5767
Ed Dir: Norman Horrocks
Mktg Dir: Amy Pratico

Publications: Textbooks, library edi-
    tions, professional books for
    teachers, librarians & school ad-
    ministrators
Electronic Programs: Librarian's Helper
    Cataloging Program, Librarian's
    Helper Online Catalog
Audience: Adult
Subjects: Art, historical dictionaries,
    drama, cinema, music, reference
    books covering all areas of the
    humanities
Discount: Bookdeals: 10%; on prepaid
    orders, 15%
Services: Catalog. Exhibit at ALA,
    others

SCHOCKEN BOOKS
Div. of Random House Inc.
201 E. 50th St., New York, NY 10022
212-572-2559, 800-638-6460; Fax:
    212-572-6030
Pres: David I. Rome
Children's Ed: Patricia Woodruff

Publications: Trade books, library edi-
    tions, paperback originals, profes-
    sional for teachers, librarians &
    school administrators
Audience: K-12, adult

Subjects: Fiction, sex education, art,
    mathematics, social studies, biogra-
    phies, picture books, crafts, religion,
    environment & energy, sciences
Discount: Inquire
Services: Catalog. Exhibit at ALA

SCHOLASTIC INC.
555 Broadway, New York, NY 10012
212-505-3000, 800-392-2179; Fax:
    212-505-3377
Orders: Box 1068, Jefferson City, MO
    65102
314-636-5271; Fax: 314-635-5881
Mkg Mgr: John Mason

Publications: Trade books, paperbacks
Imprints: Apple, Blue Ribbon, Blue Sky
    Press, Cartwheel, Little Apple,
    Mariposa, Point, Point Signature,
    Thriller
Audience: K-12
Subjects: General fiction, biography
Services: Catalog. Exhibit at ALA, IRA,
    CRA, educational conventions

SCHRODER MUSIC COMPANY
1450 Sixth St., Berkeley, CA 94710
415-524-5804
Owner: Nancy Schimmel
Mgr: Ruth Pohlman

Publications: Paperback originals.
    Audiorecords/cassettes
Audience: K-12, adult
Subjects: Music
Discount: 2-4 copies, 20%; 5 or more,
    40%

**Scientific American Books for Young
    Readers, see W. H. FREEMAN & CO.**

SCOTT, FORESMAN & CO.
1900 E. Lake Ave., Glenview, IL 60025
708-729-3000, 800-782-2665; Fax:
    708-486-3968
Pres: Kate Nyquist
Children's Ed: Tom Nieman
Mktg VP: Lesa Scott
Lib/Sch Prom Dir: Sari Factor

Publications: Textbooks, workbooks,
    computer books, professional books
    for teachers. Audiorecords/cassettes,
    filmstrips, computer software, trans-
    parencies, videotapes/cassettes,
    multimedia kits
Audience: K-12, adult
Subjects: Family life, physical
    education, social studies, auditory
    & visual, foreign countries &
    languages, poetry, driver education,
    consumer education, health, safety,
    dictionaries, language arts, sciences,
    drama, mathematics, sex
    education
Special interest: Native Americans,
    Spanish-speaking, bilingual students,
    nonsexist education

Services: Catalog. Promotional newsletter. Exhibit at IRA, NCTE, NCSS,
NABSE, NCTM, NCEA, & most national education conferences

SEAL PRESS
3131 Western Ave., Ste. 410, Seattle,
WA 98121-1028
206-283-7844; Fax: 206-285-9410
Dist. by Publisher's Group West, 4065
Hollis, Emeryville, CA 94608;
510-658-3453; Fax: 510-658-1834
Ed: Holly Morris
Mktg: Ingrid Emerick

Publications: Trade books
Subjects: Poetry & nonfiction by
women

THE SHOE STRING PRESS, INC.
925 Sherman Ave., Hamden CT 06514
203-248-6307; Fax: 203-230-9275
Publisher: Diantha C. Thorpe
Lib/Sch Prom Dir: Nancy C. McGrath

Publications: Trade books, library editions, paperback originals, professional books for teachers, librarians
& school administrators
Imprints: Library Professional Publications, Linnet Books
Audience: Preschool-12, adult
Subjects: Serious & scholarly nonfiction in humanities; professional
library literature for teachers, librarians & those who work with children;
bibliography & reference; fiction &
nonfiction for children & young
adults
Discount: Inquire
Services: Catalog. Promotional newsletter. Exhibit at ALA, AASL, MLA,
ABA

SIERRA CLUB BOOKS FOR CHILDREN
100 Bush St., San Franciscoco, CA
94101
415-291-1619; Fax: 415-291-1602
Distributed by Little, Brown & Co.,
200 West St., Waltham, MA 02254
800-759-0190
Contact: Helen Sweetland

Publications: Trade books
Audience: Children
Subjects: Picture books, fiction, non-
fiction
Special interest: Environment

**SIMON & SCHUSTER BOOKS FOR
YOUNG READERS**
Simon & Schuster, Inc.
866 Third Ave., New York, NY 10022
212-702-2000
Orders: 200 Old Tappan Rd., Old Tap-
pan, NJ 07675. 800-223-2336
Contact: Willa Perlman

Publications: Trade books, library edi-
tions, paperback reprints
Imprints: Atheneum, Macmillan, Mar-
garet K. McElderry, Little Simon,
Aladdin Paperbacks
Audience: Preschool-12
Subjects: Books in hardcover and
paperback, for children from
preschool to young teens
Discount: Inquire
Services: Catalog. Exhibit at ALA, IRA,
NCTE, ABA

SISTER VISION PRESS
Box 217, Station E, Toronto, Ontario,
M6H 4E2 Canada
416-532-2184
Contact: Makeda Silvera

Publications: Trade books
Audience: K-12
Special interest: Multicultural

Skylark, see **BANTAM DOUBLEDAY
DELL BOOKS FOR YOUNG READERS**

SMITHMARK PUBLISHERS INC.
16 E. 32nd St., New York, NY 10016
212-532-6600, 800-645-9990; Fax:
212-683-5768
Pres: Pyhilip J. Martinho

Publications: Trade books
Audience: Juvenile, adult
Subjects: Nonfiction & illustrated books

SPOKEN LANGUAGE SERVICES
Box 783, Ithaca, NY 14851-0783
607-257-0500
Pres: J. M. Cowan

Publications: Textbooks, trade books,
paperback originals & reprints,
professional books for teachers.
Audiorecords/cassettes
Audience: 8-12, adult
Subjects: Dictionaries, foreign lan-
guages
Special interest: Spanish-speaking,
bilingual students
Discount: Schools, 10%; bookstores,
20-40%
Services: Catalog

**STANDARD EDUCATIONAL
CORPORATION**
200 W. Madison St., #300, Chicago, IL
60606
312-346-7440; Fax: 312-580-7215
Pres, Mktg Dir & Lib/Sch Prom Dir:
Ken Nichol
Ed-in-Chief & Children's Ed: Douglas
W. Downey

Publications: Library editions, subscrip-
tion books, premium books
Audience: K-12, adult
Subjects: Fiction, animals, music, art,
picture books, crafts, poetry, diction-
aries, sciences
Discount: Orders to $100, 30%; over
$100, 40%
Services: Exhibit at ALA

STANDARD PUBLISHING COMPANY
8121 Hamilton Ave., Cincinnati, OH
45231
513-931-4050, 800-543-1301; Fax:
513-931-0904
Pres: Bob Dittrich
New Prod Dir: Mark Taylor
Mktg Dir: Dick LeGros

Publications: Board books for toddlers,
picture books, easy readers, devo-
tional, coloring & activity books,
classroom & learning materials,
Christian education materials
Audience: Preschool-adult
Subjects: Biblical teaching, good
values
Services: Catalog

Starfire, see **BANTAM DOUBLEDAY
DELL BOOKS FOR YOUNG READERS**

STECK-VAUGHN COMPANY
Box 26015, Austin, TX 78755
512-795-3222, 800-531-5015; Fax:
512-795-3229
Contact: Steven Korte, Walter Koss-
mann, Elaine Johnston

Publications: Textbooks, workbooks.
Computer software
Imprint: Raintree
Audience: K-12, adult
Subjects: Juvenile & young adult fic-
tion & nonfiction
Special interest: Reading disabled, ear-
ly learning, encyclopedias, science
Services: Catalog. Workshops. Exhibit
at IRA, NCTE, CEC, AAACE

STEMMER HOUSE PUBLISHERS
2627 Caves Rd., Owings Mills, MD
21117
410-363-3690; Fax: 410-363-8459
Pub, Ed, Mktg Dir & Lib/Sch Prom Dir:
Barbara Holdridge

Publications: Trade books, library editions, paperback originals. Audi-
orecords/cassettes
Audience: K-12, adult
Subjects: Family life, design,
philosophy, animals, fiction, art,
home economics, crafts, picture
books, environment & energy, social
studies
Special interest: Artists, crafts-
people
Discount: 25 or more copies, 20%
Services: Catalog. Exhibit at ALA, IRA,
NCTE

STERLING PUBLISHING CO.
387 Park Ave. S., New York, NY
  10016-8810
212-532-7160, 800-367-9692; Fax:
  212-213-2495
Pres: Burton Hobson
Children's Ed: Anne Kallem
Mktg Dir: Marty Shamus
Lib/Sch Prom Dir: Sheila Barry

Publications: Trade books, library editions, paperback originals & reprints,
  reference books. Videotapes/
  cassettes
Audience: K-12, adult
Subjects: Dance, physical education,
  vocational training, animals, health,
  picture books, military, art, hobbies,
  safety, business, home economics,
  social studies, crafts, music, sports
Discount: Schools & libraries, 20%; retail 42%
Services: Catalog. Exhibit at ALA, ABA

STEWART, TABORI & CHANG
Subs. of Brant Publications Inc.
575 Broadway, New York, NY 10012
212-941-2929, 800-722-7202; Fax:
  212-941-2982
Dist. by Workman Publishing Co.,
  675 Brighton Beach Rd., Menasha,
  WI 54952
Pub: Leslie Stoker
Mktg Dir: Margaret Orto

Publications: Trade books
Audience: Juvenile, adult
Subjects: Picture books, art books

SUCCESS PUBLISHING
Div. of Success Group
2812 Bayonne Dr., Box 30965, Palm
  Beach Gardens, FL 33420
407-626-4643, 800-330-4643; Fax:
  407-775-1693
Pres: Allan H. Smith
Children's Ed: Judith Louise
Mktg Dir: Robin Garretson

Publications: Workbooks, trade books,
  library editions, paperback originals
  & reprints
Audience: 4-12
Subjects: Family life, art, hobbies, business, career development, crafts
Discount: 12-36 copies, 50%; 36-72,
  55%; 72-108, 60%; 108-144, 70%;
  144 or more, 75%
Services: Catalog. Promotional newsletter. Exhibit at ALA

SULLIVAN ASSOCIATES
Imprint of Good Morning Teacher! Publishing Co.
819 Mitten Rd., #37, Burlingame, CA
  94010
415-697-6657
Pres: Lori Harp McGovern

Publications: Textbooks, workbooks,
  reading programs. Audiorecords/
  cassettes, computer software
Audience: Preschool-12, adult
Subjects: Picture books, foreign languages, safety, health, sciences, language arts, social studies,
  mathematics
Special interest: Spanish-speaking,
  bilingual students, reading disabled
Services: Catalog. Exhibit at IRA, ABA,
  EDSA, toy fairs

SUMMY-BIRCHARD INC.
Div. of Warner/Chappell Inc.
265 Secaucus Rd., Secaucus, NJ
  07096-2037
201-348-0700; Fax: 201-348-1782
Dir: Lynn Sengstack

Publications: Music education
  methods. Cassettes & LPs
Audience: Preschool-12, adult
Subjects: Music (Suzuki Method)
Services: Catalog

Sunburst Books, see **FARRAR,
STRAUS & GIROUX**

SUNSTONE PRESS
239 Johnson St., Box 2321, Sante Fe,
  NM 87504-2321
505-988-4418; Fax: 505-988-1025
Pres: James Clois Smith Jr.

Publications: Paperback originals
Audience: 2, 4-12, adult
Subjects: Southwestern history, biogra-
  phies, crafts, environment & energy,
  fiction
Discount: Schools, 20%
Services: Catalog. Promotional news-
  letter. Exhibit at New Mexico Library
  Assn.

SYRACUSE UNIVERSITY PRESS
1600 Jamesville Ave., Syracuse, NY
  13244-5160
315-423-2596, 800-365-8929; Fax:
  315-443-5536
Ed-in-Chief: Robert Mandell
Mktg Dir & Lib/Sch Prom Dir: Thomas
  Lavoie

Publications: Textbooks, workbooks,
  professional books for teachers &
  school administrators
Audience: 10-12, adult
Subjects: Education of learning disabled, mentally handicapped
Discount: Libraries & professionals,
  10%
Services: Catalog

TAMBOURINE BOOKS
Div. of William Morrow
1350 Ave. of the Americas, New York,
  NY 10019
212-261-6793, 800-843-9389;

Fax: 212-261-6689
Contact: Paulette Kaufmann, Jazan
  Higgins, Lori Benton

Publications: Trade books
Audience: Children
Subjects: Hardcover books for children

TAPLINGER PUBLISHING COMPANY
Box 1324, New York, NY 10185
201-432-3257; Fax: 201-432-3708
Dist. by Parkwest Publications Inc.,
  451 Communipaw Ave. Jersey City,
  NJ 07304
Pres: Louis Strick
Exec Dir: Theodore Rosenfeld

Publications: Trade books, paperback
  reprints
Audience: 10-12, adult
Subjects: Art, biographies, fiction,
  music
Special interest: Calligraphy
Discount: 20%
Services: Catalog. Exhibit at ALA

TEACHERS & WRITERS
COLLABORATIVE
5 Union Sq. W., New York, NY
  10003-3306
212-691-6590; Fax: 212-675-0171
Ed Dir: Nancy Larson Shapiro
Mktg Dir & Lib/Sch Prom Dir: Ron
  Padgett

Publications: Paperback originals,
  professional books for teachers &
  librarians
Audience: 1-12, adult
Subjects: Art, auditory & visual, dance,
  creative writing
Discount: Inquire
Services: Catalog. Exhibit at NCTE

TEACHERS COLLEGE PRESS
Teachers College, Columbia University
1234 Amsterdam Ave., New York, NY
  10027
212-678-3929; Fax: 212-678-4149
Mkt Dir & Lib/Sch Prom Dir: Mel Berk

Publications: Textbooks, trade books,
  paperback originals & reprints,
  professional books for teachers,
  librarians & school administrators,
  tests
Audience: K-12, adult
Subjects: Teacher training, art, early
  childhood, language arts, social
  studies
Discount: Inquire
Services: Catalog. Exhibit at IRA,
  NAEYC, ASCD, AERA, NCTE

TEN SPEED PRESS
Box 7123, Berkeley, CA 94707
510-559-1632, 800-841-BOOK; Fax:
  510-559-1637
Managing Ed: Nicole Geiger

Publications: Library, paperbacks, trade
books
Imprints: Tricycle Press
Audience: Preschool-6, adults
Subjects: Fiction, nonfiction
Discount: Inquire
Services: Catalog. Exhibit at ALA, ABA,
NAEYC, others

THEYTUS BOOKS, LTD.
Box 20040, Penticton, B.C., Canada
V2A 8k3
604-493-7181
Pres: Greg Young-Ing

Publications: Trade books
Audience: Children
Subjects: Fiction, nonfiction
Special interest: Native American

THIRD WORLD PRESS
Box 730, Chicago, IL 60619
312-651-0700; Fax: 312-651-7286
Pres: Haki Madhubuti

Publications: Trade books
Audience: Children, adults
Subjects: Fiction, nonfiction
Special interest: African American
literature

CHARLES C. THOMAS, PUBLISHER
2600 First St., Springfield, IL
62794-9265
217-789-8980, 800-258-8980; Fax:
217-789-9130
Adv Mgr: Michael Thomas

Publications: Textbooks, professional
books for teachers & school administrators
Audience: Adult
Subjects: Health, auditory & visual,
physical education, career development, safety, environment & energy,
sex education, family life
Special interest: Emotionally disturbed,
physically handicapped, speech disabled, blind, deaf, reading disabled,
mentally disabled
Discount: Libraries, 10%; quantity discounts, inquire

THOMASSON-GRANT PUBLISHERS
One Morton Dr., 5th Fl., Charlottesville,
VA 22903-6806
804-977-1780, 800-999-1780; Fax:
804-977-1696
Ed: Susie Shulman
Dir Mktg: Catherine Pietrow

Publications: Trade books, calendars
Audience: Juvenile, adult
Subjects: Photography, aviation, pic-
ture books
Services: Distributor for Merrybooks

THOMSON LEARNING
115 Fifth Ave., New York, NY 10003

212-979-2210, 800-880-4253; Fax:
212-979-2819

Publications: Trade books, library
editions
Audience: K-8
Subjects: Nonfiction: crafts, history,
math, art, science, geography, cultural diversity

THOR PUBLISHING COMPANY
Box 1782, Ventura, CA 93002
805-648-4560; Fax: 805-653-6359
Lib/Sch Prom Dir: Alice McGrath

Publications: Trade books, paperback
originals
Audience: 5-12, adult
Subjects: Health, physical education,
sports, self defense
Special interest: Nonsexist education
Discount: Libraries, assorted titles, 1-4
copies, 30%; 5-49, 40%; schools,
assorted titles, 10 or more, 30%

THORNDIKE PRESS
Box 159, Thorndike, ME 04986
207-948-2962, 800-223-6121; Fax:
207-948-2863
Childrens' Ed: Jamie Knoblock
Mktg Dir: Mary Kee

Publications: Large print library edi-
tions, professional books for librari-
ans. Audio books.
Audience: 7-12
Subjects: Fiction & nonfiction
Special Interest: Reading disabled,
large-print books
Discount: Inquire
Services: Catalog. Toll-free ordering.
Exhibit at ALA

TICKNOR & FIELDS
Subs. of Houghton Mifflin
215 Park Ave. S., New York, NY
10003
212-420-5800; Fax: 212-420-5850
Edit Dir: John Herman
Publicity Mgr: Irene Williams

Publications: Trade books &
paperbacks
Audience: Juvenile, adult
Subjects: Fiction & general nonfiction
Services: Exhibit at ALA

TOR BOOKS
Subs. of Tom Doherty Associates; Affil.
of St. Martin's Press
175 Fifth Ave., 14th Fl., New York, NY
10010
212-388-0100, 800-221-7945; Fax:
212-388-0191
Children's Ed: Kathleen Doherty

Publications: Trade books, mass
market & trade paperbacks
Imprints: Aerie Books, Forge Books

Audience: Juvenile, young adult, adult
Subjects: Fiction, horror, science fiction, mystery & suspense

TRAFALGAR SQUARE PUBLISHING
Box 257, North Pomfret, VT 05053
802-457-1911; Fax: 802-457-1913
Pres: Caroline Robbins
Mktg Dir: Paul Feldstein

Publications: Trade books Audience:
Juvenile, young adult, adult
Subjects: Picture books
Services: Distributor for Andersen
Press, B. T. Batsford, Canongate
Press, Hutchinson, National Trust,
Pavilion, Victor Gollancz

TRANSATLANTIC ARTS, INC.
Box 6086, Albuquerque, NM 87197
505-898-2289
Pres: Stephen Vayna

Publications: Textbooks, trade books,
paperback originals & reprints,
professional books for teachers &
librarians
Audience: K-12, adult
Subjects: Picture books, business, sex
education, dance, family life, home
economics, animals, poetry, career
development, social studies, dictionaries, fiction, language arts, art,
religion, computer software, sports,
drama, foreign countries & languages, mathematics, auditory &
visual, safety, consumer education,
vocational training, encyclopedias,
health, music, biographies, sciences,
crafts, environment & energy, hobbies, physical education
Discount: Inquire
Services: Catalog. Importer for numerous English publishers

Tricycle Press, see TEN SPEED PRESS

TRILLIUM PRESS
Box 209, Monroe, NY 10950
914-726-4444; Fax: 914-726-3824
Pres: T. M. Kemnitz
Mktg Dir: Myrna Kaye

Publications: Textbooks, workbooks,
trade books, library editions, paperback originals, computer books,
professional books for teachers &
school administrators. Audiorecords/
cassettes, computer software, transparencies, videotapes/cassettes,
multimedia kits
Audience: Preschool-12, adult
Subjects: Crafts, fiction, creativity,
leadership, futures studies, animals,
dictionaries, language arts, art, drama, mathematics, computer software, encyclopedias, music,
consumer education, environment &
energy, social studies

Special interest: Gifted children
Services: Catalog. Exhibit at IRA, NCTE, conferences on gifted children. Dist. for: KAV Books, Royal Fireworks Press

Triumph Books, see **LIGUORI PUBLICATIONS**

TROLL ASSOCIATES
100 Corporate Dr., Mahwah, NJ 07430
201-529-4000, 800-526-5289; Fax: 201-529-9347
Contact: Linda Lannon, Bonnie Brook

Publications: Trade books, library editions, paperback originals & reprints, programmed learning systems
Imprints: Bridgewater, Little Rainbow, Medallion, Rainbow Bridge, Watermill, WestWind, Whistlestop
Audience: Preschool-12
Subjects: Crafts, hobbies, social studies, animals, dictionaries, language arts, sports, biographies, environment & energy, picture books, career development, fiction, safety, computer software, foreign countries, sciences
Special interest: Native Americans, blind, deaf, Black Americans
Services: Catalog. Exhibit at ALA, IRA, AECT, NCTE

TUNDRA BOOKS
Box 1030, Plattsburgh, NY 12901
514-932-5434; Fax: 514-484-2152
Pres: May Culter

Publications: Trade books
Audience: Juvenile, adult
Subjects: Picture books

Tupelo Books, see **MORROW JUNIOR BOOKS**

CHARLES E. TUTTLE COMPANY
28 Main St., Rutland, VT 05701
802-773-8930, 802-773-8229, 800-526-2778; Fax: 802-773-6993
Ed Off: 153 Milk St., Boston, MA 07109
Pres: Peter Ackroyd
Ed-in-Chief: Kathryn Sky-Peck
Mktg Dir: Michael Kerber
Lib/Sch Prom: Desiree Zicho

Publications: Trade books, paperback originals & reprints
Audience: Preschool-12, adult
Subjects: Dance, hobbies, poetry, art, dictionaries, home economics, religion, biographies, drama, language arts, social studies, business, fiction, music, sports, crafts, foreign countries & languages (Asia), picture books, martial arts
Special interest: Bilingual students,

Asia, especially Japan, Asian art, languages & martial arts, Americana, especially New England & Hawaii, antiques, heraldry, genealogy, local history, travel guides
Discount: Trade, 1-4 copies, 40%; 5 or more, 40-50%; inquire
Services: Catalog. Exhibit at ALA, ABA

TWAYNE PUBLISHERS
866 Third Ave., New York, NY 10022
212-702-2000; Fax: 212-605-9375
Pub: Karen C. Day

Publications: Professional books for teachers & librarians
Audience: Adult
Subjects: Literature, literary criticism, author biographies

TWENTY-FIRST CENTURY BOOKS
Div. of Henry Holt, Inc.
115 W. 18th St., New York, NY 10011
212-886-9200, 800-488-5233; Fax: 212-633-0748
Pub: Jeanne Vestal
Mktg Dir: Paul Conklin

Publications: Trade books, library editions
Audience: Juvenile
Subjects: Drug & disability awareness, environment, science, social studies, biography
Services: Exhibit at ALA

TYNDALE HOUSE PUBLISHERS
336 Gundersen Dr., Wheaton, IL 60187
708-668-8300, 800-323-9400; Fax: 708-668-9092
Pres: Mark D. Taylor
Ed-in-Chief: Wendell Hawley
Mkt Dir: Dan Balow

Publications: Trade books, paperback originals & reprints. Transparencies, videotapes/cassettes
Audience: Preschool-12, adult
Subjects: Health, religious books & bibles, art, dictionaries, hobbies, biographies, encyclopedias, home economics, business, family life, picture books, career development, fiction, poetry
Discount: Quantity discount, inquire
Services: Catalog. Exhibit at CBA, NRB

UAHC PRESS
Div. of Union of American Hebrew Congregations
838 Fifth Ave., New York, NY 10021-7046
212-249-0100; Fax: 212-734-2857
Exec Dir: Stuart L. Benick
Children's Ed: Aron Hirt-Manheimer
Mktg Dir & Lib/Sch Prom Dir: Emily Wollman

Publications: Textbooks, workbooks, trade books, paperback originals, professional books for teachers & school administrators. Filmstrips, craft kits
Audience: Preschool-12, adult
Subjects: Drama, poetry, art, family life, religion, biographies, foreign countries & languages, sex education, crafts, music, social studies, dance, picture books, Bible stories, ethics, Jewish history & culture, Judaism, literature
Special interest: Bilingual students
Discount: School, 10-33%
Services: Catalog. Approval plans. Exhibit at Educators Assembly convention, Jewish conferences

UNITED STATES COMMITTEE FOR UNICEF
333 E. 38th St., New York, NY 10016
212-686-5522
Pres: Gwendolyn Calvert Baker
VP Public Affairs: Richard W. Gorman
Media Manager: Nancy Sharp-Zickerman

Publications: Trade books, professional books for teachers. Films, filmstrips, multimedia kits, games, posters, puzzles, slides
Audience: Preschool-12, adult
Subjects: Fiction, poetry, art, foreign countries, social studies, crafts, health, children's rights, cookbooks, UNICEF, drama, music, environment & energy, picture books
Services: Catalog. Promotional newsletter

UNIVERSITY OF OKLAHOMA PRESS
1005 Asp, Norman, OK 73019-0445
405-325-5111, 800-627-7377; Fax: 405-325-4000
Ed Dir: George W. Bauer
Ed: John N. Drayton
Mktg Dir: Beverly Todd
Lib/Sch Prom Dir: JoAnn Reece

Publications: Textbooks, trade books, paperback originals & reprints, professional books for teachers, librarians & school administrators
Audience: 5-12, adult
Subjects: Environment & energy, animals, foreign languages, biographies, crafts, dance
Special interest: Native Americans
Discount: Inquire
Services: Catalog, brochures. Exhibit at AAA, SAA, OAH, AIA/APA, Oklahoma & Texas library conventions, Western History, American Society for Ethnohistory & others

UNIVERSITY OF TEXAS PRESS
Box 7819, Austin, TX 78713-7819
512-471-7233; Fax: 512-320-0668

Dir: Joanna Hitchcock
Asst Dir & Exec Ed: Theresa May

Publications: Trade books
Audience: 11-12, adult
Subjects: Scholarly publications, Texas history, culture, Latin American studies, natural history, women's studies, anthropology
Services: Catalog

U.S. GOVERNMENT PRINTING OFFICE

Superintendent of Documents, Washington, DC 20402
202-783-3238
Superintendent of Documents: Wayne Kelley
Mktg Dir: Charles B. McKeown

Publications: Textbooks, workbooks, trade books, paperback originals, computer books, professional books for teachers, librarians & school administrators, subject bibliographies in elementary education, children & youth
Audience: K-12, adult
Subjects: Business, dictionaries, health, music, animals, social studies, career development, encyclopedias, hobbies, physical education, art, vocational training, computer software, environment & energy, home economics, picture books, auditory & visual, consumer education, family life, language arts, safety, biographies, crafts, foreign countries & languages, mathematics, sciences, travel
Services: Catalog. Exhibit at ALA

UTAH STATE UNIVERSITY PRESS

Logan, UT 84322-7800
801-750-1362; Fax: 801-750-1541
Ed-in-Chief: Michael Spooner
Mktg Dir: Mary Donahue
Ed: John R. Alley

Publications: Textbooks, trade books, library editions, paperback originals & reprints
Audience: 9-12, adult
Subjects: Western history, folklore
Discount: Libraries, 10%; jobbers, 20-40%; textbooks, 20%
Services: Catalog. Brochures. Exhibit at various conventions

VAN NOSTRAND REINHOLD COMPANY

115 Fifth Ave., New York, NY 10003
212-254-3232; Fax: 212-254-9499
Orders: 7625 Empire Dr., Florence, KY 41042; 606-525-6600
Pres: Brian Heer
Mktg Dir: Karen Wilner

Publicatons: Trade books, paperback originals & reprints, professional books for teachers

Audience: 1-12, adult
Subjects: Art, biographies, design, health sciences, computer science, encyclopedias, dictionaries
Discount: Inquire
Services: Catalog

VEDANTA PRESS

Vedanta Society of Southern California
1946 Vedanta Place, Hollywood, CA 90068
213-465-7114; Fax: 213-465-9568
Mktg Dir & Lib/Sch Prom Dir: R. Adjemica

Publications: Trade books, paperback originals
Audience: 2-12, adult
Subjects: Biographies, religion, folktales, philosophy
Services: Catalog. Exhibit at ABA

VIKING CHILDREN'S BOOKS

Div. of Penguin USA
375 Hudson St., New York, NY 10014
212-366-10014
Contact: Regina Hayes, Maureen Gordon, Mimi Kayden, Elena Rockman

Publications: Trade books
Audience: Preschool-12
Subjects: Picture books, business, sex education, dance, family life, home economics, animals, poetry, career development, social studies, dictionaries, fiction, language arts, art, religion, computer software, sports, drama, foreign countries & languages, mathematics, auditory & visual, safety, consumer education, vocational training, encyclopedias, health, music, biographies, sciences, crafts, environment & energy, hobbies, physical education

VOLCANO PRESS

Box 270, Volcano, CA 95689
209-296-3445; Fax: 209-296-4515
Pub: Ruth Gottstein
Business Mgr: Ann Sharkey

Publications: Trade books, paperback originals
Audience: All ages
Subjects: Domestic violence, women's health, children's titles
Special interest: Multicultural children's books
Services: Catalog. Exhibit at ALA, ABA, APA. Dist for: Down There/Yes Press, Planned Parenthood of Central California

Voyager Books, see HARCOURT BRACE & COMPANY

VSE PUBLISHER

212 S. Dexter St., Denver, CO 80222-1055

303-322-7450
Pres: Vivian Sheldon Epstein

Publications: Trade books, library editions, paperback originals
Audience: Preschool-9
Subjects: Art, social studies, science
Special interest: Nonsexist education
Discount: Retail, 33%
Services: Promotional newsletter

J. WESTON WALCH, PUBLISHER

Box 658, Portland, ME 04104-0658
207-772-2846, 800-341-6094; Fax: 207-772-3105
Pres: Suzanne S. Austin
Ed: Richard S. Kimball
Mktg Dir: M. F. Harmon

Publications: Workbooks, professional books for teachers, supplemental teaching aids, posters, spirit duplicating & photocopy masters. Audiorecords/cassettes, filmstrips, computer software, transparencies, multimedia kits
Subjects: Consumer education, foreign languages, music, sex education, art, crafts, health, physical education, social studies, business, drama, home economics, poetry, sports, career development, environment & energy, language arts, safety, vocational training, computer software, family life, mathematics, sciences
Services: Catalog. Exhibit at NCTE, NCTM, NSSEA, EDSA & other teacher conventions

WALKER & CO.

435 Hudson St., New York, NY 10014
212-727-8300, 800-AT-WALKER
Pres: Ramsey Walker
Pub: George Gibson
Children's Ed: Emily Easten
Mktg Mgr: Cheryl Peremes

Publications: Trade books, library editions, professional books for teachers
Audience: Preschool-12, adult
Subjects: Environment & energy, picture books, social studies, animals, family life, poetry, sports, art, fiction, religion, vocational training, biographies, health, sciences, career development, mathematics, sex education
Discount: Inquire
Services: Catalog. Promotional newsletter. Exhibit at ALA, IRA AASL

WARD HILL PRESS

Box 04-0424, Staten Island, NY 10301-0424
718-816-9449
Contact: Loretta Dunlap, Steven Joseph

Publications: Trade books
Audience: Juvenile, adult
Subjects: Nonfiction

Frederick Warne, see **PENGUIN USA**

WARNER BOOKS
Subs. of Time, Inc.
1271 Ave. of the Americas, New York, NY 10020
212-522-7200; Fax: 212-522-7991
Distributed by Little, Brown, & Co., 200 West St., Waltham, MA 02254. 800-759-0190
Pub: Nancy Neiman

Publications: Trade books & paperbacks
Imprints: Mysterious Press, Questar
Audience: Juvenile, young adult, adult
Subjects: Fiction & nonfiction
Services: Distributor for DC Comics Graphic Novels

WATERFRONT BOOKS
85 Crescent Rd., Burlington, VT 05401-3326
802-658-7477, 800-639-6063
Pres, Ed-in-Chief & Children's Ed: Sherrill N. Musty

Publications: Textbooks, workbooks, trade books, library editions, paperback originals & reprints, professional books for teachers, librarians & school administrators. Films
Audience: K-12
Subjects: Sex education, animals, social studies, family life, mental health, psycho-social, health, safety
Discount: 5 copies or more, 20%
Services: Catalog. Exhibit at ALA

Watermill, see **TROLL ASSOCIATES**

WATSON-GUPTILL PUBLICATIONS
1515 Broadway, New York, NY 10036
212-764-7300, 800-451-1741; Fax: 212-536-5359
VP: Glenn Heffeman
Sales Mgr: Barbara Witke

Publications: Trade books, paperback originals & reprints, computer books
Imprints: Amphoto
Audience: 9-12, adult
Subjects: Music, art, photography, computer software, crafts, hobbies
Special interest: How-to-books
Discount: Inquire
Services: Catalog. Exhibit at ALA, ABA

Wave Books, see **WESTERN PUBLISHING CO., INC.**

WESTERN PUBLISHING CO., INC.
850 Third Ave., 15th Fl., New York, NY 10022

212-753-8500; Fax 212-371-1091
VP, Publ: Robin T. Warner

Publications: Trade books, mass market books
Imprints: Artists & Writers Guild, Golden Books, Goldencraft, Golden Press, Wave Books
Audience: Preschool-young middle readers
Subjects: Fiction & nonfiction picture & storybooks
Services: Exhibit at ALA, ABA, Toy Fair

WESTMINSTER PRESS/JOHN KNOX PRESS
100 Witherspoon St., Louisville, KY 40202-1396
502-569-5043, 800-523-1631; Fax: 502-569-5018
Mng Ed: Stephanie Egnotovich
Mktg Dir: Mina Grier

Publications: Textbooks, workbooks, trade books, paperback originals, professional books, for teachers, programmed learning systems, materials for congregations. Audio-records/cassettes
Audience: 6-12, adult
Subjects: Family life, biographies, religion, crafts, social studies, drama, sports, environment & energy
Discount: Libraries, clergy, professors, 20%
Services: Catalog. Exhibit at ALA, CSLA, CBA, combined book exhibits

Westwind, see **TROLL ASSOCIATES**

WHISPERING COYOTE PRESS
480 Newbury St., Ste. 104, Danvers, MA 01923
508-281-4995; Fax: 508-777-6148
Pub: Lou Alpert

Publications: Trade books
Audience: Juvenile
Subjects: Illustrated fiction, nonfiction

Whistlestop, see **TROLL ASSOCIATES**

ALBERT WHITMAN & COMPANY
6340 Oakton St., Morton Grove, IL 60053
708-581-0033, 800-255-7675; Fax: 708-581-0039
Children's Ed: Kathleen Tucker
Mktg Dir & Lib/Sch Prom Dir: Denise Ripp

Publications: Library editions
Audience: K-8
Subjects: Crafts, sciences, animals, family life, social studies, art, fiction, biographies, health, career development, picture books
Special interest: Reading disabled, Spanish-speaking, mentally disabled,

bilingual students, physically handicapped, blind, deaf
Discount: Schools/libraries, 5 or more, 25%
Services: Catalog. Exhibit at ALA, IRA

GEORGE WHITTELL MEMORIAL PRESS
3722 South Ave., Youngstown, OH 44502
216-788-1064
Ed-in-Chief: Jean M. Kelty

Publicatons: Paperback originals, professional books for teachers & librarians
Audience: K-12, adult
Subjects: Poetry, animals, myths & fairy tales, environment & energy, fiction, picture books
Discount: School & libraries, 20%
Services: Catalog

JOHN WILEY & SONS
605 Third Ave., New York, NY 10158-0012
212-850-6000, 800-CALL-WILEY; Fax: 212-850-6799
Contact: George Stanley, John Chambers, Athena Michael, Barry Champany

Publications: Reference/trade books
Audience: 9-12, adult
Subjects: Professional, scientific & technical books/journals, computers, biography, history, finance, nature, science, nonfiction

WINDSWEPT HOUSE PUBLISHERS
Mount Desert, ME 04660-0159
207-244-7149; Fax: 207-244-3369
Pres, Ed-in-Chief: Jane Weinberger
Office Mgr: Lysa Levin
Ed Asst: Kate Whitaker

Publications: Paperback originals
Audience: Preschool-12, adult
Subjects: Animals, fiction, picture books
Discount: Schools & libraries, 20%
Services: Catalog. Exhibit at ABA

WINSTON-DEREK PUBLISHERS
1722 West End Ave., Nashville, TN 37203
615-321-0535, 800-826-1888; Fax: 615-329-4824
Contact: Matalyn Rose Peebles

Publications: Trade books
Imprints: Magpie Books, One Horn Press
Audience: Juvenile, adult
Subjects: Nonficton, poetry, education, bibles

WOMEN'S ACTION ALLIANCE, SEX EQUITY IN EDUCATION PROGRAM
370 Lexington Ave., New York, NY 10017

212-532-8330
Exec Dir: Karel R. Amaranth

Publications: Computer books, professional books for teachers & school administrators
Audience: Preschool-12, adult
Subjects: Sex equity, career development, vocational training, body image
Special interest: Nonsexist education, multiracial education
Discount: Quantity
Services: Conduct workshops, teacher training, resource lists, provide information, referrals

WORD INC.
Div. of Thomas Nelson Publishing
5221 N. O'Connor Blvd., Ste. 1000, Irving, TX 75039
214-556-1900, 800-933-9673; Fax: 214-401-2344
Pub: Kip Jordan

Publications: Trade hardcovers & paperbacks, paperback reprints
Audience: Juvenile, young adult, adult
Subjects: Religion, Bible commentaries, Christian counseling

Wordsong, see **BOYDS MILLS PRESS**

WORDWARE PUBLISHING, INC.
1506 Capital Ave., Plano, TX 75074
214-423-0090, 800-229-4949; Fax: 214-881-9147
Contact: Kenni Driver

WORKMAN PUBLISHING COMPANY
708 Broadway, New York, NY 10003
212-254-5900, 800-722-7202; Fax: 212-254-8098
Pres: Peter Workman
Ed-in-Chief: Suzanne Rafer

Publications: Trade books, paperback originals, calendars. Audiorecords/ cassettes

Audience: Preschool-12, adult
Subjects: Sciences, animals, gardening, cookbooks, career development, crafts, language arts
Discount: Inquire
Services: Catalog. Exhibit at ALA & other conferences

WORLD BOOK, INC.
Subs. of The Scott Fetzer Co.
525 W. Monroe, Chicago, IL 60661
312-258-3700, 800-621-8202; Fax: 312-258-3950
Contact: Janet T. Peterson

Publications: Reference
Audience: Preschool-12, adult
Subjects: Encyclopedias, health & science year books, pre-school learning materials, dictionaries, maps
Discount: Inquire
Services: Brochures. Exhibit at ALA, Catholic Library Assn.

WRITERS & READERS PUBLISHING INC.
Box 461, Village Sta., New York, NY 10014
212-982-3158; Fax: 212-777-4924
Pres: Glenn Thompson

Publications: Trade books
Imprints: Black Butterfly Children's Books
Audience: Juvenile, adult
Subjects: African-Americans
Services: Exhibits at ALA

WRITER'S DIGEST BOOKS
Div. of F & W Publications
1507 Dana Ave., Cincinnati, OH 45207
513-531-2222, 800-289-0963; Fax: 513-531-4744
Pres: Richard Rosenthal
Sales Dir: Jennie Berliant

Publications: Trade books, paperbacks
Imprints: Betterway Books
Audience: Children, young adult, adult

Subjects: Reference & instructional books: writing, photography, poetry, graphic design
Discount: Inquire

Yearling, see **BANTAM DOUBLEDAY DELL BOOKS FOR YOUNG READERS**

Yes Press, see **DOWN THERE PRESS**

Jane Yolen Books, see **HARCOURT BRACE & COMPANY**

Young Skylark, see **BANTAM DOUBLEDAY DELL BOOKS FOR YOUNG READERS**

Young Yearling, see **BANTAM DOUBLEDAY DELL BOOKS FOR YOUNG READERS**

ZONDERVAN PUBLISHING HOUSE
Subs. of HarperCollins Publishers
5300 Patterson Ave., SE, Grand Rapids, MI 49530
616-698-6900, 800-727-3480; Fax: 616-698-3439
Pres: Bruce E. Ryskamp
Pub, Books: Scott Bolinder
Ed-in-Chief: Stan Gundry
Mktg Dir: Chris Grant

Publications: Textbooks, trade books, hardcover & paperback originals & reprints, books for teachers & administrators. Audio & video productions
Subjects: Family life, biographies, fiction, career & personal development, health, dictionaries, sex education, encyclopedias, current issues, psychology, recovery, self-help, religious books & Bibles
Discount: Inquire
Services: Catalog. Exhibit at ABA, CBA, NAE, CMI, NRB

COMPUTER SOFTWARE PRODUCERS & DISTRIBUTORS

2

The following software companies produce and/or distribute materials for or about children and young adults. This includes CD-ROM, multimedia, interactive media, and integrated library system software. Companies are designated by three codes: a *Producer* creates programs but does not distribute them, selling through jobbers, wholesalers, or distributors; a *Distributor* does not produce software but only distributes software made by other companies. A *Producer/distributor* (majority of entries) both creates and distributes programs. A classified index to software subjects is at the end of this section.

ABC-CLIO
Box 1911, Santa Barbara, CA 93117
800-422-2546; Fax: 805-685-9685
Pres: Ron Boehm
Sales Mgr: Richard Bass

Producer/Distributor
Formats: CD-ROM
Hardware: DOS
Audience: K-12, adult
Subjects: Library reference
Availability: Direct retail (mail order)
Services: Catalog, free 60 day preview

ABC NEWS INTERACTIVE
30 Technology Dr., Warren, NJ 07059
908-668-0022; 800-524-2481

Producer/Distributor
Formats: Educational software
Hardware: Macintosh, DOS
Subjects: Health, multimedia, social studies

ACADEMIC HALLMARKS, INC.
Box 998, Durango, CO 81302
800-321-9218
Pres: R. W. Brown
Sales Mgr: R. W. Sauer
Lib/Sch Prom Dir: Vicki Strait

Producer/Distributor
Formats: Educational, test item database, and authoring systems software; copyprotected
Hardware: Apple, DOS, Macintosh
Audience: 6-12, adult
Subjects: 60,000 + multiple choice & short answer criterion-referenced test questions on Literature, English, geography, American history, world history, government, law, economics, recent events, astronomy, geology, oceanography, meteorology, physics, chemistry, health, psychology, biology, botany, zoology, general math, geometry, algebra, art, music, and construction. Also, questions for academic competitions and national academic meets
Availability: Direct retail (mail order), retail stores
Discount: Inquire
Services: Catalog, promotional newsletters, preview policy

ACTIVISION
11440 San Vicente Blvd., Ste. 300, Los Angeles, CA 90049
310-207-4500, 800-477-3650
Pres: Peter Doctorow

Producer/Distributor
Formats: Educational and entertainment software
Hardware: DOS
Audience: K-12, adult
Subjects: Mathematics, social studies, English, language arts, history, science
Availability: Retail, direct retail
Services: Catalog

ACCULAB PRODUCTS GROUP
200 California Ave., Palo Alto CA 94306-1618
415-325-5898
Pres: Ken Lew

Producer/Distributor
Formats: Educational software
Hardware: Macintosh
Audience: 4-12
Subjects: Sciences, SensorNet
Availibility: Direct retail (mail order)
Services: Catalog

ADDISON-WESLEY PUBLISHING CO., INC.
One Jacob Way, Reading, MA 01867-3999
617-944-3700, 800-447-2226; Fax: 617-944-9338
Sales: Susan Hartman, Ann Lane

Producer/Distributor
Formats: Educational software
Hardward: Macintosh
Audience: K-12
Subjects: Mathematics

ADOBE SYSTEMS
1585 Charleston Rd., Box 7900, Mountain View, CA 94039-7900
415-961-4400, 800-833-6687; Fax: 415-961-3769
Sales: Lavonne Peck

Producer/Distributor
Formats: Educational software
Hardware: DOS, Macintosh
Subjects: Art, teacher aids/instructional tools

ADVANTAGE LEARNING SYSTEMS
Dept. 1100, Box 36, Wisconsin Rapids, WI 54495-0036
800-338-4204
Pres: Harry Barfoot
Sales Mgr: Scott Knickelbine

Producer/Distributor
Formats: Educational software

Hardware: Macintosh, Windows
Audience: K-12
Subjects: Reading
Availability: Direct sales
Services: Catalog, demo disk

AGENCY FOR INSTRUCTIONAL TECHNOLOGY (AIT-THE LEARNING SOURCE)

Box A, Bloomington, IN 47402
812-339-2203; Fax: 812-333-2478
Exec Dir: Dr. Michael F. Sullivan
Dir Partnerships: Michael Stickney
Dir Marketing: Ray McKelvey
Dir Sales: Suzanne Pelletier
Mgr TV Mktg: Barbara Ravellette
Mgr Prog Acquisitions: Nancy Gray

Developer & Distributor
Formats: Videocassette, videodisc, print, software
Audience: Pre-school-community college, teacher inservice, adult
Subjects: Art, early childhood, foreign language, guidance/mental health, health/safety, language arts, mathematics, science, social studies, staff development, vocational education/tech-prep
Special Interests: K-12 curriculum, vocational education, staff development
Discounts: Volume purchases, special prices for schools in states that are members of an AIT consortium project. Regional member discounts for ITV leases
Services: Catalogs, descriptive brochures, previews. Represent programs for other producers. Exhibit at AECT/InCite, AVA, state Tech-prep mtgs, Head Start, NCCA, ASCD. Sell/lease to schools, media centers, libraries, ITV/PBS stations/networks, cable systems

ALADDIN SOFTWARE

1001 Colfax St., Danville, IL 61832
217-443-4611
Pres: Ken Horlander

Producer/Distributor
Formats: Educational, game, graphic, and computer aided instruction software
Hardware: DOS, Radio Shack
Audience: K-12
Subjects: Teacher aids, computer literacy, geography, mathematics, science
Availability: Direct retail (mail order)
Services: Catalog

ALDUS

411 First Ave. S, Seattle, WA 98104
206-628-4511; Fax: 206-343-4240
Sales Mgr: Danella Birch

Producer/Distributor
Formats: Educational software

Hardware: DOS, Macintosh
Subjects: Art, teacher aids/instructional tools

AMERICAN EDUCATIONAL

7506 N. Broadway Ext., Oklahoma City, OK 73116-9016
405-840-6031, 800-222-2811; Fax: 405-848-3960
Sales Contact: Betty Barnes

Producer/Distributor
Formats: Educational software
Hardware: Apple
Subjects: Language arts, reading

APPLE COMPUTER

#1 Infinite Loop, Cupertino, CA 95014
408-996-1010, 800-800-2775

Producer/Distributor

APPLIED OPTICAL MEDIA CORP.

1450 Boot Rd., Bldg. 400, West Chester, PA 19380
215-429-3701
Pres: John Brown
Sales Mgr: Paul Dellevigne

Producer/Distributor
Formats: CD-ROM
Hardware: Windows, Macintosh
Audience: K-12
Subjects: Dinosaurs, languages, U.S. Presidents
Availability: Direct retail (mail order)
Services: Catalog

AQUARIUS PEOPLE MATERIALS, INC.

Box 128, Indian Rocks Beach, FL 33535
813-595-7890
Pres: Phil Padol

Producer/Distributor
Formats: Educational software
Hardware: Apple, DOS
Audience: Preschool-12, adult
Subjects: Language development, grammar, mathematics, history, reading, home economics, social science, industrial arts, special education
Availability: Direct retail (mail order)
Services: Catalog, preview policy, exhibit at AECT

ARIS MULTIMEDIA ENTERTAINMENT

310 Washington Blvd., Ste. 100, Marina Del Rey, CA 90292
310-821-0234, 800-228-2747; Fax: 310-821-6463
Dir Mktg: C. W. Bottorff
(503-488-4864)

Producer
Formats: CD-ROM
Hardware: Windows, Macintosh
Audience: 3-12, adults

Subjects: Science, Americana, animals, biology
Availability: Mail order
Services: Brochures. Exhibit at trade shows (COMDEX, Intermedia)

ARIZONA STATE UNIVERSITY

Technology Based Learning & Research
Box 870111, Tempe, AZ 85287-0111
602-965-4960; Fax: 602-965-8887
Dir: Gary Bitter

Producer/Distributor
Formats: CD-ROM, training/educational software
Hardware: Macintosh, DOS
Audience: K-12, adult
Subjects: Instructional media design, mathematics, teacher education
Availability: Mail order

ARS NOVA SOFTWARE

Box 637, Kirkland, WA 98083
206-889-0927, 800-445-4866; Fax: 206-889-0359
Sales Mgr: Paul Tolo

Producer/Distributor
Formats: Educational software
Hardware: Macintosh
Subjects: Music

ARTIFICIAL INTELLIGENCE RESEARCH GROUP

921 N. La Jolla Ave., Los Angeles, CA 90046
213-656-7368
Pres: Steve Grumette

Producer/Distributor
Formats: Educational, games, and teaching aid software.
Hardware: Hewlett-Packard, Rainbow, Apple II, DOS, Texas Instruments, Commodore, Monroe, Franklin, Osborne, Heath/Zenith, Radio Shack
Audience: 3-12, adult
Subjects: Computer literacy, language development, science
Availability: Direct retail (mail order), retail stores
Services: Promotional newsletters

ATTAINMENT COMPANY, INC.

Box 930160, Verona, WI 53593-0160
608-845-7880, 800-327-4269; Fax: 608-845-8040
Pres: Don Bastian
Sales Mgr: Adele Stemler

Producer/Distributor
Formats: Educational software, video
Hardware: DOS, Apple II/Macintosh
Audience: Young Adult
Subjects: People with special needs, youth at risk
Availability: Mail order
Services: Catalog; 30-day preview; exhibit at conferences

AUDIO FORUM
On-the-Green, Guilford, CT 06437
203-453-9794, 800-243-1234
Pres: Gefferey Norton

Producer/Distributor
Formats: Educational software
Hardware: DOS, Macintosh, Apple II
Audience: K-12Subjects: Foreign language instruction
Availability: Direct retail (mail order)
Services: Catalog

AURBACH & ASSOCIATES
8233 Tulane Ave., St. Louis, MO
63132-5019
314-726-5933; Fax: 314-664-1852
Dirs: Liz & Richard Aurbach

Producer/Distributor
Formats: Educational software
Hardware: Macintosh
Subjects: Teacher aids/instructional tools, testing

AUTODESK, INC.
11911 N. Creek Pkwy., Bothell, WA
98011
206-487-2233, 800-228-3601; Fax:
206-485-0021
Sales: Irene Plantenberg

Producer/Distributor
Formats: Educational software
Hardware: DOS
Subjects: Teacher aids/instructional tools, vocational education

AUTO-GRAPHICS, INC.
3201 Temple Ave., Pomona CA 91768
714-595-7204, 800-776-6939
Pres: Robert S. Cope
Sales Mgr: Douglas K. Bisch

Producer/Distributor
Formats: CD-ROM
Hardware: DOS
Audience: K-12, adult
Subjects: Library management systems and processing services
Availability: Vendor rep., RFP
Services: Product literature, consultation

AV SYSTEMS, INC.
Box 60533, Santa Barbara, CA 93160
805-569-1618
Pres: Adrian Vance

Producer/Distributor
Formats: Educational, games, graphics, and computer-aided instruction software
Hardware: Apple II
Audience: 6-12, adult
Subjects: Teacher aids, environment and energy, history, mathematics, religion, art, foreign languages, home economics, music, science, business education, geography, industrial arts, physical education, social science, computer literacy, grammar, language development, political science, special education, economics, health education, library use, reading, spelling
Availability: Direct retail (mail order)
Services: Catalog

B5 SOFTWARE CO.
1024 Bainbridge Place, Columbus, OH
43228
614-276-2752
Pres: Glenn Bardus
Sales Mgr & Lib/Sch Prom Dir: Sharon Bardus

Producer/Distributor
Formats: Educational, authoring system and computer-aided instruction software
Hardware: Apple II, DOS
Audience: K-12, adult
Subjects: Mathematics, spelling, computer literacy, music, recordkeeping, grammar, political science, history, reading, language development, special education
Availability: Mail order, retail stores
Services: Catalog

BLS TUTORSYSTEMS
5153 W. Woodmill Dr., Ste. 18, Wilmington, DE 19808
800-545-7766; Fax: 302-633-1619
Pres: A. F. Siegfried
Sales Mgr: Sharon Stanley

Producer/Distributor
Formats: Educational and computer-aided instruction software; copyprotected; backups available
Hardware: DOS, Apple II, Novell, NetBIOS, ICLAS networks
Audience: 2-12, adult
Subjects: Reading, grammar, mathematics, business education, spelling, algebra, health education, history, drivers' education
Availability: Direct retail (mail order), local dealers
Services: Catalog, preview policy, free videos showing use in high schools and middle schools; free demo disk

BAKER & TAYLOR SOFTWARE
3850 Royal Ave., Simi Valley, CA
93063
800-775-4100; Fax: 805-522-7300
Ordering Contact: Amir Pirastehfar
Pres: Jim Warburton
Sales Mgr: Bill Hartman

Distributor
Formats: Educational & entertainment software, CD-ROM
Hardware: DOS, Apple IIE, Macintosh
Audience: Preschool-12, adult
Subjects: Geography, history, literature, art, reference
Availability: Direct retail
Services: Catalog. Exhibit at conference

BANNER BLUE SOFTWARE
Box 7865, Fremont, CA 94537
510-794-6850; Fax: 510-794-9152
Pres: Kenneth Hess
Sales Mgr: Julie Rice

Producer/Distributor
Formats: Educational, home, and business software
Hardware: DOS, Apple II
Audience: K-12, adult
Subjects: Genealogy, economics, politics, management
Availability: Direct retail (mail order), retail stores
Services: Free technical phone support

BAUDVILLE
5380 52nd St., SE, Grand Rapids, MI
49508
616-698-0888, 800-728-0880; Fax:
616-698-0554
Pres: Deb Sikanas
Sales Mgr & Lib/Sch Prom Dir: Karen Westover

Producer/Distributor
Formats: Educational software
Hardware: DOS, Apple, Macintosh
Audience: PreK-12, adult
Subjects: Art, computer literacy, music
Availability: Direct retail (mail order)
Services: Catalog, exhibit at MACUL, Micro Ideas, state education conferences

BEAR AUDIO VISUAL, INC.
1602 W. Kings Hwy., San Antonio, TX
78201
210-736-1714, 800-621-2327; Fax:
210-735-5331
Pres: Anthony Lopez
Sales Mgr: Tom Boyd

Distributor
Formats: Computer software, CD-ROM, Laser Disc
Hardware: DOS, Windows, Apple II/Macintosh
Audience: K-12
Subjects: General/educational
Availability: Mail order
Services: Catalog; exhibit at conferfences

BIGFOOT PUBLISHING (GRT Corp.)
Lofand Circle, Rockwall, TX 75087
800-888-8044
Pres: Max Andreson

Producer/Distributor
Formats: Educational and entertainment software
Hardware: DOS
Audience: K-12

Subjects: Electronic coloring books, origins, prehistory
Availability: Direct retail (mail order)
Services: Price sheet

BOGAS PRODUCTIONS

751 Laurel St., Ste. 213, San Carlos, CA 94070
415-592-5129; Fax: 415-592-5196
Sales Contact: Marie A. D'Amico

Producer/Distributor
Formats: Educational software
Hardware: Macintosh
Subjects: Music

BORLAND INTERNATIONAL

1800 Green Hills Rd., Scotts Valley, CA 95066
408-431-1000, 800-331-0877; Fax: 408-438-8696

Producer/Distributor
Formats: Educational software, courseware
Hardware: DOS
Subjects: Computer literacy, instructional tools

R.R. BOWKER ELECTRONIC PUBLISHING

121 Chanlon Rd., New Providence, NJ 07974
800-521-8110
Pres: Ira Siegel

Producer/Distributor
Formats: CD-ROM
Hardware: DOS
Audience: K-12
Subjects: Library reference
Availability: Direct retail (mail order), vendor rep.
Services: Catalog

WILLIAM K. BRADFORD PUBLISHING

310 School St., Acton, MA 01720
508-263-6996, 800-421-2009; Fax: 508-263-9375
Pres: William K. Bradford

Producer/Distributor
Formats: Educational software
Hardware: Macintosh, DOS, Apple II
Audience: K-12
Subjects: Biology, reading skills, mathematics, social studies, English, language arts, history, science
Availability: Direct retail (mail order)
Services: Catalog

BRODART COMPANY

500 Arch St., Williamsport, PA 17705
800-233-8467
Pres: Joseph Largent

Distributor
Formats: CD-ROM
Hardware: DOS, Macintosh
Audience: K-12

Subjects: Library education
Availability: Direct retail (mail order)
Services: Catalog

BRODERBUND SOFTWARE, INC.

500 Redwood Blvd., Novato, CA 94948
415-382-4400, 800-521-6263; Fax: 415-382-4419
CEO: Douglas Carlston
Pres: Ed Auer
VP Sales: Rod Haden
VP Marketing: Valorie Carpenter
VP Ed Sales & Marketing: Marylyn Rosenblum
VP Publishing: Harry Wilker

Producer/Distributor
Formats: Educational, game and productivity tool software; CD-ROM
Hardware: DOS, Macintosh
Audience: All ages
Subjects: Art, language arts, mathematics, history, geography, social studies, early learning
Avaliblity: Direct retail (mail order)
Services: Catalog

BROOKS/COLE PUBLISHING CO.

511 Forest Lodge Rd., Pacific Grove, CA 93950
408-373-0728, 800-354-9706; Fax: 408-375-6414
Sales Mgr: Mary Clark

Producer/Distributor
Formats: Educational software
Hardware: Macintosh, DOS
Audience: K-12, adult
Subjects: Chemistry, mathematics, science

BUREAU OF ELECTRONIC PUBLISHING

141 New Rd., Parsippany, NJ 07054
201-808-2700, 800-828-4766
Pres: Larry Shiller
Sales Mgr: Coleen Brady

Producer/Distributor
Formats: CD-ROM
Hardware: Macintosh, DOS, Windows
Audience: 7-12, adult
Subjects: Literature, literature study guides, history
Distribution: Baker & Taylor, Navarre, Merisel, RTM

BYTES OF LEARNING

SSI 908 Niagara Falls Blvd., North Tonawanda, NY 14120-2060
416-495-9913, 800-465-6428; Fax: 416-495-9548
Sales Mgr: A. Willer

Producer/Distributor
Formats: Educational/training software
Hardware: Apple, DOS, Macintosh
Subjects: Business education

CAERE CORPORATION

100 Cooper Ct., Los Gatos, CA 95030
408-354-2743, 800-535-7226; Fax: 408-395-7000
Sales Contact: Leann Redquist

Producer/Distributor
Formats: Ocr, document management software

CALICO INC. (Computer Assisted Library Information Co.)

Box 6190, Chesterfield, MO 63017
800-367-0416
Pres and Sales Mgr: Bill Fabian

Producer
Formats: Integrated library systems software
Hardware: DOS
Audience: K-12, adult
Availability: Vendor rep., RFP
Services: Turnkey systems, catalog, consultation

C AND C SOFTWARE

5713 Kentford Circle, Wichita, KS 67220
316-683-6056
Pres: Carol L. Clark
Lib/Sch Prom Dir: Mary Hamilton

Producer/Distributor
Formats: Educational and administration software; copyprotected
Hardware: Apple II
Audience: PreK-4, 12, adult
Subjects: Language development, mathematics, special education, teacher aids
Availability: Mail order
Services: Catalog; preview policy

CASPR, INC.

635 Vaqueros Ave., Sunnyvale, CA 94086
800-852-2777
Pres: Norman Kline
Sales Mgr: Mark Plank

Producer/Distributor
Formats: Integrated library systems software; CD-ROM
Hardware: Macintosh, MS-Windows
Audience: 6-12, adult
Subjects: Library automation
Availability: Vendor rep
Services: Catalog, demo disk

CD-ROM INC.

603 Park Point Dr., Ste. 110, Golden, CO 80401
800-821-5245; Fax: 303-526-7395
Pres: Rodger S. Hutchison, Ph.D.

Distributor
Formats: CD-ROM
Hardware: DOS, Macintosh
Audience: K-12 adult

Subjects: Art and desktop publishing, books, business, economics, law, education, literature, entertainment, medical, public domain software, shareware, science and government
Availability: Direct retail (mail order)
Services: Catalog

CE SOFTWARE
1801 Industrial Circle, Box 65580, West Des Moines, IA 50265
515-221-1801, 800-523-7638; Fax: 515-221-1806
Sales: Eric Conrad

Producer/Distributor
Formats: Education software
Hardware: DOS, Macintosh
Subjects: Business education, instructional tools

CEL EDUCATION RESOURCES
655 Third Ave., New York, NY 10017
212-557-3400, 800-235-3339; Fax: 212-557-3440
Dir Sales/Mkg: Farimah Schuerman

Producer/Distributor
Format: Laserdisk, software, CD-ROM, VHS
Audience: 2-12, adult
Subjects: Social sciences, reference
Services: Catalog. Preview for schools/libraries. Exhibit at various conferences

CENTRAL POINT SOFTWARE
15220 NW Greenbrier, Beaverton, OR 97006
503-690-8090, 800-445-4208; Fax: 503-690-8083

Producer/Distributor
Formats: Utilities software programs
Hardware: DOS, Macintosh

CHANCERY SOFTWARE
4170 Still Creek Dr., Ste. 450, Burnaby, BC, Canada V5C 6C6
604-294-1233, 800-999-9931; Fax: 604-294-2225
VP, Mktg: Rondi Shouse-Rebak

Producer/Distributor
Formats: Software for educational institutions
Hardware: Macintosh, DOS
Subjects: Administration, library programs

CHARIOT SOFTWARE GROUP
3659 India St., San Diego, CA 92103
619-298-0202, 800-242-7468; Fax: 800-800-4540
Pres: George Madden
Sales Mgr: Nancy Furlong

Producer/Distributor
Formats: Educational and entertainment software

Hardware: Macintosh, DOS, Windows
Subjects: Teachers tools
Audience: K-12, adult
Availabitity: Direct retail (mail order)
Services: Catalog

CHRONICLE GUIDANCE PUBLICA-TIONS, INC.
66 Aurora St., Moravia, NY 13118
800-622-7284
Pres: Gary Fickeisen
Exec VP: Cheryl Fickeisen
Sales & Marketing Mgr: Ray Spafford

Producer/Distributor
Formats: Educational software; CD-ROM
Hardware: Apple II, DOS
Audience: 6-12, adult
Subjects: Career education and development
Availability: Direct retail (mail order)
Discount: Inquire
Services: Catalog, promotional newsletter; free 30-Day preview policy. Exhibit at ACA, AVA, ASCA, NDPC

CLARIS SOFTWARE
5201 Patrick Henry Dr., Box 526, Santa Clara, CA 95054
408-987-7000, 800-747-7483; Fax: 408-987-7563
Sales Mgr: Karen Billings

Producer/Distributor
Formats: Educational software
Hardware: Apple, DOS, Macintosh
Subjects: Computer literacy, instructional tools, multimedia, vocational education

CODA MUSIC TECHNOLOGY
6210 Bury Dr., Eden Prarie, MN 55346-1718
800-843-2066; Fax: 612-937-9760
Sales Mgr, E Div: Roger D. Williams
Sales Mgr, W Div: Tom Johnson
Marketing Asst: Peggy Wagner

Developer/distributor
Formats: Educational software; copyprotected
Hardware: Macintosh, DOS
Audience: Preschool-12, adult
Availability: Direct retail (mail order), retail and school book stores

COLUMBIA UNIVERSITY PRESS
562 W. 113th St., New York, NY 10025
212-316-7100
Pres: John D. Moore
Sales Mgr: Ursula Bollini

Producer/Distributor
Formats: CD-ROM
Hardware: DOS
Audience: 6-12
Subjects: Poetry
Availability: Phone orders, mail orders through distributor

Services: Catalog; exhibit at midwinter and main ALA meetings as well as PLA
Distribution: Updata: 310-474-5900

COMMUNICATION SKILL BUILDERS
Box 42050, Tucson, AZ 85733
602-323-7500
Pres: Ronald H. Weintraub
VP Mkt Mgr: Sandra S. Grafton

Producer/Distributor
Formats: Educational software
Hardware: Apple, DOS, Macintosh
Audience: K-12
Subjects: Special education
Availability: Direct retail (mail order)
Services: Catalog; exhibit at ASHA
Distribution: Hartley, Edmark, Mindscope, Pelican

COMP ED
18818 N. 99th Ave., Sun City, AZ 85373
800-347-4242

Producer/Distributor
Formats: Educational software
Hardware: DOS, Apple, Macintosh, Commodore
Audience: K-6
Subjects: Mathematics, reading, science, language arts, social studies, early learning
Availability: Direct retail (mail order)
Discount: School discounts
Services: Catalog; preview policy

COMPACT PUBLISHING
Box 40310, Washington, DC 20006
202-244-4770
Pres: Robert Ellis
Sales Mgr: Mike Shulman

Producer/Distributor
Formats: CD-ROM
Hardware: DOS, Windows
Subjects: Yearbook, almanacs, current events
Audience: 5-12, adult
Availabitity: Direct retail (mail order), retail
Services: Catalog, school and library editions

COMPACT DISC PRODUCTS
272 Rte. 34, Aberdeen, NJ 07747
908-290-0048
Pres: Frank Graziano

Distributor
Formats: CD-ROM
Hardware: DOS, Macintosh
Audience: K-12
Subjects: Education
Availability: Direct retail (mail order)
Services: Catalog

COMPTON'S NEWMEDIA
2320 Camino Vida Roble, Carlsbad, CA
  92009
619-929-2500; Fax: 619-929-2690
Pres: Dr. Stanley Frank
Sales Mgr: Paul Bader

Producer/Distributor
Formats: CD-ROM
Hardware: DOS
Audience: K-12, adult
Subjects: Interactive encyclopedia
Availability: Direct retail (mail order),
  retail
Services: Catalog

COMPU-TEACH
16541 Redwood Way, Redmond, WA
  98052
206-885-0517, 800-448-3224; Fax:
  206-883-9169
Sales Contact: Lynn Rushing

Producer/Distributor
Formats: Educational software
Hardware: Apple, DOS, Macintosh
Audience: K-12, adult
Subjects: Language arts

CONDUIT
The University of Iowa, Oakdale Cam-
  pus, Iowa City, IA 52242
319-335-4100, 800-365-9774; Fax:
  319-335-4077
Director: Pete Trotter
Sales Mgr & Lib/Sch Prom Dir: James
  Leaven

Producer/Distributor
Formats: Educational software;
  copyrighted
Hardware: Apple II, DOS
Audience: K-12
Subjects: Mathematics, composition,
  music, economics, political science,
  foreign languages, science, English,
  social science
Availability: Direct retail (mail order),
  retail stores
Services: Catalog; preview policy; exhibit at NCTE, NECC, ACTCL

THE CONOVER COMPANY LTD.
Box 155, Omro, WI 54963
800-933-1933
Pres: Terry Schmitz

Producer/Distributor
Formats: Educational software;
  copyrighted
Hardware: Apple II, Macintosh, DOS,
  stand alone and network-aware
  software
Audience: 7-12, adult
Subjects: Education for employment,
  workplace literacy, transition from
  school to work
Availability: Direct sales, mail order,
  dealers
Services: Catalog. Preview policy.

Exhibit at American Vocational Assn.,
CEC, AACD, ASTD

CONTINENTAL PRESS INC.
520 E. Bainbridge St., Elizabethtown,
  PA 17022
717-367-1836; 800-233-0759
Pres: Daniel H. Raffensperger
Sales Mgr: J. Robert Zuvanich

Producer/Distributor
Formats: Educational and computer-
  aided instructional software;
  copyrighted
Hardware: Apple, Macintosh, DOS
Audience: 1-9
Subjects: Special education, computer
  literacy, grammar, mathematics,
  reading
Availability: Direct retail (mail order)
Services: Catalog; preview policy; ex-
  hibit at IRA, NCTE

COREL
Box 1252, Lake Grove, NY 11755
516-689-3500, 800-245-7355; Fax:
  516-689-3549
Pres: Marcia Friedland

Producer/Distributor
Formats: Educational software
Hardware: DOS, Apple
Audience: K-12, adult
Subjects: Math & English skills, educa-
  tional games, test preparation soft-
  ware (ACT, GED, SAT, GRE),
  Logo-Apple
Availability: Retail. Mail order
Services: Catalog. Exhibit occasionally

CREATIVE PURSUITS
10433 Wilshire Blvd., Ste. 410, Los
  Angeles, CA 90024
310-446-4111
Pres: Fran Peskoff
Sales Mgr: Bev Ellman

Producer/Distributor
Formats: Educational and entertain-
  ment software
Hardware: DOS, Windows, Macintosh
Audience: Pre-K
Subjects: Art
Availability: Direct retail (mail order)
Services: Catalog

**CREATIVE MULTIMEDIA
  CORPORATION (CMC)**
514 NW 13th Ave., Ste. 400, Portland,
  OR 97209
503-241-4351
Pres: Eric Pozzo
Sales Mgr: Len Jordan

Producer
Formats: CD-ROM
Hardware: DOS, Macintosh
Audience: K-12, adult
Subjects: Language arts, medical,
  music, entertainment

Availability: Direct retail (mail order),
  retail
Services: Catalog

**CRITICAL THINKING PRESS &
  SOFTWARE**
(Formerly MidWest Publications)
Box 448, Pacific Grove, CA 93950
408-375-2455, 800-458-4849; Fax:
  408-372-3230
Pres: Michael Baker
VP: John Baker
Sales Mgr: Liz Korver

Producer/Distributor
Formats: Educational, critical thinking
  and games software; right to copy
  available
Hardware: Apple II, IBM, Macintosh
Audience: 4-12, adult
Subjects: Critical thinking, mathemat-
  ics, language arts
Availability: Direct retail (mail order)
Services: Catalog; thirty day preview

CROSS EDUCATIONAL SOFTWARE
504 E. Kentucky Ave., Ruston, LA
  71270
318-255-8921
Pres: Mark Cross

Producer/Distributor
Formats: Teaching aids, educational,
  special education, courseware,
  games, and computer-aided instruction software
Hardware: Apple II, Macintosh, DOS
Audience: 1-12, adult
Availability: Direct retail (mail order),
  retail stores

CULTURAL RESOURCES INC.
30 Iroqouis Rd., Cranford, NJ 07016
908-709-1574; Fax: 908-709-1590
Pres: Walter Reinhold
Sales Mgr: Scott Griffith

Producer/Distributor
Formats: Educational software
Hardware: Macintosh
Audience: 9-12
Subjects: Art, multimedia history of
  U.S.
Availability: Call

CURRICULUM ASSOCIATES INC.
5 Esquire Rd., North Billerica, MA
  01862-2589
617-667-8000
Pres: Frank E. Ferguson
VP Sales: Celia Goldman

Producer/Distributor
Formats: Educational software;
  copyprotected
Hardware: Apple II, DOS, Radio Shack
Audience: 2-12, adult
Subjects: Mathematics, reading, spe-
  cial education, teacher aids, techni-
  cal preparation

Availability: Direct retail (mail order)
Services: Catalog; preview policy; exhibit at IRA, NCTE, CEC, National Council for Teachers of Math

CYGNUS SOFTWARE
8002 E. Culver, Mesa, AZ 85207
602-986-5938
Pres: Wayne Williams
Sales Mgr & Lib/Sch Prom Dir: David Williams

Producer/Distributor
Formats: Educational software; copyprotected
Hardware: Apple II
Audience: 6-12, adult
Subjects: Science
Availability: Direct retail (mail order)
Services: Catalog; preview policy

DATA COMMAND INC.
Box 548, Kankakee, IL 60901
815-933-7735, 800-528-7390
Pres: Marilyn Taylor

Producer/Distributor
Formats: Educational and teaching aids software; copyprotected
Hardware: Apple II, Commodore, DOS
Audience: K-12
Subjects: Reading, composition, science, grammar, social science, mathematics, poetry, critical thinking, geography
Availability: Direct retail (mail order)
Discount: Inquire
Services: Catalog; promotional newsletters; preview policy

DATA TREK
5838 Edison Place, Carlsbad, CA 92008
800-876-5484
Pres: Scott & David Cheatham
Sales Mgr: Mark Patterson

Producer/Distributor
Formats: Integrated library systems software
Hardware: DOS, Windows
Audience: 6-12, adult
Subjects: Library automation
Availability: Vendor rep.
Services: Catalog, demo disk, retrospective conversion

E. DAVID & ASSOCIATES
22 Russett Lane, Storrs, CT 06268
203-429-1785
Pres: E. David

Producer/Distributor
Formats: Educational spreadsheet software; copyprotected
Hardware: Radio Shack, Apple II, Commodore, DOS, PET
Audience: K-12, adult
Subjects: Reading, geography, social science, grammar, special education, language development, mathematics
Availability: Direct retail (mail order)
Services: Catalog, Preview policy

DAVIDSON & ASSOC. INC.
19840 Pioneer Ave., Box 2961, Torrance, CA 90509
310-793-0600, 800-545-7677; Fax: 310-793-0601

Producer/Distributor
Formats: Educational and entertainment software
Hardware: DOS, Macintosh
Audience: K-12, adult
Subjects: Art, mathematics, social studies, English, language arts, history, science
Availabitiy: Direct retail (mail order)
Services: Catalog

DEC COMPUTING
5307 Lynnwood Dr., West Lafayette, IN 47906
317-583-2230
Pres: Dan Clark

Producer/Distributor
Formats: Educational courseware, games, and computer-aided instruction software
Hardware: Apple II, DOS, Radio Shack
Audience: 6-12, adult
Subjects: Mathematics, science, teacher aids
Availability: Direct retail (mail order), retail stores
Discount: Inquire
Services: Catalog, preview policy

DELTAPOINT
2 Harris Ct., Ste. B-1, Monterey, CA 93940
408-648-4000, 800-367-4334; Fax: 408-648-4025
Sales Contact: Jennifer Doettling

Producer/Distributor
Formats: Educational/training software
Subjects: Instructional tools

DENEBA SYSTEMS
7400 SW 87th, Miami, FL 33173
305-596-5644, 800-622-6827; Fax: 305-273-9069
Sales Contact: Mark Hall

Producer/Distributor
Formats: Educational software
Hardware: Macintosh
Subjects: Art, vocational education

DESIGN SCIENCE INC.
4028 Broadway, Long Beach, CA 90803
310-433-0685, 800-827-0685; Fax: 310-433-6969

Producer/Distributor
Formats: Educational software

Hardware: DOS, Macintosh
Subjects: Mathematics, science

DEVWARE
12520 Kirkham Ct., Ste. 1 Paway, CA 92064
619-679-2826, 800-879-0759; Fax: 619-679-2887

Producer/Distributor
Formats: Educational software
Hardware: Amiga
Subjects: Mathematics

DIDATECH SOFTWARE
4250 Dawson, Ste. 200, Burnaby, BC, Canada V5C 4B1
604-299-4435, 800-665-0667; Fax: 604-299-2428

Producer/Distributor
Subjects: Business education, problem solving, social studies

DIGITAL IMAGING ASSOCIATES
10153 York Rd., Ste. 107, Hunt Valley, MD 21030
800-989-5353
Pres: Michael Russell
Sales Mgr: Kristin Ksrukas

Producer/Distributor
Formats: Educational software
Hardware: Macintosh
Audience: Teachers
Subjects: Authoring software (hypercard)
Availility: Direct retail, vendor rep.
Services: Catalog

DIGITAL VISION
270 Bridge St., Dedham, MA 02026
617-329-5400, 800-346-0090; Fax: 617-329-6286
Sales Contact: John Pratt

Producer/Distributor
Formats: Educational software
Hardware: DOS, Macintosh
Subjects: Teacher aids/instructional tools

DISCIS KNOWLEDGE RESEARCH, INC.
90 Sheppard Ave. E., 7th Fl., Toronto, Ontario, Canada M2N 3A1
416-250-6537, 800-567-4321; Fax: 416-250-6540

Formats: CD-ROM
Hardware: Macintosh
Audience: K-12
Subjects: Reading, education
Availability: Direct retail (mail order)
Services: Catalog

WALT DISNEY COMPUTER SOFTWARE, INC.
500 S. Buena Vista St., Burbank, CA 91521
800-271-9258

Producer/Distributor
Formats: Educational and entertainment software
Hardware: DOS, Windows, Macintosh
Audience: K-12, adult
Availability: Retail
Services: Catalog

DYNACOMP, INC.
178 Phillip Rd., Webster, NY 14580
716-265-4040
Pres: F. R. Ruckdeschel
Sales Mgr: B. Rivers

Producer/Distributor
Formats: Graphics, educational, computer-aided instruction, courseware, teaching aids, authoring systems, administration, and games software
Hardware: Apple II, DOS, Commodore
Audience: K-12, adult
Subjects: Environment & energy, history, mathematics, special education, art, foreign languages, home economics, music, spelling, business education, geography, industrial arts, political science, teacher aids, computer literacy, grammar, language development, reading, economics, health education, library use, science
Availability: Direct retail (mail order), retail stores
Discount: 5 or more, 20%
Services: Catalog. Promotional newsletters
Distribution: K-12, American Micromedia, Microphys, Spectrum, Great Games, Futurecomp

DYNIX SCHOLAR
400 W. Dynix Dr., Provo, UT
    84604-5650
800-288-1145
Pres: Bernadete Razevska

Producer
Formats: Integrated library systems software
Hardware: DOS
Audience: K-12
Subjects: Library automation
Availability: Direct retail (mail order), vendor rep.
Services: Catalog

EA*KIDS
1450 Fashion Blvd., San Mateo, CA
    94404
800-245-4525

Producer/Distributor
Formats: Educational and entertainment software
Hardware: DOS, Windows
Audience: K-12, adult
Subjects: Pre-K learning skills
Availability: Retail, direct retail
Services: Teacher's edition, lab packs

EARTHWARE COMPUTER SERVICES
2386 Spring Blvd., Box 30039, Eugene, OR 97403
503-344-3383
Pres, Sales Mgr & Lib/Sch Prom Dir:
    Donna J. Goles

Producer/Distributor
Formats: Educational, courseware, authoring systems, and games software
Hardware: Apple II, DOS
Audience: 4-12, adult
Subjects: Computer literacy, science, computer science, geology, earth science
Availability: Direct retail (mail order), retail stores
Discount: Inquire
Services: Catalog, promotional newsletters, preview policy

EASTGATE SYSTEMS
Box 1307, Cambridge, MA 02238
617-924-9044, 800-562-1638; Fax:
    617-924-9051
Sales Contact: Mark Bernstein

Producer/Distributor
Formats: Educational software
Hardware: Macintosh
Subjects: Social studies

EBOOK, INC.
32970 Alvarado-Niles Rd., Ste. 704,
    Union City, CA 94587
510-429-1331; Fax: 510-429-1331
CEO: Jessee Allread
Dir Sales: Bill Davidge
Mktg: Cathy McDermott

Producer/Distributor
Formats: CD-ROM
Hardware: Macintosh, DOS
Audience: 1-12, adult
Subjects: Education, music arts series
Availability: Retail, mail order
Services: Catalog. Exhibit at Intermedia, COMDEX, Consumer Electronics Show, others

EBSCO PUBLISHING
Box 2250, Peabody, MA, 01960
800-653-2726
Natl Sales Mgr: Sam Brooks
Asst Sales Mgr: David Mangione

Producer/Distributor
Formats: CD-ROM
Hardware: DOS, Macintosh
Audience: K-12, adult
Subjects: General academic, vocational, science, health, history, music, English
Availability: Direct retail (mail order)
Services: Preview policy; money back guarantee; promotional newsletters; exhibit at AASL, ALA and other library conventions

EDCON
30 Montauk Blvd., Oakdale, NY 11769
516-567-7227
Pres: Philip Solimene
Sales Mgr: Dale Solimene

Producer/Distributor
Formats: Educational, computer-aided instruction, teaching aids software; copyprotected
Hardware: Apple II
Audience: 2-12, adult
Subjects: Reading
Availability: Direct retail (mail order)
Services: Catalog, promotional newsletters, preview policy

EDEN INTERACTIVE
1022 Natomi St., No. 2, San Francisco, CA 94103
415-241-1450
Founders: Minoo Saboori & Matthew London

Producer/Distributor
Formats: Educational and entertainment software
Hardware: Macintosh, Windows
Audience: K-12, adult
Subjects: Sports (bicycling, golf), art, history
Availability: Retail
Services: Catalog

EDMARK CORPORATION
Box 3218, Redmond, WA 98073-3218
206-556-8440, 800-426-0856; Fax:
    206-556-8998

Producer/Distributor
Formats: Educational software
Hardware: DOS, Macintosh
Audience: K-6
Subjects: Mathematics, reading skills, computer skills
Availability: Direct retail (mail order)
Services: Catalog

EDUCATIONAL ACTIVITIES INC.
1937 Grand Ave., Baldwin, NY 11510
516-223-4666, 800-645-6739; Fax:
    516-623-9282
Pres: Al Harris
Sales Mgr: Alan Stern
Lib/Sch Prom Dir: Rosalie Dow

Producer/Distributor
Formats: Educational, courseware, computer-aided instruction, and administration software; CD-ROM; copyprotected
Hardware: DOS, Apple II, Macintosh
Audience: Preschool-12, adult
Subjects: Geography, mathematics, special education, business education, grammar, music, spelling, computer literacy, history, reading, teacher aids, economics, language development, science, early child-

hood, environment & energy, library use, social science, ESL
Availability: Direct retail (mail order)
Discount: Inquire
Services: Catalog. Promotional Newsletters. Preview policy
Exhibit at AASL, ALA, AECT, NCTE

EDUCATIONAL IMAGES
Box 3456, Westside Station, Elmira, NY 14905
607-732-1090
Pres: Charles R. Beunky
Sales Mgr: Elizabeth Sill

Producer/Distributor
Formats: Educational software; CD-ROM; copyprotected
Hardware: Apple II, DOS
Audience: 5-12, adult
Subjects: Science, environment & energy, teacher aids, geography, biology, health education, career education
Availability: Direct retail (mail order)
Services: Catalog. Preview policy
Distribution: Biolearning, Microphys

EDUCATIONAL MEDIA CORP.
Box 2311, Minneapolis, MN 55421
612-781-0088
Pres & Lib/Sch Prom Dir: Don Sorenson
Sales Mgr: Earl Sorenson

Producer/Distributor
Formats: Educational and adminstration software; copyprotected
Hardware: Apple II
Audience: 8-12, adult
Subjects: Guidance, counseling
Availability: Direct retail (mail order)
Services: Catalog. Preview policy

EDUCATIONAL RESOURCES
1550 Executive Dr., Elgin, IL 60123
708-888-8300, 800-624-2926; Fax: 708-888-8499/8689
Pres: Forrest Barbieri

Distributor
Formats: Educational software, CD-ROM, laserdisc, video
Hardware: Macintosh, DOS, Apple
Subjects: General education, science, math, reading
Availability: Mail order
Services: Catalog. Exhibit at conferences

EDUCORP
7434 Trade St., San Diego, CA 92121-2410
619-536-9999, 800-843-9497; Fax: 619-536-2345
Pres: Vahe Guzel
Sales Mgr: Suzi Nawabi

Producer/Distributor
Formats: Educational software

Hardware: DOS
Audience: K-12
Subjects: Mathematics, social studies, English, language arts, history, science
Availability: Direct retail (mail order)
Services: Catalog

EDUQUEST
4111 Northside Pkwy., Atlanta, GA 30327
800-426-4338

Producer/Distributor
Formats: Educational software
Hardware: DOS
Audience: K-12
Subjects: Language arts, mathematics, science, history/social studies, multimedia
Availability: Call

EDUSOFT
Box 2304, Berkeley, CA 94702
510-548-2304, 800-338-7638; Fax: 510-548-0755
Pres: Steven Rasmussen
VP Sales: Madeleine Mulgrew

Producer/Distributor
Formats: Educational software
Hardware: Apple II, DOS
Audience: K-12, adult
Subjects: Mathematics, teacher aids
Availability: Direct retail (mail order)
Discount: Inquire
Services: Catalog, preview policy
Distribution: Major educational companies

ELECTRONIC ARTS
Box 7530, San Mateo, CA 94403
415-571-7171, 800-245-4525; Fax: 415-513-7465
Sales Contact: Holly Hartz

Producer/Distributor
Formats: Educational software
Hardware: Apple, DOS, Macintosh, Amiga
Audience: K-12, adult
Subjects: Art, music

ELECTRONIC BOOKSHELF
5276 S. Country Rd., Ste. 700, Frankfort, IN 46041
317-324-2182, 800-327-7323; Fax: 317-324-2183

Producer/Distributor
Formats: Educational software
Hardware: Apple, DOS, Macintosh
Subjects: Language arts

ELECTRONIC COURSEWARE SYSTEMS INC.
1210 Lancaster Dr., Champaign, IL 61821
217-359-7099, 800-832-4965

Pres: G. David Peters
Sales Mgr: Jodie Varner

Producer/Distributor
Formats: Educational, games, graphics, and administration software; copyprotected
Hardware: Apple II, Atari, Commodore, DOS, Macintosh
Audience: K-12, adult
Subjects: Mathematics, geography, music, grammar, science, history, spelling, language development, teacher aids
Availability: Direct retail (mail order), retail stores
Services: Catalog. Preview policy. Exhibit at MENC

EMA SOFTWARE
Box 339, Los Altos, CA 94023
415-969-4679
Pres: R. Enenstein

Producer/Distributor
Formats: Educational and administration software
Hardware: Apple II, DOS, Macintosh
Audience: 4-12, adult
Subjects: Computer literacy, mathematics, teacher aids
Availability: Direct retail (mail order), retail
Discount: Site licenses
Services: Exhibit at various educational conventions

EMC PUBLISHING
300 York Ave., St Paul, MN 55101
612-771-1555
Pres: Paul Winter
Sales Mgr: Robert O'Reilly
Lib/Sch Prom Dir: Berry Waha

Producer/Distributor
Formats: Educational software; copyprotected
Hardware: Apple II, DOS, Tandy, Macintosh
Audience: K-12
Subjects: Home economics, special education, business education, industrial arts, spelling, economics, language development, teacher aids, foreign languages, mathematics, grammar, reading
Availability: Direct retail (mail order)
Discount: Schools & libraries, 25%
Services: Catalog. Preview policy

EME CORPORATION
Box 2805, Danbury, CT 06813-2805
203-798-2050, 800-848-2050
Pres: Thomas J. McMahon

Producer/Distributor
Formats: Educational software; CD-ROM
Hardware: Apple II, DOS, Macintosh
Audience: 2-12, adult

Subjects: Mathematics, environment & energy, science, health education
Availability: Direct retail (mail order)
Services: Catalog. Preview policy. Exhibit at NSTA

ENCYCLOPEDIA BRITANNICA EDUCATIONAL CORP.
310 S. Michigan Ave., Chicago, IL 60604
312-347-7947, 800-554-9862; Fax: 312-347-7966

Formats: Video, laser-disc, CD-ROM, books
Subjects: Educational and library materials

EUREKA MICROSKILLS III
241 26th St., Box 647, Richmond, CA 94808-0647
510-235-3883
Exec Dir: M. Sumyyal Bilal
Mktg: Jerry Laureyns (Northern CA); Lea Beth Lewis (Southern CA)

Producer/Distributor
Formats: Career information and guidance software
Hardware: DOS
Audience: 7-12, adult
Subjects: Career education
Availability: Direct retail (mail order)
Discount: Inquire
Services: Promotional catalog. Newsletters. Exhibit at American Counseling Association
Distribution: EUREKA The California Career Information System

FACTS ON FILE
460 Park Ave. S, New York, NY 10016-7382
800-322-8755
Pres: Tom Conoscenti

Producer/Distributor
Formats: CD-ROM
Hardware: DOS, Macintosh
Audience: K-12, adult
Subjects: World News, Native Americans
Availability: Direct retail (mail order), retail
Services: Catalog, printed digest

FALCON SOFTWARE
Box 200, Wentworth, NH 03282
603-764-5788; Fax: 603-764-9051
Pres: Karl Oelgeschlager
Mgr Dir: Andy Covell

Producer/Distributor
Formats: Educational software, CD-ROM
Hardware: DOS, IBM, Macintosh, Apple
Audience: 10-12, adult
Subjects: Chemistry
Availability: Mail order
Services: Catalog. Exhibit at conferences

FILMS FOR THE HUMANITIES
Box 2053, Princeton, NJ 08543
609-275-1440
Mkt Coor: Lisa-Ann Zdroda

Producer/Distributor
Formats: Educational software; copyprotected
Hardware: Apple II
Audience: K-6
Subjects: Grammar, language development, reading
Availability: Direct retail (mail order)
Services: Catalog, preview policy, exhibit at ALA, AECT, NCTE

FOCUS MEDIA
485 S. Broadway, Ste. 12, Hicksville, NY 11801
516-931-2500, 800-645-8989; Fax: 516-931-2575
Sales Contacts: Judith Balian, Seth Gremetz

Producer/Distributor
Formats: Educational software
Hardware: Apple, DOS, Macintosh
Subjects: Social studies

FOLLETT SOFTWARE COMPANY
809 N. Front St., McHenry, IL 60050
815-344-8700, 800-323-3397; Fax: 815-344-8774
Pres: Charles R. Follett, Jr.
Dir of Mkt: Andrew Larson
Advertising/Product Line Mgmt: Lisa McManaman

Producer/Distributor
Formats: Integrated library systems and textbook administration software; interactive and text-based multimedia; CD-ROM
Hardware: Apple II, DOS, Macintosh
Audience: School & public library patrons
Subjects: Library automation, education, textbook
Availability: Call
Discount: Quantity: Available by product &/or service. District discounts are available for support. 35% discount on any quantity for schools of library science
Services: Catalog; promotional newsletter; preview policy; user groups. Educational services including training and MARC workshops. Full line of data services. Automation. Celebration. Exhibit at AASL, ALA, AECT, IRA

FOUNDATION FOR LIBRARY RESEACH
505 McNeill Ave., Point Pleasant, WV 25187
304-675-4350, 304-343-6480
Pres: Carol Sue Miller

Producer
Formats: Integrated library systems software

Hardware: DOS
Audience: K-12
Subjects: Library automation
Availability: Vendor rep., call
Services: Catalog

FRAME TECHNOLOGY
1010 Rincon Circle, San Jose, CA 95131
800-843-7263
Sales Contact: Yolana Leinson

Producer/Distributor
Formats: Educational/training software
Hardware: DOS, Macintosh
Subjects: Instructional tools, language arts

FREESOFT COMPANY
105 McKinley Rd., Beaver Falls, PA 15010
412-846-2700; Fax: 412-847-4436
Sales Contact: Lisa Senkevich

Producer/Distributor
Formats: Educational software
Hardware: Macintosh
Subjects: Teacher aids/instructional tools

FRIENDLYSOFT, INC.
3638 W. Pioneer Pkwy., Arlington, TX 76013
817-277-9378
Pres: Mike Yaw
Sales Mgr: June Bunch

Producer/Distributor
Formats: Educational software, games, computer-aided instruction, teaching aids, wordprocessor. Copyprotected
Hardware: IBM (or compatible)
Audience: 2-12, adult
Subjects: Business education, composition, computer literacy, spelling
Availability: Mail order, retail stores
Discount: Schools & libraries, 10% off retail
Services: Catalog. Preview policy

GPN
Box 80669, Lincoln, NE 68501
402-472-1785, 800-228-4630; Fax: 402-472-1785

Producer/Distributor
Format: VHS video, CD-ROM, videodiscs
Audience: Preschool-3
Subjects: Social studies, reading, music, food & nutrition, arts
Special interest: Reading Rainbow
Services: Catalog

G.R.C./S.W.L.
5383 Hollister Ave., Santa Barbara, CA 93111
805-964-7724, 800-933-5383
Pres: Vickie Blades
Marketing Director: Darcy Cook

Producer
Formats: Integrated library systems software; CD-ROM
Hardware: DOS, Macintosh
Audience: K-12
Subjects: Library automation
Availability: Call, vendor rep.
Services: Catalog

GALE RESEARCH
835 Penobscot Bldg, Detroit, MI 48226-4094
800-877-4253
Pres: Keith Lassner
Sales Mgr: Judy Graham

Producer/Distributor
Formats: CD-ROM
Hardware: DOS, Macintosh
Audience: 9-12, adult
Subjects: Reference, biography, literature
Availability: Direct retail (mail order)
Services: Catalog

GAMCO
1411 E. Hwy. 350, Big Spring, TX 79720
915-267-6327, 800-351-1404
Pres: Auriel Lafond
Natl Dir/Sales & Mktg: Jerry Proffitt

Producer/Distributor
Formats: Educational software
Hardware: Macintosh, DOS, Apple II
Audience: K-12
Subjects: Math, reading, language arts, social studies, teacher tools, transition skills
Availability: Direct retail (mail order)
Services: Catalog; eduational discounts; promotional newsletters; preview policy

GESSLER EDUCATIONAL SOFTWARE
55 W. 13th St., New York, NY 10011
212-627-0099, 800-456-5825; Fax: 212-627-5948

Producer/Distributor
Formats: Educational software
Hardware: Apple
Subjects: ESL, foreign languages, social studies

GREAT WAVE
5353 Scotts Valley Dr., Scotts Valley, CA 95066
408-438-1990, 800-456-5825; Fax: 408-438-7171

Producer/Distributor
Formats: Educational software
Hardware: Macintosh
AudienceL K-12
Subjects: Language arts, music

GROLIER EDUCATIONAL CORPORATION
Old Sherman Turnpike, Danbury, CT 06816

203-797-3500, 800-356-5590; Fax: 203-797-3838
Pres: Dave Arganbright

Producer/Distributor
Formats: CD-ROM
Hardware: DOS, Macintosh
Audience: K-12
Subjects: Encyclopedia, reference
Availability: Vendor rep.
Services: Catalog
Distribution: Retail, mail order

GROUP LOGIC, INC.
1408 N. Fillmore St., Arlington, VA 22201
703-525-1555, 800-476-8781; Fax: 703-528-3296
Sales Contact: Dimitri Korahais

Producer/Distributor
Formats: Educational software
Hardware: Macintosh
Subjects: Teacher aids/instructional tools

GRYPHON
7220 Trade St., Ste. 120, San Diego, CA 92121
619-536-8815, 800-795-0981, Fax: 619-536-8932

Producer/Distributor
Formats: Educational software
Hardware: Macintosh
Subjects: Teacher aids/instructional tools

HRM SOFTWARE
(A Division of Queue Inc.)
338 Commerce Dr., Fairfield, CT 06430
203-335-0906, 800-232-2224; Fax: 203-336-2481
Sales Mgr: Lyn Scott

Producer/Distributor
Formats: Educational, courseware, and computer-aided instruction software; copyprotected
Hardware: Apple II, DOS
Audience: 4-12, adult
Subjects: Mathematics, environment & energy, physical education, geography, science, health education, language development
Availability: Direct retail (mail order)
Services: Catalog. Promotional newsletters. Preview

HARTLEY COURSEWARE, INC.
133 Bridge St., Dimondale, MI 48821
517-646-6458, 800-247-1380; Fax: 517-646-8451
VP: R. David Owens
Sales Mgr: Judith Baliar
Promotion: Telaina M. Eriksen

Producer/Distributor
Formats: Educational, authoring sys-

tem, game, computer-aided instruction, teaching aid, and adminstration software; copyprotected
Hardware: Radio Shack, Tandy 1000, Apple II, Commodore, Franklin, DOS, Macintosh
Audience: Preschool-12, adult
Subjects: Language development, social science, computer literacy, mathematics, special education, foreign languages, physical education, spelling, grammar, reading, teacher aids, history, science
Availability: Direct retail (mail order), retail
Services: Catalog. Preview policy. Exhibit at AASL, ALA, IRA, NCTE, CEC, District IRA, CRLD, CTG, CSUN

HAYES MICROCOMPUTER
5923 Peachtree Industrial, Blvd., Norcross, GA 30092
404-840-9200

HEARTSOFT
Box 691381, Tulsa, OK 74167
800-285-3475
Pres: Ben Shell Jr.
Sales Mgr: W. Steve Williams

Producer/Distributor
Formats: Educational and entertainment software
Hardware: DOS, Apple II, Macintosh
Audience: K-8
Categories: Mathematics, social studies, English, language arts, history, science
Availability: Direct retail (mail order)
Services: Catalog

HIGH TECHNOLOGY SOFTWARE PRODUCTS, INC.
Box 60406, Oklahoma City, OK 73146
405-848-0480
Pres & Sales Mgr: Charles Weddington

Producer/Distributor
Formats: Educational and business/vertical market software; copyprotected
Hardware: Apple II
Audience: K-12
Subjects: Science, physics
Availability: Retail stores
Services: Catalog. Preview policy

HOUGHTON MIFFLIN CO.
School Division
222 Berkeley St., Boston, MA 02116-3764
617-351-5000; Fax: 617-252-3145

Producer/Distributor
Formats: Educational/training software
Hardware: Apple, Macintosh
Subjects: Language arts, teacher aids/instructional tools

HUMANITIES SOFTWARE
Box 950, Hood River, OR 97031
503-386-6737, 800-245-6737; Fax:
    503-386-1410
Pres: Jon Msadian
Sales Mgr: Charlotte Arnold

Producer/Distributor
Formats: Educational software
Hardware: Macintosh, DOS, Apple II,
    Windows
Audience: K-12
Subjects: Reading skills, language,
    literature, typing
Availability: Direct retail (mail order),
    retail
Services: Catalog

HYPERBOLE STUDIOS
1756 114th Ave., SE, Ste. 204,
    Bellevue, WA 98004
206-451-7751
Dir Mgr: John Locher

Producer
Formats: CD-ROM
Hardware: Macintosh, CBM
Audience: 10-12, adult
Subjects: Interactive movies, novels,
    science-fiction (some sensitive
    language)
Availability: Mail order, retail
Services: Brochures. Exhibit at con-
    ferences

HYPERGLOT FOREIGN LANGUAGE
    SOFTWARE CO. (FLS CO.)
Box 10746, Knoxville, TN 37939-0746
615-558-8270, 800-726-5087; Fax:
    615-588-6569
Pres: Phil Bagget

Producer/Distributor
Formats: Educational and entertain-
    ment software
Hardware: DOS, Macintosh, Windows
Audience: K-12, adult
Subject: Foreign languages
Availability: Direct retail (mail order)
Services: Catalog

IBIS SOFTWARE
140 Second St., Ste. #603, San Fran-
    cisco, CA 94105
415-546-1917; Fax: 415-546-0361

Producer/Distributor
Formats: Educational software
Hardware: DOS, Windows
Audience: K-12
Subjects: Music, ear training, sight
    training, rhythm
Availability: Direct retail (mail order),
    retail
Services: Catalog

IEP
Rte. 671, Box 546, Fork Union, VA
    23055

804-842-2000
Pres: Don Cahill
Sales Mgr: Maureen Cahill

Producer/Distributor
Formats: Adminstration software
Hardware: Apple II, DOS, Macintosh
Audience: Teachers
Subjects: Special education, IEP's
Availability: Direct retail (mail order)
Services: Catalog, demo disks

IMPRESSIONS SOFTWARE
7 Melrose Dr., Farmington, CT 06032
203-676-9002

Producer/Distributor
Formats: Educational and entertain-
    ment software
Hardware: DOS, Macintosh
Audience: K-12, adult
Availability: Retail
Services: Catalog

INDIVIDUAL SOFTWARE CO.
5870 Stoneridge Dr., Pleasanton, CA
    94588
800-331-3313

Producer/Distributor
Formats: Educational and entertain-
    ment software
Hardware: DOS, Macintosh
Audience: K-12
Subjects: Mathematics, social studies,
    English, language arts, history,
    science
Availability: Retail
Services: Catalog

INET CORPORATION
8450 Central Ave., Newark, CA 94560
415-797-9600
Chairman/CEO: Herman Miller

Producer/Distributor
Formats: Educational software;
    copyprotected
Hardware: Commodore, DOS, Radio
    Shack
Audience: 3-12, adult
Subjects: Reading
Availability: Direct retail (mail order)
Discount: Inquire
Services: Catalog

INFOBASES INTERNATIONAL INC.
1875 S. State St., Ste. 7-100, Orem,
    UT 84058-8037
801-224-2223
CEO: Paul Allen
Sales Mgr: Elisa Hammond

Producer/Distributor
Formats: CD-ROM
Hardware: DOS, Windows
Subjects: History, Bible, world facts
Audience: K-12, adult
Availability: Retail
Services: Catalog

INFORMATION ACCESS
362 Lakeside Dr., Foster City, CA
    94404
415-378-5249, 800-227-8431; Fax:
    800-676-2345

Producer/Distributor
Formats: CD-ROM
Hardware: DOS
Audience: 6-12, adult
Subjects: Magazine indexes to
    newspapers and government publi-
    cations
Availability: Direct retail (mail order),
    sales rep.
Services: Toll free customer support

INLINE DESIGN
308 Main St., Lakeville, CT
    06039-1204
203-435-4995, 800-453-7671; Fax:
    203-435-1091
Sales Contact: Ruth Crowther

Producer/Distributor
Formats: Educational & entertainment
    software

INNOVATIVE DATA DESIGN
1820 Arnold Industrial Way, Concord,
    CA 94520-5311
510-680-6818; Fax: 510-680-1165

Producer/Distributor
Formats: Educational software
Hardware: DOS, Macintosh
Subjects: Teacher aids/instructional
    tools

INSPIRATION SOFTWARE
2920 SW Dolph Ct., Ste. 3, Portland,
    OR 97219
503-245-9011, 800-877-4292; Fax:
    503-246-4292
Sales Contact: Chuck Nakell

Producer/Distributor
Formats: Educational software
Hardware: Macintosh
Subjects: Language arts, teacher
    aids/instructional tools

INSTRUCTIONAL COMMUNICATIONS
    TECHNOLOGY, INC. / TAYLOR AS-
    SOCIATES
10 Stepar Place, Huntington Station,
    NY 11746
516-549-3000, 800-225-5428; Fax:
    516-549-3156
Pres: Stanford E. Taylor
Gen Mgr: Audry Carty
Lib/Sch Prom Dir: Dorothea L. Taylor

Producer/Distributor
Formats: Educational and computer-
    aided instruction software; CD-ROM;
    copyprotected
Hardware: Apple II, DOS
Audience: K-12, adult
Subjects: Special education, computer

literacy, spelling, language development, mathematics, reading
Availability: Direct retail (mail order)
Services: Catalog. Preview policy. Exhibit at IRA, ICIA, COMMTEX

INTELLIMATION
130 Cremona Dr., Santa Barbara, CA 93117
805-968-2291, 800-346-8355; Fax: 805-968-8899
Pres: Ronald J. Boehm
Sales Mgr: Paul W. Sams

Producer/Distributor
Formats: Multimedia educational software
Hardware: Macintosh
Audience: K-12
Subjects: Tools & utilities, language arts, life sciences, physical science, mathematics, social studies, arts & foreign language, multimedia
Availability: Direct retail (mail order)
Services: Catalog

INTERKOM SOFTWARE
Box 1147, Elk Grove Village, IL 60007
312-472-0713
Sales Mgr & Lib/Sch Prom Dir: Edward Swick

Producer/Distributor
Formats: Educational, authoring system, game, teaching aids, and adminstration software; copyprotected
Hardware: Apple II, Franklin
Audience: K-12, adult
Subjects: Teacher aids, foreign languages, grammar, language development
Availability: Direct retail (mail order)
Discount: Quantity
Services: Catalog, preview policy

INTERNATIONAL BUSINESS MACHINES CORP., IBM UNITED STATES
Old Orchard Rd., Armonk, NY 10504
914-765-6548

INTUIT
Box 3014, Menlo Park, CA 94026
415-592-3066

Producer/Distributor
Hardware: Apple, DOS, Macintosh
Subjects: Business education, instructional tools

K-12 MICROMEDIA
6 Arrow Rd., Ramsey, NJ 07446
201-825-8888
Pres: A. G. Schweiker
Sales Mgr: Lori McCaugey

Producer/Distributor
Formats: Educational software
Hardware: Apple II, Macintosh, DOS, Windows
Audience: K-12

Subjects: Mathematics, social studies, English, language arts, history, science
Availibility: Direct retail
Services: Catalog

KEY CURRICULUM PRESS
Box 2304, Berkeley, CA 94702
510-548-2304; 800-338-7638; Fax: 510-548-0755
Pres: Steven Rasmussen
VP Sales: Madeleine Mulgrew

Producer/Distributor
Formats: Educational software
Hardware: Macintosh, DOS
Audience: 5-12, adult
Subjects: Mathematics (high school geometry)
Availability: Direct retail (mail order)
Discount: Inquire
Services: Catalog; preview policy; exhibit at NCTM meetings, inservice
Distribution: Major educational companies

KNOWLEDGE ADVENTURE INC.
4502 Dyer St., La Crescenta, CA 91214
818-542-4200, 800-542-4240
Pres: Rod Turner
Sales Mgr: Steve Chadima

Producer/Distributor
Formats: CD-ROM
Hardware: DOS, Windows
Audience: K-12, adult
Subjects: Science, dinosaurs, beginning learning, talking books
Availability: Direct retail (mail order)
Services: catalog

KNOWLEDGE REVOLUTION
15 Brush Pl., San Francisco, CA 94103
415-553-8153, 800-766-6615; Fax: 415-553-8012

Producer/Distributor
Formats: Educational software
Hardware: Macintosh
Audience: K-12
Subject: Science

KOALA ACQUISITIONS INC.
16055 Caputo Dr., Unit H, Morgan Hill, CA 95037
408-776-8181; Fax: 408-776-8187
Sales Contact: Earl Liebich

Producer/Distributor
Subjects: Art, instructional tools

KRELL SOFTWARE
Flowerfield Bldg #7, Ste. 1D, St. James, NY 1780
516-689-3500, 800-245-7355; Fax: 800-689-3549
Pres: Marcia Friedland

Producer/Distributor
Formats: Educational, game, and test preparation software; copyprotected
Hardware: IBM (or compatible), Apple
Audience: K-12, adult
Subjects: Reading, computer literacy, science, grammar, spelling, language development, teacher aids, mathematics, standard test preparation
Availability: Mail order, retail stores
Discount: Inquire
Services: Catalog

LCSI (Logo Computer Systems, Inc.)
Box 162, Highgate Springs, VT 05460
514-331-7090, 800-321-5646; Fax: 514-331-1380
Sales Mgr: Lea Iaricci

Producer/Distributor
Formats: Educational software
Hardware: Apple, DOS, Macintosh
Audience: K-12
Subjects: Creatvity & instructional tools, language arts, mathematics

LASER LEARNING TECHNOLOGIES
120 Lakeside Ave., Ste. 240, Seattle, WA 98122-3505
Pres: Darlene Atteberry & Anne Winchester
Sales: Heather Casselman

Producer/Distributor
Formats: Educational software to accompany existing laserdiscs and teacher curriculum guides for multimedia products
Hardware: Macintosh, Apple II, DOS, 2300 Laserdisc and CD-ROM products for education from over 100 publishers
Audience: K-12, adult
Subjects: Mathematics, social studies, English, language arts, history, science
Availability: Catalog, mail order
Services: Catalog; training; educational technology. Conference exhibits

LAUREATE LEARNING SYSTEMS, INC.
110 Eastspring St., Winooski, VT 05404
802-655-4755, 800-562-6801; Fax: 802-655-4757
Pres: Mary S. Wilson
Sales Mgr & Lib/Sch Prom Dir: Steve Goodman

Producer/Distributor
Formats: Educational software; copyprotected
Hardware: Apple II & IIGS, DOS, Macintosh
Audience: Pre-K-2
Subjects: Grammar, language development, special education
Availability: Direct retail (mail order)
Services: Catalog. Promotional news-

letters. Preview policy. Exhibit at
CEC, ASHA

LAWRENCE PRODUCTIONS, INC.
1800 S. 35th St., Galesburg, MI
49053-9687
616-665-7075, 800-421-4157; Fax:
616-665-7060

Producer/Distributor
Formats: Educational and entertainment software
Hardware: DOS, Macintosh
Audience: K-12, adult
Subjects: History, geography,
mathematics
Availability: Retail Services: Catalog

LEARNCO, INC.
Box L, Exeter, NH 03833
603-778-0813, 800-542-0026
Pres: J. H. Smith

Producer/Distributor
Formats: Educational software;
copyprotected
Hardware: Apple II, DOS, Macintosh
Audience: K-12
Subjects: Composition, library use,
special education, spelling, vocabulary, economics
Availability: Direct retail (mail order)
Services: Catalog; preview policy; exhibit at IRA, NCTE

LEARNING ARTS
Box 179, Wichita, KS 67201
316-636-9274
Pres: Darryl S. Roberts

Distributor
Formats: Educational, computer-aided
instruction, courseware, adminstration, and game software
Hardware: Apple II, DOS, Macintosh,
CD-ROM
Audience: K-12, adult
Subjects: Foreign languages, political
science, teacher aids, business education, geography, language development, reading composition,
grammar, library use, science, computer literacy, health education,
mathematics, social science, economics, history, physical education,
spelling
Availability: Direct retail (mail order)
Services: Catalog

THE LEARNING COMPANY
6493 Kaiser Dr., Fremont, CA 94555
415-792-2101, 800-852-2255; Fax:
510-792-9628
Pres: Bill Dinsmore
Educatl Sales Dir: Pat Walkington

Producer/Distributor
Formats: Educational software;
copyprotected
Hardware: DOS, Tandy, Apple II,
Macintosh

Audience: K-12
Subjects: Reading, art, spelling, grammar, problem-solving, language development, mathematics
Availability: Retail stores, school
dealers
Services: Catalog. Promotional newsletters. Preview policy. Exhibit at
NECC

THE LEARNING CUBE (Educational Software Collection)
3 Pine Ridge Way, Mill Valley, CA
94941
800-733-6733
Pres: Paul Kretchmer

Distributor
Formats: Educational software;
CD-ROM
Hardware: DOS, Macintosh, Apple II
Audience: K-12
Subjects: Early childhood, creative
arts, reading, spelling, general learning, reference, music and theater,
vocabulary, social science, foreign
languages, mathematics, science
and nature, writing
Availability: Direct retail (mail order)
Services: Catalog

LEARNING TEAM
10 Long Pond Rd., Armonk, NY
10504-0217
914-273-2226, 800-793-TEAM(8326);
Fax: 914-273-2227

Producer/Distributor
Formats: Educational software, CD-ROM, video
Hardware: Macintosh, IBM
Audience: K-12
Subjects: Math, science, general
Availability: Mail order
Services: Catalog. Exhibit at conferences

LEGACY SOFTWARE
8521 Reseda Blvd., Northridge, CA
91324
818-885-5773, 800-532-7692; Fax:
818-885-5779
Sales Contact: Ariella J. Lehrer

Producer/Distributor
Formats: Educational software
Hardware: Apple, DOS, Macintosh
Subjects: Language arts, mathematics

LEGO
550 Taylor Rd., Enfield, CT 06082
203-749-2291, 800-527-8339; Fax:
203-763-2466

Producer/Distributor
Formats: Educational/training software
Hardware: Apple, DOS, Macintosh
Audience: 7-12
Subjects: Mathematics, problem-solving

LIBRARIES UNLIMITED
Box 6633, Englewood, CO 80155
303-770-1220
Pres: Bohdan S. Wynar
Sales Mgr: Dianne Dierkens

Producer/Distributor
Formats: Educational reference, clipart
Hardware: Apple II, DOS
Audience: School library media
specialists, teachers
Subjects: Reference for history,
science, books, clipart for the holidays, computers & audiovisual,
borders
Availability: Direct retail (mail order),
jobbers
Services: Catalog, exhibit at major conferences

LIBRARY CORPORATION
Research Park, Inwood, WV
25428
304-229-0100
Pres: Bob Asleson
Sales Mgr: Richard Kirk

Producer/Distributor
Formats: Integrated library systems
software; CD-ROM
Hardware: DOS, Macintosh
Audience: Adult
Subjects: Library automation, reference material
Availability: Direct retail (mail order),
vendor rep.
Services: Catalog, Demo Disk

LINGO FUN, INC.
Box 486, Westerville, OH 43081
614-882-8258, 800-745-8258; Fax:
614-882-2390
Pres: Roger Neff
Sales Mgr: Mary Whitney
Lib/Sch Prom Dir: Betty A. Neff

Producer/Distributor
Formats: Educational software;
copyprotected
Hardware: Apple II, DOS
Audience: 8-12, adult
Subjects: Foreign languages
Availability: Direct retail (mail order)
Discount: Inquire
Services: Catalog; preview policy;
exhibit at ACTFL, ECCO, national,
regional & state foreign language
conferences

LIVING SOFT
Box 970, Janesville, CA 96114-0970
916-253-2700, 800-626-1262; Fax:
916-253-2703
Sales Contact: Annette Scholfield

Producer/Distributor
Formats: Educational software
Hardware: DOS
Subjects: Vocational education

LOTUS DEVELOPMENT CORP.
55 Cambridge Pkwy., Cambridge, MA
  02142
617-577-8500, 800-343-5414; Fax:
  617-693-3899
Sales Contact: Richard Ekell

**MECC (MINNESOTA EDUCATIONAL
  COMPUTING CORP.)**
6160 N. Summit Dr., Minneapolis, MN
  55430
612-569-1500, 800-685-6322; Fax:
  612-569-1551
Pres: Dale LaFrenz
VP Mktg: Bill Wilde
VP Development: Susan Schilling
VP Finance: Don Anderson

Producer/Distributor
Formats: Educational software
Hardware: Apple II, Macintosh, MS-DOS
Audience: K-12
Subjects: Art, simulations, problem-
  solving, various fun-learning formats
Availability: Direct retail (mail order),
  retail stores, direct to schools
Discount: Institutional memberships,
  inquire
Services: Catalog; direct retail (mail
  order); preview policy; exhibit at vari-
  ous conventions

MMI CORPORATION
2950 Wyman Pkwy., Box 19907, Baltimore, MD 21211
410-866-1222; Fax: 410-366-6311
Pres & Sales Mgr: R. C. Levy

Producer/Distributor
Formats: Educational software
Hardware: Apple II, DOS
Audience: K-12, adult
Availability: Direct retail (mail order)

**MACMILLIAN NEW MEDIA (MAXWELL
  ELECTRONIC PUBLISHING)**
124 Mt. Auburn St., Ste. 320, Cambridge, MA 02138
617-661-2955
Pres: Fredrick Bowes III
VP sales: Charles Wood

Producer/Distributor
Formats: Educational software;
  CD-ROM
Hardware: DOS
Audience: K-12, adult
Subjects: Dictionary for children, col-
  lege handbook
Availability: Direct retail (mail order)
Services: Product information

MACROMEDIA, INC.
600 Townsend, Ste. 310W, San Francisco, CA 94103
800-828-6067; Fax: 410-244-2876
Sales Contact: Rees Bristol

Producer/Distributor
Formats: Educational software

Hardware: Macintosh
Audience: K-adult
Subjects: Art, music, teacher aids/in-
  structional tools

MAGIC QUEST
125 University Ave., Palo Alto, CA
  94301
415-321-5838, 800-321-8925; Fax:
  415-321-8560
Sales Contact: Paul Salzinger

Producer/Distributor
Formats: Educational software
Hardware: DOS, Macintosh
Audience: K-12
Subjects: Science

MANHATTAN GRAPHIC CORP.
250 E. Hartsdale Ave., Hartsdale, NY
  10530
916-725-2048, 800-572-6533; Fax:
  916-725-2450
Sales Contact: Martin Rosenberg

Producer/Distributor
Formats: Educational software
Hardware: Macintosh
Subjects: Teacher aids/instructional
  tools

MARSHWARE
(Division of Marshfilm Enterprises, Inc.)
Box 8082, Shawnee Mission, KS
  66208
816-523-1059, 800-821-3303 (not
  MO, HI, AK); Fax: 816-333-7421
Pres & Sales Mgr: Joan K. Marsh

Producer/Distributor
Formats: Educational, courseware, and
  computer-aided instruction software;
  copyprotected
Hardware: Apple II
Audience: K-12, adult
Subjects: Health education, physical
  education, science
Availability: Direct retail (mail order),
  retail stores
Services: Catalog; preview policy

**MATH & COMPUTER EDUCATION
  PROJECT**
Lawrence Hall of Science, University of
  California, Berkeley, CA 94720
415-642-3167
Sales Mgr: Dorothy Walker

Producer/Distributor
Formats: Educational and courseware
  software; copyprotected
Hardware: Apple II
Audience: K-12, adult
Subjects: Problem-solving, health edu-
  cation, mathematics, music, reading
Availability: Direct retail (mail order),
  retail stores
Services: Catalog.

MATHEGRAPHICS SOFTWARE
61 Cedar Rd., E. Northport, NY 11731
516-368-3781
Pres: Sheldon P. Gordon

Producer/Distributor
Formats: Educational software;
  copyprotected
Hardware: Apple II, DOS, Radio Shack
Audience: 7-12, adult
Subjects: Mathematics, science
Availability: Direct retail (mail order)
Services: Catalog

MATHSOFT, INC.
201 Broadway, Cambridge, MA
  02139-1901
617-577-1017, 800-628-4223; Fax:
  617-577-8829
Sales Contract: Ellen Koup

Producer/Distributor
Formats: Educational software
Hardware: DOS, Macintosh
Subjects: Mathematics

MAVERIC SOFTWARE
9801 Dupont Ave. S., Bloomington,
  MN 55431
612-881-3738
Pres: Gary Miller
Sales Mgr: Dave Oxford

Producer/Distributor
Formats: Educational and entertain-
  ment software
Hardware: DOS, Macintosh
Audience: K-12, adult
Subjects: Tutorials in all subject areas,
  dinosaurs
Availability: Direct retail (mail order)
Services: Catalog

MAXIS
2 Theatre Sq., Ste. 230, Orinda, CA
  94563
510-254-9700, 800-336-2947; Fax:
  510-253-3736
Sales Contact: Lois Tilles

Producer/Distributor
Formats: Educational software
Hardware: DOS, Macintosh
Subjects: Science

McGRAW-HILL INC.
Blue Ridge Summit, PA 17294-0850
717-794-2191; Fax: 800-932-0183
Producer/Distributor

Formats: CD-ROM
Hardware: Macintosh, DOS
Audience: 3-12, adult
Subjects: Reference, Encyclopedia of
  Science & Technology
Services: Catalog

MEDIA ALIVE
766 San Aleso Ave., Sunnyvale, CA
  94086

408-752-8500
Pres: Bill Liu
Sales Mgr: Karen Vigoel

Producer/Distributor
Formats: Educational and entertainment software
Hardware: DOS, Windows, Macintosh
Subjects: Travel, geography
Audience: K-12, adult
Availability: Retail
Services: Catalog, educ. discount 30%

MEDIA FLEX
Box 1107, Champlain, NY 12919
518-298-2970
Pres: Harry Cham
Sales Mgr: Al Calame

Distributor
Formats: Integrated library systems software
Hardware: DOS
Audience: K-12
Subjects: Library automation
Availability: Direct retail (mail order), vendor rep.
Services: Catalog

MEDIA VISION
47300 Bayside Pkwy., Fremont, CA 94538
510-770-8600, 800-684-6699; Fax: 510-440-8837

Formats: CD-ROM, computer software
Hardware: Macintosh, DOS
Audience: K-12, adult
Subjects: Games, "I Can Read Literature"
Availability: Mail order
Services: Catalog

MERIT AUDIO VISUAL
Box 392, New York, NY 10024
800-753-6488
Sales Mgr: Ben Weintraub

Producer/Distributor
Formats: Educational software
Hardware: Apple II, DOS
Audience: 6-12, adult
Subjects: ESL and bilingual, reading, vocabulary, writing, grammar, mathematics
Availability: Direct retail (mail order), telephone order
Services: Catalog; preview policy

METIER
1951 Davina St., Henderson, NV 89014
702-897-6795
CEO: M. Gifford
Sales Mgr: D. Pickering

Producer/Distributor
Formats: Graphics, teaching aids, test generators, test banks, and computer-aided instruction software;

workbooks on learning about computers
Hardware: DOS
Audience: 5-12, adult, teachers
Subjects: Mathematics, turtle graphics, computer science
Availability: Direct retail (mail order)
Services: Consulting (fee); order on approval; news releases; conference presentations

MICROED INC.
Box 24750, Edwina, MN 55424
612-929-2242
Pres & Sales Mgr: Thorwald Esbensen

Producer/Distributor
Formats: Educational and authoring systems software
Hardware: Apple II, Commodore, Amiga, Macintosh
Audience: Preschool-12, adult
Subjects: Health education, mathematics, science, economics, history, poetry, social science, foreign languages, home economics, political science, spelling, geography, language development, reading, grammar, library use, religion
Availability: Direct retail (mail order)
Services: Catalog. Preview policy

MICROGRAMS
1404 N. Main, Rockford, IL 61103
815-965-2464, 800-338-4726
Pres: Richard Shelain
Sales Mgr & Lib/Sch Prom Dir: Kent Holden

Producer/Distributor
Formats: Educational software; copyprotected
Hardware: Apple II, DOS
Audience: K-6
Subjects: Language development, geography, mathematics, grammar, reading, health education, science, history, spelling, problem-solving
Availability: Mail order, retail stores
Discount: Inquire
Services: Catalog; preview policy

MICRO LEARNINGWARE
Hwy. 169 S., Amboy, MN 56010-9762
507-674-3705
Pres: Fred Rennpferd

Producer/Distributor
Formats: Educational software
Hardware: Apple II, DOS
Audience: Preschool-12, adult
Subjects: History, mathematics, spelling, business education, foreign languages, home economics, composition, geography, computer literacy, grammar, language development, reading, health education, library use, science
Availability: Direct retail(mail order), retail stores
Services: Catalog

MICROPHYS
12 Bridal Way, Sparta, NJ 07871
800-832-6591
Pres: A. I. Rosen
Sales Mgr & Lib/Sch Prom Dir: A. Friedman

Producer/Distributor
Formats: Educational courseware, authoring systems, games, computer-aided instruction, and administration software; copyprotected
Hardware: Apple II, Radio Shack, Commodore, DOS
Audience: 4-12, adult
Subjects: Science, language development, spelling, teacher aids, mathematics, reading
Availability: Direct retail (mail order), retail stores
Discount: Inquire
Services: Catalog; promotional newsletters; preview policy

MICROSOFT
One Microsoft Way, Redmond, WA 98052-6399
206-882-8080, 800-426-9400; Fax: 206-936-7329
Pres: Bill Gates

Producer/Distributor
Formats: Educational software; CD-ROM
Hardware: DOS, Windows, Macintosh
Audience: K-12, adult
Subjects: Music, art, science, literature
Availability: Direct retail (mail order), retail
Services: Library and school discounts

MIDWEST SOFTWARE
22500 Orchard Lake Rd. #1, Farmington, MI 48024
313-477-0897, 800-422-0095
Pres: Norman J. Eisenberg
Sales Mgr: Sue Ault

Producer/Distributor
Formats: Educational and administration software; copyprotected
Hardware: Apple II, Commodore, DOS
Audience: Preschool-12, adult
Subjects: Language development, mathematics, teacher aids, physical education, reading, early education
Availability: Direct retail (mail order), retail stores
Services: Catalog; preview policy; exhibit at MACUL

MILLIKEN PUBLISHING CO.
1100 Research Blvd., St. Louis, MO 63132-0579
314-991-4220, 800-643-0008; Fax: 800-538-1319
Sales Contact: Robin Tinker

Producer/Distributor
Formats: Educational software

Hardware: Apple, DOS, Macintosh
Audience: K-3
Subjects: Instructional tools

MINDPLAY
3130 N. Dodge Blvd., Tucson, AZ
  85716
602-322-6365, 800-221-7911; Fax:
  602-322-0363
Pres: Judith Bliss
Sales Mgr: Brian Cambell

Producer
Formats: Educational software;
  CD-ROM
Hardware: DOS, Windows, Macintosh,
  Apple II
Audience: K-12, adult
Subjects: Readiness skills, mathemat-
  ics, language arts, vocabulary de-
  velopment, writing, puzzles, social
  studies, science
Availability: Direct retail (mail order),
  dealer rep. Services: Catalog

MINDSCAPE EDUCATIONAL
1345 Diversey Pkwy., Chicago, IL
  60614-1299
312-525-1500, 800-829-1900; Fax:
  312-525-9474
Sales Contact: Mary Dailey

Producer/Distributor
Formats: Educational software
Hardware: Apple, DOS, Macintosh
Subjects: Art, language arts, teacher
  aids/instructional tools

MISTY CITY SOFTWARE
11866 Slater Ave. NE, Kirkland, WA
  98034
206-820-5559, 800-795-0049; Fax:
  206-820-4298
Sales Contact: Roberta Spiro

Producer/Distributor
Formats: Educational software
Hardware: DOS, Macintosh
Subjects: Teacher aids/institutional
  tools

MULTIMEDIA PUBLISHERS GROUP
60 Cutter Mill Rd., Ste. 502, Great
  Neck, NY 11021
516-482-0088; Fax: 516-773-0990
Dir: Harry Fox

Distributor
Formats: CD-ROM
Hardware: Macintosh, IBM
Subjects: Education, business, refer-
  ence, entertainment
Availability: Mail order, retail outlets
Services: Catalog. Trade shows

NATIONAL BOOK COMPANY
Box 8795, Portland, OR 97207-8795
503-228-6345
Pres: Carl W. Salser

Producer/Distributor
Formats: Educational and computer-
  aided instruction software
Hardware: DOS
Audience: 7-12, adult
Subjects: Business education, com-
  puter literacy, keyboarding/typing
Availability: Direct retail (mail order)
Services: Catalog

**NATIONAL GEOGRAPHIC SOCIETY
EDUCATIONAL SERVICES**
Box 98018, Washington DC
  20090-8018
202-828-6605, 800-368-2728; Fax:
  301-921-1575

Producer/Distributor
Formats: CD-ROM
Hardware: DOS, Macintosh, Apple IIGS
Audience: K-12, adult
Subjects: Biological sciences, physical
  sciences, natural science, history
Availability: Direct retail (mail order)
Services: Catalog, 5% Volume Dis-
  counts

NATIONAL TEXTBOOK CO.
4255 W. Touhy Ave., Lincolnwood, IL
  60646
312-679-5500
Pres: S. William Pattis
Sales Mgr: Larry Rutkowski
Lib/Sch Prom Dir: Richard Knox

Producer/Distributor
Formats: Educational software;
  copyprotected
Hardware: Apple II, DOS
Audience: 3-12, adult
Subjects: Foreign languages, language
  development
Availability: Direct retail (mail order),
  retail
Discount: Schools, libraries, 25%
Services: Catalog; preview policy; ex-
  hibit at AASL, ALA, IRA, NCTE, ACTFL

NEW MEDIA SOURCE
3830 Valley Centre Dr., Box 2153,
  San Diego, CA 92130-9834
800-344-2621; Fax: 619-438-2330
Jr Sales Rep: Dan White

Distributor
Formats: CD-ROM
Hardware: IBM, Macintosh
Subjects: Education (k-3), reference,
  literature, entertainment, sports,
  music, arts & images
Availability: Mail order. Accepts pur-
  chase orders from schools, libraries,
  & govt institutions
Services: Catalog. Exhibit at ALA, PLA,
  NSBA, Intermedia Show & others

NEWSBANK
58 Pine St., New Canaan, CT
  06840-5416
800-762-8182

Producer/Distributor
Subjects: Instructional tools, library
  media

NEWSWEEK EDUCATIONAL
Box 414, Livingston, NJ 07039
201-316-2000, 800-526-2595; Fax:
  201-316-2370
Sales Contact: Richard Burch

Producer/Distributor
Formats: Educational software
Hardware: Apple, DOS, Macintosh
Subjects: Social studies

NIMCO
117 Hwy. 815, Box 9, Calhoun, KY
  42327-0009
800-962-6662; Fax: 502-273-5844
Pres: Bill Jones

Distributor
Format: VHS, filmstrips, displays,
  software
Audience: Preschool-adult
Subjects: Vocational, drug education &
  recovery, self-esteem, child care, sex
  education
Services: Catalog. 14 day preview policy. Exhibit at various conferences

OCLC/FOREST PRESS
6565 Frantz Rd., Dublin, OH
  43017-3395
800-848-5878, ext. 6237; Fax:
  614-764-6096
Pres: Peter Paulson

Producer/Distributor
Formats: CD-ROM
Hardware: DOS
Audience: Adult
Subjects: Library automation
Availibility: Direct retail (mail order)
Services: Catalog, vendor rep

ONLINE COMPUTER SYSTEMS
20251 Century Blvd., Germantown,
  MD 20874
800-922-9204; Fax: 301-428-2093

Producer/Distributor
Formats: Educational software
Hardware: DOS, Macintosh, Windows
Audience: K-12
Subjects: Mathematics, social studies,
  English, language arts, history,
  science
Availability: Direct retail (mail order)
Services: Catalog

OPTICAL DATA
30 Technology Dr., Warren, NJ
  07059
908-668-1322, 800-524-2481

Producer/Distributor
Formats: Educational software
Hardware: Apple, Macintosh
Subjects: Biology, earth science,

multimedia, problem solving, science, social studies

OPPORTUNITIES FOR LEARNING
941 Hickory Lane, Mansfield, OH 44901
419-589-1700
Pres: James Miller

Producer/Distributor
Formats: Educational, game, graphic, administration and teaching aids software; CD-ROM; Laser Disc
Hardware: Apple II, Macintosh, DOS
Audience: K-12, adult
Subjects: Geography, poetry, spelling, business education, grammar, reading teacher aids, composition, history, science, computer literacy, language development, social science, economics, mathematics, special education
Availability: Direct retail (mail order)
Services: Catalog; preview policy

OPTIMUM RESOURCE
5 Hiltech Lane, Hilton Head Island, SC 29926
803-689-8000, 800-327-1473; Fax: 803-689-8008
Pres: Richaed Hefter
Sales Mgr: David Kennaugh

Producer/Distributor
Formats: Educational software; CD-ROM, CD-I
Hardware: DOS, Apple II, Commodore, Windows, Macintosh
Audience: PreK-8
Subjects: Mathematics, language arts, science, social studies, history, foreign languages
Availability: Direct retail (mail order)
Services: Catalog

ORANGE CHERRY NEW MEDIA SCHOOLHOUSE
69 Westchester Ave., Box 390, Pound Ridge, NY 10576-0390
800-672-6002; Fax: 914-764-4104
Pres: Nicholas Vazzana

Distributor
Formats: Educational software
Hardware: Macintosh
Audience: K-12
Subjects: Early learning, history, geography, physical sciences, language arts, natural sciences, mathematics, languages
Availability: Direct retail (mail order)
Services: Catalog. 10 % discounts $300 + orders

PARADIGM SOFTWARE
Box 2995, Cambridge, MA 02141
617-576-7675; Fax: 617-576-7680

Producer/Distributor
Subjects: Computer literacy, multimedia

PARAMOUNT INTERACTIVE
700 Haven Way, Palo Alto, CA 949304-1016
415-812-8200

Producer/Distributor
Formats: Educational and entertainment software
Hardware: DOS, Windows, Macintosh
Audience: K-12, adult
Availability: Retail
Services: Catalog

PASSPORT DESIGNS, INC.
100 Stone Pine Rd., Half Moon Bay, CA 94019
415-726-0280, 800-443-3210; Fax: 415-726-2254
Pres: David Kusek
Educ Sales Mgr: Bruce Chandler

Producer/Distributor
Formats: Music printing, recording and multimedia authoring software
Hardware: Apple II, DOS with Windows, Macintosh
Audience: 7-12, adult
Subjects: Music, multimedia
Availability: Direct retail (mail order), retail stores
Discount: Inquire
Services: Catalog, promotional newsletters
Distribution: Ingram Micro, Merisel, Kenfil and Thinkware

PENTON OVERSEAS INC. (The Global Language Specialists)
2470 Impala Dr., Carlsbad, PA 9208-7226
800-748-5804

Producer/Distributor
Formats: Educational and entertainment software; CD-ROM
Hardware: DOS, Windows, Macintosh
Audience: K-12, adult
Subjects: Language learning, Spanish, French, Hebrew, German, Italian, Japanese
Availability: Retail, direct retail
Services: Catalog; discount

PERMA-BOUND
Vandallia Rd., Jacksonville, IL 62650
217-243-5451, 800-551-1169; Fax: 217-243-7505
Pres: James Orr
Mktg Director (CD-ROM): Ben Mangum

Producer/Distributor
Formats: CD-ROM
Hardware: DOS
Audience: K-12, adult
Subjects: Current events
Availability: Direct retail (mail order)
Services: Catalog

PETERSONS
202 Carnegie Center, Princeton, NJ 08543
800-338-3282

Producer/Distributor
Formats: Educational and reference software
Hardware: DOS, Macintosh
Audience: K-12
Subjects: Mathematics, social studies, English, language arts, history, science
Availability: Direct retail (mail order)
Services: Catalog; demo disk

PLUMA SOFTWARE
1116 E. Greenway, Mesa, AZ 85203
602-969-9441; Fax: 602-969-9445
Sales Contact: Patrick Ryan

Producer/Distributor
Formats: Educational software
Hardware: DOS, Macintosh
Subjects: Business education, social studies

POSTCRAFT INTERNATIONAL
27811 Hopkins, Ste. 6, Valencia, CA 91355
805-257-1759

Producer/Distributor
Hardware: Macintosh
Subjects: Art, teacher aids/instructional tools

POWER INDUSTRIES
37 Walnut St., Wellesley Hills, MA 02181
617-235-7733, 800-395-5009; Fax: 617-235-0084

Producer/Distributor
Subjects: Art, instructional tools

PRESCIENCE
939 Howard St., San Francisco, CA 94103
415-543-2252, 800-827-6284; Fax: 415-882-0530

Producer/Distributor
Formats: Educational software
Hardware: Macintosh
Subjects: Mathematics, science

PSYGNOSIS SOFTWARE
675 Massachusetts Ave., Cambridge, MA 02139
617-497-7794, 800-438-7794; Fax: 617-497-6759
Sales Contact: Phil Sandrock

Producer/Distributor
Formats: Educational/training software
Subjects: Problem solving

PUBLISHING INTERNATIONAL
Box 70790, Sunnyvale, CA 94086-0790

408-738-4311; Fax: 408-773-1791
Sales Contact: Diana Aldrich

Producer/Distributor
Formats: Educational/training software
Hardware: Apple, DOS, Macintosh
Subjects: Instructional tools, vocational education

PUTNAM NEW MEDIA
1 Grosset Dr., Kirkwood, NY 13795
607-775-1740, 800-847-5515

Distributor
Formats: CD-ROM
Hardware: DOS, Apple II/Macintosh
Audience: K-3
Subjects: "Edu-tainment": math, art, history
Availability: Mail order
Services: Catalog

QUALITY COMPUTERS
20200 Nine Mile Rd., St. Clair Shores, MI 48080
313-774-7200, 800-777-3642; Fax: 313-774-2698

QUANTA PRESS INC.
1313 Fifth St. SE, Ste. 223a, Minneapolis, MN 55414
612-379-3956; Fax: 612-623-4570
Pres: Mark Foster
Sales Mgr: Dennis Burke

Producer/Distributor
Formats: CD-ROM
Hardware: DOS, Macintosh
Audience: K-12, adult
Subjects: Art, government, natural and physical sciences
Availability: Direct retail (mail order)
Services: Catalog; 10% school discount

QUARK
1800 Grant St., Denver, CO 80203
303-894-3452, 800-676-4575; Fax: 303-894-3399
Sales Contact: Peter Warren

Producer/Distributor
Hardware: Macintosh
Subjects: Instructional tools

QUE SOFTWARE
c/o Macmillian Publishing, 201 W. 103rd St., Indianapolis, IN 46290
800-448-3804

Producer/Distributor
Subjects: Business education (Typing Tutor)

QUEUE
338 Commerce Dr., Fairfield, CT 06430
203-335-0908, 800-232-2224

Producer/Distributor

Hardware: Apple, DOS, Macintosh
Subjects: Early childhood, languages, teacher aids/instructional tools

RAYDREAM
1804 N. Shoreline Blvd., Mountain View, CA 94043
414-960-0766, 800-543-8188; Fax: 415-960-1198

Producer/Distributor
Subjects: Instructional tools

REED REFERENCE PUBLISHING
121 Chanlon Rd., New Providence, NJ 07974-1154
800-323-3288
Pres: Ira Siegel
VP Electronic Publishing: Martin Brooks
VP Sales: Robert Doran

Producer/Distributor
Formats: CD-ROM
Hardware: DOS, Apple II, Macintosh
Audience: Academic and public libraries, elementary & secondary school & college educators
Subjects: Book and serial bibliographies and critical reviews, including video and audiotapes, and biographical directories
Availability: Direct retail (mail order), direct sales
Services: Catalog; preview policy; thirty day trial; demo diskette; exhibit at ALA, SLA, A&A, and other library & book seller conventions

RESEARCH DESIGN ASSOCIATES
35 Crooked Hill Rd., Ste. 200, Commack, NY 11725
516-499-0053, 800-654-8715; Fax: 516-499-0389

RESEARCH PUBLICATIONS
12 Lunar Dr., Woodbridge, CT 06525
800-375-6508

Producer/Distributor
Formats: CD-ROM
Hardware: Macintosh
Audience: K-12, adult
Subjects: Library reference
Availability: Direct retail (mail order)
Services: Catalog; demo disk

RIGHT ON PROGRAMS
755 New York Ave., Ste. 210, Huntington, NY 11743
516-424-7777
Pres: Don Feinstein

Producer/Distributor
Formats: Educational software
Hardware: Apple II, Commodore, DOS
Audience: K-12
Subjects: Social studies, English, language arts, science
Availability: Direct retail (mail order)
Services: Catalog

SWLI—MULTIMEDIA PRODUCTS DIVISION
(Formerly General Research Corporation)
5383 Holister Ave., Santa Barbara, CA 93111
800-933-5383; Fax: 805-967-7094
Sales Mgr: Mary Stewart
Mkgt Dir: Darcy Cook

Producer/Distributor
Formats: CD-ROM
Hardware: DOS
Audience: Librarians
Subjects: Library automation, bibliographic data base
Availability: Mail order
Services: Catalog

SALEM PRESS, INC.
580 Sylvan Ave., Englewood Cliffs, NJ 07632
800-221-1592; Fax: 201-871-8668
Sales Mgr: Michael Teitelbaum

Producer/Distributor
Formats: CD-ROM
Hardware: DOS
Audience: YA, adult
Subjects: Literature, science
Availability: Mail order
Services: Catalog, brochures, Exhibit at conferences

SANCTUARY WOODS
1875 S. Grant St., Ste. 260, San Mateo, CA 94402
415-578-6340; Fax: 415-578-6344
Sales Mgr: Kristy Sager

Producers/Distributor
Formats: Educational software
Hardware: Macintosh
Subjects: Early childhood, language arts, music

SCARECROW PRESS
52 Liberty St., Box 4167, Metuchen NJ 08840
800-537-7107
Pres: Albert W. Daub

Producer
Formats: Integrated library systems software
Hardware: DOS, Apple II
Audience: K-12, adult
Subjects: Library automation
Availability: Direct retail (mail order), vendor rep
Services: Catalog, demo disk

SCHOLASTIC INC.
730 Broadway, New York, NY 10003
212-505-3000, 800-541-5513; Fax: 212-505-3310
Pres: Dick Robinson
Sales Mgr: Ellen Margolies

Producer/Distributor
Formats: Educational software
Hardware: Macintosh, Apple II, DOS
Audience: K-12
Subjects: Classroom publishing, language arts, math, problem-solving, science, social studies, computer literacy
Availability: Direct retail (mail order)
Services: Catalog

SCIENCE FOR KIDS
9950 Concord Church Rd., Lewisville, NC 27023
910-945-9000
Pres: Carolyn F. Moyer
Sales Mgr: Charles Moyer

Producer
Formats: CD-ROM
Hardware: Macintosh
Audience: K-8
Subjects: Living things, forces and motion, simple machines
Availability: Direct retail (mail order)
Services: Catalog; training price

SIERRA ON-LINE INC. (BRIGHT STAR TECHNOLOGY)
Box 93614, Coursegold, CA 93614
800-326-6654, 800-743-7725; Fax: 209-683-3633

Producer/Distributor
Formats: Educational and entertainment software; CD-ROM
Hardware: DOS, Windows, Audience: K-12, adult
Availability: Direct retail (mail order), retail
Services: Catalog

SILVERPLATTER INFORMATION, INC.
100 River Ridge Dr., Norwood, MA 02062
617-769-2599, 800-343-0064; Fax: 617-769-8763

Producer/Distributor
Formats: CD-ROM
Hardware: DOS, Macintosh
Audience: K-12, adult
Subjects: Library Reference
Availability: Direct retail (mail order)
Services: Catalog

SIRS
Box 2348, Boca Raton, FL 33427
800-232-7477
Pres: Elliot Goldstein
Sales Mgr: John Frank

Producer/Distributor
Formats: CD-ROM
Hardware: DOS, Macintosh
Audience: 6-12, adult
Subjects: Social issues, science, world affairs
Availability: Mail order
Services: Catalog; preview policy;

newsletter. Exhibit at ALA, AASL, state library conventions
Distribution: Catalog. Direct mail. Regional representative

SIR-TECH SOFTWARE, INC.
Box 245, Ogdensburg Business Center, Ste. 2E, Ogdensburg, NY 13669
315-393-6633
Pres: Norman Sirotek
Sales/Mktg: Lori Sears
Public Rel: Shari T. Mitchell

Producer/Distributor
Formats: Educational, entertainment and business applications software
Hardware: DOS, Apple II, Macintosh, Commodore, Amiga and C64/128
Audience: 7-12, adult
Subjects: Business education, computer literacy, language development, logic
Availability: Direct retail (mail order), retail stores
Services: Product profile sheets available upon request

SMARTSTUFF SOFTWARE
Box 82284, Portland, OR 97282
503-775-2821

Producer/Distributor
Hardware: Macintosh
Subjects: Instructional tools

TOM SNYDER PRODUCTION
80 Coolidge Hill Rd., Watertown, MA 02172
617-926-6000, 800-342-0236; Fax: 617-926-6223
Pres: Tom Snyder

Producer/Distributor
Formats: Educational software
Hardware: DOS, Macintosh, Laserdisc
Audience: K-12
Subjects: Critical thinking, mathematics, social studies, English, language arts, history, science
Availability: Direct retail
Services: Catalog

SOCIAL STUDIES SCHOOL SERVICE
10200 Jefferson Blvd., Culver City, CA 90232
310-839-2436, 800-421-4246
Owners: Sanford Weiner, Irwin Levin

Producer/Distributor
Formats: Educational software
Hardware: Apple II, DOS
Audience: K-12, adult
Subjects: Environment and energy, home economics, business education, geography, library use, composition, grammar, political science, computer literacy, health education, social science, economics, history, teacher aids, literature

Availability: Direct retail (mail order)
Services: Catalog; preview policy, exhibit at major conventions

SOFTERWARE, INC.
200 Office Center, Fort Washington, PA 19034
215-628-0400
Pres: Nathan Relles
Sales Mgr: Douglas Schoenberg

Producer/Distributor
Formats: Administration software
Hardware: DOS
Audience: Pre-K-K
Subjects: Adminstration
Availability: Direct retail (mail order)
Discount: Inquire
Services: Promotional newsletters; preview policy; exhibit at NAEYC

SOFTLINE INFORMATION
65 Broad St., Stamford, CT 06901
800-524-7922; Fax: 203-975-8347
Pres: Eileen Heckerling
Pub: Ralph Ferragamo

Producer/Distributor
Formats: CD-ROM
Hardware: IBM
Audience: 7-12, adult
Subjects: General reference for ethnic, full-text newspapers/magazines
Availability: Mail order
Services: Brochure. Exhibits at ALA, PLA, others

SOFTSHOPPE II
1558 E. Tara Ct., Chandler, AZ 85225
602-821-9178
Pres, Sales Mgr & Lib/Sch Prom Dir: Charles D. Bedal

Producer/Distributor
Formats: Games, computer-aided instruction, teaching aids, and administration software
Hardware: Apple II, Franklin, DOS
Audience: 7-12, adult
Subjects: Spelling, teacher aids
Availability: Direct retail (mail order)
Discount: Schools & libraries, 40%
Services: Catalog

SOFTSYNC
162 Madison Ave., New York, NY 10016
212-685-2080
Pres: Sue Currier
Sales Mgr: Andrew Jacobsen

Producer/Distributor
Formats: Educational, teaching aids, and administration software
Hardware: DOS, Apple II, Atari, Commodore, Franklin
Audience: 5-12
Subjects: Business education, music, teacher aids

Availability: Direct retail (mail order),
retail stores
Discount: Inquire
Services: Catalog

SOFTWARE MARKETING CORP.
9830 S. 51st St., Bldg. A-131,
Phoenix, AZ 85044
602-893-2400
Pres: Mikle Bates
Sales Mgrs: Wyndi Ballard, Brad
Holcomb

Producer/Distributor
Formats: Educational and entertain-
ment software; CD-ROM
Hardware: DOS, Windows, Macintosh
Audience: 7-12, adult
Subjects: Automotive, solar systems,
chemistry, human body and
reproduction, computers
Availability: Direct retail (mail
order)
Services: Catalog

SOFTWARE TOOLWORKS
60 Leveroni Ct, Novato, CA 94949
415-883-3000, 800-234-3088; Fax:
415-883-3303
Pres: Bob Goldberg
Sales Mgr: Mark Beaumont

Producer/Distributor
Formats: Educational and entertain-
ment software
Hardware: DOS, Windows, Macintosh
Audience: K-12, adult
Subjects: Mathematics, social studies,
English, language arts, history,
science
Availability: Direct retail (mail order),
retail
Services: Catalog

SOFTWARE VENTURES
2907 Claremont Ave., Berkeley, CA
94705
510-644-3232, 800-336-6477; Fax:
570-848-0885

Producer/Distributor

SOLEIL SOFTWARE, INC.
3853 Grove Ct., Palo Alto, CA 94303
415-494-0114; Fax: 415-493-6416

Producer/Distributor
Subjects: Early childhood

SOUTHWESTERN PUBLISHING
5101 Madison Rd., Cincinnati, OH
45227
513-271-8811, 800-543-7972
Sales Contact: Bryan Taylor

Producer/Distributor
Formats: Educational software
Hardware: Apple, DOS, Macintosh
Subjects: Business education

**SPECIAL LEARNING ED SOFTWARE
(SLED SOFTWARE)**
Box 16322, Minneapolis, MN 55416
612-926-5820
Pres: Helen Beaubaire
Sales Mgr: Glenn Beaubaire

Producer/Distributor
Formats: Educational software;
copyprotected
Hardware: Apple II, Commodore,
Franklin
Audience: 4-12, adult
Subjects: Spelling, grammar, language
development, reading, special edu-
cation
Availability: Direct retail (mail order)
Services: Catalog; preview policy.

SPECTRUM HOLOBYTE
2490 Mariner Sq. Loop, Alameda, CA
94501
510-522-3584, 800-695-4263; Fax:
510-522-3587

Producer/Distributor
Formats: Educational software
Hardware: Apple, DOS, Macintosh
Subjects: Language arts, mathematics

SPINNAKER SOFTWARE CORP.
201 Broadway, Cambridge, MA 02139
617-494-1200, 800-826-0706
Pres: David Seuss
Sales Mgr: Priscilla Seuss

Producer/Distributor
Formats: Educational and entertain-
ment software
Hardware: DOS, Windows
Audience: K-12, adult
Subjects: Mathematics, social studies,
English, language arts, history,
science
Availability: Retail, direct retailServices:
Catalog

STECK-VAUGHN
Box 26015, Austin, TX 78755
800-558-7264; Fax: 512-343-6854
Pres: Roy Mayers
Sales Mgr: Gunner Voltz

Producer/Distributor
Formats: Educational software,
CD-ROM
Hardware: DOS, Apple IIE
Subjects: Dinosaurs, GED, pre-GED
Availability: Mail order
Services: Catalog. Exhibit at con-
ferences

SUBLOGIC CORPORATION
713 Edgebrook Dr., Champaign, IL
61820
217-359-8482
Pres: Bruce Artwick
Sales Mgr: Von Young

Producer/Distributor

Formats: Educational, game, and
graphics software; copyprotected
Hardware: Apple II, DOS
Audience: K-12, adult
Subjects: Music, spelling
Availability: Mail order, retail stores
Services: Catalog; promotional newslet-
ters; preview policy

SYMANTEC CORPORATION
10201 Torre Ave., Cupertino, CA
95014
408-253-9600, 800-441-7234; Fax:
408-253-3968

Producer/Distributor

SYRACUSE LANGUAGE SYSTEMS
719 E. Genesee St., Syracuse, NY
13210
Pres: Martin Rothenberg
Sales Mgr: Larry Rothenberg

Producer/Distributor
Formats: Foreign language software;
CD-ROM
Hardware: MPC Computer
Audience: PreK-12, adult
Subjects: Foreign language: Spanish,
French, German, Japanese, English,
ESL
Availability: Direct retail (mail order),
retail

T/MAKER
1390 Villa St., Mountain View, CA
94941
415-962-0195
Pres: Heidi Roizen
Sales Mgr: Diane Kreyenhagen

Producer/Distributor
Formats: Educational software;
CD-ROM
Hardware: DOS, Macintosh, Windows
Audience: K-12, adult
Subjects: Zoombook, interactive book
Availability: Retail, direct retail
Services: Catalog
Distribution: EdTech

TANAGER SOFTWARE PRODUCTIONS
1933 Kavis St., Ste. 208, San Lean-
dro, CA 94577
510-430-0900, 800-841-2020; Fax:
510-430-0917
Pres: Jeff Silverman

Producer/Distributor
Formats: Educational and entertain-
ment software
Hardware: DOS, Macintosh
Audience: K-12, adult
Availability: Retail
Services: Catalog

CHIP TAYLOR COMMUNICATIONS
15 Spollett Dr., Derry, NH 03038
800-876-CHIP; Fax: 603-434-9262
Contact: Chip Taylor

Producer/Distributor
Format: VHS, software, audiotapes,
    overhead transparencies
Services: Catalog

**TEACH YOURSELF BY COMPUTER
    SOFTWARE, INC.**
3400 Monroe Ave., Rochester, NY
    14445
800-764-4691
Pres: Lois B. Bennett

Producer/Distributor
Formats: Educational, authoring sys-
    tems, and teaching aids software;
    copyprotected
Hardware: Apple II, Macintosh, DOS
Audience: K-12, adult
Subjects: Language development, spe-
    cial education, foreign languages,
    mathematics, spelling, geography,
    physical education, teacher aids,
    grammar, science, history, social
    science, clip art
Availability: Direct retail (mail order),
    retail stores
Discount: Schools & libraries, 5 or
    more, 20%
Services: Catalog; promotional newslet-
    ters; preview policy.

**TECHNICAL EDUCATIONAL CON-
    SULTANTS**
76 N. Broadway, Ste, 4009, Hicksville,
    NY 11801
516-681-1773, 800-34-STUDY
Pres: Dr. Jerrold Kleinstein
Sales Mgr & Lib/Sch Prom Dir: Arnold
    Kleinstein

Producer/Distributor
Formats: Educational and computer-
    aided instruction software;
    copyprotected
Hardware: Apple II, Franklin
Audience: 9-12, adult
Subjects: Mathematics, biology
Availability: Direct retail (mail order)
Services: Catalog; preview policy

TECHWARE
Box 151085, Altamonte, FL
    32715-1085
800-347-3224

Producer/Distributor

TERRAPIN SOFTWARE
400 Riverside St., Portland, ME 04103
207-878-8200, 800-972-8200; Fax:
    207-797-9235
Sales Contact: Tricia Paul

Producer/Distributor
Formats: Educational/training software
Hardware: Apple, DOS
Subjects: Computer literacy

TEXAS CAVIAR, INC.
3933 Steck Ave., B-115, Austin, TX
    78759

512-346-7887, 800-648-1719; Fax:
    512-346-1393
Pres: C. J. Kuhn
Sales Mgr: Richard Smith

Producer/Distributor
Formats: CD-ROM
Hardware: Apple II, DOS, Windows,
    Macintosh
Audience: 1-6
Subjects: Reading, social studies,
    music
Availability: Retail

TIME WARNER INTERACTIVE GROUP
(Formerly Warner New Media)
2210 W. Olive Ave., Burbank, CA
    91506-2626
818-955-9999, 800-482-3766
    (orders); Fax: 818-955-6499
Pres: Terry Hershey
Sales Mgr: Katie Morgan
PR Mgr: Kim Sudhalter

Producer/Distributor
Formats: Educational and entertain-
    ment CD-ROM
Hardware: DOS, Windows, Macintosh
Audience: PreK-12, adult
Subjects: Beginning learning, social
    studies, language arts, history,
    science, problem-solving skills
Availability: Retail, mail order
Services: Catalog. Exhibit at trade
    shows (CES, New Media EXPO, In-
    termedia, COMDEX)

TIMEWORKS, INC.
625 Academy Dr., Northbrook, IL
    60062
708-559-1300, 800-535-9497; Fax:
    708-559-1399

Producer/Distributor
Subjects: Foreign languages

TOP TEN SOFTWARE
40982 N. State Hwy. 41, Oakhurst, CA
    93644-9600
209-683-7577; Fax: 209-683-7566

Producer/Distributor
Formats: Educational software
Hardware: Apple, DOS
Subjects: Science

TRUE BASIC
12 Commerce Ave., West Lebanon, NH
    03784
603-298-5655, 800-872-2742; Fax:
    603-298-7015
Sales Contact: Norm Chapman

Producer/Distributor
Hardware: Apple, DOS,
    Macintosh
Audience: 7-12
Subjects: Instructional tools,
    mathematics

TROLL ASSOCIATES
100 Corporate Dr., Mahwah, NJ 07430
201-529-4000
Sales Contact: Toni Samuel

Producer/Distributor
Formats: Educational software
Subjects: Language arts

TURNER MULTIMEDIA
105 Terry Dr., Ste. 120, Newtown, PA
    18940
800-344-6219; Fax: 215-579-8589

Producer/Distributor
Formats: CD-ROM, laser disc, video
Hardware: DOS, Windows, Macintosh
Audience: K-12, adult
Subjects: Science, social studies
Availability: Mail order
Services: Catalog, preview of approval

UMI
A Bell & Howell Information Company
300 North Zeeb Rd., Ann Arbor, MI
    48106
800-521-3044

Producer
Formats: CD-ROM
Hardware: DOS
Audience: 6-12
Subjects: Newspapers, dissertation ab-
    stracts, periodical abstracts
Availability: Direct retail (mail order),
    sales rep
Services: Catalog

UPDATA PUBLICATIONS INC.
1736 Westwood Blvd., Los Angeles,
    CA 90024
800-882-2844; Fax: 310-474-4095
Pres: Herbert Sclar
Sales Mgr: George Wright

Producer/Distributor
Formats: Educational software;
    CD-ROM
Hardware: Apple II, DOS, MPC
Audience: K-12
Subjects: Mathematics, social studies,
    English, language arts, history,
    science
Availability: Direct retail (mail order)
Services: Catalog; maintains database
    on all CD-ROMs

**UPPER BROADWAY BODEGA
    SOFTWARE**
Box 5001, Manchester, CT
    06045-5001
203-647-8104
Pres: Ann Bevilacqua

Producer/Distributor
Formats: Library software (Hypercard)
Hardware: Macintosh
Audience: K-12
Subjects: Library automation
Availability: Direct retail (mail order)
Services: Catalog

VALIANT INTERNATIONAL MULTI-MEDIA CORP.

195 Bonhomme St., Hackensack, NJ
07602
201-487-6340, 800-631-0867; Fax:
201-487-1930
Pres: Shelly Boldstein
Sales Mgrs: Mike Lethbridge, Anthony
Frasca

Distributor
Formats: CD-ROM, Video
Hardware: DOS, Macintosh
Audience: K-12, adult
Subjects: Educational, foreign lan-
guage, nature, entertainment, health
& fitness, research
Availability: Mail order
Services: Catalog, exhibit at trade
shows

VIRTUAL REALITY LABORATORIES

2341 Ganador Court, San Louis
Obispo, CA 93401
805-545-8515

Producer/Distributor
Formats: Educational software
Hardware: DOS, Macintosh, Windows,
Amiga
Audience: 7-12
Subjects: Astronomy
Availability: Direct retail (mail order)
Services: Catalog

VOYAGER

1 Bridge St., Irvington, NY 10533
914-591-5500, 800-446-2001
Pres: Bob Stein
Sales Mgr: Jane Wheeler

Distributor
Formats: CD-ROM
Hardware: DOS, Macintosh
Audience: K-12, adult
Subjects: Art, history, current events,
language arts, poetry, music,
movies, etc.
Availability: Direct retail (mail order)
Services: Catalog

VENTURA EDUCATIONAL SYSTEMS

910 Ramona Ave., Grover City, CA
93433
805-473-7380, 800-336-1022; Fax:
805-473-7382
Sales Contact: Fred Ventura

Producers/Distributor
Formats: Educational software
Hardware: Apple, DOS, Macintosh
Subjects: Computer literacy,
mathematics, science

VERNIER SOFTWARE

2920 SW 89th St., Portland, OR
97225
503-297-5317; Fax: 503-297-1760
Sales Contact: Christine Vernier

Producer/Distributor
Formats: Educational software
Hardware: Apple, DOS
Audience: 7-12
Subjects: Science

VIDEODISCOVERY

1700 W. Lake Ave. N, Seattle, WA
98109-3012
206-285-5400, 800-548-3472; Fax:
206-285-9245
Sales Contact: Polly Knefick

Producer/Distributor
Formats: Educational software
Hardware: DOS, Macintosh
Subjects: Art, biology, chemistry, multi-
media, science, teacher aids/instruc-
tional tools

ROGER WAGNER PUBLISHING

1050 Pioneer Way, Ste. P, El Cajon,
CA 92020
619-442-0522, 800-421-6526; Fax:
619-442-0525

Producer/Distributor
Formats: Educational software
Hardware: Apple Macintosh
Subjects: Teacher aids/instructional
tools

H. C. WARD CO.

Box 3412, DeLand, FL 32723
904-738-3412
Pres: H. C. Ward

Producer/Distributor
Formats: Educational software;
copyprotected
Hardware: VIC-20, Apple II, Commo-
dore, DOS, Radio Shack
Audience: 5-12, adult
Subjects: Remediation, mathematics
Availability: Direct retail
Discount: Quantity
Services: Catalog; preview policy

WAYZATA TECHNOLOGY

2515 E. Hwy. 2, Box 807, Grand
Rapids, MN 55744-3271
218-326-0597, 800-735-7321; Fax:
218-326-0598
Pres: Mark Engelhardt
Sales Mgr: Jon Simonsen

Producer/Distributor
Formats: Educational software
Hardware: DOS, Macintosh, Windows
Audience: K-12
Subjects: Mathematics, social studies,
English, language arts, history,
science
Availability: Direct retail (mail order)
Services: Catalog

WENGER CORPORATION, MUSIC LEARNING DIVISION

1401 E. 79th St., Minneapolis, MN
55420
612-854-1288
Pres: Lowell Fisher
Sales Mgr: Margaret Erikson
Lib/Sch Prom Dir: Daniel Kantor

Producer/Distributor
Formats: Educational courseware,
games, computer-aided instruction,
teaching aids, and administration
software; copyprotected
Hardware: Macintosh, Amiga, Atari St.,
Apple II, Atari, Commodore, DOS
Audience: Preschool-12, adult
Subjects: Music
Availability: Direct retail (mail order),
retail stores
Services: Catalog; promotional newslet-
ters; preview policy; exhibit at music
educator conventions

WILD DUCK

979 Golf Course Dr., Rohnert Park, CA
94928
707-586-0728, 800-410-6677; Fax:
707-586-0728

Producer/Distributor
Hardware: Amiga, DOS
Subjects: Art, instructional tools

H. W. WILSON

950 University Ave., Bronx, NY 10452
800-367-6770
Pres: Leo Weins
Sales Mgr: Debby Loedin

Producer/Distributor
Formats: CD-ROM
Hardware: DOS, Macintosh
Audience: 6-12, adult
Subjects: Indexes to bibliography,
book reviews, education, science,
periodical literature
Availability: Direct retail (mail order)
Services: Catalog; vendor rep

WINGS FOR LEARNING/SUNBURST

101 Castleton St., Box 100, Pleasantville, NY 10570
914-747-3310, 800-321-7511; Fax:
914-747-4109
Pres: Sally Wood
Sales Mgr: Julie Scarpa

Producer/Distributor
Formats: Educational software
Hardware: DOS, Mcintosh, Apple II
Audience: K-12
Subjects: Art, mathematics, social
studies, English, language arts, his-
tory, science
Availability: Direct retail (mail order)
Services: Catalog; demo disk

WINNEBAGO SOFTWARE CO.

121 S. Marshall, Box 430, Caledonia,
MN 55921
507-724-5411, 800-533-5430
Pres: Jeb Griffith
Sr VP: Bob Engen

Producer/Distributor
Formats: Integrated library systems
   software; copyprotected
Hardware: Apple II, DOS,
   Macintosh
Audience: 6-12, adult
Subjects: Library automation
Availability: Direct retail (mail order)
Discount: Inquire
Services: Catalog. Promotional news-
   letters. Exhibit at AASL, ALA, state
   SSLI conferences

WORLD BOOK EDUCATIONAL PRODUCTS

A Scott Fetzer Company
101 Northwest Point Blvd., Elk Grove
   Village, IL 60007
800-621-8202; Fax: 708-290-5301

Producer/Distributor
Formats: CD-ROM, video
Hardware: DOS, Macintosh, Windows
Subjects: Educational reference
Availability: Direct Mail
Services: Brochures. Exhibit at con-
   ferences

WIZARDWORKS

5354 Parkdale Dr., Ste. 104,
   Minneapolis, MN 55416
800-7859-5645; Fax: 612-541-4973
Pres: Robert J. Armstrong
Sales Mgr: Paul D. Rinde

Producer/Distributor
Formats: Educational and entertain-
   ment software
Hardware: DOS
Audience: K-12, adult
Subjects: Mathematics, social studies,

English, language arts, history,
   science
Availability: Retail
Services: Catalog

WORDPERFECT CORPORATION

1555 N. Technology Way, Orem, UT
   84057
801-225-5000, 800-321-4566; Fax:
   801-228-5377

WORDSTAR INTERNATIONAL

Box 6113, Novato, CA 94948
415-382-8000, 800-227-5609; Fax:
   415-883-1629
Orders: Box 629000, El Dorado Hills,
   CA 95762. 800-582-8000

WORLD GAME INSTITUTE

3215 Race St., Philadelphia, PA
   19104-2597
215-387-0220; Fax: 215-387-3009
Sales Contact: Elizabeth Infield

Producer/Distributor
Formats: Educational software
Hardware: Macintosh
Subjects: Environment & energy,
   science, social studies

WORLD LIBRARY, INC.

2809 Main St., Irvine, CA
   92714
714-756-9500, 800-443-0238
VP Sales & Mktg: Valerie Hustwit
Asst Dir of Sales & Mktg: Tina
   Lamperts

Producer/Distributor
Formats: CD-ROM
Hardware: IBM, Macintosh
Audience: 7-12, adult

Subjects: Classical literature
Availability: Mail order
Services: Catalog. Exhibit at ALA, ABA,
   others

WORLDVIEW SOFTWARE

76 N. Broadway, Ste. 4009, Hicksville,
   NY 11801
516-681-1773; 800-34-STUDY; Fax:
   516-822-0950

Producer/Distributor
Formats: Educational software
Hardware: DOS, Apple II
Audience: 7-12, adult
Subjects: American history, European
   history, multicultural social studies,
   Africa, Latin America, Middle East,
   Far East
Availability: Direct retail (mail order)
Discount: Available for district-wide
   adoption
Services: Catalog; preview policy; ex-
   hibit at NCSS

XIPHIAS

8758 Venice Blvd., Los Angeles, CA
   90034
310-841-2790, 800-532-3766; Fax:
   310-841-2559
VP: Jim Blake
Mktg: Kim Devore

Producer
Formats: CD-ROM
Hardware: Windows, DOS, Macintosh
Audience: 2-12, adults
Subjects: Educational materials, gener-
   al science, arts, business & politics
Availablility: Retail
Services: Catalog. Exhibit at trade
   shows (CES, COMDEX)

SOFTWARE PRODUCERS & DISTRIBUTORS—CLASSIFIED BY SUBJECT

ART

ACADEMIC HALLMARKS, INC.
ADOBE SYSTEMS
AGENCY FOR INSTRUCTIONAL TECH-
  NOLOGY
ALDUS
AV SYSTEMS, INC.
BAKER & TAYLOR SOFTWARE
BAUDVILLE
BRODERBUND SOFTWARE
CD-ROM INC.
CLARIS
CREATIVE PURSUITS
CULTURAL RESOURCES
DAVIDSON
DENEBA SYSTEMS
DYNACOMP, INC.
EDEN INTERACTIVE
ELECTRONIC ARTS
GPN
INTELLIMATION
KOALA ACQUISITIONS
THE LEARNING COMPANY
THE LEARNING CUBE
MECC
MACROMEDIA
MICROSOFT
MINDSCAPE
NEW MEDIA SOURCE
POSTCRAFT
POWER INDUSTRIES
PUTNAM NEW MEDIA
QUANTA PRESS INC.
SCHOLASTIC
VIDEODISCOVERY
VOYAGER
WILD DUCK
XIPHIAS

ASTRONOMY

ACADEMIC HALLMARKS, INC.
VIRTUAL REALITY LABORATORIES

AUTHORING SOFTWARE

ACADEMIC HALLMARKS, INC.
B5 SOFTWARE CO.
DIGITAL IMAGING ASSOCIATES
DYNACOMP, INC.
EARTHWARE COMPUTER SERVICES
HARTLEY COURSEWARE, INC.
INTERKOM SOFTWARE
MICROED INC.
MICROPHYS
PASSPORT DESIGNS, INC.
TEACH YOURSELF BY COMPUTER
  SOFTWARE, INC.

AUTOMOTIVE

SOFTWARE MARKETING CORP.

BIBLIOGRAPHY

H. W. WILSON
REED REFERENCE PUBLISHING
SWLI - MULTIMEDIA PRODUCTS
  DIVISION

BIOGRAPHIES

GALE RESEARCH
REED REFERENCE PUBLISHING

BIOLOGY

ACADEMIC HALLMARKS, INC.
ARIS MULTIMEDIA ENTERTAINMENT
WILLIAM BRADFORD
EDUCATIONAL IMAGES
INTELLIMATION
MAGIC QUEST
MAXIS
NATIONAL GEOGRAPHIC
OPTICAL DATA
SCHOLASTIC
TOM SYNDER
TECHNICAL EDUCATIONAL CON-
  SULTANTS
TOP TEN SOFTWARE
VENTURA
VIDEODISCOVERY

BOOKS, TALKING

KNOWLEDGE ADVENTURE INC.

BOOKS, INTERACTIVE

T/MAKER

BUSINESS/BUSINESS EDUCATION

AV SYSTEMS, INC.
BLS TUTORSYSTEMS
BANNER BLUE SOFTWARE
BYTES OF LEARNING
CD-ROM, INC.
DIDATECH
DYNACOMP, INC.
EDUCATIONAL ACTIVITIES INC.
EMC PUBLISHING
FRIENDLYSOFT, INC.
HIGH TECHNOLOGY
INTUIT
LEARNING ARTS
MICRO LEARNINGWARE
MULTIMEDIA PUBLISHERS GROUP
NATIONAL BOOK COMPANY
OPPORTUNITIES FOR LEARNING
PLUMA SOFTWARE
SIR-TECH SOFTWARE, INC.
SOCIAL STUDIES SCHOOL SERVICE
SOFTSYNC
SOUTHWESTERN PUBLISHING
XIPHIAS

CAREER EDUCATION

CHRONICLE GUIDANCE PUBLICATIONS
  INC.
EDUCATIONAL IMAGES
EUREKA MICROSKILLS III

CHEMISTRY

ACADEMIC HALLMARKS, INC.
BROOKS/COLE PUBLISHING
FALCON SOFTWARE
SOFTWARE MARKETING CORP.
VIDEODISCOVERY

CLIP ART

LIBRARIES UNLIMITED
TEACH YOURSELF BY COMPUTER
  SOFTWARE, INC.

COMPOSITION

CONDUIT
DATA COMMAND INC.
FRIENDLYSOFT, INC.
LEARNCO, INC.
LEARNING ARTS
MICRO LEARNINGWARE
OPPORTUNITIES FOR LEARNING
SOCIAL STUDIES SCHOOL SERVICE

COMPUTER LITERACY

ALADDIN SOFTWARE
ARTIFICIAL INTELLIGENCE RESEARCH
  GROUP
AV SYSTEMS, INC.
B5 SOFTWARE CO
BAUDVILLE
BORLAND
CLARIS
CONTINENTAL PRESS INC.
DYNACOMP, INC.
EARTHWARE COMPUTER SERVICES
EDUCATIONAL ACTIVITIES INC.
EMA SOFTWARE
FRIENDLYSOFT, INC.
HARTLEY COURSEWARE, INC.
IBM
INSTRUCTIONAL COMMUNICATIONS
  TECHNOLOGY
INTELLIMATION
KRELL SOFTWARE
LCSI
LEARNING ARTS
LEGO
MICRO LEARNINGWARE
NATIONAL BOOK COMPANY
OPPORTUNITIES FOR LEARNING
PARADIGM
SCHOLASTIC INC.
SIR-TECH SOFTWARE, INC.
SOCIAL STUDIES SCHOOL SERVICE

TERRAPIN
VENTURA
WAYZATA

COMPUTER SCIENCE

EARTHWARE COMPUTER SERVICES
METIER

CRITICAL THINKING

CRITICAL THINKING PRESS &
   SOFTWARE
DATA COMMAND INC.
TOM SNYDER PRODUCTION

CURRENT EVENTS

COMPACT PUBLISHING
PERMA-BOUND
VOYAGER

DINOSAURS

APPLIED OPTICAL MEDIA CORP.
KNOWLEDGE ADVENTURE INC.
MAVERIC SOFTWARE
STECK-VAUGHN

DRIVER'S EDUCATION

BLS TUTORSYSTEMS

EARLY CHILDHOOD/EARLY EDUCATION

AGENCY FOR INSTRUCTIONAL TECH-
   NOLOGY
BRODERBUND
COMP ED
DAVIDSON
DISCIS
EDUCATIONAL ACTIVITIES INC.
LEARNING COMPANY
THE LEARNING CUBE
MIDWEST SOFTWARE
ORANGECHERRY NEW MEDIA
   SCHOOLHOUSE

EARTH SCIENCE

BRODERBUND
EARTHWARE COMPUTER SERVICES
MECC
MAGIC QUEST
MAXIS
NATIONAL GEOGRAPHIC
OPTICAL DATA
TOM SYNDER
TURNER MULTIMEDIA
VOYAGER
WINGS FOR LEARNING

ECONOMICS

ACADEMIC HALLMARKS, INC.
BANNER BLUE SOFTWARE
CD-ROM INC.
CONDUIT
DYNACOMP, INC.
EDUCATIONAL ACTIVITIES INC.

EMC PUBLISHING
LEARNCO, INC.
LEARNING ARTS
MICROED INC.
OPPORTUNITIES FOR LEARNING
SOCIAL STUDIES SCHOOL SERVICE

ELECTRONIC COLORING BOOKS

BIGFOOT PUBLISHING (GRT Corp)

ENCYCLOPEDIA

COMPTON'S NEWMEDIA
GROLIER EDUCATIOINAL COR-
   PORATION
ENCYCLOPEDIA BRITTANICA
WORLD BOOK

ENGLISH

ACADEMIC HALLMARKS, INC.
ACTIVISION
WILLIAM K. BRADFORD PUBLISHING
CONDUIT
COREL
DAVIDSON & ASSOC. INC.
EBSCO PUBLISHING
EDUCORP
HEARTSOFT
INDIVIDUAL SOFTWARE CO.
K-12 MICROMEDIA
LASER LEARNING TECHNOLOGIES
ONLINE COMPUTER SYSTEMS
PETERSONS
RIGHT ON PROGRAMS
TOM SNYDER PRODUCTION
SOFTWARE TOOLWORKS
SPINNAKER SOFTWARE CORP.
SYRACUSE LANGUAGE SYSTEMS
UPDATA PUBLICATIONS INC.
WAYZATA TECHNOLOGY
WINGS FOR LEARNING/SUNBURST
WIZARDWORKS

ENTERTAINMENT/ENTERTAINMENT
   SOFTWARE

ACTIVISION
BIGFOOT PUBLISHING (GRT Corp)
CD-ROM INC.
CHARIOT SOFTWARE GROUP
CREATIVE PURSUITS
CREATIVE MULTIMEDIA CORPORATION
DAVIDSON & ASSOC. INC.
EA*KIDS
EDEN INTERACTIVE
HEARTSOFT

ENVIRONMENT AND ENERGY

AV SYSTEMS, INC.
CHARIOT SOFTWARE
DYNACOMP, INC.
EDUCATIONAL ACTIVITIES INC.
EDUCATIONAL IMAGES
EME CORPORATION
HRM SOFTWARE
MECC
MAGIC QUEST

NATIONAL GEOGRAPHIC
SCHOLASTIC
TOM SYNDER
SOCIAL STUDIES SCHOOL SERVICE
TOP TEN SOFTWARE
WINGS FOR LEARNING
WORLD GAME INSTITUTE

ESL

EDUCATIONAL ACTIVITIES INC.
GESSLER EDUCATIONAL
MERIT AUDIO VISUAL
SYRACUSE LANGUAGE SYSTEMS

FOOD AND NUTRITION

GPN

FOREIGN LANGUAGES

AGENCY FOR INSTRUCTIONAL
   TECHNOLOGY
AMERICAN EDUCATIONAL
AUDIO FORUM
AV SYSTEMS, INC.
WILLIAM BRADFORD
CONDUIT
DAVIDSON
DYNACOMP, INC.
EMC PUBLISHING
EDUCATIONAL ACTIVITIES
GESSLER EDUCATIONAL
HARTLEY COURSEWARE, INC.
HYPERGLOT FOREIGN LANGUAGE
   SOFTWARE CO.
INTELLIMATION
KNOWLEDGE ADVENTURE
LEARNING ARTS
LEARNING COMPANY
THE LEARNING CUBE
LINGO FUN, INC.
MICROED INC.
MICRO LEARNINGWARE
NATIONAL TEXTBOOK CO.
OPTIMUM RESOURCE
SYRACUSE LANGUAGE SYSTEMS
TEACH YOURSELF BY COMPUTER
   SOFTWARE, INC.
TIMEWORKS
VALIANT INTERNATIONAL MULTI—
   MEDIA CORP
VOYAGER

GAMES

ARTIFICIAL INTELLIGENCE RESEARCH
   GROUP
AV SYSTEMS, INC.
BRODERBUND
COREL
CRITICAL THINKING PRESS &
   SOFTWARE
CROSS EDUCATIONAL SOFTWARE
DEC COMPUTING
DYNACOMP, INC.
EARTHWARE COMPUTER SERVICES
ELECTRONIC COURSEWARE SYSTEMS
   INC.

FRIENDLYSOFT, INC.
HARTLEY COURSEWARE, INC.
INTERKOM SOFTWARE
KRELL SOFTWARE
LEARNING ARTS
MEDIA VISION
MICROPHYS
OPPORTUNITIES FOR LEARNING
SOFTSHOPPE II
SUBLOGIC CORPORATION
WENGER CORPORATION

GED

COREL
STECK-VAUGHN

GEOLOGY

ACADEMIC HALLMARKS, INC.
EARTHWARE COMPUTER SERVICES

GENEALOGY

BANNER BLUE SOFTWARE

GEOGRAPHY

ACADEMIC HALLMARKS, INC.
ALADDIN SOFTWARE
AV SYSTEMS, INC.
BAKER & TAYLOR SOFTWARE
BRODERBUND SOFTWARE, INC.
DATA COMMAND INC.
E. DAVID & ASSOCIATES
DYNACOMP, INC.
EDUCATIONAL ACTIVITIES INC.
EDUCATIONAL IMAGES
ELECTRONIC COURSEWARE SYSTEMS
   INC.
HRM SOFTWARE
LAWRENCE PRODUCTIONS, INC.
LEARNING ARTS
MEDIA ALIVE
MICROED INC.
MICROGRAMS
MICRO LEARNINGWARE
OPPORTUNITIES FOR LEARNING
ORANGECHERRY NEW MEDIA
   SCHOOLHOUSE
SOCIAL STUDIES SCHOOL SERVICE
TEACH YOURSELF BY COMPUTER
   SOFTWARE, INC.

GOVERNMENT

ACADEMIC HALLMARKS, INC.
CD-ROM INC.
INFORMATION ACCESS
QUANTA PRESS INC.

GRAMMAR

AQUARIUS PEOPLE MATERIALS, INC.
AV SYSTEMS, INC.
B5 SOFTWARE CO.
BLS TUTORSYSTEMS
CONTINENTAL PRESS INC.
DATA COMMAND INC.
E. DAVID & ASSOCIATES

DYNACOMP, INC.
EMC PUBLISHING
EDUCATIONAL ACTIVITIES INC.
ELECTRONIC COURSEWARE SYSTEMS
   INC.
FILMS FOR THE HUMANITIES
HARTLEY COURSEWARE, INC.
INTERKOM SOFTWARE
KRELL SOFTWARE
LAUREATE LEARNING SYSTEMS, INC.
LEARNING ARTS
THE LEARNING COMPANY
MERIT AUDIO VISUAL
MICROED INC.
MICROGRAMS
MICRO LEARNINGWARE
OPPORTUNITIES FOR LEARNING
SOCIAL STUDIES SCHOOL SERVICE
SPECIAL LEARNING ED SOFTWARE
TEACH YOURSELF BY COMPUTER
   SOFTWARE, INC.

HEALTH/HEALTH EDUCATION

ABC NEWS
ACADEMIC HALLMARKS, INC.
AGENCY FOR INSTRUCTIONAL
   TECHNOLOGY
AV SYSTEMS, INC.
BLS TUTORSYSTEMS
DYNACOMP, INC.
EBSCO PUBLISHING
EDUCATIONAL IMAGES
EME CORPORATION
HRM SOFTWARE
LEARNING ARTS
MECC
MARSHWARE
MATH & COMPUTER EDUCATION
   PROJECT
MICROED INC.
MICROGRAMS
MICRO LEARNINGWARE
TOM SNYDER
SOCIAL STUDIES SCHOOL SERVICE
VALIANT INTERNATIONAL

HISTORY

ACADEMIC HALLMARKS
ACTIVISION
AQUARIUS PEOPLE MATERIALS, INC.
AV SYSTEMS, INC.
B5 SOFTWARE CO.
BLS TUTORSYSTEMS
BAKER & TAYLOR SOFTWARE
WILLIAM K. BRADFORD PUBLISHING
BRODERBUND SOFTWARE, INC.
BUREAU OF ELECTRONIC PUBLISHING
CULTURAL RESOURCES
DAVIDSON & ASSOC. INC.
DYNACOMP, INC.
EBSCO PUBLISHING
EDEN INTERACTIVE
EDUCATIONAL ACTIVITIES INC.
EDUCORP
EDUQUEST
ELECTRONIC COURSEWARE SYSTEMS
   INC.
HARTLEY COURSEWARE, INC.

HEARTSOFT
INDIVIDUAL SOFTWARE CO.
INFOBASES INTERNATIONAL INC.
K-12 MICROMEDIA
LASER LEARNING TECHNOLOGIES
LAWRENCE PRODUCTIONS, INC.
LEARNING ARTS
LIBRARIES UNLIMITED
MICROED INC.
MICROGRAMS
MICRO LEARNINGWARE
MICROSOFT
NATIONAL GEOGRAPHIC SOCIETY
ONLINE COMPUTER SYSTEMS
OPPORTUNITIES FOR LEARNING
OPTIMUM RESOURCE
ORANGECHERRY NEW MEDIA
   SCHOOLHOUSE
PETERSONS
PUTNAM NEW MEDIA
TOM SNYDER PRODUCTION
SOCIAL STUDIES SCHOOL SERVICE
SOFTWARE TOOLWORKS
SPINNAKER SOFTWARE CORP.
TEACH YOURSELF BY COMPUTER
   SOFTWARE, INC.
TIME WARNER INTERACTIVE GROUP
UPDATA PUBLICATIONS INC.
VOYAGER
WAYZATA TECHNOLOGY
WINGS FOR LEARNING/SUNBURST
WIZARDWORKS
WORLDVIEW SOFTWARE

HOME ECONOMICS

AQUARIUS PEOPLE MATERIALS, INC.
AV SYSTEMS, INC.
DYNACOMP, INC.
EMC PUBLISHING
MICROED INC.
MICRO LEARNINGWARE
SOCIAL STUDIES SCHOOL SERVICE

INDUSTRIAL ARTS

AQUARIUS PEOPLE MATERIALS, INC.
AV SYSTEMS, INC.
DYNACOMP, INC.
EMC PUBLISHING

INSTRUCTIONAL TOOLS

See TEACHER AIDS/INSTRUCTIONAL
   TOOLS

LANGUAGE ARTS

ACTIVISION
AGENCY FOR INSTRUCTIONAL TECH-
   NOLOGY
WILLIAM BRADFORD
BRODERBUND SOFTWARE, INC.
COMP ED
COMPUTEACH
CONDUIT
CREATIVE MULTIMEDIA
CRITICAL THINKING PRESS &
   SOFTWARE
DAVIDSON & ASSOC. INC.

DISCIS
EDMARK
EDUCORP
EDUQUEST
ELECTRONIC BOOKS
FRAME TECHNOLOGY
GAMCO
GREAT WAVE
HARTLEY COURSEWARE
HEARTSOFT
HOUGHTON MIFFLIN
HUMANITIES SOFTWARE
INDIVIDUAL SOFTWARE CO.
INSPIRATION SOFTWARE
INTELLIMATION
K-12 MICROMEDIA
LCSI
LASER LEARNING TECHNOLOGIES
LAUREATE LEARNING
LAWRENCE PRODUCTIONS
LEARNING COMPANY
MECC
MINDPLAY
ONLINE COMPUTER SYSTEMS
OPTIMUM RESOURCES
ORANGECHERRY NEW MEDIA
   SCHOOLHOUSE
PETERSONS
QUALITY COMPUTERS
QUEUE
RIGHT ON PROGRAMS
SANCTUARY WOODS
SCHOLASTIC INC.
SIERRA ON-LINE
TOM SNYDER PRODUCTION
SOFTWARE TOOLWORKS
SPECTRUM HOLOBYTE
SPINNAKER SOFTWARE CORP.
TIME WARNER INTERACTIVE GROUP
TROLL ASSOCIATES
UPDATA PUBLICATIONS INC.
VOYAGER
WAYZATA TECHNOLOGY
WINGS FOR LEARNING/SUNBURST
WIZARDWORKS
WORDPERFECT
WORDSTAR

LANGUAGE DEVELOPMENT

AQUARIUS PEOPLE MATERIALS, INC.
ARTIFICIAL INTELLIGENCE RESEARCH
   GROUP
AV SYSTEMS, INC.
B5 SOFTWARE CO.
C AND C SOFTWARE
DYNACOMP, INC.
E. DAVID & ASSOCIATES
EDUCATIONAL ACTIVITIES INC.
ELECTRONIC COURSEWARE SYSTEMS
   INC.
EMC PUBLISHING
FILMS FOR THE HUMANITIES
HRM SOFTWARE
HARTLEY COURSEWARE, INC.
INSTRUCTIONAL COMMUNICATIONS
   TECHNOLOGY, INC./TAYLOR AS-
   SOCIATES
INTERKOM SOFTWARE
KRELL SOFTWARE

LAUREATE LEARNING SYSTEMS, INC.
LEARNING ARTS
THE LEARNING COMPANY
MICROED INC.
MICROGRAMS
MICRO LEARNINGWARE
MICROPHYS
MIDWEST SOFTWARE
NATIONAL TEXTBOOK CO.
OPPORTUNITIES FOR LEARNING
SIR-TECH SOFTWARE, INC.
SPECIAL LEARNING ED SOFTWARE
TEACH YOURSELF BY COMPUTER
   SOFTWARE, INC.

LANGUAGES

See also FOREIGN LANGUAGES

APPLIED OPTICAL MEDIA CORP.
HUMANITIES SOFTWARE
ORANGECHERRY NEW MEDIA
   SCHOOLHOUSE
PENTON OVERSEAS INC.

LAW

ACADEMIC HALLMARKS, INC.
CD-ROM INC.

LIBRARY AUTOMATION

AUTO-GRAPHICS, INC.
CALICO Inc.
CASPR, INC.
CHANCERY SOFTWARE
DATA TREK
DYNIX SCHOLAR
FOLLETT SOFTWARE COMPANY
FOUNDATION FOR LIBRARY RESEACH
G.R.C./S.W.L.
LIBRARY CORPORATION
MEDIA FLEX
OCLC
SWLI — MULTIMEDIA
   PRODUCTS DIVISION
SCARECROW PRESS
UPPER BROADWAY BODEGA
   SOFTWARE
WINNEBAGO SOFTWARE CO.

LIBRARY MEDIA

GROLIER
INFORMATION ACCESS
MICROSOFT
NEWSBANK
SILVERPLATTER INFORMATION
TOM SNYDER
H. W. WILSON
WINGS FOR LEARNING

LIBRARY USE

AV SYSTEMS, INC.
DYNACOMP, INC.
EDUCATIONAL ACTIVITIES INC.
LEARNCO, INC.
LEARNING ARTS
MICROED INC.

MICRO LEARNINGWARE
SOCIAL STUDIES SCHOOL SERVICE

LIFE SCIENCES

INTELLIMATION

LITERATURE

BAKER & TAYLOR SOFTWARE
BUREAU OF ELECTRONIC PUBLISHING
CD-ROM INC.
GALE RESEARCH
HUMANITIES SOFTWARE
MEDIA VISION
MICROSOFT
SALEM PRESS, INC.
SOCIAL STUDIES SCHOOL SERVICE
WORLD LIBRARY, INC.

LOGIC

SIR-TECH SOFTWARE, INC.

MANAGEMENT

BANNER BLUE SOFTWARE

MATHEMATICS

ACADEMIC HALLMARKS, INC.
ACTIVISION
ADDISON WESLEY
AGENCY FOR INSTRUCTIONAL TECH-
   NOLOGY
ALADDIN SOFTWARE
AQUARIUS PEOPLE MATERIALS, INC.
AV SYSTEMS, INC.
B5 SOFTWARE CO.
BLS TUTORSYSTEMS
WILLIAM K. BRADFORD PUBLISHING
BRODERBUND SOFTWARE, INC.
BROOKS/COLE
C AND C SOFTWARE
COMP ED
CONDUIT
CONTINENTAL PRESS INC.
COREL
CRITICAL THINKING PRESS &
   SOFTWARE
CURRICULUM ASSOCIATES INC.
DATA COMMAND INC.
E. DAVID & ASSOCIATES
DAVIDSON & ASSOC. INC.
DEC COMPUTING
DESIGN SCIENCE
DEVWARE
DISCIS
DYNACOMP, INC.
EDMARK
EDUCATIONAL ACTIVITIES INC.
EDUCATIONAL RESOURCES
EDUCORP
EDUQUEST
EDUSOFT
ELECTRONIC COURSEWARE SYSTEMS
   INC.
EMA SOFTWARE
EMC PUBLISHING
EME CORPORATION

GAMCO
HRM SOFTWARE
HARTLEY COURSEWARE, INC.
HEARTSOFT
INDIVIDUAL SOFTWARE CO.
INSTRUCTIONAL COMMUNICATIONS
    TECHNOLOGY, INC./TAYLOR AS-
    SOCIATES
INTELLIMATION
K-12 MICROMEDIA
KEY CURRICULUM PRESS
KRELL SOFTWARE
LCSI
LASER LEARNING TECHNOLOGIES
LAWRENCE PRODUCTIONS, INC.
LEARNING ARTS
THE LEARNING COMPANY
THE LEARNING CUBE
LEARNING TEAM
MECC
MATH & COMPUTER EDUCATION
    PROJECT
MATHEGRAPHICS SOFTWARE
MERIT AUDIO VISUAL
METIER
MICROED INC.
MICROGRAMS
MICRO LEARNINGWARE
MICROPHYS
MIDWEST SOFTWARE
MINDPLAY
NATIONAL GEOGRAPHIC
ONLINE COMPUTER SYSTEMS
OPPORTUNITIES FOR LEARNING
OPTIMUM RESOURCE
OPTICAL DATA
ORANGECHERRY NEW MEDIA
    SCHOOLHOUSE
PETERSONS
PRESCIENCE
PUTNAM NEW MEDIA
SCHOLASTIC INC.
TOM SNYDER PRODUCTION
SOFTWARE TOOLWORKS
SPINNAKER SOFTWARE CORP.
TEACH YOURSELF BY COMPUTER
    SOFTWARE, INC.
TECHNICAL EDUCATIONAL CON-
    SULTANTS
TRUE BASIC
UPDATA PUBLICATIONS INC.
VENTURA
VIDEODISCOVERY
VOYAGER
HC WARD CO.
WAYZATA TECHNOLOGY
WINGS FOR LEARNING/SUNBURST
WIZARDWORKS

MEDICAL

CD-ROM INC.
CREATIVE MULTIMEDIA CORPORATION

METEOROLOGY

ACADEMIC HALLMARKS, INC.

MOVIES

VOYAGER

MOVIES, INTERACTIVE

HYPERBOLE STUDIOS

MULTIMEDIA

ABC NEWS
ARIS MULTIMEDIA ENTERTAINMENT
ARIZONA STATE UNIVERSITY
WILLIAM K. BRADFORD PUBLISHING
BRODERBUND
CLARIS
CREATIVE MULTIMEDIA CORPORATION
CULTURAL RESOURSES INC.
DAVIDSON
DISCIS
EMERGING TECHNOLOGY
EDUQUEST
FOLLETT SOFTWARE COMPANY
GROLIER
IBM
INTELLIMATION
LASER LEARNING TECHNOLOGIES
MACROMEDIA
MICROSOFT
MULTIMEDIA PUBLISHERS GROUP
NATIONAL GEOGRAPHIC
OPTICAL DATA
PARADIGM
PASSPORT DESIGNS, INC.
SWLI — MULTIMEDIA PRODUCTS DI-
    VISION
SCHOLASTIC
TOM SNYDER PRODUCTION
TURNER MULTIMEDIA
VIDEODISCOVERY
VOYAGER
WINGS FOR LEARNING
XIPHIAS

MUSIC

ACADEMIC HALLMARKS, INC.
ARS NOVA
AV SYSTEMS, INC.
B5 SOFTWARE CO.
BAUDVILLE
BOGAS PRODUCTIONS
BRODERBUND
CONDUIT
CREATIVE MULTIMEDIA
DYNACOMP, INC.
EBOOK, INC.
EBSCO PUBLISHING
EDUCATIONAL ACTIVITIES INC.
ELECTRONIC ARTS
ELECTRONIC COURSEWARE SYSTEMS
    INC.
GPN
GREAT WAVE
IBIS SOFTWARE
LEARNING COMPANY
THE LEARNING CUBE
MECC
MACROMEDIA
MATH & COMPUTER EDUCATION
    PROJECT
MICROSOFT
NEW MEDIA SOURCE
OPTIMUM RESOURCE

PASSPORT DESIGNS, INC.
SANCTUARY WOODS
SOFTSYNC
SUBLOGIC CORPORATION
TEXAS CAVIAR, INC.
VOYAGER
WENGER CORPORATION, MUSIC
    LEARNING DIVISION

NATURAL SCIENCES

NATIONAL GEOGRAPHIC
ORANGECHERRY NEW MEDIA
    SCHOOLHOUSE
QUANTA PRESS INC.

OCEANOGRAPHY

ACADEMIC HALLMARKS, INC.

ORIGINS

BIGFOOT PUBLISHING (GRT Corp)

PHYSICAL EDUCATION

AV SYSTEMS, INC.
HRM SOFTWARE
HARTLEY COURSEWARE, INC.
LEARNING ARTS
MARSHWARE
MIDWEST SOFTWARE
TEACH YOURSELF BY COMPUTER
    SOFTWARE, INC.

PHYSICS

ACADEMIC HALLMARKS, INC.
BRODERBUND
HIGH TECHNOLOGY SOFTWARE
    PRODUCTS, INC.
KNOWLEDGE REVOLUTION
MECC
OPTICAL DATA
VERNIER SOFTWARE
WINGS FOR LEARNING

POETRY

COLUMBIA UNIVERSITY PRESS
DATA COMMAND INC.
MICROED INC.
OPPORTUNITIES FOR LEARNING
VOYAGER

POLITICAL SCIENCE

AV SYSTEMS, INC.
B5 SOFTWARE CO.
CONDUIT
DYNACOMP, INC.
LEARNING ARTS
MICROED INC.
SOCIAL STUDIES SCHOOL SERVICE

POLITICS

BANNER BLUE SOFTWARE
XIPHIAS

PREHISTORY

BIGFOOT PUBLISHING (GRT Corp)

PROBLEM-SOLVING

ACTIVISION
BRODERBUND
CHARIOT SOFTWARE
CRITICAL THINKING
DAVIDSON
DIDATECH
HARTLEY
IBM
KNOWLEDGE REVOLUTION
LCSI
LAWRENCE PRODUCTIONS
THE LEARNING COMPANY
LEGO
MATH & COMPUTER EDUCATION
   PROJECT
MAXIS
MCGRAW-HILL
MICROGRAMS
MINNESOTA EDUCATIONAL
   COMPUTING CORP
NATIONAL GEOGRAPHIC
OPTICAL DATA
OPTIMUM RESOURCES
PARADIGM
PSYGNOSIS
RESEARCH DESIGN
SCHOLASTIC INC.
TOM SYNDER PRODUCTION
SPECTRUM
TANAGER
TIME WARNER INTERACTIVE GROUP
VOYAGER
WINGS FOR LEARNING
XIPHIAS

PSYCHOLOGY

ACADEMIC HALLMARKS, INC.

PUBLIC-DOMAIN SOFTWARE

CD-ROM INC.

PUZZLES

MINDPLAY

READING

See also LANGUAGE ARTS

ADVANTAGE LEARNING SYSTEMS
AQUARIUS PEOPLE MATERIALS, INC.
AV SYSTEMS, INC.
B5 SOFTWARE CO.
BLS TUTORSYSTEMS
WILLIAM K. BRADFORD PUBLISHING
COMP ED
CONTINENTAL PRESS INC.
CURRICULUM ASSOCIATES INC.
DATA COMMAND INC.
E. DAVID & ASSOCIATES
DISCIS KNOWLEDGE RESEARCH, INC.
DYNACOMP, INC.

EDCON
EDMARK CORPORATION
EDUCATIONAL ACTIVITIES INC.
EDUCATIONAL RESOURCES
EMC PUBLISHING
FILMS FOR THE HUMANITIES
GPN
GAMCO HARTLEY COURSEWARE, INC.
HUMANITIES SOFTWARE
INET CORPORATION
INSTRUCTIONAL COMMUNICATIONS
   TECHNOLOGY, INC./TAYLOR
   ASSOCIATES
KRELL SOFTWARE
LEARNING ARTS
THE LEARNING COMPANY
THE LEARNING CUBE
MATH & COMPUTER EDUCATION
   PROJECT
MERIT AUDIO VISUAL
MICROED INC.
MICROGRAMS
MICRO LEARNINGWARE
MICROPHYS
MIDWEST SOFTWARE
OPPORTUNITIES FOR LEARNING
SPECIAL LEARNING ED SOFTWARE
TEXAS CAVIAR, INC.

RECORDKEEPING

B5 SOFTWARE CO.
CHANCERY SOFTWARE

REFERENCE

ABC-CLIO
BAKER & TAYLOR SOFTWARE
BRODART COMPANY
CEL EDUCATION RESOURCES
GALE RESEARCH
GROLIER EDUCATIONAL CORPORATION
THE LEARNING CUBE
LIBRARIES UNLIMITED
LIBRARY CORPORATION
McGRAW-HILL INC.
MULTIMEDIA PUBLISHERS GROUP
NEW MEDIA SOURCE
PETERSONS
R.R. BOWKER ELECTRONIC
   PUBLISHING
RESEARCH PUBLICATIONS
SILVERPLATTER INFORMATION, INC.
SOFTLINE INFORMATION
WORLD BOOK EDUCATIONAL
   PRODUCTS

RELIGION

AV SYSTEMS, INC.
MICROED INC.

SCIENCE

ACTIVISION
ACCULAB PRODUCTS GROUP
AGENCY FOR INSTRUCTIONAL TECH-
   NOLOGY
ALADDIN SOFTWARE
ARIS MULTIMEDIA ENTERTAINMENT

ARTIFICIAL INTELLIGENCE RESEARCH
   GROUP
AV SYSTEMS, INC.
WILLIAM K. BRADFORD PUBLISHING
BRODERBUND
CD—ROM INC.
CHARIOT SOFTWARE
COMP ED
CONDUIT
CREATIVE MULTIMEDIA
CYGNUS SOFTWARE
DATA COMMAND INC.
DAVIDSON & ASSOC. INC.
DEC COMPUTING
DESIGN SCIENCE
DYNACOMP, INC.
EARTHWARE COMPUTER SERVICES
EBSCO PUBLISHING
EDUCATIONAL ACTIVITIES INC.
EDUCATIONAL IMAGES
EDUCATIONAL RESOURCES
EDUCORP
EDUQUEST
ELECTRONIC COURSEWARE SYSTEMS
   INC.
EME CORPORATION
EMERGING TECHNOLOGY
HRM SOFTWARE
HARTLEY COURSEWARE, INC.
HEARTSOFT
HIGH TECHNOLOGY SOFTWARE
   PRODUCTS, INC.
INDIVIDUAL SOFTWARE CO.
INTELLIMATION
K—12 MICROMEDIA
KNOWLEDGE ADVENTURE INC.
KRELL SOFTWARE
LASER LEARNING TECHNOLOGIES
LEARNING ARTS
LEARNING COMPANY
THE LEARNING CUBE
LEARNING TEAM
LEGO
LIBRARIES UNLIMITED
MECC
MAGIC QUEST
MARSHWARE
MATHEGRAPHICS SOFTWARE
MAXIS
McGRAW-HILL INC.
MICROED INC.
MICROGRAMS
MICRO LEARNINGWARE
MICROPHYS
MICROSOFT
MINDPLAY
MINDSCAPE
NATIONAL GEOGRAPHIC
ONLINE COMPUTER SYSTEMS
OPPORTUNITIES FOR LEARNING
OPTICAL DATA
OPTIMUM RESOURCE
ORANGECHERRY NEW MEDIA
   SCHOOLHOUSE
PETERSONS
PRESCIENCE
QUANTA PRESS INC.
RIGHT ON PROGRAMS
SALEM PRESS, INC.
SCHOLASTIC INC.

SCIENCE FOR KIDS
SIRS
TOM SNYDER PRODUCTION
SOFTWARE TOOLWORKS
SPINNAKER SOFTWARE CORP.
TEACH YOURSELF BY COMPUTER
  SOFTWARE, INC.
TIME WARNER INTERACTIVE GROUP
TURNER MULTIMEDIA
UPDATA PUBLICATIONS INC.
VENTURA
VERNIER
VIDEODISCOVERY
VOYAGER
WAYZATA TECHNOLOGY
H. W. WILSON
WINGS FOR LEARNING/SUNBURST
WIZARDWORKS
WORLD GAME INSTITUTE
XIPHIAS

SEX EDUCATION

NIMCO

SHAREWARE

CD-ROM INC.

SPELLING

AV SYSTEMS, INC.
B5 SOFTWARE CO
BLS TUTORSYSTEMS
DYNACOMP, INC.
EDUCATIONAL ACTIVITIES INC.
ELECTRONIC COURSEWARE SYSTEMS
  INC.
EMC PUBLISHING
FRIENDLYSOFT, INC.
HARTLEY COURSEWARE, INC.
INSTRUCTIONAL COMMUNICATIONS
  TECHNOLOGY, INC./TAYLOR
  ASSOCIATES
KRELL SOFTWARE
LEARNCO, INC.
LEARNING ARTS
THE LEARNING COMPANY
THE LEARNING CUBE
MICROED INC.
MICROGRAMS
MICRO LEARNINGWARE
MICROPHYS
OPPORTUNITIES FOR LEARNING
SOFTSHOPPE II
SPECIAL LEARNING ED SOFTWARE
SUBLOGIC CORPORATION
TEACH YOURSELF BY COMPUTER
  SOFTWARE, INC.

SOCIAL SCIENCES/SOCIAL STUDIES

ABC NEWS
ACTIVISION
AGENCY FOR INSTRUCTIONAL
  TECHNOLOGY
APPLIED OPTICAL MEDIA CORP.
AQUARIUS PEOPLE MATERIALS
AV SYSTEMS, INC.
WILLIAM K. BRADFORD PUBLISHING

BRODERBUND SOFTWARE, INC.
BUREAU OF ELECTRONIC PUBLISHING
CEL EDUCATION
COMP ED
CONDUIT
DATA COMMAND
DAVIDSON
DIDATECH
EAST GATE SYSTEMS
EDUCATIONAL ACTIVITIES
EDUCORP
EDUQUEST
GPN
GAMCO
HARTLEY COURSEWARE
HEARTSOFT
INDIVIDUAL SOFTWARE CO.
INFORMATION ACCESS
INTELLIMATION
K-12 MICROMEDIA
LCSI
LASER LEARNING TECHNOLOGIES
LAUREATE
LAWRENCE PRODUCTIONS
LEARNING ARTS
THE LEARNING CUBE
MECC
MAGIC QUEST
MAXIS
MICROED INC.
MINDPLAY
MINDSCAPE
NATIONAL GEOGRAPHIC
NEWSWEEK
ONLINE COMPUTER SYSTEMS
OPPORTUNITIES FOR LEARNING
OPTICAL DATA
OPTIMUM RESOURCE
PETERSONS
PLUMA SOFTWARE
RIGHT ON PROGRAMS
SCHOLASTIC INC.
SIRS
TOM SNYDER PRODUCTION
SOCIAL STUDIES SCHOOL SERVICE
SOFTWARE TOOLWORKS
SPINNAKER SOFTWARE CORP.
TEACH YOURSELF BY COMPUTER
TEXAS CAVIAR, INC.
TIME WARNER INTERACTIVE GROUP
TURNER MULTIMEDIA
UPDATA PUBLICATIONS INC.
VOYAGER
WAYZATA TECHNOLOGY
WINGS FOR LEARNING/SUNBURST
WIZARDWORKS
WORLD GAME INSTITUTE
WORLDVIEW SOFTWARE

SOLAR SYSTEMS

SOFTWARE MARKETING CORP.

SPECIAL EDUCATION

AQUARIUS PEOPLE MATERIALS, INC.
AV SYSTEMS, INC.
B5 SOFTWARE CO
C AND C SOFTWARE
COMMUNICATION SKILL BUILDERS

CONTINENTAL PRESS INC.
CROSS EDUCATIONAL SOFTWARE
CURRICULUM ASSOCIATES INC.
E. DAVID & ASSOCIATES
DYNACOMP, INC.
EDUCATIONAL ACTIVITIES INC.
EMC PUBLISHING
IEP
INSTRUCTIONAL COMMUNICATIONS
  TECHNOLOGY, INC./TAYLOR
  ASSOCIATES
LAUREATE LEARNING SYSTEMS, INC.
LEARNCO, INC.
OPPORTUNITIES FOR LEARNING
SPECIAL LEARNING ED SOFTWARE
TEACH YOURSELF BY COMPUTER
  SOFTWARE, INC.

SPORTS

EDEN INTERACTIVE
MICROSOFT
NEW MEDIA SOURCE

TEACHER AIDS/INSTRUCTIONAL TOOLS

ADOBE SYSTEMS
ALADDIN SOFTWARE
ALDUS
APPLE COMPUTER
AURBACH
AUTODESK
AV SYSTEMS
BAUDVILLE
WILLIAM K. BRADFORD
BRODERBUND
CAERE
C AND C SOFTWARE
CE SOFTWARE
CENTRAL POINT
CHANCERY
CHARIOT SOFTWARE
CLARIS
CONDUIT
CRITICAL THINKING
CURRICULUM ASSOCIATES
DAVIDSON
DEC COMPUTING
DELTA POINT
DYNACOMP, INC.
EDMARK
EDUCATIONAL ACTIVITIES
EDUCATIONAL IMAGES
EDUSOFT
ELECTRONIC COURSEWARE
EMA SOFTWARE
EMC PUBLISHING
FRAME TECHNOLOGY
FREESOFT
GAMCO
GROLIER
HARTLEY COURSEWARE
HAYES MICROCOMPUTER
HOUGHTON MIFFLIN
HUMANITIES SOFTWARE
IBM
INNOVATIVE DATA
INSPIRATION SOFTWARE

INTERKOM SOFTWARE
KOALA
KRELL SOFTWARE
LSCI
LEARNING ARTS
LEARNING COMPANY
LOTUS
MARCROMEDIA
MANHATTAN GRAPHIC
MICROPHYS
MICROSOFT
MIDWEST SOFTWARE
MILLIKEN PUBLISHING
MINDSCAPE
MISTY CITY SOFTWARE
NEWSBANK
OPPORTUNITIES FOR LEARNING
POSTCRAFT
POWER INDUSTRIES
PUBLISHING INTERNATIONAL
QUALITY COMPUTER
QUARK
QUEUE
RAYDREAM
SCHOLASTIC
TOM SYNDER
SOCIAL STUDIES SCHOOL SERVICE
SOFTSHOPPE II
SOFTSYNC
TEACH YOURSELF BY COMPUTER
TECHWARE
TIMEWORKS
TRUE BASIC
VIDEODISCOVERY
VOYAGER
WILD DUCK

WORD PERFECT
WORDSTAR

TEST QUESTIONS

ACADEMIC HALLMARKS, INC.
COREL
DAVIDSON
KRELL SOFTWARE
METIER
TOM SNYDER

TYPING

BRODERBUND
BYTES FOR LEARNING
DAVIDSON
HUMANITIES SOFTWARE
IBM
MECC
NATIONAL BOOK COMPANY
OPTIMUM RESOURCES
QUE SOFTWARE
SCHOLASTIC
SOUTHWESTERN PUBLISHING
WINGS FOR LEARNING

VOCATIONAL EDUCATION

AGENCY FOR INSTRUCTIONAL
   TECHNOLOGY
AUTODESK
BRODERBUND
CLARIS
THE CONOVER COMPANY LTD
DAVIDSON

DENEBA SYSTEMS
EBSCO PUBLISHING
INNOVATIVE DATA
LIVING SOFTWARE
NIMCO
POSTCRAFT
PUBLISHING INTERNATIONAL
QUEUE
WAYZATA

**WORLD NEWS/WORLD FACTS/
   WORLD AFFAIRS**

FACTS ON FILE
INFOBASES INTERNATIONAL INC.
SIRS

WRITING

THE LEARNING CUBE
MERIT AUDIO VISUAL
MINDPLAY

YEARBOOKS/ALMANACS

COMPACT PUBLISHING

YOUTH AT RISK

ATTAINMENT COMPANY, INC.

ZOOLOGY

ACADEMIC HALLMARKS, INC.

AUDIOVISUAL PRODUCERS & DISTRIBUTORS

3

The following audiovisual companies produce and/or distribute materials for or about children. Companies are designated by the following codes: a Producer creates programs but does not ditribute them, selling through jobbers, wholesalers, or distributers; a Distributor does not produce audiovisual programs but only distributes programs made by other companies; a Producer/distributor both creates and distributes programs.

Each company was asked to list subjects and any special interests. It should be noted that many of the companies produce materials on many more subjects than they listed and that, in most cases, only general topics were given. Special interests of each producer are noted in an index at the end of this chapter.

ABC MULTIMEDIA GROUP
77 W. 66th St., 21st Fl., New York, NY 10023
212-456-7746
Mgr: Pamela Schaub

Producer/Distributor
Format: 16mm films, 1/2'' videoreels, 3/4'' videocassettes
Audience: Preschool, adult
Subjects: Career development, family life, sciences, animals, consumer education, fiction, sex education, art, dance, health, social studies, biographies, drama, religion, sports, business, environment & energy safety
Special interest: Native Americans, nonsexist education
Services: Catalog. Sell/lease to schools
Distribution: Various independent producers

AGS MEDIA
(formerly Ikonographics, Inc.)
1810 Sils Ave., Louisville, KY 40205
502-451-3506
Also dist. by Harper & Row Publishers, Box 1630, Hagerstown, MD 21741
Pres: Michael Nabicht
Sales Mgr: Patrick Hayden
Sr Ed: Meryann Bowman

Producer/Distributor
Format: Sound filmstrips, 16mm files, 3/4'' videocassettes, 1/2'' videocassettes
Audience: Preschool-12, adult
Subjects: Family life, health, religion, sex education
Services: Catalog. Preview prints. Exhibit at NCEA

ALA VIDEO/LIBRARY VIDEO NETWORK
320 York Rd., Towson, MD 21204
410-887-2082; Fax: 410-887-2091

Producer/Distributor
Format: Videotapes
Audience: Adult
Subjects: Library staff training; library collections
Services: Catalog

A/V CONCEPTS CORP.
30 Montauk Blvd., Oakdale, NY 11769
516-567-7227
Pres: Philip J. Solimene
Ed: Laura Solimene

Producer/Distributor
Format: Computer software, silent filmstrips, programmed learning systems
Audience: K-12, adult
Subjects: Language arts
Special interest: Reading disabled
Services: Catalog. Preview prints. Exhibit at IRA, AECT, NAVA

ABINGDON PRESS
Div.of the United Methodist Publishing House
201 Eighth Ave. S, Nashville, TN 37202
615-749-6291
Sales Dir: Carol C. Williams
Mkg/Prom: Clarinda Bowman
Children's Ed: Peggy Augustine

Producer/Distributor
Format: Audiocassettes, videorecordings
Audience: K-12
Subjects: Family life, religion

Special interest: Reading disabled, mentally handicapped
Discount: Libraries, 25%
Services: Catalog. Promotional newsletters. Exhibit at ALA, ABA, CBA, ARC

ADAMS FILM PRODUCTIONS
706 Wayside Dr., Austin, TX 78703
512-477-8846
Pres: Louis T. Adams

Producer/Distributor
Format: 16mm films
Audience: K-6
Subjects: Animals, environment & energy, wildlife
Services: Catalog. Preview prints

AFRICAN AMERICAN IMAGES
(formerly AFRO-AM PUBLISHING/ DISTRIBUTING COMPANY)
1909 W. 95th St., Chicago, IL 60643
312-445-0322, 800-552-1991

Producer/Distributor
Format: Toys & games, puzzles, teaching aids, posters, display & study prints, plays, coloring books, comic books, records & cassettes, filmstrips, videocassettes, story books, history books, paperback collections, library collections
Audience: Pre-K through high school
Subjects: Africa, biography, child development, history, human relations, language arts, multiethnic/multiculture

AGENCY FOR INSTRUCTIONAL TECHNOLOGY (AIT-THE LEARNING SOURCE)
Box A, Bloomington, IN 47402
812-339-2203; Fax: 812-333-2478
Exec Dir: Dr. Michael F. Sullivan
Dir Partnerships: Michael Stickney
Dir Mktg: Ray McKelvey
Dir Sales: Suzanne Pelletier
Mgr TV Mktg: Barbara Ravellette
Mgr Prog Acquisitions: Nancy Gray

Developer & Distributor
Format: Videocassette, videodisc, print, software
Audience: Preschool-community college, teacher inservice, adult
Subjects: Art, early childhood, foreign language, guidance/mental health, health/safety, language arts, mathematics, science, social studies, staff development, vocational education/tech-prep
Special interest: K-12 curriculum, vocational education, staff development
Discounts: Volume purchases, special prices for schools in states that are members of an AIT consortium project. Regional member discounts for ITV leases
Services: Catalogs, descriptive brochures, previews. Represent programs for other producers. Exhibit at AECT/InCite, AVA, state Tech-prep meetings, Head Start, NCCA, ASCD. Sell/lease to schools, media centers, libraries, ITV/PBS stations/networks, cable systems

AIMS MEDIA
9710 DeSoto Ave., Chatsworth, CA 91311
800-267-2467; Fax: 818-341-6700

Producer/Distributor
Format: 1/4'' & 3/4'' videocassettes, computer software, sound & silent filmstrips, 16mm films, slides
Audience: K-12, adult
Subjects: Sciences, career development, law enforcement, crime prevention, drama, health, music, animals, sex education, computers, environment & energy, hobbies, physical education, art, social studies, consumer education, family life, home economics, poetry, biographies, sports, crafts, fiction, language arts, religion, business, vocational training, dance, foreign countries & languages, mathematics, safety
Special interest: Blind, Native Americans, deaf, Spanish-speaking, reading disabled, bilingual students, mentally handicapped, nonsexist education, African Americans
Services: Catalog. Promotional newsletters. Preview prints. Rent 16mm films. Exhibit at AECT, NAVA & many others. Sell/lease to ETV & ITV stations, schools, libraries

ALARION PRESS, INC.
Box 1882, Boulder, CO 80306
800-523-9177
Pres: Ann R. Luce
Sales Mgr: Sue Wigham

Producer/Distributor
Format: Multimedia kits, VHS
Audience: K-adult
Subjects: Art, foreign countries, social studies, gifted
Special interest: Interdisciplinary social studies, gifted/talented humanities approach; art education
Services: Catalog. Promotional newsletters. Preview prints. Exhibit at NCSS, NAEA, NG/T. Sell/lease to schools, libraries

ALL AMERICAN VIDEO PRODUCTIONS, INC.
1323 Mt. Hermon Rd., Ste. 6-A, Salisbury, MD 21801
813-473-2601; Fax: 813-473-2701
Pres: Stan Nicotera
Pub Rel: Tina Nicotera
Sales Mgr: Mike Craven

Producer/Distributor
Format: VHS, PAL
Audience: K-12 to college
Subjects: All subjects
Services: Catalog. Preview prints. Exhibits at ALA, PLADistribution: S. I. Video Sales Group

ALTANA FILMS
61 Main St., Southampton, NY 11968
516-283-8662
Pres: Dan Klugherz

Producer/Distributor
Format: 16mm films
Audience: 6-12, adult
Subjects: Family life, physical education, sports, women, aging
Special interest: Nonsexist education
Services: Preview prints. Rent & sell 16mm films, videotapes

ALTSCHUL GROUP CORPORATION
1560 Sherman Ave. Ste. 100, Evanston, IL 60201
800-323-9084; Fax: 708-328-6706
Pres: Joe Farragher

Distributor
Format: 16mm films, videorecordings, 1/2'' videoreels, 3/4'' videocassettes, laserdiscs
Audience: Preschool-12, adult
Subjects: Sex education, family life, social studies, health, vocational training, language arts, special needs education, safety, core curriculum

Discount: Inquire
Services: Catalog. Preview Prints. Rent 16mm films, all video formats. Exhibit at COMMTEX, AFF, NFM. Sell/lease to ETV & ITV stations, schools, libraries, hospitals, clinics, health departments
Distribution: 16mm films & all video formats, laserdiscs

AMERICAN BIBLE SOCIETY
1865 Broadway, New York, NY 10023
212-408-1200
Bd Chmn: James Wood
President & CEO: Dr. Eugene Habecker
Nat Prog Area: Maria Martinez

Publications: Paperback originals & reprints, audiorecords/cassettes, filmstrips, videotapes/cassettes
Audience: Children, youth, adult
Subjects: Bibles and scripture resources in many languages
Special interest: Hearing and visually impaired, heritage groups, special education
Services: Catalog

AMERICAN GUIDANCE SERVICE
4201 Woodland Rd., Circle Pines, MN 55014
612-786-4343
Dir of Sales: Rebecca Powell
Mkt Mgr: Matt Keller

Producer
Format: Computer software, multimedia kits, 1/2'' VHS videocassette
Audience: Preschool-12, adult
Subjects: Mathematics, career development, physical education, family life, home economics, language arts
Special interest: Nonsexist education, mentally handicapped, parent skills
Services: Catalog. Promotional newsletters. Preview prints. Exhibit at IRA, CEC, ASHA, NAESP, NCTM, AACD, AAMFT

AMERICAN MAP COMPANY
46-35 54th Rd., Maspeth, NY 11378
718-784-0055
Pres: Stuart Dolgins
VP: Joseph P. Scali, Jr.
Lib/Sch Prom Dir: Edward Ortiz
Children's Ed: Vera Benson

Producer/Distributor
Format: Charts, globes, maps
Audience: K-12, adult
Subjects: Business, sciences, social studies
Discount: 50-249 copies, 10%; 250 copies or more, 20%
Services: Catalog. Exhibit at ALA

AMERICAN METEORITE LABORATORY
Box 2098, Denver, CO 80201
303-428-1371
Sole Proprietor: Margaret A. Huss

Producer/Distributor
Format: Laboratory kits, realia, slides
Audience: 3-12, adult
Subjects: Meteorites
Discount: Schools, 10%; libraries, 20%
Services: Catalog

AMERICAN OPTOMETRIC AS-SOCIATION
243 N. Lindbergh Blvd., St Louis, MO 63141
314-991-4100
Dir: Reynold W. Malmer

Producer/Distributor
Format: 16mm films
Audience: Preschool-12, adult
Subjects: Career development, consumer education, eye health & safety
Special interest: Vision care, professional materials for teachers
Discount: Inquire
Services: Catalog

PAUL S. AMIDON & ASSOCIATES
1966 Benson Ave., St. Paul, MN 55116
612-690-2401
Pres: Paul C. Amidon
Sales Mgr: Beth Miller

Producer/Distributor
Format: Games, audiocassettes, multimedia kits, computer software, transparencies, filmstrips, flashcards
Audience: K-12, adult
Subjects: Environment & energy, social studies, animals, foreign languages, art, language arts, auditory & visual perception, mathematics, consumer education, sciences

KEN ANDERSON FILMS
Box 618, Winona Lake, IN 46590
219-267-5774
Pres: Ken Anderson
Adv Dir: Lane Anderson

Producer/Distributor
Format: 16mm films, video
Audience: K-12, adult
Subjects: Family life, foreign countries, religion
Special interest: Spanish-speaking
Services: Catalog. Preview prints. Rent 16mm films. Sell/lease to TV networks. Sell video

THE ANNENBERG/CPB COLLECTION
901 E St. NW, Washington, DC 20004
202-879-9655; Fax: 202-783-1036
Contact: Janice Ford

Distributor
Format: VHS
Audience: Adult
Subjects: Science, math, psychology, literature, films studies, global economics, foreign language & area studies
Services: Catalog.

APPALSHOP, INC.
306 Madison St., Whitesburg, KY 41858
606-633-0108
Sales/Mktg Dir: Carolyn Sturgill

Producer/Distributor
Format: 1/2" videocassettes, audiodiscs, filmstrips, 16mm films, 3/4" videocassettes
Audience: K-12, adult
Subjects: Environment & energy, religion, art, family life, social studies, biographies, language arts, crafts, music, drama, poetry
Special interest: Nonsexist education
Discount: Inquire
Services: Catalog. Promotional newsletters. Preview prints. Rent 16mm films. Exhibit at ALA, AECT. Sell/lease to ETV, ITV & local stations, TV networks, schools, libraries

APPLAUSE PRODUCTIONS, INC.
85 Longview Rd., Port Washington, NY 11050
516-883-2897; Fax: 516-883-7460
Pres: Vincent R. Tortora
Sales Mgr: David Cole
Lib/Sch Prom Dir: Phillip Welham
Children's Ed: Durstis Nivarote

Producer/Distributor
Format: Videocassettes, 16mm films, sound filmstrips, realia
Subjects: Fine arts
Services: Catalog. Preview prints. Exhibit at FLTA. Sell/lease to cable TV systems

ARCHITECTURAL COLOR SLIDES
187 Grant St., Lexington, MA 02173
617-862-9931
Pres: Franziska Porges

Producer/Distributor
Format: Silent filmstrips, slides
Audience: 10-12 adult
Subjects: Architecture, urban studies
Services: Catalog. Preview prints. Coordinated teaching programs. Produces filmstrips to order

AUDIO BOOK CONTRACTORS
Classic Books on Cassettes, Box 40115, Washington, DC 20016
202-363-3429
Pres, Sales Mgr, Lib/Sch Prom Dir & Children's Ed: Flo Gibson

Producer/Distributor
Format: Audiocassettes
Audience: Preschool-12, adult
Subjects: Drama, fiction, poetry unabridged

Special interest: Native Americans, blind, reading disabled
Discount: Library discount 10% for 50 or more titles, 20% for 100 or more; $7 off purchase price for visually & physically handicapped
Services: Catalog. Rent at 1/3 purchase price for 30 days
Distribution: Selected titles from Recorded Books Inc., Books on Tape

BFA EDUCATIONAL MEDIA
Div. of Phoenix Learning Group
2349 Chaffee Dr., St. Louis, MO 63146
314-569-0211
Pres: Heinz Gelles
Sales Mgr: Robert Dunlap
Lib/Sch Prom Dir: Barbara Bryant

Producer/Distributor
Format: Audiocassettes, sound & silent filmstrips, super 8mm & 16mm films, 1/2" videoreels
Audience: K-12, adult
Subjects: Career development, family life, music, sciences, animals, consumer education, foreign countries & language, physical education, social studies, art, crafts, health, poetry, sports, biographies, drama, home economics, religion, vocational training, business, environment & energy, language arts, safety, values
Special interest: Blind, Native Americans, deaf, Spanish-speaking, mentally handicapped, bilingual students, nonsexist education
Discount: Inquire
Services: Catalog. Preview prints. Rent 16mm films. Workshops for teachers. Exhibit at ALA, IRA, AECT, NAVA, NCTE, ASCD. Sell/lease to ETV, ITV & local stations, TV networks, schools, libraries

BAHA'i PUBLISHING TRUST
415 Linden Ave., Wilmette, IL 60091
312-251-1854
Mgr: Terrill Hayes
Sales Mgr: Patrick Falso
Children's Ed: Dr. Betty J. Fisher

Producer/Distributor
Format: Audiocassettes, games, videorecordings
Audience: Preschool-12, adult
Subjects: Family life, fiction, religion
Special interest: Nonsexist education
Discount: Inquire
Services: Price list. Exhibit at ALA, AAR
Distribution: Trusts of UK & Australia, plus 58 other publishers

BAPTIST HOME MISSION BOARD
1350 Spring St. NW, Atlanta, GA 30367
404-898-7000
Media Dir: Ronald J. Lawson

Mktg Dir: Rick Head
Book Editor: Joe Westbury

Producer/Distributor
Format: Video & audiocassette
Audience: K-12, adult
Special interest: Native Americans,
Spanish-speaking, deaf, African
Americans
Services: Catalog. Promotional news-
letters

BARR MEDIA
12801 Schabarum Ave., Box 7878,
Irwindale, CA 91706
800-234-7878; Fax: 818-814-2672
Pres: Alex Bell
Sales: Robert Nardi

Producer/Distributor
Format: 16mm films, 3/4'' videocassettes, Beta & VHS videocassettes
Audience: K-12, adult, college
Subjects: Animals, environment &
energy, art, family life, career development, values, substance abuse,
consumer education
Services: Catalog. Preview prints. Rent
16mm films. Exhibit at AECT.
Sell/lease to schools, libraries, health
organizations, colleges
Distribution: 16mm films, video

NORMAN BEERGER PRODUCTIONS
3217-A50, S. Arville St., Las Vegas,
NV 89102
702-876-2328
Pres, Sales Mgr & Children's Ed:
Norman Beerger

Producer/Distributor
Format: Videorecordings, 1/2'' VHS &
Beta cassettes
Audience: K-12
Subjects: Art, wilderness, nature, histo-
ry, space, environment & energy,
music, sciences
Special interest: Nonsexist education
Discount: 5 or more 10%
Services: Catalog. Sell to schools,
libraries, public
Distribution: VHS & Beta videocas-
settes

BENCHMARK FILMS
569 North State Rd., Briarcliff Manor,
NY 10510
800-438-5564
Sales Mgr: Linda Hellman, Maggie Hall,
Kristin Hunter

Producer/Distributor
Format: 16mm films, 3/4'' videocassettes, 1/2'' videocassettes,
laserdisc
Audience: Preschool-12, adult
Subjects: Business, foreign countries,
music, social studies, animals, consumer education, health, physical
education, vocational training, art,
environment & energy, home economics, religion, history, auditory &
visual perception, family life, language arts, sciences, biographies,
fiction, mathematics, sex education
Special interest: Intuit Indians,
Spanish-speaking, nonsexist education
Discount:Inquire
Services: Catalog. Preview prints. Rent
16mm films. Sell/lease
Distribution: 16mm films. National Film
Board of Canada. Zagreb Films, Joy
Adamson, ABC-TV, Swedish TV,
WNET-TV, independent producers

BERGWALL PRODUCTIONS, INC.
540 Baltimore Pike, Box 2400, Chadds
Ford, PA 19317
800-645-3565; Fax: 215-388-0405
Pres: Charles Bergwall
Sales Mgr: Bruce Bergwall

Producer/Distributor
Format: Computer software, sound
filmstrips, slides, videocassettes
Audience:7-12, adult
Subjects: Crafts, safety, animals, environment & energy, sciences, business, health, vocational training,
career development, home economics, computers, mathematics
Special interest: Native Americans,
computer materials, reading disabled
Services: Catalog. Preview prints

BERLET FILMS
1646 W. Kimmel Rd., Jackson, MI
49201
517-784-6969
Pres: Walter Berlet
Sales Mgr: Mark Snedeker

Producer/Distributor
Format: 16mm films, 3/4'' videocassettes, 1/2'', VHS, Beta videocassettes
Audience: 3-10
Subjects: Social studies, animals, conservation, natural history, environment & energy, language arts,
sciences
Special interest: Natural history
Services: Catalog. Preview prints. Rent
16mm films, VHS, Beta & 3/4''
videocassettes. Sell/lease to schools,
libraries

CHANNING L. BETE COMPANY
200 State Rd., S. Deerfield, MA 01373
413-665-7611
Pres: Channing L. Bete, Jr.
VP: Michael G. Bete
Ed Dir: Laurie Devino

Producer/Distributor
Format: Sound filmstrips, transparencies
Audience: K-12, adult
Subjects: Health, career development,
religion, consumer education, safety,
environment & energy, sex education, family life, social studies
Discount: Quantity
Services: Catalog. Preview prints. Exhibit at AACD, NAESP, NAEYC

BILINGUAL EDUCATIONAL SERVICES
2514 S. Grand Ave., Los Angeles, CA
90007
213-749-6213
Pres: Jeff Penichet
Lib/Sch Prom Dir: Helen Halladay

Producer/Distributor
Format: Maps, audiocassettes, 16mm
films, sound filmstrips, transparencies, flashcards, videocassettes,
games
Subjects: Dance, hobbies, social
studies, animals, drama, language
arts, vocational training, art, fiction,
mathematics, biographies, foreign
countries, music, career development, health, sciences
Special interest: Spanish-speaking,
bilingual students Services: Catalog.
Rent library card kits. Exhibit at National Assn for Bilingual Education
Distribution: Disney Records, Educational Enrichment Materials, United
Learning, Random House, Santilana,
Pan American Book, Ideal, Educational Masters

BILLY BUDD FILMS
235 E. 57th St., New York, NY 10022
212-755-3968
Pres: Frank Moynihan
Sales/Mktg Dir: Anne K. Moynihan

Producer/Distributor
Format: 16mm films, 1/2'' videoreels,
3/4'' videocassettes
Audience: K-12, adult
Subjects: Human emotions & values,
classics
Services: Catalog. Preview prints &
cassettes. Rent & sell 16mm films.
Exhibit at AECT

**BISIAR MUSIC PUBLISHING &
PRODUCTION**
134 Cherrywood Lane, Louisville, CO
80027
303-673-0466
Pres: Ed Bisiar

Producer/Distributor
Format: Audiocassettes, CDs, &
songbooks
Audience: Children & adult
Subjects: Eddie Spaghetti's Greatest
Hits Album
Discount: Wholesale price plus ship-
ping, net 30 days

SAMUEL R. BLATE ASSOCIATES
10331 Watkins Mill Dr., Gaithersburg,
MD 20879-2935

301-840-2248
Pres & Children's Ed: Samuel R. Blate

Producer
Format: Sound & silent filmstrips, super 8mm films, pictures, slides
Audience: 8-12, adult
Subjects: Sports, art, computers, marine, fishing, boating, environment & energy, hobbies
Special interests: Computer materials, nonsexist education
Services: Preview prints

BOOKS ON TAPE
Box 7900, Newport Beach, CA 92658-7900
800-541-5525
Pres: Duvall Hecht
Sales Mgr: Jack Griffith

Distributor
Format: Audiocassettes
Audience: Preschool-12, adult
Subjects: Biographies, family life, poetry, business, fiction, language arts, travel, music
Discount: Inquire
Services: Catalog. Exhibit at ALA. Provides books in free library albums to libraries

BUDGET FILMS
4590 Santa Monica Blvd., Los Angeles, CA 90029
213-660-0187
Pres: Albert C. Drebin
VP: Larry Fine
Sales Mgr, Lib/Sch Prom: Layne Murphy

Distributor
Format: 16mm films, 1/4'' videocassettes
Audience: Preschool-12, adult
Subjects: Safety, business, vocational training, dance, foreign countries & languages, mathematics, animals, sciences, career development, drama, health, music, art, sex education, computers, environment & energy, hobbies, physical education, auditory & visual perception, social studies, consumer education, family life, home economics, poetry, biographies, sports, crafts, fiction, language, arts, religion
Special interest: Native Americans, African Americans
Services: Catalog. Promotional news letters
Distribution: 16mm films, Warner Bros., Columbia Pictures, United Artists, Time-Life Films, American International Pictures, Pyramid Films, Phoenix Films, Bailey Films, Lucerne Films, Productions Unlimited, Learning Corporation of America, Sterling Educational Films, National Film Board of Canada, Castle Films,

Carousel Films, Republic Pictures, many foreign films

BULLFROG FILMS
Box 149, Oley, PA 19547
215-779-8226; Fax: 215-370-1978
Pres: John Abrahall
Sales Mgr: Elizabeth Stanley
Lib/Sch Prom Dir & Children's Ed: Winifred Scherrer

Distributor
Format: 1/2'' videocassettes, 3/4'' videocasettes, 16mm films, videodiscs
Audience: Pre K-12, adult
Subjects: Environment & energy, sciences, language arts, social studies, animals, family life, music, vocational training, art, health, safety, crafts, home economics, hobbies.
Special interest: Native Americans, bilingual students, special needs students, deaf, professional materials for teachers
Discount: Quantity purchases, inquire about building level discounts
Services: Catalog. Preview cassettes. Promotional newsletter, Rent 16mm films, 3/4'' U-matic & VHS videocassettes. Exhibit at ALA, NFVM. Sell/lease to ETV, ITV, & local stations, TV networks, schools, libraries, hospitals, home video

CALIFORNIA LANGUAGE LABORATORIES
10511 Castine Ave., Cupertino, CA 95014
415-327-1112, 408-736-9477, 800-327-1147; Fax: 408-749-9682
Dir: Barbara Sullivan

Producer/Distributor
Format: Audio & videocassettes
Audience: 3-12, adult
Subjects: ESL, materials in 23 different languages for students of all ages learning English. All materials are bilingual and have spoken translation. Languages include Arabic, Armenian, Khmer, Cantonese, Farsi, French, German, Hindi, Hmong, Ilocano, Italian, Japanese, Korean, Lao, Mandarin, Polish, Portuguese, Russian, Serbo-Croatian, Spanish, Tagalog, Thai, and Vietnamese. Resource books accompany materials and provide lesson plans, blackline masters, tests, etc., depending on which materials are ordered.
Services: Catalogs. Preview materials for schools & libraries

CAMBRIDGE DOCUMENTARY FILMS INC.
Box 385, Cambridge, MA 02139
617-354-3677; Fax: 617-492-7653
Pres: Margaret Lazarus

Sales Mgr & Lib/Sch Prom Dir: Alice Maurice

Producer/Distributor
Format: 16mm films, 3/4'' videocassettes, 1/2'' videocassettes
Audience: 2-6, 10-12, adult
Subjects: Fiction, sex education, social studies
Special interest: Nonsexist education
Services: Catalog. Rent 16mm films, videocassettes. Exhibit at ALA. Sell/lease to ETV stations, schools, libraries
Distribution: Diane Li Productions

CAMPUS FILM DISTRIBUTORS CORP.
24 Depot Sq., Tuckahoe, NY 10707
914-961-1900
Pres: Steve Campus
Sales Mgr: Gloria Janelli
Lib/Sch Prom Dir: Berta Salomon

Producer/Distributor
Format: Super 8mm & 16mm films, audiocassettes, slides, silent filmstrips, transparencies, multimedia kits, videodiscs, exhibits, 8mm videos
Audience: Preschool-12, adult
Subjects: Various early childhood training programs, health, language arts, mathematics, sciences
Special interest: Medical, special education, mainstreaming
Discount: Quantity purchases
Services: Catalog. Promotional newsletters. Preview prints. Rent 16mm films, videocassettes, filmstrips/cassette programs. Sell/lease to ETV, ITV, & local stations, schools, libraries, hospitals
Distribution: 16mm films & filmstrips

CANYON CINEMA
2325 Third St., Ste. 338, San Francisco, CA 94107
415-626-2255
Mgrs: David Sherman, Dominic Angerame
Sales Mgr: Dominic Angerame

Distributor
Format: Super 8mm & 16mm films
Audience: K-12, adult
Subjects: Crafts, fiction, animals, dance, music, art, drama, poetry, biographies, environment & energy, religion, computers, family life, sciences
Services: Catalog. Rent films. Sell/lease to schools, libraries

CAPITAL COMMUNICATIONS
(formerly AEE Entertainment)
Box 70188, Nashville, TN 37207
615-868-2040
Pres: James D. Springer
Sales Mgr: Suella H. Yurkee

Producer/Distributor
Format: Audiocassettes, computer software, 16mm films, 3/4" videocassettes
Subjects: Environment & energy, mathematics, sex education, animals, foreign countries & languages, physical education, social studies, art, health, religion, sports, computers, home economics, safety, drama, language arts, sciences
Special interest: Native Americans, Spanish-speaking, computer materials, deaf
Services: Catalog. Preview prints. Exhibit at MIP. Sell/lease to TV networks, schools, libraries

CAREER PUBLISHING, INC.
905 Allanson Rd., Mundelein, RI 60060
312-949-0011

Producer/Distributor
Format: Games, multimedia kits, booklets, books
Audience: K-3, 10-12, adult
Subjects: Consumer education, language arts, reference
Discount: 40% off list
Services: Catalog

CAROLINA BIOLOGICAL SUPPLY CO.
2700 York Rd., Burlington, NC 27215
919-584-0381
Pres: Thomas E. Powell III
Sales/Mrkt VP: Richard Shoe

Producer/Distributor
Format: Sound filmstrips, models, videodiscs, audiodiscs, games, pictures, 1/4" & 3/4" videocassettes, audiocassettes, globes, slides, Beta VHS & 3/4" U-matic videocassettes, charts, laboratory kits, microscopic slides, computer software, maps, transparencies
Audience: K-12, adult
Subjects: Environment & energy, physical education, animals, family life, sciences, auditory & visual perception, health, sex education, biographies, hobbies, sports, computers, mathematics
Special interest: Native Americans, computer materials
Services: Catalog. Promotional newsletters. Preview prints. Rent videotapes. Exhibit at ALA. Catalog card kits

CAROUSEL FILM & VIDEO
260 Fifth Ave., Ste. 405, New York, NY 10001
212-683-1660
Pres: David B. Dash
Sales/Mktg Dir: Michael A. Dash

Distributor
Format: 16mm films, videocassettes

Audience: 6-12, adult
Subjects: Environment & energy, social studies, biographies, family life, film-making, human relations, business, foreign countries, career development, health, compuers, sex education
Special interest: African Americans, professional materials for teachers, Spanish-speaking, bilingual students, deaf, reading disabled
Services: Catalog. Promotional newsletters. Preview prints. Exhibit at AECT, state meetings
Distribution: 16mm films, CBS News, ABC News, Granada Productions, others

CATHEDRAL FILMS, INC.
Box 4029, Westlake Village, CA 91359
800-338-3456
Pres: Rev. James Friedrich

Producer/Distributor
Format: 16mm films, 1/2" videocassettes
Audience: K-12, adult
Subjects: Religion
Services: Catalog. Sell 16mm films, videocassettes. Sell to schools, libraries, churches

CENTER FOR NEW AMERICAN MEDIA
524 Broadway, New York, NY 10012
212-925-5665
Dist by Transt Media, 22-D Hollywood Ave., Hohokus, NJ 07423
Pres: A. Mark Kolker
Sales Mgr: Victor Go
Lib/Sch Prom Dir: D. DeBeau
Children's Ed: E. Orr

Producer
Format: 3/4" videocassettes, VHS videocassettes
Audience: 9-12, adult
Subjects: Language arts, social studies, political science
Services: Preview prints. Rent 3/4" & VHS videocassettes. Exhibit at NCTE, American Dialect Assn. Sell/lease to ETV & local stations, TV networks, schools, libraries

CENTRE COMMUNICATIONS
1800 30th St. −207, Boulder, CO 80301
303-444-1166
Pres: Ron Meyer

Producer/Distributor
Format: Filmstrips, 1/2" videoreels
Audience: K-12, adult
Subjects: Safety, business, vocational training, dance, foreign countries & languages, mathematics, animals, sciences, career development, drama, health, music, art, sex education, computers, environment & energy, hobbies, physical education,

auditory & visual perception, social studies, consumer education, family life, home economics, poetry, biographies, sports, crafts, fiction, language arts, religion
Services: Catalog. Preview prints. Rent 16mm films, video. Exhibit at ALA, AECT. Sell/lease to ETV & ITV stations, TV networks, schools, libraries

CHELSEA HOUSE PUBLISHERS
1974 Sproul Rd., Ste. 400, Broomall, PA 19008-0914
215-353-5166; Fax: 215-359-1439

Producer
Format: Audiocassettes
Audience: 7-12, adult
Subjects: Language arts, art, history, urban studies, psychoactive drugs, biographies, foreign countries, health
Services: Catalog. Exhibit at ALA

CHILDREN'S TELEVISION INTERNATIONAL, INC.
8000 Forbes Place, Ste. 201, Springfield, VA 22151
800-284-4523; Fax: 703-321-8971
Pres: Ray V. Gladfelter
Dir/Cust Serv: Susan Johnson

Producer/Distributor
Format: 1/2" VHS videocassette
Audience: K-12
Subjects: Art, black folklore, computers, family life, language, arts, photography, sciences, social studies
Discount: Inquire
Services: Catalog. Preview prints for leases only, schools, libraries, and cable

THE CHRISTOPHERS
12 E. 48th St., New York, NY 10017
212-759-4050
Pres: Rev. John Catoir
Prod: Ceilia Harriendorf

Producer/Distributor
Format: VHS cassettes
Audience: 4-8
Subjects: Half-hour holiday specials: Thanksgiving, Christmas, the New Year . . . .
Services: Catalog. Lease to TV stations, cable, ITV

CHURCHILL MEDIA
12210 Nebraska Ave., Los Angeles, CA 90025-3600
800-334-7830; Fax: 310-207-1330

Producer/Distributor
Format: 16mm films, videorecordings
Audience: K-12, adult
Subjects: Consumer education, health, poetry, animals, crafts, home economics, sciences, art, environment &

energy, language arts, sex education, auditory & visual perception, family life, music, social studies, career development, foreign countries, physical education, Jacques Cousteau, feelings, history, human relations, self-awareness, values, materials for teachers, film-making
Special interest: Spanish-speaking, nonsexist education, deaf
Discount: Inquire
Services: Catalog. Preview prints. Rent 16mm films. Exhibit at ALA, AECT. Lease to schools, libraries

CINE-PIC HAWAII CORPORATION
1847 Pacific Heights Rd., Honolulu, HI 96813
808-533-2677
Pres: George Tahara
Lib/Sch Prom Dir: Doug Kaya

Producer/Distributor
Format: VHS & 16mm films
Audience: 1-12, adult
Subjects: Polynesian folktales, art, dance, drama, sports
Services: Catalog

CINEMA CONCEPTS, INC.
2461 Berlin Trnpk, Newington, CT 06111
203-667-1251
Pres: Joel G. Jacobson

Distributor
Format: 1/2" videocassettes
Audience: Preschool-12, adult
Subjects: Fiction, sports, animals, foreign countries, history, biographies, health, drama, music, environment & energy, social studies
Services: Catalog. Sell & rent videocassettes

THE CINEMA GUILD, INC.
1697 Broadway, New York, NY 10019
212-246-5522
Chairman: Philip S. Hobel
Pres: Gary Crowdus

Producer/Distributor
Format: 16mm films, 3/4" videocassettes
Audience: 1-12, adult
Subjects: Career development, health, sex education, music, social studies, art, environment & energy, physical education, sports, biographies, family life, religion, parapsychology, psychology, business, foreign countries, sciences
Special interest: Native Americans, nonsexist education
Discount: Quantity & extended payment
Services: Catalog. Preview prints. Rent 16mm films & videocassettes

CLARUS MUSIC LTD.
340 Bellevue Ave., Yonkers, NY 10703
914-591-7715
Pres: Selma Fass

Producer/Distributor
Format: Audiodiscs, audiocassettes
Audience: K-12, adult
Subjects: Art, crafts, drama, music
Services: Catalog

THE COLLEGE BOARD
45 Columbus Ave., New York, NY 10023-6992
212-713-8000
Pres: Donald M. Stewart
Sales Mgr & Lib/Sch Prom Dir: Elly Weiss
Publications Director: Carolyn Trager

Producer/Distributor
Format: Computer software, videorecordings
Audience: 9-12, adult
Subject: High school guidance
Special interest: Information on transition from high school to college
Services: Catalog. Promotional newsletter. Exhibit at IRA, NAIS, ASCD, AACD, AACROA. Offers schools, libraries, tests & counseling services, financial aid information

COLONIAL WILLIAMSBURG FOUNDATION
Box 1776, Williamsburg, VA 23187
804-229-1000
Pres: Robert Wilburn
Sales Mgr: Marina Ashton

Producer/Distributor
Format: Audiodiscs, slides, audiocassettes, 1/2" videoreels, silent filmstrips, 3/4" videocassettes, games
Audience: 3-12, adult
Subjects: Social studies, art, vocational training, crafts, music, sciences
Special interest: Native Americans
Discount: 20%
Services: Catalog. Sell to schools & libraries

COMEX SYSTEMS, INC.
The Mill Cottage, Mendham, NJ 07945
800-543-6959; Fax: 201-543-9644

Producer/Distributor
Format: Videotapes; Compact Disk Interactive (CDI)
Audience: Children/adults
Services: Catalog

COMMUNICATION FOR CHANGE, INC.
(formerly Martha Stuart Communications, Inc.)
147 W. 22nd St., New York, NY 10011
212-255-2718
Pres: Sara Stuart
Sales Mgr: Barkley Stuart

Producer/Distributor
Format: Audiocassettes, 16mm films, 3/4" & 1/2" videocassettes, 1" videoreels
Audience: 9-12, adult
Subjects: Foreign countries, business, health, career development, sex education, health, environment & energy, social studies, family life
Special interest: Nonsexist education
Discount: Inquire
Services: Preview prints. Rent all formats. Sell/lease to ETV & local stations, TV networks, schools, libraries

COMMUNICATION SKILL BUILDERS, INC.
3830 E. Bellevue, Box 42050, Tucson, AZ 85733
602-323-7500
Pres: Ronald H. Weintraub
Mktg Manager: Monika Lester
Children's Ed: Patti Hartmann

Producer/Distributor
Format: Games, audiocassettes, multimedia kits, computer software, programmed learning systems, silent filmstrips, books & activity books, flashcards
Audience: Preschool-12, adult
Subjects: Auditory & visual perception, computers, language arts
Special interest: Speech & language disorders
Services: Catalog. Exhibit at NAEYC, ASHA

COMMUNICATIONS GROUP WEST
1640 Fifth St., #202, Santa Monica, CA 90401
310-451-2525
Pres: Sidney Galanty
Sales Mgr: Mark Galanty

Producer/Distributor
Format: 8mm & 16mm films, 1/4" & 3/4" videocassettes, 1/2" videoreels
Audience: K, 5-12, adult
Subjects: Language arts, consumer education, music, dance, social studies, environment & energy, history, foreign countries & languages
Special interest: Spanish-speaking, African Americans
Discount: Quantity (inquire)
Services: Catalog. Preview prints. Rent 16mm films, U-matic, Beta & VHS videocassettes

CORNELL UNIVERSITY MEDIA SERVICES
Audio-Visual Resource Center
8 Research Park, Ithaca, NY 14850
607-255-2091
Film Libn: Richard Gray
Sales/Mktg Dir: Carol Doolittle

Producer/Distributor
Format: Videotapes, audiocassettes,

multimedia kits, 16mm films, slides
Audience: Preschool-12, adult
Subjects: Crafts, health, social studies, animals, environment & energy, home economics, vocational training, business, family life, safety, child abuse, farming, forestry, media, news writing, nutrition, urban life, career development, fiction, sciences, consumer education, foreign countries, sex education
Special interest: Professional materials for teachers, material for parents
Discount: Quantity
Services: Catalog. Preview scripts. Rent & sell 16mm films, videotapes, slides, audiotapes. Exhibit at ALA. Sell/lease to ETV, ITV & local stations, TV networks, schools, libraries

CORONET/MTI FILM & VIDEO
Subs. of Simon & Schuster
250 James St., Morristown, NJ 07960
201-285-7700, 800-777-8100
Dir. of Media: Cathy Hurwitz

Producer/Distributor
Format: 16mm films, videorecordings, Beta & 1/2" VHS videocassettes
Audience: Preschool-12, adult
Subjects: Sex education, business, drama, health, physical education, animals, social studies, career development, environment & energy, home economics, poetry, art, sports, consumer education, family life, language arts, religion, auditory & visual perception, crafts, fiction, mathematics, safety, biographies, dance, foreign countries, music, sciences
Special interest: Spanish-speaking, deaf
Services: Catalog. Preview prints. Rent 16mm films, 1/2" VHS videocassettes. Exhibit at ALA, IRA, AECT, NCTE, NSTA, NCSS, ASCD, AASA. Study guides. Sell/lease to schools, libraries

CRAIGHEAD FILMS
6532 Switzer, Box 3900, Shawnee, KS 66203
913-631-3040
Pres: Wendel Craighead

Producer/Distributor
Format: 16mm films, 1/2" videoreels, 3/4" videocassettes
Audience: K-12, adult
Subjects: Health, language arts, sciences, storytelling
Special interest: Reading disabled, mentally handicapped, physically handicapped
Services: Catalog. Preview prints. Rent 16mm films, VHS & Beta videocas-

settes. Exhibit at CEC, NAEYC, Head Start
Distribution: 16mm films, VHS, Beta & 3/4" U-matic videocassette

CUISENAIRE COMPANY OF AMERICA
10 Bank Street, White Plains, NY 10602
914-997-2600
Pres: Jeffrey Sellon
VP & Sales: Maggie Holler
Ed: Doris Hirschhorn

Producer/Distributor
Format: Computer software, games, kits, models
Audience: K-12
Subjects: Mathematics
Services: Catalog. Exhibit at NCTM, ASCD, NCEA, CEC

D4 FILM STUDIOS
749 Charles River St., Needham, MA 02192
617-235-1119
Pres: Stephen Dephoure

Distributor
Format: 16mm films, VHS tapes
Audience: K-6
Services: Preview prints and rentals are available for a charge

DCA EDUCATIONAL PRODUCTS, INC.
814 Kellers Church Rd., Box 338, Bedminster, PA 18910
215-795-2841
Pres: Diane Schneider

Producer/Distributor
Format: Transparencies
Audience: 7-12, adult
Subjects: Vocational training
Services: Catalog. Preview prints

DCM INSTRUCTIONAL SYSTEMS
(formerly Damon/Instructional Systems)
80 Wilson Way, Westwood, MA 02090
617-329-4300
Children's Eds: Robert Maddestra, Dick Watson

Producer/Distributor
Format: Flashcards, 3/4" videocassettes, audiocartridges, laboratory kits
Audience: 6-12, adult
Subjects: Sex education, business, vocational training, career development, health, sciences
Special interest: Native Americans, slow learners
Services: Catalog. Promotional newsletters. Preview prints. Rent filmstrips, slides & videos. Exhibit at NSTA, NCEA. Sell/lease to schools, libraries

DANA PRODUCTIONS
6249 Babcock Ave., North Hollywood, CA 91606
818-508-5331
Pres: Albert Saparoff
Dist Dir: Andrea Ferguson

Producer/Distributor
Format: 8mm & 16mm films, videocassettes
Audience: 2-12, adult
Subjects: Language arts, history, career development, music, dance, poetry, family life, religion, health, social studies
Special interest: Mentally handicapped, Native Americans, African Americans, Mexican Americans, Spanish-speaking, nonsexist education, deaf, drug prevention & rehabilitation
Services: Catalog. Preview prints. Rent 8mm & 16mm films, videocassettes. Exhibit at AECT, ASCD

TOM DAVENPORT FILMS
Pearlstone, Delaplane, VA 22025
703-592-3701; Fax: 703-592-3717
Pres: Tom Davenport
Dist Mgr: B. J. Fleming

Producer/Distributor
Format: 16mm films, 1/2", 1/4", & 3/4" videocassettes
Audience: K-12, adult
Subjects: Language arts, biographies, music, drama, religion, family life, social studies, foreign countries
Special interest: African Americans
Services: Catalog. Preview prints. Rent 16mm films, 3/4" VHS videocassettes. Exhibit at ALA. Sell/lease to ETV, ITV, & local stations, TV networks, schools, libraries

DAVIDSON FILMS
31 E St., Davis, CA 95616
916-753-9604; Fax: 916-753-3719
Pres: Frances W. Davidson
Mktg. Mgr: K. C. Reinking

Producer/Distributor
Format: 1/2" VHS
Audience: College, university, parent groups
Subjects: Developmental psychology, Teacher training, Infant care, Developmentally disabled
Special interest: Piaget & Erikson; developmentally appropriate teaching practices
Services: Sales. Rentals. Previews. Independent production

DIMENSION FILMS
15007 Gault St., Van Nuys, CA 91405
818-997-8065
Pres: Gary Goldsmith

Producer

Format: 16mm films, video, CD-ROM
Audience: K-12
Subjects: Social studies, family life, values, fiction, language arts, sex education
Services: Rent 16mm films. Sell/lease to ETV stations

DIRECT CINEMA LIMITED
Box 10003, Santa Monica, CA 90410-1003
310-396-4774; Fax: 310-396-3233
Pres: Mitchell W. Block
V.P.: Joan von Herrmann
Sales Mgr: Michael Pultitzer
Lib/Sch Prom Dir: Betsy A. McLane

Distributor
Format: 16mm films, 3/4'' & 1/2'' videocassettes
Audience: Preschool-12, adult
Subjects: Dance, health, poetry, social studies, art, drama, hobbies, religion, business, environment & energy, language arts, safety, career & development, family life, music, sciences, crafts, fiction, physical education, sex education
Special interest: Native Americans, nonsexist education, mentally handicapped
Discount: Inquire
Services: Catalog. Preview prints. Rent 16mm films & 1/2'' videocassettes. Sell/lease to ETV, ITV, & local stations, TV networks, schools, libraries

WALT DISNEY RECORDS
500 S. Buena Vista St., Burbank, CA 91521
818-567-5327
VP: Mark Jaffe
Sales Mgr: Barry Hafft

Producer
Format: Audiocassettes, CDs
Audience: K-12, adult
Subjects: Fiction, music

DISTRIBUTION 16
32 W. 40th St., Ste. 2L, New York, NY 10018
212-730-0280
Dist. by Lucerne Media, 37 Ground Pine Rd., Morris Plains, NJ 07950
Pres: Giuliana Nicodemi

Producer
Format: 16mm films, VHS videocassettes
Audience: K-6, adult
Subjects: Art, language arts, music
Special interest: Native Americans, deaf
Services: Catalog. Preview prints. Rent 16mm films & VHS videocassettes. Sell/lease to local TV stations, TV networks, schools, libraries

DISTRIBUTION VIDEO & AUDIO
1060 Kapp Dr., Clearwater, FL 34625
800-683-4147; Fax: 813-441-3069
Lib/Sch Prom Dir: Tara Simon

Distributor
Format: VHS
Audience: K-12
Subjects: Current releases, foreign, Disney, Nintendo, Sega
Services: Catalog

DON BOSCO MULTIMEDIA
475 North Ave., New Rochelle, NY 10802
914-576-0122
Pres: James Hurley
Sales Mgr: John Thomas

Producer/Distributor
Format: Videorecordings, filmstrips, super 8mm & 16mm films, pictures, slides
Audience: K-12, adult
Subjects: Religion, sex education

DOWNTOWN COMMUNITY TELEVISION CENTER (DCTV)
87 Lafayette St., New York, NY 10013
212-966-4510
Pres: Jon Alpert, Keiko Tsuno
Sales Mgr & Lib/Sch Prom Dir: Kristen Thomas

Producer/Distributor
Format: 1/2'' videoreels, 3/4'' videocassettes
Audience: 10-12, adult
Subjects: Social studies
Services: Catalog. Exhibit at ALA

DRAMA BOOK PUBLISHERS
200 Fifth Avenue, New York, NY 10001
212-725-5377

Producer/Distributor
Format: Audiocassettes, kits
Audience: 10-12, adult
Subjects: Drama
Services: Catalog

EME CORPORATION
Box 2805, Danbury, CT 06813
203-798-2050
Pres: T. McMahon
Children's Ed: G. Ropes

Producer
Format: VHS videocassettes, charts, computer software, videodiscs, CD-ROM
Audience: 5-12, adult
Services: Catalog. Preview prints. Exhibit at NSTA

EDUCATIONAL ACTIVITIES
1937 Grand Ave., Baldwin, NY 11510
516-223-4666
Pres: Alfred S. Harris, Jr.

Adv Dir: Rosalie Dow

Producer/Distributor
Format: 1/4'' & 3/4'' videocassettes, audiocassettes, computer software, multimedia kits, videodiscs
Audience: K-12
Subjects: Consumer education, language arts, sciences, animals, dance, mathematics, social studies, auditory & visual perception, family life, music, career & development, health, physical education, computers, home economics, safety
Special interest: Computer materials, reading disabled
Services: Catalog

EDUCATIONAL DESIGN, INC.
345 Hudson St., New York, NY 10014-4502
212-255-7900
Pres: Donn Mosenfelder
Sales Mgr: Steven N. Crocker

Producer/Distributor
Format: Audiocassettes, 1/2'' videoreels
Audience: 6-12, adult
Subjects: Social studies, career development, vocational training, consumer education, hobbies, home economics
Special interests: African Americans, bilingual students, nonsexist education, reading disabled, mentally handicapped
Services: Catalog. Preview prints. Exhibit at AVA, CEC

EDUCATIONAL IMAGES, LTD.
Box 3456, Westside Sta., Elmira, NY 14905
607-732-1090
Pres: Charles R. Belinky
Sales Mgr: Pat Baker

Producer/Distributor
Format: VHS videocassettes, computer software, sound filmstrips, slides, CD-ROM
Audience: 4-12, adult
Subjects: Sciences, animals, career development, environment & energy
Services: Catalog. Preview prints. Sell/lease to ETV, ITV & local stations, TV networks, schools, libraries
Distribution: Slides, filmstrips, computer software, VHS videocassettes, CD-ROM

EDUCATIONAL INSIGHTS
19560 S. Rancho Way, Dominguez Hills, CA 90220
213-637-2131; 800-367-5713
Pres: Jay Cutler
VP, Mktg & Sales: Jim Whitney

Producer
Format: Laboratory kits, audio-

cassettes, models, dioramas, microscopic slides, flashcards, games
Audience: K-12, adult
Subjects: Career development, language arts, social studies, arts, crafts, mathematics, auditory & visual perception, environment & energy, music, biographies, fiction, physical education, business, foreign countries & languages, sciences
Services: Catalog. Exhibit at IRA, NAESP, NAVA, NSSEA, EDSA, NCTM

EDUCATIONAL RESOURCES
1550 Executive Dr., Elgin, IL 60123
800-624-2926; Fax: 708-888-8689
Pres: Forest Barbieri

EDUCATIONAL VIDEO NETWORK, INC.
1401 19th St., Huntsville, TX 77340
409-295-5767; Fax: 409-294-0233
Pres: George Russell

Producer/Distributor
Format: VHS videocassettes, Mac CD-ROM
Audience: K-12, adult
Subjects: Career development, foreign countries & languages, physical education, social studies, animals, crafts, home economics, poetry, vocational training, art, drama, language arts, religion, biographies, environment & energy, mathematics, safety, business, fiction, music, sciences
Special interest: Bilingual studies
Services: Catalog. Preview prints. Promotional newsletters

ENCYCLOPEDIA BRITANNICA EDUCATIONAL CORPORATION
310 S. Michigan Ave., Chicago, IL 60604
312-347-7947; Fax: 312-347-7966

Producer/Distributor
Format: Programmed learning systems, computer software, 1/4'' & 3/4'' videocassettes, sound & silent filmstrips, multimedia kits, 16mm films
Audience: Preschool-12, adult
Subjects: Safety, business, vocational training, dance, foreign countries & languages, mathematics, animals, sciences, career development, drama, health, music, art, sex education, computers, environment & energy, hobbies, physical education, auditory & visual perception, social studies, consumer education, family life, home economics, poetry, biographies, sports, crafts, fiction, language arts, religion
Special interest: Blind, deaf, reading disabled, mentally handicapped
Services: Catalog. Preview prints. Rent 16mm films. Free catalog cards. Ex-

hibit at ALA, IRA, AECT, NCTE, NCEA, NCSS
Distribution: 16mm films, filmstrips

FAMILY COMMUNICATIONS, INC.
4802 Fifth Ave., Pittsburgh, PA 15213
412-687-2990
Pres: Fred Rogers
Sales Mgr: William Isler

Producer/Distributor
Format: 1/2'' & 3/4'' videocassettes, audiocassettes, sound filmstrips, kits, videorecordings
Audience: K-10
Subjects: Auditory & visual perception, consumer education, family life
Special interest: Early childhood development
Services: Catalog. Rent all formats. Sell/lease to those who purchase from catalog

FAMILY FILMS
3558 S. Jefferson, St. Louis, MO 63118
314-268-1105
Prod Mgr: Rick Johnson

Producer/Distributor
Format: 1/2'' videocassettes
Audience: K-3, 7-12, adult
Subjects: Religion, values
Special interest: Spanish-speaking
Discount: Inquire
Services: Catalog. Preview prints & video. Promotional newsletters. Sell to schools, libraries, book stores

FILMIC ARCHIVES
The Cinema Center, Botsford, CT 06404
203-261-1920
Pres & Sales Mgr: Jon Sonneborn
Lib/Sch Prom Dir & Children's Ed: Christopher Cushman

Producer/Distributor
Format: Educational posters, bookmarks, etc.
Audience: 5-12, adult
Subjects: Drama, fiction, sciences, social studies, English literature, documentaries

FILMMAKERS' COOPERATIVE
175 Lexington Ave., New York, NY 10016
212-889-3820
Pres: M. M. Serra

Distributor
Format: Super 8mm, 8mm, 16mm, 35mm films
Subjects: Safety, business, vocational training, dance, foreign countries & languages, mathematics, animals, sciences, career development, drama, health, music, art, sex education, computers, environment &

energy, hobbies, physical education, auditory & visual perception, social studies, consumer education, family life, home economics, poetry, biographies, sports, crafts, fiction, language arts, religion
Services: Catalog. Rent nonprofit rental library for experimental & independently made films

FILMS INCORPORATED
5547 N. Ravenswood, Chicago, IL 60640
800-343-4312; Fax: 312-878-0416
CEO: Charles Benton
Natl Sales Mgr/Ed: June Goss

Distributor
Format: VHS, laserdisc, multimedia
Audience: K-12, adult
Subjects: Fine & performing arts, documentaries, "Wonder Works"
Services: Catalog. Limited preview. Exhibit at conferences

FILMS FOR THE HUMANITIES & SCIENCES
Box 2053, Princeton, NJ 08543
609-275-1400, 800-257-5126; Fax: 609-275-3767
Sales Mgr & Lib/Sch Prom Dir: Lisa-Ann Zdrodowski

Producer/Distributor
Format: Filmstrips, 1/2'' videoreels, 3/4'' videocassettes, videodiscs
Audience: K-12
Subjects: Drama, health, poetry, sports, art, environment & energy, home economics, religion, vocational training, career development, family life, language arts, sciences, computers, fiction, music, sex education, consumer education, foreign countries & languages, physical education, social studies
Special interest: Native Americans, Spanish-speaking, computer materials
Services: Catalog. Preview prints. Rent all formats. Exhibit at ALA, NCTE. Sell/lease to ETV & ITV stations, schools, libraries

FILMS OF INDIA
Box 48303, Los Angeles, CA 90048
213-383-9217
Pres: R. M. Bagai

Producer/Distributor
Format: Audiodiscs, 16mm films
Audience: 8-12, adults
Subjects: Foreign countries & languages, biographies, music, dance, social studies, drama, family life
Services: Catalog. Rent & sell films & discs

FOCUS INTERNATIONAL INC.
1160 E. Jericho Tpke., Huntington, NY
  11743
516-549-5320; Fax: 516-549-2066

Producer/Distributor
Format: 16mm films, 1/2'' VHS
  videocassettes
Audience: K-12, adult
Subjects: Family life, health, sex education

FORDHAM EQUIPMENT & PUBLISHING
  COMPANY
3308 Edson Ave., Bronx, NY 10469
718-379-7300; Fax: 718-379-7300
Pres: Al Robbins
Sales Mgr: Marge Gemma

Producer/Distributor
Format: Charts, sound filmstrips, multimedia kits, transparencies
Audience: K-12
Special interest: Library research, instructional programs
Services: Exhibit at ALA, state library
  convention

FRIENDS UNITED PRESS
101 Quaker Hill Dr., Richmond, IN
  47374
317-962-7573
Mgr: Ardith Talbot
Sales Mgr: Carolyn Rhoades

Producer/Distributor
Format: Audiocassettes
Subjects: Religion
Discount: Schools, libraries, 10%
Services: Catalog. Preview prints

FRIENDSHIP PRESS
475 Riverside Dr., New York, NY
  10115
212-870-2496
Orders: Box 37844, Cincinatti, OH
  45222-0844
Exec Dir: Audrey A. Miller
Children's Ed: Margaret Larom

Producer/Distributor
Format: Multimedia kits, audiodiscs,
  maps, audiocassettes, slides, charts,
  sound & silent filmstrips
Audience: K-12, adult
Subjects: Religion, art, social studies,
  biographies, foreign countries, music
Special interest: Professional materials
  for teachers
Discount: Inquire
Services: Catalog. Preview prints. Exhibit at Church & Synagogue Library
  Assn

GPN, see **GREAT PLAINS NATIONAL**

GAMCO EDUCATION MATERIALS
Box 1911, Big Spring, TX 79721-1911
915-267-6327, 800-351-1404; Fax:
  915-267-7480
Pres: Auriel A. LaFond
Sales Mgr: Jerry Proffitt
Children's Ed: Tracy Boeker

Producer/Distributor
Format: Computer software
Audience: K-12
Subjects: Language arts, mathematics,
  social studies, early childhood, and
  teacher resource
Services: Catalog. Preview copies. Exhibit at numerous conventions
  throughout the U.S.

GATEWAY PRODUCTIONS, INC.
Box 55358, New Orleans, LA 70055
504-482-3835, 800-837-4982; Fax:
  504-833-4744
Pres: William Manschot
VP Sales: Caroline R. Ramsey

Producer/Distributor
Format: Audiocassettes, sound filmstrips
Audience: K-12
Subjects: Social studies, folklore
Services: Catalog. Preview prints

GREAT PLAINS NATIONAL (GPN)
1800 N. 33rd St., Box 80669, Lincoln,
  NE 68501-0669
402-472-2007, 800-228-4630; Fax:
  402-472-1785
Sales Mgr: Larry R. Aerni

Producer/Distributor
Format: 3/4'' videocassettes, 16mm
  films, slide, videodiscs, 1/2''
  videoreels, CD-ROM
Audience: Preschool-12, adult
Special interest: African Americans,
  professional materials for teachers,
  Native Americans, Spanish-speaking,
  bilingual students, computer
  materials
Services: Distributor of educational
  programming for elementary, secondary, post-secondary, & continuing
  education. Teacher/study guides.
  Annual catalog. Quarterly newsletters and brochures. Video conferencing

GREEN MOUNTAIN POST FILMS
Box 229, Turners Falls, MA 01376
413-863-4754; Fax: 413-863-8248
Pres: Daniel Keller
Sales Mgr: Charles Light
Lib/Sch Prom Dir: Hedy Sherman
Children's Ed: Kathleen O'Connor

Producer/Distributor

Format: 16mm films, 3/4'' videocassettes, 1/2'' audiocassettes
Audience: 4-12, adult
Subjects: Social studies, consumer
  education, drama, environment &
  energy, sciences
Special interest: Nonsexist education
Services: Catalog. Preview prints.
  Promotional newsletters. Rent 16mm
  films & 3/4'' videocassettes. Exhibit
  at EFLA. Sell/lease to ETV, ITV, & local stations, TV networks, schools,
  libraries
Distribution: Distributes 16mm films,
  videocassettes, slide shows by other
  producers

GUIDANCE ASSOCIATES
Box 1000, Mt Kisco, NY 10549
914-661-4100, 800-431-1242

Producer/Distributor
Format: Sound & silent filmstrips,
  slides, 1/2'' videoreels, 3/4''
  videocassettes, videorecordings,
  multimedia kits
Audience: K-12, adult
Subjects: Psychology, computers, environment & energy, health,
  sciences, family life, sex education,
  art, social studies, business, language arts, vocational training,
  career development, mathematics,
  drug education, child development,
  safety, consumer education, home
  economics, auditory & visual perception, biographies, foreign countries
  & languages, physical education
Special interest: Nonsexist education,
  spanish-speaking, deaf, reading disabled mentally handicapped
Services: Catalog. Preview prints.
  Promotional newsletters. Exhibit at
  ALA, NCTE, APGA, CEC, AVA, NCSS,
  NSTA, NAEYC & Head Start conferences
Distribution: The Center for Humanities, Guidance Associates, Science &
  Mankind, 16mm films from Xerox
  Films

HAMMOND INC.
515 Valley St., Maplewood, NJ 07040
201-763-6000
Pres: C. Dean Hammond
Sales/Mktg Dir: Kathleen D. Hammond
Lib/Sch Prom Dir: Gwen Baker

Producer/Distributor
Format: Map, atlases, transparencies
Audience: K-12, adult
Subjects: Social studies, atlases,
  reference
Discount: Libraries, 15%
Services: Catalog. Preview prints. Exhibit at NCSS, NJSS, CSS, ABA, ALA

HAWKHILL ASSOCIATES, INC.
125 E. Gilman St., Madison, WI 53703

608-251-3934
Pres: Bill Stonevarger
Sales Mgr: Jane Denny

Producer/Distributor
Format: Sound filmstrips, 3/4''
  videocassettes, VHS & Beta
  videocassettes
Audience:4-12, adult
Subjects: Poetry, animals, sciences,
  career development, social studies,
  environment & energy, home eco-
  nomics
Special interest: Science literacy
Services: Catalog. Preview prints.
  Promotional newsletters. Exhibit at
  Natl Science Teachers Assn

**HEALTH SERVICE CENTER FOR
EDUCATIONAL RESOURCES**
University of Washington, T252 HSC,
  SB-56, Seattle, WA 98195
206-685-1186; Fax: 206-543-8051
Distribution Coord: Marie Gary

Producer/Distributor
Format: Games, audiorecordings, kits,
  charts, pictures, computer software,
  transparencies, filmstrips
Audience: Preschool-12, adult
Subjects: Environment & energy,
  health, physical education
Discount: Quantity, inquire
Services: Catalog. Preview prints.
  Promotional newsletters. Speakers
  for schools & libraries
Distribution: Computer software & in-
  structional media

D. C. HEATH & COMPANY
125 Spring St., Lexington, MA 02173
617-862-6650
Pres: Loren Korte
Pres, School Div: Albert Bursma Jr.

Producer/Distributor
Format: Transparencies, audiocassettes, videocassettes, computer
  software, multimedia & laboratory
  kits, realia
Audience: K-12
Subjects: Language arts, computers,
  mathematics, consumer education,
  sciences, drama, social studies, foreign languages, reading
Special interest: Spanish-speaking,
  computer materials, nonsexist education
Services: Catalog. Exhibit at IRA,
  NCTE, NCTM, NSTA. Consultants provide inservice training to teachers

**HEINEMANN EDUCATIONAL BOOKS,
INC.**
(a division of Reed Publishing Inc.)
361 Hanover St., Portsmouth, NH
  03801-3912
603-431-7894, 800-541-2086
Pres: John C. Watson
Sales Mgr: Michael Gibbons

Lib/Sch Prom Dir: Lori Lampert
Ed: Toby Gordon

Producer/Distributor
Format: Filmstrips, 1/2'' & 3/4''
  videocassettes
Subjects: Language arts, whole
  language, math, science, teaching
  materials
Special interest: Literacy education
Service: Catalog. Rent 1/2'' VHS videocassettes. Exhibit at IRA, NCTE

HOMER & ASSOCIATES
1420 N. Beachwood Dr., Hollywood,
  CA 90028
213-462-4710
VP & Children's Ed: Coco Conn

Producer
Format: Motion pictures, videodiscs,
  videorecordings
Audience: Preschool-6
Subjects: Sciences, computers, self-
  sufficiency, family life, health,
  mathematics
Special interest: Computer materials,
  nonsexist education
Services: Computer conferences for
  administrators

HUBBARD SCIENTIFIC CO.
1120 Halbleib Rd., Box 760, Chippewa
  Falls, WI 54729
715-723-4427; Fax: 715-723-8021

Producer/Distributor
Format: Flashcards, pictures, audiorecordings, games, transparencies,
  charts, multimedia & laboratory kits,
  videorecordings, computer software,
  maps, sound filmstrips, models
Audience: K-12
Subjects: Environment & energy,
  health, physical education,
  sciences
Special interest: Mentally handicapped
Services: Catalog. Preview prints. Exhibit at CEC, NSTA, AAHPERD

HUMAN RELATIONS MEDIA, INC.
175 Tompkins Ave., Pleasantville, NY
  10570
914-769-6900
Pres: Anson Schloat
Lib/Sch Prom Dir: Donna Giachetti

Producer
Format: Sound filmstrips, 1/2''
  videocassettes
Audience: 5-12, adult
Subjects: Language arts, social
  studies, career development,
  mathematics, consumer education,
  physical education, environment &
  energy, sciences, family life, sex
  education
Discount: Inquire
Services: Catalog. Preview prints.
  Promotional newsletters

IDEAL SCHOOL SUPPLY COMPANY
11000 S. Lavergne Ave., Oak Lawn, IL
  60453
708-425-0805
Sales Mgr: Kazol Kulikowski

Producer
Format: Manipulatives, games, labora-
  tory kits, charts, maps, sound film-
  strips, pictures, flashcards
Audience: Preschool-12, adult
Subjects: Sciences, social studies, lan-
  guage arts, mathematics
Special interest: Special education,
  early learning
Services: Catalog

**IMPERIAL INTERNATIONAL LEARNING
CORPORATION**
30 Montauk Blvd., Oakdale, NY 11769
516-567-7227
Pres: Spencer Barnard
Children's Ed: Patsy Gunnels

Producer
Format: Games, audiocassettes, multi-
  media kits, charts, computer soft-
  ware, sound filmstrips
Audience: Preschool-12
Subjects: Sciences, auditory & visual
  perception, fiction, language arts,
  music
Special interest: Reading disabled,
  remedial math
Services: Catalog. Preview prints.
  Promotional newsletters

INDIAN HOUSE
Box 472, Taos, NM 87571
505-776-2953
Owner: Tony Isaacs
Mgr: Judy Lujan

Producer/Distributor
Format: audiocassettes
Audience: 4-12, adult
Subjects: Dance, music
Special interest: Native Americans
Discount: Inquire
Services: Catalog

**INDIANA UNIVERSITY INSTRUCTIONAL
SUPPORT SERVICES**
Bloomington, IN 47405-5901
812-855-2103; Fax: 812-855-8404
Dir, Media Resources: Beverly
  Teach

Producer/Distributor
Format: 16mm films, 1/2'' & 3/4''
  videocassettes
Audience: K-12, adult
Subjects: Social studies, language arts,
  fairy tales, folklore, health,
  mathematics, sciences
Services: Major rental library. Limited
  sale of 16mm & video with preview
  for purchase consideration. Media
  reference service

INSTRUCTIONAL/COMMUNICATIONS TECHNOLOGY, INC.
10 Stepar Place, Huntington Station, NY 11746
516-549-3000, 800-225-5428; Fax: 516-549-3156
Pres: Stanford E. Taylor
General manager: Audrey Carty
Prom Coord: Dorothea L. Taylor

Producer
Format: Audiocassettes, computer software, silent filmstrips, multimedia kits
Audience: K-12, adult
Subjects: Career development, foreign countries, sciences, animals, consumer education, health, social studies, art, environment & energy, language arts, sports, auditory & visual perception, family life, mathematics, vocational training, biographies, fiction, safety
Special interest: Deaf, Native Americans, reading disabled, bilingual students, mentally handicapped, computer materials, blind
Services: Catalog. Preview policy. Exhibit at IRA, AECT, NAVA

INTEGRATIVE LEARNING SYSTEMS
140 N. Maryland Ave., Glendale, CA 91206
818-243-2675
Pres: Edward O. Vail
Sales Mgr & Lib/Sch Prom Dir: Colleen M. Vail

Producer/Distributor
Format: Audiocassettes, audioreels, multimedia kits
Audience: 3-12, adult
Subjects: Language arts, reading, spelling, history
Special interest: Native Americans, Spanish-speaking, bilingual students, reading disabled
Services: Catalog. Consultation services. Staff development seminars. Language processing workshops. Program maintenance & evaluation

INTERNATIONAL FILM BUREAU INC.
332 S. Michigan Ave., Chicago, IL 60604-4382
312-427-4545, 800-432-2241; Fax: 312-427-4550
Chmn: Wesley H. Greene
Gen Mgr: Ben F. Hodge

Distributor
Format: Videocassettes (any size), 16mm films, sound filmstrips
Audience: K-12, adult
Subjects: Language arts, animals, sciences, mathematics, social studies, art, music, biographies, foreign countries & languages, safety, health, animated films

Special interest: Native Americans, Spanish-speaking, hearing impaired
Discount: 20% on replacement copies
Services: Catalog. Preview videos. Promotional brochures. Rent video and films. Television rights available for most titles

JACOBY/STORM PRODUCTIONS
22 Crescent Rd., Westport, CT 06880
203-227-2220
Pres: Doris Storm

Producer
Format: Audiorecordings, sound filmstrips, 16mm films, videorecordings
Audience: K-12, adult
Subjects: Vocational training, computers, environment & energy, home economics, safety, art, consumer education, family life, language arts, sciences, biographies, crafts, fiction, mathematics, sex education, business, dance, foreign countries, music, social studies, career development, drama, health, poetry, sports

JANUARY PRODUCTIONS
210 Sixth Ave., Hawthorne, NJ 07507
201-423-4666, 800-451-7450; Fax: 201-423-5569
Pres: Allan Peller
Sales Mgr & Lib/Sch Prom Dir: Carol Liess
Children's Ed: Barbara Peller

Producer/Distributor
Format: Audiocassettes, computer software, multimedia kits
Audience: Preschool-10
Subjects: Language arts, animals, sciences, biographies, social studies, computers, consumer education
Services: Catalog. Preview prints. Exhibit at ALA, SSLI. Sell/lease to schools, libraries

KAR-BEN COPIES, INC.
6800 Tildenwood Lane, Rockville, MD 20852
301-984-8733, 800-4-KARBEN; Fax: 301-881-9195
Pres & Children's Ed: Judye Groner
VP, Sales Mgr & Lib/Sch Prom Dir: Madeline Wikler

Producer/Distributor
Format: Audiocartridges
Audience: K-4
Subjects: Religion
Special interest: Jewish themes
Discount: 12-24 copies, 10%; 25 or more, 25%
Services: Catalog. Exhibit at ALA

KAW VALLEY FILMS, INC.
Box 3900, Shawnee, KS 66203
913-631-3040
Pres: James Whitefield

Sales Mgr: Al Killingsworth
Lib/Sch Prom Dir: Marg Killingsworth
Children's Ed: Beth Whitefield

Producer/Distributor
Format: 16mm films, 3/4", VHS, Beta videocassettes
Subjects: Music, art, sciences, biographies, social studies, health, history, geography, language arts
Discount: Inquire
Services: Catalog. Preview prints. Rent 16mm films. VHS videocassettes. Exhibit at AECT, NAVA, AASL. Sell/lease to ETV & local stations, schools, libraries
Distribution: 16mm films & VHS videocassettes

KENT STATE UNIVERSITY, AUDIO VISUAL SERVICES
Kent, OH 44242
216-672-3456
Sales/Prom Dir: John Whyde

Distributor
Format: 16mm films, 1/2" videocassettes
Audience: K-12, adult
Subjects: Safety, business, vocational training, dance, foreign countries & languages, mathematics, animals, sciences, career development, drama, health, music, art, sex education, computer, environment & energy, hobbies, physical education, auditory & visual perception, social studies, consumer education, family life, home economics, poetry, biographies, sports, crafts, fiction, language arts, religion
Discount: To summer camps for children
Services: Catalog. Rent films. Exhibit at state & local conventions

THE KIDS ON THE BLOCK, INC.
9385-C Gerwig Lane, Columbia, MD 21046
410-290-995, 800-368-5437; Fax: 410-290-9358
Pres: Jim Thurman
VP: Ken Male
Mktg Dir: Maggie Mullikin

Producer/Distributor
Format: Audiodiscs, audiocassettes
Audience: Grades 2-8, adult
Subjects: Disabilities, educational & medical differences, social concerns
Special interest: Disability awareness
Services: Catalog. Promotional newsletters. Book series. Live puppet performances. Sell to schools, libraries, community service groups

KIMBO EDUCATIONAL
10 N. Third Ave., Box 477, Long Branch, NJ 07740
908-229-4949

Pres: Gertrude S. Kimble
VP: James A. Kimble
Mktg Dir: Elaine Rauff

Producer/Distributor
Format: Audiocassettes,
videorecordings
Audience: Preschool-5, adult
Subjects: Physical education, dance,
early childhood, language arts,
music
Special interest: Multicultural, whole
language
Services: Catalog. Exhibit at ALA, AAH-
PER, NAEYC, ABA, NSSEA, EDSA
Distribution: Educational activities,
January Productions, Milliken Videos,
School Zone Videos, Live Oak Film-
strips, Listening Library Filmstrips,
Folkways, Elephant & Raffi Cassettes

KIRKWOOD COMMUNITY COLLEGE
Box 2068, Cedar Rapids, IA 52406
319-398-5660; Fax: 319-398-5492

Producer/Distributor
Format: Videodisc
Audience: 11-12, adult
Subjects: Accounting, musical
heritage, teleconferences on dis-
tance learning & computers in
writing
Services: Catalog

WALTER J. KLEIN COMPANY
Box 472087, 6311 Carmel Rd.,
Charlotte, NC 28247-2087
705-542-1403; Fax: 704-542-0735
Chairman: Walter J. Klein
Pres: Richard A. Klein
Distribution/Video Sales Dir: Mary
Babcock

Producer/Distributor
Format: 16mm film production; video
release
Audience: All school ages, adults
Subjects: Consumer education, health,
animals, crafts, sports, business, family life, religion, vocational training,
career development, safety values
Special interest: Nonsexist education,
professional materials for teachers
Discount: Schools, libraries for multiple
copies. Nonexclusive duplication
rights can also be purchased
Services: Catalog. Preview tapes

KNOWLEDGE UNLIMITED
Box 52, Madison, WI 53701
608-836-6660; Fax: 608-831-1570
Pres: Judith DiPrima
Sales Mgr: Jane Gilbertson
Lib/Sch Prom Dir: Barbara Roberts
Children's Ed: Jon Burack

Producer/Distributor
Format: Sound filmstrips, multimedia
kits
Audience: 3-12, adult

Subjects: Sciences, animals, social
studies, art, environment & energy,
foreign countries
Special interest: Deaf
Services: Catalog. Preview prints. Exhibit at NCSS. Sell/lease to schools

**LACLEDE COMMUNICATION SERVICES,
INC.**
2675 Scott Ave., St. Louis, MO
63103-3047
314-535-3999
Pres: George Noory
Sales Mgr: Frank Wyche
Children's Ed: Judy Leventhal

Producer/Distributor
Format: 16mm films, 1/2'' videoreels,
3/4'' videocassettes
Audience: K-12, adult
Subjects: Safety, business, vocational
training, dance, foreign countries &
languages, mathematics, animals,
sciences, career development,
drama, health, music, art, sex education, computers, environment &
energy, hobbies, physical education,
auditory & visual perception, social
studies, consumer education, family
life, home economics, poetry, biographies, sports, crafts, fiction, language arts, religion
Discount: Inquire
Services: Preview prints. Rent

LANDMARK MEDIA INC.
3450 Slade Run Dr., Falls Church, VA
22042
800-342-4336; Fax: 703-536-9540
Distributor
Format: VHS & 16mm film
Audience: K-12, adult
Subjects: Educational, cataloging
Services: Catalog. Preview prints. Ex-
hibit at conferences

LEARNING RESEARCH INC.
420 NW 5th St., Evansville, IN 47708
812-426-6377; Fax: 812-421-3270

Producer/Distributor
Format: VHS
Subjects: Reading programs

LEARNING WELL
2200 Marcus Ave., New Hyde Park, NY
11040-1042
516-621-1540
Pres: David Savitsky
Sales Mgr: Mona Russo

Producer/Distributor
Format: VHS videocassettes, audiocassettes, computer software, sound
filmstrips, games
Audience: K-12
Subjects: Mathematics, career development, poetry, computers, safety,
health, vocational training, language
arts

Special interest: Native Americans,
computer materials, reading disabled, mentally handicapped
Discount: Inquire
Services: Catalog. Preview prints. Exhibit at IRA, NAVA, NSSEA, CEC,
AASL

HAL LEONARD PUBLISHING CORP.
777 W. Bluemound Rd., Milwaukee, WI
53213
414-774-3630
Pres: Keith Mardak
Mgr, Early Childhood Publns: Melinda
Wyant

Producer/Distributor
Format: Audiocassettes, compact disc,
VHS video
Audience: Preschool-12
Subjects: Music & education
Services: Catalog. Exhibit at ABA &
NAEYC

THE LITTLE RED FILMHOUSE
Box 691083, Los Angeles, CA 90069
213-855-0241
Pres: Larry Klingman

Producer/Distributor
Format: 16mm films, 3/4'' videocassettes
Audience: Preschool-12, adult
Subjects: Language arts, art, sex education, fiction, social studies, health,
values, home economics
Discount: Volume
Services: Catalog. Preview prints. Rent
16mm films & 3/4'' videocassettes.
Exhibit at ALA, AECT, NFM, AFF, Midwest Film Conference. Sell/lease to
ETV, ITV & local stations, schools,
libraries, health & law enforcement
agencies
Distribution: 16mm films & videocassettes from various producers

LIVE OAK MEDIA
Box 652, Pine Plains, NY 12567
518-398-1010; Fax: 518-398-1070
Pres: Roy Oakley

Producer/Distributor
Format: Audiocassettes, sound film-
strips, 3/4'' videocassettes
Audience: K-9
Subjects: Language arts
Special interest: AV adaptations of
children's books
Services: Catalog. Promotional news-
letters. Catalog card kits. Preview
prints. Exhibit at ALA, IRA
Distribution: Viking Press

LONG FILMSLIDE SERVICE
7505 Fairmount, El Cerrito, CA 94530
510-524-2744
Co-Owners: Verne & Joyce Odlin

Producer/Distributor
Format: Sound & silent filmstrips,
    slides
Audience: K-12, adult
Subjects: Social studies & language
    arts
Services: Catalog. Custom slide & film-
    strip production

LUCERNE MEDIA
37 Ground Pine Rd., Morris Plains, NJ
    07950
201-538-1401, 800-341-2293; Fax:
    201-538-0855
Pres & Sales Mgr: Franklin J. Visco

Distributor
Format: 16mm films, pictures, 3/4"
    videocassettes, 1/2" VHS & Beta
    videocassettes
Audience: K-12, adult
Subjects: Career development,
    mathematics, vocational training,
    animals, crafts, safety, art, environ-
    ment & energy, sciences, biogra-
    phies, family life, sex education,
    business, health, social studies
Special interest: Nonsexist education
Discount: Inquire
Services: Catalog. Preview prints.
    Promotional newsletters. Rent 16mm
    films & 1/2" VHS videocassettes. Ex-
    hibit at ALA, AECT, NAVA. Sell/lease
    to ITV stations, schools

LYCEUM PRODUCTIONS
Box 1295, La Puente, CA 91749
310-968-6424
Pres: Mark A. Pines
VP: Jerry J. Mook

Producer/Distributor
Format: Sound filmstrips, audiocas-
    settes
Audience: 5-12, adult
Subjects: Fiction, social studies,
    animals, foreign countries, sports,
    art, language arts, photography, bi-
    ographies, poetry, environment &
    energy, sciences
Special interest: Native Americans,
    Spanish-speaking, Appalachian
    people
Services: Catalog. Preview prints

MMI CORPORATION
2950 Wyman Pkwy., Box 19907, Balti-
    more, MD 21211
410-366-1222; Fax: 410-366-6311
Pres & Sales Mgr: Ralph C. Levy

Producer/Distributor
Format: Maps, VHS & Beta video-
    cassettes, charts, models, computer
    software, realia, sound & silent film-
    strips, slides, globes, transparencies
Audience: 7-12, adult
Subjects: Astronomy, space, earth
    science
Special interest: Planetariums

Services: Catalog
Distribution: All formats

MVP
9424 Eton Ave., #C, Chatsworth, CA
    91311
800-637-3555; Fax: 818-709-7846

Producer/Distributor
Format: Video
Subjects: Instructional: musical-piano,
    guitar, read music, band. Computer
    instruction. Dance, karaoke

MAGNA SYSTEMS, INC.
West Countyline 95, Barrington, IL
    60010
312-382-6477
Pres: Wilbur S. Edwards

Producer/Distributor
Format: Computer software, 1/2"
    videoreels, 3/4" videocassettes
Audience: 7-12, adult
Subjects: Mathematics, business,
    career development, consumer edu-
    cation, health, child development
Services: Catalog. Preview prints.
    Lease-to-own option for 1/2" & 3/4"
    videocassettes. Sell/lease to ETV,
    ITV, & local stations, TV networks,
    schools, libraries

MALIBU FILMS
Box 428, Malibu, CA 90265
310-456-2859
Pres: Claire Menken
Sales/Mktg Dir: David Gregory

Producer/Distributor
Format: 16mm films
Audience: K-12, adult
Subjects: Family life, music, art, fic-
    tion, social studies, auditory & visual
    perception, foreign countries, values,
    mental health, crafts, health, en-
    vironment & energy, language arts
Special interest: Spanish-speaking,
    captioned, nonsexist education,
    nonagist education
Discount: Replacement prints, 20%;
    special lease arrangement
Services: Catalog. Preview prints. Ex-
    hibit at AECT, NCEA

MAROTEN & CO.
(formerly Film Wright)
1500 16th St., #100, San Francisco,
    CA 94103-5112
415-863-6100
Pres: Prescott J. Wright

Producer/Distributor
Format: 16mm films, videorecordings
Audience: 5-12, adult
Subjects: Environment & energy,
    sciences, filmmaking, animation
Services: Catalog. Preview prints. Rent
    16mm films
Distribution: Films, videorecordings

MARSHFILM
Box 8082, Shawnee Mission, KS
    66208
816-523-1059
Pres: Joan K. Marsh

Producer/Distributor
Format: Computer software, sound
    filmstrips, VHS videocassettes, mul-
    timedia kits
Audience: K-12, adult
Subjects: Family life, sciences,
    animals, health, sex education, busi-
    ness, physical education, social
    studies, computers, religion, environ-
    ment & energy, safety
Special interest: Computer materials,
    nonsexist education
Services: Catalog. Preview prints. Sell
    to schools, libraries

THE MEDIA GUILD
11722 Sorrento Valley Rd. E., San
    Diego, CA 92121
619-755-9191; Fax: 619-755-4931

Producer/Distributor
Format: 3/4" videocassettes, VHS
    videocassettes
Audience: 3-12, adult
Subjects: Animals, art, family life,
    values
Services: Catalog. Preview prints.
    Sell/lease to ETV & ITV stations,
    schools, libraries
Distribution: Paulist Productions, Na-
    tional Film Board of Canada, CBS-TV,
    ABC-TV, BBC-TV/Open University,
    Thames Television, and independent
    producers

MEDIA LOFT, INC.
10720 40 Ave. N., Minneapolis, MN
    55441
612-375-1086, 800-532-8457
Pres: Jeffrey Harrington
Sales Mgr: Pat Schuneman

Producer/Distributor
Format: Multimedia kits,
    videorecordings
Audience: 10-12, adult
Subjects: Art, photography
Services: Catalog. Preview prints. Ex-
    hibit at ASPE

MEDIA MATERIALS, INC.
111 Kane St., Baltimore, MD 21224
800-638-6470
Pres: Bruce B. Brown
Sales Mgr: Tim Pyle

Producer/Distributor
Format: Games, audiorecordings, kits,
    programmed learning systems, flash-
    cards, manipulatives
Audience: K-8
Subjects: Auditory & visual perception,
    language arts, social studies,

mathematics, foreign languages, safety, health sciences, reading
Special interest: Bilingual students, remedial programs, African Americans
Services: Catalog. Exhibit at NAEYC, Head Start. Offer schools, libraries 30-day approvals, 100% guarantee

MERIDIAN EDUCATIONAL CORPORATION
236 E. Front St., Bloomington, IL 61701
309-827-5455; Fax: 309-829-8621

Producer/Distributor
Format: VHS, software
Audience: K-12
Subjects: Math, drug education, antibias, career awareness, health, safety, family life, guidance, reading, library skills, behavior, child care & development, clothing & textiles, nutrition, housing, parenting, relationships, life skills
Services: Catalog. Free previews

MERIWETHER PUBLISHING LTD-CONTEMPORARY DRAMA SERVICE
Box 7710, Colorado Springs, CO 80933
303-594-4422
Pres: Arthur Zapel
Lib/Sch Prom Dir & Children's Ed: Ted Zapel

Producer/Distributor
Format: Filmstrips, videorecordings, audiorecordings, games, kits
Audience: 7-12
Subjects: Sex education, drama, speech, language arts, poetry, religion
Special interest: Native Americans
Discount: Inquire
Services: Catalog. Exhibit at ALA. Sell/lease to ETV & local stations, schools, libraries

ARTHUR MOKIN PRODUCTIONS, INC.
Box 1866, Santa Rosa, CA 95402-1866
707-542-4868
Pres: Bill Mokin

Producer/Distributor
Format: 16mm films, 3/4" videocassettes, 1/2" VHS & Beta videocassettes
Audience: K-12, adult
Subjects: Safety, business, vocational training, dance, foreign countries & languages, mathematics, animals, sciences, career development, drama, health, music, art, sex education, computers, environment & energy, hobbies, physical education, auditory & visual perception, social studies, consumer education, family life, home economics, poetry, biogra-

phies, sports, crafts, fiction, language, arts, religion
Special interest: Nonsexist education, deaf, mentally handicapped
Discount: Inquire
Services: Catalog. Preview prints. Rent 16mm films, 3/4" & VHS videocassettes. Exhibit at ALA, AECT. Sell/lease to ETV stations, schools, libraries
Distribution: 16mm films. National Film Board of Canada, Educational Broadcasting Corporation (WNET), CBS

MOODY INSTITUTE OF SCIENCE
820 N. La Salle, Chicago, IL 60610-3284
312-329-2190; Fax: 312-329-4350
Dir: Tim Willms

Producer/Distributor
Format: 16mm films, 1/2" VHS videocassettes
Audience: 3-12, adult
Subjects: Sciences, animals, social studies, environment & energy, health, mathematics
Discount: Inquire
Services: Catalog. Sell 16mm films & videocassettes to consumers, churches, schools, libraries

MULLER MEDIA, INC.
23 E.39 St., New York, NY 10016
212-683-8220
Pres & Sales Mgr: Robert B. Muller
Mgr Syndication: Daniel Mulholland

Producer/Distributor
Format: 16mm films, 1/2" videoreels
Audience: 2-11, adult
Subjects: Family life, fiction

MUSIC FOR LITTLE PEOPLE
Box 1460, Redway, CA 95560-1460
800-727-2233

Producer/Distributor
Format: Audio & video cassettes, CDs

MULISOG CORPORATION
26 W. Mission, #6, Santa Barbara, CA 93101
805-966-3187
Pres: D. R. Phillips

Producer/Distributor
Format: 16mm films
Audience: K-12, adult
Subjects: Music

NATIONAL BOOK COMPANY
Box 8795, Portland, OR 97207-8795
503-228-6345
Pres: Carl W. Salser

Producer/Distributor
Format: Multimedia kits, audiorecordings, programmed learning systems, computer software, flashcards

Audience: 7-12, adult
Subjects: Family life, mathematics, business, foreign languages, sciences, computers, health, sex education, consumer education, home economics, social studies, environment & energy, language arts, vocational training
Services: Catalog. Sell/lease to local PBS station

NATIONAL FILM BOARD OF CANADA
1251 Ave. of the Americas, 16th Fl., New York, NY 10020
212-596-1770; Fax: 212-596-1779
US Dist Rep: John Sirabella

Producer/Distributor
Format: 16mm films, 1/2" videoreels, 3/4" videocassettes
Audience: K-12, adult
Subjects: Crafts, fiction, sciences, animals, dance, foreign countries & languages, social studies, art, drama, music, biographies, environment & energy, religion, business, family life, safety
Special interest: Native Americans
Services: Catalog. Preview prints. Promotional newsletter. Rent 16mm films, 3/4" & 1/2" VHS videocassettes. Exhibit at NFM, AFVF. Sell/lease to ETV, ITV & local stations, TV networks, schools, libraries

NATIONAL GALLERY OF ART EXTENSION PROGRAMS
6th St. & Constitution Ave. NW, Washington, DC 20565
202-842-6273,6263
Dir: Earl A. Powell III
Curator-in-Charge: Ruth R. Perlin

Producer/Distributor
Format: 3/4" videocassettes, multimedia kits, 16mm films, videodiscs, 1/2" videoreels
Audience: 2-12, adult
Subjects: Social studies, art, biographies, foreign languages, crafts, music
Services: Catalog. Preview prints. Rent all programs, free loan. Exhibit at ASCD. Sell/lease to ETV, ITV & local stations, TV networks, schools, libraries

NATIONAL GEOGRAPHIC SOCIETY
1145 17th St. NW, Washington, DC 20036
202-857-7000; Fax: 202-857-7300
Mgr, Educ Svcs: Sherrie Smith
Dir, Educ Media: George A. Peterson
Dir, Educ Films: Sidney Platt

Producer/Distributor
Format: Maps, computer software, motion pictures, sound filmstrips, videodiscs, globes, 1/2" videoreels, multimedia kits, 3/4" videocassettes

Audience: Preschool-12, adult
Subjects: Foreign countries & languages, social studies, animals, health, computers, language arts, environment & energy, mathematics, family life, sciences
Special interest: Deaf
Discount: Inquire
Services: Catalog. Preview prints. Rent 16mm films. Exhibit at ALA, AECT, NSTA, NCSS, NCEA. Sell video duplication licenses to schools, libraries

NATIONAL TEACHING AIDS
1845 Highland Ave., New Hyde Park, NY 11040
516-326-2555
Pres: Aaron Becker

Format: Silent filmstrips, models
Audience: 4-12, adult
Subjects: Sciences, health
Special interest: Bilingual students, blind, deaf, special education
Services: Catalog. Preview prints. Exhibit at ASHC, NABT, NCEA, NJEA, NSTA. Sell/lease to schools, libraries

NATIONAL TEXTBOOK CO.
4255 W. Touhy Ave., Lincolnwood, IL 60646
708-679-5500
Pres: S. William Pattis
Sales Mgr: Larry Rutkowski
Lib/Sch Prom Dir: Richard Knox
Children's Ed: Keith Fry

Producer/Distributor
Format: Games, audiocassettes, multimedia kits, charts, programmed learning systems, sound filmstrips, realia, flashcards
Audience: Preschool-12, adult
Subjects: Foreign countries & languages, business, language arts, career development, consumer education, drama
Special interest: Spanish-speaking, bilingual students, ESL
Discount: Schools, libraries, 25%
Services: Catalog. Preview prints. Promotional newsletters. Exhibit at ALA, ABA, IRA, NAVA, NCTE, ACTFL. Consulting as needed. Sell/lease to schools, libraries

NEW DIMENSION FILMS
85803 Lorane Hwy., Eugene, OR 97405
503-484-7125
Pres & Lib/Sch Prom Dir: Steve Raymen
Gen Mgr: Janet Brock

Distributor
Format: 16mm films, 1/2" VHS videocassettes
Audience: Preschool-12, adult
Subjects: Environment & energy, physical education, social studies,

animals, family life, religion, art, health, safety, computers, language arts, sciences, dance, music, sex education
Special interest: Nonsexist education
Services: Catalog. Preview prints. Rent 16mm films, videocassettes. Exhibit at AECT, NCTE, National Film Market, American Film Festival. Sell/lease to schools, libraries
Distribution: National Film Board of Canada, United Nations, UNESCO, Canadian Broadcasting Corp., Film Australia, New Zealand National Film Unit, New Zealand Television, FABCO, Netherlands Information Service

NIMCO
Box 9, 117 Hwy. 815, Calhoun, KY 42327-0009
800-962-6662; Fax: 502-273-5844
Pres: Bill Jones

Distributor
Format: VHS, filmstrips, displays, software
Audience: Preschool-adult
Subjects: Vocational, drug education & recovery, self-esteem, child care, sex education
Services: Catalog. 14 day preview policy. Exhibit at various conferences

NORTHERN ILLINOIS UNIVERSITY
University Libraries Film Library, De Kalb, IL 60115
805-753-1000
Pres: John E. LaTourette
Dir: David Shavit

Producer/Distributor
Format: 3/4" videocassettes, sound filmstrips, 16mm films, slides, transparencies
Audience: 5-12, adult
Subjects: Art, auditory & visual perception, home economics, language arts

JEFFREY NORTON PUBLISHERS INC./AUDIO-FORUM, THE LANGUAGE SOURCE
On the Green, 96 Broad St., Guilford, CT 06437-2635
203-453-9794; Fax: 203-453-9774

Producer/Distributor
Format: Audiocassettes, computer software, games
Audience: K-5, 11-12, adult
Subjects: Computers, foreign languages
Special interest: Native Americans, Spanish-speaking, ESL, music
Services: Catalog. Preview prints. Exhibit at ACTFL, Northwest Conference of Foreign Language Teachers, Connecticut Assn. of Foreign Language Teachers. Sell/lease to schools, libraries
Distribution: Audiocassettes, games,

videocassettes, computer programs, books

NYSTROM
Div. of Herff Jones, Inc.
3333 N. Elston Ave., Chicago, IL 60618
312-463-1144; Fax: 312-463-0515
Pres: James J. Cerza
VP of Sales: Darrell A. Coppock
VP of Mktg: Patrick E. McKeon
Exec Ed of Science: Tina T. Garrison

Producer
Format: Sound filmstrips, multimedia & laboratory kits, maps, models, CD-ROM, videodiscs
Audience: K-12, adult
Subjects: Social studies, health, language arts, mathematics, sciences
Discount: Inquire
Services: Catalog. Preview prints. Exhibit at NCSS, NSTA, ASCD, NCEA, NAESP

OXFORD UNIVERSITY PRESS
200 Madison Ave., New York, NY 10016
212-679-7300
Pres: Edward Barry
Sales Mgr: Jonathan Weiss
Lib/Sch Prom Dir: Annie Stafford

Producer/Distributor
Format: Audiocassettes
Audience: K-4
Subjects: Poetry, songs, nursery rhymes
Discount: ALA convention offer; new books, 20%; other regular special offers
Services: Catalog. Promotional newsletter. Exhibit at ALA

PBS VIDEO
Dept. of Public Broadcasting Service
1320 Braddock Place, Alexandria, VA 22314-1698
703-739-5380, 800-424-7963 (information), 800-344-3337 (orders); Fax: 703-739-5269
Dir: Don Jalbert

Distributor
Format: 3/4" videocassettes, VHS, Beta & 1/2" videocassettes
Audience: K-12, adult
Subjects: Sciences, business, social studies, environment & energy, sports, family life, health
Special interest: Native Americans, nonsexist education, deaf, Asian Americans, African Americans, Jewish Americans
Discount: Inquire
Services: Catalog. Preview prints. Promotional newsletters. Rent 3/4" & 1/2" videocassettes. Exhibit at ALA, AECT, Technological Literacy Conference, AFF

Distribution: Central distributor for programs produced by public television stations

PACIFIC CASCADE RECORDS
Sub. of Joan Lowe Enterprises
47534 McKenzie Hwy., Vida, OR 97488
503-896-3290
Pres: Joan R. Lowe
Sales Mgr: Kendra Higgins

Producer/Distributor
Format: Audiodiscs, audiocassettes
Audience: K-6
Subjects: Language arts, music, speech therapy, concept development, personality
Special interest: Learning disabilities
Discount: Inquire
Services: Catalog. Preview prints. Exhibit at regional & educational library meetings

PAULIST PRODUCTIONS
Box 1057, Pacific Palisades, CA 90272
310-454-0688; Fax: 310-459-6549
Pres: Fr. Ellwood Kieser, CSP
Sales Mgr: Paul Weber

Producer/Distributor
Format: 16mm films, 1/2" & 3/4" videocassettes
Audience: 7-12, adult
Subjects: Family life, religion, sex education
Special interest: Native Americans, Spanish-speaking, mentally handicapped
Services: Catalog. Rent 16mm films, videocassettes. Sell/lease to local TV stations, TV networks

A. W. PELLER & ASSOC.
249 Goffle Rd., Hawthorne, NJ 07507
201-423-4666
Pres: Allan Peller
Sales Mgr & Lib/Sch Prom Dir: Carol Liess
Children's Ed: Barbara Peller

Distributor
Format: Sound filmstrips, audiodiscs, games, audiocartridges, multimedia & laboratory kits, audioreels, 1/4" videocassettes, computer software
Audience: Preschool-12, adult
Subjects: Computers, music, vocational training, animals, consumer education, safety, biographies, language arts, sciences, career development, mathematics, social studies
Services: Catalog. Preview prints. Exhibit at ALA, SSCI. Sell/lease to schools, libraries

PENNSYLVANIA STATE UNIVERSITY, AUDIO VISUAL SERVICES
Special Services Bldg, 1127 Fox Hill Rd., University Park, PA 16803-1824
814-865-6314, 800-826-0132; Fax: 814-863-2574
Dir: Robert Allen
Dist Coord: Will Covington, Tom McKenna

Producer & Distributor
Format: 16mm films, 1/2" & 3/4" videocassettes
Audience: K-12, college, adult
Subjects: Anthropology, arts, business, communications, education, health, history, life sciences, mathematics, physical sciences, psychology, sociology
Special interest: African-American studies, women's studies, behavioral sciences, diversity issues
Services: Rent videos. 16mm films. Catalogs and other publications. Reference (media source and resource location assistance)

PHOENIX FILMS
A Div. of Phoenix Learning Group
2349 Chaffe Dr., St. Louis, MO 63146
314-569-0211; Fax: 314-569-2834
Pres: H. Gelles
Sales Mgr: Robert Dunlap

Producer & Distributor
Format: Super 8mm & 16mm films, 1/2" videoreels, 3/4" videocassettes, 1/2" videocassettes, posters, laserdisc, software
Audience: Preschool-12, adult
Subjects: Business, foreign countries, music, social studies, animals, drama, health, physical education, sports, art, environment & energy, hobbies, poetry, auditory & visual perception, family life, home economics, religion, biographies, fiction, language arts, sciences
Special interest: African Americans, Native Americans, nonsexist education, deaf, reading disabled
Services: Catalog. Preview prints. Exhibit at ALA, AECT

POINT OF VIEW PRODUCTIONS
2477 Folsom St., San Francisco, CA 94110
415-821-0435; Fax: 415-931-0948
Pres: Karil Daniels

Producer/Distributor
Format: 1/2" video; 16mm films, 3/4" videocassettes, pictures, slides, transparencies
Audience: Adult
Subjects: Family life, health, water birth, gentle child birth, education
Special interest: Nonsexist education
Services: Preview prints for libraries. Rent all formats. Sell/lease to ETV, ITV & local stations, TV networks, schools, libraries

POLART
5973 Cattlemen Lane, Sarasota, FL 34232
800-278-9393; Fax: 813-378-9935
Pres: Jarek Zaremba

Distributor
Format: Video, audiotapes, CD's
Subjects: Religion, cultural history
Special interest: Polish history
Service: Catalog. Exhibit at conferences

PYRAMID FILM & VIDEO
Box 1048, Santa Monica, CA 90406
310-828-7577; Fax: 310-453-9083
Pres: David Adams
Mktg Dir: Kathy Araujo
Lib/Sch Prom Dir: Robin Kamp (Box 496, Media PA 19063; 215-565-2844)
Pub: Steve Crow

Producer & Distributor
Format: 16mm films, 3/4" videocassettes, 1/2" videocassettes
Audience: K-12, adult
Subjects: Social studies, art, sports, health, literature, guidance, language arts, safety
Discount: Quantity
Services: Catalog. Supplements. Teacher's guides. Rent 16mm films & selected U-matic videocassettes

RAINBOW EDUCATIONAL VIDEO, INC.
170 Keyland Ct, Bohemia, NY 11716
516-589-6643, 800-331-4047; Fax: 516-589-6131
Pres: Charles W. Clark, III

Producer & Distributor
Format: Videocassettes, videodiscs
Audience: K-8
Subjects: All subjects
Services: Producer & distributor of nonprint educational media. Semiannual catalog

RAMIC PRODUCTIONS, INC.
Box 9518, Newport Beach, CA 92658
714-640-9115
VP: Evan Aiken

Producer/Distributor of the Eden Ryl Behavioral Series
Format: 1/2" VHS video
Audience: All age levels
Subjects: Human behavior & motivation
Special interest: Spanish-speaking
Discount: Inquire
Services: Preview. Rental. License

RANDOM HOUSE & BULLSEYE BOOKS FOR YOUNG READERS
201 E. 50th St., New York, NY 10022
212-572-2600; Fax: 212-572-8700

Producer/DistributorFormat: Cassette
packages, videocassettes
Audience: Preschool-12
Subjects: General interest
Services: Catalog

**RESCO P/R GRAPHICS & A/V
PRODUCTIONS**
99 Draper Ave., Meriden, CT 06450
203-238-9633
Pres: Ronald F. LaVoie

Producer/Distributor
Format: Slides, audiocassettes, transparencies, audioreels, sound filmstrips, pictures
Audience: Preschool-12, adult
Subjects: Social studies, art, consumer
education, foreign countries,
sciences
Services: Exhibit at AECT, AVC

**RHYTHMS PRODUCTIONS/TOM THUMB
MUSIC**
Box 34485, Los Angeles, CA
90034-0485
310-836-4678
Pres: R. S. White

Producer
Format: Audiodiscs, audiocassettes
Audience: Preschool-12, adult
Subjects: Physical education, dance,
social studies, language arts,
mathematics, music, reading
Services: Catalog. Exhibit at NSSEA,
EDSA
Distribution: Cheviot Corp., Box
34485, Los Angeles, CA
90034-0485

S.N.A.P. PRODUCTION SERVICES
18653 Ventura, #295, Tarzana, CA
91356
818-343-0283
Pres: Barry M. Seybert

Producer/Distributor
Format: 1/2'' videoreels, 3/4''
videocassettes
Audience: K-12, adult
Subjects: Vocational training, consumer education, health, physical
education, safety

SRA SCHOOL DIVISION
Macmillan/McGraw-Hill School Publish-
ing Co.
250 Old Wilson Bridge Rd., Ste. 310,
Worthington, OH 43095
614-438-6600
Pres: Peter F. Sayeski
VP Sales: Jack A. Chapel
VP Mktg: John Virden
VP Edit: Ruth Cochrane

Producer/Distributor
Format: Computer software, multimedia, videocassettes, audiocassettes,
books

Audience: Pre-K-12
Subjects: Language arts,
speech/language, mathematics,
sciences, early childhood
Special interest: Reading disabled
Discount: Inquire
Services: Catalog. Promotional news-
letters. Exhibit at IRA, NCTM, CEC.
Sell/lease to schools

ST. PAUL'S BOOKS & MEDIA
50 St. Paul's Ave., Boston, MA 02130
617-522-8911, 800-876-4463 (orders); Fax: 617-524-8035
Pres: Sister Irene Mary

Producer/Distributor
Format: Books, music cassettes, CDs,
audiocassettes, videos
Audience: K-12, adult
Subjects: Music, religion, family life,
fiction, biography
Special interest: Spanish-speaking,
blind
Discount: Inquire
Services: Catalog. Exhibit at CBA,
RBTE, NCEA. Sell/lease to schools,
libraries, home video

**SCHOOLMASTERS/CHAMPIONS ON
FILM & VIDEO**
745 State Circle, Box 1941, Ann
Arbor, MI 48106
313-761-5175
Pres: Donald N. Canham
Sales Mgr & Lib/Sch Prom Dir: Steven
W. Canham

Producer/DistributorFormat: Globes,
VHS & Beta 1/2'' videocassettes,
charts, multimedia & laboratory kits,
computer software, maps, sound &
silent filmstrips, models, games,
transparencies
Audience: K-12, adult
Subjects: Physical education, safety,
sciences, sports

SCHRODER MUSIC CO.
1450 Sixth St., Berkeley, CA 94710
510-524-5804
Pres: Nancy Schimmel
Sales Mgr: Ruth Pohlman

Producer/Distributor
Format: Audiodiscs
Audience: K-6
Subjects: Music
Special interest: Nonsexist education
Discount: Inquire
Services: Catalog. Preview prints. Ex-
hibit at ALA
Distribution: Also dist by Children's
Small Press Collection, 719 N.
Fourth Ave., Ann Arbor, MI 48104;
313-668-8056; 800-221-8056

SCIENCE KIT
777 E. Park Dr., Tonawanda, NY
14150

716-874-6020
Pres: Rick Federico
VP of Mktg: Cary Siegel

Producer & Distributor
Format: Microscopic slides, charts,
transparencies, kits, models, pictures
Audience: K-12
Subjects: Sciences, animals, sex edu-
cation, environment & energy, family
life, health
Services: Catalog. Preview prints

SCOTT RESOURCES
Box 2121, Fort Collins, CO 80522
303-484-7445
Mktg Dir: Mark Morgan
Format: Exhibits, charts, transparen-
cies, computer software, 1/2'' VHS &
Beta videocassettes, games, labora-
tory kits
Audience: K-12
Subjects: Computers, hobbies,
mathematics, sciences
Special interest: Computer materials,
learning disabledServices: Catalog.
Preview prints. Exhibit at NCTE, CEC,
ASCD, CATM, NSSEA, NSTA, AAM,
CASt., CCTM

**SHOREWOOD FINE ART
REPRODUCTIONS**
27 Glen Rd., Sandy Hook, CT 06482
203-426-8100; Fax: 203-426-0867
Pres & Sales Mgr: John H. McGrath
Lib/Sch Prom Dir & Children's Ed:
Sandra Minck

Format: Art reproductions
Audience: K-12, adult
Subjects: Foreign countries, animals,
social studies, art, environment &
energy, family life
Services: Catalog. Sell to schools,
libraries

SIMULATION TRAINING SYSTEMS
Box 910, Delmar, CA 92014
619-755-0272; Fax: 619-792-9743
Pres: R. Garry Shirts
Mktg Dir: Jane C. Lietz

Producer
Format: Simulation games
Audience: 5-12, adult
Subjects: Cultural diversity, foreign
countries, social studies
Services: Catalog

SISTERS' CHOICE PRESS
1450 Sixth St., Berkeley, CA 94710
510-524-5804
Pres: Nancy Schimmel
Sales Mgr: Ruth Pohlman

Producer/Distributor
Format: Audiodiscs, audiocassettes,
1/2'' videoreels
Audience: Preschool-6
Subjects: Fiction, music, storytelling

Special interest: Nonsexist education, storytelling
Discount: Inquire
Services: Catalog. Preview prints. Exhibit at ALA
Distribution: Also dist. by Children's Small Press Collection, 719 Fourth Ave., Ann Arbor, MI 48104; 313-668-8056, 800-221-8056

SOCIAL STUDIES SCHOOL SERVICE
10200 Jefferson Blvd., Culver City, CA 90232-0802
310-839-2436, 800-421-4246; Fax: 310-839-2249
Co-Owners: Sanford Weiner & Irwin Levin
Ed: Cathleen Wells

Distributor
Format: Flashcards, models, charts, games, pictures, computer software, globes, transparencies, dioramas, multimedia kits, 1/4'' videocassettes, sound filmstrips, maps, CD-ROM, laserdisc
Audience: 4-12
Subjects: Environment & energy, language arts, sports, business, family life, physical education, career development, foreign countries, poetry, computers, health, sex education, consumer education, home economics, social studies
Special interest: Video
Services: Catalog. Preview prints. Exhibit at NCTE, NCSS

SOCIETY FOR VISUAL EDUCATION
1345 Diversey Pkwy., Chicago, IL 60614
312-525-1500
Pres: Suzanne Isaacs

Producer & Distributor
Format: Computer software, sound filmstrips, 1/4'' & 3/4'' videocassettes, videodiscs, CD-ROM programs
Audience: Preschool-12, adult
Subjects: Computers, foreign countries, music, social studies, animals, consumer education, health, poetry, auditory & visual perception, environment & energy, safety, biographies, family life, language arts, sciences, career development, fiction, mathematics, sex education
Special interest: Multicultural
Services: Catalog. Preview prints. Sell/lease to schools, libraries

SPOKEN ARTS INC.
801 94th Ave. N., St. Petersburg, FL 33702
813-578-7600; Fax: 813-578-3101

Producer/Distributor
Format: Audiocassettes, sound filmstrips, VHS, CD-ROM

Audience: Preschool-12, adult
Subjects: Drama, health, sciences, art, environment & energy, language arts, sex education, auditory & visual perception, family life, music, social studies, biographies, fiction, poetry, sports, computers, foreign countries & languages, religion
Special interest: Mentally handicapped, Native Americans, Spanish-speaking, computer materials, reading disabled
Services: Catalog. Preview prints of filmstrips. Exhibit at ALA, IRA, NCTE, SSLI, ABA. Sell/lease to schools, libraries, daycare centers, prisons, hospitals, dealers, stores, bookclubs

STANTON FILMS
2417 Artesia Blvd., Redondo Beach, CA 90278
310-542-6573
Owner: Phyllis A. Stanton

Format: 16mm films, videocassettes
Audience: K-12, adult
Subjects: Environment & energy, auditory & visual perception, poetry, animals, foreign countries & languages, sciences, art, health, social studies, language arts, crafts, music
Services: Catalog. Preview prints. Exhibit at AECT. Sell/lease to ETV & ITV stations, TV networks, schools, libraries

STATE UNIVERSITY OF NEW YORK AT BUFFALO
Media Library, 24 Capen Hall, Buffalo, NY 14260-1651
716-645-2802
Media Lib Supv: William E. Goll

Distributor
Format: Videorecordings, motion pictures
Audience: 9-12, adult
Subjects: Business, family life, mathematics, social studies, animals, consumer education, foreign countries & languages, music, art, dance, health, poetry, environment & energy, auditory & visual perception, drama, home economics, sciences, biographies, language arts, sex education
Services: Catalog. Rent 16mm films, VHS, U-matic videocassettes

STEMMER HOUSE PUBLISHERS, INC.
2627 Caves Rd., Owings Mills, MD 21117
301-363-3690
Pres, Sales Mgr, Lib/Sch Prom Dir & Children's Ed: Barbara Holdrige

Producer/Distributor
Format: Audiocassettes
Audience: 3-12, adult
Subjects: Auditory & visual perception, language arts, poetry, multicultural

Discount: Inquire
Services: Catalog. Exhibit at ALA, ABA

STILLPOINT PUBLISHING
Div. of Stillpoint International, Inc.
Box 640, Walpole, NH 03608
603-756-9281, 800-847-4014
Pres: Errol G. Sowers
Sales Mgr & Lib/Sch Prom Dir: Philip Conover
Children's Ed: Gisela Rank

Producer & Distributor
Format: Videorecordings, audiocassettes
Audience: Preschool-12, adult
Subjects: Health, metaphysics, human potential, spirituality
Discount: Inquire
Services: Catalog. Preview prints. Exhibit at ABA
Distribution: Publishers Group West; 800-788-3123

SUMMY-BIRCHARD INC.
265 Secaucus Rd., Secaucus, NJ 07096-2037
201-348-0700 ext. 3056/3058/3002; Fax: 201-348-1782
VP: Lynn Sengstack
Lib/Sch Prom Dir: Janine Crowley

Format: Learning programs in music & accompanying records
Subjects: Music
Services: Catalog. Exhibit at MENC & other educational venues

THE SUN GROUP
1133 Broadway, New York, NY 10010
212-255-2718
Pres: Arthur Custer

Producer
Format: Audioreels, audiocassettes, sound filmstrips
Audience: Preschool-12, adult
Subjects: Foreign languages, animals, language arts, art, biographies, fiction
Special interest: Latin & Italian-speaking, ESL, audio conversions of children's books
Services: Exhibit at ALA, TESOL

SWANK MOTION PICTURES
201 S. Jefferson, St. Louis, MO 63166
314-534-6300
Pres: P. Ray Swank

Distributor
Format: 16mm films, videotapes
Audience: K-12, adult
Subjects: Biographies, social studies
Special interest: African Americans
Services: Catalog. Promotional newsletters

CHIP TAYLOR
15 Spollett Dr., Derry, NH 03038
603-434-9262; Fax: 603-434-9262
Contact: Chip Taylor

Producer/Distributor
Format: VHS, software, audiotapes,
 overhead transparencies
Services: Catalog

TELEVISION ASSOCIATES, INC.
2410 Charleston Rd., Mt. View, CA
 94043
415-967-6040
Pres: Ed Carlstone

Producer
Format: Videodiscs, 1/2'' VHS cas-
 settes, CDI
Audience: K, 9-12, adult
Subjects: Values
Services: Promotional newsletters.
 Preview prints. Sell/lease to schools,
 libraries

TIMED EXPOSURES
79 Raymond Ave., Poughkeepsie, NY
 12601
914-485-8489
Pres: Ralph Arlyck

Producer/Distributor
Format: 16mm films, 1/2'' VHS & Beta
 videocassettes
Audience: 11-12, adult
Subjects: Art, career development, for-
 eign countries, sociology
Services: Preview prints. Rent 16mm
 films, 1/2'' VHS, 3/4'' U-matic, &
 1/2'' Beta videocassettes
Distribution: Also dist by Newday
 Films, 22D Hollywood Ave., Hohokus,
 NJ 07423

TREEHAUS COMMUNICATIONS, INC.
906 W. Loveland Ave., Loveland, OH
 45140
513-683-5716
Pres: Gerard A. Pottebaum
Customer Svc Mgr: Donna Hoffman

Producer/Distributor
Format: VHS videocassettes, books,
 periodicals
Audience: Preschool, adult
Subjects: Social studies, career de-
 velopment, family life, foreign coun-
 tries, religion
Services: Catalog. Preview prints.
 Promotional newsletters. Rent VHS
 videocassettes. Exhibit at NCEA,
 OCEA. Sell/lease to media
 centers

TRILLIUM PRESS, INC.
Box 209, Monroe, NY 10950
914-783-2999
Pres: Dr. T.M. Kemnitz
Sales Mgr: Myrna Kaye
Children's Ed: Jack Henderson

Producer & Distributor
Format: Multimedia kits, audiocassettes, 1/4'' videocassettes, computer software, flashcards, games
Audience: Preschool-12, adult
Subjects: Environment & energy, auditory & visual perception, safety, business, vocational training, dance,
 foreign countries & languages,
 mathematics, animals, sciences,
 career development, drama, health,
 music, art, sex education, computers, hobbies, physical education,
 social studies, consumer education,
 family life, home economics, poetry,
 biographies, sports, crafts, fiction,
 language arts, religion
Special interest: Gifted
Services: Catalog. Exhibit at IRA,
 NCTE, NAGC. Sell/lease to schools,
 libraries
Distribution: KAV Books, Royal Fireworks Press

TURNER MULTIMEDIA
10 N. Main St., Yardley, PA
 19067-1422
800-742-1096; Fax: 215-493-5320

Producer/Distributer
Format: CD-ROM, Laser disc, video
Audience: K-12, adult
Subjects: Science, social studies
Services: Catalog. Preview on approval
Distribution: Mail order

UAHC PRESS
Publications Department
838 Fifth Ave., New York, NY 10021
212-249-0100
Edit Dir: Stuart L. Benick
Mktg Dir: Emily Wollman

Producer/Distributor
Format: Sound filmstrips, multimedia
 kits, motion pictures, slides
Audience: Preschool-12, adult
Subjects: Religion, art, social studies,
 biographies, folk tales, family life,
 foreign countries & languages
Special interest: Spanish-speaking,
 computer materials
Discount: Inquire
Services: Catalog. Exhibit at Jewish
 conventions

UNITED LEARNING
6633 W. Howard St., Niles, IL 60714
312-647-0600, 800-424-0362
Pres: Ronald Reed
VP: Frank Marquette

Producer & Distributor
Format: 1/2'' videocassettes, video-
 strips, audiocassettes, sound filmstrips
Audience: Preschool-12, adult
Subjects: Environment & energy, auditory & visual perception, family life,
 language arts, sex education,

animals, fiction, mathematics, social
 studies, foreign countries, poetry,
 vocational training, biographies,
 health, safety, home economics,
 high risk issues
Special interest: Reading disabled
Services: Catalog. Preview prints. Exhibit at ALA, IRA, AECT, NAVA, NCEA
Distribution: Filmstrips, Moreland
 Latchford

**UNITED METHODIST
COMMUNICATIONS**
810 12 Ave. S., Nashville, TN 37203
615-742-5400
AV Dist Dir: Wilford Bane

Producer/Distributor
Format: Videorecordings, 1/2'' cas-
 settes
Audience: K-12, adult
Subjects: Family life, religion, social
 studies
Services: Catalog. Sell/lease to
 schools, libraries

UNIVERSITY OF CALIFORNIA
Extension Media Center
2176 Shattuck Ave., Berkeley, CA
 94704
510-642-0460
Dir: Mary Beth Almeda
Sales Mgr: Daniel Bickley

Distributor
Format: 16mm films, 1/2'' & 3/4''
 videocassettes
Audience: 9-12, adult
Subjects: Crafts, health, safety, art,
 dance, language arts, social studies,
 business, drama, music, sports,
 career development, environment &
 energy, physical education, consumer education, fiction, poetry
Discount: Quantity
Services: Catalog. Preview prints. Rent
 16mm films. Exhibit at COMMTEX,
 AFVF, CMLEA

UNIVERSITY OF MINNESOTA
University Film & Video, 1313 Fifth St.,
 SE, Suite 108, Minneapolis, MN
 55414
612-627-4270
Dir: Judith A. Gaston

Distributor
Format: 16mm films, videocassettes
Audience: Preschool-12, adult
Subjects: Safety, business, vocational
 training, dance, foreign countries &
 languages, mathematics, animals,
 sciences, drama, health, music, art,
 sex education, environment &
 energy, physical education, family
 life, home economics, poetry, biographies, sports, fiction, language arts,
 religion
Services: Catalog. Rent 16mm films.
 VHS videocassettes. Mediagraphics

**UNIVERSITY OF SOUTH FLORIDA
FILM/VIDEO DISTRIBUTION**
Div. of Learning Technologies
4202 Fowler Ave., Tampa, FL 33620
813-974-2874
Film Coord & Prom Dir: Jacqueline D.
Langer

Producer & Distributor
Format: 16mm films, 1/2" VHS
Audience: K-12, adult
Subjects: Environment & energy, auditory & visual perception, safety, business, vocational training, dance,
foreign countries & languages,
mathematics, animals, sciences,
career development, drama, health,
music, art, sex education, computers, hobbies, physical education,
social studies, consumer education,
family life, home economics, poetry,
biographies, sports, crafts, fiction,
language arts, religion
Special interest: Educational
materials
Services: Catalog. Promotional newsletters. Rent 16mm films, 1/2" VHS
videotapes

**THE UNIVERSITY OF TEXAS INSTI-
TUTE OF TEXAN CULTURES AT SAN
ANTONIO**
Box 1226, San Antonio, TX
78294-1226
210-558-2300, 800-776-7651 (orders)
Exec VP: Dr. Rex Ball
Mktg Dir: Lynn Catalina
Producer: Leslie Burns

Producer/Distributor
Format: 1/2" & 3/4" videocassettes,
audiocassettes, traveling exhibits,
traveling trunks, sound filmstrips,
slides, 1/2" videoreels
Audience: 5-12, adult
Subjects: Texas ethnic history &
culture
Services: Catalog. Rent slide sets.
Sell/lease to schools, libraries

UNIVERSITY OF WASHINGTON PRESS
Box 50096, Seattle, WA 98145
206-543-4050
Sales/Mktg Dir: Robert Hutchins

Producer & Distributor
Format: Models, audiocassettes, 1/2"
VHS videocassettes
Audience: 4-12, adult
Subjects: Social studies, auditory &
visual perception, dance, family life,
health
Special interest: Blind, deaf, reading
disabled, mentally handicapped
Services: Catalog. Preview prints.
Promotional newsletters. Rent 1/2"
VHS videocassettes, slides, film-
strips. Exhibit at handicapped organi-
zations, ASHA, CEC, ACLD, TASH,
AAMD

U. S. COMMITTEE FOR UNICEF
331 E. 38th St., New York, NY 10017
212-686-5522
Pres: Dr. Gwendolyn Baker

Producer/Distributor
Format: Slide, games, multimedia kits,
exhibits, pictures
Audience: K-12, adult
Subjects: Art, crafts, foreign countries,
music
Services: Catalog. Loan 16mm films,
1/2" & 3/4" videocassettes (contribution requested to cover postage &
handling). Lend to ETV, ITV & local
stations, TV networks, schools,
libraries

**VALIANT INTERNATIONAL MULTI-
MEDIA CORP.**
195 Bonhomme St., Hackensack, NJ
07602
201-487-6340, 800-631-0867; Fax:
201-487-1930
Pres: Shelly Boldstein
Sales Mgrs: Mike Lethbridge, Anthony
Frasca

Distributer
Format: CD-ROM, video
Audience: K-12, adult
Subjects: Educational, foreign lan-
guages, natures, entertainment,
health-fitness, research
Services: Catalog. Exhibit at trade
shows
Distribution: Mail order

VEDO FILMS
85 Longview Rd., Port Washington, NY
11050
516-883-2825; Fax: 516-883-7460
Pres: Vincent R. Tortora
Sales Mgr: David Cole
Lib/Sch Prom Dir: Phillip Welham
Children's Ed: Diana Nivarote

Producer/Distributor
Format: 16mm films, computer software, realia, sound filmstrips, flashcards, games
Audience: Preschool-6
Subjects: Fingerpuppets Discovery of
the World (13, 15-minute films), Candy Locks & Friends (25, 4-minute
films)
Services: Catalog. Preview prints in
16mm films. Exhibit at ALAS, AECT,
NAVA. Sell/lease to ETV & local stations, TV networks, schools

VIDEO AIDED INSTRUCTION, INC.
182 Village Rd., Roslyn Heights, NY
11577
516-621-6176
Pres: Peter Lanzer
Sales Mgr: Mona E. Lanzer

Producer/Distributor
Format: 1/2" & 3/4" videocassettes

Audience: 6-12, adult
Subjects: Language arts, mathematics,
test preparation, college prep, ESL,
civil service
Special interest: Native Americans,
bilingual students
Services: Catalog. Exhibit at ALA, ABA,
VSDA, NY Home Video International.
Sell/lease to ETV stations, schools,
libraries, cable TV

VIDEO KNOWLEDGE, INC.
29 Bramble Lane, Melville, NY 11747
516-367-4250; Fax: 516-367-1006
Pres: Sally Dubrowsky
Children's Ed: Ed Dubrowsky

Producer & Distributor
Format: VHS, Beta & 3/4" videocassettes
Audience: K-10
Subjects: Environment & energy, social
studies, animals, fiction, art, foreign
countries & languages, biographies,
language arts, consumer education
Special interest: Spanish-speaking,
bilingual students, mentally handicapped
Discount: Dealers 40%, No postage
prepaid
Services: Catalog

VINEYARD VIDEO PRODUCTIONS
Box 370, West Tisbury, MA 02575
508-693-3584
Pres, Sales Mgr & Lib/Sch Prom Dir:
Marjory Potts, Robert Potts

Producer/Distributor
Format: 1/2" VHS, 3/4" videotapes
Audience: K-12, adult
Subjects: Language arts, fiction
Special interest: Reading, performing
arts, teacher training, storytelling
Services: Catalog. Preview prints. Rent
16mm films, VHS & 3/4" videocas-
settes. Exhibit at NEFF. Sell/lease to
schools, libraries
Distribution

VISUAL EDUCATION ASSOCIATION
581 W. Leffel Lane, Box 1666, Spring-
field, OH 45501
513-864-2891 (AK, HI), 800-543-5947
(U.S.), 800-243-7070 (OH)
Pres: Richard Heckler
Sales Mgr & Lib/Sch Prom Dir: Jodi
McKinney

Producer/Distributor
Format: Software, audiocassettes,
flashcards
Audience: 9-12, adult
Subjects: Language arts, vocational
training, business, mathematics,
career development, religion, computers, sciences, foreign languages,
social studies
Special interest: Native Americans,

Spanish-speaking, bilingual students, computer materials
Discount: Schools, for 12 or more identical sets, 20%
Services: Catalog. Exhibit at NACS, National School Supply Assn

BILL WADSWORTH PRODUCTIONS
1913 W. 37th St., Austin, TX 78731
512-452-4243
Pres: Bill Wadsworth

Producer/Distributor
Format: 16mm films, 1/2" videoreels, 1/2" VHS videocassettes
Audience: 5-12
Subjects: Career development, family life, health, sex education, folk tales
Discount: Catalog. Preview prints. Rent 16mm films & VHS videocassettes. Sell/lease to schools, libraries, family planning organizations

J. WESTON WALCH, PUBLISHER
321 Valley St., Portland, ME 04104
207-772-2846, 800-341-6094
Pres: Suzanne Austin
Mktg Dir: M. F. Harmon
Ed: Richard Kimball

Producer & Distributor
Format: Multimedia kits, audiorecordings, slides, computer software, videos, transparencies, flashcards, reproducible books, copy masters, workbooks, student books
Audience: 6-12, adult
Subjects: Consumer education, home economics, poetry, art, crafts, language arts, sciences, business, family life, mathematics, sex education, career development, foreign languages, music, social studies, computers, health, physical education
Special interest: Self-esteem, multicultural
Services: Catalog. Preview prints. Exhibit at IRA, NCTE, NCTM, NSTA
Distribution: Computer software for other distributors

WARNER EDUCATIONAL PRODUCTIONS
Box 8791, Fountain Valley, CA 92708
714-968-3776, 800-394-2905
Pres: Fern S. Warner

Producer & Distributor
Format: 1/4" videocassettes, audiocassettes, VHS videocassettes, filmstrips
Audience: 7-12, adult
Subjects: Arts, crafts, history
Services: Catalog. Preview prints

WESTERN INSTRUCTIONAL TELEVISION
1438 N. Gower St., Los Angeles, CA 90028

213-466-8601
Pres: Donna Matson

Producer/Distributor
Format: 3/4", VHS videocassettes, audiocassettes, & other formats
Audience: K-9
Subjects: Social studies, art, language arts, music, sciencesServices: Catalog. Preview prints. Exhibit at AECT. Sell/lease to ETV & ITV stations, schools, libraries

WESTON WOODS STUDIOS
Weston, CT 06883
203-226-3355
Pres: Morton Schindel
VP: Linda Griffin

Producer & Distributor
Format: 3/4" videocassettes, audiodiscs, audiocassettes, sound filmstrips, 16mm films
Audience: Preschool-12, adult
Subjects: Fiction, social studies, animals, foreign countries, art, language arts, biographies, music, career development, poetry
Special interest: Spanish-speaking, deaf
Services: Catalog. Preview prints. Rent 16mm films. Exhibit at ALA, IRA, AECT, NCTE. Sell/lease to schools, libraries

WFF'N PROOF LEARNING GAMES ASSOCIATES
1490-JJ South Blvd., Ann Arbor, MI 48104-4699
313-665-2269
Pres: Layman G. Allen
Sales Mgr: Daisy H. Wren

Producer & Distributor
Format: Computer software, games
Audience: 4-12, adult
Subjects: Language arts, mathematics, sciences
Special interest: Computer materials
Services: Catalog. Preview prints. Promotional newsletters

BARBARA WILK PRODUCTIONS
29 Surf Rd., Westport, CT 06880
203-226-7669
Dist by Centre Productions, 1800 30th St., Ste. 207, Boulder, CO 80301
Pres: Barbara Wilk

Producer/Distributor
Format: 16mm films, 1/4" & 3/4" videocassettes, 1/2" videoreels
Audience: 4-12, adult
Subjects: Social studies
Special interest: Native Americans
Services: Preview prints

WISCONSIN FOUNDATION
2564 Branch St., Middleton, WI 53562
608-831-6313; Fax: 608-831-2960

Producer/Distributor
Format: Interactive videodiscs
Subjects: Math, algebra, electronics
Services: Catalog. Free preview

WOMEN MAKE MOVIES
462 Broadway, Ste. 500, New York, NY 10012
212-925-0606; Fax: 212-925-2052
Exec Dir: Debra Zimmerman
Dist Mgr: Cynthia Chris

Distributor
Format: 16mm films, 1/2" & 3/4" videocassettes
Audience: 6-12, adult
Subjects: Sex education, career development, sports, family life, vocational training, foreign countries & languages, women's studies, health, arts
Special interest: Spanish-speaking, bilingual students, nonsexist education
Discount: Inquire
Services: Catalog. Preview tapes. Promotional newsletters. Rent 16mm films, 3/4" & VHS videocassettes. Programming assistance on women's issues. Sell/lease to local TV stations, schools, libraries
Distribution: 16mm films, 3/4" & VHS videocassettes

YELLOW BALL WORKSHOP
62 Tarbell Ave., Lexington, MA 02173
617-862-4283
Pres, Sales Mgr & Lib/Sch Prom Dir: Dominic Falcone
Dir: Yvonne Andersen

Producer/Distributor
Format: 16mm films
Audience: Preschool-12, adult
Subjects: Poetry, art, environment & energy, auditory & visual perception, fiction
Special interest: Animated films made by children
Services: Catalog. Preview prints. Rent 16mm films. Children's book: "Make your own animated movies & video tapes." (Publisher: Little Brown & Co., Author: Yvonne Andersen)

ZINK ENTERTAINMENT
245 W. 19th St., New York, NY 10011
212-929-2949
Pres: Jan Morgan Zink

Producer
Format: Videocassettes
Audience: Preschool-12, adult
Subjects: Fiction, consumer education, hobbies, crafts, sports, drama, family life

ZIPPORAH FILMS
One Richdale Ave., Unit #4, Cambridge, MA 02140

617-576-3603
Exec Dir & Sales Mgr: Karen Batting
    Konicek

Producer/Distributor
Format: 16mm films, 3/4'' videocas-
    settes, 1/2'' VHS videocassettes

Audience: 10-12, adult
Subjects: Social studies, business,
    career development, family life,
    religion
Special interest: Documentary films by
    Frederick Wiseman
Discount: For 3 or more

Services: Catalog. Rent 16mm films.
    Sell video. Exhibit at AFF. Sell/lease
    to schools, libraries

AUDIOVISUAL PRODUCERS & DISTRIBUTORS—
CLASSIFIED BY SPECIAL INTEREST

Bilingual Students

Aims Media
BFA Educational Media
Bilingual Educational Services
Bullfrog Films
California Language Laboratories
Carousel Film & Video
Educational Design, Inc.
Educational Video Network, Inc.
Great Plains National
Instructional/Communications
  Technology, Inc.
Integrative Learning Systems
Media Materials, Inc.
National Teaching Aids
National Textbook Co.
Video Aided Instruction, Inc.
Video Knowledge, Inc.
Visual Education Association
Women Make Movies

Blind

Aims Media
Audio Book Contractors
BFA Educational Media
Encyclopedia Britannica Educational
  Corporation
Instructional/Communications
  Technology, Inc.
National Teaching Aids
St. Paul's Books & Media
University Of Washington Press

Computer Materials

Bergwall Productions, Inc.
Samuel R. Blate Associates
Capital Communications
Carolina Biological Supply Co.
Educational Activities
Films For The Humanities & Sciences
Great Plains National
DC Heath & Company
Homer & Assocs.
Instructional/Communications
  Technology, Inc.
Learning Well
Marshfilm
Scott Resources
Spoken Arts Inc.
UAHC Press
Visual Education Association
WFF'N Proof Learning Games
  Associates

Deaf

Aims Media
BFA Educational Media
Baptist Home Mission Board
Bullfrog Films
Capital Communications
Carousel Film & Video
Churchill Media
Coronet/MTI Film & Video

Dana Productions
Distribution 16
Encyclopedia Britannica Educational
  Corporation
Guidance Associates
Instructional/Communications
  Technology, Inc.
Knowledge Unlimited
Authur Mokin Productions, Inc.
National Geographic Society
National Teaching Aids
PBS Video
Phoenix Films
University Of Washington Press
Weston Woods Studios

Mentally Disabled

Abingdon Press
Aims Media
American Guidance Service
BFA Educational Media
Craighead Films
Dana Productions
Davidson Films
Direct Cinema Limited
Educational Design, Inc.
Encyclopedia Britannica Educational
  Corporation
Guidance Associates
Hubbard Scientific Co.
Instructional/Communications
  Technology, Inc.
Learning Well
Arthur Mokin Productions, Inc.
Paulist Productions
Spoken Arts Inc.
University Of Washington Press

Native Americans

ABC Multimedia Group
Aims Media
Audio Book Contractors
BFA Educational Media
Baptist Home Mission Board
Bergwall Productions, Inc.
Budget Films
Bullfrog Films
Capital Communications
Carolina Biological Supply Co.
The Cinema Guild, Inc.
Colonial Williamsburg Foundation
DCM Instructional Systems
Dana Productions
Direct Cinema Limited
Distribution 16
Films For The Humanities &
  Sciences
Great Plains National
Indian House
Instructional/Communications
  Technology, Inc.
Integrative Learning Systems
International Film Bureau Inc.
Learning Well
Lyceum Productions

Meriwether Publishing Ltd-
  Contemporary Drama Service
National Film Board Of Canada
Jeffrey Norton Publishers Inc/Audio-
  Forum, The Language Source
PBS Video
Paulist Productions
Phoenix Films
Spoken Arts Inc.
Video Aided Instruction, Inc.
Visual Education Association
Barbara Wilk Productions

NonSexist Education

ABC Multimedia Group
Aims Media
Altana Films
American Guidance Service
Appalshop, Inc.
BFA Educational Media
Baha'i Publishing Trust
Norman Beerger Productions
Benchmark Films
Samuel R. Blate Associates
Cambridge Documentary Films Inc.
Churchill Media
The Cinema Guild, Inc.
Communication For Change, Inc.
Dana Productions
Direct Cinema Limited
Educational Design, Inc.
Green Mountain Post Films
Guidance Associates
DC Heath & Company
Homer & Assocs.
Walter J. Klein Company
Lucerne Media
Malibu Films
Marshfilm
Arthur Mokin Productions, Inc.
New Dimension Films
PBS Video
Phoenix Films
Point Of View Productions
Schroder Music Co.
Sisters' Choice Press
Women Make Movies

Reading Disabled

A/V Concepts Corp
Abingdon Press
Aims Media
Audio Book Contractors
Bergwall Productions, Inc.
Carousel Film & Video
Craighead Films
Educational Activities
Educational Design, Inc.
Encyclopedia Britannica Educational
  Corporation
Guidance Associates
Imperial International Learning
  Corporation
Instructional/Communications
  Technology, Inc.

Integrative Learning Systems
Phoenix Films
SRA School Division Spoken Arts Inc.
United Learning
University Of Washington Press

Spanish Speaking

Aims Media
Ken Anderson Films
BFA Educational Media
Baptist Home Mission Board
Benchmark Films
Bilingual Educational Services

California Language Laboratories
Capital Communications
Carousel Film & Video
Churchill Media
Communications Group West
Coronet/MTI Film & Video
Dana Productions
Family Films
Films For The Humanities & Sciences
Great Plains National
Guidance Associates
DC Heath & Company
Integrative Learning Systems
International Film Bureau Inc.

Lyceum Productions
Malibu Films
National Textbook Co.
Jeffrey Norton Publishers Inc/Audio-
  Forum, The Language Source
Paulist Productions
Ramic Productions, Inc.
St. Paul's Books & Media
Spoken Arts Inc.
UAHC Press
Video Knowledge, Inc.
Visual Education Association
Weston Woods Studios
Women Make Movies

This section includes companies that primarily distribute children's materials as well as those that include children's materials in their services.

ALLIED BOOKS & EDUCATIONAL RESOURCES
1362 Trinity, Ste. D2208, Los Alamos, NM 87544
505-662-9705

Materials: Kits, trade books, videorecordings, paperbacks, computer software, audiorecordings, audiocassettes, filmstrips, videocassettes
Audience: Preschool-12
Subjects: Sports, dictionaries, home economics, poetry, animals, vocational training, career development, environment & energy, language arts, professional books, art, Southwestern, Native American, Spanish bilingual, English-as-a-Second-Language, holiday, cookbooks, jokes, computers, fiction, family life, mathematics, safety, auditory & visual perception, consumer education, foreign languages, music, sciences, biographies, hobbies, picture books, social studies

AMBASSADOR BOOK SERVICE
42 Chasner St, Hempstead, NY 11550
516-489-4011, 800-431-8913
Pres: Gary J. Herald
Buyer: Kaye Manson

Materials: Trade books, textbooks, paperbacks
Audience: Preschool-12
Subjects: All subjects
Book titles: 20,000
Services: Regular & prebound editions. Catalog. Exhibit at ALA, IRA, AECT, NAVA. Prepay. Binding. Special orders. Distributor

AMERICAN MEDIA CORPORATION
219 N. Milwaukee St., Milwaukee, WI 53202
414-287-4600; Fax: 414-287-4602
Pres: Laurence B. Compton
Prod Mktg: Julie Plantz

Materials: Trade books, audiocassettes videocassettes, library editions, prebound
Audience: Preschool-12
Subjects: All
Book Titles: 2,000

Services: Regular and prebound editions. Audio and videocassettes. Cataloging preprocessing. Sale list. Exhibit at regional meetings. Distributor. Import fiction & nonfiction from England & Canada

SRI AUROBINDO ASSN., INC.
(formerly Matagiri Books)
2288 Fulton St., #310, Berkeley, CA 94704-1449
510-848-1841; Fax: 510-848-8531

Materials: Trade books, paperbacks
Audience: Preschool-8
Subjects: Picture books
Book titles: 400
Services: Regular editions. Approval plan. Catalog. Exclusive distributor for Sri Aurobindo Books, Sri Aurobindo Ashram Trust, Sri Aurobindo International Centre of Education. Import fiction & nonfiction books from India

BAKER & TAYLOR
5 Lake Pointe Plaza, Ste. 500, 2709 Water Ridge Pkwy., Charlotte, NC 28217
704-357-3500, 800-775-1800; Fax: 704-329-8989
Pres: G. G. Garbacz
Sr VP, Mktg: M. E. Strauss
VP, Intl Sales & Mktg: L. C. Aubuchon
VP, Purch: J. M. Srnecz
Dir, Edit: Hal Hager
Br Off(s): Commerce Serv. Center, Mount Olive Rd., Commerce, GA 30599. 404-334-5000; Fax: 404-335-2027
Momence Serv. Center, 501 A. Gladiolus St., Momence, IL 60954. 815-472-2444; Fax: 815-472-4141
Reno Serv. Center, 308 Edison Way, Reno, NV 89564-0099.
Sales Dir: W. J. Hartman. 702-786-6700
International Sales Headquarters: 652 E. Main St., Bridgewater, NJ 08807. 908-218-0400; Fax: 908-707-4387
Sommerville Serv. Center: Somerville, NJ 08876-0734. 201-722-8000; Fax 908-722-0184

Book titles: 1.9 million (1.4 million U.S./0.5 million U.K.).
Pubns: Directions (monthly, circ 7500);

Forecast (monthly, circ 19,500); Book Alert (monthly, circ 18,500); Hot Picks in Mass Market & Trade Paper (monthly, circ 29,000); Books for Growing Minds (annual, circ 50,000); B&T Link CD-Rom Title Database (monthly); School Selection Guide (annual, circ 100,000)

THE BILINGUAL PUBLICATIONS COMPANY
270 Lafayette St., Ste. 705, New York, NY 10012
212-431-3500

Materials: Trade books, textbooks, paperbacks, audiorecordings. Specialize in Spanish materials
Audience: Preschool-12
Subjects: Foreign countries & languages, language arts
Book titles: 4000
Services: Publish a fully annotated children's catalog annually. Regular editions. Import juvenile & educational materials, primarily from Spain, Mexico, Puerto Rico & Latin America. Accept collect calls

BMI EDUCATIONAL SERVICES
26 Hay Press Rd., Dayton, NJ 08810
201-329-6991, 800-222-8100
Pres: Jerry Wagner

Materials: Filmstrips, trade books, videorecordings, textbooks, audiocassettes, paperbacks, videocassettes, audiorecordings, workbooks, supplemental reading materials, teaching guides
Audience: Preschool-12
Subjects: All subjects
Book titles: 6000
AV titles: 1000
Services: Regular & prebound editions. Cataloging. Approval plan. Catalog. Exhibit at IRA, ASCD, NCTE. Distributor

BOOK WHOLESALER'S INC.
1847 Mercer Rd., Lexington, KY 40511
606-231-9789, 800-888-4478; Fax: 800-888-6319

Materials: Tradebooks, audio & video
  materials
Audience: K-12.

BOOKAZINE COMPANY, INC.
75 Hook Rd., Bayonne, NJ 07002
201-339-7777, 800-828-2430; Fax:
  201-858-7574
Pres: Irwin Kallman
School/Lib Contact: Carmen Rivera

Materials: Videocassettes, trade books,
  textbooks, paperbacks, audiocas-
  settes
Audience: Preschool-12
Subjects: All subjects
Book titles: 100,000
Services: Regular & prebound editions.
  Preprocessing. Exhibit at ALA, IRA,
  NCTE. Import fiction and nonfiction

BOOKSMITH PROMOTIONAL CO.
100 Paterson Plank Rd., Jersey City,
  NJ 07307
201-659-2768

Materials: Trade books, textbooks,
  paperbacks, magazines/periodicals
Audience: Preschool-8
Subjects: Social studies, business, drama, health, music, animals, sports,
  computers, encyclopedias, hobbies,
  picture books, art, crafts, family life,
  home economics, safety, auditory &
  visual perception, dance, fiction, language arts, sciences, biographies,
  dictionaries, foreign countries & languages, mathematics, sex education
Book titles: 2500
Services: Regular & prebound editions.
  Catalog. Exhibit at ABA, Frankfurt &
  London bookfairs. Distributor. Exclusive distributor for Mulberry Children's Press books. Import fiction &
  nonfiction from England & South
  America

BOUND TO STAY BOUND BOOKS
1880 W. Morton Rd., Jacksonville, IL
  62650
800-637-6586
VP Sales: Bill Early

Materials: Trade Books
Audience: K-12
Subjects: All subjects
Book titles: 14,000
AV titles: 1
Services: Prebound editions, Catalog-
  ing, preprocessing. Approval plan.
  Children's catalog

BRODART
500 Arch St., Williamsport, PA 17705
800-326-2461
Gen Mgr: Richard Black
Elhi Prod Mgr: Michael Puma

Materials: Videocassettes, trade books,
paperbacks, globes, kits, reinforced
  bindings
Audience: K-12, adult
Book titles: 150,000
AV titles: 4000
Services: Regular & prebound editions.
  Cataloging, preprocessing. School
  catalog. Requisition & quotation
  service. Fund control service. Circulation system interfaces

CHARLES W. CLARK COMPANY
170 Keyland Ct., Bohemia, NY 11716
516-589-6643
Pres: Charles W. Clark III

Materials: Videocassettes, videodiscs,
  filmstrips, kits, audiocassettes/read-
  alongs
Audience: Preschool-8
Subjects: All subjects
AV titles: 2000
Services: Distributor of nonprint educational media. Publish various annual
  catalogs

CONTINENTAL BOOK COMPANY
80-00 Cooper Ave., Glendale, NY 11385
718-326-0560
Sales Mgr: Robert Louissaint
Orders: Western Continental Book Co.,
  625 E. 70 Ave., Unit #5, Denver, CO
  80229
Mgrs: Alan Hayat, Linette Hayat
  Russell

Materials: Charts, slides, trade books,
  filmstrips, videorecordings, text-
  books, games, magazines/periodi-
  cals, paperbacks, maps,
  audiocassettes, audio recordings,
  realia, videocassettes
Audience: Preschool-12, adult
Subjects: Foreign languages (French,
  Spanish, German) bilingual and ESL
Book titles: 1000
AV titles: 500
Services: Children's catalog. Import
  foreign language books from France,
  Germany, Spain, Austria, Switzerland,
  Latin America, Puerto Rico, Mexico

DEMCO INC.
Box 7488, Madison, WI 53707
800-356-1200; Fax: 800-245-1329
Pres: Greg Larson
VP Mkting: Patrick Wall

Materials: Library supplies, equipment,
  & furniture, computer support
  materials & furniture, audiovisual
  storage supplies & furniture, child-
  care books, puppets, teaching
  materials, reading promotional
  materials
Audience: Preschool-12
Subjects: All subjects
Book titles: 8,000
Services: Annual full-line catalog.

Spring and fall individual catalogs.
Book repair workshops

DEMCO MEDIA
Box 14260, Madison, WI 53707
800-448-8939; Fax: 800-828-0401
VP Sales/Mktg: Brendan Wall

Materials: Turtleback books, trade
  books in prebound paperback
  binding, periodical subscription
  service
Audience: Preschool-12, adult
Subjects: All subjects
Book titles: 12,000+
Services: Cataloging. Marc records.
  Free quotes. Order typing. Periodical
  subscription service

EASTERN BOOK CO.
Box 4540, Portland, ME 04112-4540
207-774-0331

Materials: Videorecordings, trade
  books, computer software, textbooks, periodicals, paperbacks,
  videocassettes, audiorecordings,
  audiocassettes
Audience: Preschool-12
Subjects: All subjects
Book titles: 15,000
Services: Regular & prebound editions.
  Exhibit at Northeastern Library Association. Distributor

EMERY-PRATT CO.
1966 W. Main St., Owosso, MI
  48867-1372
800-762-5683 (orders), 800-248-3887
  (customer svc.); Fax: 800-523-6379

Materials: Charts, kits, programmed
  learning systems, audiocassettes,
  trade books, filmstrips, maps, slides,
  videocassettes, transparencies,
  educational toys, paperbacks,
  games, motion pictures, videorecordings, audiorecordings,
  globes, prints, computer software
Audience: Preschool-12
Subjects: All subjects
Services: Cataloging. Catalog. Exhibit
  at ALA, PLA. Custom invoicing, free
  library aids, OCLC vendor #17354,
  publisher prepayment service, fac-
  simile transmission, free shipping,
  paperback binding, standing
  orders

FOLLETT LIBRARY BOOK CO.
4506 Northwest Hwy., Rtes. 14 & 31,
  Crystal Lake, IL 60014
800-435-6170; Fax: 800-852-5488

Materials: Trade books
Subjects: All subjects
Book titles: 45,000

FRENCH & EUROPEAN PUBLISHERS, INC.
Exec Off & Natl Dist Ctr: 115 Fifth Ave, New York, NY 10003
212-673-7400

Materials: Flashcards, audiocassettes, trade books, games, videocassettes, textbooks, maps, paperbacks, programmed learning systems, audiorecordings, videorecordings
Audience: K-12
Subjects: All subjects. Dictionaries & books in more than 100 languages, including ESL
Book titles: 50,000
AV titles: 1000
Services: Regular editions. Approval plan. Children's catalog. Import titles from France, Spain, Belgium, Mexico, Puerto Rico, Haiti, Latin America. Operate retail bookstores: La Librariae de France & La Libreria Hispanica, New York & Los Angeles

GESSLER PUBLISHING CO.
55 W. 13th St., New York, NY 10011
212-627-0099
Pres: Seth C. Levin

Materials: Flashcards, trade books, videorecordings, textbooks, computer CD-ROM software, paperbacks, videocassettes, audiorecordings
Audience: K-12
Subjects: Foreign languages
Book titles: 1500
AV titles: 500
Services: Regular editions. Publisher & Distributor. Importer of supplementary teaching materials, videos & computer software in French, Spanish, Latin, German, Italian & English as a second language

GOLDEN-LEE BOOK DISTRIBUTORS
1000 Dean St., Brooklyn, NY 11238
718-857-6333, 800-473-7475

Materials: Globes, videocassettes, trade books, maps, paperbacks, videorecordings, charts, computer software, filmstrips, audiocassettes
Audience: Preschool-12
Subjects: All subjects
Book titles: 25,000
AV titles: 500
Services: Regular editions. Approval plan. Catalog. Exhibit at ALA

GRYPHON HOUSE, INC.
Box 275, 3706 Otis St., Mt. Rainier, MD 20712
301-779-6200
Pres: Larry Rood
Sales Mgr: Leah Curry-Rood

Materials: Trade books, paperbacks
Audience: Preschool & K

Subjects: Music, art, picture books, crafts, sciences, language arts, early childhood education activity books for teachers, mathematics
Book titles: 1000
Services: Regular editions. Catalog. Exclusive distributor for Bear Creek Publications; Black Butterfly; Book Peddlers; Brethren Press; Bright Ring Publishing; Building Blocks; Chatterbox Press; Checkerboard Press; Colgin Publishing; Consortium Publishing; Dawn Sign Press; Delmar Publishers; DMC Publications; Early Educator's Press; Educational Equity Concepts; Exchange Press; Floris Books; Hawthorn Press; Kaplan Press; Learning Line, Inc; Mailman Family Press; Mercer Island Preschool Association; Miss Jackie Music; New England AEYC; New Horizons; Nova University Press; Partner Press; RPM International; Redleaf Press; School Age Notes; Steam Press; Teaching Strategies; Telshare Publishing; Ten Speed Press; Turn the Page Press; Williamson Publishing

GERARD HAMON INC.
Box 758, 525 Fenimore Rd., Mamaroneck, NY 10543
914-381-4649, 800-333-4971

Materials: French language books & periodicals, trade books, textbooks, paperbacks, magazines/periodicals
Audience: Preschool-12
Subjects: All subjects
Book titles: 1000
Services: Regular editions. Exhibit at ALA, Modern Language Assn., American Assn. of Teachers of French, South Atlantic Modern Language Assn., National Council of Teachers of French Language. Distributor. Importer of supplementary teaching materials, videos & computer software in French, Spanish, Latin, German, Italian & English as a second language

MARIUCCIA IACONI BOOK IMPORTS, INC.
1110 Mariposa, San Francisco, CA 94107
415-255-8193

Materials: Trade books, paperbacks, audiorecordings, filmstrips
Audience: K-12
Subjects: All subjects
Services: Regular editions. Approval plan. Catalog. Import foreign language books from Spain, Italy, Latin America, South America, & Mexico

INGRAM BOOK COMPANY
(Division of Ingram Distribution Group, Inc.)
One Ingram Blvd., LaVergn, IN 37086-1986
615-793-5000, 800-937-8000 (orders); Fax: 615-793-5000

Materials: Compact disks, audiocassettes, trade books, paperbacks, audiorecordings, videocassettes
Audience: Preschool-12
Subjects: All subjects
Book titles: 70,000
AV titles: 6000
Services: Regular & prebound editions. Microfiche & new title catalog. Exhibit at ALA, ABA. Special services to schools, librarires & bookstores. Distributor

INTERNATIONAL SERVICE COMPANY
333 Fourth Ave., Indialantic, FL 32903
Voice/Fax: 407-724-1443
Pres: Dennis Samuels
Man Dir: Katherine Swanberg

Materials: Educational toys, charts, globes, prints, videorecordings, trade books, school supplies, dioramas, kits, programmed learning systems, computer software, textbooks, filmstrips, maps, realia, magazines/periodicals, paperbacks, flashcards, models, slides, audiocassettes, audiorecordings, games, motion pictures, transparencies, videocassettes
Audience: Preschool-12, adult
Subjects: All subjects
Services: Regular editions. Cataloging. Educational consultant to schools, libraries & bookstores. Import nonfiction & foreign language books from all countries

KEY BOOK SERVICE, INC.
Box 1434, SMS, Fairfield, CT 06430
203-374-4936

Materials: Videocassettes, trade books, foreign titles, textbooks, paperbacks, audiorecordings
Audience: Preschool-12
Subjects: All subjects
Book titles: 100,000
Services: Regular & prebound editions. Cataloging, preprocessing. Exhibit at ALA, regional & state library associations. Out-of-print search serivce for established customers; theft detection tapes. Import from Canada, Germany, United Kingdom

KOEN BOOK DISTRIBUTORS
10 Twosome Dr., Box 600, Moorestown, NJ 08057
609-235-444, 800-257-8481
Materials: Trade hardback and paperback books; book-and-cassettes;

audiocassettes; calendars
Audience: Babies to grade 12
Subjects: Baby books, picture books, early readers, middle grade readers, young adult, history, biography, geography, science, activity and game books, teacher resource books, parenting/childcare books
Book Titles: 55,000
Services: Catalog. Newsletter. Free consulting. Free microfiche

MELTON BOOK COMPANY
Box 140990, Nashville, TN 37214-0990
615-228-3204, 800-441-0511

Materials: Trade books, paperbacks, audiorecordings, games, models, prints
Audience: K-12, adult
Subjects: Religious books, bibles
Services: Approval plan. Catalog. Distributor

MILLIGAN NEWS COMPANY
150 N. Autumn St., San Jose, CA 95110
408-286-7604, 800-873-2387; Fax: 408-298-0235
Ed Div Dir: Grady Lawyer

Materials: Trade books, paperbacks, Spanish books
Audience: K-adult
Book titles: 12,000
Services: Regular editions. Book fairs for schools & libraries. RIF supplier

MOOK & BLANCHARD
Box 1295, La Puente, CA 91749
818-968-6424, 800-875-9911
Pres: Jerry J. Mook

Materials: Trade books, publishes library editions, prebound books
Audience: K-8
Subjects: All subjects
Book titles: 12,000
Services: Catalog. Cataloging/processing. MARC/MICROLIF Diskettes. Barcoding

THE NEW ENGLAND MOBILE BOOK FAIR INC.
82 Needham St., Newton Highlands, MA 02161
617-527-5817, 800-878-4264
Pres: Beatrice Strymish
School/Lib Contact: William Leydon

Materials: Trade books, audiocassettes, paperbacks, videocassettes, globes, maps
Audience: Preschool-12
Subjects: Religion, career development, sports, dictionaries, foreign countries & languages, mathematics, animals, safety, computers, vocation-

al training, drama, health, music, art, sciences, consumer education, environment & energy, hobbies, physical education, biographies, sex education, crafts, family life, home economics, picture books, business, social studies, dance, fiction, language, arts, poetry
Book titles: 50,000
Services: Library bound editions. Cataloging. Distributor.

PREBOUND CHILDREN'S BOOKS
(Formerly Associated Libraries)
229-33 N. 63 St., Philadelphia, PA 19139
800-222-4994; Fax: 215-476-3207
Pres: Robert J. Canis Jr.

Materials: Prebound books
Audience: K-12
Subjects: All subjects
Book titles: 6700
Services: Prebound editions. Cataloging, preprocessing. Semiannual children's catalog. Exhibit at state library conventions

PUBLISHERS MEDIA
5507 Morella Ave., North Hollywood, CA 91607
818-980-2666

Materials: Paperbacks, globes, maps, reference books, English & foreign language dictionaries
Audience: K-12
Subjects: All subjects
Book titles: 1800
Services: Catalog

REGENT BOOK COMPANY
101A Rte. 46, Saddle Brook, NJ 07662
201-368-2208, 800-999-9554; Fax: 201-368-9770

Materials: Extensive collection of children's "backlist" books in library binding, kits, reference books, career books
Audience: K-12
Subjects: All subjects
Book titles: 5000
AV titles: 100
Services: Regular & prebound editions. Cataloging. Catalog

STORY HOUSE CORPORATION
Bindery Lane, Charlotteville, NY 12036
607-397-8725
Mgr: Sigurd C. Rahmas
Sales Mgr: Paul M. White

Materials: Prebound paperbacks
Audience: K-12
Subjects: All subjects
Book titles: 9000
AV titles: 60

Services: Prebound editions. Free catalog cards. Catalog. Import books from various countries. Exhibit at ALA, IRA

SUNDANCE PUBLISHERS & DISTRIBUTORS INC.
Newtown Rd., Littleton, MA 01460
508-486-9201
Pres: Fred Johnson
Sales Mgr: Dale Donovan

Materials: Paperbacks, audiocassettes, videocassettes, supplementary curriculum materials
Audience: Preschool-12
Subjects: Family life, social studies, animals, fiction, sports biographies, language arts, dictionaries, picture books, drama, poetry
Book titles: 3000
AV titles: 150-200
Services: Regular & prebound editions. Exhibit at IRA, NCTE

THAMES BOOK COMPANY, INC.
34 Truman St., New London, CT 06320
203-444-2400
Operations Mgr: Deana Hartman

Materials: Trade books, paperbacks, library bound
Audience: Preschool-12, adult
Subjects: All subjects
Book titles: 2000
Services: Cataloging, preprocessing. Booklists. Catalog. Seminars. Library Core Lists. Romance/Western Book Club. Distributor.

UNIVERSITY BOOK SERVICE
2219 Westbrooke Dr., Columbus, OH 43228-9605
800-634-4272
Orders: 518, Dublin, OH 43017

Materials: Trade books, paperbacks, remainders, library bound
Audience: Preschool-12
Subjects: All subjects
Book titles: 4000
Services: Regular & prebound editions. Cataloging. Catalog

X-S BOOKS, INC.
95 Mayhill St., Saddlebrook, NJ 07662
201-712-9266

Materials: Trade books, textbooks, paperbacks, library bound, remainders & promotional books to trade & institutional market & premium & mail order houses
Audience: K-12
Subjects: All subjects
Book titles: 560
AV titles: Regular & prebound editions. Catalog

YANKEE BOOK PEDDLER INC.
999 Maple St., Contoocook, NH
    03229-3374
603-746-3102, 800-258-3774; Fax:
    603-746-5628
CEO: John R. Secor
Mgr, Children's Bk Div: Linda Mclear
Dir Pub Rel: Helmut Schwarzer

Materials: Trade books, paperbacks,
    library bound
Audience: Preschool-12
Subjects: All subjects
Book titles: 6000
Services: Regular & prebound editions.
    Cataloging, preprocessing. Approval
    plan. Description of services. Exhibit
at ALA, regional ALA meetings. First
Copy Plan. Awards Plan. Automatic
shipment of award winning books.
Comprehensive bibliographies

5

CHILDREN'S BOOKSELLERS

Listed below geographically are bookstores designed primarily for children and parents. For the most part, they are not educational nor specifically teacher's bookstores. Chain stores or bookstores which carry adult materials as well as children's selections are not included. Services provided by the stores include, but are not limited to: issuing mail order and other catalogs; financing sales by schools through school purchase orders; arranging book fairs for schools and other institutions; story hours; author talks and book signings; and special orders. Since these may change from time to time and are often added at customer's request, it is best to contact owners and/or buyers of individual stores directly to ascertain what they are currently providing. Owner's and/or children's buyers are listed at the end of each entry.

ALASKA

WILD ABOUT BOOKS
12110 Business Blvd., Eagle River, AS 99577
907-694-7323
Barbara Ward

ALABAMA

BEARING BOOKS
219 Grant St., SE, Decatur 35601
205-340-1900
Beth Johnston

ENTREKIN BOOK CENTER
446 Azalea Rd., Mobile 36609
205-660-0505
Dee Entrekin

ARIZONA

STORYBOOKS
1356 S. Gilbert #13, Mesa 85204
602-926-7323
Lavera Meaders

DUSHOFF BOOKS
3166 E. Camelback Rd., Phoenix 85016
602-957-1176
Cindy Riordan

CHANGING HANDS BOOKS
414 Mill Ave., Tempe 85281
602-966-4019
Gayle Shanks

PAPA BEAR'S BOOKS
4401 S. Elm St., Tempe 85282
602-838-9370
Debbie Papa

BOOK MARK
5001 E. Speedway, Tucson 85712

602-881-6350
Anne Underhill

KIDS' CENTER
1725 N. Swan Rd., Tucson 85732
602-322-5437
Retha Davis

WHIZKIDS BOOKS AND TOYS
1737 E. Prince, Tucson 85719
602-795-3729
Todd & Suzanne Horst

ARKANSAS

BOOK RACK
316 W. Main, Blytheville 72315
501-763-3333
Kaye McKaskie

CALIFORNIA

PEACEABLE KINGDOM
1051 Folger Ave., Berkeley 94710
800-444-7778
Olivia Hurd

SECRET GARDEN
204 N. Victory Blvd., Burbank 91502
818-846-8038
Christy Meisner

READER'S CLUBHOUSE
18326 Susan Pl., Cerritos 90701
213-865-2788
Fran Kammel

ALICE'S WONDERLAND
975B Detroit Ave., Concord 94518
510-682-1760
Alice Arndt

OVER THE RAINBOW
440 River Rd., Ste."E", Corona 91720

714-736-7707
Sally Hoover

CHILDREN'S BOOKCASE
Box 1947, Davis 95617
916-756-541
Lorraine Barr

THROUGH A CHILD'S EYES
10519 Chaney, Downey 90241
310-862-0415
Ane Miller

PETUNIA'S PLACE
2017 W. Bullard, Fresno 93711
209-438-1561
Debbie Manning

WHALE OF A TALE
4187 Campus Dr., Irvine 92715
714-854-828
Alexandra Uhl

TOMTEN
4644 El Camino Corto, La Canada 91011
818-790-3046
Anne Browne

WHITE RABBIT
Children's Books
7755 Girard Ave., La Jolla 92037
619-454-3518
Susan Malk

CAROL DOCHEFF BOOKS
1390 Reliez Valley, Lafayette 94549
415-935-9595

A CLEAN WELL-LIGHTED PLACE FOR BOOKS
2417 Larkspur Landing Circle, Larkspur 94939
415-461-0171
Martha Jackson & Ann Seaton

LINDEN TREE CHILDREN'S BOOKS
170 State St., Los Altos 94022
415-949-3390
Dennis Ronberg

CHILDREN'S BOOK WORLD
10580 3/4 West Pico, Los Angeles
  90064
213-559-2665
Sharon Hearn

EVERY PICTURE TELLS
836 North LaBrea, Los Angeles 90038
213-962-5420
Abbie Phillips

HAPPILY EVER AFTER
2640 Griffith Park, Los Angeles 90039
213-668-1996
Emily Smythe

READING RHINOCEROS
24000 Alicia Pkwy., Mission Viejo
  92691
714-588-0898
Janelle Kennedy

ONCE UPON A TIME
2284 Honolulu Ave., Montrose 91020
818-248-9668
Jane Humphrey

CHILDREN'S BOOKSHOPPE
1831 Westcliff Dr., Newport Beach
  92660
714-675-1424
Joan Pizzo

BOOK WAGON
2765 Yorkshire Rd., Pasadena 91107
818-578-0727
Linda Keller

CHILDREN'S BOOK CART
6736 Brockton Ave., Riverside 92506
714-275-9860
Joy Hasson

I LOVE TO READ
12798 Rancho Pena, San Diego
  92129
619-538-0118
Maria Escobar-Bord

CHARLOTTE'S WEB
2278 Union St., San Francisco 94123
415-441-4700
Scott Young

HICKLEBEE'S
1378 Lincoln Ave., San Jose 95125
408-292-8880
Valerie Lewis & Monica Holmes

SAN MARINO BOOK AND TOY SHOPPE
2475 Huntington Dr., San Marino
  91108
818-795-5301
Betty Takeuchi & Pana Gelt

OVER THE RAINBOW
421 Lincoln Center, Stockton 95207
209-473-0220
Pat Charles

CHILD DREAMS
12242 1/2 Ventura, Studio City 91604
818-761-8508
Jamie Carmen

PAGES/BOOKS FOR CHILDREN
18399 Ventura Blvd., Tarzana 91356
818-342-6657
Darlene Daniel

CATCH OUR RAINBOW
3148 Pacific Coast Hwy., Torrance
  90505
213-325-1081
Shirley Russell

ADVENTURES FOR KIDS
3457 Telegraph, Ventura 93003
805-650-9688
Jody Fickes

MAGIC DRAGON
1339 S. Mooney, Visalia 93277
209-733-3126
Cathy Tantau

COLORADO

SUNNYBOOKS FOR KIDS
4233 S. Buckley Rd., Aurora 80013
303-690-9590
Rebecca Mino

PRINTED PAGE
1219 Pearl St., Boulder 80302
303-443-8450
Bal Patterson

ONCE UPON A MIND
4825 Farthing Dr., Colorado Springs
  80906
719-540-9017
Carolyn Foat

CHILDREN'S BOOKSELLER
7225 Wildridge Rd., Colorado Springs
  80908
719-495-9256
Donna Duncan

CHILDREN'S MERCANTILE COMPANY
1 Old Town Square, Ft. Collins 80524
303-484-9946
Judith Bedford

BO PEEP BOOKS
1957 S. Wadsworth, Lakewood 80227
303-989-8127
Shirley Sternola

CONNECTICUT

W. J. FANTASY
955 Connecticut, Bridgeport 06607

203-333-5212
Joan Cavanaugh

ENCHANTED TALE BEARER
2100 Dixwell, Hamden 06514
203-287-8253
Nanci Dower

DISTRICT OF COLUMBIA

CHESHIRE CAT BOOK STORE
5512 Connecticut Ave., Washington
  20015
202-244-3956
Charlotte Berman
& Jewell Stoddard

FAIRY GODMOTHER
319 7 St., SE, Washington 20003
202-547-5474
Roberta Blanchard

KIDS LIKE ME
225 Emerson St., NW, Washington
  20011
202-882-2415
Quay W. Watkins

FLORIDA

JABBERWOCKY
113 W. Rich Ave., Deland 32720
904-738-3210
Miriam Venger

A KIDS BOOK SHOP
1849 NE Miami Gardens Dr., North Miami Beach 33179
305-937-2665
Lorelei Ennis

A LIKELY STORY
5740 Sunset Dr. South Miami 33143
305-667-3730
Judy Weissman

HASLAM'S BOOKSTORE
2025 Central Ave., St. Petersburg
  33713
813-822-8616
Elizabeth Haslam & Louis Miscioslia

GEORGIA

TOY SCHOOL
5517 Chamblee, Dunwoody 30338
404-393-272
Annette Savage

HOBBIT HALL
120 Bulloch Ave., Roswell 30075
404-587-0907
Anne Ginkel

HAWAII

HAWAII CHILDREN'S BOOK WORLD
1132 Bishop St., Honolulu 96813
808-531-6245
Deloris Guttman

MAUI CHILDREN'S TOYS AND BOOKS
P.O. Box 1869, Makawau 96768
808-527-2765
Madelyn D'Enbco

IDAHO

BOOK SHOP
908 Main, Boise 83702
208-342-2659
Karen Glennon

JUDI'S BOOKS
120 Main Ave., North Twin Falls
  83301
208-734-4343
Judi Baxter

ILLINOIS

ABOUT BLACK CHILDREN
4509 S. King Dr., Chicago 60653
312-285-4568
Vanessa Mulrain

ROSE ZELL BOOKS
136 Ilehamwood, DeKalb 60115
815-756-2801
Estelle Von Zellen

BOOK VINE FOR CHILDREN
304 Lincoln, Fox River 60021
708-639-4220
Liz Smith

CROCODILE PIE
866 S. Milwaukee Ave., Libertyville
  60048
708-362-8766
Kim White

ANDERSON'S BOOKSHOP
123 W. Jefferson, Naperville 60540
312-355-2665
Jean Getzel

MAGIC TREE BOOKSTORE
141 N. Oak Park Ave., Oak Park
  60301 708-848-0770
Jan Shoup

GREAT AMAZING BOOKSTORE
858 Marshall Ct., Palatine 60074
708-359-9258
Sheree Vane

NEVER NEVER LAND
134 Front St., Wheaton 60187
708690-7909
Patty Toht

INDIANA

KIDS INK
5619 N. Illinois, Indianapolis
  46208
317-255-2598
Shirley Mullin

IOWA

PUMPKIN PATCH
302 Main St., Ames 50010
515-292-5293
Emily Munson

CHESHIRE CAT BOOKSTORE
114 North 3rd St., Clear Lake 50428
515-357-6302
Jan Marcus

KANSAS

BOOK STAR
912 Maplewood Ct, Andover 67002
316-733-0240
Irene Adams

KENTUCKY

BLUE MARBLE
1356 S. Fort Thomas, Fort Thomas
  41075
606-781-0602
Tina Moore

OWL AND THE PUSSYCAT
316 S. Ashland, Lexington 40502
606-266-7121
Elizabeth Shier

LOUISIANA

ONCE UPON A TIME
3220 Johnston St., Lafayette 70503
318-981-2255
Jeanne McKellar

MAINE

OZ BOOKS
125 Main St., Southwest 04679
207-244-9077
Sheila Wilensky-Lanford

CHILDREN'S BOOK CELLAR
5 E. Concourse, Waterville 04901
207-872-4543
Carol Wynne

MARYLAND

CHILDREN'S BOOKSTORE
737 Deepdene Rd., Baltimore 21210
301-532-2000
Joann Fruchtman

FESTIVAL OF CHILDREN'S BOOKS
1809 Reisterstown, Baltimore 21208
410-486-7406
Nancy Oppenheim

SECRET GARDEN
5309 Oakland Rd., Chevy Chase
  20815
301-652-6918
Carol Fitzsimmons

JUNIOR EDITIONS
2049 Columbia Mall, Columbia 21044
301-730-2665
Mary Grant

CRACKERJACKS
7 Washington St., South Easton
  21601
301-822-7716
Cindy Orban

MASSACHUSETTS

THE BOOK SHOP OF BEVERLY FARMS
40 West St., Beverly Farms 01915
508-927-2122
Cheryl Mazur

CHILDREN'S BOOK SHOP
237 Washington St., Brookline 02146
617-734-7323
Terri Schmitz

**EIGHT COUSINS CHILDREN'S
  BOOKSTORE**
630 Main St., Falmouth 02540
508-548-5548
Carol Chittenden

BOOK KIDS
55 Market St., Ipswich 01938
508-356-9624
Robert Gritz

LITTLE BOOK ROOM
561 Adams St., Milton 02186
617-696-0044
Suzanne Sigman

TOAD HALL BOOKSTORE
51 Main St., Rockport 01966
508-546-7323
Eleanor Hoy

MICHIGAN

CHARLOTTE'S CORNER
2394 E. Stadium Blvd., Ann Arbor
  18104
313-973-9512
Julia Chu

CHILDREN NATURALLY
31727 Sheridan Dr., Birmingham
  48009
313-642-7895
Jock Denio

POOH'S CORNER
1830 Breton Rd., SE, Grand Rapids
  49506
616-942-9887
Elsie Peterson & Alexandra Brown

PAGES FOR YOUNG AGES
47 S. Monroe, Monroe 48161
313-457-0420
Nancy Miller

LITTLE DICKENS BOOKSHOP
126 S. Main, Mt. Pleasant 48858
517-773-1074
Karen Kiefer

CHILDREN'S BOOKSHOP
29791 Northwestern Hwy., Southfield
   48034
313-356-2880
Beverly Gealer

MINNESOTA

CREATIVE KIDSTUFF
4313 Upton South, Minneapolis 55410
612-929-2431
Sonja Westby

KIDSENSE
11 E. 48th St., Minneapolis 55417
612-822-0623
Amy Sternberg

WILD RUMPUS
2720 W. 43rd St., Minneapolis 55410
612-920-5005
Collette Morgan

TREE HOUSE CHILDREN'S BOOKS
2804 W. Division St., St. Cloud 56301
612-255-1776
Gertie Geck

LEARN ME BOOKS
175 Ash St., St. Paul 55126
612-490-1805
Caron Chapman

RED BALLOON BOOKSHOP
891 Grand Ave., St. Paul 55105
612-224-8320
Carol Erdahl & Michele Poire

MISSOURI

MARYKA BOOKS FOR KIDS
7536 Forsyth, Clayton 63105
314-862-6709
Ramona Briggans

READING EXPRESS
3880 Fairway Dr., Florissant 63033
314-839-0155
Kim Simon

CHILDREN'S BOOKHOUSE
Route 6, Box 500, Joplin 64801
417-624-7680
Gregory Wilks

BOOK NOOK
948 S. Stewart, Springfield 65804
417-882-2248
Jeanne Walsh

BOOK LADY
8144 Brentwood Dr., St. Louis 63144
314-631-6672
Clementine Roeder

NEBRASKA

BOOKHOUSE
10923 Prairie Bridge Rd., Omaha
   68144
402-392-1931
Ellen Scott

NEW JERSEY

ALPHABET SOUP
405 Front St., Belvidere 07823
908-475-1914
Susan Brody

CHILDREN'S BOOKSHELF
144 Roxbord Rd., Lawrenceville 08648
609-530-1462
Janet Amiott

A CHILD'S STORY
477B Cedar Lane, Teaneck 07666
201-907-0260
Rosemary Stimola

NEW MEXICO

STORY SHOP
10900 Menaul Blvd., Albuquerque
   87112
505-291-0711
Shirley Houston

NEW YORK

LITTLE BOOK HOUSE
Stuyvesant Plaza, Albany 12203
518-489-4761
Susan Novotny

TINY TALES CHILDREN'S BOOK STORE
2048 Newbridge Rd., Bellmore 11710
516-783-9539
Karen Breen

0 TO 5 BOOKS
615 76th St., Brooklyn 11209
718-748-5770
Janet Matura

CHILDREN'S BOOK BARN
8535 Reservoir Hill, Hammondsport
   14840
607-569-2385
Judith Gardner

RABBIT HILL CHILDREN'S BOOKSTORE
1235 Broadway, Hewlett 11557
516-295-3216
Clifford Wohl

ONCE UPON A TIME
77 Quaker Ridge Rd., New Rochelle
   10804
914-632-2665
Betsy Polivy

BOOKS OF WONDER
132 Seventh Ave., New York 10011
212-989-3270
Peter Glassman

YOUNG DISCOVERY
217 Main St., Ossining 10562
914-945-0600
Michael Dillon

WHITE RABBIT
70 Main St., Pine Bush 12566
914-744-6414
Jean Eustance

CHILD'S PLAY
13 Mill Creek Rd., Port Jefferson 1777
516-473-4630
Loretta Piscatella

OPEN DOOR BOOKSTORE LTD.
128 Jay St., Schenectady 12305
318-346-2719
Janet Hutchison

NASSAU KIDS BOOKS
7952 Jericho Tpke., Woodbury 11797
516-921-9255
Ann Axelrod

NORTH CAROLINA

AUNT LOUISE'S BOOKSHOP
431 W. Franklin, Chapel Hill 27516
919-942-8143
Susan Steinfirst

ONCE UPON A LAP
215 Forbush Mountain Dr., Chapel Hill
   27514
919-932-3300
Susie Wilde

BLACK FOREST BOOKS AND TOYS
115 Cherokee Rd., Charlotte 28207
704-332-4838
Louise Sanford

KIDS' LORE
603B College Rd., Greensboro 27410
919-855-5121
Gay McCormick

MAGIC DOOR
4112-112 Pleasant Vale, Raleigh
   27612
919-783-6177
Kathleen Skaar

OHIO

MRS. LIZ'S CHILDREN'S BOOKSHOP
84 West St., Chagrin Falls 44022
216-423-0121
Liz Chojnacki

CHILDREN'S BOOKERY
1175 Smiley Ave., Cincinnati 45240
513-742-8822
Betty Miller

CREATIVITY FOR KIDS
1600 E. 23rd St., Cleveland 44114
216-589-4800
Phyllis Brody

JABBERWOCKY
2499 Lee Rd., Cleveland 44118
216-932-2419
Lissa Weller

COVER TO COVER
3337 N. High St., Columbus 43202
614-263-1624
Sally Oddi

BOOKS AND COMPANY FOR KIDS
350 E. Stroop Rd., Dayton 45429
513-297-6357
Pam Beatty

KID STUFF
123 Greene St., Mariette 45750
614-374-3114
Diana McKnight

KIDS' SHELF
521 S. Main, Mt. Vernon 43050
614-397-5586
Bonnie Pryor

YOUNG READERS
1611 Center Ridge, Rocky River
  44116
216-333-7828
Elizabeth Merritt

FULL OF THE DICKENS
105 W. Water St., Sandusky 44870
419-626-6880
Kit Wysor

OKLAHOMA

A LIKELY STORY
9231 N. Penn Place, Oklahoma City
  73132
405-840-2042
Sonja Fowler

STORYBOOK STATION
7101 N.E. Expwy., Oklahoma City
  73132
405-720-2665
Paula Horabin

CHILDREN'S BOOKS & CO.
8130C S. Lewis, Tulsa 74137
918-492-8825
Jean Ann Fausser

OREGON

CHILDREN'S BOOK BARN
4570 SW Watson, Beaverton 97005
503-641-2276
Jeanne Lybecker

GINGER AND PICKLES BOOKSTORE
425 Second St., Lake Oswego 97034

503-636-5438
Barbara O'Neil

A CHILDREN'S PLACE
1631 NE Broadway, Portland 97232
503-284-8294
Carolyn Kelly

PENNSYLVANIA

BOOKTENDERS CHILDREN'S BOOKS
62 W. State St., Doylestown 18901
215-348-7160
Ellen Mager

KIDLIT
616 E. Berger St., Emmaus 18049
215-967-3916
Allison Evrard

DRAGON'S TALE
5138 Peach St., Erie 16509
814-868-9916
Dolores Kunath

CHILDREN'S BOOK WORLD
17 Haverford Station, Haverford
  19041
215-642-6274
Hannah Schwartz

PINOCCHIO BOOKSTORE
826 S. Aiken Ave., Pittsburgh 15232
412-621-1323
Marilyn Hollinshead & Rebecca Cillo

BOOKS AND BEARS
137 W. Beaver, State College 16801
814-237-4454
Elaine Wickersham

KIDLIT
865 Duchess Dr., Yardley 19067
215-321-0688
Debbie Duchin

SOUTH CAROLINA

ONCE UPON A TIME
3795 E. North, Greenville 29615
803-292-2132
Ted Vereen

TENNESSEE

CHOO CHOO CHILDREN'S BOOKS
4615 Poplar, Memphis 38117
901-372-0128
Cathy Stauffer

TEXAS

TEAGUE'S BOOKS FOR CHILDREN
1801 Hilltop Lane, Arlington 76013
817-275-4213
Carolyn Teague

BAOBAB TREE
3736 Bee Caves Rd., Austin 78746

512-328-7636
Nancy Podio

TOAD HALL
1206 W. 38th St., Austin 78705
512-323-2665
Anne Bustard & Barbara Thomas

**RAINBOW BOOKS AND LEARNING
  CENTER**
C5 Cullen Mall, Corpus Christi 78412
512-992-0590
Barbara Flanigan

ROOTABAGA BOOKERY
6717 Snider Pl., Dallas 75205
214-361-8581
Nancy O'Connor

NEVERENDING TALES
6147 P.M.1960 West, Houston 77069
712-586-7345
Mellisa Wendt

MUNCHKIN BOOKERY
1318 Lufkin Mall, Lufkin 75901
409-637-1156
Pam Moore

YOUNG AGES
Box 867656, Plano 75086
214-867-7021
Loretta Randolph

BRYSTONE CHILDREN'S BOOKS
6101 Watauga Rd., Watauga 76148
817-485-8421
Nancy Stone

UTAH

CHILDREN'S HOUR
928 E. 900 South, Salt Lake City
  84105
801-359-4150
Diane Etherington

VERMONTONCE UPON A TIME
7 Green St., Vergennes 05491
802-658-3659
Marje Vonohlsen

VIRGINIA

STORYBOOK PALACE
9538 Old Keene Mill, Burke 22015
703-644-2300
Christine Bury

SHENANIGANS
2146 Barracks Rd., Charlottesville
  22903
804-295-4797
Marion Morrison

CHILDREN'S BOOK SHOP
5730 Union Mill Rd., Clifton 22024
703-818-7270
Linda Kostrzewa

EDWARD T. RABBIT & CO.
7029 Three Chopt Rd., Richmond
  23226
804-288-2665
Kay Remick

NARNIA BOOKS
2927 W. Cary St., Richmond 23221
804-353-5675

PURPLE CRAYON
7515 Huntsman Blvd., Springfield
  22153
703-455-6100
Debra Schroeder

WASHINGTON

MAIN STREET KIDS BOOK COMPANY
10217 Main St., Bellevue 98004
206-455-8814
Andy Pickard

TIGER TALES
420 5th Ave. S., Edmonds 98020
206-775-7405
Joan Poor

PUSS'N BOOKS, INC.
15788 Redmond Way, Redmond
  98052

206-885-6828
Magda Hitzroth

ALL FOR KIDS BOOKS
2943 NE Blakeley St., Seattle 98105
206-526-2768
Chauni Hasler

POPPETS
3124 Elliot Ave., Seattle 98121
206-285-3107
Jeanne Rea

SECRET GARDEN
7900 E. Greenlake Dr., Seattle 98103
206-522-8207
Sher Ross

CHILDREN'S CORNER
W. 814 Main Ave., Spokane 99201
509-624-4820
Susan Durrie

WEST VIRGINIA

PINOCCHIO'S BOOKS & TOYS
322 High St., Morgantown 26505
304-296-2332
Jeanne Goodman

WISCONSIN

CHILDREN'S BOOKSHOP
1600 E. Meadow Grove, Appleton
  54915
414-733-3397
Harvada Elisberg

**HARRY SCHWARTZ CHILDREN'S
  BOOKS**
17145-A West, Brookfield 53005
414-786-7565
Darlene Marazzo

STORIES'N STUFF
1345 Creston Park, Janesville 53545
608-752-7202
Joan Smoke

POOH CORNER
1843 Monroe St., Madison 53711
608-256-0558
Anne Irish

WYOMING

WHIPPERSNAPPERS
207 S. 2nd St., Laramie 82070
307-721-8853
Barb Andrews

ANTIQUARIAN BOOKSELLERS

6

The following booksellers carry a selection of rare children's books. Some deal exclusively in children's and related materials and are noted with an asterisk. Each entry, arranged geographically, includes: the business name (and owner if it is not the same as the business); the business address; telephone/fax numbers; hours of operation; and in some cases special collections are noted. Most antiquarian booksellers offer selections of American and English literature, various genres, toy books, and illustrated books.

CALIFORNIA

ROBERT ALLEN BOOKS
Box 582, Altadena, 91003
818-794-4210; Fax: 818-306-6970

By appointment only

GAIL KLEMM BOOKS
Box 518, Apple Valley, 92307
619-242-5921

By appointment only
Rare, early and modern children's books and related materials, Randolph Caldecott

*BOOKS OF WONDER
439 N. Beverly Dr., Beverly Hills, 90210
310-247-8025; Fax: 310-247-9442
Peter Glassman

Hours: Mon-Sat 10-6; Sun 11-4
Folklore and Mythology, Juvenile Fantasy, Fairy Tales, Oz and Baumiana

MONROE BOOKS
Mission Village, 359 E. Shaw Ave., Ste. 102, Fresno, 93710-7609
209-224-7000
John Monroe Perz

Hours: Mon-Sat 10-5

THE BOOK TREASURY
1535 E. Broadway, Box 20033, Long Beach, 90801
213-435-7383
Jon Gentilman

Hours: Tues-Sat 11-5
Illustrated books, Oziana and juvenile fiction

RYKKEN AND SCULL
1031 Trillium Ln., Mill Valley, 94941
415-381-5701

By appointment only

THORN BOOKS AND BINDERY
624 Moorpark Ave., Box 1244, Moorpark, 93020
805-529-7610
Lynne B. Owens

Hours: Wed-Sat 12-6 & by appointment

BOOKMINE
1015 Second St., Old Sacramento, 95814
916-441-4609; Fax: 916-441-2019
Steve Mauer

Hours: Daily 10-5
Illustrated books, Mark Twain

BOOK CASE BOOKS
Box 60457, Pasadena, 91116-0457
818-449-3443
Alice S. Lee

By appointment only
Collectible 20th century children's books

ARKADYAN BOOKS & PRINTS
926 Irving St., San Francisco, 94122
415-664-6212
Gerald L. Webb

Hours: Mon-Sat 11-6

THE BOOKSTALL
570 Sutter St., San Francisco, 94102
415-362-6353
Louise & Henry Moises

Hours: Mon-Sat 11-6 or by appointment

*URSULA C. DAVIDSON BOOKS
134 Linden Ln, San Rafael, 94901
415-454-3939; Fax: 415-454-1087

By appointment only

THE BOOK DEN
15 E. Anapamu St., Box 733, Santa Barbara, 93102
805-962-3321; Fax: 805-965-2844
Eric E. Kelley

Hours: Mon-Fri 10-9; Sat 10-6; Sun 12-5

DREW'S BOOK SHOP
Box 163, Santa Barbara, 93101
805-682-3610
Warren E. Drew

By appointment only

GARCIA-GARST BOOKSELLERS
2857 Geer Rd., #C, Turlock, 95380
209-632-5054; Fax: 209-632-0805
Beverly A. & Kenneth M. Garst

Hours: Tue-Sat 11:00-5:30; Mon-Call for appointment
Children's and illustrated books, fairy tales, folklore and mythology

CONNECTICUT

KATHLEEN AND MICHAEL LAZARE
Box 117, Sherman, 06784
203-354-4181; Fax: 203-350-1761

By appointment only

FLORIDA

WOLF'S HEAD BOOKS
48 San Marco Ave., Box 3705, St.
    Augustine 32085-3705
904-824-9357
Barbara E. Nailler
Harvey J. Wolf

Hours: Mon-Fri 11-7; Sat 11-5 or by
    appointment
Juvenile Series

*B.L. MEANS RARE BOOKS
17849 S.E. 105th Ave., Summerfield
    32691
904-245-9045

By appointment only

ILLINOIS

TITLES, INC.
1931 Sheridan Rd., Highland Park,
    60035
708-432-3690; Fax: 708-945-4644
Florence Shay

Hours: Mon-Sat 10:30-5:00

BURKWOOD BOOKS
Box 172, Urbana, 61801
217-344-1419
Robert Lee Hodges

By appointment only

MARYLAND

*DORIS FROHNSDORFF
Box 2306, Gaithersburg, 20886
301-869-1256
Ella Palmer

By appointment only
Rare and classic children's books,
    drawings and original art, illustrated
    books, miniature books, Beatrix
    Potter

MASSACHUSETTS

ANDOVER BOOKS & PRINTS
68 Park St., Andover, 01810
508-475-1645, 508-475-0468
V. David Rodger

Hours: Mon-Fri 12-5; Sat 10-5; Sun
    1-4
Sept.-May only
Illustrated books

FOLKLORE BROMER BOOKSELLERS
607 Boylston St. at Copley Square,
    Boston 02116
617-247-2818; Fax: 617-247-2975

Hours: Mon-Sat 9:30-5:30
Miniature books, Illustrated books

THE BOOK & TACKLE SHOP
29 Old Colony Rd., Chestnut Hill
    02167
617-965-0459
Summer: 7 Bay St., Watch Hill, RI
    02891
Bernard Gordon

Hours: Daily 9-9

JOSEPH A. DERMONT
Box 654, Onset 02558
508-295-4760

By appointment only

TEN EYCK BOOKS
Box 84, Southboro 01772
508-481-3517

By appointment only

HAROLD M. BURSTEIN & COMPANY
36 Riverside Dr., Waltham 02154
617-893-7974; Fax: 617-641-2918

By appointment only

MICHIGAN

*TREASURES FROM THE CASTLE
1720 N. Livernois, Rochester 48306
313-651-7317
Connie Castle

MISSOURI

COLUMBIA BOOKS
13 N. 9th St., Columbia 65201
314-449-7417
Annette Kolling Weaver

Hours: Mon-Sat 9:30-6:00

GLENN BOOKS
323 E. 55th St. Kansas City 64113
816-444-4447
Frederic M. Gilhousen

Hours: Wed-Sat 11-5; Tuesday by ap-
    pointment

NEW YORK

DANIEL HIRSCH
Box 315, Hopewell Junction 12533
914-227-9631; Fax: 914-227-9632

By appointment only
Historical children's literature,
    16th-20th century illustrated books,
    fairy tales and related literature

BAUMAN RARE BOOKS
Hotel Lobby, 301 Park Ave., New York
    10022
212-759-8300; Fax: 212-759-8350

Hours: Mon-Sat 10-7

*BOOKS OF WONDER
132 Seventh Ave., New York 10011
212-989-3270; Fax: 212-989-1203
Peter Glassman

Hours: Mon-Sat 11-7; Sun 12-6
Folklore and mythology, juvenile fan-
    tasy, fairy tales, Oz and Baumiana

IMPERIAL FINE BOOKS, INC.
790 Madison Ave., Rm. 200, New York
    10021
212-861-6620
Bibi T. Mohamed

Hours: Mon-Fri 10:00-5:30; Sat 10-5

*JUSTIN G. SCHILLER, LTD.
Place des Antiquaries, 125 E. 57th St.,
    Gallery 48, New York 10022
212-832-8231, 212-751-5450; Fax:
    212-688-1139
Raymond M. Wapner

Hours: Mon-Sat 11-6
Children's literature in all languages
    (pre 1900), related art work and
    original manuscripts, illustrated
    books

LYRICAL BALLAD BOOKSTORE
7 Philadelphia St., Saratoga Springs
    12866
518-584-8779
John J. Demarco

Hours: Daily 10-6
Illustrated books, folklore

*ALPHA-BET BOOKS, INC.
670 Waters Edge, Valley Cottage
    10989
914-268-7410; Fax: 914-268-5942
Helen and Marc Younger

By appointment only
Illustrated books, fairy tales, myths

NORTH CAROLINA

**WENTWORTH & LEGGETT RARE
    BOOKS**
905 W. Main St., Brightleaf Square,
    Durham 27701
919-688-5311, 919-941-1938
Barbara L. Wentworth

Hours: Mon-Sat 11-6 or by ap-
    pointment

OHIO

SUSAN HELLER/PAGES FOR SAGES
Box 22219, 22611 Halburton Rd.,
    Cleveland 44122
216-283-2665

By appointment only

PENNSYLVANIA

ANTONIO RAIMO, FINE BOOKS
401 Chestnut St., Columbia 17512
717-684-4111, 717-684-9411; Fax:
    717-684-3151

Hours: Daily 8:30-5:30 and by ap-
    pointment

BAUMAN RARE BOOKS
1215 Locust St., Philadelphia 19107
215-546-6466; Fax: 215-546-9064

Hours: Mon-Fri 10-5

TENNESSEE

FIRST FOLIO
R.R. 1, Box 127A, Buchanan
    38222-9768
901-644-9940
Dennis R. Melhouse

By appointment only

VERMONT

**RICHARD H. ADELSON ANTIQUARIAN
    BOOKSELLER**
North Pomfret, 05053
802-457-2608

By appointment only

VIRGINIA

*JO ANN REISLER, LTD.
360 Glyndon St., NE, Vienna 22180
703-938-2967, 703-938-2237; Fax:
    703-938-9057

By appointment only
Illustrated books, original illustrative
    art, early paper dolls, paper toys

WASHINGTON

EDWARD D. NUDELMAN
Fine and Rare Books
Box 20704, Broadway Station, Seattle
    98102
206-367-4644

By appointment only

Individual book clubs are annotated under the club name. Two or more clubs sponsored by a company are annotated under the parent company with cross references under the club name.

Arrow Book Club, *see* **SCHOLASTIC BOOK SERVICES**

Beginning Readers Program, *see* **GROLIER ENTERPRISES**

CHILDREN'S BOOK-OF-THE MONTH CLUB
Div. of Book-of-the-Month-Club, Inc.
Time & Life Bldg., 1271 Ave. of the
Americas, New York, NY 10020
212-522-4200; Fax 212-522-0303

Audience: Preschool-6
Publications: One selection a month
for four age groups

CHILDREN'S BRAILLE BOOK CLUB
National Braille Press Inc.
88 St. Stephen St., Boston, MA 02115
617-266-6160
Mktg Mgr: Diane L. Croft

Audience: Preschool-3
Access: Available to teachers, schools,
libraries & individuals
Publications: Print/braille titles
Titles: 12 annually

Disney's Small World, *see* **GROLIER ENTERPRISES**

Disney'S Wonderful World of Reading, *see* **GROLIER ENTERPRISES**

Firefly Book Club, *see* **SCHOLASTIC BOOK SERVICES**

GROLIER ENTERPRISES
Sherman Turnpike, Danbury, CT
06816
203-797-3500
Pub: Barbara Gregory

BEGINNING READERS PROGRAM
Audience: Preschool-K
Access: Available to individuals
Publications: Book club editions of
Random House publications
Titles: 45

DISNEY'S SMALL WORLD
Audience: Preschool-K
Access: Available to individuals
Publications: Book club editions of
Random House publications

DISNEY'S WONDERFUL WORLD OF READING
Audience: Preschool-K
Access: Available to individuals
Publications: Book club editions of
Random House publications
Titles: About 100

JEWISH PUBLICATION SOCIETY
1930 Chestnut St., Philadelphia, PA
19103
215-564-5925
Ed: Ellen Frankel
Mktg Mgr: Jean Sue Libkind

Audience: K-12
Access: Available to teachers & individuals
Publicatons: Hardcover & paperback
originals & reprints
Titles: 35-40 annually

Lucky Book Club, *see* **SCHOLASTIC BOOK SERVICES**

PAGES READ ALOUD BOOK CLUB
Pages School Book Fairs
801 94th Ave. N., St. Petersburg, FL
33702
813-578-7600
VP Bk Div: Chuck Elkins

Audience: Infants - preschool
Access: Individuals
Publications: Hardcover originals. Parent's newsletter
Titles: 48 annually

SCHOLASTIC BOOK SERVICES
555 Broadway, New York, NY 10012
212-343-6100
Orders: Scholastic Book Clubs, Inc.,
2931 E. McCarty St., Box 7503,
Jefferson City, MO 65102
Dir, Bk Clubs: Josalyn Moran

ARROW BOOK CLUB
Ed: Pat Brigandi
Audience: 4-6
Access: Available to teachers
Publications: Paperback originals &
reprints from various publishers.
Teachers' guides, posters, transparencies, video & software. Students' & teachers' newsletters. Free
dividends for teachers
Titles: 400 annually in 9 offers

FIREFLY BOOK CLUB
Ed: Lauren Stevens
Audience: Preschool
Access: Available to teachers
Publications: Paperback originals &
reprints. Teachers' guides, posters,
transparencies. Free bonuses for
teachers
Titles: 120 annually in 4 offers

LUCKY BOOK CLUB
Ed: Eva Moore
Audience: 2-3
Access: Available to teachers
Publications: Paperback originals &
reprints from various publishers.
Teachers' guides, cassettes, video &
software. Students' & teachers'
newsletters. Free dividends for students & teachers
Titles: 350 annually in 9 offers

see-SAW BOOK CLUB
Ed: Erin McCormack
Audience: K-1
Access: Available to teachers
Publications: Paperback originals &
reprints from various publishers.
Teachers' guides, cassettes, video,
filmstrips. Students' & teachers'
newsletter. Free dividends of games,
posters, puzzles, transparencies

TEEN AGE BOOK CLUB
Ed: Greg Holch
Audience: 6-9
Access: Available to teachers
Publications: Paperback originals &
reprints. Teachers' guides, games,
charts, posters, spirit masters, software & video. Students' & teachers'
newsletters. Free bonuses for students & teachers
Titles: 400 annually in 9 offers

See-Saw Book Club, *see* **SCHOLASTIC BOOK SERVICES**

Teen Age Book Club, *see* **SCHOLASTIC BOOK SERVICES**

TROLL BOOK CLUB
2 Lethbridge Plaza, Mahwah, NJ
07430
800-541-1097; Fax: 201-529-8382

Audience: Preschool; K-1; 2-3; 4-5; 6-9
Access: Available to schools & libraries

Publications: Hardcover & paperback originals. Occasional poster

TRUMPET CLUB
Sub. of Bantam, Doubleday, Dell Publishing Co., Inc.
Box 604, Holmes, PA 19043
800-826-0110

Audience: Preschool-K; 1-3; 4-6
Access: Available to schools and librarians

Publicatons: Paperback originals, hardcover & paperback reprints. Teachers' guides, games, posters. Students' & teachers' newsletters. Free dividends for students & teachers
Titles: Approximately 2000

WEEKLY READER CHILDREN'S BOOK CLUB
New Field Publications, Inc.
2 Corporate Dr., Shelton, CT 06484-0857

203-944-2400
Exec Ed: Fritz Luecke
Audience: K-1, 2-3, 4-6
Access: Available to individuals & teachers
Publications: Hardcover fiction originals & reprints from major juvenile publishers
Titles: 2 per division every 6 weeks

AGENTS FOR CHILDREN'S PROPERTIES

8

Agents in the following list represent authors and illustrators of books, articles, theater, film, television, and other mediums for children.

LINDA ALLEN LITERARY AGENCY
1949 Green St., Ste. 5, San Francisco, CA 94123
415-921-6437; Fax: 415-921-3733

Agents for juvenile books. No unsolicited manuscripts.

MARCIA AMSTERDAM AGENCY
41 W. 82nd St., New York, NY 10024
212-873-4945; Fax: 212-873-4945
Agent: Marcia Amsterdam

Agents for books, films, TV. Unsolicited materials accepted after query first with SASE.

AUTHOR AID ASSOCIATES
340 E. 52nd St., New York, NY 10022
212-758-4213
Edit Dir: Arthur Orrmont

Agents for juvenile books. Interested only in material for middle grades & nonfiction. Telephone queries accepted. No mail queries. No unsolicited manuscripts. No poetry collections.

BARBARA BAUER LITERARY AGENCY INC.
179 Washington Ave., Matawan, NJ 07747-2944
908-583-4988

Agents for children's & young adult books.

MEREDITH BERNSTEIN
2112 Broadway, #503A, New York, NY 10023
212-799-1007
Agents: Meredith Bernstein, Elizabeth Cavanaugh

Agents for books. Unsolicited materials accepted. $45 reading fee.

GEORGES BORCHARDT, INC.
136 E. 57th St., New York, NY 10022
212-753-5785; Fax: 212-838-6518

Pres: Georges Borchardt
Agent: Anne Borchardt

Agents for books, articles, film & TV. No unsolicited materials.

ANDREA BROWN LITERARY AGENCY INC.
Box 808, El Granada, CA 94018
415-728-1783; Fax: 415-592-8846

Agents for books & software, film & TV

CURTIS BROWN LTD.
10 Astor Place, New York, NY 10003
212-473-5400
Pres: Perry Knowlton
Book Dept: Ginger Knowlton, Marilyn E. Marlow
Film, TV, AV: Chris McKerrow

Agents for books, TV, film. Unsolicited materials accepted after query first with SASE.

PEMA BROWNE LTD.
Pine Rd., Neversink, NY 12765
914-985-2936; Fax: 914-905-7635

HOWARD BUCK AGENCY
80 Eighth Ave., Ste. 1107, New York, NY 10011
212-807-7855

Agents for juvenile fiction & nonfiction. No unsolicited manuscripts.

MARIA CARVAINIS AGENCY, INC.
235 West End Ave., New York, NY 10023
212-580-1559; Fax: 212-877-3486
Agent: Maria Carvainis

Agents for young adult & adult books, magazines films & TV. Unsolicited materials accepted after query first & SASE.

HY COHEN LITERARY AGENCY
111 W. 57th St., New York, NY 10019

212-757-5237
Pres: Hy Cohen

Agents for young adult books, films, TV. Unsolicited materials accepted with SASE.

RUTH COHEN INC., LITERARY AGENT
Box 7626, Menlo Park, CA 94025
415-854-2054
Pres: Ruth Cohen

Agents for books. No full unsolicited manuscripts accepted. Send ten sample pages plus SASE.

RICHARD CURTIS ASSOCIATES, INC.
171 E. 74th Street, Ste. 2, New York, NY 10021
212-772-7363; Fax: 212-772-7393
Agent: Richard Curtis

Agents for fiction & nonfiction books. Specialize in science fiction, action-adventure, romance. Mail queries accepted. No telephone queries, no unsolicited manuscripts, no poetry collections.

ANITA DIAMANT
310 Madison Ave., New York, NY 10017
212-687-1122
Pres: Anita Diamant
Agent: Robin Rue

Agents for books, films, TV. Unsolicited materials accepted after query first.

EDUCATIONAL DESIGN SERVICES INC.
Box 253, Wantagh, NY 11793
516-221-0995, 718-539-4107
Pres: Bertram L. Linder
Agent: Edwin Selzer

Agents for textbooks only for K-12. Unsolicited materials accepted after query first with SASE.

ANN ELMO AGENCY
60 E. 42nd St., New York, NY 10165
212-661-2880; Fax: 212-463-8718
Pres: Ann Elmo
Agent: Lettie Lee

Agents for children's & young adult books, periodicals, theater, TV, film. No unsolicited materials.

JAY GARON-BROOKE ASSOCIATES
415 Central Park W., New York, NY 10025
212-866-3654; Fax: 212-666-6016
Contact: Jay Garon, Jean Free

Agents for books. Mainly mainstream novels and popular nonfiction. No unsolicited manuscripts, no mail queries, no poetry collections. Telephone queries accepted.

GOTHAM ART & LITERARY AGENCY INC.
25 Tudor City Pl., New York, NY 10017
212-989-2737; Fax: 212-645-7731

Agents for books, film & TV.

JOHN HAWKINS & ASSOCIATES, INC.
71 W. 23rd St., Ste. 1600, New York, NY 10010
212-807-7040; Fax: 212-807-9555
Agents: William Reiss, Sharon Friedman

Agents for books, periodicals, films, TV, audio, children, young adult, & adult. Unsolicited materials accepted after query first with SASE.

VIRGINIA KIDD
U.P.S, FedEx, other carriers: 538 E. Harford St., Milford, PA 18337
U.S. Mail: Box 278, Milford, PA 18337
717-296-6205; Fax: 717-296-7266
Agent: Virginia Kidd

Agents for books. No unsolicited materials.

BERTHA KLAUSNER INTERNATIONAL LITERARY AGENCY, INC.
71 Park Ave., New York, NY 10016
212-685-2642; Fax: 212-532-8638
Agent: Bertha Klausner

Agents for books, film, TV, art, theater. No unsolicited materials without query first.

BARBARA S. KOUTS
Box 558, Bellport, NY 11713
516-286-1278; Fax: 516-286-1538
Agent: Barbara S. Kouts

Agents for books. Specialize in literary fiction & children's books. Also

represent adult fiction & nonfiction. Mail queries accepted. No telephone queries, no unsolicited manuscripts, no poetry collections.

Sidney B. Kramer, see **MEWS BOOKS LTD.**

RAY LINCOLN LITERARY AGENCY
Elkins Park House, Ste. 107-B, Elkins Park, PA 19117
215-635-0827
Agent: (Mrs.) Ray Lincoln

Agents for all types of adult & children's fiction & nonfiction. Telephone & mail queries accepted. No unsolicited manuscripts & no poetry collections.

MCINTOSH & OTIS INC.
310 Madison Ave., New York, NY 10017
212-687-7400; Fax: 212-687-6894
Juv Dept Head: Dorothy Markinko
Assoc: Renee Cho
TV, Film, Stage Rights: Evva Pryor

Agents for books, TV, film, art, theater. Unsolicited materials accepted after query.

BETTY MARKS LITERARY AGENCY
176 E. 77th St., New York, NY 10021
212-535-8388
Agent: Betty Marks

Agents for books. Reading fee for unpublished writers.

SCOTT MEREDITH LITERARY AGENCY
845 Third Ave., New York, NY 10022-6687
212-245-5500
Pres: Arthur M. Klebanoff
VPs: Joshua Bilmes, Mark Joly, Rita Neyra
Agents: William Haas, Barry Malzberg, Larry Janifer, David Hernandez, Larry Ganem, Pamela Williams

Agents for books, periodicals, theater, TV, film. Fee for unsolicited materials.

MEWS BOOKS LTD.
20 Bluewater Hill, Westport, CT 06880
203-227-1836
Pres: Sidney B. Kramer
Assoc: Fran Pollak

Agents for children's, young adult & adult books, film, TV, merchandising. Unsolicited materials accepted, query & precis first. Circulation fee for unpublished authors against royalties if manuscript accepted.

MULTIMEDIA PRODUCT DEVELOP-MENT, INC.
410 S. Michigan Ave., Chicago, IL 60605
312-922-3063
Pres: Jane Jordan Browne

Agents for established authors & films & TV based on books. No unsolicited materials.

JEAN V. NAGGAR LITERARY AGENCY
216 E. 75th St., New York, NY 10021
212-794-1082
Agent: Jean Naggar, Teresa Cavanaugh

Agents for general fiction & general-interest nonfiction. Telephone & mail queries accepted. No unsolicited manuscripts & no poetry collections.

THE NORMA-LEWIS AGENCY
521 Fifth Ave., New York, NY 10175
212-751-4955
Agent: Norma Liebert

Agents for books, films, TV, theater. Unsolicited materials accepted after query first with SASE.

NORTHEAST LITERARY AGENCY
69 Broadway, Concord, NH 03301
603-225-9162
Ed: Victor Levine
Agent: Mary Hill

Agents for books, films, TV. Unsolicited materials accepted. $125-$250 reading & evaluation fee per manuscript. Reports within ten working days.

RAY PEEKNER LITERARY AGENCY, INC.
Box 3308, Bethlehem, PA 18107
215-974-9158; Fax: 215-974-8228
Contact: Barbara Puechner

Agents for mystery, suspense, women's fiction, Western historicals. Telephone & mail queries accepted. No unsolicited manuscripts & no poetry collections.

PUBLISHERS' GRAPHICS, INC.
251 Greenwood Ave., Bethel, CT 06801
203-797-8188
Pres: Paige C. Gillies
Sales Mgr: Susan Schwarzchild

Agents for children's book illustrators.

HENRY RASOF LITERARY AGENCY
4800 Osage Dr., Apt. 24, Boulder, CO 80303
303-499-4935

Agents for children's & young adult nonfiction primarily.

JOHN R. RIINA
5905 Meadowood Rd., Baltimore, MD 21212
301-433-2305
Owner: John R. Riina

Agents for textbooks, educational materials, nonfiction trade books. No unsolicited materials. Query first with SASE.

RUSSELL & VOLKENING
50 W. 29th St., #7E, New York, NY 10001
212-684-6050; Fax: 212-889-3026
Agent: Miriam Altschuler

Agents for books, films, TV. No unsolicited materials. Query with SASE first.

EVELYN SINGER LITERARY AGENCY
Box 594, White Plains, NY 10602
914-949-1147, 914-631-5160
Pres: Evelyn Singer

Agents for books & subsidiary periodical, film, TV rights. Unsolicited materials accepted from published writers. Send outline, background, SASE.

SINGER MEDIA CORP.
Seaview Business Park
1030 Calle Cordillera, Unit 106, San Clemente, CA 92673
714-498-7227; Fax: 714-498-2162
Editor: Janis Hawkridge

Agents for books, periodicals, puzzles, brain twisters, quizzes, cartoons, any juvenile activities. Do it yourself for kids. Newspaper syndicate—worldwide. Agents for published books to be licensed to foreign book publishers.

GUNTHER STUHLMANN AUTHOR'S REPRESENTATIVE
Box 276, Becket, MA 01223
412-623-5170
Dir: Gunther Stuhlmann

Agent for adult books & subsidiary film & foreign rights. Some young adult books. No unsolicited materials accepted. Query first with SASE. No picture books.

WRITERS HOUSE
21 W. 26th St., New York, NY 10010
212-685-2400
Agents: Amy Berkower, Susan Cohen, Fran Cebowitz

Agents for books. Unsolicited materials accepted only if exclusive. Send sample chapters, synopsis, with SASE.

PERIODICALS FOR CHILDREN

9

This section lists primarily those periodicals directed to children. For a list of periodicals for parents and professionals working with children see chapter 10. For a list of review sources and services see chapter 11.

Abbreviations for indexes are: BRI - Book Review Index, CBRI - Children's Book Review Index, CLA - Children's Literature Abstracts, CIJE - Current Index to Journals in Education, CMG - Children's Magazine Guide, EdI - Education Index, LL - Library Literature, MRI - Media Review Index, RGPL - Reader's Guide to Periodical Literature, SICM - Subject Index to Children's Magazines, SSCI - Social Science Citation Index, JHMI - Junior High Magazine Index.

AMERICAN GIRL
Pleasant Company Publicatons, Inc.
8400 Fairway Pl., Middleton, WI 53562
608-836-4848; Fax: 608-836-1999
Orders: Box 620991, Middleton, WI 53562
Editor: Nancy Holyoke

6/yr; $19.95; illus; no adv; 250,000 circ
Audience: 7-12
Focus: To entertain and educate girls
Contents: Features, fiction and nonfiction, contest, paperdolls, projects
Other: Unsolicited materials accepted. Back issues available

AMERICAN HISTORY ILLUSTRATED
Cowles Magazines (Sub. of Cowles Media Co.)
6405 Flank Dr., Box 8200, Harrisburg, PA 17105-8299
717-657-9555; Fax: 717-657-9526
Eds.: Ed Holm, Geneva B. Politzer, Kathleen Doyle

16/yr; $21; adv; 140,864 circ
Audience: 10-12, teachers, professionals
Focus: To enrich knowledge of American history
Contents: Articles on American cultural, social, political & military history
Reviews: 30-40/yr, books on American history
Other: Accepts unsolicited materials, query first. Back issues available. Index in RGPL, America: History & Life, JGMA. Available on microfilm

BARBIE MAGAZINE
Welsh Publishing Group, Inc.
300 Madison Ave., New York, NY 10017
212-687-0680

Eds: Katy Dobbs, Karen Tina Harrison, Betsy Loredo

6/yr; $10.30; adv; 600,000 circ
Audience: K-6, parents
Focus: Lifestyle & fashion magazine for girls based on Barbie doll
Contents: Features & news on children & media, features for children
Reviews: 40/yr, reviews of children's books & audiovisual materials, movies, records, current attractions
Other: No unsolicited materials. Back issues & reprints available. Annual index in spring issue

BIOGRAPHY TODAY
Omnigraphics, Inc.
Penobscot Bldg, Detroit, MI 48225
800-234-1340

3/yr; $42
Audience: 3-12, teachers, librarians
Focus: Profiles 15-20 people in the news
Contents: Contemporary biography from the world of politics, entertainment, sports and literature.

BOYS' LIFE
Boy Scouts of America
Box 152070, 1325 Walnut Hill Ln., Irving, TX 75015-2079
214-659-2000
Ed: Scott Stauckey

12/yr; $7.80 (Boy Scout members); $15.60 - others; illus; adv; sample; 1,300,000 circ
Audience: 1-12, primarily members of Boy Scouts of America
Focus: To explore scouting & interests in sports, magic, hobbies, conservation & other activities
Contents: Features, how-to articles, comics, reviews

Reviews: 50/yr, reviews of children's books, reviews of computer software, records & "G" rated films of interest to boys
Other: Accepts unsolicited materials. Back issues & reprints available. Annual index issued separately in February. Indexed in CMG, JHMI. Available on microform, in braille and online through DIALOG

BREAKAWAY
Focus on the Family
8605 Explorer Dr., Colorado Springs, CO 80920
719-531-5181, 800-232-6459; Fax: 719-531-3424
Ed: Greg Johnson

12/yr; $15; adv; illus; 95,000 circ
Audience: 7-12
Focus: To reinforce Christain principles in the everyday life issues of the young adult boy
Contents: Fiction & nonfiction stories, cartoons, columns which offer advice on subjects from sports to sex, celebrities and spiritual guidance
Reviews: 12-24/yr, books, audio tapes, videos
Other: Accepts unsolicited materials. Back issues available "teenage boys; advice, humor, spiritual guidance; info about sports, celebrities, general"

BRILLIANT STAR
National Spiritual Assembly of the Baha'is of the United States
536 Sheridan Rd., Wilmette, IL 60091
708-869-9039
Ed: Candace Moore Hill

6/yr; $12; illus; sample; 2,100 circ
Audience: Preschool-7, teachers, parents

Focus: A religious periodical which identifies to children the distinctive characteristics of Baha'i life

Contents: Features for & by children, poetry, stories, puzzles, games

Reviews: 6/yr, reviews of children's books & audiovisual materials, reviews of audiovisual equipment, reviews of computer software, records, cassettes & TV

Other: Accepts unsolicited materials. Back issues available

BRIO

Focus on the Family 8605 Explorer Dr., Colorado Springs, CO 80920

719-531-5181, 800-232-6459; Fax: 719-531-3424

Ed: Susie Shellenberger

12/yr; $15; adv; illus; 140,000 circ

Audience: 7-12

Focus: To reinforce Christain principles in the everyday life issues of the young adult girl

Contents: Fiction & nonfiction stories, cartoons, columns which deal on subjects from fashion and food to fitness and faith

Reviews: 12-24/yr, books, audio tapes, videos

Other: Accepts unsolicited materials. Back issues available

CALIFORNIA WEEKLY EXPLORER

California Weekly Explorer, Inc.

285 E. Main St., Ste. 3, Tustin, CA 92680

714-730-5991

Ed: Don Oliver

Wkly in school yr; $25; illus; charts

Audience: 4-7, librarians

Focus: To present California history & geography

Contents: Features & news on children & media, features for & by children

Reviews: 35/yr, reviews of children's books & audiovisual materials, reviews of computer software, maps, globes, etc.

Other: Accepts unsolicited materials with SASE. Back issues available. Annual index in Issue 34

CAREER WORLD

Weekly Reader Corporation

3001 Cindel Dr., Delran, NJ 08370

800-446-3355; Fax: 609-786-3360

Ed: Carol Rubenstein

7/yr; $8.25 (15 or more); $16.50 (2-14); $26.95 (single); sample

Audience: 7-12, teachers

Focus: To explore careers & present vocational information

Other: Accepts unsolicited materials. Back issues available. Annual index in May. Index in CMG, RGPL. Available on microform

CHICKADEE

255 Great Arrow Ave., Buffalo, NY 14207-3082

800-387-4379

10/yr; $14.95; illus

Audience: 3-8

Focus: Science & nature magazine

Contents: Stories, activities & puzzles

CHILD LIFE

Children's Better Health Institute

1100 Waterway Blvd., Box 567, Indianapolis, IN 46206

317-636-8881, Fax: 317-684-8094

Ed: Lise Hoffman

8/yr; $14.95; illus; adv; 79,000 circ

Audience: 3-6

Focus: To entertain while teaching better health habits

Contents: Features for & by children

Other: Accepts unsolicited materials. Indexed in CMG, SICM

CHILDREN'S DIGEST

Children's Better Health Institute

1100 Waterway Blvd., Box 567, Indianapolis, IN 46202

317-636-8881; Fax: 317-684-8094

Ed: Sandra Grieshop

8/yr; $14.95; illus; adv; 103,000 circ

Audience: Preteen

Focus: To entertain children while teaching them better health & safety habits

Contents: Stories, articles, puzzles & activities with a health, nutrition, exercise or safety theme, features for children

Reviews: 12-15/yr, reviews of children's books

Other: Accepts unsolicited materials. Indexed in CMG. Available on microform

CHILDREN'S PLAYMATE

Children's Better Health Institute

1100 Waterway Blvd., Box 567, Indianapolis, IN 46206

317-636-8881, Fax: 317-684-8094

Ed: Lise Hoffman

8/yr; $14.95; illus; adv; 118,000 circ

Audience: 1-2

Focus: Entertainment & health education

Contents: Stories, articles, puzzles, activities, stressing health, safety, exercises & nutrition

Reviews: 16/yr, reviews of children's books

Other: Accepts unsolicited materials. Indexed in CMG, SICM. Available on microfilm

CLASSICAL CALLIOPE, THE MUSES' MAGAZINE FOR YOUTH

Cobblestone Publishing, Inc.

20 Grove St., Peterborough, NH 03458

603-924-7209

Eds: Rosalie Baker, Charles Baker

4/yr; $14.94; illus; 3,000 circ

Audience: 6-12, teachers, librarians, parents

Focus: To introduce young people to ancient history, literature & culture

Contents: Features for children

Other: No unsolicited materials. Back issues available

CLAVIER'S PIANO EXPLORER

Instrumentalist Co., 200 Northfield Rd., Northfield, IL 60093-3390

708-446-5559

Eds: Ann Rohner, Bill Rohner

10/yr; $6; illus; sample; 73,000 controlled circ

Audience: K-10, teachers

Focus: To supplement piano lessons for students & teachers. Each issue contains a cover story, a featured composer & instrument, compositions, music games & puzzles

Contents: Features for & by children

Other: Accepts unsolicited materials. Back issues & reprints available

CLUBHOUSE

Your Story Hour, Inc.

464 W. Ferry, Box 15, Berrien Springs, MI 49103

616-471-9009; Fax: 616-471-4661

Ed: Elaine Trumbo

6/yr; $5; sample with SASE; 10,000 circ

Audience: 4-9

Focus: Character-building stories for children. Accompanies Your Story Hour radio program

Contents: Stories, puzzles, games, crafts

Other: Accepts unsolicited materials. Back issues available

CLUBHOUSE

Focus on the Family 8605 Explorer Dr., Colorado Springs, CO 80920

719-531-5181, 800-232-6459; Fax: 719-531-3424

Ed: Linda Piepenbrink

12/yr; $12; illus; 100,000 circ

Audience: 2-6, parents

Focus: To teach children Christain principles in an entertaining format

Contents: Puzzles, activites and faith-building stories

Reviews: 12-24/yr, books, audio tapes, videos concerning Christain principles

Other: Accepts unsolicited materials. Back issues available

CLUBHOUSE JR
Focus on the Family 8605 Explorer
Dr., Colorado Springs, CO 80920
719-531-5181, 800-232-6459; Fax:
719-531-3424
Ed: Lisa Brock

12/yr; $12; illus; 90,000 circ
Audience: Preschool-2, parents
Focus: To teach children Biblical prin-
ciples in an entertaining format
Contents: Crafts, games, stories which
emphasize Christain principles in ev-
ery aspect of life
Reviews: 12-24/yr, books, audio tapes,
videos concerning Christain prin-
ciples
Other: Accepts unsolicited materials.
Back issues available

COBBLESTONE: THE HISTORY MAGA-
ZINE FOR YOUNG PEOPLE
Cobblestone Publishing, Inc.
7 School St., Peterborough, NH 03458
603-924-7209; Fax: 603-924-7380
Ed: Samuel Mead

10/yr; $22.95; 38,000 circ
Audience: 4-8
Focus: Each issue treats a specific
topic in American history
Reviews: Reviews of children's books,
films
Other: Accepts unsolicited materials,
query first with SASE. Back issues
available. Indexed in CMG, JHMA.
Separate cumulative index from
1980

CREATIVE KIDS
Prufrock Press
Box 8813, Waco, TX 76714-8813
817-756-3337

4/yr; $19.95; illus
Audience: 8-14, teachers, librarians,
parents
Focus: Creative outlet by kids for kids
Contents: Poetry, stories, puzzles,
reviews & art; teachers's guide

CRICKET MAGAZINE
Carus Corporation
315 Fifth St., Box 300, Peru, IL 61354
815-223-2520, 800-998-0868

12/yr; $29.97; illus; adv; 130,000 circ
Audience: 6-12
Focus: Literature for children
Contents: Features for & by children
Reviews: 50/yr, reviews of children's
books
Other: Accepts unsolicited materials.
Back issues available. Indexed in
CMG, JHMA. Available on microfilm

CRUSADER
Calvinist Cadet Corps
1333 Alger St., Box 7259, Grand
Rapids, MI 49510

616-241-5616; Fax: 616-241-5558
Ed: G. Richard Broene

7/yr; $7; sample with 9" x 12" SASE;
13,000 circ
Audience: 4-9
Focus: To help boys see how God is at
work in their lives & in the world
around them
Contents: Features for & by children
Other: Accepts unsolicited materials.
Back issues available

CURRENT EVENTS
Weekly Reader Corporation
3001 Cindel Dr., Delran, NJ 08370
800-446-3355; Fax: 609-786-3360
Ed: Charlie Piddock

26/yr; $7.65 (10 or more); $15.30
(2-9); $29.95 (single); illus
Audience: 7-8
Focus: To build interest in national &
world events & social studies
Contents: Features & news on children
& media, features for & by children
Reviews: Reviews of children's books
Other: No unsolicited materials. Back
issues available. Indexed in CMG,
JHMA. Available in braille & on
microfilm

CURRENT HEALTH 1: A BEGINNING
GUIDE TO HEALTH EDUCATION
Weekly Reader Corporation
3001 Cindel Dr., Delran, NJ 08370
800-446-3355; Fax: 609-786-3360
Ed: Laura Ruekberg

9/yr; $7.95 (10 or more); $15.90 (2-9);
$26.95 (single); illus; sample;
155,318 circ
Audience: 4-6, teachers
Focus: To present topical health infor-
mation for classroom use Contents:
Features for children
Other: No unsolicited materials. Back
issues & reprints available. Annual
index in May. Indexed in CMG,
JHMA, RGPL. Available on microform

CURRENT HEALTH 2
Weekly Reader Corporation
3001 Cindel Dr., Delran, NJ 08370
800-446-3355; Fax: 609-786-3360
Ed: Laura Ruekberg

9/yr; $7.95 (10 or more); $15.90 (2-9);
$26.95 (single); 249,418 circ
Audience: 7-12, teachers, librarians
Focus: The latest information on various health topics for classroom use
Contents: Features for children
Reviews: Monthly additional resource
list in teacher's guide, reviews of
children's books & audiovisual
materials
Other: No unsolicited materials. Back
issues & reprints available. Annual
index in May. Indexed in CMG,

JHMA, Health Index, Academic Index. Available on microform

CURRENT SCIENCE
Weekly Reader Corporation
3001 Cindel Dr., Delran, NJ 08370
800-466-3355; Fax: 609-786-3360
Ed: Vince Marteka

18/yr; $7.95 (10 or more); $15.90
(2-9); $29.95 (single); illus; 343,789
circ
Audience: 7-9Focus: To teach science
basics & report on latest scientific
advances
Contents: Feature articles & news
about children & media, features for
& by children
Other: No unsolicited materials. Back
issues available. Indexed in JHMA.
Available in braille & on microfilm

DISCOVERING TOGETHER
Standard Publishing Company
8121 Hamilton Ave., Cincinnati, OH
45231
513-931-4050
Ed: Christine Spence

52/yr; $9.99/5 copies of 13 issues, il-
lus, sample, 75,000 circ
Audience: Preschool, parents
Focus: Take-home leaflet supplements
Sunday School lessons
Contents: Features for children
Other: No unsolicited materials

DISNEY ADVENTURES
Walt Disney Publishing
Burbank Tower Bldg., 3800 W.
Alameda Ave., BC100, Burbank, CA
91505
818-973-4333, 800-829-5146; Fax:
818-563-9344
Ed: Tommi Lewis

12/yr; $19.95; illus; adv; 500,000 circ
Audience: 2-8
Focus: To entertain while teaching current events
Contents: Features for & by children
about science, technology, travel,
environment & sports, including
comics featuring Disney character

THE DOLPHIN LOG
The Cousteau Society
8440 Santa Monica Blvd., Los Angles,
CA 90069
312-656-4422
Ed: Pamela Stacey

6/yr; $10 membership fee; illus;
86,000 circ
Audience: 1-7, teachers, librarians,
parents
Focus: To delight, instruct & instill an
environmental ethic & understanding
of the interconnectedness of all living organisms

Contents: Features for children
Reviews: 11/yr, reviews of children's
books
Other: Accepts unsolicited materials.
Back issues available. Indexed in
CMG

FFA NEW HORIZONS
(formerly The National Future Farmer)
National FFA Organization
Box 15130, 5631 Mount Vernon
Memorial Hwy., Alexandria, VA
22309
703-360-3600; Fax: 703-360-5524
Ed.: Andrew Markwart

6/yr; $3.50; illus; adv; sample;
414,249 curc
Audience: 9-12, adult
Focus: Articles of interest to young
people planning a career in
agriculture
Contents: Features and news on chil-
dren & media
Other: Accepts unsolicited materials.
Back issues & reprints available

FACES (The Magazine About People)
Cobblestone Publishing (& Co-sponsor
of the American Museum of Natural
History)
7 School St., Peterborough, NH 03458
603-924-7209
Ed: Carolyn P. Yoder

9/yr; $21.95; illus; charts; 13,000 circ
Audience: 3-9, teachers, librarians, par-
ents, general
Focus: An anthropological magazine
published in cooperation with the
American Museum of Natural
History
Contents: Features for children
Other: No unsolicited materials. Back
issues available. Indexed in CMG

FOUR AND FIVE
(Formerly 4 & 5 Story Paper)
Standard Publishing Company
8121 Hamilton Ave., Cincinnati, OH
45231
513-931-4050; Fax: 513-931-0904
Ed: Barbara Cottrell

52/yr; $9.99/quarter; illus; sample;
14,000 circ
Audience: Preschool-K, parents
Focus: Take-home paper supplements
Sunday School lessons
Contents: Stories for children
Other: No unsolicited materials. Back
issues available

THE FRIEND
The Church of Jesus Christ of Latter-
Day Saints
50 E. North Temple, Salt Lake City, UT
84150
801-240-2947
Ed: Vivian Paulsen

12/yr; $8; illus; sample; 210,000 circ
Audience: Preschool-6, teachers,
parents
Focus: To help children understand &
live by uplifting Christian principles
as taught by the Church of Jesus
Christ of Latter-Day Saints
Contents: Features for children
Reviews: 30 annually in Nov, reviews
of children's books
Other: Accepts unsolicited materials.
Back issues available. Annual
index in December. Available in
Braille

GROUP
Group Publishing, Inc.
2890 N. Monroe, Box 481, Loveland,
Co 80539
303-669-3836
Ed Dir: Joani Schultz

8/yr, $25.95; illus; adv; sample;
57,000 circ
Audience: 9-12
Focus: To provide information on personal growth, leadership skills, Bible
studies & other topics of interest to
church youth groups
Contents: Features & news on children
& media
Reviews: 45/yr, resources for church
youth group leaders, films
Other: Back issues available

GUIDE
Review & Herald Publishing Assn.
55 W. Oak Ridge Dr., Hagerstown, MD
21740
301-791-7000
Ed: Jeannette Johnson

52/yr; $27.95; adv; 45,000 circ
Audience: 5-11
Focus: To teach Christian principles by
true stories, & articles
Contents: Features for & by children
Other: Free sample with SASE. Accepts
unsolicited materials. Back issues
available. Available on microfilm

HAPPY TIMES
Concordia Publishing House
3558 S.Jefferson Ave., St. Louis, MO
63118
314-664-7000
Ed: Earl H. Gaulke

12/yr; $6.75; illus; sample; 49,000
circ
Audience: Preschool-K
Focus: To strengthen & support Christian home training by showing
characters living with & growing in
Christian principles
Contents: Stories, prayers, poems,
puzzles, activities, games for children, features by children
Other: Back issues & reprints available. Available on microfilm

HARAMBEE
Just Us Books
301 Main St., Orange, NJ 07050
201-676-4345

6/yr; $10; illus
Audience: 9-14
Focus: To help young people better
understand black history & culture
Contents: Theme issues include arti-
cles, short stories & interviews

HIGHLIGHTS FOR CHILDREN
Highlights for Children, Inc.
Box 269, Columbus OH 43216-0269
614-486-0631; Fax: 614-486-0762
Ed: Kent L. Brown Jr.

11/yr; $21.95; illus; 2,800,000 circ
Audience: Preschool-7
Contents: Fiction, nonfiction, crafts,
verse, readers' contributions, think-
ing activities
Reviews: Occasionally, reviews of chil-
dren's books
Other: Accepts unsolicited materials.
Back issues available. Annual index
in December. Indexed in CMG, JHMA

HOPSCOTCH
Box 164, Bluffton, OH 45817
419-358-4610

6/yr; $15; illus
Audience: 1-6
Focus: To challenge and entertain
young girls
Contents: Fiction and nonfiction,
games

HUMPTY DUMPTY'S MAGAZINE
Children's Better Health Institute
1100 Waterway Blvd., Box 567, Indianapolis, IN 46206
317-636-8881, Fax: 317-684-8094
Ed: Janet Hoover

8/yr; $14.95; illus; adv; 235,000 circ
Audience: K-2
Focus: To entertain children while encouraging better health & safety
habits
Contents: Stories, articles, puzzles &
activities stressing health, nutrition,
exercise, safety & hygiene for children ages 4-6
Other: Accepts unsolicited materials.
Indexed in CMG. Available on
microfilm

INTERNATIONAL GYMNAST MAGAZINE
SundbySports, Inc.
225 Brooks, Box 2450, Oceanside, CA
92051
619-722-0030
Ed: Dwight Normile

10/yr; $20; illus; adv; 30,000 circ
Audience: Parents, gymnasts,
coaches

Focus: Information on international gymnastic events & personalities
Content: Feature articles on gymnasts
Reviews: 12/yr, reviews of children's books & audiovisual materials, reviews of audiovisual equipment, reviews of computer software
Other: Accept unsolicited materials. Back issues & reprints available. Annual index in March. Indexed in CBRI, CMG, RGPL, Physical Education Index. Available on microform

JACK & JILL
Children's Better Health Institute
1100 Waterway Blvd., Box 567, Indianapolis, IN 46206
317-636-8881, Fax: 317-684-8094
Ed: Steve Charles

8/yr; $14.95; illus; adv; 326,000 circ
Audience: 2-5, teachers, librarians
Focus: To provide entertainment & health education for children
Contents: Features for & by children
Other: Accepts unsolicited materials. Indexed in CMG, SICM

JUNIOR SCHOLASTIC
Scholastic Inc.
730 Broadway, 9th Fl., New York, NY 10003
212-505-3000; Fax: 212-5053653
Ed: Lee Baier

18/yr; $6.95; illus; adv; charts; 825,000 circ
Audience: 6-8
Focus: Classroom educational material in social studies
Contents: Features for & by children
Reviews: 10/yr, reviews of children's books
Other: Accepts unsolicited materials. Back issues available. Annual index on request. Indexed in CMG, SICM

JUNIOR TRAILS
Gospel Publishing House
1445 Boonville Ave., Springfield, MO 65802
417-862-2781
Ed: Sinda S. Zinn

52/yr; $5.20; 65,000 circ
Audience: 5-6
Focus: Sunday School supplement of stories & articles that build character & teach a moral or spiritual truth
Contents: Features on children and media, features for & by children
Other: Accepts unsolicited materials. Back issues available

KEEPING POSTED WITH NCSY
National Conference of Synagogue Youth
333 Seventh Ave., 19th Fl., New York, NY 10001-5004

212-244-2011; Fax: 212-268-6819
Ed: Renee Straussad

4/yr; $6; adv; 20,000 circ
Audience: 8-12, parents, Jewish teenagers
Contents: Features for & by children
Reviews: Reviews of children's books
Other: Accepts unsolicited materials. Back issues available

KID CITY
(formerly The Electric Company Magazine)
Children's Television Workshop
One Lincoln Plaza, New York, NY 10023
212-595-3456
Ed: Maureen Hunter-Bone

10/yr; $13.97; illus; adv; sample; 250,000 circ
Audience: 1-5
Focus: To develop children's reading skills
Contents: Games, puzzles, comics, activities, posters, articles, short stories, reviews of children's books
Other: Back issues available. Indexed in CMG

KIDS DISCOVER
Mark Levine Publishers
170 Fifth Ave., New York, NY 10010
212-242-5133; Fax: 212-242-5628
Ed: Stephen Brewer

10/yr; $17.95; illus; 260,292 circ
Audience: K-7
Focus: To stimulate interest in science & the world around students
Contents: Each issue explores a different topic (fire, pyramids, rain forests, etc) with games and charts
Other: Back issues available

KIDSPORTS
Box 8488, Coral Springs, FL 33075
800-938-5588

6/yr; $15.94
Audience: 1-8
Focus: Sports magazine for children
Contents: Feature articles, fiction, games and posters

KIND NEWS
(Kids In Nature's Defense)
Box 362, East Haddam, CT 06423-0362
203-434-8666
Exec Dir: Patty Finch

9/yr; $25 (32 in a bundle); $18 if donated; illus; sample; 500,000 circ
Audience: Primary: K-2; Junior: 3-4; Senior: 5-6
Focus: To teach students respect for one another, animals and the environment

Contents: Free teacher's aid, class poster, KIND ID cards, articles about animals and the environment

KNOW YOUR WORLD EXTRA!
Weekly Reader Corporation
3001 Cindel Dr., Delran, NJ 08370
800-446-3355; Fax: 609-786-3360
Ed: Scott Ingram

14/yr; $8.95 (10 or more); $17.90 (2-9); $9.95 (single); illus; 200,000 circ
Audience: 6-12
Focus: Current events for problem readers (reading level grades 2 & 3)
Contents: Features & news on children & media, features for & by children
Reviews: Reviews of children's books
Other: No unsolicited materials. Back issues available. Indexed in CMG. Available in braille & on microfilm

LADYBUG: THE MAGAZINE FOR YOUNG CHILDREN
Box 592, Mt. Morris, IL 61054
800-827-0227

12/yr; $29.97
Audience: 2-7
Focus: Literature for children

LISTEN
Health Connection
552 W. Oakridge Dr., Hagerstown, MD 21740
800-777-9098
Ed: Lincoln Steed

12/yr; $17.95; illus; sample; 50,000 circ
Audience: 7-12
Focus: To educate young people about the "false dependencies" of alcohol, drugs & smoking through a positive approach to health
Contents: Features for & by children
Other: Accepts unsolicited materials. Back issues & reprints available. Annual index in December

MERLYN'S PEN
Merlyn's Pen, Inc.
Dept. UPD, Box 1058, East Greenwich, RI 02818
401-885-5175; Fax: 401-885-5222
Ed: R. James Stahl

4/yr (Sept-May); $18.95; illus; adv; sample; 29,000 circ
Audience: 7-12, teachers, librarians
Focus: Publication of writing and artwork by students
Contents: Features by children
Reviews: 20/yr, book & movie & travel reviews
Other: Accepts unsolicited materials. Back issues available

MULTI MEDIA SCHOOLS
Online Inc.
462 Danbury Rd., Wilton, CT
   06897-2126
203-761-1466, 800-248-8466; Fax:
   203-761-1444

MY FRIEND: A MAGAZINE FOR BOYS
   & GIRLS
Daughters of St. Paul
50 St. Paul's Ave., Boston, MA 02130
617-522-8911; Fax: 617-524-8025
Ed: Sister Anne Joan Flanagan

10/yr; $8.50; illus; sample; 15,000
   circ
Audience: 1-6
Contents: Features on children and
   media, features for & by children
Other: Accepts unsolicited materials.
   Back issues available

NATIONAL GEOGRAPHIC WORLD
National Geographic Society
17 & M Sts, NW, Washington, DC
   20036
202-857-7000, 800-638-4077
Ed: Pat Robbins

12/yr; $12.95; illus; 1,200,000 circ
Audience: 3-7
Contents: Features & news on children
   & media, features for & by children
Other: Accepts unsolicited photographs. Back issues available. Indexed in CMG, JHMA, SICM

NATIONAL WILDLIFE
National Wildlife Federation
8925 Leesburg Pike, Vienna, VA
   22184
800-432-6564

6/yr; $16; illus
Audience: 1-12, general
Focus: Membership journal reporting
   on wild animals, conservation and
   ecology
Contents: Features on wildlife
Other: Also publishes an international
   edition, *International Wildlife*

NEW EXPRESSION
Youth Communication / Chicago
   Center
70 E. Lake St., Ste. 815, Chicago, IL
   60601-5907
312-663-0543
Ed: Susan Herr

10/yr; $12; 72,000 circ
Audience: 9-12
Focus: Produced & edited by teens for
   teens, covering education, culture,
   film, records, books, politics, self-
   help, sports & general news
Contents: Features & news on
   teenagers & media, features for &
   by teenagers

Reviews: 25-30/yr, reviews of computer software
Other: Back issues available

New Horizons, see **FFA NEW
   HORIZONS**

NEW MOON
Box 3587, Duluth, MN 55803
218-728-5507

6/yr; $25
Audience: 8-12
Focus: To help young girls develop
   their own identities
Contents: Theme issues include sto-
   ries, poems, ideas & drawings

ODYSSEY
Kalmbach Publishing Co.
1027 N. Seventh St., Milwaukee, WI
   53233
414-272-2060
Ed: Elizabeth Lindstrom

10/yr; $19.95; illus; adv; sample;
   charts; 55,000 circ
Audience: 3-9
Focus: To present information on as-
   tronomy & space science
Contents: Features for & by children
Reviews: 10/yr, reviews of children's
   books, reviews of computer software
Other: Accepts unsolicited materials.
   Back issues available. Indexed in
   CMG, JHMA. Available on microfiche

OLOMEINU-OUR WORLD
Torah Umesorah, National Society for
   Hebrew Day Schools
5723 Eighteenth Ave., Brooklyn, NY
   11204
718-259-1223; Fax: 718-259-1795
Eds: Rabbi Yaakov Fruchter, Rabbi
   Nosson Scherman

8/yr; $9; illus; 17,500 circ
Audience: 3-8
Focus: Magazine for young Jewish
   students
Content: Features for children, games,
   puzzles

ON THE LINE
Mennonite Publishing House
616 Walnut Ave., Scottdale, PA 15683
412-887-8500
Ed: Mary C. Meyer

52/yr; $17.10; illus; sample; 10,000
   circ
Audience: 5-8
Focus: To aid children in their appreciation of themselves, the natural
   world, Christianity & God
Contents: Fiction, puzzles, poetry, occasional features on children, nature
   & media
Reviews: Occasional reviews of

children's books & audiovisual
   materials
Other: Accepts unsolicited materials.
   Some back issues available

OUR LITTLE FRIEND
(Seventh Day Adventist Assn.)
Pacific Press Publishing
1350 Kings Rd., Nampa, ID 83651
208-465-2500; Fax: 208-465-2531
Ed: Aileen Andres Sox

52/yr; $17.50; illus; sample; 66,000
   circ
Audience: Preschool-1
Focus: To aid in character develop-
   ment of children of Seventh-Day Ad-
   ventist Church
Contents: Stories, poetry, puzzles, fea-
   tures for children
Other: Accepts unsolicited materials.
   Back issues available

OWL
255 Great Arrow Ave., Buffalo, NY
   14207-3082
800-387-4379

10/yr; $14.95; illus
Audience: 8-14
Focus: To promote an interest in na-
   ture, science, & the world
Contents: Articles & photographs,
   posters, puzzles & cartoons

PIONEER
Brotherhood Commission, Southern
   Baptist Convention
1548 Poplar Ave., Memphis, TN
   38104
800-727-6466
Ed: Jeno Smith

12/yr; $2.64/c mo; illus; 26,000 circ
Audience: 7-9, parents
Focus: To help boys become involved
   in missions
Contents: Features for children
Other: Available on microform

**PLAYS (The Drama Magazine for
   Young People)**
Plays, Inc.
120 Boylston St., Boston, MA
   02116-4615
617-423-3157
Ed: Sylvia K. Burack

7/yr; $27; adv; 16,000 circ
Audience: 2-12, teachers, librarians,
   parents, drama directors
Focus: To provide schools & clubs
   with new, royalty-free plays & pro-
   grams for classroom & assembly use
Contents: Plays & programs
Reviews: Reviews of children's books,
   teachers' materials
Other: Accepts unsolicited materials.
   Annual index in May. Indexed in
   CMG, SICM. Available on microform

POCKETS
The Upper Room
1908 Grand, Box 189, Nashville, TN
  37202
615-340-7333; Fax: 615-340-7006
Ed: Janet R. McNish

11/yr; $12.95; illus; sample with SASE;
  55,000 circ
Audience: 1-6
Focus: To help children lay a founda-
  tion for a vital spiritual life through
  prayer & awareness of God
Contents: Features for & by children
Other: Accepts unsolicited materials.
  Back issues available

PRIMARY TREASURE
(Seventh Day Adventist Assn.)
Pacific Press Publishing
1350 Kings Rd., Nampa, ID 83651
208-465-2500; Fax: 208-465-2531
Ed: Aileen Andres Sox

52/yr; $25.95; illus; sample; 40,000
  circ
Audience: 2-4
Focus: To aid in character develop-
  ment of children of Seventh-Day Ad-
  ventist Church
Contents: True stories, poetry, puzzles,
  features for children
Other: Accepts unsolicited materials.
  Back issues available

R-A-D-A-R
Standard Publishing Company
8121 Hamilton Ave., Cincinnati, OH
  45231
513-931-4050
Ed: Margaret Williams

52/yr, $9.99/5 copies of 13 issues; il-
  lus; sample; 100,000 circ
Audience: 3-6
Focus: Take-home paper supplements
  Sunday School lessons
Contents: Scripture study, prayer
  study, fiction, features for & by chil-
  dren, poems, drawing
Other: Accepts unsolicited materials.
  Back issues available

RANGER RICK
The National Wildlife Federation
8925 Leesburg Pike, Vienna, VA
  22184-0001
703-790-4000, 800-432-6564

12/yr; $15; illus; sample; 855,000 circ
Audience: 5-12 teachers, librarians,
  parents
Focus: To teach children to respect,
  properly use & enjoy our natural
  resources
Contents: Features for children
Other: Accepts unsolicited materials.
  Back issues & reprints available. An-
  nual index in January. Indexed in

CMG, JHMA, RGPL. Available in
microform

READ MAGAZINE
Weekly Reader Corporation
3001 Cindel Dr., Delran, NJ 08370
800-446-3355; Fax: 609-786-3360
Ed: Ted Hoey

18/yr; $7.95 (10 or more); $15.90
  (2-9); $29.95 (single); illus; 380,750
  circ
Audience: 7-9
Focus: Articles focusing on topics of
  interest to young people to build
  vocabulary & reading skills
Contents: Features & news on children
  & media, features for & by children
Reviews: 4/yr, reviews of children's
  books
Other: No unsolicited materials. Back
  issues available. Annual index in Issue 18. Indexed in CMG. Available
  on microfilm

SCHOLASTIC ACTION
Scholastic Inc.
730 Broadway, New York, NY
  10003-9538
212-505-3000; Fax: 212-505-3653
Ed: Denise Willi

14/yr; $6.95; illus; 230,000 circ
Audience: 7-12
Focus: Classroom educational material
  for slow readers (level 2-4)
Contents: Features for & by children
Reviews: Reviews of children's audio-
  visual materials
Other: Accepts unsolicited materials.
  Back issues available. Annual index
  on request. Indexed in CMG, SICM.
  Available on microform

SCHOLASTIC ART
(formerly Art & Man)
Scholastic Inc.
730 Broadway, New York, NY
  10003-9538
212-505-3000, 800-631-1586; Fax:
  212-505-3653
Ed: Margaret Howlett

6/yr; $9.95; illus; 205,000 circ
Audience: 6-12
Focus: Classroom art projects &
  educational material in art
  history
Contents: Features for children
Other: No unsolicited materials. Annual
  index on request. Indexed in CMG.
  Available on microform

SCHOLASTIC CHOICES
Scholastic Inc.
730 Broadway, New York, NY
  10003-9538
212-505-3105; Fax: 212-505-3653
Ed: Lauren Tarshis

9/yr; $5.95; illus; adv; 180,000 circ
Audience: 7-10
Focus: To encourage development of
  skills in home economics, family &
  personal relationships & decision
  making
Contents: Features for children
Reviews: Reviews of computer
  software
Other: No unsolicited materials. Indexed in CMG, MRI. Available online
  through DIALOG

SCHOLASTIC LET'S FIND OUT
Scholastic Inc.
730 Broadway, New York, NY
  10003-9538
212-505-3653; Fax: 212-505-3653
Ed: Mary Read

8/yr; $4.95 (bulk only; min 20 copies);
  illus
Audience: K
Focus: Classroom educational material
Contents: Features for children
Reviews: Reviews of children's books
  & nonprint materials
Other: No unsolicited materials. Annual
  index on request

SCHOLASTIC MATH
Scholastic Inc.
730 Broadway, New York, NY
  10003-9538
212-505-3000; Fax: 212-505-3653
Ed: Tracy Randinelli

10/yr; $6.95; 311,000 circ
Audience: 7-10
Focus: Presents students with math
  puzzles & games, math learning
  ideas, trends in math
Contents: Features for & by children
Reviews: Reviews of computer
  software
Other: Accepts unsolicited materials.
  Back issues & reprints avail-
  able

SCHOLASTIC NEWS
Scholastic Inc.
730 Broadway, New York, NY
  10003-9538
212-505-3000; Fax: 212-505-3653
Eds: Shelly Bedik (1-2), J. Safro (3-4),
  Alexandra Harding (5-6)

26/yr; illus
Audience: 1-6 (1 - SCHOLASTIC NEWS
  PILOT; 2 - SCHOLASTIC NEWS
  RANGER; 3 - SCHOLASTIC NEWS
  TRAILS; 4 - SCHOLASTIC NEWS
  EXPLORER; 5 - SCHOLASTIC
  CITIZEN; 6 - SCHOLASTIC
  NEWSTIME)
Focus: People, places & news present-
  ed in six editions corresponding to
  grades 1-6
Contents: Features for children

SCHOLASTIC SCIENCE WORLD
Scholastic Inc.
730 Broadway, New York, NY
   10003-9538
212-505-3000; Fax: 212-505-3653
Ed: Bonnie Price

14/yr; $6.95; illus; adv; sample; charts;
   550,000 circ
Audience: 7-10
Focus: Classroom educational material
   in science
Contents: Features for children
Reviews: 5/yr, reviews of children's
   books
Other: No unsolicited materials. Annual
   index in mid-May. Indexed in SICM.
   Available on microform

SCHOLASTIC SCOPE
Scholastic Inc.
730 Broadway, New York, NY
   10003-9538
212-505-3117; Fax: 212-505-3653
Ed: John Rearick

20/yr; $6.95; illus; adv
Audience: 7-9
Focus: Classroom educational materi-
   als in language arts, for slower read-
   ers (level 4-6)
Contents: Features for &
   children
Reviews: Reviews of children's audi-
   ovisual materials
Other: Accepts unsolicited materials.
   Back issues available. Annual index
   on request

SCHOLASTIC UPDATE
(Includes Scholastic Search)
Scholastic Inc.
730 Broadway, New York, NY
   10003-9538
212-505-3064
Ed: Lee Kravitz

14/yr; $6.95; illus; adv; charts;
   288,000 circ
Audience: 8-12
Focus: Classroom educational material
   in social studies (government,
   history, economics, sociology &
   world affairs)
Contents: Features for children
Reviews: TV & films
Other: Accepts unsolicited materials.
   Back issues available. Annual index
   on request. Indexed in CMG, JHMA,
   RGPL. Available on microform & on-
   line through DIOLOG

SCIENCELAND
Scienceland Inc.
501 Fifth Ave., New York, NY 10017
212-490-2180; Fax: 212-490-2187
Ed: A. H. Matano

8/yr; $42 on heavy stock; $9.95 student ed; illus; 16,000 circ

Audience: K-3, teachers, librarians,
   parents
Focus: To nurture scientific thinking &
   beginning reading in school & at
   home
Contents: Features for children
Other: Accepts unsolicited materials.
   Back issues available. Annual index
   in May. Indexed in CBRI, CMG. Available on microfiche

**SEEDLING SERIES: SHORT STORY
INTERNATIONAL**
International Cultural Exchange
6 Sheffield Rd., Great Neck, NY 11021
516-466-4166
Ed: Sylvia Tankel

4/yr, $16, illus
Audience: 4-7, teachers, librarians,
   parents
Focus: To promote & strengthen the
   reading habit by providing interest-
   ing stories written by talented, living
   authors from all lands
Contents: Short stories
Other: Accepts unsolicited materials.
   Back issues available

SESAME STREET MAGAZINE
Children's Television Workshop
One Lincoln Plaza, New York, NY
   10023
212-595-3456; 800-678-0613
Ed: Ira Wolfman

10/yr; $16.97; illus; sample;
   1,000,000 circ
Audience: Preschool, parents
Focus: To develop language arts, auditory & visual perception, self-
   expression, mathematical & reading
   skills. The Parents' Guide, included
   in each issue, focuses on child development in the preschool
   child
Contents: Activities, games, captioned
   illustrations, poster
Other: Back issues available

SEVENTEEN
KIII Magazines
850 Third Ave., New York, NY 10022
212-407-9700
Ed: Midge Richardson

12/yr; $15.95; illus; adv; 1,750,000
   circ
Audience: Teenage girls
Focus: Fashion, beauty, health, food,
   decorating
Contents: Feature articles, fiction &
   poetry for & by teenage girls
Reviews: 12-20/yr, teen books, audio-
   visual materials, reviews of computer
   software
Other: Accepts unsolicited materials.
   Back issues available. Indexed in
   Health Index, CMG, JHMA. Available
   on microform

SHOFAR
43 Northcote Dr., Melville, NY 11747
516-643-4598
Ed: Richard J. Golsan

8/yr Oct-May; $14.95; illus; sample;
   16,000 circ
Audience: 4-8, teachers, librarians, parents, general
Focus: To instill pride in their heritage
   in Jewish-American children
Contents: Features for & by children
Reviews: 20/yr, reviews of children's
   books & audiovisual materials,
   reviews of audiovisual equipment,
   reviews of computer software
Other: Accepts unsolicited materials.
   Back issues available. Annual index
   in May

SING OUT!
Sing Out Corporation
Box 5253, Bethlehem, PA
   18015-5253
212-865-5366; Fax: 215-865-5129
Ed: Mark D. Moss

4/yr; $18 indiv; $25 instit; adv; 5,000
   controlled circ
Audience: 9-12, teachers, musicians
Focus: Review of the folk music scene
   including at least 20 songs & lyrics
   with instruction in "teach-in" format.
   Excellent for use by music teachers
   interested in folk music
Contents: Features for children and
   adults
Reviews: Reviews of songs & music,
   books
Other: Accepts unsolicited materials.
   Back issues & reprints available. Indexed in Music Index, Magazine Index, New Periodicals Index. Available
   on microform

16 MAGAZINE
Sterling-MacFadden Partnership
233 Park Ave. S, New York, NY
   10003-1606
212-979-4800
Eds: Randi Reisfeld, Hedy End

12/yr; $14.95; illus; adv; 400,000 circ
Audience: 4-12
Focus: Youth-oriented entertainment
   magazine
Contents: Features on children and
   media, features for children
Reviews: Reviews of children's books
   & audiovisual materials
Other: Accepts unsolicited materials.
   Back issues & reprints available

SKIPPING STONES
Box 3939, Eugene, OR 97403
503-942-8198

4/yr; $18 indiv, $25 instit; illus
Audience: 7-13
Focus: To encourage a celebration

of cultural & environmental richness
Contents: Fiction & nonfiction from around the world, in translation where required

SPIDER
Box 639, Mt. Morris, IL 61054
800-827-0227

12/yr; $29.97; illus
Audience: 6-9
Focus: To encourage the independent reader
Contents: Stories, poems & informational articles

SPORTS ILLUSTRATED FOR KIDS
Box 830609, Birmingham, AL 35283-0609
800-827-0227

12/yr; $23.95; illus
Audience: 8-13
Focus: To entertain young sports fans of all kinds
Contents: Features & stories on all athletics and profiles of athletes

STICKERS & STUFF MAGAZINE
Ira Friedman Inc.
Ten Columbus Circle, Ste. 1300, New York, NY 10019
212-541-7300
Ed & Media Review Ed: Bob Woods

5/yr; $10;
Audience: Children, teachers, librarians, parents
Focus: Lifestyle, hobbies & interests of girls aged 12
Contents: Features & news on children & media, features for & by children
Reviews: Reviews of children's books & audiovisual materials, reviews of audiovisual equipment
Other: Accepts unsolicited materials. Back issues available. Indexed in CMG

STONE SOUP, THE MAGAZINE BY CHILDREN
Children's Art Foundation
Box 83, Santa Cruz, CA 95063
408-426-5557; Fax: 408-426-1161
Eds: Gerry Mandel

5/yr; $24; illus; 15,000 circ
Audience: 2-8, teachers, librarians, parents, general
Focus: To give children access to each other's literary & graphic work
Contents: Features by children
Reviews: 10/yr, reviews of children's books, reviewed by children
Other: Accepts unsolicited materials with SASE. Back issues available.

STORY FRIENDS
Mennonite Publishing House
616 Walnut Ave., Scottdale, PA 15683
412-887-8500; Fax: 412-887-3111
Ed: Marjorie Waybill

52/yr; $11.20; illus; sample; 9,000 circ
Audience: Preschool-4
Focus: To share Christian values in story form
Contents: Stories & features for children, features by children, puzzles, activities, children's drawings
Reviews: Occasional reviews of children's books
Other: Accepts unsolicited materials. Back issues & reprints available

STRAIGHT TALK FOR YOUNG TEENS
Standard Publishing Company
8121 Hamilton Ave., Cincinnati, OH 45231
513-931-4050
Ed: Carla Crane

52/yr; $9.99/5 copies of 13 issues; illus; sample
Audience: 7-12
Focus: Take-home paper supplements Sunday school lessons
Contents: Scripture study, prayer study, fiction, features for & by children, poems, drawings
Other: Accepts unsolicited materials. Back issues available

STUDENT SERIES: SHORT STORY INTERNATIONAL
International Cultural Exchange
6 Sheffield Rd., Great Neck, NY 11021
516-466-4166
Ed: Sylvia Tankel

4/yr; $18, illus
Audience: 8-12, teachers, librarians, parents
Focus: To promote & strengthen the reading habit by providing interesting stories written by talented, living authors from all lands.
Contents: Short stories
Other: Accepts unsolicited materials. Back issues available

SURPRISES
(formerly Surprises, Activities for Kids & Parents)
Homestyles Publishing & Marketing Co.
275 Market St., Ste. 521, Minneapolis, MN 55405-5570
612-937-0909
Ed: Jeanne Palmer

6/yr; $13; illus; adv; 105,000 controlled circ; 10,000 circ
Audience: Preschool, K-6, teachers, librarians, parents, general, grandparents, any interested adult
Focus: To provide educational activities for parents/adults & children
Contents: Features for & by children
Reviews: Reviews of children's books & audiovisual materials
Other: Accepts unsolicited materials. Back issues available, $2 each

SWIMMING WORLD & JUNIOR SWIMMER
Sports Publications, Inc.
Box 45497, Los Angeles, CA 90045
213-674-2120; Fax: 213-674-0238
Ed: Bob Ingram

12/yr; $19; adv; charts; 38,000 circ
Audience: 4-12, parents, coaches
Focus: Explores the world of competitive and sport swimming including features on outstanding athletes, news of competitions, and training tips
Contents: Features for children & adults
Reviews: Swimming films & books
Other: Back issues available. Indexed in Sports Periodicals Index. Available on microfilm

TQ (Teen Quest)
The Good News Broadcasting Association
Box 82808, Lincoln, NE 68501
402-474-4567
Ed: Chris Lyon

11/yr; $11.95; 75,817 controlled circ; 60,000 circ
Audience: 6-12
Focus: To give teenagers help in living an effective & enjoyable Christian life
Contents: Features for young adults
Reviews: 35/yr, reviews of children's books
Other: Accepts unsolicited materials. Back issues available

TAPORI
New Inc. / Fourth World Movement
7600 Willow Hill Dr., Landover, MD 20785-4658
301-336-9489; Fax: 301-336-0092
Ed: Susan M. Devins

12/yr; $7; illus; sample; 2,500 circ
Audience: 1-6, teachers, librarians, parents, general
Focus: To help children from all backgrounds learn from each other
Contents: Features for & by children
Other: Accepts unsolicited materials. Back issues & reprints available

TEENS TODAY
Nazarene Publishing House
Word Action, 6401 Paseo, Kansas City, MO 64131
816-333-7000
Ed: Karen DeSollar

52/yr; free; illus; 51,000 controlled circ
Audience: 7-12
Focus: To inspire faith in Jesus Christ, mold personal growth & development, impress ethical behavior
Contents: Features for teens
Other: Accepts unsolicited materials. Back issues & reprints available

TEXAS HISTORIAN
Texas State Historical Assn.
Sid Richardson Hall/2-306, University Station, Austin, TX 78712
512-471-1525
Ed: Ron Tyler

4/yr; $6; illus; adv; 2,500 controlled circ
Audience: 6-12, teachers
Focus: To publish award-winning essays by the Junior Historians of Texas
Contents: Features by children
Other: No unsolicited materials. Back issues available. Indexed in American History & Life, History Abstracts

3-2-1 CONTACT
Children's Television Workshop
One Lincoln Plaza, New York, NY 10023
212-595-3456
Ed: Jonathan Rosenbloom

10/yr; $11.95; illus; adv; 400,000 circ
Audience: 2-7
Focus: To demonstrate the scope of science & the processes of exploration & problem solving
Contents: Science features, reader participation features
Reviews: 60/yr, reviews of computer software
Other: indexed in CMG, JHMA

TOUCH
Calvinettes
Box 7244, Grand Rapids, MI 49510-7244
616-241-5616
Ed: Joanne Ilbrink

12/yr; $9; 16,000 controlled circ
Audience: 3-8
Focus: To help girls see how God is at work in their lives & in the world around them
Contents: Features on children and media
Reviews: Reviews of children's books
Other: Accepts unsolicited materials. Back issues available

TURTLE
Children's Better Health Institute
1100 Waterway Blvd., Box 567, Indianapolis, IN 46206
317-636-8881, Fax: 317-684-8094
Ed: Elizabeth Rinck

8/yr; $14.95; illus; 381,244
Audience: 2-5
Focus: Health and fitness
Contents: Fiction and nonfiction stories, poems
Other: Unsolicited manuscripts accepted

U*S* KIDS
Children's Better Health Institute
1100 Waterway Blvd., Box 567, Indianapolis, IN 46206
317-636-8881, Fax: 317-684-8094
Ed: Steve Charles

8/yr; $20.95; illus; 225,000 circ
Audience: 1-5
Focus: Children's health and fitness
Contents: Features & news on children & media
Other: Indexed in CMG

WEEKLY BIBLE READER
Standard Publishing Company
8121 Hamilton Ave., Cincinnati, OH 45231
513-931-4050; Fax: 513-931-0904
Ed: Ruth Davis

52/yr; $9.99; illus; sample; 104,000 circ
Audience: 1-2
Focus: Christian weekly for children-
Contents: Features for & by children
Other: No unsolicited materials

WEEKLY READER
Weekly Reader Corporation
3001 Cindel Dr., Delran, NJ 08370
800-466-3355; Fax: 609-786-3360
Eds: Wanda Haan (Pre-K); Anne Guignon (K); Sue LaBella (1); Linda Starr (2); Rick Larios (3-4); Linda Carlson Johnson (5-6)

Pre-K: 28/yr, $4.65; K: 28/yr, $3.15; 1: 26/yr, $3.15; 2: 26/yr, $3.15; 3: 26/yr, $3.35; 4: 26/yr, $3.40; 5: 26/yr, $3.60; 6: 26/yr, $3.95 - All subscriptions 5 or more
Audience: Pre-K-6 (eight separate editions)
Focus: High-interest readings on current events
Contents: Features for children
Reviews: Reviews of children's books
Other: No unsolicited materials. Back issues available

WILDLIFE CONSERVATION
(formerly Animal Kingdom)
New York Zoological Society
Zoological Park, Bronx, NY 10460
718-220-5121; Fax: 718-584-2625
Ed: Joan Downs

6/yr; $10.95; illus; adv; 137,000 circ
Audience: 7-12, teachers, librarians, parents, general
Focus: Reports on the ecology, be-

havior & presentation of wildlife around the world
Contents: Features on wildlife
Other: Accepts unsolicited materials. Back issues available. Annual index in December. Indexed in Biology Digest. Available on microfiche

WITH
Faith & Life Press
Box 347, Newton, KS 67114
316-283-5100
Eds: Eddy Hall, Carol Duerkson

8/yr; $16.95; illus; adv
Audience: 9-12
Focus: Produced for teenagers within the Anabaptist-Mennonite congregation to help them to understand the complex issues & forces that impact them directly and indirectly & to make choices that reflect Anabaptist-Mennonite understanding of living by the spirit of Christ
Contents: Features for & by teenagers
Reviews: 11/yr, reviews of children's books & audiovisual materials, music
Other: Accepts unsolicited materials. Back issues & reprints available. Annual index in December

WONDER TIME
Nazarene Publishing House
Word Action, 6401 Paseo, Kansas City, MO 64131
816-333-7000
Ed: Evelyn J. Beals

52/yr; $6.75; 37,000 circ
Audience: K-2
Focus: Stories designed to connect Sunday School lessons with daily experiences
Contents: Features for children
Other: Accepts unsolicited materials with SASE. Back issues available

WORLD NEWS MAP OF THE WEEK
Weekly Reader Corporation
3001 Cindel Dr., Delran, NJ 08370
800-446-3355; Fax: 609-786-3360
Ed: Alan Lenhoff

27/yr; $79.95; illus; adv
Audience: 6-12
Focus: To give a timely presentation of world-wide issues & events
Contents: Each issue centers on one country with large map, activities and articles
Other: Accepts unsolicited materials. Back issues available

WRITING!
Weekly Reader Corporation
3001 Cindel Dr., Delran, NJ 08370
800-446-3355; Fax: 609-786-3360
Ed: Alan Lenhoff

9/yr; $7.95 (15 or more); $15.50 (2-14); $26.95 (single)
Audience: 7-12
Focus: To encourage junior & senior high school students to write effectively
Contents: Features by children
Other: Accepts unsolicited materials. Back issues available

YABA FRAMEWORK
(formerly YABA World)
Young American Bowling Alliance
5301 S. 76th St., Greendale, WI 53129
414-421-4700; Fax: 414-421-5301
Ed: Laura Plizka

6/yr Nov-Apr; free; illus; adv; 25,000 circ
Audience: K-12
Focus: To educate, inform & entertain young bowlers
Contents: Features for children
Other: No unsolicited materials. Back issues available. Indexed in Sportsearch

YOUNG RIDER
Hunters Hill Press
Box 725, Williamsburg, VA 23187-0725

804-229-6294
Ed: Lesley Ward

6/yr; $12; illus, adv
Audience: 2-10, parents
Focus: To educate, inform & entertain young riders in English equitation & horse care
Contents: Features for children
Reviews: Occasionally
Other: Accepts unsolicited materials. Back issues available

YOUR BIG BACKYARD
National Wildlife Federation
8925 Leesburg Pike, Vienna, VA 22184
703-790-4000, 800-432-6564

12/yr; $12; illus
Audience: 3-5
Focus: To teach young children about the natural world
Contents: Stories & learning games; a parent/teacher guide is included

ZILLIONS
(formerly Penny Power)
Consumers Union
101 Truman Ave., Yonkers, NY 10763-1057

914-378-2000
Ed: Charlotte Baecher

6/yr; $15.95; illus; sample; 135,000 circ
Audience: 2-7, teachers, librarians
Focus: Consumer product ratings & other information about goods & services used by children
Contents: Features for & by children
Reviews: 10-20/yr, reviews of children's books & audiovisual materials, reviews of computer software
Other: Back issues available. Indexed in CMG, CBRI, JHMA, RGPL, SICM. Available in microform

ZOOBOOKS
9820 Willow Creek Rd., Ste. 300, San Diego, CA 92131
800-992-5034

10/yr; $16.95; illus
Audience: 5-14
Focus: To provide a zoological resource
Contents: Each issue features one animal with detailed information, photographs & poster

This section lists journals for parents, teachers, child psychologists, librarians, and others who care for or work with children.

AV GUIDE: THE LEARNING MEDIA NEWSLETTER
Scranton Gillette Communications Inc.
380 E. Northwest Hwy., Des Plaines, IL 60016-2282
708-298-6622; Fax: 708-390-0408
Ed: Natalie Ferguson

12/yr, $15, illus, adv, sample, 600 circ
Audience: Teachers, librarians
Focus: Practical information on effective ways to use audiovisual media in the classroom
Contents: Features & news on children & media
Other: Accepts unsolicited materials. Back issues available. Index: Educ. Index

AVC PRESENTATIONS DEVELOPMENT & DELIVERY
(formerly Audio-Visual Communications)
P T N Publishing Corp.
445 Hollow Rd., Ste. 21, Melville, NY 11747-4722
516-845-2700; Fax: 516-845-7109
Ed: Mike McEhany

12/yr; $60; illus; adv; charts; 40,000 circ
Audience: Teachers, librarians, business & industry, government, education
Focus: New technologies in communication
Reviews: Reviews of audiovisual equipment, technical books, films
Other: Accepts unsolicited materials. Back issues & reprints available. Indexed in BPI, Graph. Arts, Lit. Abstr.

ACCESS
American Forum for Global Education
45 John St., Ste. 908, New York, NY 10038
212-732-8606
Ed: Elizabeth Valand

8/yr; $30; adv
Audience: Teachers, librarians, general

Focus: Newsletter for those interested in global education
Reviews: 70-100/yr, reviews of children's books & audiovisual materials
Other: Accepts unsolicited materials. Back issues available

THE ALAN REVIEW
National Council of Teachers of English
Radford University, Radford, VA 24142
703-831-5439, 217-328-3870
Subscrip: 1111 Kenyon Rd., Urbana, IL 61801
Ed & Media Review Ed: Robert Small

3/yr; $15; illus; adv; 23,000
Audience: Teachers, librarians, university faculty
Focus: To review and comment upon literature for young adults
Contents: Features & news on children & media
Reviews: 100/yr, reviews of children's books; 20/yr, reviews of children's audiovisual materials
Other: Accepts unsolicited materials. Indexed in CIJE

AMERICAN EDUCATOR
American Federation of Teachers
555 New Jersey Ave., NW, Washington, DC 20001
202-879-4420
Ed: Elizabeth McPike

4/yr; $8; illus; adv; sample; 700,000 circ
Audience: Teachers, administrators
Focus: To keep members informed on current topics in American education
Contents: Features & news on children & media
Reviews: 2/yr, books
Other: Accepts unsolicited materials. Back issues & reprints available

AMERICAN MUSIC TEACHER
Music Teacher's National Assn., Inc.
617 Vine St., Ste. 1432, Cincinnati, OH 45202-2434

513-421-1420
Ed: Julie Wesling Whaley

6/yr; $16 non-members; illus; adv; sample; 27,000 circ
Audience: Teachers
Focus: Information for professional music teachers in studios, private & public schools, conservatories & institutions of higher learning; covers esthetics, American music, biographies, chamber music, composition, criticism, musicology, performance, the business aspects of teaching & original research
Reviews: 150/yr, professional books
Other: Accepts unsolicited materials. Back issues available. Annual index in June/July. Available in microform & microfiche. Indexed in Bk. Rev. Index, Child. Bk. Rev. Ind., Educ. Ind., Music Artic. Guide, Music Ind.

AMERICAN SCHOOL BOARD JOURNAL
National School Boards Assn.
1680 Duke St., Alexandria, VA 22314
703-838-6722; Fax: 703-683-7590
Ed: Gregg W. Downey

12/yr; $48; illus; adv; sample; 40,000 circ
Audience: School board members
Focus: Practical articles on administrative aspects of elementary & secondary schools
Reviews: 12/yr, reviews of audiovisual equipment, reviews of computer software, professional books
Other: Accepts unsolicited materials. Back issues & reprints available. Annual index in April. Available on microform

AMERICAN TEACHER
American Federation of Teachers
555 New Jersey Ave., NW, Washington DC 20001
202-879-4431
Ed: Trish Gorman

8/yr; $10; illus; sample; 700,000 circ

Audience: Teachers, librarians, other school employees
Focus: Membership publication of the American Federation of Teachers
Contents: News about children and media
Reviews: 10-15/yr, reviews of children's books & audiovisual materials
Other: Accepts unsolicited materials. Back issues available

APPLE EDUCATION NEWS
Apple Computer, Inc.
10381 Bandley Dr., Cupertino, CA 95014
408-974-2552
Ed: Lori Deuchar

3/yr; free; 100,000 circ
Audience: Teachers, administrators, trainers
Contents: Features on children and media
Reviews: 8/yr, reviews of computer software
Other: Accepts unsolicited materials. Back issues available

ART EDUCATION
National Art Education Association
1916 Association Dr., Reston, VA
703-860-8000
Ed: Ronald MacGregor

6/yr; $50; illus; adv; 14,000 circ
Audience: Art teachers
Focus: Trends, problems, needs in visual art education at all levels
Contents: Features & news on children & media
Reviews: 1-3/yr, books
Other: Accepts unsolicited materials. Back issues & reprints available. Indexed in Art Index, CIJE, Cont. Pg. Educ., Educ. Ind. Available on microform

ARTS & ACTIVITIES
Publishers' Development Corp.
591 Camino de la Reina, Ste. 200, San Diego, CA 92108
619-297-8520; Fax: 619-297-5353
Ed: Leven C. Leatherbury

9/yr, $20, illus, adv, 22,000 circ
Audience: Teachers, librarians, parents
Focus: Visual & performing arts, classroom information & projects
Contents: Features & news on children & media, features by children
Reviews: 45-50/yr, reviews of children's books & audiovisual materials, reviews of audiovisual equipment
Other: Accepts unsolicited materials. Back issues available. Indexed in MRI, RGPL, Educ. Ind., Inc. Child. Mag. Available on microform

ARTS EDUCATION POLICY REVIEW
(formerly Design For Arts in Education)
Heldref Publications
1319 Eighteenth St., NW, Washington, DC 20036-1802
202-296-6267; Fax: 202-296-5149
Ed: Sheila Barrows

6/yr; $54 instit; $31 individ; 2,400 circ
Audience: Teachers, librarians, administrators
Focus: Major policy issues concerning K-12 education in all the arts
Reviews: Book
Other: Accepts unsolicited materials. Back issues & reprints available. Annual index in July/August. Indexed in Art Ind., Bk. Rev. Ind. Available on microform

BOOK LINKS
50 E. Huron St., Chicago, IL 60611
800-545-2433, ext. 5718
Ed: Barbara Elleman

6/yr; $20; illus; adv
Audience: Teachers, librarians
Focus: Using books in the classroom
Contents: Bibliographies, reviews & essays

CBC FEATURES
Children's Book Council, Inc.
568 Broadway, New York, NY 10012-3225
212-966-1990
Ed: Maria Juarez

2/yr; $45; 40,000 circ
Audience: Teachers, librarians, parents, authors & illustrators
Focus: Information about publishers, trends, people, places & inexpensive materials available. Indexed in Child. Lit. Abstr.

THE CATALYST
Western Center for Microcomputers in Special Education, Inc.
1259 El Camino Real, Ste. 275, Menlo Park, CA 94025
415-326-6997, 415-855-8064
Ed: Sue Swezey

4/yr; $10 individ, $15 organization, $20 foreign, sample
Audience: Teachers, librarians, parents, professions in special ed & rehabilitation
Focus: Covers the uses of microcomputer technology in special education and rehabilitation
Contents: Features & news on children & the latest technology and the people who use it
Reviews: 4-8/yr, reviews of computer software and hardware
Other: Accepts unsolicited materials. Back issues & reprints available. Index available on request

CD•ROM WORLD
11 Ferry Lane West, Westport, CT 06880
203-226-6967; Fax: 203-454-5840
Ed: Todd Harris

11/yr; $29 individ, $87 organization, add $18 foreign; illus; adv
Audience: Professionals
Focus: CD-ROM users
Contents: CD-ROM related topics
Reviews: CD-ROM hardware & software, books
Other: Accepts unsolicited materials

CHILDHOOD EDUCATION
Association for Childhood Education International
11501 Georgia Ave., Ste. 312, Wheaton, MD 20902
301-942-2443
Ed: Lucy Prete Martin

5/yr; $45; illus; adv; sample; charts; 11,700 circ
Audience: Teachers, librarians, parents, teacher educators, administrators
Focus: To inform & support teachers & others who live & work with children
Contents: Features & news on children & media
Reviews: 200/yr, reviews of children's books & audiovisual materials, reviews of computer software, films, professional books
Other: Accepts unsolicited materials. Back issues available. Annual index in April/May. Available on microform

CHILDREN & ANIMALS
The Humane Society of the United States
Box 362, East Haddam, CT 06423
203-434-8666
Ed: Paul Dewey
Guest Review Eds: Teachers from throughout the country

4/yr, $10, illus
Audience: 2-6, teachers
Focus: Help teachers incorporate the teaching of respect for life into all areas of the curriculum
Contents: Features & news on children & media, features for & by children
Reviews: 4-30/yr, reviews of children's books & audiovisual materials, reviews of computer software
Other: Accepts unsolicited materials. Back issues & reprints available

CHILDREN'S HOUSE - CHILDREN'S WORLD
Children's House, Inc.
Box 111, Caldwell, NJ 07006
201-239-3442
Ed: Kenneth Edelson

6/yr; $10.50; illus; adv; sample; charts; 50,000 circ
Audience: Teachers, librarians, parents, children's health care professionals, learning disability therapists
Focus: Information medium for all concerned with the education & development of children, ages 3-16
Contents: Features & news on children & media. Spring children's media annual
Reviews: 360-480/yr, reviews of children's books & audiovisual equipment, reviews of computer software, plays, professional books on child development
Other: Accepts unsolicited materials. Indexed in CBRI, CLA, MRI, Exceptional Children Excerpts & Abstracts. Available on microfilm

CHILDREN'S LITERATURE
Yale University Press
302 Temple St., Box 92A, Yale Sta., New Haven, CT 06520
203-432-0940
Eds: Francelia Butler

Annual; varies; illus; 2,700 circ
Audience: Teachers, librarians, university scholars
Focus: A scholarly periodical devoted to studies of children's literature
Contents: Features on children and media
Reviews: 25/yr, reviews of children's books
Other: Accepts unsolicited materials. Back issues available. Index in every fifth issue. Indexed in Book Review Index

CHILDREN'S LITERATURE IN EDUCATION
Human Sciences Press, Inc.
233 Spring St, New York, NY 10013-1578
212-620-8000; Fax: 212-463-0742
Subscrip: Fulfillment Dept., 49 Sheridan Ave., Albany, NY 12210
US/Can Ed: Anita Moss, Geoff Fox

4/yr; $25 (K-12 schools); illus; adv; 2,500 circ
Audience: Teachers, librarians, editors & authors of children's literature
Focus: The use of children's literature by educators
Contents: Interviews with noted children's authors, literary criticism of both classic & contemporary writing for children, articles about successful classroom reading projects
Reviews: 2/yr, reviews of children's books
Other: Accepts unsolicited materials. Back issues available. Annual index in December. Indexed in CIJE, Child. Bk. Rev. Ind., Educ. Ind.

COMPUTER LITERATURE INDEX
Applied Computer Research, Inc.
Box 82260, Phoenix, AZ 85071-2260
800-234-2227
Ed: Philip C. Howard

4/yr; $195
Audience: Librarians, computer professionals
Focus: Index to about 300 periodicals & all major computer books published each year. Available on microfich

COMPUTERS & PEOPLE
Berkeley Enterprises
815 Washington St., Newtonville, MA 02160
617-332-5453
Ed: Judith P. Callahan

6/yr; $24.50; illus; sample; charts; 2,800 circ
Audience: Teachers, librarians
Focus: Non-technical evaluation of the social & industrial impact of computers & data processing information systems; occasional reprints of chapters from professional books; publishes an annual Computer Directory & Buyer's Guide
Other: Accepts unsolicited materials. Back issues & reprints available. Annual index in Jan/Feb or Mar/Apr. Indexed in Chem. Abstr, Curr. Cont.

COMPUTING TEACHER
International Society for Technology in Education
Univ. of Oregon, 1787 Agate St., Eugene, OR 97403-1923
503-346-4414; Fax: 503-346-5890
Ed: Anita Best

9/yr; $46 members; $52 nonmembers; illus; adv; charts; 12,000 circ
Audience: Teachers, librarians, parents, computer coordinators
Focus: To promote use of computers in education
Contents: Features on children and media, features by children
Reviews: 12-36/yr, reviews of computer software
Other: Accepts unsolicited materials. Back issues available. Indexed in CIJE, Educ. Teach. Abstr., ERIC

THE CREATIVE CHILD & ADULT QUARTERLY
The National Association for Creative Children & Adults
8080 Springvalley Dr., Cincinnati, OH 45236-1395
513-631-1777
Ed: Ann Fabe Isaacs

4/yr; $55; illus; adv; charts; 6,000 circ
Audience: Teachers, librarians, general
Focus: "Dedicated to helping us become the best we can through understanding & applying research on creativity."Contents: Features on lives & works of creative children & adults plus projects to promote creativity for the average child & adult
Reviews: Reviews of children's books & audiovisual materials, reviews of computer software
Other: Accepts unsolicited materials. Back issues & reprints available. Annual index in Winter. Indexed on CIJE, Educ. Ind., Psycholo. Abstr. Availalbe on microform

CREATIVE KIDS
Prufrock Press
Box 8813, Waco, TX 76714-8813
(817) 756-3337
Editor: Stephanie Stout

4/yr; $19.95; illus; 45,000 circ
Audience: Grades 3-8, teachers, librarians, parents
Focus: Designed to entertain, stimulate, and challenge the creativity of children ages 8-14, encouraging their abilities and helping them to explore their ideas, opinions and world.
Contents: Features by and for children, puzzles, games, stories, poems, pen pals, and activities.
Reviews: 8/yr., reviews (by children) of children's books and educational games

DAY CARE & EARLY EDUCATION
Human Sciences Press, Inc. (Sub. of Plenum Pub. Corp.)
233 Spring St., New York, NY 10013-1578
212-620-8000; Fax: 212-463-0742
Ed: Randa Roen Nachbar

4/yr; $105; illus; adv; 5,000 circ
Audience: Teachers, librarians, administrators, day-care personnel
Focus: To provide professional guidance on instructional methods & materials & to cover current trends in day-care & early education
Contents: Features & news on children & media
Reviews: 80/yr, reviews of children's books & audiovisual materials, reviews of audiovisual equipment, reviews of computer software
Other: Accepts unsolicited materials. Back issues & reprints available. Indexed in CIJE, Cont. Pg. Educ., Educ. Ind., Except. Child. Abstr. Available on microform

DIMENSIONS OF EARLY CHILDHOOD
Southern Early Children Association
Box 5403, Little Rock, AR 72215-5403

501-663-2114
Ed: Kay C. Powers

4/yr; $15; adv; 18,000 circ
Audience: Teachers
Focus: To provide curriculum ideas, based on theory & research, for teachers & caregivers of children under six
Reviews: 75/yr, reviews of children's books & audiovisual materials, reviews of computer software, new products, professional books
Other: No unsolicited materials. Back issues & reprints available. Annual index in October

ETV NEWSLETTER
Box 597, Ridgefield, CT 06877
203-454-2618; Fax: 203-458-2618
Publisher: Charles Tepfer

26/yr; $185; sample; charts
Audience: Teachers, public TV & instructional TV professionals
Focus: News on funding, technology, programs, & general items on educational & instructional TV & video, including home video. Occasional in-depth pieces on ITV
Reviews: 26/yr, reviews of children's audiovisual materials, videocassettes
Other: No unsolicited materials. Back issues & reprints available. Annual index in February

EDUCATION
Project Innovation
1362 Santa Cruz Ct., Chula Vista, CA 91910
619-421-9377
Ed: Russell N. Cassel

4/yr; $20 indiv; $26 instit
Audience: Teachers, librarians, parents, general
Focus: To publish worthwhile theory & research related to learning & education
Contents: Features for children
Other: Accepts unsolicited materials. Back issues & reprints available. Annual index in spring. Indexed in RGPL, Education Index

EDUCATION DIGEST
Prakken Publications
Box 8623, Ann Arbor, MI 48107
313-769-1211; Fax: 313-769-8383
Ed: Kenneth C. Schroeder

9/yr; $36; adv; sample; 26,000 circ
Audience: Teachers, librarians & school administrators, particularly superintendents & principals of elementary & secondary schools
Focus: To provide educators with condensed articles, speeches & reports, selected from all published journals

Contents: Condensed features, news briefs on education
Reviews: 50/yr, reviews of children's books & audiovisual materials, reviews of computer software, professional books & materials. Also publishes lists of materials
Other: No unsolicited materials. Some back issues & reprints available. Annual index in May. Indexed in Education Index, Except. Child. Available on CD-ROM

EDUCATION LEADERSHIP
Assn. for Supervision & Curriculum Development
1250 N. Pitt St., Alexandria, VA 22314
703-549-9110
Ed: Dr. Ronald Brandt
Exec Mgr Ed: Marge Scherer

8/yr; $32 to nonmembers, illus, adv, sample, 150,000 circ
Audience: Teachers, supervisors, curriculum administrators, educators
Focus: To provide materials for the professional development of educators involved with supervision & curriculum development
Reviews: 12/yr, book reviews
Other: Accepts unsolicited materials. Back issues & reprints available.

EDUCATION TECHNOLOGY
(formerly Education Computer News)
Business Publishers Inc.
951 Pershing Dr., Silver Spring, MD 20910
301-587-6300
Ed: David Ritchie

26/yr, $194.72
Audience: Teachers, software & hardware producers
Focus: Newsletter covering classroom computer use at all levels, emphasis on secondary schools, includes trends, products, legislation, applications & research in educational technology
Reviews: 5/yr, reviews of computer software
Other: No unsolicited materials. Back issues available

EDUCATIONAL TECHNOLOGY
Educational Technology Publications, Inc.
720 Palisade Ave., Englewood Cliffs, NJ 07632
201-871-4007; Fax: 201-871-4009
Ed: Laurence Lipsitz

12/yr; $119; illus; adv; sample; 5,000 circ
Audience: Teachers, librarians
Focus: Information about educational technology
Contents: Features & news on children & media

Reviews: 100/yr, reviews of children's audiovisual materials, reviews of audiovisual equipment, reviews of computer software, films
Other: Accepts unsolicited materials. Back issues & reprints available. Annual index in December. Indexed in MRI, Education Index, CIJE, Except. Child, Educ. Abstr. Available on microfilm

THE ELEMENTARY SCHOOL JOURNAL
Center for Research in Social Behavior
Univ of Chicago Press Journals Division, 5720 S. Woodlawn Ave., Chicago, IL 60637
312-753-3347; Fax: 312-753-0811
Subscrip: Box 37005, Chicago, IL 60637
Ed: Thomas L. Good

5/yr; $28.50 indiv; $52 instit; illus; adv; sample; 6,000 circ
Audience: Teachers, school administrators, educational researchers, teacher educators
Focus: To report on the implications of research & theory for teaching practice in elementary schools
Contents: Original studies, reviews of research, conceptual analysis
Other: Back issues available. Annual index in May. Indexed in Education Index, Educational Administration Abstracts, Language & Language Behavior Abstracts, Sociology of Education Abstracts, Current Contents - Social & Behavioral Sciences. Indexed in CIJE. Available on microform

ENGLISH JOURNAL
National Council of Teachers of English
111 W. Kenyon Rd., Urbana, IL 61801-1096
217-328-3870; Fax: 217-328-9645
Ed: Ben Nelms

8/yr; $50 instit; $40 individ; illus; adv; 57,500 circ
Audience: Teachers, librarians, consultants, counselors
Focus: Topics of interest to teachers of English, grades 7-12
Contents: Features & news on children & media
Reviews: 80-100/yr, reviews of children's books & audiovisual materials, reviews of computer software, books, poetry, short stories
Other: Accepts unsolicited materials. Back issues & reprints available. Annual index in December. Indexed in CIJE, Excep. Child. Educ. Abstr., Jun. High Mag. Abstr.

EQUITY & EXCELLENCE IN EDUCATION
Greenwood Press, Inc., 88 Post Rd. W, Westport, CT 06881

203-226-3571; Fax: 203-222-1502
Ed: Byrd Jones

3/yr; $60; illus; sample; 3,000 circ
Audience: Teachers, librarians, coun-
  selors, administrators
Focus: The effects of race, ethnicity,
  gender, social class, court decisions,
  & related social & psychological fac-
  tors & processes on education
Contents: Features & news on children
  & media
Reviews: Professional books
Other Accepts unsolicited materials.
  Back issues available. Indexed in
  EdI, CIJE, Ed Admin Ab

THE EXCEPTIONAL PARENT
Psy-Ed Corporation
1170 Commonwealth Ave., Boston, MA
  02134-4646
617-730-5800; Fax: 617-730-8742
Subscrip: Dept. E P, Box 3000, Denville, NJ 07834
800-561-1973
Ed: Stanley D. Klein

8/yr; $18 indiv; $24 instit; illus; adv;
  7,000 controlled circ; 42,000 paid
  circ
Audience: Teachers, parents, professionals
Focus: To provide practical guidance
  for parents & professionals concerned with children with disabilities
Contents: Features & news on children
  & media, features for children
Reviews: 8/yr, reviews of children's
  books reviews of computer software.
  Indexed on CIJE, Educ. Ind., Except.
  Child., Educ. Ind. Available on
  microfilm

EXECUTIVE EDUCATOR
National School Boards Assn.
1680 Duke St., Alexandria, VA 22314
703-838-6722; Fax: 703-683-7590
Ed: Gregg W. Downey

12/yr; $53; illus; adv; sample; 18,000
  circ
Audience: School superintendents,
  principals
Focus: Practical articles on administrative aspects of elementary & secondary schools
Reviews: Reviews of audiovisual equipment, reviews of computer
  software
Other: Accepts unsolicited materials.
  Back issues & reprints available. Indexed in CIJE. Available on
  microfiche

GPN NEWSLETTER
Great Plains National Instructional TV
  Library
Box 80669, Lincoln, NE 68501-0669
402-472-2007, 800-228-4630
Ed: Richard L. Spence

4/yr, free, sample, controlled circ
Audience: Teachers, librarians
Focus: To provide information about
  new audiovisual instructional aids
  distributed by GPN
Reviews: Reprints reviews from other
  periodicals
Other: No unsolicited materials. Back
  issues & reprints available

GIFTED CHILD QUARTERLY
National Association for Gifted Children
1155 Fifthteen St., NW, Ste. 1002,
  Washington, DC 20005-2706
202-785-4268
Ed: John Feldhusen

4/yr; $45; 6,500 controlled circ
Audience: Teachers, librarians, par-
  ents, members
Focus: Educational & psychological
  aspects of nurturing gifted children
Contents: Features on children and
  media
Reviews: Reviews of children's books,
  reviews of computer software,
  educational practices
Other: Accepts unsolicited materials.
  Back issues available. Indexed in
  CIJE, Educ. Ind., Except. Child. Educ.
  Abstr. Available on microfilm

GIFTED CHILD TODAY
Prufrock Press
Box 8813, Waco, TX 76714-8813
817-756-3337; Fax: 817-756-3339
Ed: Stephanie Stout

6/yr; $29.95; illus; adv; 15,000 circ
Audience: Teachers, librarians, parents, teacher trainers, gifted coordinators
Focus: Practical advice and information for parents and teachers of gifted children
Contents: Articles on the latest trends
  in gifted education and information
  on meeting the social and emotional
  needs of gifted students
Reviews: 25-30/yr, reviews of children's books & audiovisual materials, computer software, activity
  books & texts
Other: Accepts unsolicited materials.
  Indexed in Exceptional Child Education Resource, Gifted Education
  Review, ERIC

HOME EDUCATION MAGAZINE
Home Education Press, Box 1083,
  Tonasket, WA 98855
509-486-1351
Eds: Mark J. Hegener, Helen E.
  Hegener

12/yr; $24; illus; adv; 5,200 circ
Audience: Teachers, parents,
  general
Focus: To help families schooling children at home

Contents: Features & news on children
  & media, features for children
Reviews: 48/yr, reviews of children's
  books & audiovisual equipment,
  reviews of computer software
Other: Accepts unsolicited materials.
  Back issues & reprints available

HOME OFFICE COMPUTING
(formerly Family Computing)
Scholastic, Inc.
730 Broadway, New York, NY 10003
212-505-3000; 212-505-4223
Ed: Claudia Cohl

12/yr, $19.97, 435,000 controlled circ
Audience: 4-12, teachers, parents,
  general
Focus: Family oriented ideas for using
  the computer for learning & fun
Reviews: Reviews of computer
  software
Other: No unsolicited materials. Back
  issues & reprints available

INDEPENDENT SCHOOL
National Association of Independent
  Schools
75 Federal St., Boston, MA
  02110-1904
617-451-2444
Ed: Blair McElroy

3/yr; $17.50; adv; 7,000 circ
Audience: Teachers, librarians, parents, school administrators
Focus: To exchange information &
  opinion about secondary & elementary education, especially in independent schools
Contents: Features & news on children
  & media, articles on teaching
  methods & innovations, school
  management
Reviews: Books of interest to teachers,
  administrators, librarians, business
  managers
Other: Accepts unsolicited materials.
  Reprints available from University
  Microfilms. Annual index in May. Indexed in CIJE, Educ. Ind., Media Rev.
  Dig. Available on microfilm

INSTRUCTOR
Scholastic Inc.
730 Broadway, New York, NY 10003
212-505-3000
Subscrip: 1 E. First St., Duluth MN
  55802
Ed: Deborah Martorell

9/yr; $14.95; illus; adv; sample;
  254,361 circ
Audience: Teachers, librarians, principals
Focus: A use magazine for elementary
  teachers
Reviews: 500/yr, reviews of children's
  books & audiovisual materials,
  professional books, film & filmstrips
  for teachers

Other: Indexed in CIJE, Child. Bk. Rev. Ind., Educ. Ind., Excep. Child. Ed. Ind., Jun. High Mag. Abstr. Available on microform

INTERFACE: THE COMPUTER EDUCATION QUARTERLY

Mitchell Publishing, Inc.
55 Penny Lane, Ste. 103, Watsonville, CA 95076
408-724-0195
Eds: Erika Berg, John Ambrose

4/yr; $26 instit; $14 indiv; illus; adv; sample; charts; 2,000 circ
Audience: Teachers, computer department heads
Focus: Articles by & for people in the educational computer field
Reviews: 40-50/yr, reviews of computer software, technical books
Other: Accepts unsolicited materials. Back uses & reprints available

INTERRACIAL BOOKS FOR CHILDREN BULLETIN

Council on Interracial Books for Children
1841 Broadway, New York, NY 10023-7648
212-757-5339

8/yr; $16 indiv; $24 instit; 7,500 circ
Audience: Adults
Focus: Organ of the Council to stimulate awareness of the subtleties of racism & sexism in children's learning materials
Contents: Guidelines & criteria, sources of alternative teaching materials, analysis of textbooks, reviews of recent children's trade & supplemental text books
Services: Back issues, $2.95 single issue, $3.95 double issue. Indexed in Alt. Press Ind., Bk. Rev. Ind., Child. Bk. Rev., Educ. Ind., Lib. Lit. Available on microfilm

JOURNAL OF COMPUTERS IN MATHEMATICS & SCIENCE TEACHING

Assoc. for the Advancement of Computing in Education
Box 2966, Charlottesville, VA 22902-2966
804-973-3987
Ed: Dan Shepardson

4/yr; $65; illus; adv; sample; 3,500 circ
Audience: Teachers, librarians
Focus: Presents comprehensive practical & theoretical information to help teach math & science with computers at all levels
Contents: Features & news on children & media
Reviews: 30/yr, reviews of children's books, reviews of computer software

Other: Accepts unsolicited materials. Back issues available. Annual index in Summer. Indexed in CIJE, Educ. Ind., ERIC. Available on microfiche

JOURNAL OF EDUCATIONAL TECHNOLOGY SYSTEMS

Society for Applied Learning Technology
Baywood Publishing, Inc., 26 Austin Ave., Box 337, Amityville, NY 11701
516-691-1270; Fax: 516-691-1770
Eds: Thomas T. Liao, David C. Miller

4/yr; $107; illus; charts; 1,000 circ
Audience: Teachers, academic researchers, graduate students
Focus: Scholarly journal to help educators make optimum use of computer & related advanced technologies
Reviews: 2-3/yr, reviews of computer software, technical books
Other: Accepts unsolicited materials. Back issues & reprints available. Annual index in June. Indexed in CIJE, Computer Literature Index, Information Science Abstracts, Telscan

JOURNAL OF READING

International Reading Assn.
800 Barksdale Rd., Box 8139, Newark, DE 19714-8139
302-731-1600; Fax: 302-731-1057
Ed: Janet Ramage Binkley

8/yr; $38; illus; adv; 20,000 circ
Audience: Teachers, librarians
Focus: Professional journal for reading & English teachers in junior & senior high schools
Reviews: 50-100/yr, reviews of children's books, reviews of computer software, reviews of teachers' professional books
Other: Accepts unsolicited materials. Back issues & reprints available. Annual index in May. Indexed in CIJE, Excep. Child. Ed. Abstr., Educ. Ind. Available on microform

JOURNAL OF READING BEHAVIOR

National Reading Conference Inc.
11 E. Hubbard, Ste. 200, Chicago, IL 60611
312-329-2512
Ed: John Readence

4/yr; $45; 2,000 circ
Audience: Reading researchers, literacy researchers
Focus: Original studies, conceptual analyses & reviews of research in reading diagnosis & instruction in the classroom & clinic, the cognitive processes of reading, the development of literacy, & the materials & patterns of written communication
Reviews: 8-12/yr, scholarly works
Other: Accepts unsolicited materials. Back issues available. Indexed in

CIJE, EdI, SSCI, Psychological Abstracts, ERIC. Available on microform

JOURNAL OF SECONDARY GIFTED EDUCATION

Prufrock Press
Box 8813, Waco, TX 76714-8813
817-756-3337; Fax: 817-756-3339
Ed: Stephanie Stout

4/yr; $35; tables; graphs; 7,000 circ
Audience: Counselors, researchers, teachers
Focus: Secondary gifted educators
Contents: Empirical research on critical theory in the field of educating secondary gifted students

JOURNAL OF VISUAL IMPAIRMENT & BLINDNESS

American Foundation for the Blind
15 W. 16th St., New York, NY 10011
Fax: 212-620-2105
Ed-in-Chief: Mary Ellen Mulholland

10/yr; $60; illus; adv; 3,500 circ
Audience: Teachers, agency administrators, rehabilitation professionals
Focus: Information for practitioners & researchers who work with visually impaired & blind children & adults; special sections for consumers: available in braille, print & cassette
Contents: News & features on technology for visually impaired & early childhood intervention
Reviews: 8/yr, reviews of children's books & audiovisual equipment, CCTV for visually impaired, reviews of computer software, large print books, cassettes
Other: Accepts unsolicited materials. Back issues & reprints available. Separate annual index in March. Indexed in University Microfiche

JOURNAL OF YOUTH SERVICES IN LIBRARIES

Assn. for Library Service to Children & Young Adult Library Services Association, American Library Association
50 E. Huron St, Chicago, IL 60611-2795
312-944-6780, 800-545-2433; Fax: 312-440-7374
Eds: Donald Kenney (Virginia Tech, Blacksburg, VA), Linda J. Wilson (Radford University, Radford, VA)

4/yr; $40; illus; adv; 9,500 circ
Audience: Teachers, librarians
Focus: Continuing education for librarians working with children & young adults
Contents: Features & news on children & media
Reviews: 40/yr, professional books for teachers & librarians
Other: Accepts unsolicitied materials. Back issues & reprints available. An-

nual index in Fall. Indexed in LL. Library & Information Sciences Abstracts, Book Rev. Ind., CIJE

JUMP CUT (A Review of Contemporary Media)
Jump Cut Associates
Box 865, Berkeley, CA 94701
510-658-4482
Eds: John Hess, Chuck Kleinhaus, Julia Lesage

1-2/yr; $20/4 issues; illus; adv; 9,500 circ
Audience: Teachers, general, people involved in media studies
Focus: political impact of film & electronic media
Reviews: 20/yr, films, books on film & media
Other: Accepts unsolicited materials. Back issues available

LANGUAGE ARTS
National Council of teachers of English
1111 Kenyon Rd., Urbana, IL 61801-1096
217-328-3870; Fax: 217-328-9645
Ed: William Teale

8/yr; $40 indiv; $50 instit; illus; adv; 21,000 circ
Audience: Teachers & supervisors of language arts at the elementary level
Focus: To provide theory & practice for helping children grow as listeners, speakers, readers & writers
Contents: Features on children and media, occasional features by children
Reviews: 300/yr reviews of children's books & audiovisual materials, professional books, films
Other: Accepts unsolicited materials. Back issues & reprints available. Indexed CIJE. Available on microform

LEARNING DISABILITY QUARTERLY
Council for Learning Disabilities
Box 40303, Overland Park, KS 66204
913-492-8755
Ed: H. Lee Swanson

4/yr; $50; adv; 5,500 circ
Audience: Teachers
Focus: To provide theoretical & practical information about educating learning disabled individuals, publishes articles, reports on original research & interpretative reviews of professional literature
Reviews: Professional materials
Other: Accepts unsolicited materials. Back issues & reprints available. Annual index in fall. Indexed in CIJE, Excep. Child. Educ. Abstr.

LEARNING MAGAZINE
Springhouse Corp.
1111 Bethlehem Pike, Box 908, Springhouse, PA 19477-0908
215-646-8700
Ed & Assoc Pub: Charlene Gaynor

8/yr; $20; illus; adv; sample; 260,000 circ
Audience: Teachers for levels K-8
Focus: Practical suggestions for activites to involve students in learning
Contents: Featues on children & media
Reviews: Occasional reviews of audiovisual materials, computer software, new children's products
Other: Accepts unsolicited materials. Back issues & reprints available. Index in CIJE, EdI

LOGO EXCHANGE
International Society for Technology in Education
Special Interest group for Logo-Using, 1787 Agate St., Eugene, OR 97403-1923
503-346-4414; Fax: 503-346-5890
Ed: Sharon Yoder

9/yr; $30; illus; adv; 2,000 circ
Audience: Teachers, librarians
Focus: Information in logo software activities worldwide
Contents: Features on children and media
Reviews: 500/yr, reviews of children's books & audiovisual materials, reviews of computer software
Other: Accepts unsolicited materials. Back issues & reprints available. Indexed ERIC. Available on microform

MATHEMATICS TEACHER
National Council of Teachers of Mathematics
1906 Association Dr., Reston, VA 22091
703-620-9840; Fax: 703-476-2970
Ed: Harry B. Tunis

9/yr; $45 member; $50 instit; illus; adv
Audience: Teachers
Focus: To help teachers improve mathematics instruction in junior & senior high schools, two-year colleges, & teacher-education colleges
Reviews: 100/yr, reviews of childen's books, reviews of computer software
Other: Accepts unsolicited materials. Back issues & reprints available. Annual index in December. Indexed in Biog. Ind., CIJE, Educ. Ind. Available on microform

MEDIA & METHODS
American Society for Educators
1429 Walnut St., Philadelphia, PA 19102

215-563-3501; Fax: 215-563-1588
Ed: Michele Sokoloff

6/yr; $29; illus; adv; 42,000 circ
Audience: 4-12, teachers in language arts & media. librarians, media specialists
Focus: The use of media & electronic devices to increase classroom effectiveness
Contents: Resource articles
Reviews: 40/yr, children's & professional books & audiovisual materials. Also lists materials recommended by test centers
Other: Accepts unsolicited materials. Some back issues. Available on microfilm from Xerox University Microfilms. Indexed in Educ. Ind., Media Rev. Digest

MICROCOMPUTER INDEX
Learned Information Inc.
143 Old Marlton Pike, Medford, NJ 08055
609-654-6266; Fax: 609-654-4309
Eds: Lisa Jasper, William Spence

6/yr; $159
Audience: Librarians, general
Focus: Abstracts & index of about 70 microcomputer periodicals; inclduing about 12 oriented to all levels of education
Reviews: Abstracts of software reviews
Other: Back issues available. Separate annual cumulative index in early April

MIDDLE SCHOOL JOURNAL
National Middle School Assn.
4807 Evanswood Dr., Columbus, OH 43229-6292
614-848-8211; Fax: 614-848-4301
Ed: Tom Dickinson

5/yr; $35; illus; adv; charts; 17,000 circ
Audience: Teachers, librarians, parents, principals & asst principals
Focus: To provide information about middle level education & help teachers & principals develop better programs
Contents: Features by children
Reviews: 10/yr, reviews of children's books, professional materials
Other: Accepts unsolicited materials. Back issues available.
Index bi- or triannually in November. Indexed in CIJE. Available on microform

MONTESSORI LIFE
(formerly Constructive Triangle)
17583 Oak St., Fountain Valley, CA 92708
714-968-0107; Fax: 714-964-0800
Ed: Joy Turner

4/yr; $29; illus; adv; sample; 12,000 circ
Audience: Teachers, librarians, parents, school administrators
Focus: Official publication of the AMS, a nonprofit organization to encourage the exchange of ideas about the Montessori method of early childhood education
Contents: Features & news on children & media
Reviews: 3/yr, reviews of children's books & audiovisual materials, reviews of computer software, professional books
Other: Accepts unsolicited materials. Back issues available (contact the American Montessori Society, 150 Fifth Ave., New York, NY 10011; 212-924-3209)

THE NEW ADVOCATE
Christopher-Gordon Publishers, Inc.
480 Washington St., Norwood, MA 02062
617-762-5577
Ed: Dr. Joel Taxel, University of Georgia
Media Review Ed: M. Jean Greenlaw, University of North Texas

4/yr; $45; illus; adv; 7,500 circ
Audience: Teachers, librarians
Focus: To foster more frequent & effective use of children's literature in K-8 classrooms
Contents: Features & news on children & media
Reviews: Reviews of children's books & audiovisual materials, articles on children's writers & illustrators
Other: Accepts unsolicited materials. Reprints available. Indexed in Bk. Rev. Index

NEWMEDIA MAGAZINE
HyperMedia Publications, Inc.
901 Mariner's Island Blvd., Ste. 365, San Mateo, CA 94404
415-573-5170; Fax: 415-573-5131
Ed: David Bunnell

13/yr; $48, free to qualified new media professionals in the U.S.; illus; adv
Audience: Professionals, current and prospective users of multimedia hardware and software
Focus: Multimedia
Contents: Topics related to multimedia
Reviews: Hardware and software

PHI DELTA KAPPAN
PDK, Inc.
Box 789, Bloomington, IN 47402-0789
812-339-1156; Fax: 812-339-0018
Ed: Pauline B. Gough

10/yr; $35; illus; adv; sample; 150,000 circ
Audience: Teachers, teacher trainers, administrators
Focus: Educational research, service & leadership, issues, trends & policy are emphasized
Contents: Features on children and media
Reviews: 15-20/yr, professional books (not textbooks)
Other: Accepts unsolicited materials. Back issues & reprints available. Annual index in June. Indexed in CIJE, EdI, Excep. Child. Educ. Abstr., SSCI

PSYCHOLOGY IN THE SCHOOLS
Clinical Psychology Publishing Company
4 Conant Sq., Brandon, VT 05733
802-247-6871; Fax: 802-247-6853
Ed-in-Chief: Gerald B. Fuller
Children's Book Review Ed: Gilbert Gredler

4/yr; $35 indiv; $100 instit; illus; adv; 1,700 circ
Audience: Teachers, school psychologists
Focus: Devoted to research, practice & opinion concerning psychological evaluation & assessment, educational practices & problems, & strategies in behavioral change of school children, from elementary to college level
Reviews: 20/yr, books about childhood education & psychology
Other: Back issues & reprints available. Annual index in October. Indexed in CIJE, Educ. Ind., Except. Child. Educ. Abstr., SSCI, Psychol. Abstr. Available on microform

PUPPETRY JOURNAL
Puppeteers of America
8005 Swallow Dr., Macedonia, OH 44056
314-825-2526
Eds: George Latshaw, Pat Latshaw

4/yr; $25 indiv; $20 libraries; membership fee; adv; 2,500 controlled circ
Audience: Teachers, librarians, parents, general
Focus: Puppetry
Contents: 6-8/yr, books on puppetry
Other: Accepts unsolicited materials. Available on microform

READ, AMERICA!
The Place In The Woods
3900 Glenwood Ave., Golden Valley, MN 55422-5302
612-374-2120; Fax: 612-593-5593
Ed: Roger A. Hammer

4/yr; $25; illus; adv; 10,000 circ
Audience: Teachers, librarians, parents, general, reading coordinators

Focus: To promote exchange of information & ideas among reading coordinators serving Reading is Fundamental (RIF), Head Start, Migrant Education & IRA children's programs
Contents: Features & news on children & media
Reviews: 4-12/yr, reviews of children's books
Other: Accepts unsolicited materials. Back issues & reprints available

READING IMPROVEMENT
Project Innovation of Mobile
Box 8508, Spring Hills Sta., Mobile, AL 36608
205-343-7802
Ed: Phil Feldman

4/yr; $20 instit; $15 indiv; 2,500 circ
Audience: Children, teachers, librarians, parents, general
Focus: To publish worthwhile theory & research related to reading & special education
Contents: News about children and media, features for children
Reviews: 20-40/yr, reviews of children's books
Other: Accepts unsolicited materials. Back issues & reprints available. Annual index in winter. Indexed in RGPL, Ed Index. Available on microform

THE READING TEACHER
International Reading Association
Box 8139, 800 Barksdale Rd., Newark, DE 19714-8139
302-731-1600; Fax: 301-731-1057
Eds: Nancy Paduk, Tim Rasinski
Adv Contact: Linda Hunter

8/yr; $38; adv; charts; 65,000 circ
Audience: Teachers, reading specialists
Focus: An open forum for information on the teaching & learning of reading
Contents: Feature articles on theory, practice, & research in reading
Reviews: 80-100/yr, reviews of children's books & audiovisual materials, reviews of computer software, educational software. Indexed in CIJE, Excep. Child. Educ. Abstr., Educ. Ind.

SCHOLASTIC COACH
Scholastic Inc.
730 Broadway, New York, NY 10003
212-505-3000
Subscrip: Box 644, Lyndhurst, NJ 07071-9985
Ed: Herman L. Masin

10/yr; $14.95; illus; adv; 42,000 circ
Audience: High school coaches, phys ed teachers

Contents: Features & news on children & media, sports techniques
Other: Accepts unsolicited materials. Back issues available. Annual index on request. Available on microform

SCHOOL LIBRARY MEDIA ACTIVITIES MONTHLY

LMS Associates
17 E. Henrietta St., Baltimore MD 21230
410-685-8621
Eds: H. Thomas Walker, Paula Montgomery

10/yr; $44; illus; adv; sample; 11,000 circ
Audience: Teachers, librarians
Focus: To provide ideas & activities for K-8 school library media specialists
Contents: Features & news on children & media
Reviews: 40-60/yr, reviews of children's books & audiovisual materials, reviews of computer software, library skills materials
Other: Accepts unsolicited materials. Back issues available. Annual index in June. Indexed in CIJE

SCHOOL LIBRARY MEDIA QUARTERLY

American Association of School Librarians
50 E. Huron St., Chicago, IL 60611-2795
312-933-6780, 800-545-2433; Fax: 312-440-9374
Ed: Marilyn W. Greenberg, Div of Curriculum & Instruction, California State University, Los Angeles, Los Angeles, CA 90032
Media Review Eds: Judith F. Davis, Joanne Troutner

4/yr; $15 members; $30 nonmembers; illus; adv; sample; 7,400 circ
Audience: AASL members, school librarians, faculty members, library school administrators
Focus: To inform AASL membership about organizational news & encourage school library media specialists to share ideas for worthwhile activities
Contents: Features on children and media, the administration of school media centers, collection development, news on school media & idea exchanges
Reviews: 100/yr, books, periodicals & audiovisual materials for the professional
Other: Accepts unsolicited materials. Back issues & reprints available. Cumulative index every 5 years. Indexed or abstracted in CIJE, Book Review Index, Current Contents: Sociological & Behavioral Sciences, Exceptional Child Education Abstracts, Information Science Abstracts,

Library Literature, Media Review Digest & Reference Services Review

SCHOOL SCIENCE AND MATHEMATICS

School Science & Math Assn., Inc.
Memorial Gym 300 B, Virginia Tech. C & I, Blacksburg, VA 24061
703-231-5558; Fax: 703-231-3717
Ed: Robert Underhill

8/yr; $32; illus; adv; 4,000 circ
Audience: Teachers
Focus: On practical methods for teaching at elementary & secondary school levels
Reviews: 30-40 book reviews, 30-40 software reviews, reviews of children's books, reviews of computer software
Other: Accepts unsolicited materials. Back issues available. Annual index in December. Indexed in CIJE

SCIENCE ACTIVITIES

Heldref Publications
1319 Eighteenth St., NW, Washington, DC 20036-1802
202-296-6267; Fax: 202-296-5149
Ed: Claire M. Wilson

4/yr; $29; illus; adv; charts; 1,500 circ
Audience: Teachers, administrators, college professors
Focus: Provides ideas for science activities for teachers
Reviews: Reviews of children's books & audiovisual materials, reviews of computer software, films
Other: Accepts unsolicited materials. Back issues & reprints available. Annual index in November/December. Indexed in CIJE, Educ. Ind. Available on microform

SCIENCE & CHILDREN

National Science Teachers Association
1742 Connecticut Ave., NW, Washington, DC 20009
202-328-5800
Ed: Phyllis R. Marcuccio

8/yr; $50 instit; $33 members; illus; adv; charts; 24,000 circ
Audience: Teachers
Focus: To aid elementary & middle school teachers in teaching science
Reviews: 400-500/yr, reviews of children's books & audiovisual materials, reviews of audiovisual equipment, reviews of computer software. Available on microfilm. Indexed in CIJE, Educ. Ind., Except. Child. Index

THE SCIENCE TEACHER

National Science Teachers Association
1742 Connecticut Ave., NW, Washington, DC 20009
202-328-5800
Ed: Juliana Texley

9/yr; $50; illus; adv; charts; 26,000 circ
Audience: Teachers, librarians
Focus: To inform junior & senior high schools science educators on new developments in science & science teaching
Contents: Science news & features, occasional news about children & media, occasional features for & by children
Reviews: 300/yr, reviews of children's books & audiovisual materials, professional materials
Other: Accepts unsolicited materials. Back issues available. Annual index in December. Indexed in CIJE, EI, International Index to Multimedia Education, Biol. Ind., Media Rev. Dig. Available on microfilm

SOCIAL EDUCATION

National Council for the Social Studies
3501 Newark St., NW, Washington DC 20016
202-966-7840
Ed: Salvatore J. Natoli

7/yr; $55; illus; adv; 28,000 circ
Audience: Teachers
Focus: Topical material on teaching methods, problems, curriculum at all educational levels; includes regular section on instructional media
Reviews: 125/yr, reviews of children's audiovisual materials, reviews of audiovisual equipment, reviews of computer software, professional books
Other: No unsolicited materials. Back issues available. Annual index in December. Indexed in CIJE, EdI, Educ. Ind., SSCI. Available on microform

TEACHING & COMPUTERS

Scholastic, Inc.
730 Broadway, New York, NY 10003-9538
212-505-3000
Subscrip: 1290 Wall St. W, Lyndhurst, NJ 07071
Ed: Mickey Revenaugh

6/yr; $23.95; illus; adv; sample; 45,000 circ
Audience: Teachers, librarians
Focus: Gives K-8 teachers ideas on how to use computers in their classrooms
Contents: Features & news on children & media
Reviews: 50/yr, reviews of children's books, reviews of computer software, other computer products
Other: Accepts unsolicited materials. Back issues & reprints available. Indexed in LL, MRI. Available on microfilm

TEACHING EXCEPTIONAL CHILDREN
Council for Exceptional Children
1920 Association Dr., Reston, VA
   22091
703-620-3660; Fax: 703-264-9494
Eds: Harold W. Heller, Fred Spooner

4/yr; $30; illus; adv; sample; charts;
   55,000 circ
Audience: Teachers, administrators
Focus: Practical methods & materials
   for classroom use by teachers with
   handicapped or gifted students: not
   research oriented, but includes database descriptions of special techniques, equipment & procedures
Reviews: 40-50/yr, reviews of children's books & audiovisual equipment, reviews of computer software
Other: Accepts unsolicited materials.
   Back issue available. Annual index in
   May. Indexed in CIJE, EdI, Excep.
   Child. Educ. Abstr. Available on
   microform

TEACHING K-8
Early Years, Inc.
40 Richards Ave., Norwalk, CT
   06854-2309
203-855-2650; Fax: 203-855-2656
Subscrip: Box 54805, Boulder, CO
   80323-4805
Ed: Allen Raymond

8/yr; $19.77; illus; adv; 132,986 circ
Audience: Elementary teachers, school
   librarians
Contents: Articles for teachers

Reviews: 100/yr, reviews of children's
   books & audiovisual materials, cur-
   riculum materials, basal textbooks
Other: Accepts unsolicited materials.
   Back issues & reprints available.
   Indexed in Educ. Ind., Excep. Child.
   Educ. Ind. Available on micro-
   form

TECHNOLOGY & LEARNING
Peter Li, Inc.
330 Progress Rd., Dayton, OH 45449
415-457-4333
Ed: Holly Brady

8/yr; $24.00; illus; adv
Audience: Teachers, librarians
Contents: Using technology creatively
   in the classroom
Reviews: Educational software reviews
Other: SASE must accompany un-
   solicited materials

TECHTRENDS
Association for Educational Communications & Technology
1025 Vermont Ave., NW, Ste. 820,
   Washington DC 20005-3516
202-347-7834; Fax: 202-347-7839
Ed: Nancy A. Klinck

6/yr; $36; illus; adv; 9,000 controlled
   circ, 5,000 paid circ
Audience: Teachers, librarians, media
   professionals
Focus: To provide practical & timely information to educators & others
   concerned with improvement of in-

struction through the effective use of
   media & technology
Contents: Features on children and
   media
Reviews: 12-15/yr, books of education
   communications & technology
Other: Accepts unsolicited materials.
   Back issues available. Annual index
   in December. Indexed in CIJE, EI,
   Current Contents, INSPEC Science
   Abstracts, International Index to
   Multi-Media Information, Exceptional
   Child Abstracts

T.H.E. JOURNAL (TECHNOLOGICAL HORIZONS IN EDUCATION)
150 El Camino Real, Tustin, CA
   92680-3670
714-730-4011; Fax: 714-730-3739
Ed: Sylvia Charp

11/yr; $29; free to qualified education-
   al administrators; adv; charts; stat;
   126,000 circ
Audience: Educational administrators
Focus: Use of high technology in delivery & administration of education at
   all levels
Contents: Features & news on children
   & media
Reviews: 500/yr, reviews of audiovisual
   equipment, reviews of computer
   software
Other: Accepts unsolicited materials.
   Back issues & reprints available. Annual index in June. Indexed in CIJE,
   Educ. Ind. Available on microform

REVIEW JOURNALS, SERVICES & INDEXES

11

This section lists principal sources of children's media reviews and also includes publications which do not regularly cover children's media but do devote special issues to children's reviews.

APPRAISAL: SCIENCE BOOKS FOR YOUNG PEOPLE
Children's Science Book Review Committee
605 Commonwealth Ave., Boston, MA 02215
617-353-4150
Ed: Diane Holzheimer

4/yr; $20; sample; 2000 controlled circ
Audience: Teachers, librarians, science supervisors
Focus: Reviews juvenile science books. Each book is reviewed by a librarian & by a science specialist
Reviews: 240/yr, reviews of children's books, YA books
Other: Back issues available. Annual index in fall issue. Indexed in CBRI

THE BOOK REPORT
Linworth Publishing, Inc.
480 E. Wilson Bridge Rd., Ste. L, Worthington, OH 43085
614-436-7107, Fax: 614-436-9490
Ed: Carolyn Hamilton

6/yr; $39; adv; sample; 11,900 circ
Audience: Librarians
Focus: A journal for school librarians
Reviews: 500/yr, reviews of children's books, audiovisual materials, computer software
Other: Back issues & reprints available. Annual index in March/April. Index in CBRI, CMG, BRI. Available on microfilm

BOOK REVIEW DIGEST
The H. W. Wilson Co.
950 University Ave., Bronx, NY 10452
212-588-8400, 800-367-6770; Fax: 718-590-1617
Ed: Martha Mooney

10/yr; price varies;
Audience: 6-12, teachers, librarians,

parents, general, specialists in humanities & social science
Focus: Provides excerpts of & citations to reviews of current US & Canadian fiction & nonfiction
Reviews: 2,700/yr of 900 books, reviews of children's books, books about children or children's literature
Other: No unsolicited materials. Back issues available. Bound cumulated annual volume. Available on CD-ROM

BOOK WORLD
The Washington Post
1150 15 St., NW, Washington, DC 20071
202-334-6000, Fax: 202-334-5549
Ed: Nina King

52/yr; $26; illus; adv; 1,165,567 circ
Audience: General
Focus: Reviews of hardcover & paperback books
Contents: Features on children and media, news about children and media, features & news abut books, author interviews, books on tape column. Fall Children's Books & Spring Children's Books published mid-Nov & mid-May respectively.
Reviews: 120/yr, children's books

BOOKLIST
American Library Association
50 E. Huron St., Chicago, IL 60611
312-944-6780, 800-545-2433; Fax: 312-44-9374
Ed: Bill Ott

22/yr; $60; illus; adv; sample; 32,000 circ
Audience: Teachers, librarians
Focus: To review books & nonprint materials recommended for library purchase
Reviews: 6,200/yr, reviews of children's books & audiovisual

materials, reviews of computer software, YA books
Other: Back issues available. Annual index in August. Indexed in CBRI, CLA, LL, MRI, RGPL. Available on microform

BOOKS FOR CHILDREN
Department of English & Office of Public Information
Clemson University, Clemson, SC 29631-1503
803-656-5414
Ed: Malcolm Usrey
Media Review Ed: Primarily English faculty; occasionally other professors

51/yr; syndicated newspaper features
Audience: Parents, general
Focus: A public service for newspapers to help guide their readers to some of the fine books available for children
Reviews: 51/yr, reviews of children's books
Other: Accept unsolicited materials

BULLETIN OF THE CENTER FOR CHILDREN'S BOOKS
University of Illinois Press
325 S. Oak St., Champaign, IL 61820
217-244-6856
Ed: Roger Sutton

11/yr; $23; sample; 8,000 controlled circ; 7,700 paid circ
Audience: Teachers, librarians, parents, general
Focus: Critical & analytical review journal for children's & YA books
Reviews: 800/yr, children's & YA books, professional books about children's literature
Other: Back issues & reprints available. Annual index in July/August. Indexed in CBRI, CLA, Children's Literature Review

CATHOLIC LIBRARY WORLD
Catholic Library Association
461 W. Lancaster Ave., Haverford, PA
    19041
215-649-5250
Ed: Anthony Prete

4/yr; $10; illus; adv; sample; 3,000
    controlled circ; 3,251 circ
Audience: Librarians
Focus: Each issue features an in-depth
    study of a specific library concern
Contents: Features & news on children
    & media, features for librarians. Spe-
    cial issue on children's literature,
    print & nonprint, published annually
    in Sept
Reviews: 150/yr, reviews of children's
    books & audiovisual materials,
    reviews of computer software,
    professional books for librarians
Other: Accepts unsolicited materials.
    Back issues available. Annual index
    in May/June. Indexed in LL, MRI,
    RGPL, CIJE, Book Review Index,
    Catholic Periodical & Literary Index,
    Library Science Abstracts

CHILDREN'S BOOK REVIEW INDEX
Gale Research Company
835 Penobscot Bldg., Detroit, MI
    48226
313-961-2242; Fax: 313-961-6083
Eds: Neal E. Walker, Beverly Baer

Annual compilation $103
Audience: Teachers, librarians, espe-
    cially school librarians
Focus: An index to children's books
    reviews
Contents: Author's name, book title,
    where & when reviewed
Other: Back issues from date of origin
    (1975) available

CHILDREN'S BOOKS REVIEW SERVICE
220 Berkeley Place, No. 1 D, Brooklyn,
    NY 11217
718-622-4036; Fax: 718-622-4036
Ed: Ann L. Kalkhoff

14/yr; $40; sample; 300 circ
Audience: Teachers, librarians, parents
Focus: To provide concise reviews of
    children's books which reflect the
    reading needs of today's children
Contents: 800/yr, reviews of children's
    books
Other: No unsolicited materials. Back
    issues available. Indexed in Book
    Review Index, Children's Book
    Review Index

CHILDREN'S LITERATURE REVIEW
Gale Research Company
835 Penobscot Bldg, Detroit, MI
    48226
313-961-2242; Fax: 313-961-6083
Ed: Gerard J. Senick

Irreg; $99; illus; Audience: 9-12,
    teachers, librarians & college
    students
Reviews: Excerpts from critiques
Other: Back volumes available

COMPUTER BOOK REVIEW
735 Ekekela Place, Honolulu, HI
    96817
808-595-7089
Ed: Carlene Char

6/yr; $30; sample; adv
Audience: Teachers, librarians, DP
    professionals
Focus: Reviews of new, noteworthy
    computer-related books
Reviews: 600/yr, reviews of children's
    books
Other: Accepts unsolicited materials.
    Back issues & reprints available. An-
    nual index published separately. In-
    dexed in BRI, CBRI. Available
    through DIALOG

CURRICULUM PRODUCT NEWS
(formerly Curriculum Product Review)
Educational Media, Inc.
922 S. High Ridge Rd., Stamford, CT
    06905
203-322-1300; Fax: 203-328-9177
Ed: Jane Y. Woodward

10/yr; free; illus; adv; 50,000 con-
    trolled circ
Audience: District-level education ex-
    ecutives
Focus: Provides district-level education
    executives with brief summaries of
    new products & services for the
    K-12 education market
Reviews: 900/yr, reviews of children's
    books & audiovisual materials,
    reviews of audiovisual equipment,
    reviews of films & plays, reviews of
    computer software, professional
    materials for educators

THE HORN BOOK MAGAZINE
Horn Book, Inc.
11 Beacon St., Ste. 1000, Boston MA
    02108-3704
617-227-1555
Ed: Anita Silvey

6/yr; $35 individual, $42 instit.; illus;
    adv; sample; 24,000 circ
Audience: Teachers, librarians, par-
    ents, booksellers
Focus: To uphold standards of excel-
    lence for children's books
Contents: Reviews of children's & YA
    books, book-related audiorecordings,
    articles about children's literature
Reviews: 400/yr, children's & YA
    books & nonprint materials
Other: Accepts unsolicited materials.
    Back issues & reprints available. In-
    dexed in LL, Book Review Digest,

Book Review Index, CIJE, Media
    Review Digest, Children's Magazine
    Guide, Cumulative Monthly Periodical
    Index. Available on microfilm

KIRKUS REVIEWS
The Kirkus Service
200 Park Ave. S, New York, NY 10003
212-777-4554
Ed: Anne Larsen

24/yr; $60; adv; 5,000 circ
Audience: Librarians
Contents: Book reviews
Review: 1200/yr, reviews of children's
    books
Other: Back issues available. Annual in-
    dex January 1 or 15. Indexed in
    Book Review Index, CBRI. Available
    on microform

KLIATT
(formerly Young Adult Paperback Book
    Guide)
Kliatt Paperback Book Guide
33 Bay State Rd., Wellesley, MA
    02181-3244
617-237-7577

6/yr; $36; adv; sample; 2,300 con-
    trolled circ
Audience: Teachers, librarians
Reviews: 1400/yr, reviews of young
    adults' books
Other: Back issues & reprints
    available. Index in January, April,
    September. Indexed in Book Review
    Index, CBRI. Available on micro-
    form

THE KOBRIN LETTER
732 Greer Rd., Palo Alto, CA 94303
415-856-6658
Ed: Beverly Kobrin

7/yr; $12; illus
Audience: Teachers, librarians, par-
    ents, school administrators,
    university professors, bookstore
    owners
Focus: Reviews & recommends nonfic-
    tion books & ways to use them
Reviews: 140/yr, reviews of children's
    books

LANDERS FILM REVIEWS
Lander Associates
Box 69760, Los Angeles, CA 90069
213-657-1686

4/yr; $180; sample; 3,000 controlled
    circ
Audience: Teachers, librarians, par-
    ents, other film users
Contents: In-depth reviews, evaluation
    & information on educational &
    documentary films & multimedia
    materials for all ages
Reviews: 500-600/yr, reviews of chil-

dren's audiovisual materials, 16mm films, 1/2'' videocassettes
Other: Back issues available. Annual index in June. Indexed in MRI

LIBRARY JOURNAL
Cahners/R. R. Bowker Magazine Group
249 W. 17th St., New York, NY 10011
212-645-0067, 800-669-1002; Fax:
212-468-6734
Subscrip: Box 1977, Marion, OH
43305-1977
Ed: Francine Fialkoff

20/yr; $79; illus; adv; bilbio; 24,145
circ
Audience: Teachers, librarians, parents, general
Reviews: 4,000/yr; reviews of audiovisual equipment, reviews of computer software, books for educators, teachers, on subjects ranging from educational games & contents to child development & books for gifted readers. Annual index. Indexed in BRD, BRI, CIJE, CBRI. Available on microform

LIBRARY LITERATURE
The H. W. Wilson Co.
950 University Ave., Bronx, NY 10452
212-588-8400, 800-367-6770; Fax:
718-590-1617
Ed: Cathy Rentschler

6/yr
Audience: Teachers, librarians, researchers
Focus: Index to material in library & information science; also available online
Contents: Features & news on children & media
Reviews: 2200/yr, reference & professional books on children's literature & media
Other: Accepts unsolicited materials. Back issues available. Index in separate bound volume

LIBRARY TALK
Linworth/Publishing
480 E. Wilson Bridge Rd., Ste. L,
Worthington, OH 43085
614-436-7107; Fax: 614-436-9490

5/yr; $39; adv
Audience: Elementary school librarians & teachers
Contents: Author profiles, reviews, creative activities & articles
Reviews: Children's books, audiovisual materials, computer software
Other: Index in CMG

LOS ANGELES TIMES BOOK REVIEW
Los Angeles Times, Inc.
Times Mirror Sq., Los Angeles, CA
90053

213-237-7777
Ed: Sonja Bolle

52/yr; illus; adv
Audience: General
Reviews: 52/yr, reviews of children's books
Other: Indexed in BRI, CBRI. Available on microform. Index available

MEDIA REVIEW
Education Funding Research Council
1611 N. Kent St., Ste. 508, Arlington,
VA 22209
703-528-1000
Ed: Frank Legato

10/yr; $99
Focus: Evaluates & rates classroom instructional material for all education levels in newsletter format
Reviews: Reviews of children's audiovisual materials, reviews of computer software

MEDIA REVIEW DIGEST
Pierian Press
Box 1808, Ann Arbor, MI 48106
313-434-5530; Fax: 313-434-6409
Ed: Mary K. Hashman

Annual; $245
Focus: Indexes & abstracts reviews of educational & feature films, video, filmstrips & other audiovisual resources, with numerous indexes to the volumes' contents
Other: Back issues available

NEW YORK TIMES BOOK REVIEW
New York Times Co.
229 W. 43rd St., New York, NY 10036
212-556-1234, 800-631-2580
Subscrip: Box 5792, GPO, New York,
NY 10087
Ed: Mitchel Levitas

52/yr; $78.40; illus; 60,000 circ
Audience: 7-12, teachers, librarians, parents, general
Focus: Includes reviews of books for & about children
Reviews: 80-120/yr, reviews of children's books
Other: Indexed in BRI, CBRI. Available on microform

PARENTS' CHOICE
Parents' Choice Foundation
Box 185, Waban, MA 02168
617-965-5913
Ed: Diana Huss Green

4/yr; $18; illus; adv; 75,000 controlled circ
Audience: Teachers, librarians, parents
Focus: To review children's media
Contents: Features & news on children & media
Reviews: 360/yr, reviews of children's

books & audiovisual materials, films & video, reviews of computer software
Other: Accepts unsolicited materials. Back issues & reprints available. Indexed in RGPL

PUBLISHERS WEEKLY
Cahners/R. R. Bowker Co.
249 W. 17th St., New York, NY 10011
212-645-0067, 800-842-1669; Fax:
212-242-7216
Subscrip: Box 1979, Marion, OH
43302
Ed: Nora Rawlinson

51/yr; $129; adv; illus; biblio; 38,349
circ
Audience: Librarians, booksellers, publishers
Focus: Publishing industry trade journal
Contents: Features on children and media. Children's Book Scene appears in the last issue of every month. It includes articles on children's book publishing, interviews with authors and editors, features on industry trends & development
Reviews: 1,000/yr, reviews of children's books
Other: Accepts unsolicited materials. Back issues & reprints available. Indexed in CBRI, LL, RGPL, BRI. Available on microform

SAN FRANCISCO CHRONICLE REVIEW
San Francisco Chronicle
901 Mission St., San Francisco, CA
94119
415-777-7042
Ed: Patricia Holt

52/yr; illus' adv
Audience: General
Reviews: 200/yr, reviews of children's books. Special issue in Christmas, Spring

SCHOOL LIBRARY JOURNAL
A Cahners/R. R. Bowker Publication
249 W. 17th St., New York, NY 10011
212-463-6759, 800-669-1002; Fax:
212-463-6734
Subscrip: Box 1978, Marion, OH
43305-1978
Ed: Lillian N. Gerhardt

12/yr; $67; adv; charts; 41,265 circ
Audience: Librarians
Focus: For children's, YA, & school library specialists
Contents: Special issue in April covers films, records, filmstrips, audio & videocassettes
Reviews: 3,800/yr, children's books, professional books for librarians, educational AV & microcomputer software reviews

Other: Indexed in CMG, LL, Book
Review Digest; BRI, CBRI, CIJE. Available on microform

SCIENCE BOOKS & FILMS
American Association for the Advancement of Science
AAAS Science Books & Films, 1333 H
St., NW, Washington, DC 20005
202-326-6454
Subscrip: Dept. SBF, Box 3000,
Denville, NJ 07834
Ed: Maria Sosa

9/yr; $40; adv; sample; 4500 circ
Audience: Teachers, librarians
Focus: To evaluate children's science
books & films for appeal & accuracy.
November/December issue includes
an annotated list of the year's best
science trade books for children
Other: Indexed in BRI, CBRI. Available
on microform

SHOW-BOOK WEEK
Chicago Sun-Times
401 N. Wabash Ave., Chicago, IL
60611
312-321-3000
Media Review Ed: Deborah Abbott

Audience: 4-6

Content: Review column For Children
appears 12 times each year
Reviews: 5-75/yr

TRIBUNE BOOKS
Chicago Tribune
435 N. Michigan Ave., Chicago, IL
60611
312-222-3232
Bk Rev Ed: Diane Donovan

12/yr; illus/ adv
Audience: General
Focus: Reviews of current literature
Contents: Children's book reviews, features on books
Reviews: 150/yr, children's books
Other: No unsolicited materials. Back
issues available

VOYA (VOICE OF YOUTH ADVOCATES)
Scarecrow Press
Box 4167, Metuchen, NJ 08840
201-548-8600, 800-537-7107; Fax:
908-548-5767
Ed: Dorothy M. Broderick

6/yr; $32.50; illus; adv; sample; charts;
3,500 circ
Focus: For people working with adolescents in schools, public libraries &
youth service agencies

Contents: Features & news on young
adults & media
Reviews: 1200-1500/yr, reviews of
young adult books & audiovisual
materials
Other: Accepts unsolicited materials.
Indexed in Book Review Digest,
CBRI, CLA. Index available. Available
on microform

WILSON LIBRARY BULLETIN
The H. W. Wilson Co.
950 University Ave., Bronx, NY 10452
212-588-8400, 800-367-6770; Fax:
718-590-1617
Ed: L. Mark

10/yr; $52; illus; adv; sample; biblio;
25,000 circ
Audience: Teachers, librarians
Focus: To report & comment on the
world of librarianship, including
books & reading
Contents: Features & news on children
& media
Reviews: 100/yr, reviews of children's
books, reviews of computer software
Other: Back issues available. Indexed
in CBRI, LL, RGPL, CLA. Available on
microform. Available through DIALOG

The Internet is a global network of computer networks started by the government over 20 years ago to futher military research. Soon researchers were exchanging electronic mail (e-mail). It uses the high-speed capability of the National Science Foundation's NSFnet to link various networks. Many network educational services use the Internet, while others are providing gateways.

States currently providing low cost or free access to the Internet for educational purposes are: California (CORE), Florida (FIRN), North Dakota (SENDIT), Texas (TENET), and Virginia (VaPEN).

This section is an alphabetical listing of cooperative networks, LISTSERV's and newsgroups that deal with K-12 education.

ACADEMY ONE
6330 Lincoln Ave., Ste. 117, Cypress, CA 90630
714-821-4472

Internet access to Academy One is offered through the Cleveland FreeNet Telenet to:
FREENET-IN-A.CWRU.EDU;
FREENET-IN-B.CWRU.EDU;
FREENET-IN-C.CWRU.EDU.
Affiliated with the National Public Telecomputing Network (NTPN) and the Cleveland Free-Net, this program aims to create a "national online information cooperative for K-12 telecomputing activities." Academy One allows schools throughout the world to access the resources of their community computer systems and participate in a variety of online projects and events. One publishes a free newsletter during the school year.

APPLE LINK
Apple Computer, Inc., #1 Infinite Loop, Cupertino, CA 95014
408-996-1010

Access to the K-12 Education Area is through general AppleLink membership.

This official online information resource of the Apple Computer community offers a K-12 Education Area with special information for classroom teachers and computer coordinators. Menu selections include reviews of Macintosh education software; a discussion forum for dialogues and news; listing of conferences and other events for K-12 educators; news about education-related Apple products; and other resources, including grant opportunities, lesson plans, and research results.

AT&T LEARNING NETWORK
Box 6391, Parsipanny, NJ 07054
800-367-7225

This curriculum-based telecommunications program for grades K-12 matches students and teachers in "learning circles" with eight to ten other classes around the world. The program reinforces collaborative learning through a structured, committed partnership between all matched classes.

CALIFORNIA TECHNOLOGY PROJECT
800-272-8743 (CA), 310-985-9631 (other states)

This project, operated collaboratively by the California State University system and the California Dept. of Education, sponsors the California Online Resources for Education (CORE). CORE provides K-12 teachers with electronic access to e-mail, the Internet, and education-related curriculum materials. Currently, 6,000 teachers use CORE, dialing into 20 California State University campuses. The California Technology Project has also developed a Graphical User Interface Design for Educators (GUIDE) to help teachers access e-mail, Netnews, and databases in a windows-type environment rather than with commands. The GUIDE is available for Macintosh and IMB personal computers.

CENTER FOR CHILDREN AND TECHNOLOGY
Bank Street College of Education, 610 W. 112th St., New York, NY 10025
212-875-4560

This research center also serves as the National Center for Technology in Education, a project of the Office of Educational Research and Improvement, U.S. Dept. of Education. The center investigates the roles of technology in children's lives—both in the classroom and in general—and the design and development of prototypical software that supports engaged, active learning. It offers a free quarterly newsletter and low-cost publications.

CONSORTIUM FOR SCHOOL NETWORKING (CoSN)
Box 65193, Washington, DC 20035-5193
202-466-6296

CoSN is a community of organizations, government agencies, corporations, and individuals with an interest in K-12 education. Through computer networking, CoSN helps educators and students increase their productivity, professional competence, and opportunities for learning and collaborative work.

EDUCOM K-12 NETWORKING PROJECT

1112 16th St. NW, Ste. 600, Washington, DC 20036
202-872-4200

This project aims to link practitioners in primary and secondary education through computer-mediated communication networks, and, with this connectivity, to develop networked resources to support curriculum reform and institutional restructuring. Current and planned activities include developing directories of K-12 people and resources and a user orientation packet, including primers and guides to training resources; seeking avenues for business and industry collaboration; and conducting outreach to key practitioners and policy makers.

ELECTRONIC FRONTIER FOUNDATION (EFF)

666 Pennsylvania Ave. SE, Washington, DC 20003
202-544-9237
Internet: EFF@EFF.ORG

This membership organization focuses on policy issues related to national networking. In the K-12 context, EFF concerns itself with policies for determining the resources to which students will have access. EFF publishes a free newletter, *EFFector Online,* on general Internet topics.

ERIC CLEARINGHOUSE ON INFORMATION RESOURCES (ERIC/IR)

303 Huntington Hall, Syracuse University, Syracuse, NY 1234-2340
315-443-3640
Internet: ERIC@SUVM.ACS.SYR.EDU.

ERIC/IR is one of 16 clearinghouses in the ERIC system, which is sponsored by the Office of Educational Research and Improvement, U.S. Dept. of Education. ERIC/IR specializes in educational technology and library/information science and processes documents in these areas for the ERIC database. The clearinghouse also provides user services and publications related to its scope areas, including the *ERIC Networker,* electronic "help sheets" for using ERIC resources on the Internet.

FREDMAIL NETWORK

Box 243, Bonita, CA 91908
615-475-4852

This cooperative consortium maintains a distributed and low-cost telecommunications network for public agencies such as schools, libraries, cities, and community service organizations. FrEdMail is dedicated to K-12 education, helping teachers and students partici-

pate in a wide variety of learning experiences and exchange information freely and simply. FrEdMail features learning projects that motivate students to become better learners and writers. It also lets teachers share experiences, ideas, and materials as well as information for professional development, and provides a gateway to the Internet. FrEdMail publishes a quarterly newletter and guides to help teachers implement telecomputing.

FLORIDA INFORMATION RESOURCE NETWORK (FIRN)

Florida Education Ctr., Rm. B 114, 325 W. Gaines St., Tallahassee, FL 32399
904-487-0911

More than 3,000 teachers and administrators in Florida have set up free accounts for e-mail on FIRN. FIRN users also can access the ERIC database and library card catalogs of several colleges and universities in Florida through the network. To aid teachers in instructional planning, FIRN posts curriculum guides for using resources such as CNN, Newsweek, and the Discovery Channel in the classroom.

FREE-NETS

Free-Nets are free, community sponsored and maintained computer bulletin board systems. General services are available such as e-mail, Usenet news and often limited Internet access. Most maintain community services such as library and city government information. (Currently available in Buffalo, Cleveland, Chicago, Denver, Lorain Co., OH, Minneapolis/St.Paul, Philadelphia, Summit, NJ, Tuscaloosa, Washington, DC, and Oregon).

IBM/NATIONAL EDUCATION ASSOCIATION (NEA) SCHOOL RENEWAL NETWORK

NEA National Center for Innovation, 1201 16th St. NW, Washington, DC 20036
202-822-7783

Dedicated to school reform, this electronic network is intended to create a research base by a community of actively engaged practitioners and researchers. Participants include partners in the NEA National Center for Innovation's programs, federally funded research and development laboratories and centers, several research universities, and schools from other national school reform efforts.

INTERNATIONAL SOCIETY FOR TECHNOLOGY IN EDUCATION (ISTE) SPECIAL INTEREST GROUP FOR TELECOMMUNICATIONS (SIG/TEL)

1787 Agate St., Eugene, OR 97403-1923
503-346-4141
Internet: ISTE@UOREGON.EDU.

The largest international nonprofit professional organization serving computer-using educators, ISTE is dedicated to the improvement of education through the use and integration of technology. ISTE-Net, an online computer network for ISTE members, is available through GTE Education Services (1-800-927-3000). The Special Interest Group for telecommunications publishes a newsletter about telecommunications in education, *T.I.E. News.*

K12NET

1151 SW Vermont St., Portland, OR 92719
503-280-5280

This network is a system of more than 250 linked bulletin boards carrying thousands of messages each week among sites around the world. Participants access many subject-specific conferences and also collaborate on projects. Developed as a grassroots project, K12NET is a collaborative effort available free to anyone who can access it through a bulletin board.

KIDSNET

This is a global Internet electronic discussion group for children and their teachers. Ongoing discussions deal with general questions about computer networks and user interfaces and specific projects linking groups of children in one school or another. A spinoff of the KIDSNET list is another list called KIDS, which allows children to post messages to other children. To subscribe, send an e-mail request to JOINKIDS@VMS.PITT.EDU.

LISTSERVS

These are electronic discussion groups on the Internet. They provide a way for network users to share ideas on a specified topic. Known also as newsgroups, discussion groups, bulletin boards and mailing lists, E-mail messages are sent to a central address and then sent to all participants of the group. An unmoderated list allows free-flowing discussion. There is no restriction on who can particiapte or the number of messages or the content. A moderated list has a moderator who screens messages. If the message is appropriate, it is then posted. To subscribe to a list, send a mail message to the LISTSERV host machine (listser@hostname). Leave the subject line blank. In the text of the message type: subscribe (lisserv name) (your firstname lastname).

The name of the LISTSERV is first, followed by hostname and an explanation of the function of the discussion.

AACL (@auvm)
Association for the Advancement of Computing

ABILITY (@asuacad)
Study and advancement of academically, artistically and athletically able

ALTLEARN (@sjuvm.bitnet)
Sharing of alternative learning strategies for physically handicapped

BEHAVIOR (@asuacad.bitnet)
Discussion of children with ADD, ADHD & autism

BGEDU-L (@ukcc.uky.edu)
Discussion on the quality of education

CHEMED'L (@uwf)
Forum of topics for chemistry teachers at high school and college level

CHEMISTRYTM
(chemistrytm-request@dhvx20.csudh.edu)
Unmoderated list for high school and college students and their teachers. Fosters exchange of ideas and information on chemistry

CSAC (@uvmvm.bitnet)
Computing Strategies Across the Curriculum

COSNDISC (@bitnic)
Consortium for School Networking discussion

CSRNOT-L (@uiucvmd)
Center for the Study of Reading List

CURRICUL (@saturn.rowan.edu)
Curriculum development issues, higher education, K-12

DINOSAUR
(request@donald.wichitaks,ncr.com DISC-L)
Advanced listings and curriculum material for educational programming on the Discovery Channel and The Learning Channel(@sendit.no-dak.edu)

ECENET (@uiucvmd)
Early childhood education — 0-8 years

ECEOL-L (@maine.edu)
Discussion of early childhood education

EDISTA (@usachvml.bitnet)
Discussion of distance education

EDNET (@nic.umass.edu)
Discussion of educational potential of the Internet

ELED-L (@ksuvm)
Elementary education list

HOME-ED
(home-ed-request@think.com)
Home education discussion list

IECC (@iecc-equest@stolaf.edu)
International e-mail classroom connections list for teachers seeking penpals. Not intended to find individual penpals.

INFED-L (@accsun.unicamp.br)
Uses of computers in education

K12ADMIN (@suvm)
K-12 educators interested in educational administration

KIDCAFE (@ndsuvml)
Youth dialogue

KIDLINK (@ansuvml)
Kidlink project list

KIDLIT-L (@bingvmb)
Children's literature discussion list

KIDS (joinkids@vms.cis.pitt.edu)
Spinoff of KIDSPHERE for children to post messages for other children around the world

KIDSPHERE (formerly Kidsnet)
(kidsphere-request@vms.cis.pitt.edu)
Global network for K-12 students, teachers, school administrators and scientists

LIBER (@uvmvm)
Library/media services

LM__NET (@suvm)
School library media network

MIDDLE-L (listserv@vmd.cso.uiuc.edu)
Discussion group for middle school education topics

MSPROJ (@msu)
Annenberg/CPB Math-Science Project

MULTI-L (@barilvm)
Language & education in multi-lingual settings

PHYSHARE (@psuvm)
Resources for high school physics

PUBYAC (@lis.pitt.edu)
Children & young adult library services

SAIS-L (@unbvml.bitnet)
Discussion on science awareness and promotion

SUSIG (@miamiu)
Discussion on teaching math

T321-L (@mizzoul)
Teaching science in elementary schools

TAG-L (@ndsuvml)
Discussion of education for talented and gifted

TEACHNET (@acadvnl.uottawa.ca)
Discussion for technical support staff covering technical support for education and research

TESL-L (@cunyvm)
Teaching English as a second language

Y-RIGHTS (@sjuvm)
Children's rights

YOUTHNET (@indycms)
Youth network

MERIT/NSF INFORMATION SERVICES
Merit Network, Inc., 2901 Hubbard, Pod G, Ann Arbor, MI 48105-2016
800-66-MERIT, 313-936-3000
Internet: NSFNET-INFO@MERIT.EDU

Merit Network, Inc., which operates the NSFNet backbone, also provides information support services to the networking community through e-mail or telephone. Staff offer help in using the Internet and information about K-12 connections and resources. Merit publishes a free newsletter, Link Letter, which can be requested through e-mail to NSFNET-LINKLETTER-REQUEST@MERIT.EDU. To obtain hard copies, write to the organization.

NATIONAL GEOGRAPHIC KIDS NETWORK
National Geographic Society, Educational Services, Washington, DC 20036
800-368-2728

Kids Network is an international telecommunications-based science and geography curriculum for fourth through sixth-graders createdby the National Geographic Society and Technical Education Research Centers, Inc. Students at schools in 50 states and more than 20 countries are assigned to research teams composed of 10 to 15 different classes. They investigate topics such as the water supply, weather, pollution, nutrition, and solar energy on the local level, then compare data with other members of their research team. Scientists help them trace geographic patterns in the data through letters, maps, and graphs. A Spanish-language version of the curriculum is being piloted.

NATIONAL SCIENCE FOUNDATION'S NETWORK SERVICE CENTER (NNSC)
10 Moulton St., Cambridge, MA 02138
617-873-3400
Internet: NNSC@NNSC.NSF.NET

The mission of NNSC is to collect, maintain, and distribute information about NSF-Net and provide assistance to networking end users. NNSC maintains the Internet Resource Guide, which is available through anonymous file transfer protocol at NNSC.NSF.NET, directory resource-guide. This and other resources can also be obtained by sending e-mail to INFO-SERVER@NNSC.NSF.NET, and typing in the body of the message: Request: info Topic: help
NNSC also offers network assistance through e-mail and a telephone hotline.

NEW YORK STATE EDUCATION AND RESEARCH NETWORK (NYSERNet)
111 College Place, Syracuse, NY 1324
   4100
315-443-4120
Internet: INFO@NYSERNET.ORG

NYSERNet is a regional network of the National Science Foundation's NSFNet and the Internet. NYSERNet links more than 70 state institutions of higher education, industries, government agencies, libraries, and schools to each other and to the Internet. It includes a K-12 networking interest group.

NEWSNET

Newsnet is a collection of over 5,000 discussion groups. These differ from LISTSERVs in that it is not necessary to subscribe to a group to read or respond to it. Each group centers on a single topic. Having access to the Internet does not automatically give access to the Usenets. Ask your systems administrator. If the answer is affirmative, ask which newsreader to use. This program acts as an interface. The newsreader presents the articles one at a time for you to read. Groups, divided into categories named hier-

archies, are constantly being created and dissolved. Each hierarchy is devoted to a particular area. There are 36 newsgroups in the K-12 hierarchy.

k12.chat.elementary
Students grades K-5

k12.chat.junior
Students grades 6-8

k12.chat.senior
High school students

k12.chat.teacher
Teacher forum

k12.ed.art
Art curriculum

k12.ed.business
Business education curriculumk

12.ed.comp.literacy
Computer literacy

k12.ed.health-pe
Health and physical education

k12.ed.life-skills
Home economics and career education

k12.ed.math
Mathematics

k12.ed.music
Music and performing arts

k12.ed.science
Science

k12.ed.soc-studies
Social studies and history

k12.ed.special
Students with disabilities or special needs

k12.ed.tag
Talented and gifted students

k12.ed.tech
Industrial arts and vocational education

k12.lang.art
Language arts

k12.lang.deutsch.eng
German/English practice with native speakers

k12.lang.esp-eng
Spanish/English practice with native speakers

k12.lang.francais
French/English practice with native speakers

k12.lang.russian
Russian/English practice with native speakers

k12.library
Libraries and librarians

k12.sys.channel0
Forum for teachers

k12.sys.channel1
Forum for teachers

k12.sys.channel2
Forum for teachers

k12.sys.channel3
Forum for teachers

k12.sys.channel4
Forum for teachers

k12.sys.channel5
Forum for teachers

k12.sys.channel6
Forum for teachers

k12.sys.channel7
Forum for teachers

k12.sys.channel8
Forum for teachers

k12.sys.channel9
Forum for teachers

k12.sys.channel10
Forum for teachers

k12.sys.channel11
Forum for teachers

k12.sys.channel12
Forum for teachers

k12.sys.projects
Teaching projects

NORTHWEST REGIONAL EDUCATIONAL LABORATORY (NWREL)
101 SW Main St., Ste. 500, Portland, OR 97204
503-275-9500

A program of the Office of Educational Research and Improvement, U.S. Dept. of Education, NWREL seeks to improve schools and classroom instruction in the states of the Northwest. NWREL has a special interest in education technology and networking, and offers publications and a free newsletter, the *Northwest Report*, to a national audience.

PBS LEARNING LINK
PBS ONLINE, 1320 Braddock Place, Alexandria, VA 22314
703-739-8464

PBS Learning Link is a computer-based, interactive communication system for K-12 educators, students, adult learners, and public television viewers. It features databases and information resources, message centers, e-mail and gateways to remote sites. Its services are locally managed and operated by public broadcasting stations, education agencies, or community organizations in 20 states. A national version is available to those who do not have access to the local version. PBS provides technical support and national content; site operators tailor the services to meet community needs.

SENDIT

Box 5164, NDSU Computer Center, Fargo, ND 58105
701-237-8109

SENDIT is a pilot K-12 computer network for North Dakota educators and students developed by the North Dakota State University (NDSU) School of Education and Computer Center. Currently, the host NeXT computer may be accessed through six toll-free and four local numbers in North Dakota. More than 70 forums have been established for topical discussions; educators also have limited access to the Internet.

SOUTHEASTERN REGIONAL VISION FOR EDUCATION (SERVE)

41 Marietta St. NW, Ste. 1000, Atlanta, GA 30303
800-659-3204

A program of the Office of Educational Research and Improvement, U.S. Dept. of Education, SERVE focuses on improving education in the southeastern region of the country. SERVE-Line is an online information system offering educators news and product announcements, instructional software that can be downloaded ("shareware"), discussion groups, and e-mail. Users may also request a free ERIC search; results will be mailed in approximately 2 weeks. Nonmembers with telecommunications software and a modem can get limited access to SERVE-Line through 1-800-487-7605.

SPECIALNET

GTE Education Services, GTE Place, W. Airfield Dr., Box 619810, Dallas/Fort Worth Airport, TX 75261-9810
800-927-3000

In operation since 1981, this information network offers educators and administrators e-mail, bulletin boards, conferencing, and databases that address various topics in special education. Sponsored by the National Association of State Directors of Special Education, it includes a variety of bulletin boards maintained by editors with expertise in the fields covered, including learning disabilities, parent involvement programs, and special education litigation.

TECHNICAL EDUCATION RESEARCH CENTERS (TERC)

2067 Massachusetts Ave., Cambridge, MA 02140
617-547-0430

This program researches, develops, and disseminates innovative programs for educators. A special interest is curriculum projects involving telecomputing. Services include outreach, technical assistance, curriculum guides, and information dissemination.

TERC also publishes a free newsletter, *Hands On!*

TEXAS EDUCATION NETWORK (TENET)

Texas Education Agency, 1701 N. Congress Ave., Austin, TX 78701
512-463-9091

TENET currently links more than 15,000 K-12 educators and administrators who use the network for e-mail, resource sharing, and access to databases via the Internet. Among the offerings made available to TENET users are news services, reference materials, and full-text ERIC Digests. As TENET expands, users will be able to access the Internet through a local call to one of sixteen sites across the state or through a toll-free number.

VIRGINIA'S PEN

Virginia Dept. of Education, 101 N. 14th St., 22nd, Richmond, VA 23219
Internet:
HCATHERN@VDOE386.VAK12ED.EDU

Approximately 6,000 educators currently have accounts on Virginia's statewide network. They can access Virginia's Pen via a local call to one of several sites across the state or through a toll-free line if they are located in a remote area. Network offerings include various discussion groups, topical news reports, study skills guides, and curriculum resources. Through History Online, students and teachers can pose questions to designated historians who will respond in the character of key historical figures, including Thomas Jefferson and James Madison.

CULTURAL DIVERSITY RESOURCES

13

The following organizations provide information or resources related to different cultures. They offer children's and youth programs, information services and resources, bibliographies, and general assistance to teachers and students.

African American Cultural Center
2560 W. 54th St., Los Angeles, CA 90008
213-299-6124

African Studies Center
Univ. of Wisconsin, 1454 Van Hise Hall, Madison, WI 53706
608-263-2171

The African Studies Center has recognized specialists in African history on the staff.

AFS Intercultural Programs
313 E. 43rd St., New York, NY 10017
212-949-4242

This organization is an international, nongovernmental student exchange program. It is also a founding member of the Council on Standards for International Educational Travel (CSIET).

Akwesasne Communication Society
Box 140, Rooseveltown, NY 13683
613-938-1113

The Akwesasne Communication Society distributes interviews of Native Americans on cassettes.

All Dolled Up
3318 W. Martin Luther King, Jr. Blvd., Los Angeles, CA 90008
213-969-1740

This company is a vendor of books and dolls and a source of information about black doll making.

American Association for Chinese Studies
Ohio State Univ., 300 Bricker Hall, Columbus, OH 43210
614-292-6681

The American Association for Chinese Studies publishes a biannual journal en-titled the American Journal of Chinese Studies and promotes Chinese studies in American colleges and universities.

American Community Cultural Center Association
19 Foothills Dr., Pompton Plains, NJ 07444
201-835-2661

The American Community Cultural Center Association encourages participation in the arts by everyone. It offers programs and workshops ranging from theater to writing skills. The programs are held in schools and theaters interstate.

American Historical Society of Germans from Russia (AHSGR)
AHSGR Heritage Center, 631 D St., Lincoln, NE 68502-1199
402-474-3363

The purpose of this organization is to promote a better understanding and appreciation of Germans from Russia. It is for researchers, librarians, historians, educators, genealogists, biographers and all descendants of Germans from Russia. It has chapters throughout the United States and maintains over 3,200 books, manuscripts, journals, family histories, maps and other publications.

American Indian Culture Research Center (AICRC)
Blue Cloud Abbey, Box 98, Marvin, SD 57251
605-432-5528
Founded in 1967, the American Indian Culture Research Center (AICRC) distributes books, films, records, and tapes. It involves men and women from the fourteen upper midwest reservations and supports Indian leaders and educators in rebuilding the Indian community. The AICRC educates nonIndian public in Indian culture and philosophy and advises reservation school and community groups. In conjunction with the Blue Cloud Abbey, the AICRC offers the services of a video editing studio to reservation people.

American Indian Heritage Foundation (AIHF)
6051 Arlington Blvd., Falls Church, VA 22044
202-463-4267

Founded in 1973, the American Indian Heritage Foundation (AIHF) is dedicated to inspiring Indian youth to excel. It educates nonIndians in Indian culture and heritage. It also sponsors scholarships, grants and loans to Indian youth. The AIHF strives to preserve Indian culture of all kinds.

American Indian Studies Center and Library
Univ. of California, Los Angeles, 405 Hilgard Ave., 3220 Campbell Hall, Los Angeles, CA 90024

The American Indian Studies Center and Library has an extensive library and resource center. It publishes the *American Indian Studies Culture and Research Journal* and also publishes books. It coordinates education, research and action-oriented programs and sponsors lectures and workshops.

American Irish Historical Society (AIHS)
991 Fifth Ave., New York, NY 10028
212-288-2263

Founded in 1897, this organization is dedicated to the preservation of Irish culture and heritage. The society maintains a library of over 30,000 items and has lectures, readings, musical presentations, and art exhibitions.

American Israel Friendship League (AIFL)
134 E. 39th St., New York, NY 10016
212-213-8630

Founded in 1971, this organization is committed to sustaining and developing friendship between the U.S. and Israel. It provides educational and cultural programs and sponsors student and youth exchange programs.

American Jewish Historical Society (AJHS)
Two Thornton Rd., Waltham, MA 02514
617-891-8110

Founded in 1892, this society is dedicated to the collection, preservation, and dissemination of information on the history of Jewish Americans. It has a library of 80,000 volumes, over seven million manuscripts, 250 art objects, 500 American Yiddish film and theater posters and a collection of restored American Yiddish films. Some genealogical resources are also available. In addition, it sponsors an America-Israel high school student educational exchange program.

American Study Program for Educational and Cultural Training (ASPECT)
26 Third St., 5th Fl., San Francisco, CA 94103
415-777-4348/1-800-USYOUTH

This organization is a nonprofit cultural exchange organization bringing students from 21 countries around the world to study at the high school and college level in American high schools, community and junior colleges. The students in the college program can choose to stay with a family through the host family program or can live in dormitories on campus. There is also an international language school program.

ARBA Sicula (AS)
St. John's Univ., Jamaica, NY 11439
718-998-5990

Founded in 1978, the ARBA Sicula is interested in the preservation and promotion of Sicilian culture and language. It offers publications in the Sicilian language. It also provides a bilingual newsletter which includes articles about Sicilian folklore, art, history, cuisine, and literature.

ARC Associates, Inc.
310 Eighth St., Ste. 220, Oakland, CA 94607
415-834-9455

ARC Associates publishes and disseminates curriculum materials on Chinese language arts and social studies as well as bilingual storybooks.

Armenian General Benevolent Union (AGBU)
31 W. 52nd St., New York, NY 10019
212-765-8260

Founded in 1906, the Armenian General Benevolent Union (AGBU) is an international organization that promotes Armenian heritage through educational, humanitarian and cultural programs. It operates 22 elementary, secondary and prep schools and provides scholarship grants and loans for the American Univ. of Armenia. It also sponsors summer career internships, Armenian language study, and international athletic games.

Armenian Students Association of America (ASA)
395 Concord Ave., Belmont, MA 02178
617-484-9548

Founded in 1910, this organization provides 60 grants of amounts ranging from $500-$1500 on a yearly basis. (Applicants must be of Armenian ancestry and a full time student at an American college or university.) It also maintains a speakers bureau and gives annual awards to Armenian-American achievers.

Asia Society
725 Park Ave., New York, NY 10021
212-288-6400

The Asia Society has educational programs, multimedia curriculum publications and videos.

Asian Cinevision
32 E. Broadway, New York, NY 10002
212-925-8685

Founded in 1976, the Asian Cinevision is a venue for the portrayal of Asian-American life. It sponsors film festivals, exhibitions, series, and workshops. It has a media archive/library, media information, and production services. It also has an artist in residence program. In addition, it produces a comprehensive, annotated guide entitled *The Asian American Media Reference Guide*. It serves as a resource catalogue of film and video programs by, for, or about Asian Americans. Over 570 works are included.

Association of Student & Professional Italian-Americans (ASPI)
Box 531, Village Station, New York, NY 10014
212-242-3215

Founded in 1957, this organization promotes and preserves Italian culture through cultural activities. It offers assistance to Italian exchange students and Italian American students and professionals. It sponsors cultural activities, lectures, discussions, theater, and opera activities.

Assembly of Turkish American Associations (ATAA)
1601 Connecticut Ave., N.W., Ste. 303, Washington, DC 20009
202-483-9090

Founded in 1979, this organization seeks to act as a liaison between Turkey and the U.S. Its goal is to promote awareness and education. It provides programs in charity, education, job placement, cultural activities, and Turkish history and heritage. It maintains an archive, statistics, a library of 1500 + items, and a computer database.

Association of Teachers of Latin American Studies (ATLAS)
252-58 63rd Ave., Flushing, NY 11362-2406
718-428-1237

Founded in 1970, this organization strives to provide an accurate portrayal of Latin American customs, heritage, languages and people. It publishes curriculum guides on Argentina, Brazil, Chile, Ecuador and Mexico. The association consists of educators and others interested in promoting the study of Latin America in U.S. educational institutions.

Austrian Cultural Institute
11 E. 52nd St., New York, NY 10022-5390
212-759-5165

This organization provides free brochures and folders to educators and students. It is a cultural agency of the Austrian Foreign Ministry and has a reference library consisting of about 8,000 volumes of materials relating to Austria. It has a film, video, and slide lending service and traveling exhibitions are available to educational institutions free of charge.

Avery Institute of Afro-American History & Culture
58 George St., Box 2262 Charleston, SC 29401
803-792-5742

The Avery Institute has a library specializing in South Carolina Afro-American history.

Belarusan-American Association, Inc.
National Headquarters, 166-34 Gothic Drive, Jamaica, NY 11432

Belarusan-American Women Association (BAWA)
146 Sussex Drive, Manhasset, NY 11030
516-627-9195

Founded in 1956, this association is for women of Belarusan birth, descent or association by marriage. The association strives to preserve Belarusan culture and heritage and has Belurusan language classes, school programs and cultural events.

Brazilian-American Cultural Institution
4103 Connecticut Ave., N.W., Washington, DC 20008
202-362-8334

Founded in 1964, this bi-national organization promotes cultural exchange between the U.S. and Brazil. It sponsors programs such as art exhibitions, recitals, lectures, and films. Its 6000 volume library is available to members and it has a music library with Brazilian classical and popular music. It also has a language laboratory for teaching the Portuguese language.

Brooklyn Museum of Art
Dept of African, Oceanic & New World Art
200 Eastern Parkway, Brooklyn, NY 11238
918-638-5000

The Brooklyn Museum of Art has over 125,000 volumes in its collection.

Bureau of Indian Affairs
18th & C Sts., NW, Washington, DC 20245-0001
202-343-7445

The Bureau of Indian Affairs publishes a variety of materials about Native Americans including books, maps, posters and pamphlets.

Center for Cuban Studies
124 W. 23rd St., New York, NY 10011
212-242-0559

Founded in 1972, the Center for Cuban Studies strives to narrow the informational and relational gap between Cuba and the U.S. It runs an Information Exchange Program, sponsors cultural exchanges, and maintains a library and graphics/photographic ar-

chives. It offers film showings, lectures, seminars, conferences, exhibits, and concerts.

Center for Japanese Studies
223 Fulton St., Room 500, Berkeley, CA 94720
412-642-3156

Center for Korean Studies
Institute of East Asian Studies
Univ. of California, 2223 Fulton St., Room 512, Berkeley, CA 94720
415-642-5674

Center for Southeast Asia Studies
Univ. of California, Berkeley, 260 Stephens Hall, Berkeley, CA 94720
415-642-3608

Cherokee National Historical Society (CNHS)
Box 515, Tahlequah, OK 74465
918-456-6007

Founded in 1963, this society is dedicated to preserving the history and culture of the Cherokee nation. It runs the Cherokee National Museum and the Ancient Village, a living 16th century village. It conducts the Trail of Tears Outdoor Drama and houses the official archives of the Cherokee nation. It has a full time education director. The Cherokee National Museum Library, located on site, has a genealogy service for tracing Cherokee ancestry.

Chinese American Civic Council (CACC)
Box 166082, Chicago, IL 60616-6082
312-225-0234

Founded in 1951, this organization works for the participation in and contribution to American way of life by Chinese Americans. Its special emphasis is on youth programs.

Chinese American Forum
606 Brantford Ave., Silver Spring, MD 20904
301-622-3053

The *Chinese American Forum* is a quarterly magazine in English by Chinese Americans devoted to culture bridging and nationwide communication. It intends to nourish the harmonious bicultural life and promote full participation in the American system.

Chicano Studies Research Center
Univ. of California, 3121 Campbell Hall, Los Angeles, CA 90024
213-825-2363

Congress for Jewish Culture (CJC)
25 E. 21st St., New York, NY 10010
212-505-8040

Founded in 1948, the Congress for Jewish Culture works for the preservation of Yiddish. It offers a wide variety of programs including lectures, art exhibits, concerts, research, conferences and publications.

Czech Heritage Foundation (CHF)
Box 761, Cedar Rapids, IA 52406
319-365-0868

Founded in 1974, this organization facilitates ethnic festivals, concerts, cultural events and maintains a speakers bureau. It is for individuals interested in Czech and Slovakian history, culture and traditions.

Danish Sisterhood of America (DSA)
3429 Columbus Dr., Holiday, Fl 34691-1027

Founded in 1883, the Danish Sisterhood of America works to preserve Danish heritage and traditions. It awards scholarships and camp grants and operates the Junior American Danish Auxiliary (JADA) lodges that teach Danish language, dances, crafts, and heritage.

DQ University Library
Box 409, Davis, CA 95616
916-758-0470

The DQ University is run by Native Americans and sponsors educational and social events. The library has an extensive collection on Native American culture.

El Bireh Palestine Society of the U.S.A. (EBPSUSA)
c/o Rafeek Farah, M.D., 2105 West Rd., Trenton, MI 48183
313-675-7777

Founded in 1981, this organization was formed by people originally from the town of El Bireh, Palestine. Its goal is to preserve Palestinian culture. It has programs for education, scholarships, refugee assistance, children's services, and cultural programs.

Federation of Turkish-American Societies (FTAS)
821 United Nations Plaza, 2nd Fl., New York, NY 10017
212-682-7688

Founded in 1956, this federation is an association of over 35 Turkish American Associations in the U.S. It represents the Turkish American community and promotes Turkish-American friendship. It maintains a library of 500 volumes and celebrates Ataturks Commemoration Day (Nov.10), Youth and Sports Day (May 19) and Children's Day (Apr.23.).

Finnish-American Historical Society of the West

Box 5522, Portland, OR 97208
503-654-0448

This is a nonprofit organization dedicated to preserving the cultural heritage of America's Finnish settlers. It maintains a reference library of works about Finland, the American West and Finnish immigrants. It has books and magazines in both Finnish and English.

German Society of Pennsylvania (GSP)

611 Spring Garden St., Philadelphia, PA 19123
215-627-2332

Founded in 1764, the German Society of Pennsylvania strives to preserve German cultural heritage. It offers German language instruction, conversation opportunity, and scholarships for German majors at area colleges. It maintains the largest private German library in the U.S., with holdings of over 100,000 books, 100 audio tapes, 19th century newspapers, and various archival records. About 90% of the items are in German. It sponsors programs of German culture, drama, music and celebrations.

Global Organization of People of Indian Origin

60 Bradley Place, Stanford, CT 06905
203-329-8010

Founded in 1980, this organization works for the advancement of Indians in the U.S. and provides communication among various Indian organizations and groups in the U.S. It strives to preserve Indian culture and for that purpose organizes cultural, social and educational affairs nationwide. It also seeks to establish and maintain friendly ties between the U.S. and India and maintains contact with the government concerning matters important to its constituency. It operates seminars, a speakers bureau, compiles statistics and bestows awards.

Goethe House

1014 Fifth Ave., New York, NY 10028
212-439-8700

The Goethe House offers monthly cultural programs geared toward teachers of the German language. It has a library of about 11,000 volumes (approximately 80% in German), 130 periodicals and numerous A/V materials (500 audiocassettes, 280 videos and a small number of CD's). The audiocassettes include German pop music and jazz, a large number of recordings of texts by German authors, radio plays, and cassettes for children. The video collection consists primarily of documentary films on German art, literature, history, geography and includes a selection of recent feature films by contemporary German directors. The library is open to the public. It presents films, exhibitions and various cultural activities.

Hola Kumba Ya!

Box 50173, Philadelphia, PA 19132
215-848-5118

This organization seeks to preserve oral storytelling and other aspects of folk art, such as dance, music and song. It presents group and solo performances in various public venues across the U.S. Other programs include workshops, lectures, consultations and resource information.

Information Center on Children's Culture

331 E. 38th St., New York, NY 10016
212-686-5522

The Information Center on Children's Culture is a source of information on Hispanic children.

Institute of Chinese Culture

86 Riverside Dr., New York, NY 10024
212-787-6969

Founded in 1943, this organization's goal is to promote traditional Chinese culture and to foster better understanding and friendship between the Chinese and the American peoples through cultural exchanges. In cooperation with other organizations such as the Association of Chinese Calligraphy and the Chinese Consolidated Benevolent Association, the Institute sponsors activities such as the Chinese Calligraphy and Art exhibits, sport events and lectures for Chinese youth and for Americans. In conjunction with the Asian Speakers' Bureau, it provides well known speakers for the American public and mass media (fees are charged for speakers). It helped establish the Chinatown Cultural Service Center located at the Confucius Plaza in Chinatown, New York City. The Center is open to the public, has over 15,000 books and has news reels and films from Free China and Hong Kong.

Instituto Italiano Di Cultura (Italian Cultural Institute)

686 Park Ave., New York, NY 10021
212-879-4242

Founded in 1850, this is a cultural branch of the Consulate General of Italy, administered by the Department for Cultural Relations at the Ministry for Foreign Affairs. It promotes cultural ties between Italy and the U.S. It maintains a library, has a reading room, an information office and A/V materials. It organizes lectures by Italian and American scholars on various aspects of Italian culture and provides information on academic exchanges. Other Italian Cultural Institute offices can be found in the following cities:

International Romani Union

Manchaca, TX 78652-0822
512-282-1268

This organization is an umbrella organization that coordinates a number of regional and national bodies in about 30 countries throughout the world. One of its activities is to provide educational materials about Gypsy peoples to non-gypsy peoples. It compiles statistics, operates a speakers' bureau and maintains a library of over 1,500 items including books, videos and audiocassettes.

Italian Cultural Institute

500 N. Michigan Ave., Ste. 1850, Chicago, IL 60611
312-822-9545

Italian Cultural Institute

12400 Wilshire Blvd., Ste. 300, Los Angeles, CA 90025
213-207-4937

Italian Cultural Institute

1 Charlton Court, Ste. 102, San Francisco, CA 94123
415-922-4178

Italian Cultural Institute

1601 Fuller St., NW, Washington, DC 20009
202-328-5500

Japan Foundation (JF)

152 W. 57th St., 39th Fl., New York, NY 10019
212-489-0299

Founded in 1972, the Japan Foundation strives to promote educational and cultural exchange between U.S. and Japan. It assists libraries in the expansion of Japan related materials.

Japanese American Citizens League (JACL)
1765 Sutter St., San Francisco, CA 94115
415-921-5225

This organization is dedicated to ending bigotry, especially anti-Asian sentiment. A handbook on anti-Asian sentiment is available from them and the Education Committee is compiling a bibliography of Japanese American history. The organization also has regional offices in the following areas: Washington, D.C.; Chicago; Los Angeles; Seattle and Fresno.

Japanese American Library
Box 590598, San Francisco, CA 94159
415-567-5006

The Japanese American Library is a research center dedicated to preserving Japanese American heritage.

Korean Cultural Service
5505 Wilshire Blvd., Los Angeles, CA 90036
213-936-7141

The Korean Cultural Service maintains a Korean materials library, promotes cultural programs and exhibits.

Kurdish Heritage Foundation of America
345 Park Place, Brooklyn, NY 11238
718-783-7930

This organization was founded in 1981. Its purpose is to promote an awareness of the existence of Kurds as an ethnic group through cultural and educational activities. The Kurdish Library was established in 1986 and is the only repository of its kind in the Western Hemisphere housing a comprehensive collection of resources on the Kurds of the Middle East. The Library includes over 2,000 volumes, periodicals, newspapers, articles and reports in English and a variety of foreign languages. It includes maps, slides, photographs, audiocassettes and videos. The audio collection consists of traditional and contemporary Kurdish music. The Kurdish Museum houses costumes, village jewelry, artifacts and examples of Kurdish carpets. It also maintains a speakers' bureau and compiles statistics.

Laotian Cultural & Research Center
1413 Meriday Lane, Santa Ana, CA 92706
714-541-4533

This organization was founded in 1983 and is interested in preserving Laotian culture by collecting documents which illustrate the history of Laos. It maintains a library of over 500 items on the history of Laos.

Latin American Studies Association (LASA)
Univ. of Pittsburgh, William Pitt Union, 9th Fl., Pittsburgh, PA 15260
412-648-7929

Founded in 1966, the Latin American Studies Association seeks to promote teaching and research in Latin American studies. It encourages the increase of library materials on Latin America and encourages research and publication. It also distributes the Kalman Silvert Award and LASA Media Awards.

Luso-American Education Foundation (LAEF)
Box 1768, Oakland, CA 94604
415-452-4465

This organization strives to preserve the culture of Portuguese Americans. It provides advisory and reference services and assists teachers and school districts in setting up Portuguese language and literature courses. Services are free and available to California residents only.

Mexican American Studies Research Center
Univ. of Arizona, Modern Language Bldg., Tucson, AZ 85721

This is a source of information on Chicano culture.

Museum of the American Indian
Broadway at 155th St., New York, NY 10032
212-283-2420

National Asian American Telecommunications Association (NAATA)
346 Ninth St., Second Fl., San Francisco, CA 94103
415-863-0814

NAATA distributes Asian American films and videos as well as radio works by Asian Americans.

National Association for the Advancement of Colored People (NAACP)
4805 Mt. Hope Dr., Baltimore, MD 21215
301-358-8900

National Association of Black Storytellers
Box 27456, Philadelphia, PA 19118
215-844-8463

National Association of Japan-America Societies
New York, NY

This is a nonprofit, national organization, formed in 1979 to provide a cooperative network among independent Japan-America Societies located throughout the United States. Following is a list of its 25 member organizations. These organizations can serve as a resource for programs on Japan for the city in which the society is located. Contact the individual organization to determine other (if any) resources that may be available through that organization.

Japan America Society of Alabama
600 N. 18th St., Rm. 7N-0015, Birmingham, AL 35291-0015
205-250-2077

Japan Society of Boston, Inc.
22 Batterymarch St., Boston, MA 02109
617-451-0726

Japan-America Society of Central Florida, Inc.
Box 23744, Tampa, FL 33623
813-289-6283

Japan America Society of Chicago, Inc.
225 W. Wacker Dr., Ste. 2250, Chicago, IL 60606
312-263-3049

Japan-America Society of Greater Cincinnati
300 Carew Tower, 441 Vine St., Cincinnati, OH 45202-2812
513-579-3114

Japan America Society of Colorado
707 Seventeenth St., Ste. 2300, Denver, CO 80202
303-295-8862

Japan America Society of Georgia
South Tower, 225 Peachtree St. NE, Ste. 710, Atlanta, GA 30303
404-524-7399

Greater Detroit & Windsor Japan-America Society
150 W. Jefferson, Ste. 1500, Detroit, MI 48226
313-963-1988

Japan-America Society of Hawaii
Box 1412, Honolulu, HI 96806
808-524-4450

Japan-America Society of Houston
1360 Post Oak Blvd., Ste. 1760,
  Houston, TX 77056
713-963-0121

Japan-America Society of Indiana, Inc.
First Indiana Plaza, 135 N.
  Pennsylvania St., Ste. 1570, Indianapolis, IN 46204-2491
317-635-0123

Japan America Society of Kentucky
Box 333, Lexington, KY 40584
606-231-7533

Japan America Society of New Hampshire
Box 1226, Portsmouth, NH
  03802-1226
603-433-1360

Japan Society
333 E. 47th St., New York, NY 10017
212-832-1155

Founded in 1907, the Japan Society
promotes American understanding of
Japan, its culture, economy, history,
and people. It seeks to do the same
about Americans for Japanese people.
It sponsors cultural and educational
programs and cultural exchanges.

Japan Society of Northern California
31 Geary St., San Francisco, CA
  94104
415-986-4383/1-800-67JAPAN

Japan America Society of Oregon
221 NW Second Ave., Portland, OR
  97209
503-228-9411 x235, 236

Japan America Society of Pennsylvania
500 Wood St., Ste. 1614, Pittsburgh,
  PA 15222
412-281-4440

Japan America Society of Phoenix
4635 E. Lake Shore Dr., Ste. 116,
  Tempe, AZ 85282
602-893-0599

Japan America Society of Southern California
ARCO Plaza, 505 S. Flower St., Level
  C, Los Angeles, CA 90071
213-627-6217

Japan Society of South Florida
World Trade Center, 80 SW 8th St.,
  Ste. 2809, Miami, FL 33130
305-358-6006

Japan America Society of St. Louis, Inc.
25 N. Brentwood Blvd., St. Louis, MO
  63105
314-726-6822

Japan America Society of the State of Washington
One Union Sq. Bldg., 600 University
  St., Ste. 2420, Seattle, WA
  98101-3163
206-623-7900

Japan Virginia Society
830 E. Main St., Ste. 304, Richmond,
  VA 23219
804-783-0740

Japan America Society of Washington, Inc. (DC)
Dacor-Bacon House Mews, 606 18th
  St., NW, Washington, DC 20006
202-289-8290

Japan America Society of Wisconsin, Inc.
The Wisconsin World Trade Center,
  424 E. Wisconsin Ave., Milwaukee,
  WI 53202-4406
414-272-5160

National Council for Languages and International Studies (NCLIS)
300 I St., NE, Ste. 211, Washington,
  DC 20002
202-546-7855

Founded in 1982, the National Council
for Languages and International
Studies emphasizes the need for
foreign language education in U.S.
schools. It keeps contact with
legislators and lawmakers to further
the ends of language and international studies and monitors related
legislative action. (It has helped create
32 federal programs since 1981.) In
addition, it represents 36 national and
regional organizations encompassing
the major and less commonly taught
modern languages, the classics, linguistics, bilingual education, exchanges, international business
education, and educational technology.

National Federation of Indian American Associations
Box 462, Wakefield Station, Bronx, NY
  10466
203-329-8010

This umbrella organization was founded in 1980 and has 11 regional
groups. It consists primarily of Asian
Indian organizations whose purpose
is to represent and advance the interests of Indians in the United States.
It coordinates cultural, educational,
social and economic activities for
Asian Indians in North America. It
operates a speakers' bureau, disseminates information and compiles
statistics.

National Italian American Foundation (NIAF)
666 11th St., NW, Ste. 800,
  Washington, DC 20001
202-638-0220

Founded in 1975, this organization is
interested in research and education in
all areas of Italian culture. It maintains
contact with Congress and other
governmental entities. It also bestows
awards and scholarships and has a
program for educational exchange. It
operates an information referral service and collects statistics.

National Native American Cooperative
Box 5000, San Carlos, AZ
  85550-0301
602-230-3399

Founded in 1969, the National Native
American Cooperative publishes the
Native American Directory and encourages Native American artists in
their crafts. It sponsors Pow Wows
and cultural festivals and also sponsors information services.

National Organization of Italian-American Women
445 W. 59th St., Rm. 1248, New York,
  NY 10019
212-237-8574

Founded in 1980, this organization
promotes the ethnic pride of Italian
American women. It seeks to encourage education and accomplish-
ments for Italian American women and
defuse stereotypes. It offers educational programs on various topics,
maintains a youth outreach program
and awards scholarships to Italian
American women pursuing higher education.

Native American Newspapers Collection
815 State St., Madison, WI 53706
608-262-9584

Native American Public Broadcasting Consortium
Box 8311, Lincoln, NE 68501
402-472-3522

The Native American Public Broadcasting Consortium has many authentic
educational video programs available
for public use.

Native American Research Information Service
American Indian Institute, 555 Constitution Ave., Norman, OK 73037
405-325-1711

The Native American Research Information Service computer database has

over 6,000 items. It covers 1969 to the present and provides information on native culture, natural resources, economic and human resources.

Netherland-America Foundation
54 W. 39th St., New York, NY 10018
212-767-1616

This organization offers interest free study loans to qualified Dutch students studying in the U.S. and American students studying in the Netherlands in higher education.

Philippine Resource Center
2288 Fulton, Ste. 103, Box 40090, Berkeley, CA 94704
415-548-2546

The Philippine Resource Center maintains a library of Philippine materials.

POLART
5973 Cattlemen Lane, Sarasota, FL 34232
813-378-9393

POLART is a supplier of Polish films, music and literature. They have a catalogue of videos of feature films, musical performances, sporting events, children's features, travel and documentaries as well as compact discs of classical, folk, jazz and popular music.

Polish Institute of Arts & Sciences of America
208 E. 30th St., New York, NY 10016
212-686-4164

This organization was founded in 1942. It operates the Alfred Jurzykowski Memorial Library, a specialized reference library on Polish studies, which contains over 20,000 volumes. It is a center of research, documentation and information on Polish American culture and history.

Polish Museum of America (PMA)
984 N. Milwaukee Ave., Chicago, IL 60622
312-384-3352

Founded in 1937, this organization promotes the knowledge and study of Polish history and culture. It publishes Polish culture bibliographies and various books. It has programs which include lectures, concerts, movie/slide presentations, plays, and scholarly conferences. It maintains a library of 60,000 volumes, 250 periodicals and A/V materials.

Popular Culture Library
Bowling Green State Univ., Bowling Green, OH 43403-0600
419-372-2450

Created in 1969, the Popular Culture Library is an internationally known repository dedicated to acquiring and preserving primary research materials on 19th and 20th century American popular culture. It is the leading popular culture library in the United States. It contains a wide variety of materials which support culturally diverse research and teaching programs, particularly the collections of underground/counter-culture periodicals, genre periodicals and popular fiction.

Portuguese Continental Union of the United States of America (PCU)
899 Boylston St., Boston, MA 02115
617-536-2916

Founded in 1925, this organization promotes Portuguese culture. It offers scholarships and assistance to exchange students, and bestows annual awards for assistance to Portuguese people. It also has a library of 4000 volumes.

Project ASIA (Asian Shared Information & Access)
2225 W. Commonwealth Ave., Ste. 315, Alhambra, CA 91803
818-284-7744

This organization provides cataloging and selection services for Chinese, Japanese, Korean and Vietnamese materials.

REFORMA (National Association to Promote Library Services to the Spanish Speaking)
c/o American Library Association, Office of Library Outreach Services, 50 E. Huron St., Chicago, IL 60611
800-545-2433

This organization is committed to the improvement of library and information services for Spanish speaking and Hispanic people in the United States.

SALALM (Seminar on the Acquisition of Latin American Library Materials)
University of Wisconsin, Secretariat, Memorial Library, Madison, WI 53706
608-262-3240

SALALM disseminates bibliographic information about all types of Latin American and Caribbean publications.

Scottish Historic and Research Society of Delaware Valley (SHRSDV)
102 St. Paul's Rd., Ardmore, PA 19003
215-649-4144

Founded in 1964, provides access to a library of Scottish materials available

by appointment and also has some genealogical material and papers aimed at primary and secondary students.

Sino-American Amity Fund (SAAF)
86 Riverside Dr., New York, NY 10024
212-787-6969

Founded in 1956, this educational and charitable organization is dedicated to promoting better understanding between American and Chinese people. It assists Chinese students with higher education costs in the U.S. and seeks to promote peace by establishing leadership models for young Chinese people, with the goal of lasting good relations between the U.S. and China.

Sino Broadcasting
137 Waverly Place, San Francisco, CA 94108
415-433-3340

Radio, television and magazines in Chinese languages.

Society for French American Cultural Services and Educational Aid
972 Fifth Ave., New York, NY 10021
212-439-1439; 800-937-3624

This is a lending agency for materials relating to French culture and history. It offers French feature films on video and documentaries on 16mm. It also has French books and music on CD's and cassettes.

Society for German-American Studies
c/o Dr. Don Heinrich Tolzmann, Central Library, M.L. 33, Univ. of Cincinnati, Cincinnati, OH 45221
513-556-1859

This society exists for the purpose of studying and promoting interest in all aspects of German American culture including history, linguistics, folklore, genealogy, literature, theater, music and other creative art forms. It strives to publish and present information and findings in the interest of public education and service. It assists researchers, teachers, and students and also seeks to improve cross cultural relations between German speaking nations and the Americas.

Sons of Norway
1455 W. Lake St., Minneapolis, Mn 55408
612-827-3611

Founded in 1895, the Sons of Norway is dedicated to the preservation and promotion of Norwegian culture. It tries to strengthen ties between the U.S. and Norway. It maintains a library of slides, videos, musical CD's, and other items for use free of charge to members and for a nominal fee to nonmembers. It also has travel, cultural and sports programs and a scholarship program for educational exchange.

St. David's Society of the State of New York (SDS)
71 W. 23rd St., New York, NY 10010
212-924-8415; 212-924-3945

Founded in 1801, this society was formed to preserve Welsh culture and to assist Welsh immigrants or those of Welsh ancestry. It awards 80 scholarships and grants to students of the arts, music, literature, and drama and bestows awards and offers classes in the Welsh language.

Swedish Council of America
2600 Park Ave., Minneapolis, MN 55407
612-871-0593

The Swedish Council of America was formed in 1972. Over 107 Swedish-American (and some Scandinavian-American) societies and organizations in various parts of the United States and Sweden are affiliate members of the Council. The Council serves as a clearinghouse of information regarding the availability of Swedish and Swedish-American cultural resources, including lecturers, exhibits, folk dance troupes, choirs, etc.

Urasenke Tea Ceremony Society (UCTS)
153 E.69th St., New York, NY 10021
212-988-6161

Founded in 1980, the Urasenke Tea Ceremony Society seeks to promote intercultural understanding through the ceremonial sharing of tea. It offers classes in chanoyu, or tea ceremony, and also offers lecture/tour/demonstrations to school groups.

Vietnamese American Social & Cultural Council
Vietnamese American Good Neighborhood Committee
1115 E. Santa Clara St., San Jose, CA 95116
408-971-8281

This is a source for English as A Second Language materials related to the Vietnamese language.

Visual Communications
Southern California Asian American Studies Center, Inc.
263 S. Los Angeles St., Rm. 307, Los Angeles, CA 90012
213-680-4462

The Visual Communications organization produces programs on Asian American themes. It also has an extensive photograph collection.

Welsh Library
c/o The Welsh Guild,
Arch Street Presbyterian Church, 1724 Arch St., Philadelphia, PA 19103

World Around Songs
5790 Hwy.80 S., Burnsville, NC 28714
704-675-5343

This organization offers a catalog of a variety of pocket-sized songbooks. The songbooks range from multicultural folk songs to rounds and carols to spirituals and hymns.

MUSEUMS

14

The museums included in this section are primarily geared to children. Unusual and noteworthy exhibits are noted.

ALABAMA

CENTER FOR CULTURAL ARTS
501 Broad St., Gadsden, AL 35901
205-543-2787; Fax: 205-546-7435
Dir/Curator: Bobby Welch

Founded: 1990
Hours: M-F 9:00-5:00, Sa 10:00-6:00,
Su 1:00-5:00
Includes children's museum

CHILDREN'S HANDS-ON MUSEUM
2213 University Blvd., Tuscaloosa, AL
35403
205-349-4235
Dir/Curator: Kathleen HughesD

Founded 1984
Hours: Tu-F 9:00-5:00, Sa 1:00-5:00
Choctaw Indian village, planetarium,
T.V. studio and other special exhibits

DISCOVERY PLACE
1320 22nd St. S,, Birmingham, AL
35205
205-939-1177; Fax: 205-933-4111
Mailing Address: 1421 22nd St. S, Birmingham, AL 35205
Dir/Curator: John L. Mackay

Founded: 1981
Hours: M-F 9:00-3:00, Sa 10:00-4:00,
Su 1:00-4:00
Hands-on children's science museum.
Interactive exhibits on the human
body, communications, and elec-
tricity.

ALASKA

THE IMAGINARIUM
725 W. 5th, Anchorage, AK 99501
907-276-3179; Fax: 907-258-4306
Exec Dir: Nancy Hoke

Founded: 1986
Hours: M-Sa 10:00-6:00, Su
12:00-5:00
Science, discovery center and museum; exhibits include wetlands, rain
forest, marine life, galaxy room.

ARIZONA

ARIZONA MUSEUM FOR YOUTH
35 N. Robson, Mesa, AZ 85201

602-644-2468
Dir/Curator: Barbara Meyerson

Founded: 1978
Hours: Tu-F 1:00-5:00, Sa 10:00-5:00,
Su 1:00-5:00

TUCSON CHILDREN'S MUSEUM
200 S. 6th Ave., Tucson, AZ 85702
602-792-9985; Fax: 602-792-0639
Dir/Curator: Beth LaRoche

Founded: 1986
Hours: call 884-7511
Exhibits include Turn it On, Turn it
Off!; Bubble Factory, Firehouse,
Science Gallery, and ME room. Also,
hands-on electricity and energy con-
servation exhibit.

ARKANSAS

CHILDREN'S MUSEUM OF ARKANSAS
1400 W. Markham, Ste. 200, Little
Rock, AR 72201
501-374-6655; Fax: 501-374-4746
Exec Dir: Putter Bert

Founded 1991
Hours: Tu-Su 10:00-5:00; F
10:00-9:00
Exhibits include Farmers Market and
Railroad Observation Deck.

CALIFORNIA

BAY AREA DISCOVERY MUSEUM
557 E. Fort Baker, Sausalito, CA
94965
415-332-9646; Fax: 415-332-9671
Dir/Curator: Diane Frankel

Founded: 1985
Hours: W-Su 10:00-5:00, open Tu in
Summer
Hands on museum with exhibits for
children ages 1-12 including media
center, science lab, art studio, ceramic studio and theater. Also exhibits on architecture and industry of
the Bay Area.

LORI BROCK CHILDREN'S MUSEUM
3803 Chester Ave., Bakersfield, CA
93301
805-395-1201
Ed. Svcs Coord.: Marsha Carlson

Founded: 1976
Hours: M-F 8:00-4:30, Sa 10:00-4:00,
Sun 1:00-4:00

CHILDREN'S DISCOVERY MUSEUM OF SAN JOSE
180 Woz Way, San Jose, CA
95110-2780
408-298-5437; Fax: 408-298-6826
Exec Dir: Sally Oberg

Founded: 1983
Hours: Tu-Sa 10:00-5:00, Su
12:00-5:00
Features include early childhood
resource center, Brandenburg Theater, Children's Garden and rotating
exhibits of vehicles.

CHILDREN'S DISCOVERY MUSEUM OF THE DESERT
42-501 Rancho Mirage Lane, Rancho
Mirage, CA 92270
619-346-2900
Dir/Curator: Karen Riley

Founded: 1987
Hours: Tu-Sa 9:00-3:00, closed Su, M
Features garden, art recycle center,
doctor's office

CHILDREN'S MUSEUM AT LA HABRA
301 E. Euclid, La Habra, CA 90631
310-905-9693
Dir/Curator: Catherine Michaels

Founded: 1977
Hours: M-Sa 10:00-5:00, Su 1:00-5:00

CHILDREN'S MUSEUM OF SAN DIEGO
200 West Island Ave., San Diego, Ca
92101
619-233-8792; Fax: 619-233-8796
Exec. Dir: Robert L. Sain

Founded: 1983
Hours: Tu-Sa 10:00-4:30, Su
12:00-4:30
Hands-on interactive exhibits for children ages 2-12

COYOTE POINT MUSEUM FOR EN-VIRONMENTAL EDUCATION
1651 Coyote Point Dr., San Mateo, CA
94401
415-342-7755
Dir/Curator: Linda Liebes

Founded: 1954
Hours: Tu-Sa 10:00-5:00, Su
12:00-5:00. Open some holidays
Environmental hall depicts six ecological zones found in the San Francisco Bay area, and features computer games, films, exhibits, and graphics. The adjacent Wildlife Habitats houses animals, amphibians, birds and reptiles native to the area.

DISCOVERY CENTER
1944 N. Winery Ave., Fresno, CA
93703
209-251-5533
Dir: John Houseman

Founded: 1956
Hours: daily 11:00-4:00
Various hands-on exhibits.

EXPLORATORIUM
3601 Lyon St., San Francisco, CA
94123
415-561-0360

Hours: Summer M-Su 10:00-5:00 (W
10:00-9:30). Closed M during non-summer hours
First and foremost interactive museum housed in the Palace of Fine Arts. 650 hand's-on exhibits including: tornado, electrical current, finger paint, and Tactile Dome sensory journey.

HAYWARD SHORELINE INTERPRETIVE CENTER
4901 Breakwater, Hayward, CA 94545
510-881-6751
Dir/Curator: Michael E. Koslosky

Hours: M-Su 10:00-5:00
Goal is to introduce visitors to the natural history and ecology of the San Francisco Bay. Education programs for school groups, weekend interpretive events for families/general visitors.

JUNIOR ARTS CENTER
Barnsdall Art Park
4814 Hollywood Blvd., Los Angeles,
CA 90027
213-485-4474; Fax: 213-485-8396
Dir: Harriet S. Miller

Founded: 1967
Hours: Office M-F, 9:00-4:30; Gallery
Tu-Su, 12:30-5:00
International art collection has 3,500 original works by children from fifty countries. Museum exhibits, classes and workshops emphasize the importance of children's viewing and responding to original works of art.

KIDSPACE MUSEUM
390 S. El Molino Ave., Pasadena, CA
91101

818-449-9144
Exec. Dir: Kristi Williamson

Founded 1979
Hours: school year W 2:00-5:00, Sa-Su
12:30-5:00; Summer/holidays Tu-F
1:00-5:00, Sa-Su 12:30-5:00
Participatory museum for children. Exhibits include Eco-beach, Planetarium, Critter Caverns and International Masks.

THE LINDSAY MUSEUM
1931 First Ave., Walnut Creek, CA
94596
510-935-1978
Dir/Curator: Stephen Barbata

Founded: 1955
Hours: W-Su 1:00-5:00

LONG BEACH CHILDREN'S MUSEUM
445 Long Beach Blvd., #60, Long
Beach, CA 90802
310-495-1653; Fax: 310-495-2188
Exec Dir: Liz Miramontes-Kennard

Founded: 1985
Hours: Th-Sa 11:00-4:00, Su
12:00-4:00
Exhibits include art cafe, TRW computer station, GTE shadow room, Penelope's hospital room, granny's attic, Vons mini mart and "Goin Fishin."

LOS ANGELES CHILDREN'S MUSEUM
310 N. Main St., Los Angeles, CA
90012
213-687-8801
Exec. Dir: Vincent Beggs

Founded: 1979
Hours: Call for hours

JOSEPHINE RANDALL JUNIOR MUSEUM
199 Museum Way, San Francisco, CA
94114
415-554-9600
Dir: Amy Dawson

Hours: Tu-Sa 10:00-5:00

SULPHUR CREEK NATURE CENTER
1801 D. St., Hayward, CA 94541
510-881-6747
Dir/Curator: Michael E. Koslosky

Founded: 1964
Hours: Tu-Su 10:00-4:00
Goal is to introduce visitors to local wildlife. Live animals, interactive displays, special education programs for school children and families.

YOUTH SCIENCE INSTITUTE, ALUM ROCK DISCOVERY CENTER
16260 Alum Rock Ave., San Jose, CA
95127

408-258-4322
Dir: David Johnston

Founded: 1953
Hours: Tu-F 12:00-4:00, Sa
12:00-4:30; Summer, also Su
10:30-4:30
Children's Natural History Museum. Exhibits of live animals and birds.

YOUTH SCIENCE INSTITUTE, SANBORN DISCOVERY CENTER
16055 Sanborn Rd., Sanborn-Skyline
Park, Saratoga, CA 95070
408-867-6940
Dir: David Johnston

Founded: 1953
Hours: March-Oct, W-F 9:00-4:30, Sa-Su 12:00-4:30.
Small insect zoo, earthquake display, Ohlone Indian display, redwood ecology.

COLORADO

CHILDREN'S MUSEUM OF COLORADO SPRINGS
750 Citadel Dr. E., #3044, Colorado
Springs, CO 80909
719-574-0077; Fax: 719-591-5519
Exec Dir: Richard Conway

Founded: 1988
Hours: Tu-Su 10:00-5:00
Exhibits include children's hospital, opera stage, art studio and computer station.

CHILDREN'S MUSEUM OF DENVER
2121 Children's Museum Dr., Denver,
CO 80211-5221
303-433-7444
Exec. Dir: Jim Brickey

Founded: 1973
Hours: Tu-Su 10:00-5:00, except Fri
10:00-8:00

COLLAGE CHILDREN'S MUSEUM
2065 30th St., Boulder, CO 80306
303-440-0053
Exec Dir: Alison Moore

Founded: 1989
Hours: W-Sa 10:00-5:00, Su 1:00-5:00
Exhibits include Mirrors and Me, Color My Shadow, Dragons of the Dump and Ball Maze.

HALL OF LIFE HEALTH EDUCATION CENTER
(Dept. of the Denver Museum of Natural History)
City Park, 2001 Colorado Blvd., Denver, CO 80205
303-329-5433; Fax: 303-331-6492
Manager: Sue Palmer

Founded: 1975

Hours: daily 9:00-5:00 except
Christmas
Interactive health and wellness exhibits
on "How Life Begins," anatomy genetics, five-senses, fitness, stress,
substance abuse. Children's health
classes and workshops available
year-round.

CONNECTICUT

LUTZ CHILDREN'S MUSEUM
247 S. Main St., Manchester, CT
06040
203-643-0949
Dir/Curator: Vivian F. Zoe

Founded: 1953
Hours: Tu-W 2:00-5:00, Th-F
9:30-5:00, Sa-Su 12:00-5:00; closed
M and major holidays

NEW BRITAIN YOUTH MUSEUM
30 High St., New Britain, CT 06051
203-225-3020
Dir: Michele Deasy

Founded: 1956
Hours: Tu-F 1:00-5:00, Sa 10:00-4:00

SCIENCE CENTER OF CONNECTICUT
950 Trout Brook Dr., West Hartford,
CT 06119
203-231-2824
Dir: Robert F. Content

Founded: 1927
Hours: Tu-Sa 10:00-5:00, Su
12:00-5:00, M 10:00-5:00 throughout the summer and Monday school
holidays

DISTRICT OF COLUMBIA

CAPITAL CHILDREN'S MUSEUM
800 Third St. NE, Washington, DC
20002
202-543-8600
Dir/Curator: Ann W. Lewin

Founded: 1974
Hours: M-Su 10:00-5:00
A hands-on learning institution.

CHILDREN'S MUSEUM OF
WASHINGTON, INC.
4954 MacArthur Blvd., NW, Washington, DC 20007
202-337-4954
Dir/Curator: Susan Seligmann

Founded: 1941
Hours: Closed for renovations, due to
open in 1995
Hands-on science and history
exhibits.

ROCK CREEK NATURE CENTER
5200 Glover Rd. NW, Washington, DC
20015

202-426-6829
Mgr: Dave Smith

Founded: 1960
Hours: Tu-Su 9:00-5:00

FLORIDA

BOCA CHILDREN'S MUSEUM
498 Crawford Blvd., Boca Raton, FL
33432
407-368-6875
Dir: Dr. Hugh M. Murphy

Founded: 1979
Hours: Tu-Sa 12:00-4:00
New exhibits 5 times a year.

BREVARD MUSEUM
2201 Michigan Ave., Cocoa, FL 32926
407-632-1830; Fax: 407-631-7551
Dir/Curator: Rachel C. Moehle

Founded: 1975
Hours: Tu-Sa 10:00-4:00, Su
1:00-4:00; closed M
Exhibits of shells, fossils, Indian
habitat dioramas, aquariums, work-
ing bee-hive, Children's hands-on
Discovery Room, 22 acre Nature
Center.

CHILDREN'S MUSEUM OF TAMPA
7550 North Blvd., Tampa, FL 33604
813-935-8441
Dir/Curator: Marian Winters

Founded: 1985
Hours: M-Th 9:00-4:30, F 9:00-3:00,
Sa 10:00-5:00, Su 1:00-5:00

DISCOVERY SCIENCE CENTER OF
CENTRAL FLORIDA
50 S. Magnolia Ave., Ocala, FL 32670
904-620-2555
Dir/Curator: Margaret Spontak

Founded: 1990
Hours: Tu-Sa 9:00-5:00, Su 1:00-5:00
Hands-on exhibits.

JUNIOR MUSEUM OF BAY COUNTY
1731 Jenks Ave., Panama City, FL
32405
904-769-6128
Dir: Mary N. Sandlin

Founded: 1969
Hours: Tu-F 10:00-4:00, Sa
10:00-4:00
Hands-on science museum, Discovery
Depot, Body Works, Nature Corner,
Imagine Me. Also nature trail,
locomotive and farmstead exhibits.

MARINELIFE CENTER OF JUNO BEACH
1200 U.S. Hwy 1, Loggerhead Park,
Juno Beach, FL 33408
407-627-8280
Dir/Curator: Larry Wood

Founded: 1980
Hours: Tu-Sa 10:00-4:00, Su
12:00-3:00
Tours, aquariums, reptiles, birds, plus
a live shark and ray exhibit.

MIAMI YOUTH MUSEUM
5701 Sunset Dr., Miami, FL
33143
305-661-3046; Fax: 305-669-0917
Exec. Dir: Barbara Zohlman

Founded: 1985
Hours: M-F 10:00-5:00, Sa-Su
11:00-5:00
Features include hands-on interactive
exhibits. Kidscape exhibit: Winn-Dixie
Supermarket, Dr. Smile's Dental
Office, Metro-Dade Fire Dept. exhibit,
Tot Spot and Creation Station. Also
Channel 4 TV's working newsroom.

SOUTH FLORIDA SCIENCE MUSEUM
4801 Dreher Trail N., West Palm
Beach, FL 33405
407-832-1988; Fax: 407-833-0551
Dir/Curator: Charles D. Smith

Founded: 1959
Hours: Sa-Th 10:00-5:00, F
10:00-10:00
Aldrin Planetarium, Gibson Observato-
ry, Aquarium, various hands-on
exhibits. Annual Renaissance
Festival.

TALLAHASSEE MUSEUM OF HISTORY
AND NATURAL SCIENCE
3945 Museum Dr., Tallahassee, FL
32304
904-575-8684
Dir/Curator: Russell Daws

Hours: M-Sa 9:00-5:00, Su 12:30-5:00

YOUNG AT ART CHILDREN'S MUSEUM,
A UNIQUE CHILDREN'S MUSEUM
801 S. University Dr., Plantation, FL
33324 305-424-0085
Dirs: Esther Shrago and Mindy Shrago
Spechler

Founded: 1985
Hours: Tu-Sa 11:00-5:00, Su
12:00-5:00; closed Mondays except
on school holidays.
Hands-on art activities.

GEORGIA

COBB COUNTY YOUTH MUSEUM
649 Cheatham Hill Dr., Marietta, GA
30064
404-427-2563
Dir: Elizabeth Rhodes

Founded: 1964
Hours: March-June, Oct-Nov first Su
2:00-4:00; School tours M-F
9:30-1:30 during school year.

GEORGIA SOUTHERN UNIVERSITY MUSEUM
Rosenwald Bldg., Georgia Southern
  University, Statesboro, GA
  30460
912-681-5444
Dir/Curator: Dr. Delma Presley

Founded: 1980
Hours: Tu-F 9:00-5:00, Su 2:00-5:00

UNCLE REMUS MUSEUM
214 Oak St., Eatonton, GA 31024
706-485-6856
Dir/Curator: Norma Watterson

Founded: 1963
Hours: M-Sa 10:00-5:00 (closed one
  hour for lunch), Su 2:00-5:00; closed
  Tu, Sept thru May
Exhibits include Old Slave Cabin, wood
  carvings of "De Critters," Joel Chan-
  dler Harris First Editions and Uncle
  Remus mementos.

HAWAII

HAWAII CHILDREN'S MUSEUM
650 Iwilei Rd., Honolulu, HI 96817
808-592-5437; Fax: 808-592-5433
Pres: Loretta Yajima

Founded: 1985
Hours: Tu-F 9:00-1:00, Sa & Su
  10:00-4:00

ILLINOIS

ARTIFACT CENTER AT SPERDUS MUSEUM
618 S. Michigan Ave., Chicago, IL
  60605
312-922-9012; Fax: 312-922-6406
Dir/Curator: Susan Bass Marcus

Founded: March 1989
Hours: Su-Th 1:30-4:30
Hands on exhibit geared for children
  and families to explore the ancient
  Near East as archaeologists. Includes activity stations, an illustrated timeline and an Israelite
  house.

CHICAGO CHILDREN'S MUSEUM
465 E. Illinois St., 2nd Fl, Chicago, IL
  60611
312-527-1000; Fax: 312-527-9082
Dir/Curator: Dianne L. Sautter

Founded: 1982
Hours: Tu-F 12:30-4:30, Sa-Su
  10:00-4:30; Tu-F 10:00-12:30
  (preschool exhibit only)
Hands-on interactive exhibits such as
  "Magic and Masquerade" (about
  West African artifacts), "The Stinking
  Truth About Garbage," (about recy-
  cling) and an exhibition grandpar-
  ent/grandchild relations.

DISCOVERY CENTER
711 N. Main St., Rockford, IL 61103
815-963-6769; Fax: 815-965-0642
Exec Dir: Sarah Wolf

Founded: 1984
Hours: Tu-Sa 11:00-5:00, Su
  12:00-5:00
Exhibits are devoted to electricity and
  magnets, simple machines, color &
  light, chemistry, math and puzzles,
  among others.

DUPAGE CHILDREN'S MUSEUM
1777 S. Blanchard Rd., Wheaton, IL
  60187
708-260-9907; Fax: 708-690-5516
Exec Dir: Susan Broad

Founded: 1987
Hours: Tu-Sa 9:30-4:30, Su 1:00-4:00
Exhibits include Ramps & Rollers,
  Waterworks, Young Explorers, Con-
  struction House and Textile Art.

EXPLORATION STATION—A CHIL-DREN'S MUSEUM
396 N. Kennedy Dr., Bradley, IL
  60915
815-935-5665
Dir/Curator: Marilyn O'Flaherty

Founded: 1987
Hours: Fall, Winter: Tu 12:00-5:00;
  W,F,Sa 10:00-5:00, Th 12:00-8:00,
  Su 1:00-5:00; Summer: M-W,F,Sa
  10:00-5:00, Th 10:00-8:00, Su
  1:00-5:00
Features two-story castle, part of sailing ship, sight and soundspace shut-
  tle exhibit and live animals exhibit.

KOHL CHILDREN'S MUSEUM
165 Green Bay Rd., Wilmette, IL
  60091
708-256-6056; Fax: 708-256-2921
Dir/Curator: Linda Kay

Founded: 1985
Hours: Tu-Su 10:00-5:00, closed M
Miniature grocery store, Long Ago and
  Far Away—exhibit includes castle
  and sailing ship. Hands-on exhibits.

INDIANA

CHILDREN'S MUSEUM OF INDIANAPOLIS
3000 N. Meridian, Indianapolis, IN
  46208
317-924-5431; Fax: 317-921-4019
President: Peter Sterling

Founded: 1926
Hours: Tu,W,F,Sa 10:00-5:00; Th
  10:00-8:00, Su 12:00-5:00; M in
  summer 10:00-5:00
Housed in 5 story brick building.
  Largest and fourth oldest children's
  museum. Exhibits on physical and

natural sciences, history, foreign cultures, and the arts. Includes world's
  tallest water clock, SpaceQuest
  Planetarium, Lilly Theater, and a
  turn-of-the-century carousel. Programs and activities also offered.

HANNAH LINDAHL CHILDREN'S MUSEUM
1402 S. Main St., Mishawaka, IN
  46544
219-258-3056
Dir/Curator: Peggy A. Marker

Founded: 1946
Hours: Tu-F 9:00-12:00, 1:00-4:00

MUNCIE CHILDREN'S MUSEUM
306 S. Walnut, Muncie, IN 47305
317-286-1660; Fax: 317-286-1662
Dir/Curator: Mary K. Raggio

Founded: 1977
Hours: Tu-Sa 10:00-5:00, Su
  1:00-5:00; closed holidays

IOWA

CHILDREN'S MUSEUM
533 16th St., Bettendorf, IA 52722
319-344-4106
Dir/Curator: Tracey Kuehl

Founded: 1974
Hours: W 10:00-5:00, Th-F
  10:00-8:00, Sa 10:00-5:00, Su
  12:00-5:00
Hands-on activities on farm-life, a
  heart exhibit, nature room and other
  traveling exhibits

SCIENCE STATION
427 First St., SE, Cedar Rapids, IA
  54201
319-366-0968
CEO: John F. Karn

Founded: 1986
Hours: Tu-Sa 9:00-5:00, Su 1:00-4:00
Features full size hot air balloon.

KANSAS

CHILDREN'S MUSEUM OF KANSAS CITY
4601 State Ave., Kansas City, KS
  66102
913-287-8888
Dir: Mary Kay Inginthron

Founded: 1984
Hours: Tu-F 9:30-4:30, Sa-Su
  1:00-4:30
Slice of the City: a hands on exhibit
  showing how things in the home and
  in cities work.

WONDERSCOPE CHILDREN'S MUSEUM
16000 W. 65th St., Shawnee Mission,
  KS 66217

913-268-8130; Fax: 913-268-4608
Exec Dir: Cindy Kolkin

Founded: 1990
Hours: Tu-Sa 10:00-5:00, Su
12:00-5:00
Exhibits include an ecology room, TV
studio/weather station, circus room,
grocery store, and science labs.

KENTUCKY

LEXINGTON CHILDREN'S MUSEUM
401 W. Main St., Lexington, KY 40507
606-258-3253; Fax: 606-258-3255
Dir: Roger L. Paige

Founded: 1990
Hours: Labor Day-Memorial Day M-F
10:00-6:00, Sa 10:00-5:00, Su
1:00-5:00.
Hands-on interactive museum with
seven galleries and over 90 exhibits.

LIVING ARTS AND SCIENCE CENTER
362 N. Martin Luther King Blvd., Lexington, KY 40508
606-252-5222
Dir/Curator: Marty Henton

Founded: 1968
Hours: Sept-May M-F 9:00-4:00, Sa
10:00-2:00; Summer M-F 9:00-4:00

LOUISVILLE VISUAL ART AS-
SOCIATION
3005 Upper Rd., Louisville, KY 40207
502-896-2146
Dir/Curator: John Bagley

Founded: 1909
Hours: M-F 9:00-5:00, Sa 10:00-3:00,
Su 4:00-12:00
Gallery and historic landmark. Art
classes offered for ages 4 to adult.

LOUISIANA

CHILDREN'S MUSEUM OF LAKE
CHARLES
925 Enterprise Blvd., Lake Charles, LA
70601
318-433-9420
Dir/Curator: D.C. Flynt

Founded: 1988
Hours: Tu-Sa 10:00-5:00, Su
2:00-5:00
Features Kid's Town, U.S.A.

LOUISIANA ARTS AND SCIENCE
CENTER
100 S. River Rd., Baton Rouge, LA
70802
504-344-5272; Fax: 504-344-9477
Exec. Dir: Carol Gikas

Founded: 1960
Hours: Tu-F 10:00-3:00, Sa
10:00-4:00, Su 1:00-4:00

Exhibits include Discovery Depot (children's hands-on room), Science Station (hands' on science gallery),
Egyptian collection, Train City, LASC
train (5 renovated railroad cars from
the 1920s-1940s, and changing exhibits.

LOUISIANA CHILDREN'S MUSEUM
428 Julia St., New Orleans, LA 70130
504-586-0725; Fax: 504-529-3666
Dir/Curator: Bonnie Conway

Founded: 1986
Hours: Tu-Sa 9:30-4:30; Summer: daily
9:30-4:30
Includes exhibit on Cajun culture,
Shadow Trap, Bernoulli Blower, Vor-
tex, Arch Bridge, Echo Tube-Delayed
Sound Exhibit.

MAINE

CHILDREN'S DISCOVERY MUSEUM
265 Water St., Box 5056, Augusta,
ME 04330
207-622-2209

Founded: 1983
Hours: Tu-F 9:00-2:00, Sa 10:00-4:00,
Su 1:00-4:00

CHILDREN'S MUSEUM OF MAINE
142 Free St., Portland, ME 04101
207-828-1234
Dir/Curator: Cynthia Baldwin

Founded: 1977
Hours: M,W,Th 10:00-5:00; F
10:00-8:00; Tu, Su 12:00-5:00

MARYLAND

BALTIMORE CHILDREN'S MUSEUM
10440 Falls Rd., Brooklandville, MD
21022
410-823-2551; Fax: 410-337-4914
Exec Dir: Beatrice Taylor

Founded: 1977
Hours: W-Sa 10:00-4:00, Su
12:00-4:00
Exhibits include Youcan Toucan Theat-
er, Family Folklore, Native American
Tipi, and New Game on the Block.

BALTIMORE CITY LIFE MUSEUMS
800 E. Lombard St., Baltimore, MD
21202
410-396-3524; Fax: 410-396-1806
Curator: Victoria Hawkins

Founded: 1935
Hours: Tu-Sa 10:00-4:00, Su
1:00-4:00 (open until 5:00 during
daylight savings hours).
Area museums include Carroll Man-
sion, Center for Urban Archeology,
1840 House, Courtyard Exhibition
Center, and Brewer's Park, as well

as the Peale Museum and H.L. Men-
cken House.

MASSACHUSETTS

THORNTON W. BURGESS MUSEUM
4 Water St., Sandwich, MA 02563
508-888-4668
Exec Dir: Jeanne Johnson

Founded: 1976
Hours: M-Sa 10:00-4:00, Su 1:00-4:00
Exhibits concern the naturalist/author
Thornton W. Burgess.

CHILDREN'S MUSEUM
Museum Wharf
300 Congress St., Boston, MA 02210
617-426-6500
Acting Dir: Pat Steuert

Hours: Sa-Su, Tu-Th 10:00-5:00, F
10:00-5:00; closed M from Labor
Day to June except school vacation
weeks and holidays

CHILDREN'S MUSEUM AT HOLYOKE
444 Dwight St., Holyoke, MA 01040
413-536-7048

Founded: 1981
Hours: M-Sa 10:00-4:30, Su
12:00-5:00
Participatory exhibits for ages 2-12, including science activities.

THE CHILDREN'S MUSEUM, INC. IN
DARTMOUTH
276 Gulf Rd., S. Dartmouth, MA
02748
508-993-3361
Dir/Curator: Neale Birdsall

Founded: 1952
Hours: Tu-Sa 10:00-5:00, Su & major
holidays 1:00-5:00
First Friday night of each month is Family Night and the museum is open
free of charge 5:00-8:00 p.m.

CHILDREN'S MUSEUM IN EASTON
9 Sullivan Ave., North Easton, MA
02356
508-230-3789
Dir/Curator: Rose Scanlon

Founded: 1988
Hours: Tu-Sa 10:00-5:00, Su
12:00-5:00
Housed in old fire station. Hands on
activities include performance
center, train room and craft projects.

THE DISCOVERY MUSEUMS
177 Main St., Acton, MA 01720
508-264-4201; Fax: 508-264-0210
Dir/Curator: Rob Moir

Founded: Children's Museum-1982;
Science Museum-1987

Hours: During school year: Tu,Th,F
   1:00-4:30; W,Sa,Su 9:00-4:30.
   Science Museum: Tu,Th,F 1:00-4:30,
   W 1:00-6:00 Sa-Su 9:00-4:30; Summer Tu-Su 9:00-4:30, W 9:00-6:00
Two museums: creative children's museum is housed in 100 year old Victorian house with ten exhibit areas
   for children one-six. Science museum is filled with science theme
   spaces for exploration and experimentation by school age children.

MICHIGAN

ANN ARBOR HANDS-ON MUSEUM
219 E. Huron, Ann Arbor, MI 48104
313-995-5437
Dir/Curator: Cynthia Yao

Founded: 1979
Hours: Tu-F 10:00-5:30, Sa
   10:00-5:00, Su 1:00-5:00

CHILDREN'S MUSEUM/DETROIT
PUBLIC SCHOOLS
67 E. Kirby, Detroit, MI 48202
313-494-1210; Fax: 313-873-3384
Dir/Curator: Beatrice Parsons

Founded: 1917
Hours: M-F class tours 9:00-4:00; public 1:00-4:00, Sa 9:00-4:00 (Oct-May)

CURIOUS KIDS' MUSEUM
415 Lake Blvd., St. Joseph, MI 49085
616-983-2543; Fax: 616-983-3317
Dir: Mary Baske

Founded: 1988
Hours: W-Su 10:00-5:00

KINGMAN MUSEUM OF NATURAL
HISTORY
W. Michigan Ave. & 20th St., Battle
   Creek, MI 49017
616-965-5117
Dir/Curator: Robert Learner

Founded: 1869
Hours: Tu-Sa 9:00-5:00, Su 1:00-5:00;
   Jul & Aug M 9:00-5:00

YOUR HERITAGE HOUSE
110 E. Ferry Ave., Detroit, MI 48202
313-871-1667
Dir/Curator: Josephine H. Love

Founded: 1969
Hours: M-F 10:00-4:00
African heritage room, doll & puppetry
   collection; housed in 19th century
   residence and carriage house.

MINNESOTA

A.M. CHISHOLM MUSEUM/DULUTH
CHILDREN'S MUSEUM
506 W. Michigan St., Duluth, MN
   55802

218-722-8563
Dir: Bonnie A. Cusick

Founded: 1930
Hours: May 1-Oct 15, daily
   10:00-5:00; other months: M-Sa
   10:00-5:00, Su 1:00-5:00
Features cultural and natural history
   exhibits.

LAURA INGALLS WILDER MUSEUM
AND TOURIST CENTER
Walnut Grove, MN 56180
507-859-2358 or 507-859-2155
Dir/Curator: Shirley Knakmuhs

Founded: 1974
Hours: May-Aug 10:00-7:00, Apr, Sept,
   Oct 10:00-5:00 or by appt. during
   the year

MINNESOTA CHILDREN'S MUSEUM
1217 Bandana Blvd., N, St. Paul, MN
   55108
612-644-5305; Fax: 612-644-4708
Dir: Ann L. Bitter

Founded: 1979
Hours: Tu 9:00-5:00, W-Sa 9:00-8:00,
   Su 12:00-5:00, M 9:00-5:00 (June -
   Aug. only)
Twelve interactive hands-on exhibits including crawl-through adventure
   maze, hospital exhibit, 5000 sq. ft.
   outdoor garden, electro-magnetic
   crane.

MISSOURI

BABLER STATE PARK, RIVER HILLS
VISITOR CENTER
800 Guy Park Dr. (just off. Hwy 109),
   Chesterfield, MO 63005
314-458-3813
Park Naturalist: Dale Kannaworf

Founded: 1989
Hours: M-F 8:30-4:00, Sa-Su & holi-
   days 9:00-4:00; closed Christmas,
   Thanksgiving and New Year's
   Day.
Features dioramas of the area, also
   touch tables with microscopes. Spe-
   cial programs offered—contact Park
   Naturalist.

EUGENE FIELD HOUSE AND TOY
MUSEUM
634 S. Broadway, St. Louis, MO
   63102
314-421-4689
Dir/Curator: Frances Kerber Walrond

Founded: 1936
Hours: W-Sa 10:00-4:00, Su
   12:00-5:00
Childhood home of Eugene Field, the
   "Children's Poet," the home of
   Roswell M. Field, lawyer for Dred
   Scott.

HISTORIC HERMANN INC. MUSEUM
Fourth & Schiller, Hermann, MO 65041
314-486-2017 or 2781
Dir/Curator: Gennie Tesson

Founded: 1956
Hours: Apr-Oct 10:00-5:00
A museum on German culture.

LAURA INGALLS WILDER HOME AND
MUSEUM
Rte. 1, Box 24, Mansfield, MO 65704
417-924-3626
President: Jean Coday

Founded: 1957
Hours: March 15-May 20: M-Sa
   10:00-4:00, Su 1:30-4:00; May
   21-Sept 5: M-Sa 9:30-5:30, Su
   1:30-5:30; Sept 6-Oct 30: M-Sa
   10:00-4:00, Su 1:30-4:00 (dates
   vary slightly each year)

KALEIDOSCOPE
Box 414580, #132, Kansas City, MO
   64141
816-274-8300; Fax: 816-274-3148
Dir/Curator: Ms. Regi Ahrens

Founded: 1969
Hours: call for information
Creative art exhibit for children ages
   5-12.

THE MAGIC HOUSE, ST. LOUIS
CHILDREN'S MUSEUM
516 S. Kirkwood Rd., St. Louis, MO
   63122
314-822-8900; Fax: 314-822-8930
Dir/Curator: Elizabeth Fitzgerald

Founded: 1979
Hours: School year: Tu-Th 1:00-9:00, F
   1:00-9:00, Sa 9:30-5:30, Su
   11:30-5:30. Summer: Tu-Th, Sa
   9:30-5:30, F 9:30-9:00, Su
   11:30-5:30.
Over 60 hands-on exhibits focusing on
   science and art. Special area for
   children 1-7 years old. Learning Lab
   ("Expericenter") contains science lab,
   art studio, workshop and kitchen
   area.

MARK TWAIN BOYHOOD HOME &
MUSEUM
208 Hill St., Hannibal, MO 63401
314-221-9010
Dir/Curator: Henry Sweets

Founded: 1912
Hours: 7 days, winter 10:00-4:00;
   summer 8:00-6:00; closed Thanksgiving, Christmas, New Year's day.
Home consists of restored rooms
   where Clements family once lived.
   Museum exhibits memorabilia concerning Mark Twain. Includes au-
   dio/visual programs. Site contains 5
   buildings.

MONTANA

DOUG ALLARD'S FLATHEAD INDIAN MUSEUM AND TRADING POST
#1 Museum Lane, Box 460, St. Ignatius, MT 59865
406-745-2951, 800-821-3318; Fax: 406-745-2961
Dir/Curator: Jeanine M. Allard

Founded: 1973
Hours: Winter (Oct.-Apr.) daily 9:00-5:30 Summer (May-Sept.) daily 9:00-9:00 pm
Exhibits of beaded clothing of Flathead Indians, wild rocky mountainanimal mounts, Buffalo exhibit (history and use), eagle feather regalia, pottery, baskets and jewelry of other U.S. Indians.

NEBRASKA

LINCOLN CHILDREN'S MUSEUM
121 S. 13th St., Lincoln Sq., Lincoln, NE 68506
402-477-0128
Exec Dir: Marilyn Gorham

Founded: 1987
Hours: Su & M 1:00-5:00, Tu, Th & Sa 10:00-5:00, F 9:30-5:00
Exhibits include grocery store, lunar lander, tractor and fire engine.

OMAHA CHILDREN'S MUSEUM
500 S. 20th St., Omaha, NE 68102
402-342-6164
Dir: Elizabeth T. Browning

Founded: 1975
Hours: Tu-Sa 10:00-5:00, Su 1:00-5:00

NEVADA

LAS VEGAS NATURAL HISTORY MUSEUM
900 Las Vegas Blvd., N, Las Vegas, NV 89101
702-384-DINO; Fax: 702-384-5343
Dir/Curator: Marilyn Gillespie

Founded: 1991
Hours: daily 9:00-4:00; closed Thanksgiving and Christmas
Features interactive children's room, international wildlife room, exhibits on marine life including sharks and live specimens. Also exhibits on birds, prehistoric animals (including animated dinosaurs).

LIED DISCOVERY MUSEUM
833 Las Vegas Blvd., N, Las Vegas, NV 89101
702-382-3445; Fax: 702-382-0592
Dir/Curator: Suzanne Leblanc

Founded: 1990

Hours: Tu, Th-Sa 10:00-5:00, W 10:00-7:00, Su 12:00-5:00
Over 100 interactive exhibits exploring the wonders of the arts and sciences. Also features an ongoing program of activities, workshops and performances for children of all ages.

NEW HAMPSHIRE

CHILDREN'S MUSEUM OF PORTSMOUTH
280 Marcy St., Portsmouth, NH 03801
603-436-3853
Dir/Curator: Denise Doleac

Founded: 1983
Hours: Tu-Sa 10:00-5:00, Su 1:00-5:00

NASHUA CENTER FOR THE ARTS
14 Court St., Nashua, NH 03060
603-673-4475; Fax: 603-882-7705
Dir/Curator: Robert Daniels

Founded: 1966
Hours: M-Th 9:00-9:00, F-Sa 9:00-5:00
Art classes, dance, live performances for both adults and children, rotating exhibits, computer classes.

NEW JERSEY

CORA HARTSHORN ARBORETUM
324 Forest Dr. S, Short Hills, NJ 07078
201-376-3587
Dir/Curator: Elizabeth Naughton

Founded: 1961
Hours: Tu-Th 2:30-4:30, Sa 9:30-11:00; Oct & May Su 3:00-5:00

MONMOUTH MUSEUM
Newman Springs Rd., Lincroft, NJ 07738
908-747-2266
Dir/Curator: Dorothy V. Morehouse

Founded: 1963
Hours: Tu-Sa 10:00-4:30, Su 1:00-5:00

NEW MEXICO

ALBUQUERQUE CHILDREN'S MUSEUM
800 Rio Grande N.W., #10, Albuquerque, NM 87110
505-842-1537; Fax: 505-842-5915
Dir: Lisa Gorence

Founded: 1991
Hours: Tu-Sa 10:00-5:00, Su 12:00-5:00
Activities and discovery workshops, exhibits and teaching theater program.

DEMING LUNA MIMBRES MUSEUM
301 S. Silver St., Deming, NM 88030

505-546-2382
Dir: Ruth Russell

Founded: 1957
Hours: M-Sa 9:00-4:00, Su 1:30-4:00
Louise Southerland Toys & Dolls Collection including over 800 dolls; Gem & Mineral Society Collection, other exhibits of authentic clothes, toys, military artifacts and a blacksmith exhibit.

SANTA FE CHILDREN'S MUSEUM
1050 Old Pecos Trail, Santa Fe, NM 87501
505-989-8359
Pres.: Doug McDowell

Founded: 1985
Hours: Winter: Th-Sa 10:00-5:00, Su 12:00-5:00; Summer: W-Sa 10:00-5:00, Su 12:00-5:00
Interactive exhibits.

NEW YORK

BROOKLYN CHILDREN'S MUSEUM
145 Brooklyn Ave., Brooklyn, NY 11213
718-735-4400
Dir: Mindy Duitz
Asst Dir for External Affairs: Barbara Perlow

Hours: W-F 2:00-5:00; Sa, Su & holidays 12:00-5:00; closed M, Tu

CHILDREN'S MUSEUM OF HISTORY, NATURAL HISTORY, & SCIENCE
311 Main St., Utica, NY 13501
315-724-6128 or 9129
Dir/Curator: Jeffrey Chard

Founded: 1963
Hours: During school year W, Sa, Su 10:00-4:30, Th-F 12:00-4:30, Closed M. Summer: Tu-Sa 10:00-4:30

CHILDREN'S MUSEUM OF MANHATTAN
212 W. 83rd St., New York, NY 10024
212-721-1234
Dir/Curator: Andrew Ackerman

Hours: M,W,Th 1:30-5:30; F-Su 10:00-5:00; closed Tu

CHILDEN'S MUSEUM OF THE ARTS
72 Spring St., New York, NY 10012
212-274-0986; Fax: 212-274-1776

DISCOVERY CENTER OF THE SOUTHERN TIER
60 Morgan Rd., Binghamton, NY 13903
607-773-8661
Dir/Curator: Pokey Crocker

Founded: 1983
Hours: Tu-F 10:00-4:00, Sa 10:00-5:00, Su 12:00-5:00

HISTORIC RICHMOND TOWN
441 Clarke Ave., Staten Island, NY
   10306
718-351-1611; Fax: 718-351-6057
Exec. Dir: Barnett Shepherd

Founded: 1955
Hours: W-Su 1:00-5:00 (April-Dec); W-F
   1:00-5:00 (Jan-Mar)
Authentic village and museum complex
   interpreting three centuries of daily
   life and culture on Staten Island.
   Many buildings restored and open to
   the public. Authentic interiors, formal
   exhibits and demonstrations of daily
   activities.

THE JUNIOR MUSEUM
282 Fifth Ave., Troy, NY 12182
518-235-2120
Dir: Ralph Pascale

Founded: 1954
Hours: Group tours: M-F 9:00-5:00;
   Gen public visiting: W-F 1:00-5:00,
   Sa-Su 11:00-4:30
Hands-on exhibits focusing on science,
   history and the arts. Log cabin,
   planetarium, Iroquois Indian exhibit,
   live animals, Discovery Room and
   Environmental exhibits.

METROPOLITAN MUSEUM OF ART
1000 Fifth Ave., New York, NY
   10028-0198
212-570-3961; Fax: 212-570-3972
Assoc Dir for Educ: Kent Lydecker

Founded: 1870
Hours: Tu-Th and Su 9:30-5:15, F-Sa
   9:30-8:45
The Charles H. Tally Lecture Series is
   designed for children, ages 6-12,
   and parents for exploring works of
   art in the Museum's galleries
   through discussions and sketching.
   Lectures are held Fridays 6:00-7:00
   and 7:30-8:30. Program contents
   vary. Also various programs for students in grades 6 through 12.

**SCI-TECH CENTER OF NORTHERN NEW
   YORK**
154 Stone St., Watertown, NY 13601
315-788-1340
Exec Dir: Lance Evans

Founded: 1982
Hours: Tu-Sa 10:00-4:00 or by appt,
   open some school holidays
Over 35 exhibits including shadow
   room, binary number machine, video
   yard stick, sand pendulum.

**SCOTIA-GLENVILLE CHILDREN'S
   MUSEUM**
102 N. Ballston Ave., Scotia, NY
   12302
518-346-1764
Dir/Curator: Joan Gould

Founded: 1978

**STATEN ISLAND CHILDREN'S
   MUSEUM**
1000 Richmond Terrace, Staten
   Island, NY 10301
718-273-2060; Fax: 718-273-2836
Exec Dir: Kate Bennett

Founded: 1974
Hours: Tu-Su 12:00-5:00

VICTORIAN DOLL MUSEUM
4332 Buffalo Rd., North Chili, NY
   14514
716-247-0130
Dir/Curator: Linda Greenfield

Founded: 1970
Hours: Tu-Sa 10:00-4:30, Su
   1:00-4:30; closed Mondays, holidays
   and in Jan.
Displays of collector dolls including;
   Kewpie dolls, paper dolls, Schoenhut
   Dolls & Circus, Noah's Ark, toys and
   an action puppet theater. Also exhibits of dolls representing famous
   personalities of comics, literature,
   movies, history and fashion. Located
   near Rochester, NY.

NORTH CAROLINA

**COMMUNITY COUNCIL FOR THE ARTS
   CHILDREN'S MUSEUM**
Box 3554, Kinston, NC 28502
919-527-2517
Dir/Curator: Mark Brown

Founded: 1966
Hours: Tu-Sa 9:00-5:00, or by appt.

DISCOVERY PLACE, INC.
301 N. Tryon St., Charlotte, NC
   28202
704-372-6261, 800-935-0553
Dir/Curator: Freda H. Nicholson

Founded: 1947
Hours: M-F 9:00-5:00, Sa 9:00-6:00,
   Su 1:00-6:00; closed Thanksgiving
   and Christmas
Uses "open storage" to allow visitors
   to see collections of minerals, shells,
   insects, butterflies, and assorted artifacts, and to see actual preparation
   of specimens. Omnimax Theater and
   Planetarium.

HEALTH ADVENTURE
2 South Park Square, Asheville, NC
   28801
704-254-6373
Dir/Curator: Dr. Barry M. Buxton

Founded: 1968
Hours: Tu-Sa 10:00-5:00, Su (Jun-Oct)
   1:00-5:00
Oversize models dramatize function of
   the body's systems.

**NATURAL SCIENCE CENTER OF
   GREENSBORO**
4301 Lawndale Dr., Greensboro, NC
   27455
910-288-3769; Fax: 910-288-0545
Pres: Edward Von Der Lippe

Founded: 1957
Hours: M-Sa 9:00-5:00, Su 12:30-5:00
Exhibits include petting area and zoo,
   sea lab, planetarium, livingstream
   garden, and botanical courtyard.

THE NATURE MUSEUM
1658 Sterling Rd., Charlotte, NC
   28204
704-337-2665; Fax: 704-337-2670
Naturalist: Robert Cline

Founded: 1949
Hours: M-F 9:00-5:00, Sa 10:00-5:00,
   Su 1:00-5:00
Live animal room, puppet theater,
   earth science hall, lake life room,
   and Nature Trail.

**ROCKY MOUNTAIN CHILDREN'S
   MUSEUM**
1610 Gay St., Rocky Mount, NC
   27804
919-972-1168
Dir/Curator: Karl L. McKinnon

Founded: 1953
Hours: M-F 10:00-5:00, Sa 12:00-5:00,
   Su 2:00-5:00 (Apr-Oct)

NORTH DAKOTA

**CHILDREN'S MUSEUM AT YUNKER
   FARM**
1201 28th Ave. N, Fargo, ND 58102
701-232-6102
Dir/Curator: Tom Espel and Paula
   Carlson

Founded: 1989
Hours: T,W,F,Sa 10:00-5:00, Th
   1:00-8:00; Summer: same hours as
   above, but also M 10:00-5:00
Interactive exhibits for children ages
   toddler to 12.

OHIO

CLEVELAND CHILDREN'S MUSEUM
10730 Euclid Ave., Cleveland, OH
   44106-2200
216-791-7114; Fax: 216-791-8838
Exec Dir: Nancy King Smith

Founded: 1986
Hours: Summer (Mid-June-Labor Day)
   M-F 11:00-5:00, except Tu:
   9:00-12:00 Preschool Prime Time,
   Sa 10:00-5:00, Su 1:00-5:00; School
   Year (Labor Day to Mid-June) W-F &
   Su 1:00-5:00, Sa 10:00-5:00, Tu
   9:00-12:00 Preschool Prime Time;

Open Memorial Day, July 4th and
Labor Day 1:00-5:00; closed Thanks-
giving, Christmas and New Year's
Day.

LITTLE RED SCHOOLHOUSE
73 S. Professor St., Oberlin, OH
   44074
216-774-1700
Dir: Patricia Murphy

Founded: 1836
Hours: 1st Sat. of every month
   1:00-3:00, every Tu 1:00-3:00 or by
   appt. Site has 1836 school house
   and James Monroe house.

OREGON

CHILDREN'S MUSEUM
Operated by the Southern Oregon
   Historical Society
206 N. 5th St., Jacksonville, OR
   97501
503-773-6536; Fax: 503-776-7994
Mailing Address: 106 N. Central Ave.,
   Medford, OR 97501
Exec. Dir: Samuel J. Wegner

Founded: 1979
Hours: W-Sa 10:00-5:00; Su-Tu
   12:00-5:00
24 lifelike settings depicting daily life
   and ways of American Indians and
   pioneer settlers of southern Oregon
   from the 1840s to 1920s. Most exhibits have hands-on reproductions.

CHILDREN'S MUSEUM
3037 SW Second, Portland, OR 97212
503-823-2227
Dir/Curator: Robert Bridgeford

Founded: 1949
Hours: M-Su 9:00-5:00

THE GILBERT HOUSE CHILDREN'S
   MUSEUM
116 Marion St., NE, Salem, OR 97301
503-371-3631
Dir/Curator: Dr. Martin A. Morris

Founded: 1987
Hours: Tu-Sa 10:00-5:00, Su
   12:00-4:00
Housed in two historic homes. All
   hands-on exhibits in sciences, arts
   and humanities.

WONDER WORKS, A CHILDREN'S
   MUSEUM
419 E. Second, The Dalles, OR
   97058
503-296-2444
Dir: Carolyn Thomas

Founded: 1977
Hours: W-Sa 10:00-5:00
Features Oregon Trail exhibit and
   exhibit on the Norway Olympics.

PENNSYLVANIA

CHILDVENTURE MUSEUM AND SHOP
3364 Susquehanna Rd., Dresher, PA
   19025
215-643-9906
Dirs: Nina Kardon and Beverly Levine

Founded: 1989
Hours: Tu-Sa 10:00-4:00, Su
   12:00-4:00
Hands-on exhibits and cultural exhibits.

HANDS-ON HOUSE, CHILDREN'S
   MUSEUM OF LANCASTER
2380 Kissel Hill Rd., Lancaster, PA
   17601
717-569-kids
Dir/Curator: Lynne Morrison

Founded: 1987
Hours: Winter Tu-Th 11:00-4:00, F
   11:00-8:00, Sa 10:00-5:00, Su
   10:00-5:00; June 15-Sept. 15 Tu-Th
   10:00-4:00, F 10:00-8:00, Sa
   10:00-5:00, Su 10:00-5:00
Eight exhibit rooms, all with changing
   exhibits.

MARY MERRITT DOLL MUSEUM
Rte 2, Douglassville, PA 19518
215-385-3809
Dir/Curator: Marjorie Darrah

Founded: 1963
Hours: M-Sa 10:00-5:00, Su
   1:00-5:00; closed holidays

PETER J. MCGOVERN LITTLE LEAGUE
   BASEBALL MUSEUM
Rte. 15 S, Williamsport, PA 17701
717-326-3607
Dir/Curator: Cynthia Stearns

Founded: 1982
Hours: Labor Day-Memorial Day M-Sa
   9:00-5:00, Su 12:00-5:00; Summer
   M-Sa 9:00-7:00, Su 12:00-7:00
Features batting and pitching cages
   with video replay.

PITTSBURGH CHILDREN'S MUSEUM
10 Children's Way, Pittsburgh, PA
   15212-5250
412-322-5059; Fax: 412-322-4932
Exec. Dir: Maggie Forbes

Founded: 1983
Hours: School year: Tu-Sa 10:00-5:00,
   Su 12:00-5:00; Summer: M-Sa
   10:00-5:00, Su 12:00-5:00
Longterm exhibits include: Playpath,
   Luckey's Climber, Human Machine,
   Riverscape, Looking at You, Stuffee,
   Andy Warhol's "Myths," Sky, and
   other permanent exhibits.

PLEASE TOUCH MUSEUM
210 N. 21st St., Philadelphia, PA
   19103

215-963-0667
Dir: Nancy D. Kolb

Founded: 1976
Hours: M-Su 9:00-4:30, closed Thanks-
   giving, Christmas and New Year's
   Day

QUIET VALLEY LIVING HISTORICAL
   FARM
1000 Turkey Hill Rd., Stroudsburg, PA
   18360
717-992-6161
Dir/Curator: Ron Mishkin

Founded: 1963
Hours: June 20-Labor Day: M-Sa
   9:30-5:30, Su 1:00-5:30; groups by
   appt. (Apr 1-June 19 and in Sept
   and last two weeks of October).
Farm Animal Frolic last two weekends
   in May. Other scheduled activities
   year-round (e.g. Old Time Christmas).

TOY TRAIN MUSEUM
300 Paradise Lane, Strasburg, PA
   17579
717-687-8976
Dir/Curator: Anthony D'Alessandro

Founded: 1977
Hours: Apr, Nov, Dec weekends; May
   1-Oct 31 daily; Christmas week
   Hours always 10:00-5:00

RHODE ISLAND

CHILDREN'S MUSEUM OF RHODE
   ISLAND
58 Walcott St., Pawtucket, RI 02860
401-726-2591
Dir/Curator: Janice O'Donnell

Founded: 1977
Hours: Tu-Sa 9:30-5:00, Su 1:00-5:00
Exhibits include "Our House," a fas-
   cinating architecture exhibit, and
   "Great Grandmother's Kitchen," a
   real 1800's kitchen.

SOUTH DAKOTA

ENCHANTED WORLD DOLL MUSEUM
615 N. Main, Mitchell, SD 57301
605-996-9896
Dir: Valerie LeBreche
Curator: Eunice Reece

Founded: 1977
Hours: Summer 8:00-8:00; closed Dec
   1-Mar 31

TENNESSEE

CHILDREN'S MUSEUM AT OAK
   RIDGE
461 W. Outer, Oak Ridge, TN 37830
615-482-1074
Dir/Curator: Selma Shapiro

Founded: 1973
Hours: M-F 9:00-5:00, Sa & Su
1:30-4:30

CHILDREN'S MUSEUM OF MEMPHIS

2525 Central Ave., Memphis, TN
38104
901-458-2678; Fax: 901-458-4033
Exec. Dir: Jeanne Finan

Founded: 1987
Hours: Tu-Sa 9:00-5:00, Su
12:00-5:00
The museum is a child-sized city called
CityScape containing a bank, grocery
store, garage, health center, toddler
"playpark", recycle exhibit, vertical
maze, and clocktower. Changing exhibits also featured. All exhibits
designed for hands-on activities.

EAST TENNESSEE DISCOVERY CENTER

516 N. Beaman St., Box 6204, Knoxville, TN 37914-0204
615-637-1192
Admin Dir: Susan Elder
Educ. Facilitator: Lynn Blair

Hours: M-F 9:00-5:00, Sa 1:00-5:00

LOG CABIN CHILDREN'S MUSEUM

1638 Crescent Dr., Kingsport, TN
37064
615-246-6635
Dir/Curator: Muriel C. Spoden

Founded: 1981
Hours: Sa-M afternoons, Apr-Oct by ap-
pointment
Frontier American settlement.

TEXAS

AUSTIN CHILDREN'S MUSEUM

1501 W. 5th St., Austin, TX 78703
512-472-2499; Fax: 512-472-2495
Dir/Curator: Dr. Deborah Edward

Founded: 1983
Hours: Tu-Sa 10:00-5:00, Su
12:00-5:00
Permanent features include Whole
Foods Market, Playscape, Health
Lab, Studio Stage, Creation Station,
City Works.

CHILDREN'S MUSEUM OF HOUSTON

1500 Binz, Houston, TX 77004-7112
713-522-1138; Fax: 713-522-5747
Exec Dir: Jane Jerry

Founded: 1980
Hours: Tu-Sa 9:00-5:00, Su
12:00-5:00. Museum is closed on
Mon.
Exhibits in the Kresge Foundation
Kaleidoscope, Edward Rudge Allen,
Jr. Inspirations Gallery and Expres-
sions (an art activity room for chil-

dren), Meadows Environmental
Gallery (exhibit on recycling - "Our
Small Planet"), New Perspectives
Gallery (hands-on experience in daily
life of other countries - "Yalahag, A
Mountain Village in Mexico" and
"Ta-hsi, A Market Town in Taiwan"),
Cullen Investigations Gallery (exhibits
on archeology and site preservation
in "Dig It: Houston's History Under-
ground" and on farmers and cus-
tomers in "Farm to Market"),
Technikids Gallery (hands-on exhibit,
"How Does It Work? The Science
Behind the Automobile,") Kid TV Stu-
dio and Tot Spot Gallery.

DEPOT MUSEUM

514 N. High St., Henderson, TX 75652
903-657-4303
Dir/Curator: Susan Weaver

Founded 1978
Hours: M-F 9:00-12:00, 1:00-5:00, Su
9:00-1:00
Historic county buildings and artifacts.

DON HARRINGTON DISCOVERY CENTER

1200 Streit Dr., Amarillo, TX 79106
806-355-9547; Fax: 806-355-5703
Dir: Jack N. McKinney

Founded: 1968
Hours: Tu-Sa 9:00-5:00, Su 1:00-5:00;
Summer hours vary
Special summer exhibits.

HOUSTON FIRE MUSEUM

2403 Milam St., Houston, TX 77006
713-524-2526; Fax: 713-520-7566
Dir: Tom McDonald

Founded: 1981
Hours: Tu-Sa 10:00-4:00
Permanent hands-on teaching collec-
tion of the history of fire fighting in
Houston and America in general.
Programs for children on fire safety
at school and at home.

MUSEUM OF THE SOUTHWEST

1705 W. Missouri Ave., Midland, TX
79701-6516
915-689-2882; Fax: 915-570-7077
Dir/Curator: Wendell Ott and Melanie
Mathewes

Founded: 1965
Hours: Tu-Sa 10:00-5:00, Su
2:00-5:00
Includes Fredda Turner Durham Children's Museum and the Marion
Blakemore Planetarium. Collections
include archeological artifacts and
art of the Southwest. Courses for
adults and children offered.

MUSEUMS OF ABILENE

102 Cypress, Abilene, TX 79601

915-673-4587
Dir: Dr. Paul Lack

Founded: 1937
Hours: Tu-Sa 10:00-5:00 (Th until
8:30), Su 1:00-5:00
Hands-on projects.

UTAH

THE CHILDREN'S MUSEUM OF UTAH

840 N. 300 W., Salt Lake City, UT
84103
801-328-3383; Fax: 801-328-3384
Dir/Curator: Richard R. Morris

Founded: 1983
Hours: M 9:30-9:00, T-Sa 9:30-5:00, S
12:00-5:00
Hands on and experiential learning
permanent and long-term exhibits
for children. Permanent exhibts include the "Utah Jazz Basketball Exhibit" addressing basketball history,
the skeletal system and the vascular
system; "Primary Children's Medical
Center" including Jarvik artificial
heart equipment and a giant stetho-
scope; "Live Animal Display"; "Light
Touch" with seven exhibits exploring
light, color, vision and perception
and "727 Jet Plane Cockpit" with
training simulator.

MCCURDY HISTORICAL DOLL MUSEUM

246 N. 100 East, Provo, UT 84601
801-377-9935
Dir/Curator: Shirley B. Paxman

Founded: 1979
Hours: Tu-Sa 12:00-6:00

VERMONT

DISCOVERY MUSEUM

51 Park St., Essex Junction, VT 05452
802-878-8687
Dir/Curator: Rae Dushway

Founded: 1974
Hours: Sept-Jun Tu, W 11:00-4:00; Th-
Sa 10:00-5:00; Su 1:00-5:00, closed
M; July & Aug Tu-Sa 10:00-5:00, Su
1:00-5:00

VIRGINIA

CHESAPEAKE PLANETARIUM

Box 15204, Chesapeake, VA 23328
804-547-0153 ext. 281
Dir/Curator: Robert J. Hitt, Jr.

Founded: 1963
Hours: M-F 8:00-4:00 & Th evening
(reservations only)

CHILDREN'S MUSEUM, PRIMARY CARE CENTER

Box 231, Lee St. and Park Place,
Charlottesville, VA 22908

804-924-1593
Dir/Curator: Ellen Vaughan

Founded: 1982
Hours: M-F 9:00-4:00
Programs and hands on health exhibits
to familiarize children with medicine
and human anatomy including, Five-
senses model.

PORTSMOUTH CHILDREN'S MUSEUM
420 High St., Portsmouth, VA 23704
804-393-8393
Dir: Betty Burnell
Curator: Trish Pfeifer

Hours: Tu-Sa 10:00-5:00, Su
1:00-5:00; closed M

RICHMOND CHILDREN'S MUSEUM
740 Navy Hill Dr., Richmond, VA
23219
804-788-4949
Dir/Curator: Nan Miller

Founded: 1977
Hours: Tu-F 10:00-4:30, Sa
10:00-5:00, Su 1:00-5:00; Summer:
M-F 10:00-4:30, Sa 10:00-5:00, Su
1:00-5:00
Art studio, playworks area (hands-on
occupational exhibits), stage play
area, The Cave—a re-creation of a
real-life cave.

VIRGINIA DISCOVERY MUSEUM
Box 1128, Charlottesville, VA 22902
804-977-1025
Dir: Peppy G. Linden

Founded: 1981
Hours: Tu-Sa 10:00-5:00, Su
1:00-5:00
Walk-in kaleidoscope, log cabin, art
studio, bee-hive and dress up area.

VIRGINIA LIVING MUSEUM
524 J. Clyde Morris Blvd., Newport
News, VA 23601
804-595-1900
Dir/Curator: Robert P. Sullivan

Founded: 1966
Hours: Winter M-Sa 9:00-5:00, Su
1:00-5:00; Summer M-Sa 9:00-6:00,
Su 10:00-6:00, Th 7:00-9:00

WASHINGTON

CHILDREN'S MUSEUM
305 Harrison St., Seattle Ctr, Seattle,
WA 98109-4645

206-441-1768; Fax: 206-488-0910
Dir/Curator: Dr. Michael Herschensohn

Founded: 1971
Hours: Memorial Day-Labor Day daily
10:00-5:00; otherwise Tu-Su
10:00-5:00
Child-sized neighborhood where children can role play in doctor's office,
grocery store, fire engine, Metro
bus, theater and cafe. Daily hands-
on workshops and drop-in art
studio. Temporary exhibits introduce children to life in other
lands.

KARSHNER MEMORIAL MUSEUM
309 Fourth St. NE, Puyallup, WA
98372
206-841-8748
Dir/Curator: Rosemary Eckerson

Founded: 1930
Hours: Open to student groups M-F;
first Sat. of month (Oct-May) to
public.
Exhibits include Native Americans and
natural history.

**PIONEER FARM MUSEUM AND OHOP
VILLAGE**
7716 Ohop Valley Rd., Eatonville, WA
98328
206-832-6300
Dir/Curator: Carol Ford

Founded: 1975
Hours: Summer: daily 11:00-5:30

WEST VIRGINIA

**SUNRISE MUSEUM/SUNRISE SCIENCE
HALL**
746 Myrtle Rd., Charleston, WV
25314
304-344-8035
Dir/Curator: Ross McGuire

Founded: 1961
Hours: W-Sa 11:00-5:00, Su
12:00-5:00; closed M, Tu

**YOUTH MUSEUM OF SOUTHERN WEST
VIRGINIA**
Box 1815, Beckley, WV 25802-
1815
304-252-3730
Exec Dir: Sandi Parker

Founded: 1977
Hours: daily 10:00-5:00

WISCONSIN

**CLOWN HALL OF FAME & RESEARCH
CENTER**
114 N. 3rd St., Delavan, WI 53115
414-728-9075
Dir/Curator: Lynne Thornegate

Founded: 1986
Hours: daily 10:00-4:00
Clown shows and historical exhibits.

FOX CITIES CHILDREN'S MUSEUM
10 College Ave., Appleton, WI 54911
414-734-3226; Fax: 414-734-0677
Exec Dir: Denise Pannebaker

Founded: 1991
Hours: M-Th & Sa 10:00-5:00, F
10:00-8:00, Su 12:00-5:00
Exhibits include Grandma's Attic,
Science Spectrum, Passport to the
World, and Construction Junction.

**WISCONSIN CHILDREN'S
CENTER/MADISON CHILDREN'S
MUSEUM**
100 State St., Madison, WI 53703
608-256-6445; Fax: 608-256-3226
Exec. Dir: Georgia Heise

Founded: 1981
Hours: Tu-Sa 10:00-5:00, Su
1:00-5:00
Hands-on exhibits, including the
Shadow Room; Cows, Curds and
Their Whey (an exhibit about the
dairy industry) and Hands on Health
(about hospitals and health).

WYOMING

**WYOMING CHILDREN'S MUSEUM &
NATURE CENTER**
710 Garfield St., Laramie, WY 82070
307-745-6332
Exec Dir: Rika Clement

Founded: 1988
Hours: Tu 8:30-12:30, Th 1:00-5:00,
Sa 10:00-4:00; W&F 1:00-5:00
(summer)

Professional and general associations for educators, librarians, and child care workers are listed alphabetically. A full calendar of events and conferences sponsored by these associations will be found in chapter 20 and awards for children's media offered by many of these associations and other sponsors appear in chapter 19.

ACADEMY OF FAMILY FILMS AND FAMILY TELEVISION

334 W. 54th St., Los Angeles, CA 90037
213-752-5811
Exec Dir: Dr. Donald A. Reed

Founded: 1980
Membership: 300 teachers, students, librarians, film makers & general public
Purpose: To help improve the quality of current motion pictures & television; to award the achievements of individuals in the industry
Services: Sponsors seminars for children, teachers, librarians & members. Annual conferences held which include workshops on children's film and TV programs. Also holds annual awards ceremony & film screenings (free to members)
Media: Publishes newsletter (quarterly) free to members

AGENCY FOR INSTRUCTIONAL TECHNOLOGY

Box A, Bloomington, IN, 47402-0120
812-339-2203, 800-457-4507; Fax: 812-333-4318
Internet: technos@linknet.com
Exec Dir: Michael F. Sullivan

Founded: 1962
Purpose: A nonprofit US-Canadian corporation established to foster learning by developing, acquiring & distributing quality electronic technology-based resources & services; & by providing leadership to the educational technology policy community
Services: Develops, acquires, distributes instructional media, including videotape, interactive videodiscs, computer software, & supporting print. Offers staff training & workshops.
Media: *TECHNOS: Quarterly for Education & Technology* and *Catalog of Instructional Resources* (annual)

AMERICAN ASSOCIATION OF SCHOOL ADMINISTRATORS

1801 N. Moore St., Arlington, VA 22209-9988
703-528-0700
Exec Dir: Richard Miller

Founded: 1865
Membership: 18,000 school administrators
Purpose: To ensure high standards of educational leadership for the nation's schools
Services: Provide workshops, seminars & conventions for school administrators, school board members & the general public. Sponsors annual conference. Offers online information network on relevant issues, pending legislation, job openings & resources for handling problems
Media: Publishes *The School Administrator* (monthly) & an association newspaper, *Leadership News* (bimonthly) free to members. Also publishes a wide variety of books, reports & pamphlets on all aspects of school administration. Produce videotapes, slides & cassettes

AMERICAN ASSOCIATION OF SCHOOL LIBRARIANS (AASL)

Division of the American Library Association
50 E. Huron St., Chicago, IL 60611
312-944-6780; 800-545-2433
Exec Dir: Ann Carlson Weeks

Membership: 7,625 school librarians & students in the field
Purpose: Concerned with the general improvement & extension of library services for young people
Services: Charged by the ALA for planning a program of study & service toward the improvement & extension of library media services in elementary & secondary schools as a means of strengthening the complete educational environment. Develops criteria for the evaluation, selection, interpretation & utilization of media as used in the context of the school program. Works to stimulate research in the library field in conjunction with other units of the ALA. Interprets the role of school libraries for other professionals & lay groups. Works to improve the status & encourage the professional development of school librarians. Conducts activities & projects for improvement & extension of service in the school library when such projects are beyond the scope of type-of-activity divisions, after specific approval by the ALA council
Media: Publishes *School Library Media Quarterly*, $30, free to members

AMERICAN ASSOCIATION OF TEACHERS OF SPANISH AND PORTUGUESE

University of Northern Colorado
Gunter Hall, Room 106, Greeley, Colorado 80639
303-351-1090; Fax: 303-351-1095
Exec Dir: Dr. Lynn A. Sandstedt

Membership: 12,500 teachers
Purpose: To serve membership via publications & the annual meeting to assist in the teaching of Spanish & Portuguese. Membership includes teachers/professors from all over the U.S. & abroad
Services: Offers educational workshops & sponsors contests & awards for children's media; also sponsors annual conferences
Media: Publishes *Hispania* (four/year), *Enlace* (three/year), membership fee $30, basic registration fee $20, renewal fee $15, foreign subscribers $12/year for postage

AMERICAN CHORAL DIRECTORS ASSOCIATION

Box 6310, Lawton, OK 73506
405-355-8161
Exec Dir: Dr. Gene Brooks

Founded: 1959
Membership: 16,000

Purpose: To serve the needs of choral directors & to promote the development of choral music in all ways, including performance, composition, publication & research

Services: ACDA has numerous national committees engaged in exploring choral music materials, techniques & standards, including committees representing children's, junior & senior high school choirs. Sponsors festivals, clinics & workshops on the state level as well as division & national conventions for choral directors from schools, universities, churches & community groups. Biennial convention held March 8-11, 1995, Washington, DC. Maintains student chapters in many high schools, colleges & universities

Media: Publishes *The Choral Journal* (ten/year), $25. Also publishes books & pamphlets for choral conductors

AMERICAN COLLEGE OF MUSICIANS/NATIONAL GUILD OF PIANO TEACHERS

Box 1807, Austin, TX 78767
512-478-5575
Pres: Richard Allison

Founded: 1929
Membership: 12,000 teachers
Purpose: To encourage the serious study of music & piano for all ages
Services: Gives music examinations, auditions, awards, scholarships
Media: *Piano Guild Notes*, a bimonthly journal, $15/year; also publishes books & produces videorecordings geared for teachers

AMERICAN EDUCATIONAL RESEARCH ASSOCIATION (AERA)

1230 17th St., NW, Washington, DC 20036
202-223-9485
Exec Dir: William J. Russell

Founded: 1915
Membership: 20,000 professors, state & local school system research directors, research specialists, graduate students of education & educators in foreign countries
Purpose: To improve the educational process by encouraging scholarly inquiry related to education, dissemination of research results & their practical applications
Services: Conducts curriculum development studies; postsecondary education, school evaluation & program development
Media: Publishes *Educational Researcher* (ten/year); *American Educational Research Journal* (quarterly); *Contemporary Education Review* (quarterly); *Educational Evaluation & Policy Analysis* (quarterly);

Journal of Educational Statistics (quarterly); *Review of Educational Research* (quarterly); *Review of Research in Education* (annual); *Encyclopedia of Educational Research*; *Handbook of Research on Teaching*; several other handbooks & a membership directory

AMERICAN FEDERATION OF TEACHERS

555 New Jersey Ave., NW, Washington, DC 20001-
202-879-4400
Pres: Albert Shanker

Founded: 1916
Membership: 830,000 public & professional employees including public & private school teachers, paraprofessionals & school-related personnel (PSRPs), higher education faculty, staff & nurses & other health professionals
Purpose: To improve the educational environment, both for students & teachers; to promote the interests & concerns of its members
Services: Offers educational programs for members. Sponsors special conferences dealing with specific aspects of the educational process. Holds biennial conventions & biennial Quality Educational Standards in Teaching (QuEST), July 27-30, 1995 in Washington, D.C.
Media: Publishes *American Teacher*—monthly newspaper, & *American Educator*—quarterly professional journal, as well as various newsletters geared for specific membership constituencies. Maintains a publications division specializing in other professional resources for teachers. Catalog

AMERICAN FILM & VIDEO ASSOCIATION

(formerly Educational Film & Video Association)
Box 48659, 8050 Millawake, Niles, IL 60714
708-698-6440; Fax: 708-352-7528

Founded: 1943
Membership: 1400
Purpose: To inform educational institutions, commercial organizations & individuals interested in 16mm film & video of outstanding productions. Presents Blue Ribbon Awards to films & videotapes at the American Film & Video Festival, sponsored by AFVA.
Services: Maintains a library of 16mm films & videos
Media: Publishes AFVA Bulletin, bimonthly, with research news & calendar of events; also *Sightlines* (quarterly). Publishes evaluations of

films, videotapes, books & pamphlets on aspects of audiovisual education. Conference in May or June

AMERICAN FOUNDATION FOR THE BLIND

15 W. 16th St., New York, NY 10011
212-620-2000
President: Carl R. Augusto

Founded: 1921
Purpose: To enable persons who are blind or visually impaired to achieve equality of access & opportunity that will ensure freedom of choice in their lives
Services: Provide schools, agencies & organizations the professional services of national & regional staff, who provide expertise in areas such as education, employment, aging, & access to the environment. Record & duplicate approximately 400 Talking Book titles each year. Provide technical assistance, develop staff training, & provide information & referral services. Educate the public about blindness & visual impairment. Administer the National Technology Center. House the M.C. Migel Memorial Library. Maintain & preserve the Helen Keller Archives. Evaluate & sell special devices & consumer products to help blind & visually impaired people. Conduct, evaluate, & publish social research on visual impairment & blindness. Maintain a governmental relations office in Washington, DC. Process & make available an identification card for legally blind people
Media: Publishes *AFB News* (three/year), free; *Journal of Visual Impairment & Blindness* (bimonthly), $75/year institutional; $45/year individual. AFB Press publishes books, pamphlets, and videos for teachers, researchers & other professionals concerned with people who are blind or visually impaired

AMERICAN LIBRARY ASSOCIATION

50 E. Huron St., Chicago, IL 60611
312-944-6780
Exec Dir: Elizabeth Martinez

Founded: 1876
Membership: 55,836
Purpose: To provide leadership for the development, promotion, & improvement of library & information services & the profession of librarianship in order to enhance learning & ensure access to information for all
Services: Promotes the use of books & information services. Establishes standards of service, support, educational qualifications & welfare for libraries. Accredits library schools. Lobbies for legislation affecting

libraries & serves as a liaison with government agencies. Maintains a Washington office. Sponsors National Library Week. Functions as a watchdog in matters of intellectual freedom & censorship. Holds an annual convention in Summer & an annual meeting in Winter

Media: Publishes *American Libraries* (11/year), $60; *Booklist* (22/year), $60; *Choice* (11/year), $160, & other periodicals. Publication division also publishes numerous books & pamphlets

AMERICAN MONTESSORI SOCIETY

150 Fifth Ave., New York, NY 10011
212-924-3209
National Dir: Michael Earnes

Founded: 1960
Membership: 10,000 teachers & parents, affiliated schools, training programs, libraries
Purpose: Devoted to promotion of philosophy & techniques of Dr. Maria Montessori in early education
Services: Sponsors institutes & offers workshops, seminars & printed materials to members, librarians, school administrators & the general public. Also sponsors annual conferences in April (April 22-24, 1994, Dearborn, MI)
Media: Publishes *Constructive Triangle Magazine* (quarterly), $30/year or $10/copy

AMERICAN SOCIETY FOR DEAF CHILDREN

E. 10th & Tahlequah, Sulphur, OK 73086
800-942-ASDC
Attn: Kathy Witchey

Founded: 1967
Membership: Approximately 20,000 parents, family members, friends & professionals
Purpose: Provides information & support to parents & families with hearing-impaired or deaf children
Services: Provides information on childhood hearing impairment & its effect on families, options & programs available to deaf children, as well as opportunities for children & their families to live with deafness while leading fulfilling, productive lives. Sponsors biennial conference
Media: Publishes *The Endeavor* (quarterly), free; also publishes reports resulting from conventions & workshops

AMERICAN THEATER ARTS FOR YOUTH

1429 Walnut St., Philadelphia, PA 19102-3218
215-563-3501; 800-523-4540;

Fax: 215-563-1588
Exec Dir: Laurie Wagman

Founded: 1970
Purpose: To provide children of all ages with high quality film & theater performances as part of their education
Services: Sponsors film & theater programs to children & the general public
Media: Publishes *Media & Methods* magazine. Also produces films for children.

AMERICAS BOYCHOIR FEDERATION

120 S. 3rd St., Connellsville, PA 15425
412-628-8000; Fax: 412-628-0682
Pres: Rodelfo Torres

Founded: 1968
Membership: 1300 boy choirs
Purpose: A professional society devloted to improving the quality of boy choirs & their directors & to foster the interchange of information among boy choirs across the country
Services: Offers workshops for children & holds an annual festival. Sponsors annual conferences which include workshops & seminars
Media: *ABF Newsletter* (quarterly)

ASSOCIATION FOR CHILDHOOD EDUCATION INTERNATIONAL

11501 Georgia Ave., Ste. 312, Wheaton, MD 20902
301-942-2443, 800-423-3563
Exec Dir: Gerald Odland

Founded: 1931
Memberships: 17,000 teachers, librarians, parents & students
Purpose: To work for the education & well-being of children from birth through age 14; to raise the standard of training of teachers & others concerned with children; to inform the public about children's needs & ways schools programs can be adjusted to meet those needs
Services: Offers workshops & seminars for teachers, librarians & general public; cosponsors educational programs. Annual study conference
Media: Publishes *Childhood Education* (5/yr), *ACEI Exchange* (bimonthly), *Journal of Research in Childhood Education* (biennial) Also publishes books, booklets, pamphlets, audiocassettes & videotapes. Catalog

ASSOCIATION FOR EDUCATIONAL COMMUNICATIONS & TECHNOLOGY (AECT)

1025 Vermont Ave., Ste. 820, Washington, DC 20005

202-347-7834
Exec Dir: Stan Zener

Founded: 1923
Membership: 5,000 media specialists, media techonologists & librarians
Purpose: To improve instruction through the effective use of media & technology
Services: Develops certification guidelines for media personnel. Makes recommendations for media programs in schools & in teacher education. Monitors acitivtes of governmental agencies & Congress in area of educational communications. Sponsors ECT Foundation, a charitable organization devoted to the support of leadership, scholarship & research activities in educational communications & technology. Sponsors workshops & seminars on children's media at annual convention. Sponsors an International Student Media Festival which showcases all types of student-produced media
Media: Publishes *Educational Technology Research & Development* (quarterly), $30 for members, $45/yr for nonmembers; *Tech Trends* (6/yr), $30/yr for nonmembers

ASSOCIATION FOR LIBRARY SERVICE TO CHILDREN

Division of American Library Association
50 E. Huron St., Chicago, IL 60611
312-280-2163
Exec Dir: Susan Roman

Membership: 4,000 librarians, library science educators, & others interested in library services to youth
Purpose: Dedicated to the improvement & extension of library service to children (preschool-grade 8) in all types of libraries. Charged by ALA with the evaluation & selection of media for children & improvement of techniques of library services to children
Services: Sponsors workshops, seminars & institutes for teachers, librarians & the general public. Topics include various aspects of children's literature & media. Conducts children's media programs at the annual ALA convention. Sponsors annual Arbuthnot Lecture. Presents three awards annually: the Newbery Medal to the author of the most distinguished contribution to American Literature for Children; the Mildred L. Batchelder Award to the publisher of the most outstanding children's book originally published in a foreign language & subsequently published in English. The Laura Ingalls Wilder Award is given every five years to an

author or illustrator whose books have made a substantial contribution to children' literature over a period of years

Media: Publishes *Journal of Youth Services in Libraries* (quarterly), $40 & ALSC Newsletter (quarterly), free to members. Also publishes books & pamphlets related to children's literature & library services for children. Checklist

ASSOCIATION OF JEWISH LIBRARIES
c/o National Foundation for Jewish Culture
330 Seventh Ave., 21st Fl., New York, NY 10001
216-381-6440
Pres: Dr. Ralph Simon

Founded: 1965
Membership: 1000 librarians
Purpose: To foster Judaica librarianship & promote awareness of Judai literature among children & adults
Services: Sponsors annual conferences featuring seminars on children's materials.
Media: Publishes *AJL Newsletter* (quarterly) & *Judaica Librarianship* (semiannual)

AVKO EDUCATIONAL RESEARCH FOUNDATION, INC.
3084 W. Willard Rd., Clio, MI 48420
810-686-9283
Exec Dir: Don McCabe

Founded: 1974
Membership: 500 teachers, librarians, parents, & students
Purpose: To develop materials & techniques for reading/spelling education geared to all students, including the dyslexic & learning disabled
Services: Offers workshops & seminars to teachers, members & the general public. Also sponsors annual conferences. Sells reference works & text books based on AVKO's research. Catalog

ALEXANDER GRAHAM BELL ASSOCIATION FOR THE DEAF
3417 Volta Place, NW, Washington, DC 20007
202-337-5220 Voice/TT
Exec Dir: Donna Dickman, Ph.D
Dir of Membership/Mktg/Publn Sales: Elizabeth Quigley

Founded: 1890
Membership: 4,400
Purpose: To promote universal rights & optimal opportunities—from infancy through adulthood—to learn, use, maintain & process both spoken & written language
Services: Conferences, conventions, lending library, information ser-

vices, publication sales, & periodicals
Media: Periodicals division publishes *The Volta Review*, a scientific journal, & *Volta Voices*, a magazine both available to schools & libraries for $42/yr. Also publishes textbooks, workbooks, videotapes, etc. for children with impaired hearing, their parents, & professionals. Catalog

BOY SCOUTS OF AMERICA
1325 Walnut Hill Lane, Box 152079, Irving, TX 75015-2079
214-580-2000
Exec Dir: Jere Ratcliffe

Founded: 1910
Membership: 5,339,660 adults & youth ages 7-20 (including young women ages 14-20)
Purpose: To serve others by helping instill values in young people &, in other ways, to prepare them to make ethical decisions during their lifetime
Services: Leads in organizing youth groups, conducts adult leader training programs, sponsors outdoor learning experiences, & publishes training & support materials
Media: Publishes *Boy's Life* (monthly), $15.60 annual subscription; *Scouting Magazine* (6 times a year), for adult volunteers; *Exploring Magazine* (4 times a year), for youth ages 14-20. Produces a wide range of books, pamphlets, & videotapes for teachers, librarians, adult leaders, children, youth, & the general public, with the majority of materials geared for BSA's programs & membership. Publications include: merit badge pamphlets, a series of 122 titles designed to help boys ages 11-17 learn about hobbies, sports, the outdoors, & careers ($1.85 ea); sports & academic books for boys ages 8-10 ($1.35 ea); videotapes & printed materials aimed at child abuse & drug abuse. Catalog

BOYS & GIRLS CLUBS OF AMERICA
771 First Ave., New York, NY 10017
212-351-5900; Fax: 212-351-5972
Chairman: C.J. Silas
Pres: Thomas G. Garth

Founded: 1906
Purpose: A national organization which helps boys & girls of all backgrounds, with special concern for those from disadvantaged circumstances, develop the qualities needed to become responsible citizens & leaders
Services: Boys & Girls Clubs of America assists existing clubs: to hire, train, & retain highly qualified professional staff; to identify, recruit,

& train local boards; by providing fundraising & marketing consultation/training; by consulting on facility design/construction/safety & maintenance; by providing a full complement of resource literature & supplies; by conducting workshops, conferences & training events for professionals in Clubs, including an annual National Conference, Administrative Conferences & Program Institutes; & by developing programs in six core program areas. Programs address issues such as juvenile delinquency prevention, vocational guidance & career education, health care, alcohol abuse prevention, environmental education, family life & community service. Leadership training through the National Youth of the Year Program & Keystone Clubs
Media: *Connections Magazine*: distributed quarterly to Executive Directors & Board Presidents of Member Clubs. Subscriptions are available for $10. Single copy is $3

BRAILLE INSTITUTE
741 N. Vermont, Los Angeles, CA 90029
213-663-1111, 800-BRAILLE
Exec Dir: Russell Kirbey

Purpose: To provide services to the blind
Services: Offers educational programs for visually impaired children & adults. Regional library (affiliated with National Library Service for Blind & Physically Disabled) has braille & talking books for children
Media: Publishes *Expectations* (annual) free to blind children; The *Braille Mirror* (ten/year), free to blind adults. Also publishes books in braille

BOYS & GIRLS CAMP FIRE
(formerly Camp Fire, Inc.)
4601 Madison Ave., Kansas City, MO 64112-1278
816-756-1950
Exec Dir: K. Russell Weathers

Founded: 1910
Membership: 600,000 children & adultsPurpose: To provide an informal education program for youth, focused on children ages 5-18
Services: Provides recreational & educational activities in group programs. Emphasizes the development of skills for out-of-door living, crafts, health, self-reliance, child care & interpersonal relations. Provides day care centers, special interest courses, adult leadership workshops, parenting classes, co-ed activites, drop-in programs, cooperative projects with other agencies & demonstration projects.

Biennial Congress of Camp Fire Councils.
Media: Publishes books, pamphlets, posters & loose leaf training materials for children, adult leaders & council staff; some materials are in Spanish & Braille. Catalog. Publishes *Camp Fire - Annual Report; Program Prospects* (quarterly); *Teens in Action* (quarterly)

LEWIS CARROLL SOCIETY OF NORTH AMERICA
617 Rockford Rd., Silver Springs, MD 20902
301-593-7077
Exec Dir: Charles Lovett

Founded: 1974
Membership: 400 librarians, book collectors & dealers, general public
Purpose: To promote interest & studies in the work of Lewis Carroll & his continuing effect on our culture
Services: Sponsors exhibitions featuring original manuscripts of Carroll's work with original illustrations by Tenniel. Also sponsors expeditions to Carroll Country, England. Holds annual conferences semi-annualy
Media: Publishes *The Knight Letter* newsletter (semi-annual), free to members or $2 each; Carroll studies pamphlet series (annual), $20-$35. Also publishes occasional catalog

CATHOLIC LIBRARY ASSOCIATION
461 W. Lancaster Ave., Haverford, PA 19041
215-649-5250; Fax: 215-896-1191
Exec Dir: Anthony Prete

Founded: 1921
Membership: 3100
Purpose: To promote Catholic principles through the improvement of library services & cooperative programs in publishing, education & information management. Provides inspiration & practical aid to librarians engaged in work with children, from preschool through the elementary level in institutions & in specialized libraries
Services: Sponsors conferences & institutes. Annual conference. Awards Regina Medal annually to honor a lifetime dedication to children's literature
Media: Publishes *Catholic Library World* (quarterly), $60 to nonmembers; *Catholic Periodical & Literature Index* (bimonthly), $80

CENTER FOR EARLY ADOLESCENCE
University of North Carolina at Chapel Hill
D-2 Carr Mill Town Center, Carrboro, NC 27510

919-966-1148
Dir: Frank A. Loda, M.D.

Founded: 1978
Purpose: To help policymakers & service providers understand the important period of early adolescence & to increase the effectiveness of agencies & professionals in dealing with children in this age group
Services: Serves as a clearinghouse of information on school improvement, parenting, responsive community services & other related issues. Trains volunteers & professionals to work with 10-15 year olds, including two- and three-day intensive training sessions in parent education & program planning for adolescents
Media: Publishes *Common Focus* (occasional), free upon request. Publication division produces numerous curricula books & pamphlets geared to teachers, librarians, policymakers, trainers & youth-service professionals. Catalog

CHARACTER EDUCATION INSTITUTE
Dimension II Building
8918 Tesoro, Ste. 220, San Antonio, TX 78217
210-829-1727
Exec Dir: Ray S. Erlandson, Sr.

Founded: 1970
Purpose: To promote instruction & testing in basic human values such as honesty, patriotism, self-respect & kindnessServices: Produces a character-development curriculum for use in the classroom (grades K-middle school). The program is used in 32,000 classrooms nationwide
Media: Publishes *Character Education Today* (quarterly), free. Publication division produces instructional kits

CHILD WELFARE LEAGUE OF AMERICA
440 First St., NW, Ste. 310, Washington, DC 20001
202-638-2952
Exec Dir: David S. Liederman

Founded: 1920
Membership: 700 agencies involved with children's services
Purpose: A nonsectarian, privately supported organization devoted to improving child care & services for deprived, neglected & dependent children & their families
Services: Offers workshops, seminars & training conferences to members & agency executives & childcare workers. Also sponsors annual conference in Washington, DC
Media: Publishes *Child Welfare* (bimonthly), $50 individual, $60 institutional, $35 student; *Children's Voice* (9/yr), $35 individual, $50 institutional; *Washington Social Legislation*

Bulletin (biweekly), $65. Publication division produces films as part of its training curricula, books & pamphlets. Catalog

CHILDREN'S ART FOUNDATION
Box 83, Santa Cruz, CA 95063
408-426-5557, 800-447-4569
Exec Dir: William Rubel

Founded: 1973
Membership: 18,000 teachers, librarians, parents & students
Purpose: To encourage children, ages 3 to 13, to express themselves through quality writing & art
Services: Operates a children's art museum, maintains a research archive of children's writing & art, runs an innovative after school program
Media: Publishes *Stone Soup, the Magazine by Children* (5/year), free to members, $4.95/copy for nonmembers/$24 for one year

THE CHILDREN'S BOOK COUNCIL
568 Broadway, New York, NY 10012
212-966-1990; Fax: 212-966-2073
Pres: Paula Quint

Founded: 1945
Membership: 60 publishers of trade books for children
Purpose: To promote the reading & enjoyment of children's books
Services: Conducts workshops & speakers programs in conunction with conferences of other associations with which it has formal liaison committees; sponsors Children's Book Week & year-round Reading Programs. Also maintains a noncirculating library, open to the public, of children's books published by members over the past two years
Media: Publishes *CBC Features* (8/year), $45/lifetime subscription. Produces booklists, posters & other materials for Children's Book Week & Reading Programs & a series of taped sessions covering topics related to bringing children & books together. Also *Children's Books: Awards & Prizes,* featuring domestic & international awards, $57.50 softcover, $85 hardcover. Also publishes a variety of free pamphlets.

CHILDREN'S LITERATURE ASSOCIATION
Box 138, Battle Creek, MI 49016
616-965-8180
Pres: Sarah Smedman

Founded: 1972
Membership: 700 scholars, teachers, librarians, professors & graduate students
Purpose: To encourage & disseminate

scholarship in children's literature & to encourage high standards of literary excellence in this genre

Services: Sponsors workshops of teaching literary criticism to children, kindergarten through grade eight; awards fellowships to assist members in research & provides a research service to answer questions about children's literature. Holds annual conference (June 1995: Durham, NH) Also sponsors annual awards for work in research & literary criticism to members & adolescents

Media: *Children's Literature: An International Journal* (quarterly). Publications division publishes numerous books & pamphlets for teachers & librarians. Catalog

CHILDREN'S READING ROUND TABLE OF CHICAGO

2045 N. Seminary Ave., Chicago, IL 60631

312-525-7257

Founded: 1931

Membership: 925 authors, illustrators, educators, librarians, publishers, booksellers

Purpose: Nonprofit organizations, supports activities that foster & enlarge children's & young people's interest in books & reading; promotes fellowship among persons actively involved in juvenile books

Services: Sponsors in even-numbered years Children's Literature Conference at Loyola Univ. Sheridan Rd. Campus, Chicago, open to all. In odd-numbered years, sponsors 3-day seminar for writers & illustrators, also at Loyola Univ. Campus. Annual program, second Thursday of May, features trade books by CRRT & Midwest authors published in preceding year

Media: Publishes *CRRT Bulletin* (7/year) & *Member Yearbook*, both free to members. Offers brochure listing writers & artists available for school & library programs

CHILDREN'S TELEVISION WORKSHOP

One Lincoln Plaza, New York, NY 10023

212-595-3456

Pres: David V. B. Britt

Founded: 1963

Purpose: To reach all children, particularly those of poor & rural communities, with CTW-produced educational television programs & related activites

Services: Produces "Sesame Street," & "3-2-1 Contact" educational programs. Community Education Services Division is responsible for

encouraging the use of CTW productions as aids in education; assists in-service programs for schools & other organizations involved in education. Helps in the design of supplemental programs to meet the needs of rural & urban poor children, as well as children of migrant families. CES also establishes special viewing centers where children not enrolled in preschool programs can view productions. Provides training workshops for paraprofessionals, parents, day care & Head Start personnel, college students & others. Sponsors a course on television as a teaching tool. Works with the Illinois Migrant Council to train migrants in early childhood education. Special efforts are made to reach Spanish-speaking children. Conducts childhood education training programs for prison inmates

Media: Besides producing regular television broadcasts, CTW publishes *Sesame Street Magazine* (10/year), *3-2-1 Contact Magazine* (10/year) & *Kid City* (10/year). Publishes books, bibliographies, films, filmstrips, & supplementary materials on CTW programs. With Guidance Associates, developed a primary grades social studies program & with National Textbook Company, produced a multimedia bilingual curriculum

CHRISTIAN SCHOOLS INTERNATIONAL

3350 E. Paris Ave. SE, Box 8709, Grand Rapids, MI 49512

616-957-1070

Exec Dir: Sheri D. Haan

Founded: 1920

Membership: 450 school board members, administrators

Purpose: Service organization for member schools

Services: Sponsors seminars, workshops & conferences for members, teachers, students, librarians & the general public. Annual conference for school principals & board members (always in August)

Media: Publishes *Christian School Administrator* (quarterly); *Christian Home & School: A Magazine for Contemporary Christian Families* (6/year). Also publishes textbooks, workbooks & other educational materials for students, teachers & other related professionals

CHURCH AND SYNAGOGUE LIBRARY ASSOCIATION

Box 19357, Portland, OR 97280-0357

503-244-6919

Exec Dir: Dorothy J. Rodda

Founded: 1967

Membership: 1,850 church & syna-

gogue librarians, educators, & publishers

Purpose: To provide education & guidance in establishing high standards of library service & materials selection for churches & synagogues

Services: Sponsors seminars & workshops for librarians & members. Offers consultation to individual libraries nationwide & provides ongoing services through local chapters. Also sponsors annual three-day conferences & awards for outstanding contributions to librarianship & literature, including the Helen Keating Ott Award for contributions in children's literature

Media: Publishes *Church and Synagogue libraries* (bimonthly), free to members, $15 to nonmembers. Also publishes several books geared to librarians

COLUMBIA SCHOLASTIC PRESS ASSOCIATION

Box 11, Central Mail, Columbia University, New York, NY 10027

212-854-9400; Fax: 212-854-9401

Exec Dir: Edmund J. Sullivan

Founded: 1925

Membership: 2,200 staff involved in the production of student publications

Purpose: To encourage writing skills through the medium of school publications, by evaluating school newspapers, magazines & yearbooks

Services: Educational workshops are held during annual convention in March & conference in November in New York City. Also sponsors Summer workshops. Awards for excellence are given to school newspapers, magazines, & yearbooks

Media: Publishes *Student Press Review* (quarterly), $16; also publishes books for students & teachers

COMIC MAGAZINE ASSOCIATION OF AMERICA

355 Lexington Ave., 17th Fl., New York, NY 10017

212-661-4261; Fax: 212-370-9047

Exec Dir: Stephen Changaris

Founded: 1954

Membership: 12 publishers, engravers, printers, & distributors

Purpose: To promote dialog on the interests of professionals engaged in the production & distribution of comic magazines in the U.S.; to improve the educational & artistic standards of the industry in the interest of children, who constitute a large percentage of comic magazine readers

Services: Provides a network for

professionals concerned with the status & content of comic magazines, especially in terms of their educational potential

Media: Publishes the Code of the Comics Magazine Association (periodically)

CONSORTIUM OF COLLEGE & UNIVERSITY MEDIA CENTERS

Executive Office, CCUMC, Iowa State University, 121 Pearson Hall — MRC, Ames, IA 50011
515-294-1811
Exec Dir: Don Reck

Founded: 1971
Membership: 400 administrators of film & video libraries, film/video producers & distributors
Purpose: To facilitate the management of media collections & the use of media in education & training
Media: Publishes Leader (biannual), free to members

COUNCIL FOR CHILDREN WITH BEHAVIORAL DISORDERS

Division of Council for Exceptional Children
1920 Association Dr., Reston, VA 22091-1589
703-620-3660 (voice/TDD); Fax: 703-264-9494

Founded: 1962
Membership: 8,500 teachers, special administrators, college & university professors, parents, mental health personnel, & other professionals
Purpose: To promote & facilitate the education & general welfare of children & youth with behavioral & emotional disorders
Services: Actively pursues quality educational services & program alternatives for persons with behavioral disorders, advocates for the needs of such children & youth, emphasizes research & professional growth as vehicles for better understanding behavioral disorders, & provides professional support for persons who are involved with & serve youth with behavioral disorders
Media: Publishes Behavioral Disorders journal (quarterly) free to members, also available by subscription; CCBD Newsletter (quarterly) free to members; Beyond Behavior magazine (three times per year) free to members, also available by subscription; and monographs on behavioral disorders of children and adolescents

COUNCIL FOR ELEMENTARY SCIENCE INTERNATIONAL

University of Missouri, 212 Townsend Hall, Columbia, MO 65211

317-274-6813

Founded: 1920
Membership: 500 teachers & school administrators
Purpose: To promote science education at the elementary school level
Services: Offers workshops & seminars to teachers & members. Sponsors annual conference in conjunction with the National Science Teachers Association
Media: Publishes CESI News (quarterly) free to members. Also publishes sourcebooks, monographs, books & pamphlets geared for educators. Catalog

COUNCIL FOR INDIAN EDUCATION

Box 31215, Billings, MT 59107
406-252-7451
Exec Dir: Dr. Hap Gilliland

Founded: 1970
Purpose: To improve the quality of educational materials & training for teachers of Native American children
Services: Offers workshops & seminars for teachers
Media: Publishes a range of books on Native American culture & history

THE COUNCIL OF THE GREAT CITY SCHOOLS

1413 K St., NW, Ste. 400, Washington, DC 20005
202-371-0163
Exec Dir: Michael D. Casserly

Founded: 1961
Membership: 45 superintendents & board of education representatives
Purpose: To study, develop, implement & evaluate programs designed to ensure quality education & equality of educational opportunity for urban children
Services: Sponsors annual conference (always in Autumn)
Media: Publishes Urban Educator (monthly); Council Directory (annual); Legislative Activity Report (biweekly). Publications division publishes research geared to teachers & other educational professionals. Catalog

COUNCIL ON INTERRACIAL BOOKS FOR CHILDREN

1841 Broadway, Room 608, New York, NY 10023
212-757-5339
Exec Dir: Melba Johnson Kgositsile

Founded: 1965
Membership: Educators, editors & parents
Purpose: To promote antiracist & antisexist children's literature, textbooks & other learning materials by focus-

ing on their hidden & not so hidden messages
Services: Operates the Racism & Sexism Resource Center for Educators which offers workshops, seminars & institutes for teachers & librarians (fee). Also evaluates textbooks & storybooks for race & sex bias & develops antiracist, antisexist curricula, lesson plans, syllabi, bibliographies, etc., for school & library programs. Cosponsors programs with Teachers College, Columbia University & with the National Council of Churches
Media: Publishes Interracial Books for Children Bulletin (8/year), $16/year to individuals; $24 to institutions. Also publishes books, pamphlets, monographs & print & audiovisual materials for teachers, librarians & the general public. Annual board meeting. Catalog

THE JOHN DEWEY SOCIETY FOR THE STUDY OF EDUCATION AND CULTURE

c/o Dr. Robert C. Morris, School of Education, 1400 E. Hanna Ave., Indianapolis, IN 46227
317-788-3286
Sec Treas: Dr. Robert C. Morris

Founded: 1935
Membership: Approximately 400 librarians, professors of education, teachers, students, general public
Purpose: Seeks to focus attention on issues related to education & society
Services: Sponsors seminars & research projects for teachers, librarians, members & college professors. Also sponsors an annual meeting in conjunction with the American Association of Colleges for Teacher Education
Media: Publishes Current Issues in Education (periodic); Insights (periodic). Also publishes nubmerous books & pamphlets for librarians, teachers, education professionals & individuals interested in educational issues

DIRECTION SPORTS, INC.

600 Wilshire Blvd., Ste. 320, Los Angeles, CA 90017-3215
213-627-9861
Exec Dir: Tulley N. Brown

Founded: 1968
Membership: 1,000 elementary, primary & secondary students & teachers
Purpose: To service the educational & attitudinal needs of disadvantaged youth through an afterschool program of group sports & reading/math lessons
Services: Offers workshops & seminars for students; a planned afterschool program run by community

teenagers under the mentorship of college & graduate students

Media: Publishes *Direction Sports* (biannual) free. Also publishes pamphlets & reproduces videorecordings from network television for use for other youth programs, with children, teachers, librarians & general public

THE EDUCATIONAL PRODUCTS INFORMATION EXCHANGE (EPIE INSTITUTE)

103-3 W. Montauk Hwy., Hampton
    Bays, NY 11946
516-728-9100
Pres: Kenneth Komoski

Founded: 1967
Membership: Schools, school districts, state agencies & individuals involved in education
Purpose: To supply educators with objective, independently researched purchasing information on teaching materials, allowing educators to compare & evaluate products before purchase & to identify materials which most closely fit their school's curriculum
Services: Sponsors workshops in textbook & software selection; provides a Curriculum Alignment Service for Educators (CASE) to help them match K-8 math texts with standardized achievement tests, state mandated tests & state curricula
Media: Publishes TESS Educational Software Selector (annual); EPIE-gram Newsletters covering equipment & materials (monthly) $65, online information service on microcomputing products via CompuServe

EDUCATIONAL RESEARCH SERVICE

2000 Clarendon Blvd., Arlington, VA
    22201
703-243-2100
Pres: Glen E. Robinson

Founded: 1973
Membership: 2600 school districts
Purpose: A nonprofit research organization serving the information needs of school administrators
Services: Functions as a national clearinghouse for research in education & school administration. Provides on-call information service for specific educational problems or topics to members. Conducts studies, surveys & searches on problems facing school administrators
Media: Publishes *ERS Bulletin* (3/year) & *ERS Exchange* (3/year). Also provides reports, monographs, researach briefs, research memos & information aids to members

FUTURE PROBLEM SOLVING PROGRAM

315 W. Huron, Ste. 140B, Ann Arbor,
    MI 48103-4203
313-998-7377; Fax: 313-998-7663
Exec Dir: James Alvino

Founded: 1974
Membership: 200,00 students & teachers
Purpose: To motivate & assist students in developing creative thinking, problem-solving & teamwork skills, increase their communication skills, develop critical & analytical skills & increase awareness & interest in the future
Services: Offers educational workshops composed of teams of students at various grade levels who work with instructors on research & problem-solving in selected areas of study. Also offers Future Problem Solving Bowls for students who excel in these workshops, as well as other competitions for students at all grade levels. Sponsors seminars & institutes for teachers, librarians, & the general public. Annual international conference (always in June)
Media: Publishes *Creative Express* (quarterly), $18/year; *Future Problem Solving Newsletter* (quarterly); *Resource Manual* (annual), $25. Also publishes several books & educational support materials for teachers, librarians & the general public. Also produces videorecordings & slide tapes

GIRL SCOUTS OF THE USA

420 Fifth Ave., New York, NY
    10018-2702
212-940-7500
Exec Dir: Mary Rose Main

Founded: 1912
Purpose: Nonprofit association of girls & women from all segments of American society established to help members develop their potential, make friends & become a vital part of their communityServices: Provides programs of informal education & skills training through local Girl Scout Councils throughout the country. Programs are structured to serve five age levels for girls 5-17 years of age. Also offers leadership & management training for adult Girl Scout volunteers & executives
Media: Publishes *Girl Scout Leader* (quarterly), plus a variety of books & pamphlets to assist in advocating the Girl Scout programs. Also produces video & audio tapes, films & slide presentations in support of training & promotional programs

GIRLS, INC.

(formerly Girls Club of America, Inc.)
30 E. 33rd St., New York, NY 10016
212-689-3700
Dir.: Margaret Gates, Thomas G. Garth

Founded: 1945
Membership: 250,000; girls ages 6-18
Purpose: To help girls from all backgrounds establish their individual identities & develop to their fullest potential
Services: Offers workshops & seminars to children, teachers & girl's club staff members. Sponsors annual confernce in April
Media: Publishes books & pamphlets for children, teachers & the general public. Also *Girl's Clubs of America - Annual Report* (free); *Girl's INK*, 6/year (free), concerning drug abuse, teenage pregnancy. Catalog

GREAT BOOKS FOUNDATION

35 W. Wacker Dr., Ste. 2300, Chicago,
    IL 60601-2298
312-332-5870; 800-222-5870
Pres: Alice Owens

Founded: 1947
Members: 800,000
Purpose: To provide people of all ages with a lifelong program of liberal education through reading & discussion of great works of literature, philosophy, psychology & history
Services: Trains more than 18,000 teachers, librarians, parents & others to conduct junior & adult courses in interpretation & critical analysis of literature
Media: Publishes Junior Great Books Reading Aloud Program Series (Gr:K-1; 2-9; 10-12); Great Books Reading & Discussion Program (for adults). Also publishes newsletters, journals & pamphlets for teachers, librarians & the general public. *Leader Notes* (quarterly); *An Introduction to Shared Inquiry* paperback reading series, reader & leader aids. Catalog

HIGH/SCOPE EDUCATIONAL RESEARCH FOUNDATION

600 N. River St., Ypsilanti, MI
    48198-2898
318-485-2000
Pres: David P. Weikart

Founded: 1970
Membership: 38 administrators, researchers, educational consultants & support staff
Purpose: To promote the learning & development of children from infancy through adolescence & to support parents & teachers in helping them develop & learn
Services: Offers workshops & seminars

to teachers & all those who work with children in developing, selecting, improving & evaluating curricula & teaching methods. Also provides individual consultation. Sponsors annual conference. Publications catalog. Conducts research

Media: Publishes High Scope ReSource newsletter (3/year) free; Extensions (6/year), $30. Publications division produces numerous books, articles & papers, films & filmstrips, videorecordings, records & cassettes

HOME ECONOMICS EDUCATION ASSOCIATION
Box 603, Gainesville, VA 22065
703-349-4676
Exec Dir: Stephanie H. Price, Ph.D

Purpose: To promote a better understanding of family & community life, to improve the quality of home economics instruction & to broaden the scope of the curriculum
Services: Promotes programs in home economics education. Supplements existing services available to home economics educators
Media: Publishes newsletters, books & pamphlets for the teacher & home economics student. List

INSTITUTE FOR CHILDHOOD RESOURCES
220 Montgomery St., #2811, San Francisco, CA 94104
415-864-1169
Dir: Stevanne Auerbach
Founded: 1975

Purpose: To provide parents & professionals with resources & methods to enable parents to participate in educating their children
Services: Offers educational programs to children, teachers, librarians & parents. Maintains a resource center which reviews products for family-based education
Media: Publications division produces books, pamphlets, films & filmstrips geared for children & parents. Produces Whole Child: A Sourcebook, Choosing Childcare, The Toy Chest, and others

INTERNATIONAL ASSOCIATION OF SCHOOL LIBRARIANSHIP
Box 1486, Kalamazoo, MI 49005
616-343-5728
Exec Sec: Jean E. Lowrie

Founded: 1971
Membership: 875 school librarians, educators & libraries
Purpose: To encourage the development of school libraries & library programs throughout the world
Services: Offers workshops to

librarians & sponsors annual conference
Media: Publishes quarterly newsletter with membership. Also publishes annual conference proceedings

INTERNATIONAL DEAF/TEK, INC.
Box 2431, Framingham, MA 01701-0404
508-620-1777
Pres: Brenda Monene, M.Ed.

Founded: 1983
Membership: By subscription
Purpose: International electronic mail service (Deaftek.USA) dedicated totally to the deaf & hard of hearing managed by International Deaf/Tek, Inc. The service resides on SprintMail & provides access to Internet/Bitnet & all services with X400 interconnections, send-only fax, & other electronic services
Services: Offers a full electronic mail service which includes announcements & news of interest to the deaf community. Provides electronic mail for research projects & opportunities for communication & discussion of issues important to deaf people. Also gives technical consultation on telecommunication to other groups serving deaf and hard of hearing people. Subscribers are the major organizations, agencies, individuals, professionals & service providers in the field of deafness. International Deaf/Tek, Inc. gives workshops at deafness related conventions & conferences and personnel are trained in the field of deafness

INTERNATIONAL FEDERATION OF CHILDREN'S CHOIRS
120 S. 3rd St., Shallway Bldg., Connellsville, PA 15425
412-628-8000
Pres: Fielding L. Fry

Founded: 1969
Membership: 600 children's choirs
Purpose: To encourage information interchange among children's choirs & their directors around the world
Services: Sponsors workshops for children & teachers. Also holds annual conferences

INTERNATIONAL FILM BUREAU INC.
332 S. Michigan Ave., Chicago, IL 60604-4382
312-427-4545, 800-432-2241
Chmn: Wesley H. Greene
Gen. Mgr & CEO: Ben F. Hodge

Founded: 1957
Purpose: Distributes audiovisual programs for children, young adults & adults

Services: Offers audiovisual materials to teachers, librarians, AV directors & media directors
Media: Distributes a wide variety of films, filmstrips, & videorecordings for children on subjects ranging from literature to careers

INTERNATIONAL READING ASSOCIATION
800 Barksdale Rd., Box 8139, Newark, DE 19711
302-731-1600; Fax: 302-731-1057
Exec Dir: Alan Farstrup

Founded: 1956
Membership: 94,000 classroom teachers, reading specialists, college professors, administrators, supervisors, researchers, librarians, media specialists, parents, & students
Purpose: To improve the quality of reading instruction & to promote literacy worldwide
Services: Publishes books & journals on teaching reading. Sponsors an annual convention each spring, a biennial world congress, an adolescent & adult literacy conference, & regional conferences throughout the year. Has over 40 special interest groups. Sponsors awards, including the IRA Children's Book Award. Publishes reading lists for children & adolescents. Has local & state/national councils/affiliates throughout the world

INTERNATIONAL SOCIETY FOR TECHNOLOGY IN EDUCATION (ISTE)
(Merged with International Association for Computing in Education & International Council for Computers in Education)
1787 Agate St., Eugene, OR 97403-1923
503-346-4414; 800-336-5191 (orders); Fax: 503-346-5890
Exec Sec: Maia S. Howes

Purpose: To advance the effective use of computers in education (primary & secondary) through information & assistance in planning, evaluating, coordinating & teaching classes which incorporate computers
Services: Offers educational programs, regional workshops for teachers, members, & the general public. Sponsors an annual conference (National Educational Computing Conference)
Media: Publishes Computing Teacher (8/year); Journal of Reasearch on Computers in Education (quarterly); Update (8/year). Also publishes several books, monographs & instruction manuals for teachers, teacher educators & students. Catalog

JEWISH BOOK COUNCIL OF THE JEWISH COMMUNITY CENTER ASSOCIATION OF NORTH AMERICA
(formerly Jewish Book Council)
15 E. 26th St., New York, NY 10010
212-532-4949

Founded: 1925
Purpose: To promote & disseminate Jewish books
Services: Serves as a clearinghouse for information & guidance of Jewish books. Holds an annual awards ceremony (Jewish Book Award) to an author who combines literary merit with an affirmative expression of Jewish values in the areas of children's literature & illustrated children's books
Media: Publishes *Jewish Book Annual: The American Yearbook of Jewish Literary Creativity* ($33.50); *Jewish Book World* (quarterly). Also publishes books, pamphlets, posters & bibliographies for children, teachers, librarians & the general public

JEWISH PUBLICATION SOCIETY
1930 Chestnut St., Philadelphia, PA 19103-4599
212-564-5925
Exec Dir: Rabbi Michael Monson

Founded: 1888
Membership: 16,500 teachers, librarians, parents & students
Purpose: To perpetuate Jewish culture & tradition through literature
Services: Sponsors annual conference in Philadelphia, first week of June
Media: Publishes books & catalogs for children & adults on such subjects as history, scripture, poetry & art

THE KIDS ON THE BLOCK, INC.
9385 C. Gerwig Lane, Columbia, MD 21046
410-290-9095, 800-368-KIDS
Exec Dir: James S. Thurman

Founded: 1977
Membership: 16 educators, administrators, puppet makers
Purpose: To teach children about the social, emotional, physical & environmental differences & disabilities of different groups & individuals in our society & to encourage interaction & mutual understanding
Services: Offers workshops & performances to children, teachers, librarians & organizations serving special populations
Media: Publishes *Keeping Up with the Kids* (biannual), free to purchasers. Produces puppets, scripts, props, educational materials & teacher's guides on subjects such as mental retardation, divorce, drug abuse & physical disabilities

LEARNING DISABILITIES ASSOCIATION OF AMERICA
4156 Library Rd., Pittsburgh, PA 15234
412-341-1515
Exec Dir: Jean Petersen

Founded: 1963
Membership: 60,000 parents, educators, libraries, professionals
Purpose: To define & find solutions for the broad spectrum of learning problems
Services: Provides information & referrals to parents & professionals seeking help for children with learning disabilities. Works with schools in implementing programs for early identification & treatment. Also works with correctional authorities & jurists to develop comprehensive approaches to education & employment of the learning disabled delinquent. Operates a resource center. Sponsors seminars & workshops for teachers, librarians, members & the general public. Holds international conference annually. Local chapters sponsor art exhibits & awards
Media: Publishes ACLD *Newsbriefs* (bimonthly), $5. Also produces books & pamphlets & distributes films & videorecordings for the professional & general public. Catalog

MATH/SCIENCE NETWORK
Preservation Park, 678 13th St., Ste. 100, Oakland, CA 94612
510-893-6284

Founded: 1975
Membership: 275 teachers, scientists, mathematicians, engineers, sex equity specialists, career counselors & parents
Purpose: To increase the participation of girls & women in math & science education & careers, including vocational education & nontraditional occupations
Services: Conducts workshops & seminars on sex equity in math & science education & employment for children, teachers, parents & the general public.
Media: Publishes *Broadcast* (quarterly). Publications division produces pamphlets, reprints, videorecordings & monographs for teachers, researchers, career counselors & interested individuals

NATIONAL ART EDUCATION ASSOCIATION
1916 Association Dr., Reston, VA 22091-1590
703-860-8000; Fax: 703-860-2960
Exec Dir: Dr. Thomas Hatfield

Founded: 1947
Membership: 14,000 art teachers at all levels, art supervisors, museum art educators, anyone concerned with education in the visual arts
Purpose: To promote art education at all levels, encourage innovation & research, provide a forum for the exchange of ideas among members & serve as an advocate for quality art education to educational decision makers & arts organizations
Services: Maintains a library & research center for members. Special programs & awards for students. Sponsors travel to world cultural centers. Holds an annual conference in April. Sponsors national programs of honorary, scholastic & monetary awards
Media: Publishes *Art Education* (6/year), $50, free to members; *NAEA News* (6/year); *Studies in Art Education*, a research journal (4/year), $25, free to members. Publishes a bibliography of books & pamphlets. Distributes t-shirts, buttons, posters

NATIONAL ASSOCIATION FOR BILINGUAL EDUCATION
Union Center Plaza, 810 1st St. NE, 3rd Fl., Washington, DC 20002
202-898-1829; Fax: 202-789-2866
Exec Dir: James J. Lyons

Founded: 1975
Membership: 3,000 teachers, librarians, parents & students
Purpose: To work for educational & occupational equity for language-minority groups & to foster bilingualism in all facets of American culture
Services: Coordinates & disseminates information which supports bilingual educational policies. Identifies & publicizes exemplary bilingual education programs & sponsors research in language & multicultural education
Media: Publishes journals, newsletters & research papers on bilingual education, legislation & other issues of interest to educators, parents, legislators & the general public.

NATIONAL ASSOCIATION FOR CREATIVE CHILDREN & ADULTS
8080 Springvalley Dr., Cincinnati, OH 45236-1395
513-631-1777
Chief Exec Off: Ann Fabe Issacs

Purpose: To help the creative to treasure & respect their productive potentialities & harmonize their uniqueness with their need to fit into society
Services: Annual conference. Projects

for home, school, office. Annual workshops; creativity counseling; field terms for children, parents, teachers, & inservice training for teachers

Media: Publishes *Creative Child & Adult Quarterly*, $55

NATIONAL ASSOCIATION FOR GIFTED CHILDREN

1155 15th St. NW, #1002, Washington, DC 20005-2706
202-785-4268
Exec Dir: Peter Rosenstein

Founded: 1954
Membership: 7000 teachers, librarians, parents & university professors
Purpose: To further the education of gifted students so as to enhance their potential creativity
Services: Sponsors training institutes & an annual conference for educators & parents
Media: Publishes the *Gifted Child Quarterly*, $45/year. Publications division also issues pamphlets, monographs & a newsletter, *National Association for Gifted Children Communique* (quarterly)

NATIONAL ASSOCIATION FOR THE EDUCATION OF YOUNG CHILDREN

1509 16th St., NW, Washington, DC 20036-1426
202-232-8777, 800-424-2460
Exec Dir: Marilyn M. Smith

Membership: Nearly 90,000
Purpose: To serve & act on behalf of the needs & rights of young children with primary focus on the provision of educational services & resources to adults who work with & for children
Services: Sponsors an annual conference which attracts approximately 20,000 participants from every aspect of children's services. Provides affiliate group legislative committees with the most up-to-date information on laws & regulations pertaining to children's services. Plans & conducts public education activities to focus attention on needs & issues related to young children in communities throughout this nation during the Week of the Young Child. Produces video training tapes for early childhood teachers & maintains a computerized child care information service
Media: *Young Children* (bimonthly), spotlights current projects theory & research in early childhood as well as practical articles. Available through membership, $25 or subscription, $30. NAEYC publishes books & pamphlets on a wide range of topics. Free catalog

NATIONAL ASSOCIATION FOR THE PRESERVATION AND PERPETUATION OF STORYTELLING

Box 309, Jonesborough, TN 37659
615-753-2171
Exec Dir: Jimmy Neal Smith

Founded: 1975
Membership: 5000 teachers, librarians, folklorists, students, storytellers & arts organizations
Purpose: To provide information on the art of storytelling, its meaning, importance & applications in contemporary American culture
Services: Offers consultation & technical assistance in organizing storytelling activities, workshops, seminars, field recording & collection; training programs for librarians, members & the general public, including ministers & businessmen who wish to improve their public speaking. Maintains an archive of audio & video recordings of contemporary storytelling for researchers. Members are entitled to group health insurance. Also sponsors an annual 3-day storytelling festival in Jonesborough the first full weekend of October & an annual conference (always in July)
Media: Publishes *National Catalog of Storytelling* (annual); *Storytelling Magazine*. Publications division produces a variety of books, albums & cassettes geared to all age groups & applications. Catalog

NATIONAL ASSOCIATION FOR VISUALLY HANDICAPPED

22 W. 21st St., New York, NY 10010
212-889-3141
Exec Dir: Lorraine H. Marchi

Founded: 1954
Membership: 20,000 educators, librarians, parents & students
Purpose: To serve the partially seeing (all ages)
Services: Provides information & referral for low vision services from public & private sources. Offers various types of visual aids, ranging from simple magnifiers to closed circuit TVS. Conducts educational programs for the medical & allied fields & educators who work with the partially seeing. Serves as consultant to publishers seeking to enter the large print field (both adult & children's books). Offers guidance, counselling, & educational materials to parents & educators of partially seeing children.
Media: Publishes *In Focus* (semi-annual), free. Publications division offers large type textbooks, testing materials & literature for young people, as well as numerous booklets & educational materials concerning the partially seeing for professionals & laypersons. Catalog

NATIONAL ASSOCIATION OF DRAMATIC & SPEECH ARTS

208 Cherokee Dr., Blacksburg, VA 24060
703-231-5805
Exec Dir: Dr. H. D. Flowers, II

Founded: 1936
Membership: 500 teachers, students, professionals in theater, children & community members
Purpose: To develop & promote black theater among members & encourage interest within the community
Services: Offers workshops, seminars & institutes for children, teachers, librarians & the general public. Sponsors annual conference, always late March or early April
Media: Publishes *NADS Newsletter* (quarterly; *Encore* (semi-annual), $5/ea for nonmembers. Publications division produces several books, pamphlets, videorecordings, filmstrips & slides geared for children, teachers, librarians & the public

NATIONAL ASSOCIATION OF ELEMENTARY SCHOOL PRINCIPALS

1615 Duke St., Alexandria, VA 22314-3483
703-684-3345
Exec Dir: Dr. Samuel G. Sava

Purpose: Devoted to improving the image & self-esteem of each child through improvement & advancement of elementary & middle school principals
Services: Monitors & promotes legislation affecting elementary & middle schools. Provides workshops & training programs for elementary & middle school principals.
Media: Publishes *Principal* (4/year) & *Communicator* (8/year), free to members

NATIONAL ASSOCIATION OF THE DEAF

814 Thayer Ave., Silver Spring, MD 20910
301-587-1788
Exec Dir: Nancy Block

Founded: 1880
Membership: Over 20,000 teachers, librarians, parents, students, organizations & interpreters
Purpose: To promote the interests & well being of hearing imparied persons
Services: Provides information on deafness & related topics. Actively opposes employment & educational

discrimination, via the Legal Defense Fund. Conducts deaf leadership training programs, as well as training & rehabilitation programs for disadvantaged deaf persons. Biennial conference, always in the summer; (1996: Portland, OR; 1998: San Antonio, TX)

Media: Publishes the *Deaf American* (periodic), $20/year to nonmembers. Also publishes books, pamphlets, films, videotapes & kits for & about deaf children & adults as well as publications on research developments, professional education & community awareness.

NATIONAL BLACK CHILD DEVELOPMENT INSTITUTE

(formerly Black Child Development Institute)
1023 15th St. NW, Ste. 600, Washington, DC 20005
202-387-1281; Fax: 202-234-1738
Exec Dir: Evelyn K. Moore

Founded: 1970
Membership: 3,250
Purpose: Established by the Black Womens' Community Development Foundation to provide a national vehicle to meet the comprehensive developmental needs of black children, youth, & families
Services: Monitors legislation, regulations, policies & programs that have direct impact on black children & families on the federal, state & local levels. Disseminates legislative reviews & analyses to local groups. Gives technical assistance to affiliate groups in the planning of child care services & adoption. Provides an information & referral service. Sponsors regional conferences & workshops on topics such as adoption, foster care, child welfare, child development policies, family services, & public schools. Sponsors workshop on the media & their impact on children at annual conference. Sponsors week-long Public Policy Institute for the presidents of local affiliates. Annual conference in October
Media: Publishes *The Black Child Advocate* (4/year) $12.50; a quarterly newsletter, *Child Health Talk* ($8.00). Publishes books & seminar papers on services to & the status of black children & youth, position papers, legislative updates & analyses, bibliographies of children's books & book reviews

NATIONAL BRAILLE ASSOCIATION, INC.

3 Townline Circle, Rochester, NY 14623-2513
716-427-8260; Fax: 716-427-0263

Founded: 1945
Membership: 2,000 volunteers & professional educators
Purpose: To develop & distribute materials for the visually impaired in all three media: braille, large type & tape. Also acts as a national clearinghouse for the exchange of ideas & suggestions on improving transcription techniques
Services: Offers continuing education seminars & workshops to those who produce & transcribe reading materials. Also maintains a depository of braille books for college students & adults interested in various careers. Conferences held twice yearly
Media: Publishes NBA Bulletin (quarterly), $30. Manuals, guidelines & workshop reprints are available for sale

NATIONAL CAPTIONING INSTITUTE

5203 Leesburg Pike, Falls Church, VA 22041
703-998-2400, 800-533-9673 (voice), 800-321-8337 (TDD)
Pres: Philip W. Bravin

Founded: 1979
Purpose: To provide closed captioned television for the benefit of hearing-impaired
Services: Provides captioned programming & technology for millions of people who can benefit from captioned television. Also distributes TeleCaption™ decoders to hundreds of retail locations across the country. Handles responsibility for decoder development, consumer research, public awareness, providing counsel to Congress on captioning-related issues, decoder giveaway programs for low-income families, & many other activities
Media: Publishes research geared to teachers, librarians, & the general public

NATIONAL CENTER FOR HEALTH EDUCATION

72 Spring St., Ste. 208, New York, NY 10012
212-334-9470; Fax: 212-334-9845
Act Pres: Janic Nittoli

Founded: 1975
Membership: 1,800 health care professionals
Purpose: To promote health education, especially among young people
Services: Develops health care curricula, public-awareness programs & resources for elementary through high school education. Sponsors an annual conference

NATIONAL COMMITTEE FOR PREVENTION OF CHILD ABUSE (NCPCA)

332 S. Michigan Ave., Ste. 1600, Chicago, IL 60604-4357
312-663-3520
Exec Dir: Anne H. Cohn Donnelly

Purpose: NCPCA is dedicated to involving concerned citizens in actions to prevent child abuse. While the organization is concerned with both primary & secondary prevention, its principal focus is on primary prevention
Services: NCPCA is a privately funded organization promoting public awareness of child abuse & community based programs to prevent child abuse; has 67 chapters nationwide; & publishes educational materials that deal with child abuse, child abuse prevention, & parenting
Media: A brochure that describes NCPCA's programs & catalog that describes educational materials published by the organization are available free upon request

NATIONAL COUNCIL FOR GEOGRAPHIC EDUCATION (NCGE)

Indiana University of Pennsylvania, 16A Leonard Hall, Indiana, PA 15705
412-357-6290; Fax: 412-357-7708
Exec Dir: Ruth I. Shiny

Founded: 1915
Membership: 3,800 geographers, teachers, librarians, educational institutions
Purpose: NCGE works to enhance the status & quality of geography teaching & learning
Services: Annual meetings: Lexington, KY, Nov. 2-5, 1994; San Antonio, TX, Oct. 25-28, 1995. National Geography Olympiad. NCGE has developed various awards to promote excellence in geographic education
Media: Publishes *Journal of Geography* (6/year), $15 to students, $60 to libraries, $35 to K-12 teachers; regular subscription included in membership; *Perspective* (5/year) included in membership, $10/year to others. Also produces slides for geography courses, available to librarians, teachers, & the general public. Publishes books, pamphlets, catalog

NATIONAL COUNCIL OF TEACHERS OF ENGLISH (NCTE)

1111 W. Kenyon Rd., Urbana, IL 61801-1096
217-328-3870
Pres: Jane Hydrick
Pres-Elect: Miriam Chaplin

Exec Dir: Miles Myers
Dir Pubns Svcs: Clifford N. Maduzia
PR Asst: Lori Bianchini

Founded: 1911
Membership: 68,000 teachers at all
levels, school administrators &
librarians
Purpose: To improve the quality of English & language arts instruction for
students at all levels of education
Services: Serves as a clearinghouse of
ideas on subject matter of English &
its teaching. Provides counseling &
teaching aids to members. Lobbies
at local, state, & national levels
through SLATE (Support for the
Learning & Teaching of English). Annual conventions : Nov. 16-21,
1994, Orlando, FL; Nov. 15-20,
1995, San Diego, CA. Sponsors
study sessions at various conferences on aspects of children's literature & the teaching of English.
Sponsors workshops, seminars & institutes for teachers, librarians & the
general public. Maintains NCTE archives & library of 1200 books &
200 periodicals for children's professionals for use on the premises.
Presents award for Poetry for Children every three years in Spring, at
National Language Arts Conference,
to an outstanding children's poet
(medallion plaque). Presents Achievement Awards in Writing annually to
outstanding senior high school students of English, & Promising Young
Writers Award annually to 8th grade
students. Administers programs to
recognize excellence in student literary magazines annually for junior,
middle, & high schools
Media: Publishes Language Arts
(8/year), Primary Voices K-6 (quarterly), English Journal (9/year), & Notes
Plus (quarterly) for member
teachers, elementary & middle-
junior-senior high, respectively.
English Leadership Quarterly is for
English Department heads. Also publishes Research in the Teaching of
English (quarterly), $15 to individu-
als. Publications division offers
books & pamphlets geared primarily
for teachers, & cassette tapes of
conference speeches. Catalog

NATIONAL COUNCIL OF TEACHERS OF MATHEMATICS

1906 Association Dr., Reston, VA
22091-1593
703-620-9840; Fax: 703-476-7560
Exec Dir: Dr. James D. Gates

Founded: 1920
Membership: 98,000 teachers of
mathematics & institutions
Purpose: To assist in promoting the interests of mathematics in America,

especially in elementary & secondary
fields & to bring the interest of
mathematics to the attention of the
education world
Services: Maintains a mathematics
education library & resource center,
conducts public & government relations programs, sponsors annual national competitions for students,
regional meetings, & sponsors an
annual conference (Apr. 6-9, 1995:
Boston, MA; Apr. 25-28, 1996: San
Diego, CA; Apr. 17-20, 1997: Minneapolis, MN)
Media: Publishes a bimonthly newsletter, topical yearbooks, educational
materials & journals: Mathematics
Teacher (9/year), Arithmetic Teacher
(9/year), National Council of
Teachers of Mathematics - Yearbook
($14.40 to members; $18 for nonmembers)

NATIONAL EDUCATION ASSOCIATION

1201 16th St., NW, Washington, DC
20036
202-833-4000
Exec Dir: Don Cameron

Founded: 1857
Membership: 2,000,000; elementary &
secondary teachers, higher education faculty, retired educators &
educational support personnel
Services: Through various program
units, NEA services its members,
local & state affiliates & governance
bodies with information about legislation, instructional needs, problems
of educational employees & state &
national developments related to instructional issues. Maintains six
regional offices. Operates an education research center to provide its
members, media, lawmakers & other
organizations with in-depth data &
research publications. Works to effect education reform, equity in education employee compensation & to
attract the brightest and best to the
teaching profession. Maintains close
relationship with teachers in other
countries through the World Con-
federation of Organizations of the
Teaching Profession (WCOTP). Conducts local, regional, state & national workshops, conferences & training
seminars. Works to increase the involvement of educational employees
in the election of pro-education can-
didates. Provides assistance to affiliates preparing to implement special
projects. Provides trained professional staff to help affiliates in areas of
crises, human relations, instructional
development, training, community
action, organizing & political action.
Annual conference
Media: Publishes Today's Education &
NEA Today (8/year). Also publishes

books, cassettes, pamphlets & multimedia packets dealing with issues
related to education, in-service training of teachers, parent/community
involvement & instruction development through the NEA Professional
Library, the largest publisher of
teacher in-service materials in the
world. Operates a Broadcast Services Center to keep its memebers,
affiliates & the public informed of
new uses of technology in education. Provides training in video
production and use. Catalog

NATIONAL INDIAN YOUTH COUNCIL

318 Elm St., SE, Albuquerque, NM
87102
505-247-2251
Exec Dir: Gerald Wilkinson

Founded: 1961
Membership: 46,000 Native Americans
Purpose: To advance & improve the
status of Native Americans by
promoting educational & employment opportunities for youth & encouraging media that reflects Native
American culture
Services: Sponsors seminars & workshops for members, teachers, &
young people
Media: Publishes a newsletter for
members, pamphlets for children,
teachers, & the general public.
Catalog

NATIONAL INFORMATION CENTER FOR EDUCATIONAL MEDIA

Box 40130, Albuquerque, NM 87196
505-265-3591
Managing Dir: Patrick Sauer

Founded: 1966
Purpose: Established as bibliographic
reference source for educational
audiovisual materials & citations
Services: Print indexes, online files,
CD-ROMs, custom search & product
delivery

NATIONAL MIDDLE SCHOOL ASSOCIATION

4807 Evanswood Dr., Columbus, OH
43229-6292
614-8484-8211; Fax: 614-848-4301
Exec Dir: Ron Williamson

Founded: 1973
Membership: 10,000 teachers, librarians, administrators, college & university students
Purpose: To promote the development
& growth of middle schools as dis-
tinct & necessary in their contribution to American education
Services: Sponsors institutes & holds
annual conferences in November
Media: Publishes the Middle School
Journal 5/year, $30; Target on the

Middle (occasional), free to members; *Middle Ground* (semi-annual), free to members. Publications division produces books, videorecordings & audiotapes for teachers

NATIONAL SCHOOL ORCHESTRA ASSOCIATION

345 Maxwell Dr., Pittsburgh, PA 15236-2067
412-882-6996; Fax: 614-848-4301
Exec Sec: Norman Mellin

Founded: 1958
Membership: Approximately 10,000 orchestra directors, primarily in public schools
Purpose: To foster better orchestras throughout the public schools & improve students' musical knowledge & composition skills
Services: Workshops offered to members; sponsors NSOA compostion contest for original musical compositions created by school groups. Holds annual conferences
Media: Publishes *NSOA Bulletin* (4/year)

NATIONAL SCIENCE SUPERVISORS ASSOCIATION

82 Deepwood Dr., East Hartford, CT 06118-2411
Exec Dir: Kenneth R. Roy, Ph.D.

Founded: 1959
Membership: 1100 leaders in science education
Purpose: To improve science education through leadership development
Services: Workshops, seminars, institutes, miniconferences, publications, scholarship programs, resource materials. Annual conference held early April each year
Media: Publishes newsletter, *Science Leadership Trend Notes*, source book, directory, journal & more

NATIONAL SCIENCE TEACHERS ASSOCIATION (NSTA)

1742 Connecticut Ave., NW, Washington, DC 20009-1171
202-328-5800
Exec Sec: Bill G. Aldridge

Founded: 1895
Membership: 63,000 science teachers, colleges, libraries & secondary schools
Purpose: To promote excellence in science teaching
Services: Provides liaison with government agencies, legislative alerts & Congressional testimony, issues position statements & conducts national surveys, sets certification standards for science teachers & institutions that train them, offers annual awards recognizing students &

teachers for outstanding work: Presidential Awards for Math & Science Teaching & 17 other programs; offers curriculum & student assessment. Sponsors teachers honors workshops, NASA education workshops, computer camps, short courses, & educational tours. Sponsors regional seminars & meetings & an annual conference. Affiliated with the American Association of Science
Media: Publishes numerous periodicals, journals & reports, computer software, teaching aids, educational books, posters & examinations, including: *Energy & Education Newsletter* (bimonthly), $9/year; *Journal of College Science Teaching* (bimonthly); *NSTA Report* (quarterly); *Science & Children* (8/year); *Science Scope* (7/year); *Science Teacher* (9/year)

NATIONAL/STATE LEADERSHIP TRAINING INSTITUTE ON THE GIFTED/TALENTED

Hilton Center, 900 Wilshire Bldg., Ste. 1142, Los Angeles, CA 90017-3311
213-489-7470
Dir: Irving S. Sato

Founded: 1972
Services: Sponsors workshops & institutes for teachers, librarians & the general public. Holds several national conferences yearly on curriculum for the gifted & on creativity & the gifted
Media: Publishes quarterly bulletin. Publications division publishes books & produces filmstrips for teachers, librarians & other educators. Catalog

NATIONAL STORY LEAGUE

c/o Virginia Dare Shope, 1342 4th Ave., Juniata, Altoona, PA 16601
814-942-3449
Pres: Virginia Shope

Founded: 1903
Membership: 15,000 teachers, librarians, parents, business women, & students
Purpose: The League seeks to instill appreciation for the concepts of love, peace & morals through programs in storytelling that incorporate education & entertainment
Services: Offers education programs in storytelling technique for children, teachers, librarians & the general public. Programs include workshops, seminars & institutes. Conducts meetings & conventions throughout the year at various locations. Conferences feature seminars in children's media. Sponsors an annual short-story competition for children & awards cash prizes to three winners
Media: Publishes *Story Art Magazine* (quarterly), 5/year to non-members;

Story Art Yearbook. A publications division publishes books & pamphlets on storytelling skills for children, teachers, librarians, & parents

NATIONAL TELEMEDIA COUNCIL (NTC)

120 E. Wilson St., Madison, WI 53703
608-257-7712; Fax: 608-257-7714
Exec Dir: Marieli Rowe

Founded: 1953
Purpose: The National Telemedia Council is a nonprofit educational organization which promotes media literacy for children & youth through teachers, librarians/media specialists, parents & other caregivers, media professionals, researchers, & others. NTC links & supports their efforts to help our young people to be "in," rather than "under" the control of the media they consume
Services: NTC serves as the clearinghouse & center for media literacy education & is currently developing computerized database designed specifically for tracking media education resources & information. Conferences, symposiums & workshops are also developed & offered by NTC.
Media: Publishes *Telemedium* (4/year), free to members. Variety of other educational/informational materials are available. Subscribership to the Media Literacy Clearinghouse & Center is being established

THE NATIVE AMERICAN PUBLIC BROADCASTING CONSORTIUM

Box 83111, Lincoln, NE 68501
402-472-3522
Dir: Frank Blythe

Founded: 1977
Membership: 65 tribal organizations, public television stations, educational organizations, individuals
Purpose: To encourage the creation, production & distribution of quality programming by, for & about native Americans of all age groups
Services: Offers workshops, seminars & instructional videotapes to teachers, librarians & the public. Also holds annual conferences which often include chidren's media workshops & awards for children's media
Media: Publishes *NAPBC Newsletter* (quarterly). Produces films & videorecordings for teachers, children, librarians & the general public

THE 92ND ST. YOUNG MEN'S & YOUNG WOMEN'S HEBREW ASSOCIATION

1395 Lexington Ave., New York, NY 10128
212-415-5600
Exec Dir: Sol Adler

Founded: 1874

Purpose: A cultural & community organization for children, adolescents, & families

Services: Offers workshops & seminars for children & the general public. Also sponsors parent-child programs

Media: Books, journals, videocassettes & workbooks based on YM-YWHA programs now under development

OLYMPIC MEDIA INFORMATION

Box 190, West Park, NY 12493

201-963-1600

Exec Dir: Walt Carroll

Founded: 1968

Membership: Approximately 1,000 teachers & librarians

Purpose: Provides media reference & review service

Media: Publishes Educational Media Catalogs on Microfiche (semi-annual), $87.50. Also produces numerous films, videorecordings, slides & filmstrips for teachers, students, librarians, & the general public. Catalog

ORCHARD HOUSE, LOUISA MAY ALCOTT MEMORIAL ASSOCIATION

Box 343, Concord, MA 01742-0343

508-369-4118

Dir: Stephanie Upton

Founded: 1911

Membership: 500

Purpose: To preserve for public enjoyment & education the home where Louisa May Alcott wrote her famous novel, *Little Women,* in 1868

Services: Provides educational programs, including guided tours & living history activities for students, teachers, librarians, & the general public

Media: Publishes Alcott *NEWSNOTES & PORTFOLIO* for members, $25 individual, $35 family membership yearly. Other publications include pamphlets, booklets & educational packets for all age groups. Gift shop catalog & educational materials order form available

PARENT COOPERATIVE PRESCHOOLS INTERNATIONAL

c/o Kathy Mensel, Box 90410, Indianapolis, IN 46290

317-849-0992

Exec Sec: Kathy Mensel

Founded: 1960

Membership: 12,500 teachers & parents

Purpose: To strengthen community appreciation of parent education & to promote interchange of information & support among parent cooperative nursery schools, kindergarten &

other parent-sponsored preschool programs

Services: Offers workshops & courses in teacher training for cooperative schools. Provides consultation & support services to cooperative preschools & holds annual conferences in all areas of the US & Canada. Also studies & promotes legislation to further the health & well-being of children & families

Media: Publishes *Cooperatively Speaking* (3/year), $15. Publications division produces a bibliography of materials useful to cooperatives, several pamphlets & guidelines, plus videorecordings for teachers & parents

PUPPETEERS OF AMERICA

Five Cricklewood Path, Pasadena, CA 91107

818-797-5748

Chairperson: Gayle G. Schluter

Founded: 1937

Membership: 2100 teachers, librarians, parents, students

Purpose: Dedicated to promoting & developing the art of puppetry

Services: Brings together both professional & amateur puppeteers from all over the world. Provides consulting services & information on puppetry activities & events. Holds national puppetry festivals (biennially) which include performances, workshops, exhibits, film & video shows & a puppetry exchange. Also maintains an audiovisual library & a puppetry store

Media; Publishes *The Puppetry Journal* (quarterly), plus an annual membership directory & bimonthly newsletters

READING REFORM FOUNDATION

Box 98785, Tacoma, WA 98498-0785

206-588-3436

Exec Dir: Marian Hinds

Founded: 1961

Membership: 3,000 teachers, administrators, parents

Purpose: To combat illiteracy in America by working to restore intensive phonics in reading education

Services: Sponsors workshops, seminars, college instructional courses & meeting. Disseminates information on intensive phonics & coordinates education programs. Sponsors annual conference in July & occasional contests for children

Media: Publishes *The Reading Informer* (quarterly) & *Sounds of Reading* (8/year). Also publishes pamphlets, books & bibliography of phonics texts for teachers, librarians & the general public

SCHOOL SCIENCE & MATHEMATICS ASSOCIATION

Bloomsburg University, 400 E. Second St., Bloomsburg, PA 17815-1301

717-389-4915; Fax: 717-389-3894

Exec Dir: Donald L. Pratt

Founded: 1901

Membership: 1,000 teachers & librarians

Purpose: To improve the teaching of science & mathematics

Services: Provides educational workshops & seminars to teachers, sponsors media workshops, contests, & awards for children. Annual conference

Media: Publishes monthly periodical *School Science and Mathematics,* $30 domestic, $35 foreign; newsletters, journals, & books geared for teachers

SOCIETY OF CHILDREN'S BOOK WRITERS AND ILLUSTRATORS

22736 Vanowen St., West Hills, CA 91306

Pres: Stephen Mooser

Exec Dir: Lin Oliver

Purpose: To assist authors, illustrators, editors, agents, children's librarians, educators who work with children's books, & writers & producers for children's television

Services: Serves as a clearinghouse for the exchange of information on children's media. Lobbies for legislation promoting members' interests. Administers a free manuscript exchange through which members can seek professional criticism of their work. Annual conference on children's literature held in Los Angeles, CA, in August. Awards three Golden Kite Statuettes & three Honor Book Certificates annually to most outstanding fiction, nonfiction & illustrated children's books written by members

Media: Publishes *SCBW Bulletin* (bimonthly), to members only

SOUTHERN ASSOCIATION OF COLLEGES AND SCHOOLS

1866 Southern Lane, Decatur, GA 30033

404-789-4500; Fax: 404-329-6598

Interim Dir: John Davis

Founded: 1895

Membership: 11,811 educational institutions

Purpose: Accreditation of educational institutions; provides standards & guidance for accreditation of elementary, secondary & occupational institutions & colleges

Services: Holds workshops & seminars at annual meetings

Media: Publishes *Proceedings* (6/year) & a wide variety of brochures, reports, guidelines, study materials, & policies on accreditation of educational institutions & issues related to teaching & education. Conference in December

SOUTHERN ASSOCIATION ON CHILDREN UNDER SIX

Box 6130, Little Rock, AR 72215-6130
501-663-0353
Exec Dir: Rose A. Adams

Founded: 1948
Membership: Over 18,000 early childhood educators, daycare providers, program administrators, researchers, teacher trainers, parents
Purpose: To provide a central clearinghouse for local, state, & federal issues affecting young children & their families; to explore child development & early education issues
Services: Provides training, presents awards. Annual conferences
Media: Publishes *Dimensions* (quarterly), publishes curriculum & training materials. Also publishes position papers. Each of 14 state affiliate groups publishes a newsletter & holds separate annual conferences. Resource catalog available

TEACHERS & WRITERS COLLABORATIVE

Five Union Sq. W., New York, NY 10003-3306
212-691-6590
Exec Dir: Nancy Larson-Shapiro

Founded: 1967
Purpose: To encourage innovative methods of teaching creative writing & the arts
Services: Conducts workshops on educational techniques in creative writing & the arts for children at all grade levels. Also sends professional writers & artists to public schools to demonstrate their art forms
Media: Publishes a magazine (bimonthly) and books for teachers, writers, & other members

TECHNOLOGY EDUCATION FOR CHILDREN COUNCIL (TECC)

1914 Association Dr., Reston, VA 22091-1502
703-860-2100
Pres: Lewis Kieft

Founded: 1963
Membership: 250 teachers, technology education consultants, teacher educators, & school administrators
Purpose: To foster technology education by providing resource materials for professional use, stimulating

research & discussion among educators in the field & encouraging active use of computers & other technology by elementary school students
Services: Provides workshops & seminars to members. Also sponsors an annual conference: March 26-28, 1995, Nashville, TN; March 31-April 2, 1996, Phoenix, AZ
Media: *TECC Newsletter* (semi-annual), $8/year included with membership fees. Also publishes several monographs, films & project idea sets

TECHNOLOGY STUDENT ASSOCIATION

(formerly American Industrial Arts Student Association)
1914 Association Dr., Reston, VA 22091
703-860-9000
Exec Dir: Rosanne T. White

Founded: 1978
Membership: 75,000 students
Purpose: An association of technology & industrial-arts students established to promote educational programs & to develop leadership in the field
Services: Offers educational programs to students & teachers in technology & industrial arts disciplines. Conducts competitive events at state & national conferences. Annual conference in June
Media: Publishes two newsletters: *School Scene (3/year)* & *Advisor Update (3/year)*. Publication division offers books, pamphlets, slides & videorecordings for students in technology & industrial arts. Catalog

TOY MANUFACTURERS OF AMERICA, INC.

200 Fifth Ave., Ste. 740, New York, NY 10010
212-675-1141
Pres: David Miller

Founded: 1916
Membership: 250 toy manufacturers & importers, toy testing labs & design firms
Purpose: To promote the sale & appropriate selection of toys & games
Media: Publishes two pamphlets: *Toy Industry Fact Book* and *The TMA Guide to Toys & Play*

U.S. COMMITTEE FOR UNITED NATIONS CHILDREN'S FUND

333 E. 38th St., New York, NY 10036
212-686-5522

Founded: 1947
Purpose: To support UNICEF-assisted projects in developing countries through fundraising activities & to inform the American people about the lives & needs of these children
Services: Offers workshops to students, teachers, librarians & the

general public on children in Third World countries. Also maintains The Information Center on Children's Cultures, which provides lists of primary source materials & answers basic questions on childhood in countries worldwide. The center also loans a limited number of art exhibits
Media: Publishes *News of the World's Children* (3/year). Publications division produces numberous books, pamphlets, films, videorecordings, games & puzzles

U.S. SECTION OF INTERNATIONAL BOARD ON BOOKS FOR YOUNG PEOPLE

Box 8139, 800 Barksdale Rd., Newark, DE 19714
Exec Dir: Alida von Krough Cutts

Founded: 1984
Membership: 400 authors, illustrators, publishers, teachers & librarians
Purpose: To promote the development of quality reading materials for young people around the world. The board works in cooperation with other organizations to facilitate the exchange of information on reading programs & children's media throughout the world
Services: Assists in promoting international book exhibits, developing directories of institutions in the field of children's literature, & financing international literacy programs. Participates in the Hans Christian Andersen Awards program. Biennial IBBY conventions held
Media: Publishes the *USBBY Newsletter* (semi-annual) free to members

UNITED SYNAGOGUE OF CONSERVATIVE JUDAISM

Commission on Jewish Education
155 Fifth Ave., New York, NY 10010-6802
Dir: Robert Abramson

Founded: 1945
Membership: Educators representing the various organizational arms of the Conservative Movement in Judaism
Purpose: To promote & supervise education in Conservative Judaism, particularly of children at the elementary & secondary levels
Services: Sponsors workshops, seminars & institutes for teachers, rabbis, & lay leaders. Also sponsors an overseas program in Israel for educators
Media: Publishes *Your Child* (3 issues), $7 subscription, & *Tov L' Horot* (free to affiliated educators). Publication division produces appropriate books, pamphlets, films, slides, & videorecordings. Catalog

WOMEN'S NATIONAL BOOK ASSOCIATION

160 Fifth Ave., Room 604, New York, NY 10010
212-675-7805
Exec Off: Sandra K. Paul

Founded: 1917
Membership: 1000 publishers, authors, librarians, editors, illustrators, designers, educators, critics, booksellers
Purpose: A network for all professionals in the publishing field, providing a forum for exchanging ideas & information, generating contacts in the industry, as well as promoting recognition of women's achievements at all levels in the field
Services: Conducts meetings at local chapters featuring speakers, workshops & discussion groups. Sponsors luncheons & dinners for authors & offers seminars on aspects of publishing. Also sponsors awards for industry achievements, including the Lucile Micheels Pannell Award for children's books. Annual conference held at American Library Association annual convention
Media: Publishes *The Bookwoman* (3/year), $8 to nonmembers

WORLD AROUND SONGS, INC.

20 Colberts Creek Rd., Burnsville, NC 28714
704-675-5343
Exec Dir: Paul Cope

Founded: 1976
Services: Distributes pocket books of songs from around the world, primarily for children, individuals, & groups. Publishes custom made songbooks available in quantity for schools, camps, churches, & other organizations

WORLD EDUCATION FELLOWSHIP, U.S. SECTION

c/o Dr. Mildred Haipt, College of New Rochelle, 29 Castle Pl., New Rochelle, NY 10805

914-654-5578
Pres: Dr. Hildred Haipt

Founded: 1921
Membership: 15,000 worldwide, approximately 75 U.S. members
Purpose: To promote global understanding for a more peaceful world through educational innovation & lifelong learning in the arts
Services: Produces curriculum materials for children & adults to develop skills in painting, music dance, literary expression & all the arts. Also offers seminars, conferences & workshops to members & the general public. Annual conferences held in the spring
Media: Publishes *The New Era* (quarterly); *Worldscope* (periodic); also publishes pamphlets for teachers and the public

YOUNG ADULT LIBRARY SERVICES ASSOCIATION

Division of the American Library Association
50 E. Huron St., Chicago, IL 60611
312-280-4390
Exec Dir: Ann Weeks

Membership: 2,129 librarians, educators, & others interested in library services to youth
Purpose: Dedicated to the improvement & extension of library services to young adults (12-18 years) in all types of libraries. Charged by ALA with the evaluation & selection of media for young adults & improvement of techniques employed in library services for young adults
Services: Sponsors workshops & seminars on materials & services for young adults at the annual ALA convention. Selects Best Books for Young Adults annually & lists Selected Films & Video for Young Adults each year at ALA Midwinter Meeting
Media: Publishes *Journal of Youth Services in Libraries* (quarterly), $25. Also publishes books & pamphlets

for librarians & young adults. Checklist

YOUNG AUDIENCES

115 E. 92nd St., New York, NY 10128
212-831-8110
Exec Dir: Richard Bell

Purpose: To connect the arts with the education of children in elementary & secondary schools
Services: Sends local professional performing artists & artist ensembles into schools to give educational performances, workshops, & residencies
Media: Publishes: *Young Audiences Newsletter* & an annual report. Also issues arts & education materials for artists working in schools

YOUNG MEN'S CHRISTIAN ASSOCIATION

101 N. Wacker Dr., Chicago, IL 60606
312-977-0031
Exec Dir: David R. Mercer

Founded: 1851 (in the U.S.)
Membership: Serves 14 million girls, boys, women, and men annually
Purpose: Provides preventive, value-based programs that promote the healthy development of children, build positive behavior in teens, & give families the support they need to succeed
Services: The YMCA meets community needs through programs ranging from child care to job training to teen centers to health & fitness for people of all ages, incomes, & abilities
Media: Publishes *Discovery YMCA* (quarterly), free to volunteers & staff members; *Executive Notes* (6/year), free. Brochures, videotapes, & other materials for YMCA staff, board members, volunteers, & the general public

STATE LIBRARY & MEDIA ASSOCIATIONS

16

State and regional library and media associations are listed alphabetically.

ALABAMA

ALABAMA INSTRUCTIONAL MEDIA ASSOCIATION
President: Darnell Whited, Oneonta City Schools, (H) 606 Ridgeway Dr., Oneonta, AL 35121; 205-274-0918; Fax: 205-274-2910
President-elect: Bernice Young, (H) 312 Brown Ave., Eutaw, AL 35462

ALABAMA LIBRARY ASSOCIATION
President: Margaret Blake, 2569 Old Dobbins Rd., Mobile, AL 36695; 205-690-8377; Fax: 205-690-8015
President-elect: Jack F. Bulow, 2100 Park Place, Birmingham, AL 35203; 205-226-3613
Publication: *Alabama Librarian*

ALASKA

ALASKA TECHNOLOGY ROUNDTABLE OF THE ALASKA LIBRARY ASSOCIATION
President: Lois Stiegemeier, Alaska Department of Education, P.O. Box F, Juneau, AK 99811; 907-465-2644.
President-elect: Marilyn P. Clark, Juneau School District, 10014; Crazy Horse Drive, Juneau, AK 99801; 907-463-1850; Fax: 907-463-1828.

ALASKA LIBRARY ASSOCIATION
President: Rita Dursi Johnson, University of Alaska Southeast, William Eagan Library, 11120 Glacier Hwy., Juneau, AK 99801-8676; 907-465-6285.
President-elect: Greg Hill, Noel Wien Public Library, 1215 Cowles Street, Fairbanks, AK 99701; 907-459-1020
Publications: *Sourdough; Newspoke*

ARIZONA

ARIZONA EDUCATIONAL MEDIA ASSOCIATION
President: Caryl Ellis, Prescott Unified School District #1, 146 S. Granite St., Prescott, AZ 86302; 602-445-5400; Fax: 602-776-0243.
President-elect: John Barnard, Arizona State University, University Media Systems, Tempe, AZ 85287-2304; 602-965-6137; Fax: 602-965-1738

ARIZONA STATE LIBRARY ASSOCIATION
President: Jean Collins, Northern Arizona University, Cline Library, Box 6022, Flagstaff, AZ 86011-6022; 602-523-6802; Fax: 602-523-3770.
Publication: *ASLA Newsletter*

ARKANSAS

ARKANSAS ASSOCIATION OF INSTRUCTIONAL MEDIA
President: John Cheek, Arkansas Educational Television Network, 350 S. Donaghey, Conway, AR 72032; 501-682-4185; Fax: 501-682-4122.
President-elect: David Spillers, University of Arkansas at Little Rock, 2801 S. University, Little Rock, AR 72204; 501-569-3269.

ARKANSAS LIBRARY ASSOCIATION
President: Jenelle Stephens, Arkansas State Library, 1 Capitol Mall, Little Rock, AR 72201; 501-682-2550; Fax: 501-682-1529.
Publication: *Arkansas Libraries*

CALIFORNIA

CALIFORNIA MEDIA AND LIBRARY EDUCATORS ASSOCIATION
President: Robert Skapura, Los Medanos College, 2700 E. Leland Dr., Pittsburg, CA 94565; 510-439-2181 Ext. 220; Fax: 510-427-6384
President-elect: John McGinnis, Cerritos College, 11110 Alondra Blvd, Norwalk, CA 90650; 310-860-2451; Fax: 310-467-5002

CALIFORNIA LIBRARY ASSOCIATION
President: Mary Jo Levy, Palo Alto City Library, Downtown Branch, 270 Forest Ave., Palo Alto, CA 94301-2512; 415-329-2516.
Publication: *California Libraries*

COLORADO

COLORADO EDUCATIONAL MEDIA ASSOCIATION
President: Su Eckhardt, Smoky Hill H.jS. Media Center, 16100 East Smoky Hill Rd., Aurora, CO 80015; 303-693-1700 ext. 5590; Fax: 303-693-1700 ext. 5561.
President-elect: (Ms.) Billy Wolter, Arvada Middle School Media Center, (H) 6495 Happy Canyon Rd., #3, Denver, CO 80237; 303-423-1553; Fax: 303-423-5213

COLORADO LIBRARY ASSOCIATION
President: Margaret Owens, Jefferson County Public Library, 10200 W. 20th Ave., Lakewood, CO 80215; 303-275-2216; Fax: 303-275-2225.
Publications: *Colorado Libraries; CLA News*

CONNECTICUT

CONNECTICUT EDUCATIONAL MEDIA ASSOCIATION

President: Carolyn Marcato, Fairfield High School, (H) 155 Catalpa Rd., Wilton, CT 06897; 203-255-8451; Fax: 203-284-1506

President-elect: I.A. (Tally) Negroni, Stamford High School, (H) 53 Blueberry Hill, Weston, CT 06883; 203-977-4931; 203-358-0128

CONNECTICUT LIBRARY ASSOCIATION

President: Jan Vail-Day, Woodbridge Town Library, 10 Newton Rd, Woodbridge, CT 06525; 203-389-3433; Fax: 203-389-3457

President-elect: Maxine Bleiweiss, Lucy Robbins Wells Library, 95 Cedar St., Newington, CT 06111-2603; Fax: 203-667-1255

Publication: *Connecticut Libraries*

DELAWARE

DELAWARE LIBRARY ASSOCIATION

President: Jonathan Jeffery, University of Delaware, Hugh M. Morris Library, Reference Department, Newark, DE 19717-5267; 302-831-2432

President-elect: Patricia Woods, Sussex Tech High School, Box 351, Georgetown, DE 19947-0351; 302-856-0961

Publication: *DLA Bulletin*

DISTRICT OF COLUMBIA

DISTRICT OF COLUMBIA LIBRARY ASSOCIATION

President: Trellis Wright, 8298 Quill Point Dr., Bowie, MD 20720; 202-707-2441; Fax: 202-707-8366

President-elect: Dan Clemmer, 5527 Trent St., Chevy Chase, MD 20815-5511; 202-647-3002

Publication: *Intercom*

FLORIDA

FLORIDA ASSOCIATION FOR MEDIA IN EDUCATION

President: Helen Tallman, Mast Academy, Dade County Schools, (H),7601 SW 94th Ave., Miami, FL 33173; 305-365-6278

President-elect: Linda Schroeder, Buchholz High School, Alachua County Schools, (H) 4249 NW 56th Way, Gainesville, FL 32606; 904-955-6702

FLORIDA LIBRARY ASSOCIATION

President: Helen Moeller, Leon County Public Library; 200 W. Park Ave., Tallahassee, Fl 32301; 904-487-2665

President-elect: Elizabeth Curry, SEFLIN, 100 S. Andrews Ave., Ft. Lauderdale, FL 33301; 305-357-7318

Publication: *Florida Libraries*

GEORGIA

GEORGIA ASSOCIATION FOR INSTRUCTIONAL TECHNOLOGY

President: Catherine Price, Valdosta State College, Dept. of Secondary Education, Valdosta, GA 31698; 912-333-5927; 912-333-7167

President-elect: Gordon Baker, Eagles Landing High School, 301 Tunis Rd., McDonough, GA 30253; 404-954-9515; Fax: 404-914-9789

GEORGIA LIBRARY ASSOCIATION

President: Donna D. Mancini, Dekalb County Public Library, 215 Sycamore St., Decatur, GA 30030, 404-370-8450; Fax: 404-370-8469

President-elect: Sue Hatfield, Director Library Services, Dekalb College; Pantherville Rd., Decatur, GA 30034; 404-299-4273

Publication: *Georgia Librarian*

GUAM

GUAM LIBRARY ASSOCIATION

President: Chih Wang, Dean; Learning Resources, University of Guam, Mangilao, GU 96923, 671-734-2482; Fax: 671-734-6882

President-elect: Maxine Becker, Micronesian Health Archives; School of Nursing & Allied Health, University of Guam, Mangilao, GU 96923; 671-734-9218; Fax: 671-734-8379.

HAWAII

HAWAII LIBRARY ASSOCIATION

President: Jean Ehrhorn, 507 Koko Isle Circle, Honolulu, HI 96825; 808-956-2472

President-elect: Diane Eddy, 4823 Kolohala St., Honolulu, HI 96816; 808-689-8392

Publications: *HLA Journal; HLA Newsletter*

IDAHO

IDAHO ASSOCIATION FOR EDUCATIONAL COMMUNICATIONS AND TECHNOLOGY

President: David Peck, School Dostrict #25, 3115 Pole Line Rd., Pocatello, ID 83204; 208-235-3222; Fax: 208-235-3280

IDAHO LIBRARY ASSOCIATION

President: Karen Strege, 633 E. 25th Ave. Spokane, WA 99203; 509-455-6697

Publication: *Idaho Librarian*

ILLINOIS

ILLINOIS ASSOCIATION FOR EDUCATIONAL COMMUNICATIONS AND TECHNOLOGY

President: Jim Bradford, Illinois State University, Instructional Technology Services, Normal, IL 61790-6370; 309-438-3694; Fax: 309-438-8788

ILLINOIS LIBRARY ASSOCIATION

President: Lee Logan, Illinois Valley Library System, 845 Brenkman Dr., Pekin, IL 61554-1522; 309-353-4110

President-elect: Sue Stroyan, Illinois Wesleyan University, Box 2899, Bloomington, IL 61702-2900; 309-556-0125; Fax: 309-556-3261

Publication: *ILA Reporter*

INDIANA

ASSOCIATION FOR INDIANA MEDIA EDUCATORS

President: Bonnie Grimble, Cannel High School, 520 E. Main St., Cannel, IN 46032; 317-846-7721; Fax: 317-571-4066

President-elect: Dennis LeLoup, Indiana Dept. of Eduction, Learning Resources Unit, (H) 4324 Clovelly Ct., Indianapolis, IN 46254; 317-232-9119; Fax: 317-232-9121

INDIANA LIBRARY FEDERATION

President: Diane Bever, 6160 N. Forest Ave., Forest, IN 46039-9547; 317-453-2000

President-elect: Laura Johnson, 4129 Cranbrook, Indianapolis, IN 46250; 317-269-1850

Publications: *Focus on Indiana Libraries; Indiana Libraries*

IOWA

IOWA EDUCATIONAL MEDIA ASSOCIATION

President: Lucille Lettow, University of Northern Iowa, (H) 1516 College St., Cedar Falls, IA 50613; 319-273-6167

IOWA LIBRARY ASSOCIATION

President: Catherine Rod, Grinnell College, Burling Library, Grinnell, IA 50112; 515-269-3353; Fax: 515-269-4283

Publication: *Catalyst*

KANSAS

KANSAS ASSOCIATION FOR EDUCATIONAL COMMUNICATIONS AND TECHNOLOGY

President: Susanne Bradley, Concordia Jr.-Sr. High School, 436 W. 10th, Concordia, KS 66901; 913-243-2453

KANSAS LIBRARY ASSOCIATION
President: Virginia Prither, Ellinwood School & Community Library, 210 N. Shiller, Ellinwood, KS 67526-1651; 316-564-2606
President-elect: Rowena Olson, McPherson College, Box 1402, McPherson, KS 67460-1402; 316-241-0731 x 1213
Publication: *KLA Newsletter*

KENTUCKY

KENTUCKY ASSOCIATION FOR COMMUNCATIONS AND TECHNOLOGY
President: Fred. C. Kolloff, Eastern Kentucky University, 102 Perkins Bldg., Richmond, KY 40475-3127; 606-622-2474; Fax: 606-622-6276
President-elect: George Pfotenhauer, Eastern Kentucky University, 112 Library, Richmond, KY 40475-3121; 606-622-1070; Fax: 606-622-1174

KENTUCKY LIBRARY ASSOCIATION
President: June Martin, John Grant Crabbe Library, Eastern Kentucky University; Richmond, KY 40475-3121; 606-622-6176; Fax: 606-622-1174
Publication: *Kentucky Libraries*

LOUISIANA

LOUISIANA ASSOCIATION FOR EDUCATIONAL COMMUNICATIONS AND TECHNOLOGY
President: Gail G. Griffin, A.C. Steere Elementary, 4009 Youree Dr., Shreveport, LA 71105; 318-865-5675; Fax: 318-631-5241
President-elect: Dr. Dan Jordan, University of Southwestern Louisiana, Lafayette, IA 70501

LOUISIANA LIBRARY ASSOCIATION
President: Dr. Walter Wicker, 5027 Stow Creek, Ruston, LA 71270; 318-257-2577
President-elect: Marvene Dearman, 1471 Chevelle Dr., Baton Rouge, LA 70806; 504-357-6464
Publication: *LLA Bulletin*

MAINE

MAINE EDUCATIONAL MEDIA ASSOCIATION
President: David W. Anderson, Thomton Academy, 438 Main St., Saco, ME 03909; 207-363-3621
First Vice President: Linda Lord, Mount View High School, RR 2, Box 180, Thomdike, ME 04986; 207-568-3255

MAINE LIBRARY ASSOCIATION
President: Valerie Osborne, Old Town Public Library, 64 Middle St., Old Town, ME 04468; 207-827-3972
Vice-president: Karen Reilly, Libn., Eastern Maine Tech. College, 364 Hogan Rd., Bangor, ME 04401; 207-941-4600 x 4640; Fax 207-941-4641
Publications: *Maine Entry; Maine Memo*

MARYLAND

MARYLAND EDUCATIONAL MEDIA ORGANIZATION
President: Fred Thomas, Cecil Co. Public Schools, 201 Booth St., Elkton, MD 21921; 410-996-5400

MARYLAND LIBRARY ASSOCIATION
President: Joyce Demmitt, Information Services; Howard County Library; 10375 Little Patuxent Pkwy., Columbia, MD 21044; 410-313-7800
President-elect: William G. Wilson, College of Lib. & Inf. Sci., University of Maryland, College Park, MD 20742; 301-405-2067
Publication: *The Crab*

MASSACHUSETTS

MASSACHUSETTS SCHOOL LIBRARY MEDIA ASSOCIATION
President: Rolf Erikson, Minuteman Regional Voc. Tech., 758 Marrett Rd., Lexington, MA 02173; 617-861-6500 Ext. 263; Fax: 617-862-6010
President-elect: Gail Gunn, Algonquin Regional High School, Bartlett Street, Northborough, MA 01532; 508-582-4115; Fax: 508-351-7049

MASSACHUSETTS LIBRARY ASSOCIATION
President: Ellen Rainville, J.V. Fletcher Library; 50 Main St., Westford, MA 01886; 508-692-5555
President-elect: Ellen Rauch, Eastern Mass. Regl. Lib. Sys., c/o Boston Public Library, Copley Square, Boston, MA 02115; 617-536-5400
Publication: *Bay State Librarian*

MICHIGAN

MICHIGAN ASSOCIATION FOR MEDIA IN EDUCATION
President: Victoria DeFields, Bridgman Public Schools, 9964 Gast Rd., Bridgman, MI 49106; 616-466-0229; Fax: 616-460-0229
President-elect: Susan Schwartz, REMC 13, Ingham ISD, 210 State St., Masson , MI 48854; 517-676-1051; Fax: 517-676-9726

MICHIGAN LIBRARY ASSOCIATION
President: Sandra Scherba, Cromaine Library, 3688 N. Hartland Rd., Hartland, MI 48353-0950; 313-632-5200; Fax: 313-632-5279
President-elect: Martha Stilwell, Kellogg Community College, 450 North Ave., Battle Creek, MI 49017-3306; 612-965-4122; Fax: 612-965-4133
Publication: *Michigan Librarian* Newsletter

MINNESOTA

MINNESOTA EDUCATIONAL MEDIA ORGANIZATION
President: Jim Marshall, Minnesota Center for Arts Education, 205 Birnanwood Dr., Bumsville, MN 55337; 612-591-4742; Fax: 612-591-4747
President-elect: Margaret H. Schelbe, College of St. Scholastica, 1200 Kenwood Ave., Duluth, MN 55811; 218-723-6562; Fax: 218-723-6290

MINNESOTA LIBRARY ASSOCIATION
President: Mark Ranum, East Central Regional Library, 244 S. Birch, Cambridge, MN 55008-1521; 612-689-1901; Fax: 612-689-9605
Publication: *MLA Newsletter*

MISSISSIPPI

MISSISSIPPI EDUCATIONAL COMMUNICATIONS AND TECHNOLOGY ROUNDTABLE
President: Becky Dailey, Thomas St. School, 901 S. Thomas, Tupelo, MS 38801; (601) 841-8602; Fax: 601-841-8887
President-elect: Tommy Saunders, Pass Christian Elementary, 703 W. North St., Pass Christian, MS 39571; 601-452-4397

MISSISSIPPI LIBRARY ASSOCIATION
President: Charline Longino, Biloxi Library, Harrison County Library System, 139 Laheuse St., Biloxi, MS 39530; 601-374-0330
Publication: *Mississippi Libraries*

MISSOURI

MISSOURI ASSOCIATION FOR EDUCATIONAL COMMUNICATIONS AND TECHNOLOGY
President: Hal Gardner, Missouri School Service Center, (H) 318 Grover, Warrensburg, MO 64093; 816-543-4261
President-elect: Donald Greer, U.M., St. Louis, 8001 Natural Bridge Rd., Marilac 263, St. Louis, MO 63121; 314-553-6519

MISSOURI LIBRARY ASSOCIATION
President: Beth Eckles, Wolfner
    Library, Missouri State Library, 600
    W. Maine, Jefferson City, MO 65101;
    314-751-8720
Publication: *MO Info*

MONTANA

MONTANA LIBRARY ASSOCIATION
President: Susan Nissen, Montana
    Power Company, Law Library, 40 E.
    Broadway, Butte, MT 59701;
    406-496-5000
President-elect: Mary Bushing, Renne
    Library, Montana State University,
    Bozeman, MT 59717; 406-994-
    4994; Fax: 406-994-4117
Publication: *Library Focus*

NEBRASKA

**NEBRASKA EDUCATIONAL MEDIA
ASSOCIATION**
President: Phyllis Brunken, Education
    Service Unit (ESU) #7, 2657 44th
    Ave., Colombus, NE 68601; 402-
    564-5753; Fax: 402-563-1121
President-elect: Steve Davis, (H) 8
    Seminole Lane, Kearney, NE 68847;
    308-236-5940

NEBRASKA LIBRARY ASSOCIATION
President: Rod Wagner, Nebraska
    Library Commission, 1200 N Street,
    Ste. 120; Lincoln, NE 63508-2006;
    800-307-2665; Fax: 404-471-2083
Publication: *NLAQ*

NEVADA

NEVADA LIBRARY ASSOCIATION
President: Karen Albrethson, Spring
    Creek Elementary School, 7 Spring
    Creek Pkwy, Elko, NV 89801;
    702-753-6881
Publication: *Highroller*

NEW HAMPSHIRE

**NEW HAMPSHIRE EDUCATIONAL
MEDIA ASSOCIATION**
President: Deirdre Angwin, McKelvie
    Middle School, 108 Liberty Hill Rd.,
    Bedford, NH 03110; 603-472-3729
President-elect: Kim Carter, Souhegan
    High School, 412 Boston Post Rd.,
    Amherst, NH 03031; 603-673-9940
    Ext. 249; Fax: 603-673-0318

**NEW HAMPSHIRE LIBRARY
ASSOCIATION**
President: Randy Brough, Franklin Pub-
    lic Library, 310 Central St., Franklin,
    NH 03235; 603-934-2911
President-elect: Nancy Urtz, St. Anselm
    College, Geisel Library, 100 St. An-
    selm Dr., Manchester, NH
    03102-1310; 603-641-7300
Publication: *NHLA Newsletter*

NEW JERSEY

**EDUCATIONAL MEDIA ASSOCIATION
OF NEW JERSEY**
President: Pam Chesky, Woodbridge
    Township School, (H) 135 Midwood
    Way, Colonia, NJ 07067
President-elect: Dagmar Finkle, (H) 81
    Lisa Dr., Chatham, NJ 07928-1010

NEW JERSEY LIBRARY ASSOCIATION
President: Mary Lou Abrams, Paramus
    Public Library, E 116 Century Rd.,
    Paramus, NJ 07652; 201-599-1302
President-elect: Tim Murphy, Maurice
    M. Pine Free Public Library, 10-01
    Fair Lawn Ave., Fair Lawn, NH
    07410; 201-796-3400; Fax: 201-
    794-6344
Publications: *New Jersey Libraries*;
    NJLA Newsletter

NEW MEXICO

**EDUCATIONAL TECHNOLOGY/NEW
MEXICO AECT, a Roundtable of New
Mexico Library Association**
President: Kathy Flanary, New Mexico
    Military Institute, 101 W. College
    Blvd., Roswell, NM 88201-5173;
    505-624-8384; Fax: 505-624-8390
President-elect: Richard Bell, Raton
    Middle School, 500 S. 3rd St.,
    Raton, NM 87740; 505-445-8032;
    Fax: 505-445-5641

NEW MEXICO LIBRARY ASSOCIATION
President: Barbara Billey, San Juan
    College Library, 4601 College Ave.,
    Farmington, NM 87401; 505-599-
    0256; Fax: 505-599-0385
President-elect: Kathy Flannery, New
    Mexico School for the Visually Han-
    dicapped, 1900 White Sands Blvd.,
    Alamogordo, NM 88310; 505-437-
    3505 Ext. 129
Publication: *NMLA Newsletter*

NEW YORK

NEW YORK LIBRARY ASSOCIATION
President: Rhonna Goodman, New York
    Academy of Medicine, 2 E. 103rd
    St., New York, NY 10029;
    212-876-8200 Ext. 312

NORTH CAROLINA

**NORTH CAROLINA ASSOCIATION FOR
EDUCATIONAL COMMUNICATIONS
AND TECHNOLOGY**
President: Libby Gray, McClintock
    Junior High School, (H) 6900 Ronda
    Ave., Charlotte, NC 28211; 704-
    343-6425; Fax: 704-343-6509
President-elect: Mary-Jane Crum,
    Eastern Guilford High School, 415
    Peeden St, Gibsonville, NC 27249;
    910-271-3290; Fax: 910-449-
    7392

**NORTH CAROLINA LIBRARY
ASSOCIATION**
President: Gwendolyn Jackson,
    Southeast Tech Assistance Center,
    2013 Lejeune Blvd., Jacksonville, NC
    28546-7027; 919-577-8920; Fax:
    919-577-1427
President-elect: David Ferguson, For-
    syth County Public Library; 660 W.
    Fifth St., Winston-Salem, NC
    27101-2705; 919-727-2556; Fax:
    919-727-2549
Publication: *North Carolina Libraries*

NORTH DAKOTA

**NORTH DAKOTA LIBRARY
ASSOCIATION**
President: Kathy Walders, Bismarck
    Public Library, 515 N. 5th St., Bis-
    marck, ND 58501; 701-222-6410

OHIO

**OHIO EDUCATIONAL LIBRARY MEDIA
ASSOCIATION**
President: Lynda Sadowski, Mentor
    High School, 6477 Center St., Men-
    tor, OH 44060; 216-974-5348
President-elect: Kimberley Miller-Smith,
    12904 Coventry Ave., Pickerington,
    OH 43147; 614-861-6873

OHIO LIBRARY COUNCIL
President: Alan Hall, Public Library of
    Steubenville, Jefferson County, 407
    S. 4th St., Steubenville, OH 43952;
    614-282-9782; Fax: 614-282-2919
Publication: *Ohio Libraries*

OKLAHOMA

OKLAHOMA LIBRARY ASSOCIATION
President: Robert Swisher, University
    of Oklahoma, School of Lib & Info
    Studies, 401 W. Brooks, Norman, OK
    73019; 405-325-3921
President-elect: Jane Sanders, Bartles-
    ville Public Library, 600 S. John-
    stone, Bartlesville, OK 74003;
    918-337-5353
Publication: *Oklahoma Librarian*

OREGON

**OREGON EDUCATIONAL MEDIA
ASSOCIAITON**
President: Dr. Richard Forcier, Western
    Oregon State College, (H) 25335 SW
    Neill Rd., Sherwood, OR 97140,
    503-838-8441, 503-838-8474
President-elect: Diane Claus-Smith,
    North Salem H.S., (H) 750 Stewart
    NE, Salem, OR 97301;
    503-399-3241

OREGON LIBRARY ASSOCIATION
President: Ann Billeter, Jackson County
    Library System, 413 W. Main, Med-
    ford, OR 97501-2730; 503-776-

7285; Fax: 503-776-7290
PublicationN: *Oregon Library News*

PACIFIC NORTH WEST LIBRARY ASSOCIATION

President: Audrey Kolb, 2471 NW Williams Loop, Redmond, OR 97756

President-elect: Anne Haley, Walls Walls Public Library; 238 E. Aller Street, Walls Walls, WA 99362-1967; 509-545-6549; Fax: 509-527-3748

PENNSYLVANIA

PENNSYLVANIA ASSOCIATION FOR EDUCATIONAL COMMUNICATIONS & TECHNOLOGY

President: Kyle Peck, Penn State University, 270 Chambers Bldg., University Park, PA 16802; 814-863-4316; Fax: 814-863-7602

President-elect: Kathleen Smith, Clarion University, 123 Stevens Hall, Clarion, PA 16214; 814-226-2404; Fax: 814-226-2039

PENNSYLVANIA LIBRARY ASSOCIATION

President: Kathy Kennedy, Monroeville Public Library; 2615 Mosside Blvd., Monroeville, PA 15146; 412-372-0500

Publication: *PLA Bulletin*

PUERTO RICO

ASSOCIATION FOR EDUCATIONAL COMMUNCIATIONS AND TECHNOLOGY OF PUERTO RICO

President: Roberto Velez-Santiago, Bayamon Central University, Box 1725, Bayamon, P.R. 00960-1725; 809-786-3030 Ext. 216; Fax: 809-269-5480

President-elect: Maria de Lourdes Lopez-Maldonado, Instituo de Educacion Universal, Box 3818, San Jose Station, Hato Rey, P.R. 00930; 809-767-2000 Ext. 57; Fax: 809-250-1921

RHODE ISLAND

RHODE ISLAND EDUCATIONAL MEDIA ASSOCIATION

President: Susan Bryan, Warwick Veterans High School, 2401 West Shore Rd., Warwick, RI 02886; 401-737-3300 Ext. 5329

President-elect: Paul E. Venancio, Middletown School Department, Aquidneck Ave., Middletown, RI 02842; 401-846-6395; Fax: 401-849-7170

RHODE ISLAND LIBRARY ASSOCIATION

President: James Giles, Cranston Public Library, 140 Sockanossett Cross

Rd., Cranston, RI 02920; 401-943-9080; Fax: 401-943-5079
Publication: *RILA Bulletin*

SOUTH CAROLINA

ASSOCIATION FOR EDUCATIONAL COMMUNICATIONS AND TECHNOLOGY OF SOUTH CAROLINA

President: Tami Clyburn, Lugoff-Elgin Middle School, Box 68, Lugoff, SC 29078; 803-438-3591; Fax: 803-438-8027

President-elect: A. Jeanie McNamara, USC, Davis College, Columbia, SC 29208; 803-777-3164; Fax: 803-777-7938

SOUTH CAROLINA LIBRARY ASSOCIATION

President: Mary L. Smalls; 7313 State Unversity, Orangeburg, SC 29117; 803-536-8825; Fax: 803-536-8902
Publication: *News & Views of the SCLA*

SOUTH DAKOTA

SOUTH DAKOTA ASSOCIATION FOR COMMUNCIATIONS AND TECHNOLOGY

President: Mary Schwartz, Redfield School District, Box 560, Redfield, SD 57469-0560, 605-472-0560; Fax: 605-472-2316

President-elect: Jean Dietrich, Custer High School, 527 Montgomery St., Custer, SD 57730-1199; 605-673-4473; Fax: 605-673-5607

SOUTH DAKOTA LIBRARY ASSOCIATION

President: Elvita Landau, Brookings Public Library; 515 3rd St., Brookings, SD 57006
Publication: *Book Marks*

TENNESSEE

TENNESSEE LIBRARY ASSOCIATION

President: John B. Evans, Head Circulation, Memphis State University, Library, Memphis, TN 30152; 901-678-4485

President-elect: Lynnette Sloan, Blue Grass Public Library, 104 E. 6th St., Columbia, TN 38401; 615-388-9282
Publications: *Tennessee Librarian; TLA Newsletter*

TEXAS

TEXAS ASSOCIATION FOR EDUCATIONAL TECHNOLOGY

President: Doug Rogers, Center for Educational Technology, Baylor University College of Education, Box 97314, Waco, TX 76798-7314; 817-755-3111; Fax: 817-755-3265

Presidenr-elect: Sandy Sharps, Plano

ISD, 1706 Canadian Trail, Plano, TX 75023; 214-519-8212; Fax: 214-519-8215

TEXAS LIBRARY ASSOCIATION

President: Ruth Dahlstrom, Goliad Independent School Dist., Box 830, Goliad, TX 77963; 512-645-3257

President-elect: Barbara Gubbin, Houston Public Library, 500 McKinney, Houston, TX 77002-2534; 713-247-1651; Fax: 713-247-3531
Publications: *Texas Library Journal;* TLA/CAST

UTAH

UTAH EDUCATIONAL LIBRARY MEDIA ASSOCIATION

President: David Walton, Instructional Technology, Alpine School District, 50 North Center, American Fork, UT 84003; 801-756-8400; Fax: 801-756-8404

President-elect: Margaret Blackham, Library Media, Rock Canyon Elementary School, 2405 N. 650 East, Provo, UT 84604; 801-245-4935

UTAH LIBRARY ASSOCIATION

President: Pete J. Giacoma, 365 Emery, Salt Lake City, UT 84104; 801-451-2322

President-elect: Julie Farnsworth, 8577 S. Autumn Gold Circle, W. Jordan, UT 84088; 801-943-4636
Publication: *Utah Libraries/News*

VERMONT

VERMONT EDUCATIONAL MEDIA ASSOCIATION

President: Karen Hennig, Craftsbury Academy, R.R. 1, Box 94, Craftsbury Common, VT 05827; 802-586-7706

President-elect: Mary Prior, Bamet School, Bamet, VT 05821; 802-663-4498

VERMONT LIBRARY ASSOCIATION

President: Nancy Wilson, Lawrence Public Library; 40 North St., Briston, VT 05443; 802-453-2366

President-elect: Albert Joy, University of Vermont, Bailey Howe Library, Burlington, VT 05405-0036; 802-656-2020; Fax: 802-656-4038
Publication: *VLA News*

VIRGINIA

VIRGINIA EDUCATIONAL MEDIA ASSOCIATION

President: Vickie Pearce, Norfolk Public Schools, (H) 1077 Lord Dunmore Dr., Virginia Beach, VA 23464; 804-441-1916; 804-441-2430

President-elect: Verley Sue Dodson, Hurley High School, Box 156, Hurley, VA 24620; 703-566-8334; Fax: 703-566-7738

VIRGINIA LIBRARY ASSOCIATION
President: Linda Farynk, Ratford University, McConnell Library, Ratford, VA 24142; 703-831-5471; Fax: 703-831-6104
Publications: *VLA Newsletter; Virginia Librarian*

WASHINGTON

WASHINGTON LIBRARY MEDIA ASSOCIATION
President: Susan Baker, Bremerton School District, (H) 304 White Pine Dr., Bremerton, WA 98310; 206-478-0753 Ext. 3232; Fax: 206-478-5061
President-elect: Elden (Denny) Bond, Olympic ESD 114, 105 National Ave., N., Bremerton, WA 98312; 206-479-2752; Fax: 206-576-6399

WASHINGTON LIBRARY ASSOCIATION
President: Sharon Hammer, Fort Vancouver Regional Library, 1007 E. Mill Plain Blvd., Vancouver, WA 98603-3504; 206-695-1561; Fax: 206-693-2681
Publications: *ALKI: The Washington Library Association Journal; The Link*

WEST VIRGINIA

WEST VIRGINIA EDUCATIONAL MEDIA ASSOCIATION
President: Lynne Curran, Doddridge County Middle School, (H) 408 1/2 Pennsylvania Ave., Nutter Fort, WV 26301; 304-873-2390; Fax: 304-873-2541
President-elect: Janet Underwood, Salem T., (H) Rt. 2, Box 79, Bristol, WV 26332; 304-782-5232

WEST VIRGINIA LIBRARY ASSOCIATION
President: Dr. Charles Julian, National Tech Transfer Center, Div. of Education & Training, Wheeling Jesuit College, 1108 W. Washington Ave., Wheeling, WV 26003; 304-243-2595
Publication: *West Virginia Libraries*

WISCONSIN

WISCONSIN EDUCATIONAL MEDIA ASSOCIATION
President: Terri Iverson, CESA#3, 1835 Ridgeview Acres, Platteville, WI 53818; 608-822-3276; Fax: 608-263-2046

WISCONSIN LIBRARY ASSOCIATION
President: Venora McKinney; Milwaukee Public Library; 814 W. Wisconsin Ave., Milwaukee, WI 53233-2385; 414-286-3025; Fax: 414-286-2794
Publication: *WLA Newsletter*

WYOMING

WYOMING EDUCATIONAL MEDIA ASSOCIATION
President: Douglas Hinkle, Wheatland High School, 13th & Oak Sts., Wheatland, WY 82201; 307-322-2075; Fax: 307-322-2084
President-elect: Rodney Knudson, Huleu School, Box 127, 401 Sagar St., Hulen, WY 82720; 307-467-5947; Fax: 307-467-5280

WYOMING LIBRARY ASSOCIATION
President: Kathy Carlson, Wyoming State Law Library, Supreme Court Bldg., Cheyenne, WY 82002; 307-777-7509
Publication: *WLA Newsletter*

The school media office for each state is listed alphabetically. Where an appropriate director's name is available it is listed first.

ALABAMA

JANE BANDY SMITH
Coordinator Instruction Assistance
  Section
Alabama Department of Education
Student Instructional Services Division
Gordon Persons Bldg., Rm 3340
50 North St.
Montgomery AL 36130

Serves 1,247 schools with student
  population approx. 774,000
Selection: Print, non-print & computer
  software suggested at state level.
  Encourage faculty on a school by
  school basis to help w/selection.
Services: Consultants, publish guidelines on collection suggestions,
  media schedules & facilities

ALASKA

School Library/Media coordinator
State of Alaska Department of Education, Div. of State Libraries
344 W. 3rd Ave., Ste. 125, Anchorage,
  AK 99501
907-269-6568

ARIZONA

C. DIANE BISHOP
State Superintendent of Public School
Educational Information Center
Arizona Department of Education
1535 West Jefferson
Phoenix, AZ 85007
602-542-5416
Fax: 602-542-5283

Approx. 1,080 schools. Approx. student pop. 732, 306
Selection: Print & nonprint at district
  level
Services: In-service training at district
  level

ARKANSAS

SUE McKENZIE
Arkansas Department of Education

405-B State Education Bldg.
Little Rock, AR 72201-1071
501-682-4593

Serves 312 schools (Elem/Secondary)
Selection: Print (State level)

CALIFORNIA

GLEN THOMAS
Director
Curriculum Frameworks & Instructional
  Resources Office
560 J St., Ste. 290, Sacramento, CA
  95814
916-445-2731

Oversees the review of instructional
  resources for state adoption, and social content (legal compliance
  reviews) for 58 counties; 1006 districts
Evaluation: Print & nonprint materials
Selection: Print & nonprint selected at
  local level
Services: In-service training, liaison
  with community agencies

COLORADO

LYNDA WELBORN
Sr. Consultant, School Library Media
Colorado Department of Education
201 E. Colfax, Rm 309, Denver, CO
  80203
303-866-6730

CONNECTICUT

LINDA NAIMI
Consultant Computer Technology
Connecticut Department of
  Education
Box 2219, Hartford, CT 06145
203-566-5658

BETTY V. GOYETTE
Consultant, Instructional Media
Connecticut Department of
  Education
Box 2219, Hartford, CT 06145
203-566-6660

Serve approx 1,000 schools with total
  population of 500,000
Selection: Print, nonprint & computer
  software at local level; textbooks at
  local level
Services: In-service training, liaison
  with community agencies, publication of newsletter & bibliographies,
  instructional television

CHARLES R. WHITE
Consultant, Educational media for
  Vocational & Technical Education
25 Industrial Park Rd., Middletown, CT
  06457
203-638-4110

DELAWARE

THOMAS F. BRENNAN
Supervisor
State Department of Public Instruction
Standards & Curriculum Branch
John G. Townsend Bldg., Box 1402,
  Dover, DE 19903
303-739-3902

Pop 27,630
Selection: Print, nonprint & software
Services: State level

DISTRICT OF COLUMBIA

Dr. BESTER BONNER
District of Columbia Public Schools
1709 3rd St. NE, 4th Fl.
Washington DC 20002
202-576-8654

FLORIDA

REBECCA AUGUSTYNIAK
Coordinator
Educational Services Program
  (Formerly Florida Educational
  Information Service)
251 Sliger Bldg., 2035 E. Dirac,
  Tallahassee, FL 32310

Pop 124,773
Selection: Print, nonprint & software
Services: State level

GEORGIA

NANCY V. PAYSINGER
Director, Media Services Unit
Georgia Department of Education
Atlanta, GA 30334-5040
404-656-2418
Coordinates 1800 schools with a total
 population of 1 million
Evaluation: Print, nonprint & computer
 software
Selection: Nonprint & computer software at state, district & local level;
 textbooks at state, district & local
 level
Services: In-service training, liaison
 with community agencies, publication of newsletters & bibliographies,
 statewide distribution of video titles,
 consultation on media, program &
 facility design

HAWAII

PATSY M. IZUMO
Director
Special Instructional Programs & Ser-
 vices Branch
808-733-9143
FRANCINE M. GRUDZIAS
ShS Specialist III
School Library Services
808-733-9134
State of Hawaii
Department of Education
Special Instructional Programs & Serv-
 ices Branch
2530 10th Ave., Rm A-20
Honolulu, HI 96816

Pop Served: 1,257, 600 (state)
Selection: Print/nonprint
Publications: *Honolulu Star Bulletin*
 (index)

IDAHO

State Department of Education
Les B. Jordan Office Bldg.,
650 W. State St., Boise, ID 83720
208-334-3300

Pop Served: 1, 006, 749 (state level)
Selection: Print/nonprint
Publications: *Idaho Library Directory*,
 newsletter (monthly), Public Library
 Statistics

ILLINOIS

DR. LAWRENCE K. WERNER
Principal Consultant
School Improvement Planning & As-
 sistance
Illinois State Board of Education
Dept. of School Improvement &
 Services
100 N. First St., Springfield, IL
 62777-001
217-782-2826

State Pub Sch K-12: 1,893,077
Pop (Non-Pub) 217,102
PS district #923
Decisions made at local level

INDIANA

PHYLLIS LAND USHER
Senior Officer
JACQUELINE G. MORRIS
Manager, Learning Resources
Center for School Improvement,
 Indiana Department of Education Rm
 229, State House, Indianapolis, IN
 46204
317-232-9127

IOWA

BETTY JO BUCKINGHAM
Consultant, Educational Media
Iowa Department of Education
Grimes State Office Bldg., Des Moines,
 IA 50319-0146
515-281-3707; Fax: 515-242-
 6025

Supervises 397 districts (1555
 schools) with total population
 492,520; 205 approved nonpublic
 schools with population of 45,341;
 and 15 Area Education Media
 Centers (AEAMCs) which serve the
 public & approved nonpublic schools
 in their area
Evaluation: Print. AEAMC may provide
 evaluation service for either print or
 nonprint
Selection: Print, nonprint & computer
 software, and textbooks are selected
 at district or local school level.
 AEAMCs also select for their own
 collections & may provide for
 previews, joint purchase, or licensed
 duplication
Services: In-service training (generally
 in conjunction with AEAMCs), publication of newsletters, manuals,
 guides & bibliographies
Examination Center: Some AEAMCs
 provide this service as part of their
 mandated curriculum labs

KANSAS

JACQUELINE LAKIN
Information Management Education
 Program Specialist
Kansas State Board of Education
120 Southeast 10th Ave., Topeka, KS
 66612-1182
913-296-2144

Pop Served 2,461,000 (State)
Selection: Print/nonprint/software
Publications: *Kansas Libraries*
 (newsletter), *Kansas State Pub.
 Lib. Statistics* (manual)

KENTUCKY

JACKIE WHITE
Information Resources Consultant
KY Department of Education
500 Mero St., Frankfort, KY 40601
502-564-7168; Fax: 502-564-6470

Supervises 1,363 schools with total
 population of 644,421
Selection: Print, nonprint & computer
 software at local level; textbooks at
 district level. Textbooks selected un-
 der direction of Div of Textbook
 Services, same address
Examination center: Anne McConnell,
 Univ of Kentucky, Patterson Office
 Tower, 4th flr, Lexington, KY

LOUISIANA

Louisiana Department of Education
Box 94064
Baton Rouge, LA 70804-9064
504-342-3464

Pop. Served 4,192,781
Selection: Print/nonprint
Pub: *Book Beat: A Young Adult Serices
 Manual for LA Pub. Lib.*; directories,
 newsletter

MAINE

WALTER J. TARANKO
Media Coordinator
Maine State Library
State House Station #64, Maine State
 Library, Augusta, ME 04333
207-287-5620

Serve 800 schools with total population of 220,000
Evaluation: Print, nonprint & computer
 software
Selection: Print, nonprint & computer
 software at state, district & local
 level
Services: In-service training, special
 reading programs, liaison with community agencies, publication of
 newsletters, approved lists of materials & bibliographies

MARYLAND

GAIL C. BAILEY
Chief, School Library Media Services
 and State Media Services
Branch
Maryland Department of
 Education
200 W. Baltimore St., Baltimore, MD
 21201-2595
410-333-2125

Selection: Print, nonprint & computer software at district & local
 level; textbooks at district & local
 level

MASSACHUSETTS

CANDACE BOYDEN
Director
Education Technology Bureau
Massachusetts Department of Education
1385 Hancock St., Quincy, MA 02169

MICHIGAN

ROSEMARY CARY
Coordinator
Michigan Department of Education
Library Media & Telecommunciations
Box 30008, Lansing, MI 48909
517-373-1806

MINNESOTA

JOAN WALLIN
Supervisor, Media & Techonology
MARY S. DALBOTTEN
School Library Specialist
Minnesota Department of Education
550 Cedar St., St Paul, MN 55101
612-296-1570

Serve 1,501 schools with total population of 786,413
Selection: Print, nonprint & computer software at local level; textbooks at local level
Examination center: Doris Pagel, Director, Center for Children's & Young Adult Books, Mankato, MN 56002

MISSISSIPPI

Mississippi Department of Education
Educational Media Service
Box 771, Ste. 604
Jackson. MS 39205
601-359-3778

Pop Served 2,618,700
Selection: Print/nonprint
Pub: MS State Govt. Publication (index), Reading Light, The Packet

MISSOURI

JOHN MILLER
Direter, Teacher Certification
CARL F. SITZE
Learning Resources Supervisor
EPRA FINLEY
Supv. Instructional Improvement Resources
STEVEN BARR
Asst. Director, Learning Resources
Missouri Department of Elementary & Secondary Education
Box 480, Jefferson City, MO 65101
314-751-4445
Supervises 545 schools with total population of 795,107
Selection: Print, nonprint & computer software at local level; textbooks at local level
Services: In-service training
Examination center: Missouri State Library, Truman State Office Bldg., Jefferson City, MO 65101

MONTANA

DIANA LOBLE
Library Media Specialist
Office of Public Instruction
Rm. 106, State Capitol, Helena, MT 59620
406-444-2979

Supervises state schools with total population of 157,000
Evaluation: Print, nonprint & computer software
Selection: Print, nonprint & computer software at state level
Services: In-service training, publication of newsletters

NEBRASKA

WAYNE FISHER
Consultant Instructional Technology
Nebraska Department of Education
301 Centennial Mall S., Lincoln, NE 68509-4987
402-471-2295

Pop served 1,584,617
Selection: Print/nonprint/software
Pub: Film/AV catalog, Interchange, NEBASE News, Cassette Books, NE Lib directory

NEVADA

Nevada Department of Education
Education Branch
400 W. King, Capital Complex, Carson City, NV 89710
702-687-5160

Pop Served: 1,342, 090
Selection: Print/nonprint
Pub: Info Connection, NV Lib. Dir & Statistics, Silver Lining (Talking Books)

NEW HAMPSHIRE

SUSAN SNIDER
Curriculum Supervisor for Library Media Services
New Hampshire Department of Education
101 Pleasant St., Concord, NH 03301
603-271-2632
Pop Served: 1,109,252
Selection: Print/nonprint
Pub: Granite Bits (Irregular), Granite State Libraries (bi-monthly newsletter)

NEW JERSEY

NOVIS SAUNDERS
Department of Education
Center for Occupation Education
Experimentation and Demonstration Library
223 Broadway, Newark, NJ 07104
201-648-2121; Fax: 201-648-3144

NEW MEXICO

MARY JANE VINELLA
Director, Instruction Materials
New Mexico Department of Education
Education Bldg., Santa Fe, NM 87501-2786
505-827-6504

Pop Served: 1,515,069
Selection: Print/nonprint/software
Pub: Annual Statistical Report, Hitchhiker, Kaleidescope, Lib Directory

NEW YORK

ROBERT E. BARRON
Bureau Chief
NYS Education Department
Bureau of School Library Media Programs, Rm 676 EBA, Albany, NY 12234
518-474-2468

Selection:Print/nonprint for state
Pub: Checklist of Official Publications of the State of New York, The Bookmark

NORTH CAROLINA

ELSIE L. BRUMBACK
Director, Media & Techonology Support Team
CECILIA SNEED
Chief Consultant for Media Evaluation Services
North Carolina Department of Public Instruction
301 N. Wilmington St., Education Bldg., Raleigh, NC 27201-2825
919-715-1530

Supervises approximately 2,000 schools with total population of 1,387,763
Evaluation: Print & nonprint & computer software
Selection: Print & nonprint & computer software at local level; textbooks at state level with local system making final selection
Services: In-service training, publication of newsletters, approved lists of materials & bibliographies, hands-on examination of software
Examination center: Media Evaluation Ctr, same address

NORTH DAKOTA

DR. WAYNE G. SANSTEAD
Superintendent, Department of Public
  Instruction
PATRICIA HERBAL
Director Elementary Education
ND Department of Public Instruction
600 E. Boulevard Ave., Bismarck, ND
  58505-0440
701-224-2295, Fax: 701-224-4770

Works with 473 elementary schools
Selection: Print, nonprint & computer
  software at local level; textbooks at
  local level
Services: Liaison with community
  agencies; in-service training

OHIO

THERESA M. FREDERICKA
Coordinator, Library/Media Services
Lakewood City Schools
1470 Warren, Lakewood, OH 44107
CARL C. CARTER
Library Media Consultant
Ohio Dept. of Education
65 S. Front St., Rm 611, Columbus,
  OH 43266-0308
614-466-9272

Consultant for 615 school districts;
  coordinator of statewide library automation project, INFOHIO
Services: Provides information related
  to library/media programs & automation

OKLAHOMA

JEANIE JOHNSON
Director, Library Media/ITV
JOANNE HOPE
Coordinator, Library Media/ITV
PAULA WALKER
Coordinator, Library Media/ITV
2500 N. Lincoln Blvd., Rm 215, Okla-
  homa City, OK 73105-4599
405-521-2956

Supervises 554 branches with total
  population of 604,188
Evaluation: Print, nonprint & computer
  software
Selection: Print, nonprint & computer
  software at district & local level
Examination center: Oklahoma Dept. of
  Libraries, 200 NE 18th, Oklahoma
  City, OK 73105

OREGON

JAMES W. SANNER
Coordinator, Instructional Technology
Oregon Department of Education
Instructional Technology Unit
700 Pringle Pkwy., SE, Salem, OR
  97310-0290
503-378-4974

Pop 107,786
Selection: Print & nonprint at local
  level

PENNSYLVANIA

JOHN L. EMERICK
Director, School Library Media Services
Pennsylvania Department of Education
333 Market St, Box 911, Harrisburg,
  PA 17126-0333
717-787-6704

Supervises 501 schools with total
  population of 2,500,000
Selection: Print, nonprint & computer
  software at local level; textbooks at
  local level
Services: In-service training, liaison
  with community agencies, computer
  networking, retrospective conversion, grant writing
Examination center: Eastern Area
  Branch, Frankford & Castor Aves,
  Philadelphia, PA 19124; Western
  Area Branch, 2 Allegheny Ctr, Ste
  1300, Pittsburgh, PA 15212; Northeastern Area Branch, 368 Tioga
  Ave., Kingston, PA 18704

RHODE ISLAND

RICHARD LATHAM
Coordinator, Grant Programs
State Department of Education
22 Hays St., Providence, RI 02908
401-277-2617

SOUTH CAROLINA

LINDA C. BARTONE
Education Associate: Library Media
South Carolina State Department of
  Education
801 Rutledge Bldg., 1429 Senate St.,
  Columbia, SC 29201

Provides support, services & advocacy
  for school library media programs in
  1,109 schools serving 633,418
  students
Evaluation: Library media center books
  & audiovisual software
Selection: Library media center
  resources at local level, instruction
  materials - state, district, & local level under the direction of Joey Hill,
  Office of Instructional Techonology
  Development, 1108 Rutledge Bldg.,
  1429 Senate St., Columbia, SC
  29201
Services: Provides leadership, direct
  services, assessment & coordination
  statewide for public school library
  media programs & serves as a liaison to other offices within the agency as well as to other agencies &
  organizations

SOUTH DAKOTA

DONNA GILLILAND
School Library/Media Coordinator
South Dakota State Library
800 Governors Dr., Pierre, SD
  57501-2294
605-773-3131; Fax: 605-773-4950

Supervises over 400 libraries in approximately 840 schools. There are
  226.4 FTE library media specialists
  in the 1993-94 school year. Total
  state enrollment: 148,804 students
Evaluation: Occasional evaluation of
  print, nonprint, & computer software
Selection: All selection of print, nonprint, & computer software takes
  place at district & local level. Textbooks also at local level
Services: In-service training, liaison
  with professional & community organizations, publish newsletters, bibliographies, guidelines, curriculum
  guides, compile statistics, evaluate
  libraries upon request, review district
  library development plans for accreditation office
Examination centers: TIE Office, 1925
  Plaza Blvd., Rapid City, SD
  57707-9357 (Dir: Jim Parry - computer software)

TENNESEE

PHYSSIS E. PARDUE
TEN Administrative Coordinator
Office of Education Technology
Tennessee Dept. of Education
7th Fl. Gateway Plaza, 710 James
  Robertson Pkwy., Nashville, TN
  37243-0381
615-532-1242, 800-538-1497; Fax:
  615-741-6236

Supervises 1,800 schools with total
  population of 900,000
Evaluation: Print
Selection: Print at district & local level;
  textbooks at local level from state
  approved list
Services: In-service training, publication of newsletters

TEXAS

TEXAS EDUCATION AGENCY
1701 N. Congress, Austin, TX
  78701—1494
512-463-9734

Supervises 1047 districts, 6,184 campuses with a population of approximately 3,535,000
Selection: Print & nonprint at state,
  district & local level; textbooks at
  state level

Services: In-service training, liaison with community agencies

UTAH

BONNIE MORGAN
Director
Utah State Office of Education, Curriculum Division
250 E. 500 South St., Salt Lake City, UT 84111
801-538-7774

Supervises 738 schools
Evaluation: Print, nonprint, textbooks
Selection: Print & nonprint at district & local level; textbooks at state & district level
Services: In-service training, publication of newsletter & approved lists of materials

VERMONT

LEDA SCHUBERT
School Media Coordinator
Vermont Department of Education
120 State St., Montpelier, VT 05620
802-828-3111

Supervises 400 schools with total population of 100,000
Evaluation: Print & nonprint
Selection: Print & nonprint at local level; textbooks at local level
Services: In-service training, special reading programs, liaison with community agencies, publication of newsletter & bibliographies, techical assistance, school improvement

VIRGINIA

GLORIA K. BARBER
Associate Specialist, Library Media

Virginia Department of Education
Box 2120, Richmond, VA 23216-2120
804-225-2539; Fax: 804-736-1703

Supervises: 133 school divisions (1800 schools); consultant services; technical assistance
Evaluation: Computer software under leadership of JoyceFaye White, Associate Specialist Instructional Technology (804-225-2598); Computer hardware, Richard Schley (804-371-6882); Distance Education, William C. Rodgers (804-225-2833)
Services: In-service training, liaison with state and community agencies, teleconferences, workshops, newsletters, projects

WASHINGTON

DEBORAH L. KOSS-WARNER
Supervisor, Learning Resources
Office of State Superintendent of Public Instruction
Old Capital Bldg., Olympia, WA 98504
206-753-6723

Serves staff, schools & limited service to other agencies
Publ: SPI Publication

WEST VIRGINIA

BRENDA L. WILLIAMS
Assistant Director
Office of Technology & Information Systems
WV Department of Education
Bldg. 6, Rm 346, 1900 Kanawha Blvd. East, Charleston, WV 25305-0330
304-558-7880; Fax: 304-558-2584

Supervises 970 schools with total population of 310,000
Evaluation: Print, nonprint & computer software
Selection: Print, nonprint, & computer software at district & local level

WISCONSIN

RICHARD J. SORENSON
School Library Media Consultant
Wisconsin Department of Public Instruction
125 S. Webster St., Box 7841, Madison, WI 53707
608-266-1924

Pop 191,262
Selection: Print & nonprint & software at state and local level

WYOMING

JACK PRINCE
Applied Techonology Consultant
Wyoming Department of Education
Hathaway Bldg., Cheyenne, WY 82002
307-777-5883

Supervises 250 schools with total population of 95,000
Selection: Print, nonprint & computer software at district & local level; textbooks at local level. State Dept. computer software/hardware selected under direction of Steve King, Technology Coord, Wyoming Dept. of Educ, Hathaway Bldg., Cheyenne, WY 82002
Services: In-service training & technical assistance

FEDERAL GRANTS FOR CHILDREN'S PROGRAMS

18

This chapter lists federal funding sources for children's programs and services. Entries are arranged numerically according to program numbers, which follow the program title and correspond to OMB catalog numbers. For further information, consult the *Catalog of Federal Domestic Assistance* and *The Federal Register,* citing the OMB number.

SCHOOL BREAKFAST PROGRAM - 10.553

OBJECTIVES: To assist States in providing a nutritious nonprofit breakfast service for school students, through cash grants and food donations.

TYPES OF ASSISTANCE: Formula Grants. FY 94 est $980,352,000.

ELIGIBILITY REQUIREMENTS: State and U.S. Territory agencies; public and nonprofit private schools of high school grade and under; public and nonprofit private residential child care institutions, except Job Corps Centers; residential summer camps that participate in the Summer Food Service Program for Children; and private foster homes. Schools desiring to participate must agree to operate a nonprofit breakfast program that is available to all children regardless of race, sex, color, national origin, age, or handicap.

INFORMATION CONTACTS: For regional or local office contact: Director, Child Nutrition Division, Food and Nutrition Service, Department of Agriculture, Alexandria, VA 22302. Telephone: (703) 305-2590. (Use same 7-digit number for FTS.) Contact: Stanley C. Garnett, Director.

NATIONAL SCHOOL LUNCH PROGRAM - 10.555

OBJECTIVES: To assist States, through cash grants and food donations, in making the school lunch program available to school students and to encourage the domestic consumption of nutritious agricultural commodities.

TYPES OF ASSISTANCE: Formula Grants. FY 94 est $4,328,214,000.

ELIGIBILITY REQUIREMENTS: State and U.S. Territory agencies, public and nonprofit private schools of high school grade and under; public and nonprofit private residential child care institutions, except Job Corps Centers, residential summer camps that participate in the Summer Food Service Program for children and private foster homes. Schools and residential child care institutions desiring to participate must agree to operate a nonprofit food service that is available to all children regardless of race, sex, color, national origin, age, or handicap.

INFORMATION CONTACTS: For regional or local office contact: Director, Child Nutrition Division, Food and Nutrition Service, Department of Agriculture, Alexandria, VA 22302. Telephone: (703) 305-2590 (Same for FTS). Contact: Stanley C. Garnett, Director.

SPECIAL MILK PROGRAM FOR CHILDREN - 10.556

OBJECTIVES: To provide subsidies to schools and institutions to encourage the consumption of fluid milk by children.

TYPES OF ASSISTANCE: Formula Grants. FY 94 est $20,531,000.

ELIGIBILITY REQUIREMENTS: Any State or U.S. Territory (except territories subject to the requirements of the Compact of Free Association) agency, public and nonprofit private school or child care institution of high school grade or under, except Job Corps Centers, may participate in the Special Milk Program upon request if it does not participate in a meal service program authorized under the National School Lunch Act or the Child Nutrition Act of 1966. This generally includes nonprofit nursery schools, child-care centers, settlement houses and summer camps. Nonprofit schools with split session kindergarten and pre-kindergarten programs can receive subsidies for milk served to students in the split session kindergartens and pre-kindergartens who do not have access to the meal service program operating in the school. All schools and child care institutions which participate must agree to operate the program on a nonprofit basis for all students without regard to race, sex, color or national origin, age or handicap.

INFORMATION CONTACTS: For regional or local office contact: Director, Child Nutrition Division, Food and Nutrition Service, Department of Agriculture, Alexandria, VA 22302. Contact: Stanley C. Garnett, Director. Telephone: (703) 305-2590. (Same for FTS.)

CHILD AND ADULT CARE FOOD PROGRAM - 10.558

OBJECTIVES: To assist States, through grants-in-aid and other means, maintain nonprofit food service programs for children and elderly or impaired adults in public and private nonprofit non-residential institutions providing care; family day care homes for children; and private for-profit centers that receive compensation under Title XX for at least 25 percent of the enrolled children, or 25% of licensed capacity, and under Title XIX or Title XX for at least 25 percent of the adults, who are enrolled in non-residential day-care services.

TYPES OF ASSISTANCE: Formula Grants; Sale, Exchange, or Donation of Property and Goods. FY 94 est $1,528,446,000.

ELIGIBILITY REQUIREMENTS: The State or U.S. Territory Educational Agency or other designated agency within the State or U.S. Territory applies for, and signs an annual agreement to receive Federal funds for disbursement, except in States where such agency is not permitted to disburse funds to any institution. In that case, institutions may receive funds directly from the Department of Agriculture.

INFORMATION CONTACTS: For regional or local office contact: Director, Child Nutrition Division, Food and Nutrition Service, Department of Agriculture, Alexandria, VA 22302. Contact: Stanley C. Garnett, Director. Telephone: (703) 305-2590. (Use same 7-digit number for FTS.)

SUMMER FOOD SERVICE PROGRAM FOR CHILDREN - 10.559

OBJECTIVES: To assist States, through grants-in-aid and other means, to conduct nonprofit food service programs for needy children during the summer months and at other approved times, when area schools are closed for vacation.

TYPES OF ASSISTANCE: Formula Grants. FY 94 est $254,612,000 and donated commodities including bonus commodities: FY 94 est $1,576,600.

ELIGIBILITY REQUIREMENTS: The State and U.S. Territory agency applies for and signs an annual agreement to receive Federal funds for disbursement; where the State does not administer the program, the institution may sign an agreement and receive funds directly from the Department of Agriculture.

INFORMATION CONTACTS: For regional or local office contact: Director, Child Nutrition Division, Food and Nutrition Service, Department of Agriculture, Alexandria, VA 22302. Contact: Stanley C. Garnett, Director. Telephone: (703) 305-2590. (Use same 7-digit number for FTS.)

INDIAN SOCIAL SERVICES - CHILD WELFARE ASSISTANCE -15.103

OBJECTIVES: To provide foster home care and appropriate institutional (non-medical) care for dependent, neglected, and handicapped Indian children in need of protection residing on or near reservations, including those children living in Bureau of Indian Affairs service area jurisdictions in Alaska and Oklahoma, when

these services are not available from State or local public agencies.

TYPES OF ASSISTANCE: Direct Payments for Specified Use. FY 94 est $22,000,000.

ELIGIBILITY REQUIREMENTS: Dependent, neglected, and handicapped Indian children in need of protection whose families live on or near Indian reservations or in Bureau of Indian Affairs service area jurisdictions in Alaska and Oklahoma, and who are not eligible for similar Federal, State or county funded programs. Written application may be made by a parent, guardian or person having custody of the child, or by court referral.

INFORMATION CONTACTS: Regional or Local Office: Information can be secured from the Agency Superintendents, and from Area Directors. Applications for child welfare assistance are made at the local agency or tribal level. Headquarters Office: Division of Social Services, Office of Tribal Services, Bureau of Indian Affairs, MS-310 SIB, 1849 C Street, NW, Washington, DC 20245. Telephone: (202) 208-2721. Contact: Betty Tippeconnic.

INDIAN EDUCATION - ASSISTANCE TO SCHOOLS - 15.130

OBJECTIVES: To provide supplemental education programs for eligible Indian students attending public schools.

TYPES OF ASSISTANCE: Direct Payments for Specified Use. FY 94 est $22,826,000.

ELIGIBILITY REQUIREMENTS: Tribal organizations, Indian Corporations, school districts or State which have eligible Indian children attending public school districts and have established Indian Education Committees to approve supplementary programs beneficial to Indian students.

INFORMATION CONTACTS: For regional or local office contact: Division of Education Programs, Office of Indian Education Programs, Bureau of Indian Affairs, 1849 C Street, NW, Washington, DC 20240. Telephone: (202) 208-4190. Contact: Dr. Dennis Fox.

JUVENILE JUSTICE AND DELINQUENCY PREVENTION - SPECIAL EMPHASIS - 16.541

OBJECTIVES: To develop and implement programs that design, test, and demonstrate effective approaches, techniques and methods for preventing and controlling juvenile delinquency such as community based-alternatives to institutional confinement; developing and

implementing effective means of diverting juveniles from the traditional juvenile justice and correctional system; programs stressing advocacy activities aimed at improving services to youth impacted by the juvenile justice system; model programs to strengthen and maintain the family unit; prevention and treatment programs relating to juveniles who commit serious crimes; programs to prevent hate crimes; and a national law-related education program of delinquency prevention.

TYPES OF ASSISTANCE: Project Grants (Cooperative Agreements or Contracts); Provision of Specialized Services. Grants: FY 94 est $23,500,000. Technical Assistance: FY 94 est $0.

ELIGIBILITY REQUIREMENTS: Special Emphasis funds are available under the Juvenile Justice and Delinquency Prevention Act of 1974, as amended, to public and private nonprofit agencies, organizations, individuals, State and local units of government, combinations of State or local units.

INFORMATION CONTACTS: Office of Juvenile Justice and Delinquency Prevention, Office of Justice Programs, Department of Justice, Washington, DC 20531. Telephone: (202) 307-5914.

MISSING CHILDREN'S ASSISTANCE - 16.543

OBJECTIVES: To ensure that there is effective coordination among all federally funded programs related to missing children. Establish and maintain a national resource center and clearinghouse to: (1) provide technical assistance to local and State governments, public and private nonprofit agencies and individuals in locating and recovering missing children; (2) coordinate public and private programs to locate and recover missing children; (3) disseminate nationally, information on innovative missing childrens' programs, services, and legislation; and (4) provide technical assistance to law enforcement agencies, private nonprofit agencies, and individuals in the prevention, investigation, prosecution and treatment of the missing or exploited child case. Periodically conduct national incidence studies to determine the actual number of children reported missing each year, the number of children who are victims of stranger abductions, the number of children who are victims of parental kidnappings, and the number of missing children who are recovered each year. Compile, analyze, publish and disseminate an annual summary of research currently being conducted on missing children, which will include an annual comprehensive plan for assuring cooperation and coordination among all agencies and organizations with responsibilities related to missing children. Provide a program to establish and maintain a national 24-hour toll-free telephone line where individuals may report information regarding the location of missing children.

TYPES OF ASSISTANCE: Project Grants (Cooperative Agreements). FY 94 est $5,971,000.

ELIGIBILITY REQUIREMENTS: Missing Children's funds are available under the Juvenile Justice and Delinquency Prevention Act of 1974, as amended, to public and private nonprofit agencies, organizations, individuals, State and local units of government, combinations of State or local units.

INFORMATION CONTACTS: Office of Juvenile Justice and Delinquency Prevention, Department of Justice, Washington, DC 20531. Telephone: (202) 307-0598.

PART D - JUVENILE GANGS AND DRUG ABUSE AND DRUG TRAFFICKING - 16.544

OBJECTIVES: To establish and support programs and activities that involve families and communities that are designed to: (1) reduce the participation of juveniles in drug-related crimes, particularly in elementary and secondary schools; (2) develop within the juvenile adjudicatory and correctional systems new and innovative means to address the problems of juveniles convicted of serious drug-related and gang-related offenses; (3) reduce juvenile involvement in gang-related activity, particularly activities that involve the distribution of drugs by or to juveniles; (4) promote the involvement of juveniles in lawful activities in geographical areas in which gangs commit crimes; (5) provide treatment to juveniles who are members of such gangs, including members who are accused of committing a serious crime and members who have been adjudicated as being delinquent; (6) support activities to inform juveniles of the availability of treatment and services for which financial assistance is provided under this program; (7) facilitate Federal and State cooperation with local officials to assist juveniles who are likely to participate in the activities of gangs that commit crimes and to establish and support programs that facilitate coordination and cooperation among local education, juvenile justice, employment and social services agen-

cies, for the purpose of preventing or reducing the participation of juveniles in activities of gangs that commit crimes; (8) provide personnel, personnel training, equipment and supplies in conjunction with programs and activities designed to prevent or reduce the participation of juveniles in unlawful gang activities or unlawful drug activities, to assist in improving the adjudicative and correctional components of the juvenile justice system; (9) provide pre- and post-trial drug abuse treatment to juveniles in the juvenile justice system; and (10) provide abuse education, prevention and treatment involving police and juvenile officials in demand reduction programs.

TYPES OF ASSISTANCE: Project Grants (Cooperative Agreements orContracts). FY 94 est $5,450,000.

ELIGIBILITY REQUIREMENTS: Part D funds are available under the Juvenile Justice and Delinquency Prevention Act of 1974, as amended, to public or private nonprofit agencies, organizations or individuals.

INFORMATION CONTACTS: Office of Juvenile Justice and Delinquency Prevention, Office of Justice Programs, Department of Justice, Washington, DC 20531. Telephone: (202) 307-0751.

CHILDREN'S JUSTICE ACT DISCRETIONARY GRANTS FOR NATIVE AMERICAN INDIAN TRIBES - 16.583

OBJECTIVES: Fifteen percent of the first $4.5 million of funds from the Crime Victims Fund that are transferred to the Department of Health and Human Services as part of the Children's Justice Act are to be statutorily reserved by the Office for Victims of Crime (OVC) to make grants for the purpose of assisting Native American Indian tribes in developing, establishing, and operating programs designed to improve the handling of child abuse cases, particularly cases of child sexual abuse, in a manner which limits additional trauma to the child victim and improves the investigation and prosecution of cases of child abuse.

TYPES OF ASSISTANCE: Project Grants; Direct Payments for Specified Use. FY 94 est $675,000.

ELIGIBILITY REQUIREMENTS: Federally recognized Indian tribal governments and nonprofit organizations that provide services to Native Americans. Specific criteria will vary depending on the grant.

INFORMATION CONTACTS: Cathy Sanders, Program Specialist, Federal Crime Victims Division, Office for

Victims of Crime, Office of Justice Programs, Department of Justice, 633 Indiana Avenue, N.W., Washington, DC 20531. Telephone: (202) 514-6445.

APPALACHIAN CHILD DEVELOPMENT - 23.013

OBJECTIVES: To provide child care services throughout the region which meet the needs of industry and its employees.

TYPES OF ASSISTANCE: Project Grants. FY 94 est $0.

ELIGIBILITY REQUIREMENTS: Public and private nonprofit organizations are eligible, if the projects are consistent with the ARDA, the ARC Code and State Plan and priorities.

INFORMATION CONTACTS: Inquiries and proposals for projects should be submitted first to the Appalachian State office designated by the Governor. Other inquiries may be addressed to: Executive Director, Appalachian Regional Commission, 1666 Connecticut Avenue, NW, Washington, DC 20235. Telephone: (202) 673-7874.

PROMOTION OF THE ARTS - ARTS IN EDUCATION - 45.003

OBJECTIVES: To encourage State and local arts agencies to develop long-term strategies to help establish the arts as basic to the education of students prekindergarten through twelfth grade; to encourage State and local education agencies to develop and implement sequential arts education programs; to encourage the involvement of artists and cultural organizations in enhancing arts in education for a broad segment of the population; to encourage the career development of excellent teachers and professional artists involved in education; to develop and stimulate research to teach quality education in the arts; to encourage the development of improved curriculum materials, evaluation, and assessment of arts education programs; to foster cooperative programs with the U.S. Department of Education; and to encourage dissemination of information and research about current and past successful arts education programs.

TYPES OF ASSISTANCE: Project Grants. FY 94 est $7,800,000.

ELIGIBILITY REQUIREMENTS: Arts Education Partnership grants, the only grant category at this time, are available for State Arts Agencies only. The AIE Program also supports initiatives depending on the priorities of the Agency and funds available. Depending on the type of initiative, grants, or cooperative agreements may be made to nonprofit organizations if donations to such organizations qualify as a charitable deduction under Section 170(c) of the Internal Revenue Code of 1954. This definition also includes State and local governments.

INFORMATION CONTACTS: Arts in Education Program, Room 602, National Endowment for the Arts, The Nancy Hanks Center, 1100 Pennsylvania Avenue, NW., Washington, DC 20506. Telephone for Guidelines (202)682-5797; for other information; (202) 682-5426 (use same 7-digit number for FTS). TDD: (202) 682-5496.

PROMOTION OF THE HUMANITIES - HUMANITIES PROJECTS IN MEDIA - 45.104

OBJECTIVES: To encourage and support radio and television production that: 1) Advances public understanding and appreciation of the humanities by adults and young people of junior high and high school age; 2) is of the highest professional caliber both in terms of scholarship in the humanities and in terms of technical production; and 3) is suitable for national television broadcast and distribution, or for national, regional or local radio broadcast.

TYPES OF ASSISTANCE: Project Grants. FY 94 est $10,500,000.

ELIGIBILITY REQUIREMENTS: State and local governments, sponsored organizations, public and private nonprofit institutions/organizations, other public institutions/organizations, Federally recognized Indian tribal governments, Native American organizations, U.S. Territories, nongovernment-general, minority organizations and other specialized groups, quasi-public nonprofit institutions.

INFORMATION CONTACTS: Division of Public Programs, Humanities Projects in Media, National Endowment for the Humanities, Room 420, Washington, DC 20506. Telephone: (202) 606-8278.

PROMOTION OF THE HUMANITIES - ELEMENTARY AND SECONDARY EDUCATION IN THE HUMANITIES - 45.127

OBJECTIVES: To increase the effectiveness of humanities teaching in our Nation's elementary, middle, and secondary schools. The purpose of the program is to strengthen instruction principally through faculty development. Applicants may be individual schools, school systems, colleges, universities, museums, libraries, or groups of institutions working in collaboration. A proposal is expected to demonstrate a com-

mitment to increasing the teachers' knowledge in the fields of the humanities and to strengthening the intellectual capabilities imparted by effective study of the humanities.

TYPES OF ASSISTANCE: Project Grants. FY 94 est $8,415,000.

ELIGIBILITY REQUIREMENTS: State and local governments; sponsored organizations; public and private nonprofit institutions/organizations; other public institutions/organizations; Federally recognized Indian tribal governments; Native American organizations; U.S. Territories; nongovernment-general; minority organizations; other specialized groups; and quasi-public nonprofit institutions.

INFORMATION CONTACTS: Elementary and Secondary Education in the Humanities, National Endowment for the Humanities, Room 302, Washington, DC 20506. Telephone: (202) 606-8377.

PROMOTION OF THE HUMANITIES - NEH/READER'S DIGEST TEACHER-SCHOLAR PROGRAM - 45.154

OBJECTIVES: To increase the effectiveness of humanities teaching in our Nation's elementary, middle, and secondary schools. The purpose of the program is to strengthen instruction through a year of full-time study in one of the disciplines of the humanities. Applicants must be full-time teachers with at least three years of classroom experience who intend to return to teaching for at least two years after completing the project. A proposal is expected to demonstrate a commitment to increasing the teacher's knowledge in the fields of the humanities and to strengthening the intellectual capabilities imparted by effective study of the humanities.

TYPES OF ASSISTANCE: Project Grants. FY 94 est $0 (awards will be supported entirely out of gifts and matching funds).

ELIGIBILITY REQUIREMENTS: Teachers that: (1) Are employed full-time in elementary, middle, or high schools; (2) have teaching responsibilities primarily in the humanities; (3) have completed at least three years of full-time teaching at the time of application; (4) intend to return to teaching after completing the project; and (5) are not past recipients of the Teacher-Scholar award may apply. Librarians may apply if they spend more than 50 percent of their time directly teaching humanities courses.

INFORMATION CONTACTS: Elementary and Secondary Education in the Humanities, National Endowment for

the Humanities, Room 302, Washington, DC 20506. Telephone: (202) 606-8377.

EDUCATION AND HUMAN RESOURCES - 47.076

OBJECTIVES: To provide leadership and support to the Nation's efforts to improve the quality and effectiveness of science, mathematics and engineering education; with the ultimate goal being a scientifically literate society, a technically competent workforce and a body of well-educated scientists and engineers adequate to the Nation's needs. The program supports activities in the following areas: systemic reform; elementary, secondary and informal science education; undergraduate education; graduate education and research development; human resource development; and research, evaluation and dissemination.

TYPES OF ASSISTANCE: Project Grants. FY 93 est $487,500,000; FY 94 est not yet available.

ELIGIBILITY REQUIREMENTS: Public and private colleges (2-year and 4-year) and universities, State and local educational agencies, nonprofit and private organizations, professional societies, science academies and centers, science museums and zoological parks, research laboratories, and other institutions with an educational mission.

INFORMATION CONTACTS: Assistant Director, Education and Human Resources, National Science Foundation, Room 516, 1800 G Street, NW., Washington, DC 20550. Telephone: (202) 357-7557.

FOSTER GRANDPARENT PROGRAM - 72.001

OBJECTIVES: Dual purposes of the program are: (1) to provide part-time volunteer service opportunities for low-income persons age 60 and over and (2) to give supportive person-to-person service in health, education, welfare and related settings to help alleviate the physical, mental, and emotional problems of infants, children, or youth having special or exceptional needs. In addition, eligible agencies or organizations may, under a Memorandum of Agreement with ACTION, receive technical assistance and materials to aid in establishing and operating a non-ACTION funded Foster Grandparent Program project using local funds.

TYPES OF ASSISTANCE: Project Grants. FY 94 est $66,301,000.

ELIGIBILITY REQUIREMENTS: Grants are made only to State and local government agencies and private nonprofit organizations.

INFORMATION CONTACTS: Regional or Local Office: ACTION Regional and State Program Offices. Headquarters Office: Program Officer, Foster Grandparent Program, ACTION, 1100 Vermont Avenue, NW., Washington, DC 20525. Telephone: (202) 606-4849.

BILINGUAL EDUCATION - 84.003

OBJECTIVES: To develop and carry out programs of bilingual education in elementary and secondary schools, including activities at the preschool level, which are designed to meet the educational needs of children of limited English proficiency; to demonstrate effective ways of providing such children with instruction designed to enable them, while using their native language, to achieve competence in English; or to develop alternative instruction programs that need not use the native language; to develop the human and material resources required for such programs; and to build the capacity of grantees to continue programs of bilingual education when assistance under this program is reduced or no longer available.

TYPES OF ASSISTANCE: Project Grants; Direct Payments for Specified Use. FY 94 est $153,738,000.

ELIGIBILITY REQUIREMENTS: Local educational agencies and in some cases institutions of higher education; private nonprofit and for-profit organizations; and nonprofit institutions or organizations of Indian tribes that operate elementary or secondary schools may apply.

INFORMATION CONTACTS: Office of Bilingual Education and Minority Languages Affairs, Department of Education, 330 C Street, SW., Room 5086, Washington, DC 20202. Contact: Rudolph Munis, Division Director, Division of State and Local Programs. Telephone: (202) 205-9700.

CHAPTER 1 PROGRAMS - LOCAL EDUCATIONAL AGENCIES - 84.010

OBJECTIVES: To improve the educational opportunities of educationally deprived children by helping them succeed in the regular school program, attain grade level proficiency, and improve achievement in basic and more advanced skills.

TYPES OF ASSISTANCE: Formula Grants. FY 94 est $6,500,000,000.

ELIGIBILITY REQUIREMENTS: State educational agencies (SEAs) and the Secretary of the Interior may apply. Local educational agencies (LEAs)

and Indian tribal Schools are subgrantees.

INFORMATION CONTACTS: Compensatory Education Programs, Office of Elementary and Secondary Education, Department of Education, 400 Maryland Avenue, SW., Room 2043, Washington, DC 20202-6132. Contact: Mary Jean LeTendre. Telephone: (202) 401-1682.

FOLLOW THROUGH - 84.014

OBJECTIVES: To sustain and augment in primary grades the gains that children from low-income families make in Head Start and other quality preschool programs. Follow Through provides special programs of instruction as well as health, nutrition, and other related services that will aid in the continued development of children to their full potential. Active participation of parents is stressed. Emphasis is placed on the demonstration and dissemination of effective approaches specifically designed to improve the school performance of children from low-income families and the provision of comprehensive services.

ELIGIBILITY REQUIREMENTS: Discretionary project grants are made to specified local educational agencies and public and private institutions of higher education or educational regional laboratories or other appropriate public or private nonprofit agencies, organizations, or institutions.

TYPES OF ASSISTANCE: Project Grants. FY 94 est $8,478,000.

INFORMATION CONTACTS: Compensatory Education Programs, Office of Elementary and Secondary Education, Department of Education, 400 Maryland Avenue, SW., Rm. 2043, Washington, DC 20202-6132. Contact: Robert Alexander. Telephone: (202) 401-1692.

SPECIAL EDUCATION - INNOVATION AND DEVELOPMENT - 84.023

OBJECTIVES: To improve the education of children with disabilities through research and development projects and model programs (demonstrations).

TYPES OF ASSISTANCE: Project Grants; Project Grants (Contracts); Project Grants (Cooperative Agreements). FY 94 est $20,635,000.

ELIGIBILITY REQUIREMENTS: State or local educational agencies, institutions of higher education, and other public or private educational or research agencies and organizations may apply. Only nonprofit organizations are eligible for awards except under 20 U.S.C. 1442.

INFORMATION CONTACTS: Division of

Innovation and Development, Office of Assistant Secretary for Special Education and Rehabilitative Services, Department of Education, 400 Maryland Avenue, SW., Washington, DC 20202. Contact: Martha Coutinho. Telephone: (202) 205-8156.

EARLY EDUCATION FOR CHILDREN WITH DISABILITIES - 84.024

OBJECTIVES: To support demonstration, dissemination, and implementation of effective approaches to preschool and early childhood education for children with disabilities.

TYPES OF ASSISTANCE: Project Grants; Project Grants (Cooperative Agreements); Project Grants (Contracts). FY 94 est $25,167,000.

INFORMATION CONTACTS: Division of Educational Services, Special education Programs, Office of Assistant Secretary for Special Education and Rehabilitative Services, Department of Education, 400 Maryland Avenue, SW., Washington, DC 20202. Contact: James Hamilton. Telephone: (202) 205-9084.

SERVICES FOR CHILDREN WITH DEAF-BLINDNESS - 84.025

OBJECTIVES: To provide technical assistance to State education agencies and to improve services to deaf-blind children and youth.

TYPES OF ASSISTANCE: Project Grants; Project Grants (Cooperative Agreements); Project Grants (Contracts). FY 94 est $12,832,000.

ELIGIBILITY REQUIREMENTS: Public or private nonprofit agencies, organizations, or institutions may apply.

INFORMATION CONTACTS: Division of Educational Services, Office of Special Education Programs, Assistant Secretary for Special Education and Rehabilitative Services, Department of Education, 400 Maryland Avenue, SW., Washington, DC 20202. Contact: Dawn Hunter. Telephone: (202) 205-5809.

MEDIA AND CAPTIONING FOR INDIVIDUALS WITH DISABILITIES - 84.026

OBJECTIVES: To maintain a free loan service of captioned films for the deaf and instructional media for the educational, cultural, and vocational enrichment of the disabled. Provide for acquisition and distribution of media materials and equipment; provide contracts and grants for research into the use of media and technology, train teachers, parents, and others in media and technology utilization.

TYPES OF ASSISTANCE: Project Grants; Project Grants (Cooperative Agreements); Project Grants

(Contracts). FY 94 est $17,892,000.

ELIGIBILITY REQUIREMENTS: Profit and nonprofit, public and private agencies, organizations, or institutions may apply.

INFORMATION CONTACTS: Division of Educational Services, Special Education Programs, Office of Assistant Secretary for Special Education and Rehabilitative Services, Department of Education, Washington, DC 20202. Contact: Ernest Hairston. Telephone: (202) 205-9172; 205-8170 - TDD.

INDIAN EDUCATION - FORMULA GRANTS TO LOCAL EDUCATIONAL AGENCIES - 84.060

OBJECTIVES: To develop and carry out supplementary elementary and secondary school programs designed to meet the special educational and culturally related academic needs of Indian children, for example to: 1) Improve academic performance, 2) reduce school dropout rates and improve attendance, and 3) integrate the value of cultural education into the school curriculum for Indian children.

TYPES OF ASSISTANCE: Project Grants. FY 94 est $60,905,000.

ELIGIBILITY REQUIREMENTS: Local educational agencies (LEAs) that enroll at least 10 Indian children or in which Indians constitute at least 50 percent of the total enrollment. These requirements do not apply to LEAs serving Indian children in Alaska, California, and Oklahoma or located on, or in proximity to, an Indian reservation. An Indian tribe that operates a school in accordance with standards established by the Bureau of Indian Affairs under Section 1121 of the Education Amendments of 1978 (25 U.S.C. 2001) or under contract with the Bureau of Indian Affairs according to Public Law 93-638 is deemed to be an LEA for the purposes of this program. Schools operated by the Bureau of Indian Affairs (BIA), Department of the Interior, are eligible only if funds are available in accordance with Section 5312(b)(3) of the Act.

INFORMATION CONTACTS: Office of Indian Education, Office of Elementary and Secondary Education, Department of Education, 400 Maryland Avenue, SW., Room 2177, Washington, DC 20202. Contact: Cathie Martin, Branch Chief, Grants Administration Branch. Telephone: (202) 401-1902.

INDIAN EDUCATION - SPECIAL PROGRAMS AND PROJECTS - 84.061

OBJECTIVES: To plan, develop, and implement programs and projects for the improvement of educational opportunities for Indian children, programs that serve gifted and talented Indian students, prepare and improve qualifications of persons serving Indian students in educational personnel positions, encourage Indian students to acquire a higher education, and reduce the incidence of dropping out of school among elementary and secondary school students.

TYPES OF ASSISTANCE: Project Grants. FY 94 est $8,150,000.

ELIGIBILITY REQUIREMENTS: Eligible applicants include: State and local educational agencies, federally supported elementary and secondary schools for Indian children, Indian tribes, Indian organizations, Indian institutions, and institutions of higher education. Priority is given to Indian tribes, Indian organizations, Indian institutions, and consortia of higher education institutions, LEAs, SEAs, Indian tribes and Indian organizations.

INFORMATION CONTACTS: Office of Indian Education, Department of Education, 400 Maryland Avenue, SW., Room 2177, Washington, DC 20202. Contact: Cathie Martin, Branch Chief, Grants Administration Branch. Telephone: (202) 401-1902.

INDIAN EDUCATION - GRANTS TO INDIAN-CONTROLLED SCHOOLS - 84.072

OBJECTIVES: To provide financial assistance to Indian-controlled schools to develop and implement cultural enrichment programs for elementary and secondary schools that are designed to meet the special educational needs of Indian children. The schools must be located on or near a reservation and must be governed by an Indian tribe or tribally sanctioned organization.

TYPES OF ASSISTANCE: Project Grants. FY 94 est $3,125,000.

ELIGIBILITY REQUIREMENTS: An Indian tribe or Indian organization, or an LEA that will have been an LEA for not more than three years at the beginning of the proposed project period is eligible if it operates a school for Indian children that is located on or near a reservation. However, the requirement that a school be located on or near a reservation does not apply to any school serving Indian children in Alaska, California, or Oklahoma.

INFORMATION CONTACTS: Office of Indian Education, Department of Education, Office of Elementary and Secondary Education, 400 Maryland Avenue, SW., Room 2177, Washing-ton, DC 20202. Contact: Cathie Martin, Branch Chief, Grants Administration Branch. Telephone: (202) 401-1902.

WOMEN'S EDUCATIONAL EQUITY - 84.083

OBJECTIVES: 1) To promote educational equity for women in the United States; (2) to promote educational equity for women who suffer multiple discrimination, bias, or stereotyping based on (i) sex; and (ii) race, ethnic origin, disability, or age; and (3) to enable educational agencies and institutions to meet the requirements of Title IX of the Education Amendments of 1972 relating to nondiscrimination on the basis of sex in federally assisted educational programs.

TYPES OF ASSISTANCE: Project Grants. FY 94 est $1,984,000.

ELIGIBILITY REQUIREMENTS: Through a nationwide competition, public and private nonprofit agencies, institutions, and organizations including student and community groups and individuals may apply.

INFORMATION CONTACTS: Equity and Educational Excellence Division, Office of Elementary and Secondary Education, Department of Education, 400 Maryland Avenue, SW., Washington, DC 20202-6246. Contact: Ms. Carolyn N. Andrews. Telephone: (202) 401-1342.

LAW-RELATED EDUCATION - 84.123

OBJECTIVES: (1) To support new and ongoing programs at the elementary and secondary schools, adult education, community organizations, and institutions of higher education, by developing and implementing model projects designed to institutionalize law-related education (LRE); (2) provide assistance from established LRE programs to other State and local agencies; and (3) to support projects to develop, test, demonstrate, and disseminate new approaches or techniques.

TYPES OF ASSISTANCE: Project Grants; Project Grants (Contracts). FY 94 est $3,000,000.

ELIGIBILITY REQUIREMENTS: State educational agencies, local educational agencies, public or private nonprofit agencies, organizations, and institutions may apply.

INFORMATION CONTACTS: Equity and Educational Excellence Division, Office of Elementary and Secondary Education, 400 Maryland Avenue, SW., Washington, DC 20202-6440. Contact: Alice Ford. Telephone: (202) 401-1342.

DRUG-FREE SCHOOLS AND COMMUNITIES - NATIONAL PROGRAMS - 84.184

OBJECTIVES: To assist in drug and alcohol abuse education and prevention activities as authorized by the Drug-Free Schools and Communities Act of 1986, as amended.

TYPES OF ASSISTANCE: Project Grants (Contracts); Project Grants (Cooperative Agreements). Project Grants (Discretionary). FY 94 est $15,000,000.

ELIGIBILITY REQUIREMENTS: Institutions of higher education. SEAs, LEAs, and nonprofits are eligible.

INFORMATION CONTACTS: Director, Division of Drug-Free Schools and Communities, Department of Education, Office of Elementary and Secondary Education, 400 Maryland Avenue, SW., Washington, DC 20202-6439. Contact: Seledia Shephard and Gail Beaumont. Telephone: (202) 401-1258.

EDUCATION FOR HOMELESS CHILDREN AND YOUTH - GRANTS FOR STATE AND LOCAL ACTIVITIES - 84.196

OBJECTIVES: To carry out the policies set forth in Section 721 of the Act, to provide activities for and services to homeless children and homeless youths to enroll in, attend, and achieve in school, to establish or designate an office in each State educational agency (SEA) and Outlying Area for the coordination of education for homeless children and youth; to develop and carry out a State or area plan for the education of homeless children and youth; to develop and implement programs for school personnel to heighten awareness of specific problems of homeless children and youth; and to provide grants to local educational agencies.

TYPES OF ASSISTANCE: Formula Grants. FY 94 est $25,470,000.

ELIGIBILITY REQUIREMENTS: Departments of education in the 50 States, the District of Columbia, Puerto Rico, the Outlying Areas, and schools serving Indian students that are funded by the Secretary of the Interior may apply. Only LEA's are eligible for State subgrants.

INFORMATION CONTACTS: Compensatory Education Programs, Office of Elementary and Secondary Education, Department of Education, 400 Maryland Avenue, SW., Rm. 2043, Washington, DC 20202-6132. Contact: Robert Alexander. Telephone: (202) 401-1692.

STAR SCHOOLS PROGRAM - 84.203

OBJECTIVES: To provide grants to eligible telecommunications partnerships to develop, construct and acquire audio and visual facilities and equipment, to develop and acquire instructional programming, and to obtain technical assistance for the use of such facilities and instructional programming, in order to encourage improved instruction in mathematics, science, literacy skills and foreign language as well as other subjects such as vocational education. To serve underserved populations including the disadvantaged, illiterate, limited-English proficient, and disabled.

TYPES OF ASSISTANCE: Project Grants. FY 94 est $27,000,000.

ELIGIBILITY REQUIREMENTS: Eligible partnerships may take the form of either: (1) A public agency or corporation established for the purpose of developing and operating telecommunications networks to enhance educational opportunities, or (2) a partnership that includes three or more of the following, at least one of which must be an agency as described in (a) or (b): (a) A local education agency with a significant number of elementary and secondary schools that are eligible for assistance under Chapter 1 funds or elementary and secondary schools operated for Indian children by the Department of the Interior; (b) a State education agency; (c) an institution of higher education or State higher education agency; (d) a teacher training center; (e) a public or private agency with experience or expertise in the planning or operation of telecommunications networks or academy or a public broadcasting entity; or (f) a public or private elementary or secondary school.

INFORMATION CONTACTS: Office of Educational Research and Improvement, Department of Education, Washington, DC 20208-5644. Cheryl Garnette. Telephone: (202) 219-2267 or Joseph Wilkes. Telephone: (202) 219-2186.

JACOB K. JAVITS GIFTED AND TALENTED STUDENTS EDUCATION GRANT PROGRAM - 84.206

OBJECTIVES: To provide financial assistance to state and local educational agencies, institutions of higher education, and other public and private agencies and organizations, to stimulate research, development, training, and similar activities designed to build a nationwide capability in elementary and secondary schools to meet the special educational needs of gifted and talented students. To supplement the use of state, local, and Chapter 2 funds for the education of gifted and talented students.

TYPES OF ASSISTANCE: Project Grants. FY 94 est $7,437,000. Note: In FY 94 $1,750,000 will support the National Center.

ELIGIBILITY REQUIREMENTS: State and local education agencies, institutions of higher education, other public and private agencies, and organizations (including Indian tribes and organizations as defined by the Indian Self-Determination and Education Assistance Act and Hawaiian Native organizations) may apply. Only institutions of higher education and State educational agencies or a combination of them are eligible to apply to operate the National Center authorized under Section 4104 (c).

INFORMATION CONTACTS: Research Applications Division, Programs for the Improvement of Practice, Department of Education, 555 New Jersey Ave., NW., Washington, DC 20208-5644. Contact: Norma Lindsay (Project Grants). Telephone: (202) 219-1719, and Ivor Pritchard (Research Center). Telephone: (202) 219-2223.

FIRST SCHOOLS AND TEACHERS - 84.211

OBJECTIVES: To support projects to improve educational opportunities for and the performance of elementary and secondary school students and teachers.

TYPES OF ASSISTANCE: Project Grants. FY 94 est $5,396,000.

ELIGIBILITY REQUIREMENTS: Departments of education in the 50 states, the District of Columbia, Puerto Rico, the Outlying Areas, and schools serving Indian students that are funded by the Secretary of the Interior may apply. Only LEA's are eligible for state subgrants.

INFORMATION CONTACTS: Department of Education, FIRST, Office of Educational Research and Improvement, Washington, DC 20208-5524. Telephone: (202) 219-1496.

FIRST FAMILY SCHOOL PARTNERSHIP - 84.212

OBJECTIVES: To increase the involvement of families in improving the educational achievement of their children in preschool, elementary and secondary schools.

TYPES OF ASSISTANCE: Project Grants. FY 94 est $3,687,000.

ELIGIBILITY REQUIREMENTS: Local educational agencies eligible to receive Chapter 1 funds may apply.

INFORMATION CONTACTS: Department of Education, FIRST, Office of Educational Research and Improvement,

Washington, DC 20208-5524. Telephone: (202) 219-1496.

EVEN START - STATE EDUCATIONAL AGENCIES - 84.213

OBJECTIVES: To provide family-centered education projects to help parents become full partners in the education of their children, to assist children in reaching their full potential as learners, and to provide literacy training for their parents.

TYPES OF ASSISTANCE: Formula Grants. FY 94 est $102,300,000.

ELIGIBILITY REQUIREMENTS: State educational agencies (SEA). The subgrantees are local educational agencies (LEAs) applying to their SEAs in collaboration with community-based organizations, public agencies, institutions of higher education or other nonprofit organizations. Any of the latter, with demonstrated quality, may apply in collaboration with a LEA.

INFORMATION CONTACTS: Department of Education, Compensatory Education Programs, Office of Elementary and Secondary Education, 400 Maryland Avenue, SW., Washington, DC 20202-6132. Contact: Letitia Rennings. Telephone: (202) 401-1692.

THE SECRETARY'S FUND FOR INNOVATION IN EDUCATION - 84.215

OBJECTIVES: To conduct programs and projects that show promise of identifying and disseminating innovative educational approaches.

TYPES OF ASSISTANCE: Project Grants. FY 94 est $40,000,000.

ELIGIBILITY REQUIREMENTS: State educational agencies, local educational agencies, institutions of higher education, public and private organizations and institutions may apply.

INFORMATION CONTACTS: Department of Education, FIRST, Office of Educational Research and Improvement, Washington, DC 20208-5524. Telephone: (202) 219-1496.

EDUCATIONAL PARTNERSHIPS - 84.228

OBJECTIVES: To encourage the creation of alliances between public elementary and secondary schools or institutions of higher education and the private sector in order to: (1) Apply the resources of the private and nonprofit sectors of the community to the needs of elementary and secondary schools or institutions of higher education in that community to encourage excellence in education; (2) encourage businesses to work with educationally disadvantaged students and with

gifted students; (3) apply the resources of communities for the improvement of elementary and secondary education or higher education; and (4) enrich the career awareness of secondary or postsecondary school students and provide exposures to the work of the private sector.

TYPES OF ASSISTANCE: Project Grants; Project Grants (Contracts). FY 94 est $2,120,000.

ELIGIBILITY REQUIREMENTS: To apply for a grant an applicant must be an eligible partnership. An eligible partnership must include one or more local educational agencies or institutions of higher education, or both, and one or more of the following (1) A business concern; (2) A community-based organization; (3) A nonprofit private organization; (4) A museum; (5) A library; (6) An educational television or radio station; and (7) an appropriate state agency.

INFORMATION CONTACTS: Educational Networks Division, Room 502, 555 New Jersey Avenue, NW., Washington, DC 20208-5644. Telephone: (202) 219-2116.

CHILDREN AND YOUTH WITH SERIOUS EMOTIONAL DISTURBANCE - 84.237

OBJECTIVES: To establish projects for the purpose of improving special education and related services to children and youth with serious emotional disturbance.

TYPES OF ASSISTANCE: Project Grants; Project Grants (Contracts); Project Grants (Cooperative Agreements). FY 94 est $4,147,000.

ELIGIBILITY REQUIREMENTS: Institutions of higher education, state and local educational agencies, and other appropriate public and private nonprofit institutions or agencies may apply.

INFORMATION CONTACTS: Contact: Martha Coutinho. Telephone: (202) 205-8156.

EVEN START - INDIAN TRIBES AND TRIBAL ORGANIZATIONS - 84.258

OBJECTIVES: To provide family-centered education projects to help parents become full partners in the education of their children, to assist children in reaching their full potential as learners, and to provide literacy training for their parents.

TYPES OF ASSISTANCE: Project Grants (Discretionary). FY 94 est $1,500,000.

ELIGIBILITY REQUIREMENTS: Federally recognized Indian tribes, and tribal organizations as defined in the Indian Self-Determination and Education Assistance Act, Section 4, may apply.

INFORMATION CONTACTS: Department of Education, Compensatory Education Programs, Office of Elementary and Secondary Education, 400 Maryland Avenue, SW., Washington, DC 20202-6132. Contact: Donna Conforti. Telephone: (202) 401-1692.

DEMONSTRATION GRANTS FOR THE PREVENTION OF ALCOHOL AND OTHER DRUG ABUSE AMONG HIGH-RISK YOUTH - 93.144

OBJECTIVES: To support client oriented prevention demonstration programs that will develop client and/or service systems targeted toward: (1) decreasing the incidence and prevalence of drug and alcohol use among high-risk youth; (2) identifying and reducing factors in the individual, in the parents and extended family, school, peer group and neighborhood placing youth at high risk for using alcohol and other drugs; and (3) increasing resiliency/protective factors within high-risk youth, peer groups, and families reduce the likelihood that youths will use alcohol and other drugs. The specific goals and objectives of an applicant need not address all of these program goals. However, proposed projects should be consonant with one or more of them.

TYPES OF ASSISTANCE: Project Grants. FY 94 est $65,300,000.

ELIGIBILITY REQUIREMENTS: Any public (including governmental bodies) or nonprofit private entity is eligible to apply for grant support.

INFORMATION CONTACTS: Program Contacts: Ms. Rose C. Kittrell, Chief, High Risk Youth Branch, Division of Demonstrations for High Risk Populations, Center for Substance Abuse Prevention, Substance Abuse and Mental Health Services Administration, Public Health Service, Department of Health and Human Services, Rockwall II Building, 5600 Fishers Lane, Rockville, MD 20857. Telephone: (301) 443-0353. Grants Management Contact: Ms. Margaret Heydrick, Grants Management Officer, Center for Substance Abuse Prevention, Substance Abuse and Mental Health Services Administration, Public Health Service, Department of Health and Human Services, Rockwall II Building, 5600 Fishers Lane, Rockville, MD 20857. Telephone: (301) 443-3958. (Use same numbers for FTS.)

CHILDHOOD LEAD POISONING PREVENTION PROJECTS - STATE AND COMMUNITY-BASED CHILDHOOD LEAD POISONING PREVENTION PROGRAM - 93.197

OBJECTIVES: (1) To screen and identify infants and young children for lead poisoning; (2) to identify their possible sources of lead exposure; (3) to monitor medical and environmental management of lead-poisoned children; (4) to provide information on childhood lead poisoning, its prevention, and management to the public, health professionals, and policy and decision makers; and (5) to encourage community action programs directed to the goal of eliminating childhood lead poisoning.
TYPES OF ASSISTANCE: Project Grants. FY 94 est $41,409,000.
ELIGIBILITY REQUIREMENTS: Eligible applicants are State health departments or other State health agencies or departments deemed most appropriate by the State to lead and coordinate the State's childhood lead poisoning prevention program, and agencies or units of local government that serve jurisdictional populations greater than 500,000. This eligibility includes health departments or other official organizational authority (agency or instrumentality) of the District of Columbia, the Commonwealth of Puerto Rico, and any Territory or possession of the United States. Also eligible are federally-recognized Indian Tribal governments. If a State agency applying for grant funds is other than the official State health department, written concurrence by the State health department must be provided. Eligible applicants may enter into contracts, including consortia agreements as necessary, to meet the requirements of the program and strengthen the overall application.
INFORMATION CONTACTS: Program Contact: Mr. David L. Forney, Lead Poisoning Prevention Branch, Division of Environmental Hazards and Health Effects, National Center for Environmental Health, Centers for Disease Control and Prevention, MSF-42, Public Health Service, 4770 Buford Highway, Atlanta, GA 30341. Telephone: (404) 488-7330. Grants Management Contact: Mr. Henry S. Cassell III, Procurement and Grants Office, Centers for Disease Control and Prevention, Public Health Service, 255 East Paces Ferry Road, NE., Atlanta, GA 30305. Telephone: (404) 842-6630. (Use same numbers for FTS.)

HEAD START - 93.600
OBJECTIVES: To provide comprehensive health, educational, nutritional, social and other services primarily to economically disadvantaged preschool children, including Indian children on federally-recognized reservations, and children of migratory workers and their families; and to involve parents in activities with their children so that the children will attain overall social competence.
TYPES OF ASSISTANCE: Project Grants. FY 94 est $2,851,244,604. (NOTE: The funds in this program are also available for program contracts. The amounts which can be used for such contracts cannot be predetermined.)
ELIGIBILITY REQUIREMENTS: Any local government, federally-recognized Indian tribe, or public or private nonprofit agency which meets the requirements may apply for a grant. However, application will be considered only when submitted in response to a specific announcement, published in the Federal Register, which solicits proposals to establish new Head Start Programs. Grantee agencies may subcontract with other child-serving agencies to provide services to Head Start children.
INFORMATION CONTACTS: For regional or local office: Administration for Children and Families/Head Start, Department of Health and Human Services, P.O. Box 1182, Washington, DC 20013. Telephone: (202) 205-8569.

CHILD WELFARE RESEARCH AND DEMONSTRATION - 93.608
OBJECTIVES: To provide financial support for research and demonstration projects in the area of child and family development and welfare.
TYPES OF ASSISTANCE: Project Grants. FY 94 est $6,466,744. (NOTE: The funds in this program are also available for program contracts. The amounts which can be used for such contracts cannot be predetermined.)
ELIGIBILITY REQUIREMENTS: Grants: State and local governments or other nonprofit agencies, institutions of higher learning, and other organizations engaged in research or child welfare activities. Contracts: Any public or private organizations.
INFORMATION CONTACTS: Penny Maza, Ph.D, Assistance Branch, Children's Bureau, Administration for Children and Families, P.O. Box 1182, Washington, DC 20013. Telephone: (202) 205-8172.

RUNAWAY AND HOMELESS YOUTH - 93.623
OBJECTIVES: To establish and operate local centers to address the immediate needs of runaway and homeless youth and their families.
TYPES OF ASSISTANCE: Project Grants. FY 94 est $35,109,856.
ELIGIBILITY REQUIREMENTS: Grants are available to State and local governments, for-profit or nonprofit private agencies, and coordinated networks of such agencies.
INFORMATION CONTACTS: For regional or local office: Associate Commissioner, Family and Youth Services Bureau, Administration for Children and Families, Department of Health and Human Services, P. O. Box 1182, Washington, DC 20013. Telephone: (202) 205-8102.

ADOPTION OPPORTUNITIES - 93.652
OBJECTIVES: To provide financial support for demonstration projects to improve adoption practices; to gather information on adoptions; and to provide training and technical assistance to improve adoption services.
TYPES OF ASSISTANCE: Project Grants. FY 94 est $12,162,520. (NOTE: The funds in this program are also available for program contracts. The amounts which can be used for such contracts cannot be predetermined.)
ELIGIBILITY REQUIREMENTS: Grants: State or local government or nonprofit institutions of higher learning, State and local government or nonprofit organizations engaged in adoption services or research in child welfare activities. Contracts: Public and private nonprofit agencies and organizations.
INFORMATION CONTACTS: Delmar Weathers, Children's Bureau, Administration for Children and Families P.O. Box 1182, Washington, DC 20013. Telephone: (202) 205-8671. (Use same number for FTS.)

DRUG ABUSE PREVENTION AND EDUCATION RELATING TO YOUTH GANGS - 93.660
OBJECTIVES: To prevent and reduce the participation of youth in gangs that engage in illicit drug-related activities; to promote involvement of youth in lawful activities; to prevent the abuse of drugs by youth; to support coordination of activities of local police departments, education, employment and social service agencies; to provide information on the treatment and rehabilitation options available to youth; to coordinate support between schools and State and Federal governments; and to provide technical assistance to eligible organizations.
TYPES OF ASSISTANCE: Project Grants; Project Grants (Contracts). FY 94 est $10,647,328.
ELIGIBILITY REQUIREMENTS: State and local governments, federally-

recognized Indian Tribal Governments, U.S. Territories and possessions, public and nonprofit private agencies, organizations (including community-based organizations with demonstrated experience in the field), institutions, and individuals.

INFORMATION CONTACTS: Maria Candamil, Family and Youth Services Bureau, Administration for Children and Families, P.O. Box 1182, Washington, DC 20013. Telephone: (202) 205-8078 or (202) 205-8054.

COMPREHENSIVE CHILD DEVELOPMENT CENTERS - 93.666

OBJECTIVES: To plan for and carry out projects for a five-year period to provide intensive, comprehensive, integrated and continuous supportive services for infants, toddlers, and pre-schoolers from low-income families to enhance their intellectual, social, emotional and physical development and provide support to their parents and other family members.

TYPES OF ASSISTANCE: Project Grants. FY 94 est $48,789,648.

ELIGIBILITY REQUIREMENTS: Applications are only accepted after the publication of a request for proposal through a Federal Register Announcement. Eligible entities include: (1) a Head Start agency; (2) an agency that is eligible to be designated as a Head Start agency under Section 641 of the Head Start Act; (3) a community based organization as defined under Section 4 (5) of the Job Training Partnership Act (29 U.S.C. 1303(5); (4) an institution of higher education as defined under Section 1201 (a) of the Higher Education Act of 1965 (20 U.S.C. 11411); (5) a public hospital as defined under 42 U.S.C. 2910(c); (6) a community development corporation as defined under Section 681 (a)(2)(A) of the Community Services Block Grant Act (42 U.S.C. 9910 (a)(2)(A)); or (7) a public or private nonprofit agency or organization specializing in delivering social services to infants or young children (i.e., toddlers and pre-schoolers).

INFORMATION CONTACTS: Allen Smith, Administration for Children and Families, P.O. Box 1182, Washington, DC 20013. Telephone: (202) 205-8566.

CHILD ABUSE AND NEGLECT DISCRETIONARY ACTIVITIES - 93.670

OBJECTIVES: To improve the national, state, community and family activities for the prevention, identification, and treatment of child abuse and neglect through research, demonstration service improvement, information dissemination, and technical assistance. A specific portion of funds each year is made available for projects in the area of child sexual abuse.

TYPES OF ASSISTANCE: Project Grants (Contracts). FY 94 est $16,227,239.

ELIGIBILITY REQUIREMENTS: Grants: State, local governments, nonprofit institutions and organizations engaged in activities related to the prevention, identification, and treatment of child abuse and neglect. Contracts: Public and private agencies.

INFORMATION CONTACTS: Director, National Center on Child Abuse and Neglect (NCCAN), P.O. Box 1182, Washington, DC 20013. Telephone: (202) 205-8586.

RESEARCH FOR MOTHERS AND CHILDREN - 93.865

OBJECTIVES: To stimulate, coordinate, and support fundamental and clinical, biomedical, and behavioral research and research training associated with normal development from conception to maturity and those factors or special health problems that may delay or interfere with normal development. The Center for Research for Mothers and Children (CRMC) supports research for mothers, children, and families, and is designed to: (1) advance knowledge about fetal development, pregnancy, and birth; (2) identify the prerequisites of optimal growth and development through infancy, childhood, and adolescence; and (3) contribute to the prevention and treatment of mental retardation, developmental disabilities, and other childhood and adolescent problems. Small Business Innovation Research (SBIR): to stimulate technological innovation; to use small business to meet Federal research and development needs; to increase private sector commercialization of innovations derived from Federal research and development; and to foster and encourage participation by minority and disadvantaged persons in technological innovation. Small Instrumentation Program: To support the purchase of relatively low-cost pieces of research equipment that generally are not funded in research project grants and which also do not qualify for support under the National Institutes of Health's (NIH) larger shared instrumentation program.

TYPES OF ASSISTANCE: Project Grants. FY 94 est $233,741,000. ELIGIBILITY REQUIREMENTS: Grants: Universities, colleges, medical, dental and nursing schools, schools of public health, laboratories, hospitals, state and local health departments, other public or private institutions, both nonprofit and for-profit, and individuals. National Research Service Award: Support is provided for academic and research training only, in health and health-related areas which are periodically specified by the National Institutes of Health. Individuals with a professional or scientific degree are eligible (M.D., Ph.D., D.D.S., D.O., D.V.M., Sc.D., D.Eng., or equivalent domestic or foreign degree). Predoctoral research training grants to institutions are also supported. Proposed study must result in biomedical or behavioral research training in a specified shortage area and which may offer opportunity to research health scientists, research clinicians, etc., to broaden their scientific background or to extend their potential for research in health-related areas. Applicants must be citizens of the United States or be admitted to the United States for permanent residency; they also must be nominated and sponsored by a public or private institution having staff and facilities suitable to the proposed research training. Domestic nonprofit organizations may apply for the institutional NRS grant. SBIR: SBIR grants can be awarded only to domestic small businesses (entities that are independently owned and operated for profit, are not dominant in the field in which research is proposed, and have no more than 500 employees). Primary employment (more than one-half time) of the principal investigator must be with the small business at the time of award and during the conduct of the proposed project. In both Phase I and Phase II, the research must be performed in the U.S. or its possessions. To be eligible for funding, a grant application must be approved for scientific merit and program relevance by a scientific review group and a national advisory council. Small Instrumentation Grants Program: Eligible institutions or institutional components are those domestic, nonprofit organizations that: (1) received at least three NIH research grants totaling at least $200,000 but not exceeding $2,924,000 in the previous fiscal year, and (2) have active NIH research grant support. Only those organizations or organizational components receiving a letter of invitation to apply from the NIH are eligible for this program. Only one application may be submitted by each eligible organization or organizational component.

INFORMATION CONTACTS: Program

Contact: Ms. Hildegard P. Topper, National Institute of Child Health and Human Development, National Institutes of Health, Public Health Service, Department of Health and Human Services, Building 31, Room 2A04, Bethesda, MD 20892. Telephone: (301) 496-1848. Grants Management Contact: Donald E. Clark, Chief, Office of Grants and Contracts, National Institute of Child Health and Human Development, National Institutes of Health, Public Health Service, Department of Health and Human Services, Executive Plaza North, Rockville, MD 20892. Telephone: (301) 496-5001. (Use same numbers for FTS.)

COOPERATIVE AGREEMENTS TO SUPPORT SCHOOL HEALTH EDUCATION TO PREVENT THE SPREAD OF ACQUIRED IMMUNODEFICIENCY SYNDROME - 93.938

OBJECTIVES: To support the development and implementation of effective health education for human immunodeficiency virus (HIV) and other important health problems for school-age populations (elementary through college-age youth, parents, and relevant school, health, and education personnel).

TYPES OF ASSISTANCE: Project Grants (Cooperative Agreements). FY 94 est $28,654,000.

ELIGIBILITY REQUIREMENTS: Eligible applicants are official State health and education agencies (SEA) in States and territories of the United States (including the District of Columbia, the Commonwealth of Puerto Rico, the Virgin Islands, and Guam), nonprofit organizations, and universities.

INFORMATION CONTACTS: Program Contact: Mr. Peter Cortace, Program Development and Services Branch, Division of Adolescent and School Health, National Center for Chronic Disease Prevention and Health Promotion, Centers for Disease Control and Prevention, Public Health Service, Department of Health and Human Services, 4770 Burford Highway, Mailstop K31, Atlanta, Georgia 30333. Telephone: (404) 488-5365. Grants Management Contact for State and Local Programs: Mr. Edwin Lin Dixon, Grants Management Officer, Grants Management Branch, Procurement and Grants Office, Centers for Disease Control, Public Health Service, Department of Health and Human Services, 255 E. Paces Ferry Road, NE., Mailstop E-15, Atlanta, GA 30333. Telephone: (404) 842-6508 or FTS 236-6508. Grants Management Contact for National, Private Sector Organizations: Ms. Clara Jenkins, Grants Management Officer, Grants Management Branch, Procurement and Grants Office, Centers for Disease Control, Public Health Service, Department of Health and Human Services, 255 E. Pace Ferry Road, NE., Mailstop E-15, Atlanta, GA 30305. Telephone: (404) 842-6575.

NATIONAL AWARDS

The following is a list of national awards given to recognize and honor those people involved in the creation, production, and promotion of outstanding children's media.

JANE ADDAMS CHILDREN'S BOOK AWARD

Women's International League for Peace and Freedom & the Jane Addams Peace Association
777 UN Plaza, New York, NY 10017
212-682-8830

Recognizes: The author of a book of the preceding year that most effectively promotes peace, social justice, world community & the equality of the sexes and all races
Announced: Annually on Jane Addams' birthday, September 6, usually in Baltimore
Prize: Hand-illuminated scroll & silver book seal; honor scrolls are also awarded

AMERICAN ASSOCIATION OF SCHOOL LIBRARIANS DISTINGUISHED SERVICE AWARD

American Association of School Librarians & Baker & Taylor
50 E. Huron St., Chicago, IL 60611
312-944-6780
Awards Prgm Asst: Marie-Louise Settem

Recognizes: A member of the library profession who has made an outstanding national or international contribution to school librarianship and school library development
Announced: Annually at the American Library Association conference
Prize: $2000

HANS CHRISTIAN ANDERSEN AWARDS

International Board on Books for Young People (IBBY)

Recognizes: Every 2 years, an author and an illustrator, living at the time of nomination, who are judged to have made a lasting contribution of outstanding value to literature for children and young people

MILDRED L. BATCHELDER AWARD

American Library Association; Association for Library Service to Children

50 E. Huron St., Chicago, IL 60611-2795
312-280-2163, 800-545-2433 Ext. 2163, 312-440-9374; TELEX 4909992082 ALA UI

Recognizes: An American publisher for translating an outstanding children's book into English.
Announced: In January at the ALA Midwinter Meeting
Prize: Citation

THE L. FRANK BAUM MEMORIAL AWARD

The International Wizard of Oz Club., Inc., Box 95, Kinderhook, IL 62345

Recognizes: A person making an outstanding contribution to the saga of Oz in writing, illustrating, research, editing, & club activities.
Announced: Third weekend in June at the Ozmopolitan Convention
Prize: Plaque

IRMA S. AND JAMES H. BLACK BOOK AWARD

Bank Street College of Education
610 W. 112th St., New York, NY 10025
212-875-4452
Librarian: Linda Greengrass

Recognizes: An outstanding book for young children, published during the previous year, which combines excellence in story-line, language & illustration.
Announced: Annually in spring
Prize: Scroll & book seal

BOSTON GLOBE-HORN BOOK AWARD

Boston Globe Newspaper & Horn Book Magazine
Morrisey Blvd., Boston, MA 02107
617-929-2000

Recognizes: Outstanding authors and illustrators of quality books for children
Announced: In September at the New England Library Association's annual meeting
Prize: Honor books in each of three categories

CBC HONORS PROGRAM

The Children's Book Council
568 Broadway, Ste. 404, New York, NY 10012
212-966-1990
Pres: Paula Quint

Recognizes: A person whose work in communications, over a sustained period of time, warrants special recognition
Announced: Occasionally
Prize: Commemorative momento

CALDECOTT MEDAL

American Library Association; Association for Library Service to Children
50 E. Huron St., Chicago, IL 60611-2795
312-280-2163, 800-545-2433 Ext. 2163
Exec Dir: Susan Roman

Recognizes: The artist of the most distinguished American children's picture book during the preceding year
Announced: At the annual ALA Midwinter Meeting
Prize: Medal & book seal

THE CARNEGIE AWARD

American Library Association; Association for Library Service to Children
50 E. Huron St., Chicago, IL 60611-2795
312-280-2163; 800-545-2433 Ext. 2163

Recognizes: An American producer for the outstanding video production of the previous calendar year
Announced: At the Newbery/Caldecott press conference during the ALA Midwinter Meeting
Prize: A medal to be awarded in June during the ALA Annual Conference

CHILDREN'S BOOK AWARD

International Reading Association
800 Barksdale Rd., Newark, DE 19711
Exec Dir: Alan E. Farstrup

Recognizes: A new author (first or second book) of promise
Announced: Annually, in May
Prize: $1000

CHILDREN'S READING ROUND TABLE AWARD

Children's Reading Round Table of Chicago
2045 N. Seminary Ave., Chicago, IL 60614
Contact person: Diana Myers

Recognizes: Long-term contributions to children's books, honoring either authors, illustrators, book reviewers, professors of children's literature, librarians and/or editors
Announced: Annually in October
Prize: Scroll, check from CRRT Award Fund

THE CHRISTOPHER AWARDS

The Christophers
12 E. 48th St., New York, NY 10017
212-759-4050
Award Coord: Peggy Flanagan
Asst. Coord: Mary Jeanne Mazzoni

Recognizes: Producers, directors & writers of TV specials, full-length motion pictures and books for children & adults who reflect the highest human & spiritual values
Prize: Bronze medallion

MARGARET A. EDWARDS AWARD

(formerly the YASD/SLJ Author Achievement Award)
American Library Association, Young Adult Services Division, & Association for Library Service to Children
50 E. Huron St., Chicago, IL 60611-2795

Recognizes: An author whose work has been taken to heart by young adults over a period of years & provides an "authentic voice that continues to illuminate their experiences & emotions, giving insight into their lives"
Presented: During ALA Annual Conference
Prize: Citation & $1000

EMMY AWARDS

Academy of Television Arts & Sciences
5220 Lankershim, North Hollywood, CA 91601
818-953-7575
Exec Dir: James Loper
Children's Prog Spec: John Leverence

Recognizes: Outstanding achievement in television
Announced: Annually in the fall
Prize: Statuette

GOLDEN HEART

Romance Writers of America
13700 Veterans Memorial Dr., Ste. 315, Houston, TX 77014
713-440-6885
Office Supervisor: Linda Fisher
Recognizes: The author of the best un published manuscript for young adult romance
Announced: Annually at the summer conference
Prize: Golden Heart Medallion

CORETTA SCOTT KING AWARDS

American Library Association, Social Responsibilities Round Table, & Coretta Scott King Task Force
50 E. Huron St., Chicago, IL 60611-2795

Recognizes: Outstanding books by African-American authors & illustrators whose works promote an understanding & appreciation of all cultures
Prize: Framed citation, honorarium of $250, set of Encylopaedia Britannica or World Book encyclopaedias

GOLDEN KITE AWARD

Society of Children's Book Writers and Illustrators
22736 Vanowon St., Ste. 106, West Hills, CA 91307
Exec Dir: Lin Oliver

Recognizes: The most outstanding children's books written and illustrated during the year by the Society of Children's Book Writers and Illustrators
Announced: April 15
Prize: Three statuettes & three honor book plaques

EVA L. GORDON AWARD FOR CHILDREN'S SCIENCE LITERATURE

American Nature Study Society
231 Wildwood, Ann Arbor, MI 48103
Awards Chr: Janet Naher-Snowden, 541 Tamaimi Tail, Akron, OH 44303

Recognizes: An author of children's science books of outstanding quality
Announced: At ANSS meeting in the spring
Prize: Certificate

GRAMMY

National Academy of Recording Arts & Sciences
303 N. Glenoaks Blvd., Burbank, CA 91502
231-849-1313
Exec Dir: Christine M. Farnon

Recognizes: The producer, featured artist(s), or individual rendering the greatest creative contribution to the best children's recording of the year
Announced: Annually in mid-winter in Los Angeles
Prize: Statuette

UNICEF-EZRA JACK KEATS INTERNATIONAL AWARD FOR EXCELLENCE IN CHILDREN'S BOOK ILLUSTRATION

Ezra Jack Keats Foundation & UNICEF Greeting Cards Operation
UNICEF House, 3 United Nations Plaza, New York, NY 10017

Recognizes: Illustrators new to children's books (no more than five published books)
Prize: $5000 & silver medal

NATIONAL JEWISH BOOK AWARD FOR CHILDREN'S LITERATURE

Jewish Book Council
15 E. 26th St., New York, NY 10010
212-532-4949
Exec Dir: Paula Gribetz Gottlieb
Children's Prog Spec: Marcia W. Posner

Recognizes: Authors of Jewish children's books
Announced: Annually, late spring
Prize: $750 & a certificate

NATIONAL JEWISH BOOK AWARD FOR ILLUSTRATED CHILDREN'S BOOKS

Jewish Book Council
15 E. 26th St., New York, NY 10010
212-532-4949
Exec Dir: Paula Gribetz Gottlieb
Children's Prog Spec: Marcia W. Posner

Recognizes: Illustrators of high quality Jewish children's books
Announced: Annually, late spring
Prize: $750 & a certificate

NEWBERY MEDAL

American Library Association, Association for Library Service to Children
50 E. Huron St., Chicago, IL 60611
312-944-6780
Exec Dir: Susan Roman

Recognizes: The most distinguished contribution to American literature for children during preceding year
Announced: At annual ALA Midwinter Meeting
Prize: Medal

SCOTT O'DELL AWARD FOR HISTORICAL FICTION

100 E. 57th St., Chicago, IL 60637
312-752-7880
Awards Chr: Zena Sutherland

Recognizes: Both new & established authors who create historical fiction for children & young people
Prize: $5000

ORBIS PICTUS AWARD

National Council of Teachers of English (NCTE)

1111 Kenyon Rd., Urbana, IL 61801
217-328-3870

Recognizes: Outstanding nonfiction for children.

HELEN KEATING OTT AWARD FOR OUTSTANDING CONTRIBUTION TO CHILDREN'S LITERATURE

Church & Synagogue Library Association
Box 19357, Portland, OR 97280

Recognizes: A person or organization for a significant contribution to high moral and ethical values in children's literature
Announced: Annually at conference held in different cities each year in June

LUCILE MICHEELS PANNELL AWARD

Sponsored by Women's National Book Association
c/o Children's Book Council, 568 Broadway, Ste. 404, New York, NY 10012
212-966-1990; Fax: 212-966-2073
Pannell Award Coord: Allan Marshall

Recognizes: A bookseller's creative efforts to bring children & books together
Announced: At the American Booksellers Association Convention
Prize: $2500 and an original children's book illustration to each winner

THE PHOENIX AWARD

Children's Literature Association
Box 138, Battle Creek, MI 49016
Contact: Marianne Gessner

Recognizes: Works of merit published 20 years ago that were not honored then
Announced: Annually at May conference
Prize: Brass statue

SCIENCE-WRITING AWARD IN PHYSICS & ASTRONOMY FOR ARTICLES OR BOOKS INTENDED FOR CHILDREN

American Institue of Physics
335 E. 45th St., New York, NY 10017
212-661-9404

Recognizes: Distinguished writing that improves children's understanding and appreciation of physics & astronomy
Prize: $3000, certificate, inscribed Windsor chair

EDGAR ALLAN POE AWARD

Mystery Writers of America
236 W. 27th St., New York, NY 10001
212-888-8171

Recognizes: The best juvenile or young adult mystery of the preceding year
Announced: In the spring (submissions deadline December 1)
Prize: Ceramic bust of Edgar Allan Poe, nominees receive scrolls

REGINA MEDAL

Catholic Library Association
St. Mary's College of Minnesota, 700 Terrace Heights, Winona, MN 55987-1399

Recognizes: A lifetime dedication to children's literature
Announced: Annually on February 1
Prize: Silver Medal

RITA AWARD

Romance Writers of America
13700 Veterans Memorial Dr., Ste. 315, Houston, TX 77014
713-440-6885
Office Supervisor: Linda Fisher

Recognizes: The author of the best published young adult romance
Announced: Annually at the summer conference
Prize: Rita Statuette

SYDNEY TAYLOR MANUSCRIPT AWARD CONTEST

15 Goldsmith St., Providence, RI 02906
c/o Lillian Schwartz

Recognizes: The author of the best manuscript of a children's book for ages 8 to 11 by an unpublished author
Announced: Annually at the June AJL convention
Prize: $1000

THE WASHINGTON POST/CHILDREN'S BOOK GUILD NONFICTION AWARD

4405 W St., NW, Washington, DC 23185-1626

Recognizes: A body of work in children's nonfiction
Announced: Annually in November at the Children's Book Week luncheon in Washington, DC
Prize: Monetary award & crystal cube

LAURA INGALLS WILDER MEDAL

Association for Library Service to Children, American Library Association
50 E. Huron St., Chicago, IL 60611
312-944-6780

Recognizes: A US author or illustrator whose books have made a substantial contribution to children's literature over a period of years (given every three years)

Announced: During American Library Association's mid-winter conference & presented at the annual conference in the summer
Prize: Citation

PAUL A. WITTY SHORT STORY AWARD

International Reading Association
800 Barksdale Rd., Box 8139, Newark, DE 19714-8139

Recognizes: The author of an original short story published for the first time during the previous year which encourages young readers to read periodicals

WRANGLER AWARD (WESTERN HERITAGE AWARDS PROGRAM)

National Cowboy Hall of Fame
1700 NE 63rd St., Oklahoma City, OK 73111
405-478-2250
Exec Dir: Byron Price
Children's Prog Spec: Ms. M.J. Van Deventer, Dir of Publications

Recognizes: Authors who tell the great stories of the West & organizations and individuals who have made outstanding contributions to Western heritage
Announced: Annually in April at the Cowboy Hall of Fame
Prize: Bronze replicas of a Charles M. Russell sculpture

YOUNG PEOPLES'S LITERATURE AWARDS

Friends of American Writers
3000 N. Sheridan Rd, Apt. 6A, Chicago, IL 60657
Chr: Mrs. Ruth B. Wiener

Recognizes: An author who has lived in or lives in or whose story takes place in Arkansas, Illinois, Indiana, Iowa, Kansas, Kentucky, Michigan, Minnesota, Mississippi, North Dakota, Nebraska, Ohio, Oklahoma, South Dakota, Tennessee, or Wisconsin
Announced: Annually in spring in Chicago
Prize: $500 and certificate of merit

YOUNG READER'S CHOICE AWARD

Pacific Northwest Library Conference
Graduate School of Library & Information Science
FM-30, University of Washington, Seattle, WA 98195

Recognizes: An elementary & senior high list of outstanding books chosen by children of Pacific Northwest States
Announced: Annually at the April WLA convention

STATE AWARDS

The following state awards recognize outstanding children's books and other children's media as well as media facilitators. Many of these honors are voted on by the children themselves.

ARKANSAS

CHARLIE MAY SIMON CHILDREN'S BOOK AWARD

Arkansas Elementary School Council
Arkansas Dept. of Educ., 4 State Capitol Mall, Room 302-B, Little Rock, AR 72201
501-682-4371
Sec/Treas: James A. Hester
AESC Chair: Dr. Carol Snelson

Recognizes: Reading encouragement in grades 4 to 6
Announced: In April
Prize: Medallion
First runner-up prize: Honor trophy

CALIFORNIA

COMMONWEALTH CLUB SILVER BOOK AWARD - JUVENILE CATEGORY

The Commonwealth Club of California
595 Market St., San Francisco, CA 94105
415-597-6700
Exec Dir: James D. Rosenthal

Recognizes: California authors
Announced: In June in San Francisco
Prize: Silver medal

FLORIDA

SUNSHINE STATE YOUNG READER'S AWARD

Co-sponsored by the Florida Association for Media in Educ. and the School Library Media Service Office, Florida Dept. of Educ.
FAME, Box 13119, Tallahassee, FL 32317
305-671-4746
Dept. of Educ., 522 Florida Educ. Center, Tallahassee, FL 32399
904-488-8184

Recognizes: Quality literature for young readers and reading for pleasure
Announced: In the spring
Prize: Specially designed book ends and seal for books

GEORGIA

GEORGIA CHILDREN'S BOOK AWARD

College of Education, University of Georgia
125 Aderhold, Athens, GA 30602

404-542-4520
Exec Dir: Carol J. Fisher

Announced: Annually in May at the Georgia Center for Continuing Education

HAWAII

NENE BOOK AWARD

Hawaii Association of School Librarians, Hawaii Library Association, Children's Section
Box 23019, Honolulu, HI 96822

Recognizes: The best book of fiction suitable for grades 4 to 6
Announced: During National Library Week at the spring meeting of HASL
Prize: Carved Koa wood platter

ILLINOIS

CARL SANDBURG LITERARY ARTS AWARD

Friends of the Chicago Public Library
400 S. State St., 9S-7, Chicago, IL 60605
312-747-4907

Recognizes: Outstanding achievement in literature for children by a Chicago author
Announced: In the fall at the Literary Arts Ball
Prize: $1000

INDIANA

YOUNG HOOSIER BOOK AWARD

Association for Indiana Media Educators
1908 E. 64th, South Dr., Indianapolis, IN 46220-2104
317-257-8558
Children's Prog Spec: Dr. Karen G. Burch

Recognizes: The importance of recreational reading by kindergarten, upper elementary, & junior high school children and encourages cooperation among administrators, schol media specialists, & teachers in broadening the reading program
Announced: In the spring at AIME conference

Prize: Plaques for each winner in four categories—Picture Book, K-3, grades 4-6, and 6 to 8

IOWA

IOWA CHILDREN'S CHOICE AWARD

Iowa Educational Media Association
2306 Sixth, Harlan, IA 51537
Exec Sec: Paula Behrendt

Recognizes: Outstanding authors, and promotes an avenue for communication between children, teachers, and parents
Prize: Engraved school bell

IOWA TEEN AWARD

Iowa Educational Media Association
2306 Sixth, Harlan, IA 51537
Exec Sec: Paula Brehrendt

Recognizes: The favorite author of students in grades 6 to 9
Announced: Annually on April 1
Prize: Brass apple

KANSAS

WILLIAM ALLEN WHITE CHILDREN'S BOOK AWARD

Emporia State University, Emporia, KS 66801
316-341-5208
Exec Dir: Henry R. Stewart

Recognizes: In the memory of one of the state's most distinguished citizens encouragment of children of Kansas to read and enjoy good books
Announced: Annually after April 1 at the William Allen White Library at ESU
Prize: Bronze medal

KENTUCKY

KENTUCKY BLUEGRASS AWARD

Northern Kentucky University, Learning Resource Center, 268 BEP, Highland, KY 41099
606-572-5439
Exec Dir: Jennifer Smith

Recognizes: A favorite book selected from a list of recently published titles and chosen by Kentucky children in grades K to 8
Announced: Annually in March;

presented to author at KBA Conference on Children's Literature
Prize: Certificate

LOUISIANA

SUE HEFLEY EDUCATOR OF THE YEAR AWARD
Louisiana Association of School Librarians
Box 3058, Baton Rouge, LA 70821

Recognizes: An outstanding school librarian in Louisiana
Announced: Annually, if merited
Prize: Engraved plaque

MARYLAND

MARYLAND SCHOOL FILM FESTIVAL
Maryland Educational Media Organization & Maryland State Department of Educ.
Box 21127, Baltimore, MD 21228
301-744-0915

Recognizes: Student media production skills
Announced: In May
Prize: Certificate

MINNESOTA

KERLAN AWARD
University of Minnesota
109 Walter Library, Minneapolis, MN 55455
612-624-4576
Exec Dir & Children's Prog Spec.: Karen Nelson Hoyle

Recognizes: Singular attainments in children's literature and in appreciation for a generous donation of unique resources to the Kerlan Collection for the study of children's literature
Announced: Annually in April
Prize: Plaque

MAUD HART LOVELACE AWARD
Youth Reading Awards, Inc.
Frank White Elementary Library, Huntsinger Ave.,Park Rapids, MN 56470
218-732-3333 Ext. 206
Contact: Leann Hess

Recognizes: A contribution to children's literature in grades 3 to 8
Announced: Annually in April
Prize: Plaque

MILKWEED PRIZE FOR CHILDREN'S LITERATURE
Milkweed Prize for Children's Literature
430 First Ave. N., Ste. 400, Minneapolis, MN 55401-1743

Recognizes: Excellence in literature for children in the middle grades
Prize: Publication by Milkweed Editions, $3,000

MISSISSIPPI

THE UNIVERSITY OF SOUTHERN MISSISSIPPI CHILDREN'S BOOK FESTIVAL MEDALLION
School of Library Science, Southern Station, Box 5146, Hattiesburg, MS 39406-5146
601-266-4228
Dir: Onva Boshears

Recognizes: An outstanding author and/or artist for contributions to children's literature
Announced: Annually in March at the Children's Book Festival, University of Southern Mississippi
Prize: Silver Medallion

MISSOURI

THE MARK TWAIN AWARD
Missouri Association of School Librarians
5552 S. Kinghighway, St. Louis, MO 63109-3258
314-352-1958

Recognizes: Books chosen for their quality & potential popularity with Missouri's 4th to 8th graders
Announced: Annually in April at the spring MASL conference
Prize: Bronze bust of Mark Twain sculpted by Barbar Shanklin

NEBRASKA

THE GOLDEN SOWER: NEBRASKA CHILDREN'S BOOK AWARD
Nebraska Library Association
Henzlik Hall, University of Nebraska, Lincoln, NE 68588-0355
402-472-2231

Recognizes: A work chosen for its popularity with state's children
Announced: Annually
Prize: Plaque

NEW JERSEY

GARDEN STATE CHILDREN'S BOOK AWARD
New Jersey Library Association
Box 1534, Trenton, NJ 08067

Recognizes: Books for early & middle grades on basis of literary merit & popularity with readers. Three categories: easy-to-read, fiction (Gr: 2-5), nonfiction (Gr: 2-5). Awards to

authors & illustrators.
Announced: At Spring Conference of NJLA

NEW JERSEY AUTHOR AWARD
New Jersey Institute of Technology, Alumni Association, 323 King, Newark, NJ 07102
201-596-3441
Exec Dir: Herman A. Estrin

Recognizes: New Jersey children's book authors
Announced: Annually at the NJIT Student Center, New Jersey Institute of Technology, Newark
Prize: Citation and luncheon

NEW YORK

EMPIRE STATE AWARD FOR EXCELLENCE IN LITERATURE FOR YOUNG PEOPLE
New York Library Association
Youth Services Section
252 Hudson Ave., Albany, NY 11210

Recognizes: A body of work that represents excellence in Children's or Young Adult literature and has made a significant contribution to literature for young people
Announced: During the NYLA Annual Conference

PIED PIPER AWARD
New York Library Association
Youth Services Section
252 Hudson Ave., Albany, NY 12210
518-432-6952
Exec Dir: Nancy Lian

Recognizes: Excellence in printed materials furthering library services to youth in, by, or for a New York state library
Announced: Annually in the fall at NYLA conference
Prize: Certificate and token of recognition

WOODWARD PARK SCHOOL ANNUAL BOOK AWARD
Woodward Park School, 50 Prospect Park W., Brooklyn, NY 11215
718-768-1103
Children's Prog Spec: Beth Schneider

Recognzies: Author who makes children critically aware of human relations through literature
Announced: Annually in October
Prize: Monetary contribution to a children's organization of the author's choice

NORTH CAROLINA

ANNETTE LEWIS PHINAZEE AWARD
School of Library & Information
  Sciences
North Carolina Central University,
  Durham, NC 27707
919-560-6485
Exec Dir: Benjamin F. Speller

Recognizes: A North Carolina librarian
  who has made a significant contribution to promoting the use of black
  children's literature
Announced: Biannually during the
  Charlemae Hill Rollins Colloquium in
  Durham
Prize: Monetary award, medal and engraved plaque housed in the library
  school

NORTH DAKOTA

**FLICKER TALE CHILDREN'S BOOK
  AWARD**
Youth Services Section/North Dakota
  Library Association
515 North Fifth St., Bismarck, ND
  58501
701-222-6410
Pres: Jan Hendrickson (changes yearly)

Recognizes: The author of North Dakota childrens' favorite book
Announced: Annually in April. Authors
  invited to NDLA conference to
  receive award from classrooms of local children
Prize: State plaque

OHIO

BUCKEYE CHILDREN'S BOOK AWARD
State Library of Ohio, 65 S. Front St.,
  Columbus, OH 43266-0334
614-644-6906
Awards Consultant: Floyd C. Dickman

Recognizes: Outstanding recent children's books, thereby encouraging
  critical reading of literature and
  promoting teacher/librarian involvement in children's reading programs
Announced: Biannually in April
Prize: Certificate in three categories:
  grades K to 2, 3 to 5, and 6 to 8

OHIOANA BOOK AWARD
Ohioana Library Association, 1105
  Ohio Depts. Bldg., 65 S. Front St.,
  Columbus, OH 43266-0334
614-466-3831

Publicizes books by Ohioans or about
  Ohio. Those born in Ohio or who
  have lived there for at least 5 years
  are eligible. Five awards are given
  each year for children's and adult
  books.

Announced: In the fall at the annual
  meeting of the association
Prize: Certificates and art glass

OKLAHOMA

**SEQUOYAH CHILDREN'S BOOK
  AWARD**
Oklahoma Library Association, 300
  Hardy Dr., Edmond, OK 73034
405-348-0506

Recognizes: Reading & interest in
  books by encouraging children in
  grades 3 to 6 to vote for their
  favorite title.

OREGON

EVELYN SIBLEY LAMPMAN AWARD
Children's Services Division, Oregon
  Library Association
Coos Bay Public Library, 525 N.
  Anderson, Coos Bay, OR 97420
503-269-1101
Pres: Brian Bond

Recognizes: An individual's contribu-
  tion to the children of Oregon and
  the Pacific Northwest in the fields of
  literature, library service
Announced: At the Oregon Library
  Association spring conference in
  April
Prize: Plaque

PENNSYLVANIA

DREXEL CITATION
Drexel College of Information
  Studies & The Free Library of
  Philadelphia
Drexel University, Philadelphia, PA
  19104
215-895-2447
Exec Dir: Dr. Shelley G. McNamara

Recognizes: Authors, illustrators, publishers or others who have made
  outstanding contributions to the field
  of children's literature for the children of Philadelphia
Announced: In advance of the annual conference about children's
  literature co-sponsored by the
  library and university in Philadelphia
Prize: Hand-lettered and illustrated citation

**OUTSTANDING PENNSYLVANIA
  AUTHOR AWARD**
Pennsylvania School Librarians
  Association
c/o Susan Wolfe, 1201 Yverdon Dr.
  A7, Camp Hill, PA 17011

Recognizes: An author living in or writing about Pennsylvania

Announced: At the annual conference
Prize: Certificate

**PLEASE TOUCH MUSEUM BOOK
  AWARD**
Please Touch Museum
210 N. 21st St., Philadelphia, PA
  19103
215-963-0067
Exec Dir: Nancy D. Kolb

Recognizes: An outstanding concept
  book for young children by a first
  time American author
Announced: Annually in the fall
Prize: Framed certificate

SOUTH CAROLINA

CHILDREN'S BOOK AWARD
South Carolina Association of School
  Librarians
Box 2442, Columbia, SC 29202
803-796-8427

Recognizes: The author of an out-
  standing children's book (grades 3-6)
Announced: In April in Greenville, SC
Prize: Medal

JUNIOR BOOK AWARD
South Carolina Association of School
  Librarians, Box 2442, Columbia, SC
  29202
803-796-8427

Recognizes: The author of an outstanding book for young adults
  (grades 6-9)
Announced: Annually in the spring
Prize: Medal

YOUNG ADULT BOOK AWARD
South Carolina Association of School
  Librarians, Box 2442, Columbia, SC
  29202
803-796-8427

Recognizes: The author of an outstanding book for young adults
  (grades 9-12)
Announced: Annually in the spring
Prize: Medal

SOUTH DAKOTA

**PRAIRIE PASQUE CHILDREN'S BOOK
  AWARD**
South Dakota Library Association
800 Governor's Dr., Pierre, SD 57501

Recognizes: Reading and interest in
  books by encouraging children in
  grade 4 to 6 to vote for their
  favorite title.

TEXAS

TEXAS BLUEBONNET AWARD
Texas Library Association, Texas

Association of School Libraries,
Children's Round Table
3355 Bee Cave Rd., Ste. 401, Austin,
TX 78746
512-328-1518
Exec Dir: Patricia Smith
TBA Coord: Christina Woll

Recognizes: Reading and interest in
books by encouraging children in
grades 3 to 6 to vote for their
favorite title
Announced: Annually in April at the
TLA annual conference
Prize: Desk ornament

VERMONT

DOROTHY CANFIELD FISHER AWARD
Vermont Congress of Parents &
Teachers/Vermont Department of
Libraries
138 Main St., Montpelier, VT 05602

Recognizes: Enthusiastic and dis-
criminating readers who honor the
ideals of Dorothy Canfield Fisher
Announced: Annually in late spring
Prize: Illuminated scroll

WASHINGTON

WASHINGTON CHILDREN'S CHOICE PICTURE BOOK AWARD
WCCPBA, Box 1413, Bothell, WA
98041
Coord: Rebecca Miller

Recognizes: Outstanding picture books
chosen by children in grades K-3
Announced: Annually in April at the
WLA annual conference

WISCONSIN

GOLDEN ARCHER AWARD
Dept. of Library & Learning Resources
University of Wisconsin-Oshkosh
Oshkosh, WI 54901

Recognizes: A fiction of nonfiction title
chosen by children of Wisconsin in
grades 4 through 8
Announced: Annually in the spring
Prize: Hand-crafted bronze medal &
certificate

LITTLE ARCHER AWARD
Dept. of Library & Learning Resources

University of Wisconsin-Oshkosh
Oshkosh, WI 54901

Recognizes: A title chosen by children
of Wisconsin in grades K to 3
Announced: Annually in the spring
Prize: Hand-crafted bronze medal

ELIZABETH BURR AWARD
Children's Book Award Committee,
Wisconsin Library Association, 4785
Hayes Rd., Madison, WI 53704

Recognizes: Distinguished achievement in children's literature

WYOMING

INDIAN PAINTBRUSH BOOK AWARD
Wyoming Library Association
Box 1387, Cheyenne, WY 82003

Recognizes: An author whose book
was voted best by 4th to 6th grade
students statewide
Announced: In the spring; presented at
WLA fall convention

1995

February

3-9   Philadelphia, PA. Midwinter Annual Conference. **American Library Association**

7-11   Austin, TX. 15th Annual State Conference. **Texas Computer Education Association (TCEA)**

8-12   Anaheim, CA. **Association for Educational Communications & Technology**

8-12   Atlanta, GA. **Music Library Association**

10-13   New Orleans, LA. Annual Convention. **American Association of School Administrators (AASA)**

16-18   Colorado Springs, CO. Annual Conference. **Colorado Educational Media Association. (CEMA)**

22-24   Myrtly Beach, SC. **South Carolina Library Association**

23-26   Philadelphia, PA. National Convention. **National Science Teachers Association (NTSA)**

25-26   Louisville, KY. Annual Spring Conference. **Kentucky Council of Teachers of English/Language Arts**

March

3-5   Traverse City, MI. Winter Conference. **Michigan Association for Media in Education (MAME)**

7-10   Lafayette, LA. Annual Conference. **Louisiana Library Association**

8-11   Washington, DC. National Convention. **American Choral Directors Association**

10-14   Juneau, AK. Annual Conference. **Alaska Library Association**

12   National Girl Scout Birthday. **Girl Scouts of the USA**

15-18   Salt Lake City, UT. Annual Conference. **Utah Library Association**

March 1995

16-18   Indianapolis, IN. Annual Conference. **Association for Indiana Media Educators (AIME)**

22-24   Topeka, KS. Kansas Triconference: **Kansas Library Association, Kansas Association for Educational Communications & Technology, Kansas Association of School Librarians**

24-25   Oahu, HI. **Hawaii Library Association.**

27-30   Cincinnati, OH. **Catholic Library Association** (joint with National Catholic Education Association)

27-
April 1   Orlando, FL. **Southern Association for Children Under Six (SACUS)**

April

4-8   Dallas, TX. Conference. **Texas Library Association (TLA)**

5-8   Spokane, WA. **Idaho Library Association** (joint with **Washington Library Association**)

5-9   Indianapolis, IN. Annual Convention. **Council for Exceptional Children (CEC)**

6-9   Boston, MA. 73rd Annual Meeting. **National Council of Teachers of Mathematics (NCTM)**

8-12   San Diego, CA. **National Association of Elementary School Principals**

9-15   National Library Week. **American Library Association (ALA)**

11-12   Cromwell, CT. **Connecticut Library Association**

20-23   Portland, OR. National Conference. **Young Audiences**

22   Nat'l Girl Scout Leader's Day. **Girl Scouts of the USA**

25-28   Indianapolis, IN. **Indiana Library Federation**

26-28   Auburn, AL. **Alabama Library Association.**

April 1995

26-29   Billings, MT. **Montana Library Association**

26-29   Tulsa, OK. **Oklahoma Library Association**

26-29   Ruidoso, NM. **New Mexico Library Association**

26-29   Portland, OR. **Oregon Library Association**

27-29   Logan, UT. Spring Conference. **Consortium of College & University Media Centers (CCUMC)**

30-   Anaheim, CA. 40th Annual Convention. **International Reading Association (IRA)**
May 4

May

1-2   Sturbridge, MA. **Massachusetts Library Association**

2-4   Atlantic City, NJ. **New Jersey Library Association**

3-6   Ocean City, MD. **Maryland Library Association**

3-6   Peoria, IL. **Illinois Library Association**

5-7   Rochester, NY. 23rd National Conference. **National Braille Association Inc. (NBA)**

9-13   Ft. Lauderdale, FL. **Florida Library Association**

17-18   Burlington, VT. **Vermont Library Association**

21-23   Orono, ME. **Maine Library Association**

June

3-6   Chicago, IL. **American Booksellers Association**

10-15   Montreal, PQ. **Special Libraries Association**

15-18   Calgary, AB. **Canadian Library Association**

16-19   Baltimore, MD. **National Educational Computing Conference**

22-29   Chicago, IL. Annual Conference. **American Library Association (ALA)**

June 1995

22-29   Chicago, IL. **Association for Library Services to Children**

July

20-22   Memphis, TN. Annual Conference. **Tennessee Association of School Librarians**

August

22-26   Istanbul, Turkey. **International Federation of Library Associations & Institutions (IFLA)**

September

Library Card Sign-Up Month. **American Library Association (ALA)**

6-8   Dayton, OH. **Ohio Library Council**

29-
Oct. 2   Aspen, CO. **Colorado Library Association**

October

1st
weekend   Jonesborough, TN. 23rd National Storytelling Festival. **National Association for the Preservation & Perpetuation of Storytelling (NAPPS)**

Winnemucca, NV. **Nevada Library Association**

1-3   Providence, RI. **New England Library Association**

3-6   Greenboro, NC. **North Carolina Library Association**

3-7   Pittsburgh, PA. **Pennsylvania Library Association**

4-6   Kansas City, MO. **Missouri Library Association**

4-7   Sioux Falls, SD. **Mountain Plains Library Association** (joint conference **North Dakota Library Association/South Dakota Library Association**)

11-13   Mankato, MN. **Minnesota Library Association**

13-16   Ft. Smith, AK. **Arkansas Library Association**

18-20   Des Moines, IA. **Iowa Library Association**

18-20   Lansing, MI. **Michigan Library Association**

October 1995

   18-22   Milwaukee, WI. **Oral History Association**

   19-21   Buffalo, NY. **Literacy Volunteers of America**

   19-21   Davis, WV. **West Virginia Library Association**

   25-27   Kentucky, NB. **Nebraska Library Association**

   25-27   Appleton, WI. **Wisconsin Library Association**

   25-27   Jackson, MS. **Mississippi Library Association**

   25-28   San Antonio, TX. Annual Meeting. **National Council for Geographic Education (NCGE)**

   25-29   Rochester, NY. **New York Library Association**

   26-28   Jekyll Island, GA. **Georgia Library Association**

November

   8-12   Tampa, FL. **National Association for Gifted Children**

   11-14   Santa Clara, CA. **California Library Association**

   15-20   San Diego, CA. **National Council of Teachers of English**

   17-19   St. Louis, MO. **Theatre Library Association**

   29-
   Dec. 2.   New Orleans, LA. Annual Conference. **National Reading Conference**

1996

January

   16-19   San Antonio, TX. **Association for Library and Information Science Education**

   19-25   San Antonio, TX. Midwinter Meeting. **American Library Association (ALA)**

   19-25   San Antonio, TX. **Association for Library Services to Children**

January 1996

31-   San Antonio, TX. **Association for Educational Communication and Technology**
Feb. 4

February

6-10   Austin, TX. 16th Annual State Conference. **Texas Computer Education Association (TCEA)**

14-17   Seattle, WA. **Music Library Association**

March

8-11   San Diego, CA. Annual Convention. **American Association of School Administrators (AASA)**

12   National Girl Scout Birthday. **Girl Scouts of the USA**

19-22   Alexandria, LA. **Louisiana Library Association**

24-27   Portland, OR. **Oregon Library Association**

26-30   Portland, OR. **Public Library Association/ALA**

26-27   Washington, DC. **National Association of Elementary School Principals**

28-31   St. Louis, MO. National Convention. **National Science Teachers Association (NTSA)**

April

1-5   Orlando, FL. Annual Convention. **Council for Exceptional Children (CEC)**

10-12   Wichita, KS. **Kansas Triconference/KLA, KAECT, KASL**

14-20   National Library Week. **American Library Association (ALA)**

16-18   Tampa, FL. **Florida Library Association**

21-24   Helena, MT. **Montana Library Association**

22   National Girl Scout Leader's Day. **Girl Scouts of the USA**

April 1996

23-27   Houston, TX. Conference. **Texas Library Association**

25-28   San Diego, CA. 74th Annual Meeting. **National Council of Teachers of Mathematics (NCTM)**

28-
May 2   New Orleans, LA. 41th Annual Convention. **International Reading Association (IRA)**

May

13-17   Chicago, IL. **Illinois Library Association**

25-28   Los Angeles, CA. Convention & Trade Show. **American Booksellers Association, Inc. (ABA)**

June

6-9   Halifax, NS. **Canadian Library Association**

8-13   Boston, MA. **Special Libraries Association**

24   Orlando, FL. **Theater Library Association**

July

4-10   New York, NY. Annual Conference. **American Library Association (ALA)**

4-10   New York, NY. **Association for Library Services to Children**

August

7-10   Fairbanks, AK. **Pacific Northwest Library Association** (joint with **Alaska Library Association**)

16-18   Denver, CO. **Colorado Library Association**

19-24   Beijing, China. **International Federation of Library Associations**

September

Library Card Sign-Up Month. **American Library Association**

October

2-4   St. Cloud, MN. **Minnesota Library Association**

2-5   Nampa, ID. **Idaho Library Association**

October 1996

6-9   Lancaster, PA. **Pennsylvania Library Association**

8-10   Waterloo, IA. **Iowa Library Association**

9-12   Spearfish, SD. **South Dakota Library Association**

9-11   St. Louis, MO. **Missouri Library Association**

16-18 Dearborn, MI. **Michigan Library Association**

22-26 Lexington, KY. **Southeastern Library Association** (joint with **Kentucky Library Association**)

22-27 Saratoga Springs, NY. **New York Library Association**

23-25 Lincoln, NB. **Nebraska Library Association**

November

1-16   Middleton, WI. **Wisconsin Library Association**

13-16 Santa Barbara, CA. Annual Meeting. **National Council for Geographic Education (NCGE)**

BIBLIOGRAPHY OF SELECTION TOOLS

This bibliography annotates basic selection tools and reference guides for children's media collections and services.

A TO ZOO: SUBJECT ACCESS TO CHILDREN'S PICTURE BOOKS
By Carolyn W. Lima & John A. Lima. 4th ed. Bowker, 1993. 1,000 pp.

This nonevaluative listing provides 15,000 fiction and nonfiction picture books for preschool through second grade. Complete bibliographic information is provided and separate author, title and illustrator indexes provide access to main sections. Caldecott Award winners are noted and ISBNs are provided for new entries.

ACL DISTINGUISHED BOOKS REVIEWED IN 1992
The Association of Childrens Libraries of Northern California, 1993. 26 pp.

The 96 titles selected and annotated for this guide are those reviewed in *Bay Views* in 1992 and considered to have ''outstanding literary merit, high quality of illustration and design, and for their contribution to a child's understanding of the world.''

ADVENTURE GAMES FOR MICROCOMPUTERS: AN ANNOTATED DIRECTORY OF INTERACTIVE FICTION, 1991
By Patrick R. Dewey. Meckler, 1991. 170 pp.

Over 300 interactive software adventure games are included in this directory. Each entry specifies a description of the game, the level of graphic and textual sophistication, and details on software producers and prices.

ADVENTURING WITH BOOKS: A BOOKLIST FOR PRE-K—GRADE 6
Edited by Julie M. Jensen & Nancy L. Roser. 10th ed. National Council of Teachers of English, 1993. 603 pp.

This annotated bibliography profiles books of interest (published between 1988 to 1992) to children prekindergarten through grade 6. Award books are included as well as author, title and subject indexes.

AGAINST BORDERS: PROMOTING BOOKS FOR A MULTICULTURAL WORLD
By Hazel Rochman. American Library Association, 1993. 280 pp.

This book features *Booklist* bibliographical information on specific ethnic groups and multicultural issues primarily for grades 6-12. Themes such as outsiders, family, friends, family survival, fathers and love are included in the fiction and nonfiction titles.

ALL EARS: HOW TO USE AND CHOOSE RECORDED MUSIC FOR CHILDREN
By Jill Jarrow. Viking, 1991. 206 pp.

This annotated guide describes recordings for children by more than 75 artists.

AMERICAN AS STORY: HISTORICAL FICTION FOR SECONDARY SCHOOLS
By Elizabeth F. Howard. American Library Association, 1988. 137 pp.

This guide profiles 150 novels portraying the impressions of people living through significant periods in American history.

AMERICAN HISTORY: A GUIDE TO THE REFERENCE LITERATURE
By Ron Blazek & Anna H. Perrault. Libraries Unlimited, 1993. 400 pp.

This work identifies and describes reference books pertaining to American history copyrighted through 1992. Electronic databases and microform sources are included when available.

AMERICAN HISTORY FOR CHILDREN AND YOUNG ADULTS: AN ANNOTATED BIBLIOGRAPHIC INDEX
By Vandelia VanMeter. Libraries Unlimited, 1990. 324 pp.

This index of over 2,000 citations of the best books about people and events in American history includes both fiction and nonfiction arranged by time period. The guide is available on computer disc.

AMERICAN INDIAN REFERENCE BOOKS FOR CHILDREN AND YOUNG ADULTS
By Barbara J. Kuipers. Libraries Unlimited, 1991. 176 pp.

This annotated bibliography provides more than 200 recommended reference books on American Indians for grades 3-1-2. Included is a checklist for evaluating materials on American Indians.

THE ART OF CHILDREN'S PICTURE BOOKS: A SELECTIVE REFERENCE GUIDE
By Sylvia S. Marantz & Kenneth A. Marantz. Garland, 1988. 165 pp.

This annotated bibliography identifies books, ERIC documents, articles and unpublished dissertations published since 1960.

AUDIOCASSETTE FINDER. 3RD ED.
National Information Center for Educational Media, 1993.

This reference tool provides information about 40,000 educational materials recorded on audiocassettes. Each entry includes a description of content, audience level, format, running time, date of release, rental/purchase source.

AWARD-WINNING BOOKS FOR CHILDREN AND YOUNG ADULTS, 1990-1991

By Betty L. Criscoe & Philip J. Lanasa, III. Scarecrow Press, 1993. 714 pp.

Covering books written and published in English-speaking countries, this guide summarizes the number of awards received by books, authors, and publishers in 1990 and 1991. Each title includes the name of the award; background and selection criteria for each award; author; title; review; photograph of each book cover; interest/reading level; name and address of publisher; number of pages; cost; and ISBN. Seven indexes including a subject index and four appendixes are part of this guide.

BEACHUM'S GUIDE TO LITERATURE FOR YOUNG ADULTS

Edited by Kirk Beetz & Suzanne Niemeyer. Beachum, 1990. 4 vols.

This guide analyzes over 200 outstanding books for young adults. A thematic index is included in the alphabetical index.

BEGINNING WITH BOOKS: LIBRARY PROGRAMMING FOR INFANTS, TODDLERS, AND PRESCHOOLERS

By Nancy N. DeSalvo. Shoe String Press, 1993. 186 pp.

Programs designed for the child from infancy to age five are explained in twenty-four structured book experiences. Board books, flap books, fingerplays, recordings, videos, and toys are included. Books, films and tapes are related to specific toys.

BEST BOOKS FOR CHILDREN: PRESCHOOL THROUGH GRADE 6

By John T. Gillespie & Corinne J. Naden. 4th ed. Bowker, 1990. 1,002 pp.

This evaluative listing provides 11,299 "best" curriculum-related books recommended in leading journals for children from preschool to grade 6. Included are author, title, illustrator, subject indexes and reading level recommendations.

BEST BOOKS FOR JUNIOR HIGH READERS

By John T. Gillespie. Bowker, 1991. 567 pp.

This volume recommends 5,674 books from leading journals for junior high readers. An appendix lists over 750 challenging titles for advanced young teenagers.

BEST BOOKS FOR SENIOR HIGH READERS

By John T. Gillespie. Bowker, 1991. 931 pp.

This annotated listing for senior high readers offers over 10,000 books recommended in reviews from journal sources.

THE BEST HIGH/LOW BOOKS FOR RELUCTANT READERS

By Joni Richards Bodart. Libraries Unlimited, 1990. 100 pp.

This bibliography, available in book form or discs, includes both books in print, as well as old favorites for grades 3-12, for reluctant readers.

BEST SCIENCE BOOKS AND AV MATERIALS FOR CHILDREN

By Susan M. O'Connell, et al. American Association for the Advancement of Science, 1988. 350 pp.

This bibliography is "an annotated list of science and mathematics books, films, filmstrips, and video cassettes for children ages five through twelve selected from the pages of *Science Books & Films* magazine." Indexes for both book and audiovisual materials are found under author, title, subject, series titles and AV distribution.

BEST-VIDEOS FOR CHILDREN AND YOUNG ADULTS: A CORE COLLECTION FOR LIBRARIANS

By Jennifer Jung Gallant. ABC-CLIO, 1990. 185 pp.

This selective annotated list provides over 350 of the most notable VHS video titles available for children and young adults. All videos included in this bibliography have won awards or have been favorably reviewed.

THE BEST YEARS OF THEIR LIVES: A RESOURCE GUIDE FOR TEENAGERS IN CRISIS

By Stephanie Zvirin. American Library Association, 1992. 122 pp.

This resource guide presents critical reviews of 200 nonfiction titles for teenagers in crisis, ages 12-18, as well as brief descriptions of fiction and video titles. Age level designations are provided for all entries.

BEYOND PICTURE BOOKS: A GUIDE TO FIRST READERS

By Barbara Barstow & Judith Riggle. Bowker, 1989. 354 pp.

The 1,600 first readers profiled offer a plot synopsis, critical evaluation and comments about the illustrations. A list of 200 outstanding first readers are included with readability assessments based on the Spache formula. Subject, title, illustrator and series indexes are included.

BIBLIOGRAPHY OF BOOKS FOR CHILDREN

Association for Childhood Education International, 1989. 128 pp.

This bibliography offers over 1,500 annotations for selecting children's books. Title and author indexes are provided including appropriate age levels.

BIOGRAPHY AND CHILDREN: A STUDY OF BIOGRAPHY FOR CHILDREN AND CHILDHOOD IN BIOGRAPHY

By Stuart Hannabuss, et al. Unipub, 1993. 160 pp.

This volume examines the value of biographical information for children. Contents include: childhood in literature, the use of biographical material, a bibliography of primary material, and one for secondary sources.

BLACK AMERICAN WOMEN IN LITERATURE: A BIBLIOGRAPHY 1976 THROUGH 1987

By Ronda Glikin. McFarland, 1989. 263 pp.

This comprehensive bibliography focuses on works by 300 black American women published from 1976 through 1987.

BLACK EXPERIENCE IN CHILDREN'S LITERATURE

New York Public Library, 1989. 64 pp.

This paperbound index lists an assortment of fiction and nonfiction titles depicting the black experience in children's literature.

BOOK BAIT: DETAILED NOTES ON ADULT BOOKS POPULAR WITH YOUNG PEOPLE

By Eleanor Walker. American Library Association, 1988. 166 pp.

This annotated bibliography for librarians working with seventh to ninth grade students provides information on adult books recommended by young adults. Main entries consist of plot summaries, background information about the author and the story. Subject and title indexes are included.

THE BOOK BUYER'S ADVISOR: THE DEFINITIVE GUIDE TO DISCOVERING THE YEAR'S BEST BOOKS

By Bill Ott. American Library Association, 1990. 450 pp.

This volume, arranged by genre, is screened each year in *Booklist*. Separate author and title indexes are provided.

THE BOOKFINDER, VOL. 4: A GUIDE TO CHILDREN'S LITERATURE ABOUT THE NEEDS AND PROBLEMS OF YOUTH AGED 2-15.

Edited by Sharon Spredemann Dreyer. American Guidance Service, 1989. 642 pp.

This annotated guide of 3,200 titles is designed to locate books for children as they cope with problems in their lives and to serve as a bibliotherapy tool. Some 450 psychological, behavioral and developmental themes are utilized in this volume.

BOOKS BY AFRICAN-AMERICAN AUTHORS AND ILLUSTRATORS FOR CHILDREN AND YOUNG ADULTS

By Helen E. Williams. American Library Association, 1991. 270 pp.

This volume identifies books written and illustrated by black authors and illustrators which are appropriate for children and young adults.

BOOKS FOR CHILDREN AND YOUNG ADULTS ABOUT WAR AND PEACE

By Virginia A. Walter. Oryx Press, 1993. 160 pp.

A positive method is presented for exposing young people to the complexities of moral and political issues surrounding war. Specific books and methods are used to introduce the subject of war to varying age groups. A list of resources for adults on war and peace is included.

BOOKS FOR CHILDREN TO READ ALONE: A GUIDE FOR PARENTS AND LIBRARIANS

By George Wilson & Joyce Moss. Bowker, 1988. 178 pp.

This annotated list provides over 350 fiction and nonfiction books chosen for their appeal to young readers. All titles are analyzed for readability under the Spache & Fry readability formula.

BOOKS FOR THE GIFTED CHILD. VOL. 2

By Paula Hauser & Gail A. Nelson. Bowker, 1988. 244 pp.

This volume covers 195 challenging fiction and nonfiction titles for the gifted child. Each entry provides complete bibliographic information, reading level, and evaluation of plot, characters and style.

BOOKS IN SPANISH FOR CHILDREN AND YOUNG ADULTS, SERIES V/ LIBROS INFANTILES Y JUVENILES EN ESPAÑOL, SERIE NO. V.: AN ANNOTATED GUIDE/UNA GUIA ANOTADA

By Isabel Schon. Scarecrow Press, 1989. 180 pp.

This guide provides books written in Spanish for students from preschool to high school. Most of the books, which have been published since 1986 come from Argentina, Belgium, Chile, Colombia, Costa Rica, Cuba, Honduras, Mexico, Nicaragua, Puerto Rico, Spain, United States, Uruguay, and Venezuela. Appendices include book dealers, author, and title indexes.

BOOKS KIDS WILL SIT STILL FOR: THE COMPLETE READ-ALOUD GUIDE. 2ND ED

By Judy Freeman. Bowker, 1990. 660 pp.

The annotated read-aloud guide contains 2,100 recommended titles tested through the author's experience as a school librarian. Includes author, title, illustrator and subject indexes.

BOOKS FOR THE JUNIOR HIGH YEARS

Edited by James E. Davis & Hazel K. Davis. National Council of Teachers of English, 1989. 115 pp.

This guide is devoted to literature suitable for the junior high/middle school student. A list of the best books from the 1988 edition of *Your Reading* is included.

BOOKS FOR THE TEENAGE

New York Public Library. Annual

Young adult librarians provide a collection of book titles written for teenagers and arranged by subject.

BOOKS FOR YOU: A BOOKLIST FOR SENIOR HIGH STUDENTS

Edited by Shirley Wurth. 11th ed. National Council of Teachers of English, 1992. 257 pp.

This annotated bibliography profiles books of interest to the young adult on subjects from Adventure to Westerns. Included are author, title and subject indexes.

BOOKS TO HELP CHILDREN COPE WITH SEPARATION AND LOSS: AN ANNOTATED BIBLIOGRAPHY. 4TH ED

By Marsha Rudman, et al. Bowker, 1993. 500 pp.

This annotated bibliography profiles 750 fiction and nonfiction books focusing on separation and loss.

BOOKS TO READ ALOUD WITH CHILDREN THROUGH AGE 8

By Child Study Children's Book Committee. Bank Street College, 1989. 59 pp.

Books to read aloud to young children are the focus of this book. All selections are chosen to foster the love of reading.

BOWKERS COMPLETE VIDEO DIRECTORY

Bowker, 1990. 2 vols.

Over 120,000 programs on 75,000 videos comprise this detailed reference work. Title, genre, cost, and director indexes are included.

BROOKLINE (MA) PUBLIC SCHOOLS READING LIST 1991/92

Brookline School Committee, 1990. 67 pp.

This list provides students, grades K-8, a reading list of recommended titles.

BUILDING THE REFERENCE COLLECTION: A HOW-TO-DO-IT MANUAL FOR SCHOOL AND PUBLIC LIBRARIANS

By Gay D. Patrick. Neal-Schuman, 1992. 150 pp.

This guide is divided into two sections. The first section deals with identifying users and their needs; selection criteria; tools for selection and review; budget allocations; and online reference services. The second section lists approximately 300 annotations in four categories: a core list for all school levels and three lists for elementary, intermediate, and high school levels.

CANADIAN BOOKS FOR CHILDREN: GUIDE TO AUTHORS AND ILLUSTRATORS

By Jon C. Stoh & R.E. Jones. Harcourt Brace Jovanovich, 1988. 246 pp.

A complete guide to works of 105 Canadian authors and illustrators are profiled in this volume. A selective list of recommended Canadian books for kindergarten through grade 8 is provided as well as a list of award books.

CANADIAN BOOKS FOR YOUNG PEOPLE. LIVRES CANADIANA POUR LA JEUNESSE. 4TH ED.
Edited by Andre Gagnon & Ann Gagnon. University of Toronto, 1988. 186 pp.

This collection of over 2,500 Canadian (both English and French) books for preschool through high school includes bibliographic and order information and a brief annotation in the language of the publisher. Indexes by author, title and illustrator are included.

CD-ROM COLLECTION BUILDER'S TOOL KIT. THE COMPLETE HANDBOOK OF TOOLS FOR EVALUATING CD-ROMS
By Paul T. Nicholls. Pemberton Press, 1990. 180 pp.

Over 67 CD-ROM products are profiled in this handbook. Profiles include publisher, hardware request, software, evaluative descriptions, frequency of update, and citation of other reviews. Other features include a list of directories and catalogs, an extensive bibliography, newsletters, a list of journals and selection tools.

CD-ROM INFORMATION PRODUCTS: AN EVALUATIVE GUIDE AND DIRECTORY
Edited by C. J. Armstrong & J. A. Large. Gower Publishing Company, 1990. 3 vols.

This guide evaluates CD-ROM products in Part 1 and provides a list of products arranged by broad subject headings in Part 2. A directory of company addresses where products can be purchased is provided.

CD-ROM 1992: AN ANNOTATED BIBLIOGRAPHY OF RESOURCES
By Jennifer Langlois. Meckler, 1992. 300 pp.

This source gives an annotated bibliography of CD-ROM books and periodicals dealing with library science and educational technology.

CD-ROMS FOR SCHOOL LIBRARIES: AN EVALUATIVE GUIDE TO COLLECTION BUILDING
By Catherine Murphy. Meckler, 1993. 200 pp.

This annotated and evaluative guide lists the ''best CD-ROMs available for use in the K-12 curriculum. Bibliographic databases, full text archives, directories, utilities, and subject-special collections are included.

CD-ROMS IN PRINT: AN INTERNATIONAL GUIDE TO CD-ROM, CD-I, CDTV & ELECTRONIC BOOK PRODUCTS (PRINT VERSION)
Meckler, 1993. 700 pp.

CD-ROM products, providers, and distributors are available in this comprehensive list. Over 3,500 products are arranged alphabetically by title. Each entry includes hardware requirements, search software, application type, update frequency, price, and the necessary CD-ROM player.

CD-ROMS IN PRINT: AN INTERNATIONAL GUIDE TO CD-ROM, CD-I, CDTV & ELECTRONIC BOOK PRODUCTS (CD-ROM VERSION)
Meckler, 1993.

There are over 3,500 title records and over 3,500 company records that are searchable in this guide. 512K of RAM and DOS 3.0 or greater are required to run the DOS version of this CD-ROM product. A Macintosh-format CD is also available.

CELEBRATING THE DREAM
New York Public Library, 1990. 31 pp.

This collection consists of a variety of books written by black authors for high school students.

CHILDREN'S BOOKS: AWARDS AND PRIZES
Rev. ed. Children's Book Council, 1993. 404 pp.

This book provides coverage of nearly 200 children's books receiving awards and prizes from their inception through 1992.

CHILDREN'S BOOKS OF THE YEAR
The Child Study Children's Book Committee. Bank Street College, Annual.

This annotated annual guide lists the best 600 book titles for children, ages preschool to 14. Books of outstanding merit and those for high interest easy reading are noted. Tips for parents to use to guide their children's reading are included.

CHILDREN'S CATALOG
16th ed. H. W. Wilson, 1991. 1,346 pp.

A subscription includes a hardbound index of over 6,000 nonfiction and fiction books. Each of the four annual supplements offers 500 additional annotated citations. Entries are arranged by Dewey Decimal.

CHILDREN'S FICTION SOURCEBOOK
By Margaret Hobson, et al. Ashgate, 1992. 296 pp.

A source for fiction for those concerned with children's reading. Included are indexes by title, series, age range and genre. A section on classics describes available editions.

CHILDREN'S LITERATURE AWARDS AND WINNERS
Compiled and edited by Delores Blythe Jones. 3rd ed. Gale, 1994. 678 pp.

This single volume index provides a comprehensive list of 5,000 award winning children's book titles. Almost 7,000 authors and illustrators are listed in separate indexes.

CHOICES: A CORE COLLECTION FOR YOUNG RELUCTANT READERS. VOL. 2
Edited by Julie Cummins and Blair Cummins. Evanston, IL: John Gordon Burke, 1990. 544 pp.

This supplement to volume one describes 275 titles published between 1983 and 1988 that are recommended for reluctant readers for grades 1-6.

CHOOSING BOOKS FOR CHILDREN: A COMMONSENSE GUIDE. REV. ED.
By Betty Hearne. Delacorte/Dell, 1990. 228 pp.

This annotated guide includes over 300 selections of children's books published from 1970 to 1990 plus some old favorites. Author/illustrator and subject indexes are included.

THE COMPLETE DIRECTORY OF LARGE PRINT BOOKS AND SERIALS
Bowker. Annual.

This directory offers order information for over 6,500 large print books by author, title, or subject. Some 65 large-print periodicals and newspapers are included in the serials index.

CORE LIST OF BOOKS AND JOURNALS IN EDUCATION
Edited by Nancy Patricia O'Brien & Emily Fabiano. Oryx Press, 1991. 136 pp.

The 979 entries presented in this volume represent education sources needed to complete research projects or to serve as a good reference collection.

COUNTING BOOKS ARE MORE THAN NUMBERS: AN ANNOTATED ACTION BIBLIOGRAPHY

By Patricia L. Roberts. Shoe String Press, 1990. 270 pp.

This bibliography profiles 350 picture books that introduce mathematical skills and concepts to K-2 grade children. The appendix includes a list of titles by the mathematical skill taught.

CULTURALLY DIVERSE LIBRARY COLLECTIONS FOR CHILDREN

By Herman L. Totten & Risa W. Brown. Neal-Schuman, 1994. 250 pp.

This index enables librarians to ethnically balance their school library collections to include African, Hispanic, Asian and Native Americans.

CURRENT ISSUES RESOURCE BUILDER: FREE AND INEXPENSIVE MATERIALS FOR LIBRARIANS AND TEACHERS

By Carol Smallwood. McFarland, 1989. 414 pp.

This resource lists free and inexpensive sources for information on 280 different topics. A variety of multimedia materials are included.

DEALING WITH DIVERSITY THROUGH MULTICULTURAL FICTION: LIBRARY-CLASSROOM PARTNERSHIPS

By Laurie Johnson & Sally Smith. American Library Association, 1993. 140 pp.

This book focuses on using the multicultural fiction collection for grades 5-8. Selection criteria for evaluating books which realistically reflect diversity are included.

DEATH AND DYING IN CHILDREN'S AND YOUNG PEOPLE'S LITERATURE: A SURVEY AND BIBLIOGRAPHY

By Marian S. Pyles. McFarland, 1988. 187 pp.

This bibliography provides books for children and young people on death and dying.

DEVELOPING RESILIENCY THROUGH CHILDREN'S LITERATURE: A GUIDE FOR TEACHERS AND LIBRARIANS, K-8

By Nancy L. Cecil & Patricia L. Roberts. McFarland, 1992. 224 pp.

This book details about 200 selections from children's literature featuring characters who demonstrate positive coping behaviors. The selections are divided into four parts: folk literature, historical fiction, biographies, and contemporary fiction.

DICTIONARIES FOR ADULTS AND CHILDREN

Edited by Sandy Whiteley. American Library Association, 1991. 46 pp.

This resource provides reviews of 19 current dictionaries for children arranged by age group and 9 college/desk dictionaries as an aid to selection for public and school librarians.

DOGS, CATS, AND HORSES: A RESOURCE GUIDE TO THE LITERATURE FOR YOUNG PEOPLE

By Charlene Strickland. Libraries Unlimited, 1990. 225 pp.

This resource guide profiles 630 fiction and nonfiction titles for grades 1 to 12 on dogs, cats and horses published since 1920. A disc version is available.

E FOR ENVIRONMENT: AN ANNOTATED BIBLIOGRAPHY OF CHILDREN'S BOOKS WITH ENVIRONMENTAL THEMES

By Patti Sinclair. Bowker, 1992. 292 pp.

This annotated bibliography describes over 500 children's books that focus on environmental themes. Indexed by author, title, subject, reading level and illustrator.

EASY READING: BOOK SERIES AND PERIODICALS FOR LESS ABLE READERS 2nd Ed.

International Reading Association, 1989. 90 pp.

Recommendations of books for the less able reader are included in this bibliography which critically reviews 44 book serials and 15 periodicals. Indexes by genre, ethnicity, and reading/interest level are included.

EDUCATING THE GIFTED: A SOURCEBOOK

By M. Jean Greenlaw & Margaret E. McIntosh. American Library Association, 1988. 512 pp.

This sourcebook provides more than 2,000 bibliographic entries for educating the gifted. Each chapter is followed by an annotated bibliography.

EDUCATION: A GUIDE TO REFERENCE AND INFORMATION SOURCES

By Lois J. Buttlar. Libraries Unlimited, 1989. 258 pp.

This guide provides coverage of reference materials in the field of education encompassing all general reference and social sciences reference sources that have a direct or overlapping relationship with education.

EDUCATIONAL FILM & VIDEO LOCATOR. 4TH Ed.

Bowker, 1990. 3,361 pp. (2 vols.)

An annotated bibliography describes 52,000 videos and films for viewers of all ages. Entries indicate running time, format, color, production date, former titles, and series. A separate subject, title and audience level index locates rentals under more than 621 subject headings.

EDUCATIONAL SOFTWARE PREVIEW GUIDE, 1990-91

Edited by Ed Hancock, et al. International Society for Technology in Education, 1991. 98 pp.

This guide lists over 500 software titles favorably reviewed for grades K-12.

EDUCATORS GUIDE TO FREE FILMS

Educators Progress Service. Annual.

This annotated guide, updated annually, provides a listing of film titles available for free loan to educational institutions. Title, subject and source indexes are provided.

EDUCATORS GUIDE TO FREE FILMSTRIPS AND SLIDES

Educators Progress Service. Annual.

Free-loan filmstrips and slides are listed in this annually updated guide under curriculum-related subjects. Title, subject and source indexes are provided.

EDUCATOR'S GUIDE TO FREE SCIENCE MATERIALS

Educators Progress Service. Annual.

This annual guide describes over 1,700 audiovisual materials related to the life and physical sciences. Most items are free and some are available on loan.

EDUCATOR'S GUIDE TO FREE TEACHING AIDS

Educators Progress Service. Annual.

This annotated guide provides 2,123 of the best free printed materials and five sample teaching units—all in a loose-leaf binder for ease of use (or sharing)

EDUCATOR'S GUIDE TO FREE VIDEOTAPES

Educators Progress Service. Annual.

This annotated guide lists 2,481 free videotapes including VHS, 3/4'' and Beta formats.

EDUCATOR'S INDEX OF FREE MATERIALS
Educators Progress Service. Annual.

This annotated guide lists 2,659 printed materials for high school students and above.

THE ELEMENTARY SCHOOL LIBRARY COLLECTION: A GUIDE TO BOOKS AND OTHER MEDIA. 18TH Ed.
Edited by Lauren K. Lee & Gary D. Hoyle. Brodart, 1992. 1,242 pp.

This resource of 10,847 titles provides librarians, establishing a new media center, a core collection for prekindergarten to sixth grade children as well as a tool for maintaining existing collections. Author, title and subject indexes are included.

ELEMENTARY TEACHERS GUIDE TO FREE CURRICULAR MATERIALS
Educators Progress Service. Annual.

This annual guide provides an annotated listing of free teaching aids sponsored by companies, foreign countries, professional organizations and associations.

EL-HI TEXTBOOKS AND SERIALS IN PRINT 1993. 121ST Ed.
Bowker, 1993. 1,555 pp.

This volume contains more than 71,000 titles (5,000 new entries) of texts, workbooks, periodicals, tests, programmed learning materials, teaching aids, professional books, AV materials, posters and other resources. Annual updates are provided.

EQUIPMENT DIRECTORY OF AUDIO, VISUAL, COMPUTER AND VIDEO PRODUCTS. 37TH Ed.
International Communicators Industry Association, 1991. 600 pp.

This directory provides details for selecting video, audiovisual and computer equipment. Comparisons in prices and sizes of products is easily done using this guide.

EXPLORERS AND EXPLORATION: THE BEST RESOURCES FOR GRADES 5 THROUGH 9
By Ann Welton. Oryx Press, 1993. 192 pp.

Each of the ten chapters in this resource concludes with a detailed annotated bibliography of fiction and

nonfiction books covering explorations that occurred over the last 1,000 years.

EXPLORING THE UNITED STATES THROUGH LITERATURE SERIES
Series Ed. Kathy Latrobe. Oryx Press.

This seven-volume series describes print and nonprint materials that teachers can use with students to study individual states. Volumes cover the Great Lakes States, the Pacific States, the Southwest States, Southeast States, Northeast States, the Mountain States and the Plains States.

EYEOPENERS! HOW TO CHOOSE AND USE CHILDREN'S BOOKS ABOUT REAL PEOPLE, PLACES AND THINGS
By Beverly Korbin. Viking Penguin, 1988. 317 pp.

Over 500 nonfiction books are cited in this volume and projects are suggested to link books to the child's life.

FAMILIES IN TRANSITION: AN ANNOTATED BIBLIOGRAPHY
By Judith De Board Sadler. Archon Books, 1988. 251 pp.

The transitional family is the focus of this annotated bibliography. One chapter is devoted to 134 books for children and young adults.

FANTASY LITERATURE FOR CHILDREN AND YOUNG ADULTS: AN ANNOTATED BIBLIOGRAPHY
By Ruth N. Lynn. Bowker, 1988. 771 pp.

This annotated guide recommends over 3,300 English and American fantasy novels and collections for children and young adults.

FICTION CATALOG. 12TH ED.
H.W. Wilson, 1991. 956 pp.

This annotated list of more than 5,200 fiction titles serves as an aid to collection development and maintenance as well as a resource for readers' advisors. Author, title, subject indexes and a directory of publishers are provided.

FICTION FOR YOUTH: A GUIDE TO RECOMMENDED BOOKS. 3RD ED.
Edited by Lillian L. Shapiro & Barbara Stein. Neal-Schuman, 1992. 292 pp.

This annotated resource of fiction titles offers parents and teachers a list of books that will motivate capable young adult readers to read more and

better books, especially the college-bound student.

FICTION INDEX FOR READERS 10 TO 16. SUBJECT ACCESS TO OVER 8,200 BOOKS (1960-1990)
By Vicki Anderson. McFarland, 1992. 488 pp.

This index lists and briefly annotates over 8,200 fiction titles for readers age 10-16 commonly found in school and public libraries. Subject and author/title indexes are provided.

FICTION SEQUELS FOR READERS 10 TO 16: AN ANNOTATED BIBLIOGRAPHY OF BOOKS IN SUCCESSION
By Vicki Anderson. McFarland, 1990. 158 pp.

This annotated bibliography details about 1,500 fiction sequels for readers ages 10 to 16.

FILM & VIDEO FINDER. 4TH ED.
Edited by Stephanie Korney. National Information Center for Education Media, 1989. 3 vols.

This three-volume guide covers information on over 110,000 films and videos. Each entry includes a description of content, audience level, format, running time, date of release, and rental/purchase source.

FILMS FOR LEARNING, THINKING AND DOING: DEVELOPING LIBRARY SKILLS
By Mary D. Lankford. Libraries Unlimited, 1992. 228 pp.

This resource provides films for learning, thinking and doing on the elementary and secondary levels. Also included is a bibliography of books on film, directory of film producers, photographs and an index.

FREE MAGAZINES FOR LIBRARIANS. 3RD ED.
By Adeline Mercer Smith & Diane Rovena Jones. McFarland, 1989. 238 pp.

This source of free magazines provides a basic list for small to medium-sized libraries.

FREE RESOURCE BUILDER FOR LIBRARIANS AND TEACHERS. 2ND ED
By Carol Smallwood. McFarland, 1992. 319 pp.

This resource, grouped by broad topics, provides access to numerous free materials for library and classroom use. Current information sources useful to educators (addresses, phone numbers) include nonprofit organizations, businesses and government. A subject index is provided.

FUN FOR KIDS II: AN INDEX TO CRAFT BOOKS

By Marion F. Gallivan. Scarecrow Press, 1992. 482 pp.

Over 300 books, published since 1981, list information on crafts for different grade levels. Books are indexed by author and title. An alphabetical craft index is arranged by name of project, by type of material, and by nationality and holiday.

GENRE FAVORITES FOR YOUNG ADULTS

By Sally Estes. American Library Association, 1993. 64 pp.

This compilation of popular young adult bibliographies compiled from *Booklist* reviews published from 1980 through 1991 focuses on genre favorites for young adults. Some adult titles with young adult appeal are included.

GENREFLECTING: A GUIDE TO READING INTERESTS IN GENRE FICTION. 3RD. ED

By Betty Rosenberg & Diana T. Herald. Libraries Unlimited, 1991. 345 pp.

This selected annotated biblioigrapy provides information on the newest popular genre fiction including a history and criticism of each genre.

GLOBAL BEAT

New York Public Library, 1992. 16 pp.

This index contains books for teenagers who are interested in global literature pertaining to Latin America, the Caribbean, Africa, India, the Far East, and Native Americans.

GOOD READING: A GUIDE FOR SERIOUS READERS. 23RD ED.

By Arthur Waldhorn, et. al. Bowker, 1990. 465 pp.

A reading list for the serious adult reader is the focus of this book. A core list of "101 significant books" is supplemented with new lists of books to be read before entering college, while on vacation, and after retirement.

GOVERNMENT PUBLICATIONS FOR SCHOOL LIBRARIES: A BIBLIOGRAPHIC GUIDE AND RECOMMENDED CORE COLLECTION

By Donald J. Voorhees. New York Library Association, 1988. 32 pp.

This guide offers a suggested list of government and New York State documents that could enhance a school library collection. Annotations provide complete bibliographies. Information is given on how to order the pamphlets.

GROWING PAINS: HELPING CHILDREN DEAL WITH EVERYDAY PROBLEMS THROUGH READING

By Maureen Cuddigan & Mary Beth Hanson. American Library Association., 1988. 165 pp.

This bibliography provides a listing of books to help children deal with everyday problems through reading. Author/title and subject indexes are included.

GUIDE TO FREE COMPUTER MATERIALS

Educators Progress Service. Annual.

Over 250 free computer programs, demonstration software, and brochures are listed in this annual nonevaluative guide. Title, subject and source indexes are included.

GUIDE TO POPULAR U.S. GOVERNMENT PUBLICATIONS. 2ND ED.

By William G. Bailey. Libraries Unlimited, 1990. 314 pp.

This guide identifies and describes some 2,500 U.S. Government documents published between 1985-1989.

GUIDE TO REFERENCE BOOKS FOR SCHOOL MEDIA CENTERS. 4TH ED.

By Margaret Irby Nichols. Libraries Unlimited, 1992. 463 pp.

This comprehensive guide provides over 2,000 entries to current reference materials for school media centers, including microcomputer software selection aids.

GUIDE TO RESOURCES IN ENVIRONMENTAL EDUCATION. 11TH ED.

Edited by P.S. Berry & C. Lynford. Lanher, MD: Unipub, 1991. 325 pp.

This listing of over 10,000 resources relating to the environment includes books and audiovisual materials such as computer software, games, videos, cassettes, films and slides. Level of suitability is included for primary grades through college.

A GUIDE TO TEACHING MIDDLE GRADES ABOUT WAR

By Phyllis K. Kennemer. Oryx Press, 1992. 176 pp.

A variety of materials and resources is available about the Revolutionary War, Civil War, World War I, World War II, and the Vietnam War. This guide includes a selected chronology for each war; recommended books such as picture books, factual books, biographies, and fiction books; a sample lesson plan for each unit; suggested questions and activities; and glossary. New opportunities are presented for stimulating high-level thinking skills and class discussions.

GUIDE TO VIDEOCASSETTES FOR CHILDREN

By Diana Green, et al. Consumers Union, 1989. 270 pp.

This annotated guide reviews over 300 videocassettes for children. Appendices include a directory of sources for videocassettes, an age-range index and a title index.

HANDBOOK OF CONTEMPORARY FICTION FOR PUBLIC LIBRARIES AND SCHOOL LIBRARIES

By Mary K. Biagini. Scarecrow Press, 1989. 257 pp.

Novels and short stories by more than 1,100 authors are listed chronologically. The most popular genres and authors of world literature are included.

HEALTH RESOURCE BUILDER: FREE AND INEXPENSIVE MATERIALS FOR LIBRARIANS AND TEACHERS

By Carol Smallwood. McFarland, 1988. 263 pp.

This resource provides sources for obtaining inexpensive materials on health, mental health and safety.

HIGH INTEREST-EASY READING: A BOOKLIST FOR JUNIOR AND SENIOR HIGH SCHOOL STUDENTS

Edited by William G. McBride. National Council of Teachers of English, 1990. 133 pp.

Almost 400 annotations describe current titles that can be used to motivate reluctant young adult readers. Although this index was written for students, educators and parents will also find it to be a valuable selection tool.

HIGH INTEREST EASY READING FOR JUNIOR AND SENIOR HIGH SCHOOL STUDENTS. 5TH ED.

National Council of Teachers of English, 1988. 115 pp.

This annotated bibliography provides books selected to appeal to the reluctant reader.

HIGH/LOW HANDBOOK: ENCOURAGING LITERACY IN THE 1990S. 3RD ED.

Compiled & edited by Ellen V. LiBretto. Bowker, 1990. 304 pp.

This resource provides a core collection of over 400 recommended books, magazines, software, and nonprint materials for reluctant or disabled readers. Subject, title, reading level and interest level indexes are included.

HIGHSCOPE SURVEY OF EARLY CHILDHOOD SOFTWARE

By Warren Buckleitner, High Scope Press, 1989. 187 pp.

This listing of 355 software programs for young children is designed to assist parents and educators to locate developmentally appropriate software for children aged three to six.

A HISPANIC HERITAGE, SERIES IV: A GUIDE TO JUVENILE BOOKS ABOUT HISPANIC PEOPLE AND CULTURES

By Isabel Schon. Scarecrow Press, 1991. 173 pp.

Students in kindergarten through high school can better understand and appreciate the political, social, and economic problems of many Hispanic people in Argentina, Bolivia, Chile, Colombia, Costa Rica, Cuba, Ecuador, El Salvador, Guatemala, Honduras, Mexico, Nicaragua, Panama, Peru, Puerto Rico, Spain, Venezuela, and the Hispanic people of the United States. Author, subject, and title indexes are included.

THE HUMANITIES: A SELECTIVE GUIDE TO INFORMATION SOURCES. 3RD ED.

By Ron Blazek & Elizabeth S. Aversa. Libraries Unlimited, 1988. 382 pp.

This guide covers reference works and computerized databases in the humanities. A guide to serial publications in each discipline is provided.

INDEX TO COLLECTIVE BIOGRAPHIES FOR YOUNG READERS. 4TH ED.

Edited by Karen Breen. Bowker, 1988. 494 pp.

This volume indexes over 1,100 collective biographies of over 10,000 prominent figures by name of the biographees, occupation, and by title of the collective work.

INFORMATION BOOKS FOR CHILDREN

Edited by Keith Barker. Ashgate, 1991. 258 pp.

A guide designed for children's librarians and teachers looking for informa-

tion books for children provides over 470 titles for children between the ages of 3 and 16. Detailed subject and author/title indexes are included.

THE INTEGRATED CURRICULUM: BOOKS FOR RELUCTANT READERS, GRADES 2-5

By Anthony D. Fredericks. Libraries Unlimited, 1992. 187 pp.

This book contains 40 books selected to motivate reluctant readers. A section on resources and booklists completes the volume.

INTERNATIONAL GUIDE TO LITERATURE ON FILM

Edited by Tom Costello. K.G. Saur, 1992. 416 pp.

This index focuses on foreign and domestic literary films produced between 1930 and 1990. All 5,000 entries are arranged alphabetically by author and film title, and include complete bibliographies.

INTRODUCING BOOK PLOTS 3: A BOOK TALK GUIDE FOR USE WITH READERS AGES 8-12

By Diana L. Spirt. Bowker, 1988. 352 pp.

Ninety fiction and nonfiction titles are summarized and analyzed in this volume. Selection aids are recommended and related titles are listed.

INTRODUCTION TO THE WORLD OF CHILDREN'S BOOKS. 2ND ED.

By Margaret R. Marshall. Ashgate, 1988. 327 pp.

Books in this volume provide a "multinational view of the children's book scene." Included is a bibliography and an index.

JUNIOR HIGH SCHOOL LIBRARY CATALOG. 6TH ED.

H. W. Wilson, 1990. 802 pp.

This annotated catalog organizes 3,200 fiction and nonfiction titles by subject area and Dewey Decimal Classification. Each book indexed is written for grades 7-9.

JUNIORPLOTS 4: A BOOKTALK GUIDE FOR USE WITH READERS AGES 12-16

By John T. Gillespie & Corinne J. Naden. Bowker, 1992. 450 pp.

This booktalk guide provides entries for 80 contemporary fiction and nonfiction books arranged by genre. Additional selections of 500 related books are included.

KLIATT AUDIOBOOK GUIDE

By Jean B. Palmer. Libraries Unlimited, 1993. 250 pp.

This collection of 400 reviews of recommended audiobooks can be used for working with visually impaired, learning disabled, and reluctant readers.

THE LATEST AND GREATEST READALOUDS

By Sharron L. McElmeel. Libraries Unlimited, 1993. 200 pp.

This resource focuses on the best readaloud books for the elementary and middle school classroom. Reading level/ listening level by both grade and age is provided.

LEARNING AIDS: AN INFORMATION RESOURCE DIRECTORY. 2ND ED.

Edited by Trish Halleron, et al. Bowker, 1989. 280 pp.

This educational resource on AIDs is directed at educators and other professionals concerned with selecting appropriate materials for their clients. Included are tools for use in educational settings.

LIBROS EN ESPANOL PARA LOS PEQUENOS

New York Public Library, 1990. 32 pp.

This unique index is a collection of picture books and fairy tales that are written in Spanish and translated into English.

LITERATURE-BASED ART & MUSIC: CHILDREN'S BOOKS AND ACTIVITIES TO ENRICH THE K-5 CURRICULUM

By Mildred Knight Laughlin & Terri Parker Street. Oryx Press, 1992. 168 pp.

Step-by-step explanations of activities are included in this interdisciplinary program for art and music. All items are described in relation to selected stories and books.

LITERATURE-BASED MORAL EDUCATION: CHILDREN'S BOOKS AND ACTIVITIES FOR TEACHING VALUES, RESPONSIBILITY, AND GOOD JUDGEMENT IN THE ELEMENTARY SCHOOL

By Linda Leonard Lamme & Suzanne Lowell Krogh, with Kathy A. Yachmetz. Oryx Press, 1992. 168 pp.

Values, social skills, and good judgement can be taught through children's fiction. Nine values are discussed that are important for a child's moral development. Each of the nine value chapters is divided into rationale, classroom vignette, book reviews and curricular extensions, and summary.

LITERATURE-BASED READING: CHILDREN'S BOOKS AND ACTIVITIES TO ENRICH THE K-5 CURRICULUM
By Mildred Knight Laughlin & Claudia Lisman Swisher. Oryx Press, 1990. 168 pp.

Literary works provide reading experiences and activities that reinforce and enhance the process of acquiring language skills. Teachers are encouraged to help their students become independent, self-confident readers.

LITERATURE-BASED SOCIAL STUDIES: CHILDREN'S BOOKS AND ACTIVITIES TO ENRICH THE K-5 CURRICULUM
By Mildred Knight Laughlin & Patricia Payne Kardaleff. Oryx Press, 1991. 160 pp.

The Curriculum Task Force of the National Commission on Social Studies in Schools was used as a guide to set student goals for each grade level and to state the desired comprehension levels for each of the social studies subjects discussed. Subjects include families, friendship, world neighbors, American citizens, and the U.S. today and tomorrow.

THE LITERATURE OF DELIGHT: A CRITICAL GUIDE TO HUMOROUS BOOKS FOR CHILDREN
By Kimberly O. Fakih. Bowker, 1993. 352 pp.

Some 800 humorous titles are identified-both fiction and nonfiction. Author, title and subject indexes are provided as well as character and grade level. Entries are critcally annotated and range from first books to novels.

MAGAZINES FOR CHILDREN: A GUIDE FOR PARENTS, TEACHERS, AND LIBRARIANS. 2ND ED.
By Selma K. Richardson. American Library Association, 1991. 87 pp.

This annotated list profiles some 90 magazines for children preschool through eighth grade. Included are appendices for religious publishers, editions for the visually impaired, classification by age and grade level, and a subject index.

MAGAZINES FOR LIBRARIANS. 6TH ED.
By Bill Katz & Linda Sternberg Katz. Bowker, 1989. 1,159 pp.

This guide provides a description of 6,521 magazines and periodicals listed under 139 subject headings.

MAGAZINES FOR YOUNG PEOPLE: A CHILDREN'S MAGAZINE GUIDE COMPANION VOLUME. 2ND ED.
By Bill Katz & Linda Sternberg Katz. Bowker, 1991. 361 pp.

This volume describes and evaluates over 1,100 magazines for young people in 74 subjects. Updates are triennial.

MEDIA REVIEW DIGEST
Pieran Press. Annual updates.

This guide serves as a core media reference tool and a standard catalog for media information. The guide is divided into four sections: film and video, filmstrips, audio, and miscellaneous.

MICROCOMPUTER SOFTWARE SOURCES: A GUIDE FOR BUYERS, LIBRARIANS, PROGRAMMERS, BUSINESS PEOPLE, AND EDUCATORS.
Libraries Unlimited, 1990. 176 pp.

Sources for microcomputer software is profiled in 8 sections: the software industry and its sources; applications in business, education, and library; machine-specific software; guides to free and inexpensive software; and citations for directories, handbooks, journals, and newsletters.

MIRRORS OF AMERICAN CULTURE: CHILDREN'S FICTION SERIES IN THE TWENTIETH CENTURY.
By Paul Deane. Scarecrow Press, 1991. 275 pp.

Children's fiction series are some of the most popular and best-selling children's books. This study includes a historical survey, an examination of critical attitudes, an investigation of children's reading motives, and an analysis of style and methods.

MORE CREATIVE USES OF CHILDREN'S LITERATURE: VOLUME 1: INTRODUCING BOOKS IN ALL KINDS OF WAYS
By Mary Ann Paulin. Shoe String Press, 1992. 621 pp.

Titles published from 1980 to 1990 are listed in the annotated bibliographies that are arranged by subject and

genre. Booktalking, multimedia methods, and literature-based reading are discussed in detail. Indexes are included for author, title, subject, and nonprint formats.

MORE EXCITING, FUNNY, SCARY, SHORT, DIFFERENT AND SAD BOOKS, KIDS LIKE ABOUT ANIMALS, SCIENCE, SPORTS, FAMILIES, SONGS, AND OTHER THINGS
By Frances Laverne Carroll & Mary Meacham. American Library Association, 1992. 192 pp.

This briefly annotated bibliography of both fiction and nonfiction titles provides guidance for the most common subject requests received from children in libraries.

MORE STORY STRETCHERS
By Shirley C. Raines & Robert J. Canady. Association for Childhood Education International, 1991.

More than 90 well-loved children's books are used as the basis for teaching in this book.

MOTHER GOOSE COMES FIRST: AN ANNOTATED GUIDE TO THE BEST BOOKS AND RECORDINGS FOR YOUR PRE-SCHOOL CHILD
By Lois Winkel & S. Kimmel. Henry Holt, 1990. 194 pp.

This volume identifies over 700 book titles and recordings worthwhile for the preschool child. Author/illustrator/performer and title indexes are included.

MULTICULTURAL CHILDREN'S AND YOUNG ADULT LITERATURE: A SELECTED LISTING OF BOOKS PUBLISHED BETWEEN 1980-1988. 2ND ED.
Cooperative Children's Book Center, University of Wisconsin-Madison, 1989. 38 pp.

This annotated bibliography profiles a selected list of multicultural materials published between 1980-1988 in the United States and Canada.

THE MUSEUM OF SCIENCE AND INDUSTRY BASIC LIST OF CHILDREN'S SCIENCE BOOKS
By Bernice Richter and Duane Wenzel. American Library Association. Annual.

This basic booklist features the best trade science books published annually for children K-12. Annual supplements update the initial work. Also included are sections that cite adult sourcebooks, children's science magazines, a directory of publishers, review journals, science education journals, and author/title indexes.

MY COUNTRY TIS OF ME: HELPING CHILDREN DISCOVER CITIZENSHIP THROUGH CULTURAL HERITAGE

By Rita Kohn, et al. McFarland, 1988. 175 pp.

This book provides ideas for classroom explorations of family and community identity. An extensive annotated bibliography of resources is provided.

MY NAME IN BOOKS: AN ANNOTATED GUIDE TO CHILDREN'S LITERATURE

By Katharyn Puckett. Libraries Unlimited, 1993. 200 pp.

This guide helps users locate books by character names. It includes 2,000 entries with publication information, type of book, number of pages and a brief annotation.

NEAL-SCHUMAN INDEX TO FINGERPLAYS

Compiled by Kay Cooper, Edited by Jim Roginski. Neal-Schuman, 1993. 319 pp.

This index includes more than 1600 fingerplays that can be found in over 60 sources. Early childhood specialists, parents, librarians, and storytellers will find this to be a very valuable resource.

NEAL-SCHUMAN INDEX TO PERFORMING AND CREATIVE ARTISTS IN COLLECTIVE BIOGRAPHIES

By Susan Poorman. Neal-Schuman, 1991. 155 pp.

Children and young adults will find this index very useful. Biographies about thousands of performing artists such as dancers, actors, comedians, and musicians appear alphabetically in the main index. Each entry indicates the length of the biography and if it contains illustrations and photographs.

NEAL-SCHUMAN INDEX TO SPORTS FIGURES IN COLLECTIVE BIOGRAPHIES

By Paulette Bochnig Sharkey. Neal-Schuman, 1991. 167 pp.

This index lists 250 collective biographies that were published between 1965 and 1988. Each entry includes the athletes' nickname, birthdate, sport specialty, and length of biography.

THE NEWBERY AND CALDECOTT AWARDS: A GUIDE TO THE MEDAL AND HONOR BOOKS

By Association for Library Services to Children. Chicago: American Library Association. Annual.

The annual guide contains a listing of all Newbery and Caldecott award winning books and honor titles from 1922 through 1993. Brief descriptive annotations are provided.

NEWBERY AND CALDECOTT MEDAL AND HONOR BOOKS IN OTHER MEDIA

Compiled by Paulette Bochnig Sharkey. Neal-Schuman, 1992. 142 pp.

Now children with reading disabilities will enjoy listening to and reading award winning stories. This index provides a list of the classics that have been converted into braille and other audio-visual formats.

THE NEW YORK TIMES PARENT'S GUIDE TO THE BEST BOOKS FOR CHILDREN

By Eden Ross Lipson. Times Books, 1988. 448 pp.

This annotated bibliography, designed for parents, lists 956 books for children. Author, title and illustrator indexes are provided as well as those for read aloud, age-appropriate, and special subject indexes.

NONFICTION BOOKS FOR CHILDREN: ACTIVITIES FOR THINKING, LEARNING, AND DOING

By Carol Doll. Libraries Unlimited, 1990. 117 pp.

This book suggests creative ways for teachers to use some 60 nonfiction books for elementary curriculum enrichment. Indexes are provided by grade level and subject/activity.

NONFICTION FOR YOUNG ADULTS: FROM DELIGHT TO WISDOM

By Betty Carter & Richard F. Abrahamson. Oryx Press, 1990. 248 pp.

The uses of nonfiction books are explained to motivate young adults to utilize them in the classroom and the library. Interviews with seven well-known authors enhance the understanding of the creative process necessary in writing nonfiction.

NOW READ ON: A GUIDE TO CONTEMPORARY POPULAR FICTION

By Mandy Hicken & Ray Plytherch. Ashgate, 1990. 328 pp.

This comprehensive guide profiles modern English language fiction divided into eighteen genres. An author index and a list of characters are included.

100 WORLD-CLASS THIN BOOKS; OR WHAT TO READ WHEN YOUR BOOK REPORT IS DUE TOMORRROW!

By Joni Richards Bodart. Libraries Unlimited, 1993. 300 pp.

This volume reviews 100 books, each with 200 pages or less. Entries include bibliographic information, genre, grade level, subjects, characters, main themes, readability and ideas of how to write a book report or booktalk.

101 DESKTOP PUBLISHING AND GRAPHICS PROGRAMS

By Patrick R. Dewey. American Library Association, 1993. 225 pp.

This volume provides information about approximately 300 different desktop publishing and graphics software programs. A list of clip art collections are given to enhance graphics and font collections are described to reveal available type faces. Vendor information and a glossary are appended.

ONLY THE BEST: THE ANNUAL GUIDE TO THE HIGHEST-RATED EDUCATIONAL SOFTWARE PRESCHOOL - GRADE 12

Bowker, Annual

This selection guide profiles the best educational software programs indicated by 37 authoritative sources. Entries include a brief description, grade level recommendations and a listing of magazine reviews. A mid-year ALERT service provides an update on new programs available. Volume 1 (1985-1989) recommends the best 500 software programs on the market. The 1991 annual adds another 183 programs.

OUR FAMILY, OUR FRIENDS, OUR WORLD: AN ANNOTATED GUIDE TO SIGNIFICANT MULTICULTURAL BOOKS FOR CHILDREN AND TEENAGERS

By Lyn Miller-Lachmann, Bowker, 1991. 400 pp.

This guide is an annotated bibliography of the '' best fiction and nonfiction focusing on the life and character of ethnic and minority people living in the U. S. and Canada'' and other lands. Attention is given to age and reading levels.

OUT OF THE CLOSET AND INTO THE CLASSROOM: HOMOSEXUALITY IN BOOKS FOR YOUNG PEOPLE

By Laurel A. Clyde and Marjorie Lobban. Bowker, 1992. 150 pp.

This selection tool deals with homosexuality in books for young people, providing insight into the ways in which sexual preference and sexuality are presented to young people.

PAPERBACK BOOKS FOR CHILDREN: A SELECTED LIST TO AGE 13.

Child Study Book Committee. Bank Street College, 1988.

This annotated guide profiles over 500 paperback titles for children arranged by age and interest.

PARENT'S CHOICE MAGAZINE GUIDE TO VIDEOCASSETTES FOR CHILDREN

Edited by Diana Huss Green. Consumers Report Book, 1989. 270 pp.

This annotated guide lists "children videocassettes that will help expand their lives, their vision, and their sense that everything is possible." Included in the annotations are age levels and length of films. Appendices provide a list of videocassette services and a title index.

PEOPLES OF THE AMERICAN WEST: HISTORICAL PERSPECTIVES THROUGH CHILDREN'S LITERATURE

By Mary Hurlbut Cordier & Maria A. Perez-Stable. Scarecrow Press, 1989. 244 pp.

Over 100 historical fiction books are annotated in this bibliography about the American West dating from the 1530's to the early 1900's. Criteria for selection include realism of setting and events, nonsexist and nonracist character portrayals, literary qualities and availability.

PICTURE BOOKS FOR CHILDREN. 3RD ED.

American Library Association, 1990. 243 pp.

This resource guide is provided for "teachers of children from nursery school through junior high, for day care personnel, for librarians, school and public libraries, for parents and for other adults concerned with the selection of well-written, imaginatively illustrated picture books that are of interest to children of all ages and backgrounds." Author, title and illustrator indexes are included.

PICTURE BOOKS FOR LOOKING & LEARNING: AWAKENING VISUAL PERCEPTIONS THROUGH THE ART OF CHILDREN'S BOOKS

By Sylvia S. Marantz. Oryx Press, 1992. 248 pp.

The use of art in children's books is introduced by discussing the various media used and techniques employed by illustrators. Over 40 award-winning books are arranged by age group for the purposes of instruction.

PLAY, LEARN AND GROW: AN ANNOTATED GUIDE TO THE BEST BOOKS AND MATERIALS FOR YOUNG CHILDREN

By James L. Thomas. Bowker, 1992. 439pp.

This guide provides a full range of multimedia resources that will stimulate visual and auditory development in children. This highly evaluative resource lists over 1,100 print and nonprint materials. Each entry includes complete bibliographic information, age level, a brief annotation and a priority purchase ranking for each entry.

POPULAR READING FOR CHILDREN III: A COLLECTION OF BOOKLIST COLUMNS

Edited by Sally Estes. American Library Association, 1992. 64 pp.

This third compilation of popular reading lists that have been approved in *Booklist* includes a mix of genres and subjects that appeal to a variety of reading abilities and tastes.

PORTRAYING PERSONS WITH DISABILITIES: AN ANNOTATED BIBLIOGRAPHY OF FICTION FOR CHILDREN AND TEENAGERS

By Debra Robertson. Bowker, 1992. 482 pp.

This selective annotated bibliography includes more than 650 fiction books that promote understanding of the disabled. Titles are grouped by broad disability categories.

PORTRAYING PERSONS WITH DISABILITIES: AN ANNOTATED BIBLIOGRAPHY OF NONFICTION FOR CHILDREN AND TEENAGERS

By Joan Brest Friedberg, et al. Bowker, 1992. 385 pp.

This selective bibliography describes and evaluates over 350 nonfiction titles published between 1984-1991 which encourage readers to develop open attitudes about people with dis-

abilities. Titles are grouped by broad disability categories.

PRIMARYPLOTS 2: A BOOK TALK GUIDE FOR USE WITH READERS AGES 4-8

By Rebecca L. Thomas. Bowker, 1993. 400 pp.

This booktalk guide profiles 150 of the best picture books published 1988-1992.

PROMINENT SCIENTISTS: AN INDEX TO COLLECTIVE BIOGRAPHIES. 3RD ED.

By Paul A. Pelletier. Neal-Schuman, 1994. 353 pp.

This index lists 330 collective biographies that have been published since 1960. Readers will find over 14,000 biographies of famous scientists.

REACHING CHILDREN-AT-RISK: MULTIMEDIA RESOURCES

By Grady Sue Saxon, et al. Bowker, 1992. 400 pp.

This tool is an annotated bibliography of source materials (both print and nonprint) for teachers working with children at risk.

READ ALL YOUR LIFE: A SUBJECT GUIDE TO FICTION

By Barbara Kerr Davis. McFarland. 296 pp.

This book, intended for book discussion groups, provides a subject guide to fiction books appropriate for adults and recommended for high school students.

RECORDING FOR THE BLIND

Catalog of Recorded Books. Princeton, NJ: Recording for the Blind. Irregular.

This catalog lists free educational books on tapes for the visually handicapped and over 60,000 textbook titles available in cassette format.

RECOMMENDED REFERENCE BOOKS FOR SMALL AND MEDIUM-SIZED LIBRARIES AND MEDIA CENTERS. 12TH ED.

Edited by Bohdan S. Wynar. Libraries Unlimited, 1993. 300 pp.

This volume reviews 546 titles chosen to be the most valuable reference books published during 1991.

RECOMMENDED REFERENCE BOOKS IN PAPERBACK. 2ND ED.

By Andrew L. March, Libraries Unlimited, 1992. 263 pp.

Nearly 1,000 in-print paperback reference books are provided in this volume.

REFERENCE BOOKS FOR CHILDREN

By Carolyn Sue Peterson and Ann D. Fenton. 4th ed. Scarecrow Press, 1992. 415 pp.

Over 1,000 titles are included in this buying guide for both public and school libraries. The materials cover a wide range of interests, curriculum needs, and levels of difficulty through middle school.

REFERENCE BOOKS FOR CHILDREN'S COLLECTIONS

New York Public Library, 1991. 109 pp.

Librarians and teachers can select from over 400 titles to find books suitable for almost any reading level. A vast number of subjects are covered from general reference to language, sports, literature and art.

REFERENCE BOOKS FOR YOUNG READERS: AUTHORITATIVE EVALUATIONS OF ENCYCLOPEDIAS, ATLASES, AND DICTIONARIES

Edited by Marian Sader. Bowker, 1988. 627 pp.

This volume provides evaluations for encyclopedias, atlases and dictionaries and allows comparisons of similar reference services.

REFERENCE GUIDE TO SCIENCE FICTION, FANTASY AND HORROR

By Michael Burgess. Libraries Unlimited, 1992. 404 pp.

This compilation provides an overview of reference materials in the genre of science fiction, fantasy and horror. Included are bibliographies, dictionaries, encyclopedias, directories and indexes.

REFERENCE SOURCES FOR SMALL AND MEDIUM SIZED LIBRARIES. 5TH ED.

American Library Association, 1992. 352 pp.

This annotated bibliography updates the reference sources needed for small and medium sized libraries covering all Dewey Decimal classification fields including traditional materials for children and young people. Included are sources of microfilm, on-line databases, and CD-ROM products.

RELIGIOUS BOOKS FOR CHILDREN: AN ANNOTATED BIBLIOGRAPHY

By Patricia Pearl. Church and Synagogue Library Association, 1988. 36 pp.

This annotated bibliography provides a core collection of over 400 books on religion for preschool through grade 6.

RIP-ROARING READS FOR RELUCTANT TEEN READERS. 2ND ED

By Gale W. Sherman & Bette D. Ammon. Libraries Unlimited, 1993. 150 pp.

This volume provides 40 (20 for grades 5-8 and 20 for grades 9-12) contemporary titles for reluctant teen readers.

THE SCHOOL LIBRARIAN'S SOURCEBOOK

By Claire Rudin. Bowker, 1990. 504 pp.

A bibliography of professional resources for the school media specialist. Entries include a description of the book's purpose, information about the author(s) or editors and a final comment.

SCIENCE & TECHNOLOGY: A PURCHASE GUIDE FOR LIBRARIES

The Carnegie Library of Pittsburgh, 1992. (Annual).

This annotated bibliography of over 1,000 new books received by the Carnegie Library of Pittsburgh for both students and adults, provides books of interest to the general reader on the subject of science and technology.

SCIENCE & TECHNOLOGY IN FACT AND FICTION: A GUIDE TO CHILDREN'S BOOKS

By DayAnn Kennedy, et. al. Bowker, 1990. 331 pp.

This resource lists scientific, technological, and futuristic works selected from top professional journals recommended by teachers and librarians. Author, title, illustrator, subject and readability indexes are included.

SCIENCE & TECHNOLOGY IN FACT AND FICTION: A GUIDE TO YOUNG ADULT BOOKS

By DayAnn Kennedy, et al. Bowker, 1990. 363 pp.

This evaluative annotated bibliography of both fiction and nonfiction titles helps to satisfy the teenagers curiosity about science.

SCIENCE BOOK AND FILMS' BEST BOOKS FOR CHILDREN, 1988-1991

Edited by Maria Sosa & Shirley M. Malcom. Association for the Advancement of Applied Science, 1992. 300 pp.

This volume contains all books recommended in *Science Books and Films* from 1988-1991. The books annotated are arranged alphabetically within broad subject headings.

SCIENCE FICTION AND FANTASY REFERENCE INDEX 1985-1991

By Hal W. Hall. Libraries Unlimited, 1993. 675 pp.

This work provides 14,000 books, articles, and news reports in the science fiction, fantasy, and horror genres.

SCIENCE FOR CHILDREN: RESOURCES FOR TEACHERS

By the National Science Research Center. National Academy Press, 1988. 176 pp.

This resource guide provides access to a large collection of science materials for children.

SENIOR HIGH SCHOOL LIBRARY CATALOG. 14 ED.

H. W. Wilson, 1992. 1,464 pp.

This research tool serves as a guide for a high school library in collection development and maintenance. Over 6,000 fiction and nonfiction titles are represented as essential to a senior high school collection grades 9-12.

SENIORPLOTS: A BOOK TALK GUIDE FOR USE WITH READERS AGES 15-18

By John T. Gillespie and Corinne J. Naden. Bowker, 1989. 386 pp.

This booktalk guide groups 1,050 best books under a dozen themes and genres popular with teenagers. Highlighted are 80 contemporary fiction and nonfiction works.

SENSITIVE ISSUES: AN ANNOTATED GUIDE TO CHILDREN'S LITERATURE K-6

By Timothy V. Rasinski & Cindy S. Gillespie. Oryx Press, 1992. 176 pp.

This whole-language guide deals with such subjects as divorce, substance abuse, death and dying, home environments, child abuse, prejudice and cultural differences, moving, illness, and disability. The acting strategies, high-interest activities, resources for teachers and parents, and a directory of publishers are included.

SEQUELS: AN ANNOTATED GUIDE TO NOVELS IN SERIES. 2ND ED.

By Janet Husband & Jonathan F. Husband. American Library Association, 1990. 576 pp.

This volume provides recreational reading sources for novels in series. This edition offers expanded coverage of mystery and detective fiction and updated entries for prolific authors included in the first edition.

THE SINGLE - PARENT FAMILY IN CHILDREN'S BOOKS: AN ANNOTATED BIBLIOGRAPHY. 2ND ED.
By Catherine Townsend Horner. Scarecrow, 1988. 339 pp.

This annotated bibliography of more than 600 fiction and nonfiction titles features topics related to single parent families such as divorce, separation and desertion. Author, title and subject indexes are provided.

SLIDE BUYERS' GUIDE: AN INTERNATIONAL DIRECTORY OF SLIDE SOURCES FOR ART AND ARCHITECTURE. 6TH ED.
Edited by Norine D. Cashman. Libraries Unlimited, 1990. 190 pp.

This guide offers slide sources in the U. S., Canada, and foreign countries for art and architecture. Included are individuals, companies, museums, and institutions that have slides for sale, rent or exchange.

SOFTWARE INFORMATION FOR APPLE II COMPUTERS
Pittsburgh, PA: Black Box, 1990. 829 pp.

This volume lists 12,000 programs for Apple II Computers. This directory is available through Applelink and Dialog.

SOFTWARE REVIEWS ON FILE
Facts on File.

This monthly review file profiles over 600 software programs per year published in 125 journals. Indexing by subject and computer is provided.

SOURCES OF INFORMATION FOR HISTORICAL RESEARCH
By Thomas P. Slavens. Neal-Schuman, 1994. 577 pp.

Students, researches, and librarians are directed on how to use archives and biographies to find global historical information. Entries are fully annotated.

STORY STRETCHERS FOR THE PRIMARY GRADES
By Shirley C. Raines & Robert J. Canady. Gryphon House, 1991.

This volume provides 90 children's book titles for the primary grades K-3 for teachers to use in their lesson plans.

THE STORYTIME SOURCEBOOK: A COMPENDIUM OF IDEAS AND RESOURCES FOR STORYTELLERS
By Carolyn N. Cullum. Neal-Schuman, 1990. 177 pp.

Listed are picture books and audio-visual materials recommended for 3 - 7 year olds. Suggestions for story hour activities such as fingerplays, games and craft projects are provided under each entry.

A SUBJECT BIBLIOGRAPHY OF THE FIRST WORLD WAR: BOOKS IN ENGLISH, 1914-1987
By A. G. S. Enser. Ashgate, 1990. 520 pp.

This reference guide contains 6,800 entries about World War I which are indexed by author, title and listed under 350 subject headings.

A SUBJECT BIBLIOGRAPHY OF THE SECOND WORLD WAR AND THE AFTERMATH: BOOKS IN ENGLISH 1975-1987
By A. G. S. Enser. 2nd. ed. Ashgate, 1990. 287 pp.

This bibliography includes over 1,600 entries about World War II. An author and title index are included.

SUBJECT GUIDE TO CHILDREN'S BOOKS IN PRINT 1994
Bowker, 1994. 856 pp Annual.

Subject information for every available fiction and nonfiction children's book in print is provided in this source. Full bibliographic information for each entry is furnished. Annual updates are maintained.

SUBSTANCE ABUSE: A RESOURCE GUIDE FOR SECONDARY SCHOOLS
By Sally L. Myers & Blanche Woolls. Libraries Unlimited, 1991. 168 pp.

This annotated bibliography of books and media offers coverage to titles about alcohol, drugs, tobacco, steroids, caffeine and other substances. A core collection of items for the school media center is included.

SUPERNATURAL FICTION FOR TEENS: MORE THAN 1300 GOOD PAPERBACKS TO READ FOR WONDERMENT, FEAR, AND FUN. 2ND ED.
By Cosette Kies. Libraries Unlimited, 1992. 267 pp.

This collection contains 1,300 paperback books of supernatural fiction for teens. Appendices include "books in series" and "movie list."

T.E.S.S. THE EDUCATIONAL SOFTWARE SELECTION
EPIE Institute. Annual.

This tool lists available educational software plus a group of "classic" programs. Descriptions are provided in terms of educational philosophy, hardware requirements, instruction methods and subject/grade levels. This list is available through CompuServe and is updated bimonthly.

TRIED AND TRUE: 500 NONFICTION BOOKS CHILDREN WANT TO READ
By George Wilson and Joyce Moss. Bowker, 1992. 300 pp.

This 500 item selective annotated bibliography details the best child-tested nonfiction. Books are grouped for reading pleasure, research and subject-specific titles. Entries contain full bibliographic information, reading level and a brief description.

TWINS IN CHILDREN'S AND ADOLESCENT LITERATURE: AN ANNOTATED BIBLIOGRAPHY
By Dee Storey. Scarecrow Press. 1993 410 pp.

Over 300 books published between 1904 and 1992 that feature twins as the main topic. Each annotation describes the characters and their feelings about being twins. Authors' comments are included regarding their reasons for writing about twins.

202(+) MICROCOMPUTER SOFTWARE PACKAGES TO USE IN YOUR LIBRARY: DESCRIPTIONS, EVALUATIONS AND PRACTICAL ADVICE. 2ND ED.
By Patrick R. Dewey. American Library Association, 1992. 180 pp.

More than 250 software packages are recommended in this second edition. Packages are fully described and programs are identified by function.

UNDERSTANDING ABILITIES, DISABILITIES, AND CAPABILITIES: A GUIDE TO CHILDREN'S LITERATURE
By Margaret F. Carlin, et al. Libraries Unlimited, 1991. 114 pp.

A bibliography of titles appropriate for children, ages 2-18, is provided to address over 40 handicapping conditions in books, films and other nonprint media.

U.S. GOVERNMENT BOOKS
Government Printing Office. Quarterly.

This free annotated guide lists over 1,000 government publications arranged by topics such as business and industry, careers, agriculture and consumer aids.

U. S. GOVERNMENT PUBLICATIONS FOR THE SCHOOL LIBRARY MEDIA CENTER. 2ND ED.
By Leticia T. Ekhaml & Alice J. Wittig. Libraries Unlimited, 1991. 156 pp.

This quick-reference guide and checklist describes U. S. government documents in a format that reflects curriculum needs for a school library media center. A list of basic selection tools is also included.

U.S. HISTORY: A RESOURCE BOOK FOR SECONDARY SCHOOLS, VOLUME I, 1450-1865; U.S. HISTORY: A RESOURCE BOOK FOR SECONDARY SCHOOLS, VOLUME 2, 1865-PRESENT
By James R. Giese & Laurel R. Singleton. ABC-CLIO, 1989. 347 pp.

This two-volume set provides secondary school students and high school teachers involved with the study of the history of the United States an abundance of primary and information sources. All print and nonprint citations are annotated. A glossary and detailed index are included.

USING CHILDREN'S BOOKS IN READING/LANGUAGE ARTS PROGRAMS
By Diane D. Canavan & Lavonne H. Sanborn. Neal-Schuman, 1992. 216 pp.

This bibliography is recommended for finding children's books that support instructional objectives for reading and language arts theories.

USING GOVERNMENT DOCUMENTS: A HOW-TO-DO-IT MANUAL FOR SCHOOL LIBRARIANS
By Melody S. Kelly. Neal-Schuman, 1992. 176 pp.

Elementary and secondary school librarians can turn here to find out how to obtain inexpensive or free government documents. The U.S. government publishes maps, charts, posters, software, and other multimedia materials that can be used to support the curriculum.

USING MEDIA TO MAKE KIDS FEEL GOOD
By Maureen Gaffney. Oryx, 1988. 253 pp.

This book is an annotated guide to 62 short films for elementary school children. Many films are suitable for children with limited English proficiency and the learning disabled. Age and theme indexes are provided.

USING NONFICTION TRADE BOOKS IN THE ELEMENTARY CLASSROOM: FROM ANTS TO ZEPPELINS
By Evelyn B. Freeman & Diane Goetz Person, Editors. National Council of Teachers of English, 1992. 183 pp.

Elementary school teachers will find numerous nonfiction book titles to suit a specific topic or use in a complete unit of study. This practical collection provides comprehensive bibliographies, as well as recommended classroom activities that complement the curriculum.

USING PICTURE STORYBOOKS TO TEACH LITERARY DEVICES: RECOMMENDED BOOKS FOR CHILDREN AND YOUNG ADULTS
By Susan Hall. Oryx Press, 1990. 176 pp.

Picture storybooks can be used successfully from second grade children through young adults. This guide describes 273 picture storybooks published between 1980 and 1988 that illustrate allusion, puns, imagery, paradox, simile, analogy, satire, and other literary devices.

UNIVERSITY PRESS BOOKS FOR PUBLIC AND SECONDARY SCHOOL LIBRARIES
Association of American University Presses, 1991. 114 pp.

This annotated bibliography provides access to over 500 titles for public and secondary school libraries published by university presses. Arranged by the Dewey Decimal System, the entries contain complete bibliographic information, a short annotation, and reading level/appeal coding. Author, title and a directory of contributing publishers' indexes are included.

VARIETY'S VIDEO DIRECTORY PLUS
Bowker. Annual.

This online guide includes 62,000 videos searchable by 20 search criteria to find exact titles. Searches may display or print out over 2,500 full text, critical reviews. A MacIntosh version is available.

VENTURE INTO CULTURES: A RESOURCE BOOK OF MULTICULTURAL MATERIALS AND PROGRAMS
Edited by Carla D. Hayden. American Library Association, 1992. 165 pp.

This annotated bibliography offers multicultural titles, including those in native languages.

VERTICAL FILE INDEX: GUIDE TO PAMPHLETS AND REFERENCES TO CURRENT TOPICS
H. W. Wilson, Monthly except August

This index, arranged alphabetically by subject, lists free and inexpensive materials on current topics from kindergarten to adult. A title index is also provided.

VIDEO FOR LIBRARIANS: SPECIAL INTEREST VIDEOS FOR SMALL AND MEDIUM-SIZED PUBLIC LIBRARIES
Edited by Sally Mason & James C. Schotz. American Library Association, 1988. 163 pp.

This list designed for public librarians includes videos recommended for children and young adults. Children's titles are arranged alphabetically and young adult books are identified with YA symbols.

THE VIDEO SOURCE BOOK. 13TH ED.
Edited by Julie C. Furtaw. Gale Research, 1992. 2 vols.

This listing of over 126,000 available video programs describes subject areas from a wide range of educational tapes. Programs available for lease or purchase in a variety of video formats are included. Access to the programs are provided through video program listings, or indexes by subject, credits, videodisc, 8 mm or captioned. A distribution list is included.

VIDEOS FOR UNDERSTANDING DIVERSITY: A CORE SELECTION AND EVALUATION GUIDE
By George I. Stevens. American Library Association, 1993. 300 pp.

This guide profiles 126 feature and documentary videos selected for classroom use. Technical and production data for each video are provided.

WALFORD GUIDE TO REFERENCE MATERIAL. VOL. 1: SCIENCE AND TECHNOLOGY. 6TH ED.
Edited by Marilyn Mullay & Priscilla Schicke. Unipub, 1993. 796 pp.

This volume contains reference materials on the subject of science and technology covering such subjects as optics, genetics, wildlife conservation, medicine, agriculture and textiles.

WALFORD GUIDE TO REFERENCE MATERIAL. VOL. 3: GENERALIA, LANGUAGE AND LITERATURE, AND THE ARTS. 5TH ED.
By A. Chalcraft, et al. Unipub, 1991. 1,035 pp.

This volume provides over 8,800 reference materials on generalists, language, literature and the arts.

WAR AND PEACE LITERATURE FOR CHILDREN AND YOUNG ADULTS: A RESOURCE GUIDE TO SIGNIFICANT ISSUES
By Virginia A. Walter. Oryx Press, 1993. 184 pp.

The quality titles in this index cover a wide range of reading levels from preschool children to ninth graders. Teachers will be able to find books about historical and fictional wars. Annotations provide an analytical approach to the literary themes which explore the ambiguity and resolutions of human conflicts.

WHAT DO CHILDREN READ NEXT?
Edited by Candy Colborn. Gale Research, 1993. 800 pp.

This selection aid lists 2,000 modern and classic book titles. Entries are listed in alphabetical order by author and include complete bibliographies. Ten indexes are provided for the user to gain easy access to books of interest.

WHAT DO YOUNG ADULTS READ NEXT?
Edited by Pam Spencer. Gale Research, 1993. 700 pp.

Young adults will find a list of 1,500 book titles of interest to them. This easy to use selection aid arranges the entries in alphabetical order according to the author's name. Ten indexes are provided to assist the user in locating a particular book. Entries include detailed bibliographies.

WOMEN'S ISSUES: AN ANNOTATED BIBLIOGRAPHY

By Laura Stemel Mumfor. Salem Press, 1989. 163 pp.

This annotated bibliography, designed for high school students and college undergraduates, profiles materials on womens issues.

THE WONDERFUL WORLD OF MATHEMATICS: A CRITICALLY ANNOTATED LIST OF CHILDREN'S BOOKS IN MATHEMATICS
Edited by Diane Thiessen & Margaret Matthias. National Council of Teachers of Mathematics, 1992. 241 pp.

This guide reviews 500 mathematics books for children. The reviews "describe each books content and accuracy, its illustrations and their appropriateness, the author's writing style, and the activities, if any, in the book."

WORDLESS/ALMOST WORDLESS PICTURE BOOKS: A GUIDE
By Virginia H. Richey & Katharyn E. Pucket. Libraries Unlimited, 1992. 223 pp.

This annotated bibliography covers books in which the illustrations provide the complete story - alphabet and number books, concept books, and books with minimal text. Indexes are provided for both subject and themes which make this a valuable source for whole language classrooms.

WORDS ON CASSETTE
Bowker. Annual.

This annual publication lists more than 49,000 spoken-word audio cassettes in numerous subject areas such as art, business, education, and literature. Indexing is provided for author, title, subject, producer/distributor and reader. More than 900 producers and distributors are listed.

WORLD HISTORY FOR CHILDREN AND YOUNG ADULTS: AN ANNOTATED BIBLIOGRAPHIC INDEX
By Vandelia VanMeter. Libraries Unlimited, 1992. 425 pp.

This index identifies and describes hundreds of books on world events, both fiction and nonfiction, for elementary and secondary students. Books are arranged by time periods, subdivided by subject, and indexed by grade level.

YOUNG ADULT BOOK REVIEW INDEX
Edited by Barbara Beach. Gale Research, 1988. Annual.

This index offers 16,800 reviews of 6,300 books and periodicals that are recommended for ages 11 to 17. Full-length audio books are also reviewed.

YOUNG ADULT READER'S ADVISOR. 2 VOLS
Bowker, 1992. 1,702 pp.

A two-volume resource features 17,000 bibliographic entries and over 850 biographical profiles providing guidance in selecting classroom reading material and books for pleasure reading. Books suited for grades 6-8 are noted and brief annotations are provided when necessary.

YOUNG PEOPLE'S BOOKS IN SERIES
By Judith K. Rosenberg & C. Allen Nichols. Libraries Unlimited, 1992. 424 pp.

This volume contains every series published from 1976-1990 from early elementary grades through high school. A disc version is also available.

YOUR READING: A BOOKLIST FOR JUNIOR HIGH AND MIDDLE SCHOOL
Edited by C. Anne Webb. 9th ed. National Council of Teachers of English, 1993. 250 pp.

This annotated bibliography of titles published between 1991 and 1992 is divided into 4 sections: Imagining, Exploring, Learning and Understanding, and offers an appendix of suggested readings.

NAMES & NUMBERS INDEX TO CHILDREN'S MEDIA SOURCES

A Child's Story, 477B Cedar Lane, Teaneck, NJ 07666. 201-907-0260.
(5)

A Children's Place, 1631 N. E. Broadway, Portland 97232. 503-284-
8294. (5)

A Clean Well-Lighted Place For Books,
2417 Larkspur Landing Circle, Larkspur, CA 94939. 415-461-0171.
(5)

A Kids Book Shop, 1849 NE Miami
Gardens Dr., North Miami Beach, FL
33179. 305-937-2665. (5)

A Likely Story, 5740 Sunset Drive,
South Miami, FL 33143. 305-667-
3730. (5)

A Likely Story, 9231 N. Penn Place,
Oklahoma City, OK 73132. 405-840-
2042. (5)

Abbeville Press, 488 Madison Ave.,
New York, NY 10022. 212-888-
1969, 800-227-7210; Fax: 212-
644-5085. (1)

ABC-CLIO, Box 1911, Santa Barbara,
CA 93117. 800-422-2546; Fax:
805-685-9685. (2)

ABC Multimedia Group, 77 W. 66th
St., 21st Fl., New York, NY 10023.
212-456-7746. (3)

ABC News Interactive, 30 Technology
Dr., Warren, NJ 07059. (2)

Abingdon Press, Box 801, Nashville,
TN 37202-0801. 615-749-6290,
800-251-3320; Fax: 615-749-6512.
(1)

Abingdon Press, Div. of the United
Methodist Publishing House, 201
Eighth Ave. S, Nashville, TN 37202.
615-749-6291. (3)

About Black Children, 4509 S. King
Dr., Chicago, IL 60653.
312-285-4568. (5)

Harry N. Abrams, 100 Fifth Ave., New
York, NY 10011. 212-206-7715,
800-345-1359. (1)

Academic Hallmarks, Inc., Box 998,
Durango, CO 81302. 800-321-9218.
(2)

Academic Therapy Publications, 20
Commercial Blvd., Novato, CA
94949-6191. 415-883-3314, 800-
422-7249 (orders outside CA); Fax:
415-883-3720. (1)

Academy Chicago Publishers, 363 W.
Erie St., Chicago, IL 60610-3125.
312-751-7300, 800-248-7323
(orders-outside IL only); Fax:
312-751-7306. (1)

Academy Of Family Films And Family
Television, 334 W. 54th St., Los
Angeles, CA 90037. 213-752-5811.
(15)

Academy One, 6330 Lincoln Ave., Ste.
117, Cypress, CA 90630. 714-821-
4472. (12)

Accent Publications, 12100 W. Sixth
Ave., Denver, CO 80215. 303-988-
5300; Fax: 303-989-7737. (1)

Access, American Forum for Global
Education, 45 John St., Ste. 908,
New York, NY 10038. 212-732-
8606. (10)

Acculab Products Group, 200 California Ave., Palo Alto, CA 94306-1618.
415-325-5898. (2)

Activision, 11440 San Vicente Blvd.,
Ste. 300, Los Angeles, CA 90049.
310-207-4500, 800-477-3650. (2)

Adams Film Productions, 706 Wayside
Dr., Austin, TX 78703.
512-477-8846. (3)

Addison-Wesley Publishing Co., Inc.,
One Jacob Way, Reading, MA 01867-
3999. 617-944-3700, 800-447-
2226; Fax: 617-944-9338. (1, 2)

Richard H. Adelson Antiquarian Bookseller, North Pomfret, VT 05053.
802-457-2608. (6)

Adobe Systems, 1585 Charleston Rd.,
Box 7900, Mountain View, CA
94039-7900. 415-961-4400, 800-
833-6687; Fax: 415-961-3769. (2)

Advantage Learning Systems, Dept.
1100, Box 36, Wisconsin Rapids, WI
54495-0036. 800-338-4204. (2)

Adventures For Kids, 3457 Telegraph,
Ventura, CA 93003. 805-650-9688.
(5)

Africa World Press, Box 1892, Trenton, NJ 08607. 609-771-2666; Fax:
609-771-1616. (1)

African American Cultural Center,
2560 W. 54th St., Los Angeles, CA
90008. 213-299-6124. (13)

African American Images, 1909 W.
95th St., Chicago, IL 60643. 312-

445-0322; Fax: 312-445-9844. (1, 3)

African Studies Center, Univ. of Wisconsin, 1454 Van Hise Hall, Madison, WI 53706. 608-263-2171. (13)

AFS Intercultural Programs, 313 E.
43rd St., New York, NY 10017.
212-949-4242. (13)

Agency For Instructional Technology,
(AIT-THE LEARNING SOURCE), Box A,
Bloomington, IN 47402. 812-339-
2203; Fax: 812-333-2478. (2, 3, 15)

AGS Media, (formerly Ikonographics,
Inc), 1810 Sils Ave., Louisville, KY
40205. 502-451-3506. (3)

Aims Media, 9710 DeSoto Ave., Chatsworth, CA 91311. 800-267-2467;
Fax: 818-341-6700. (3)

Akiba Press, Box 13086, Oakland, CA
94661. (1)

Akwesasne Communication Society,
Box 140, Rooseveltown, NY 13683.
613-938-1113. (13)

ALA Video/Library Video Network, 320,
York Rd., Towson, MD 21204. 410-
887-2082. Fax: 410-887-2091. (3)

Alabama Department of Education,
Student Instructional Services Division, Gordon Persons Bldg., Rm.
3340, 50 North St., Montgomery, AL
36130. (17)

Alabama Instructional Media Associa-
tion, C/O Darnell Whited, Oneonta
City Schools, (H) 606 Ridgeway Dr.,
Oneonta, AL 35121. 205-274-0918;
Fax: 205-274-2910. (16)

Alabama Library Association, C/O Mar-
garet Blake, 2569 Old Dobbins Rd.,
Mobile, AL 36695. 205-690-8377;
Fax: 205-690-8015. (16)

Aladdin Software, 1001 Colfax St.,
Danville, IL 61832. 217-443-4611.
(2)

The Alan Review, National Council of
Teachers of English, Radford University, Radford, VA 24142. 703-831-
5439, 217-328-3890. (10)

Alarion Press, Inc., Box 1882, Boulder,
CO 80306. 800-523-9177. (3)

Alaska Library Association, c/o Rita
Dursi Johnson, University of Alaska
Southeast, William Eagan Library,
11120 Glacier Hwy., Juneau, AK
99801-8676. 907-465-6285. (16)

Alaska Technology Roundtable Of The Alaska Library Association, c/o Lois Stiegemeier, Alaska Department of Education, Box F, Juneau, AK 99811. 907-465-2644. (16).

Albuquerque Children's Museum, 800 Rio Grande N.W., #10, Albuquerque, NM 87110. 505-842-1537; Fax: 505-842-5915. (14)

Aldus, 411 First Ave. S, Seattle, WA 98104. 206-628-4511; Fax: 206-343-4240. (2)

Aleph-Bet Books, Inc., 670 Waters Edge, Valley Cottage, NY 10989. 914-268-7410; Fax: 914-268-5942. (6)

Alexander Graham Bell Association For The Deaf, 3417 Volta Place, NW, Washington, DC 20007. 202-337-5220 Voice/TT. (1, 15)

Alfred Publishing Company, 16380 Roscoe Blvd., Ste. 200, Box 10003, Van Nuys, CA 91410-0003. 818-891-5999, 800-292-6122; Fax: 818-891-2182. (1)

Alice's Wonderland, 975B Detroit Ave., Concord, CA 94518. 510-682-1760. (5)

All American Video Productions, Inc., 1323 Mt. Hermon Rd., Ste. 6-A, Salisbury, MD 21801. 813-473-2601; Fax: 813-473-2701. (3)

All Dolled Up, 3318 W. Martin Luther King, Jr. Blvd., Los Angeles, CA 90008. 213-969-1740. (13)

All For Kids Books, 2943 N.E. Blakeley St., Seattle, WA 98105. 206-526-2768. (5)

Doug Allard's Flathead Indian Museum and Trading Post, #1 Museum Lane, Box 460, St. Ignatius, MT 59865. 406-745-2951, 800-821-3318; Fax: 406-745-2961. (14)

Robert Allen Books, Box 582, Altadena, CA 91003. 818-794-4210; Fax: 818-306-6970. (6)

Allied Books & Educational Resources, 1362 Trinity, Ste. D2208, Los Alamos, NM 87544. 505-662-9705. (4)

Alphabet Soup, 405 Front St., Belvidere, NJ 07823. 908-475-1914. (5)

Altana Films, 61 Main St., Southampton, NY 11968. 516-283-8662. (3)

Altschul Group Corporation, 1560 Sherman Ave. Ste. 100, Evanston, Il

60201. 800-323-9084; Fax: 708-328-6706. (3)

Alyson Publications, 40 Plympton St., Boston, MA 02118. 617-542-5679. (1)

Ambassador Book Service, 42 Chasner St, Hempstead, NY 11550. 516-489-4011; 800-431-8913. (4)

American Association for Chinese Studies, 300 Bricker Hall, Ohio State Univ., Columbus, OH 43210. 614-292-6681. (13)

American Association Of School Administrators, 1801 N. Moore St., Arlington, VA 22209-9988. 703-528-0700. (15)

American Association Of School Librarians (AASL), Division of the American Library Association, 50 E. Huron St., Chicago, IL 60611. 312-944-6780; 800-545-2433. (15)

American Association Of Teachers Of Spanish And Portuguese, University of Northern Colorado, Gunter Hall, Room 106, Greeley, Colorado 80639. 303-351-1090; Fax: 303-351-1095. (15)

American Bible Society, 1865 Broadway, New York, NY 10023. 212-408-1200. (1, 3)

American Choral Directors Association, Box 6310, Lawton, OK 73506. 405-355-8161. (15)

American College Of Musicians/ National Guild Of Piano Teachers, Box 1807, Austin, TX 78767. 512-478-5575. (15)

American Community Cultural Center Association, 19 Foothills Dr., Pompton Plains, NJ 07444. 201-835-2661. (13)

American Educational, 7506 N. Broadway Ext., Oklahoma City, OK 73116-9016. 405-840-6031, 800-222-2811; Fax: 405-848-3960. (2)

American Educational Research Association (AERA), 1230 17th St., NW, Washington, DC 20036. 202-223-9485. (15)

American Educator, American Federation of Teachers, 555 New Jersey Ave., NW, Washington, DC 20001. 202-879-4420. (10)

American Federation Of Teachers, 555 New Jersey Ave., NW, Washington, DC 20001. 202-879-4400. (15)

American Film & Video Association, (formerly Educational Film & Video Association), Box 48659, 8050 Millawake, Niles, IL 60714. 708-698-6440; Fax: 708-352-7528. (15)

American Foundation For The Blind, AFB Press, 15 W. 16th St., New York, NY 10011. 212-620-2000, 800-232-5463; Fax: 212-620-2105. (1, 15)

American Girl, Pleasant Company Publicatons, Inc., 8400 Fairway Pl, Middleton, WI 53562. 608-836-4848; Fax: 608-836-1999. (9)

American Guidance Service, 4201 Woodland Road, Circle Pines, MN 55014. 612-786-4343. (3)

American Historical Society of Germans from Russia (AHSGR), AHSGR Heritage Center, 631 D St., Lincoln, NE 68502-1199. 402-474-3363. (13)

American History Illustrated, Cowles Magazines (Sub. of Cowles Media Co.), 6405 Flank Dr., Box 8200, Harrisburg, PA 17105-8299. 717-657-9555; Fax: 717-657-9526. (9)

American Indian Culture Research Center (AICRC), Box 98, Blue Cloud Abbey, Marvin, SD 57251. 605-432-5528. (13)

American Indian Heritage Foundation (AIHF), 6051 Arlington Blvd., Falls Church, VA 22044. 202-463-4267. (13)

American Indian Studies Center and Library, Univ. of California, Los Angeles, 405 Hilgard Ave., 3220 Campbell Hall, Los Angeles, CA 90024. (13)

American Irish Historical Society (AIHS), 991 Fifth Ave., New York, NY 10028. 212-288-2263. (13)

American Israel Friendship League (AIFL), 134 E.39th St., New York, NY 10016. 212-213-8630. (13)

American Jewish Historical Society (AJHS), Two Thornton Rd., Waltham, MA 02514. 617-891-8110. (13)

American Library Association, 50 E. Huron St., Chicago, IL 60611. 312-944-6780. (15)

American Library Association/ALA Editions, 50 E. Huron St., Chicago, IL 60611-2790. 312-944-6780, 800-545-2433; Fax: 312-944-8741. (1)

American Library Publishing Co., Inc., Box 4272, Sedona, AZ 86340-4272. 602-282-4922. (1)

American Map Company, 46-35 54th Rd. Maspeth, NY 11378. 718-784-0055. (3)

American Media Corporation, 219 N. Milwaukee St., Milwaukee, WI 53202. 414-287-4600; Fax: 414-287-4602. (4)

American Meteorite Laboratory, Box 2098, Denver, CO 80201. 303-428-1371. (3)

American Montessori Society, 150 Fifth Ave., New York, NY 10011. 212-924-3209. (15)

American Music Teacher, Music Teacher's National Assn., Inc., Ste. 1432, 617 Vine St., Cincinnati, OH 45202-2434. 513-421-1420. (10)

American Optometric Association, 243 N. Lindbergh Blvd., St. Louis. MO 63141. 314-991-4100. (3)

American School Board Journal, National School Boards Assn., 1680 Duke St., Alexandria, VA 22314. 703-838-6722; Fax: 703-683-7590. (10)

American Society For Deaf Children, E. 10th & Tahlequah, Sulphur, OK 73086. 800-942-ASDC. (15)

American Study Program for Educational and Cultural Training (ASPECT), 26 Third St., 5th Fl., San Francisco, CA 94103. 415-777-4348/1-800-USYOUTH. (13)

American Teacher, American Federation of Teachers, 555 New Jersey Ave., NW, Washington DC 20001. 202-879-4431. (10)

American Theater Arts For Youth, 1429 Walnut St., Philadelphia, PA 19102-3218. 215-563-3501, 800-523-4540; Fax: 215-563-1588. (15)

Americas Boychoir Federation, 120 S. 3rd St., Connellsville, PA 15425. 412-628-8000; Fax: 412-628-0682. (15)

Paul S. Amidon & Associates, 1966 Benson Ave., St. Paul, MN 55116. 612-690-2401. (3)

Amsco School Publications, 315 Hudson St., New York, NY 10013. 212-675-7000; Fax: 212-675-7010. (1)

Marcia Amsterdam Agency, 41 W. 82nd St., New York, NY 10024. 212-873-4945; Fax: 212-873-4945. (8)

Anchorage Press, Inc., Box 8067, New Orleans, LA 70182. 504-283-8868; Fax: 504-866-0502. (1)

Ken Anderson Films, Box 618, Winona Lake, IN 46590. 219-267-5774. (3)

Anderson's Bookshop, 123 W. Jefferson, Naperville, IL 60540. 312-355-2665. (5)

Andover Books & Prints, 68 Park St., Andover, MA 01810. 508-475-1645, 508-475-0468. (6)

Andrews & McMeel, 4900 Main St., Kansas City, MO 64112. 816-932-6700, 800-286-4216; Fax: 816-932-6706. (1)

Ann Arbor Hands-On Museum, 219 E. Huron, Ann Arbor, MI 48104. 313-995-5437. (14)

The Annenberg/CPB Collection, 901 E. St. NW, Washington, DC 20004. 202-879-9655; Fax: 202-783-1036. (3)

Appalshop, Inc., 306 Madison St., Whitesburg, KY 41858. 606-633-0108. (3)

Applause Productions, Inc. 85 Longview Rd., Port Washington, NY 11050. 516-883-2897; Fax: 516-883-7460. (3)

Apple Computer, #1 Infinite Loop, Cupertino, CA 95014. 408-996-1010, 800-800-2775. (2)

Apple Education News, Apple Computer, Inc., 10381 Bandley Dr., Cupertino, CA 95014. 408-974-2552. (10)

Apple Island Books, Box 276, Shapleigh, ME 04076. 207-324-9453. (1)

Apple Link, Apple Computer, Inc., #1 Infinite Loop, Cupertino, CA 95014. 408-996-1010. (12)

Applied Optical Media Corp., 1450 Boot Rd., Bldg. 400, West Chester, PA 19380. 215-429-3701. (2)

Appraisal: Science Books For Young People, Children's Science Book Review Committee, 605 Commonwealth Ave., Boston, MA 02215. 617-353-4150. (11)

Aquarius People Materials, Inc., Box 128, Indian Rocks Beach, FL 33535. 813-595-7890. (2)

ARBA Sicula (AS), St. John's Univ., Jamaica, NY 11439. 718-998-5990. (13)

ARC Associates, Inc., 310 Eighth St., Ste. 220, Oakland, CA 94607. 415-834-9455. (13)

Arcade Publishing Inc., 141 Fifth Ave., New York, NY 10010. 212-475-2633; Fax: 212-353-8148. (1)

Architectural Color Slides, 187 Grant St., Lexington, MA 02173. 617-862-9931. (3)

Aris Multimedia Entertainment, 310 Washington Blvd., Ste. 100, Marina Del Rey, CA 90292. 310-821-0234, 800-228-2747; Fax: 310-821-6463. (2)

Arizona Department of Education, 1535 W. Jefferson, Phoenix, AZ 85007. 602-542-5416, Fax: 602-542-5283. (17)

Arizona Educational Media Association, c/o Caryl Ellis, Prescott Unified School District #1, 146 S. Granite St., Prescott, AZ 86302. 602-445-5400; Fax: 602-776-0243. (16)

Arizona Museum For Youth, 35 N. Robson, Mesa, AZ 85201. 602-644-2468. (14)

Arizona State Library Association, c/o Jean Collins, Northern Arizona University, Cline Library, Box 6022, Flagstaff, AZ 86011-6022. 602-523-6802; Fax: 602-523-3770. (16)

Arizona State University, Technology Based Learning & Research, Box 870111, Tempe, AZ 85287-0111. 602-965-4960; Fax: 602-965-8887. (2)

Arkadyan Books & Prints, 926 Irving St., San Francisco, CA 94122. 415-664-6212. (6)

Arkansas Association Of Instructional Media, c/o John Cheek, Arkansas Educational Television Network, 350 S. Donaghey, Conway, AR 72032. 501-682-4185; Fax: 501-682-4122. (16)

Arkansas Department of Education, 405-B State Education Bldg., Little Rock, AR 72201-1071. 501-682-4593. (17)

Arkansas Library Association, c/o Jenelle Stephens, Arkansas State Library, 1 Capitol Mall, Little Rock, AR 72201. 501-682-2550; Fax: 501-682-1529. (16)

Armenian General Benevolent Union (AGBU), 31 W. 52nd St., New York, NY 10019. 212-765-8260. (13)

Armenian Students Association of America (ASA), 395 Concord Ave., Belmont, MA 02178. 617-484-9548. (13)

ARO Publishing Co., Box 193, Provo, UT 84603. 801-377-8218, 800-338-7317. (1)

Ars Nova Software, Box 637, Kirkland, WA 98083. 206-889-0927, 800-445-4866; Fax: 206-889-0359. (2)

Art Education, National Art Education Association, 1916 Association Dr., Reston, VA 22091. 703-860-8000. (10)

Arte Publico Press, University of Houston, 4800 Calhoun #429 AH, Houston, TX 77004. 713-749-4768, 800-633-ARTE; Fax: 713-743-2847. (1)

Artifact Center At Sperdus Museum, 618 S. Michigan Ave., Chicago, IL 60605. 312-922-9012; Fax: 312-922-6406. (14)

Artificial Intelligence Research Group, 921 N. La Jolla Ave., Los Angeles, CA 90046. 213-656-7368. (2)

A.R.T.S., 32 Market St., New York, NY 10002. 212-962-8231. (1)

Arts & Activities, Publishers' Development Corp, 591 Camino de la Reina, Ste. 200, San Diego, CA 92108. 619-297-8520; Fax: 619-297-5353. (10)

Arts Education Policy Review, (formerly Design For Arts in Education), Heldref Publications, 1319 Eighteenth St., NW, Washington, DC 20036-1802. 202-296-6267; Fax: 202-296-5149. (10)

Asia Resource Center, Box 15375, Washington, DC 20003. 202-547-1114. (1)

Asia Society, 725 Park Ave., New York, NY 10021. 212-288-6400. (13)

Asian Cinevision, 32 E. Broadway, New York, NY 10002. 212-925-8685. (13)

Assembly of Turkish American Associations (ATAA), 1601 Connecticut Ave. N.W., Ste. #303, Washington, D.C. 20009. 202-483-9090. (13)

Associated Publishers Group, 1501 County Hospital Rd., Nashville, TN 37218. 615-254-2450; Fax: 615-254-2456. (1)

Association For Childhood Education International, 11501 Georgia Ave., Ste. 35, Wheaton, MD 20902. 301-942-2443. (1, 15)

Association For Educational Communications & Technology (AECT), 1025 Vermont Ave., Ste. 820, Washington, DC 20005. 202-347-7834. (15)

Association For Educational Communciations And Technology Of Puerto Rico, c/o Roberto Velez-Santiago, Bayamon Central University, Box 1725, Bayamon, P.R. 00960-1725. 809-786-3030 Ext. 216; Fax: 809-269-5480. (16)

Association For Educational Communciations And Technology Of South Carolina, c/o Tami Clyburn, Lugoff-Elgin Middle School, Box 68, Lugoff, SC 29078. 803-438-3591; Fax: 803-438-8027. (16)

Association For Indiana Media Educators, c/o Bonnie Grimble, Cannel High School, 52 E. Main St., Cannel, IN 46032. 317-846-7721; Fax: 317-571-4066. (16)

Association For Library Service To Children, Division of American Library Association, 50 E. Huron St., Chicago, IL 60611. 312-280-2163. (15)

Association Of Jewish Libraries, c/o National Foundation for Jewish Culture, 330 Seventh Ave., 21st Fl., New York, NY 10001. 216-381-6440. (15)

Association of Student and Professional Italian-Americans (ASPI), Box 531, Village Station, New York, NY 10014. 212-242-3215. (13)

Association of Teachers of Latin American Studies (ATLAS), 252-58 63rd Ave., Flushing, NY 11362-2406. 718-428-1237. (13)

AT&T Learning Network, Box 6391, Parsipanny, NJ 07054. 800-367-7225. (12)

Attainment Company, Inc., Box 930160, Verona, WI 53593-0160. 608-845-7880, 800-327-4269; Fax: 608-845-8040. (2)

Audio Book Contractors, Classic Books on Cassettes, Box 40115, Washington, DC 20016. 202-363-3429. (3)

Audio Forum, On-the-Green, Guilford, CT 06437. 203-453-9794, 800-243-1234. (2)

Augsburg Fortress Publishers, 426 S. Fifth St., Box 1209, Minneapolis MN 55440-1209. 612-330-3300, 800-328-4648; Fax: 612-330-3455. (1)

August House Publishers Inc., Box 3223, Little Rock, AR 72203. 501-372-5450, 800-284-8784; Fax: 501-372-5579. (1)

Aunt Louise's Bookshop, 431 W. Franklin, Chapel Hill, NC 27516. 919-942-8143. (5)

Aurbach & Associates, 8233 Tulane Ave., St. Louis, MO 63132-5019. 314-726-5933; Fax: 314-664-1852. (2)

Sri Aurobindo Assn., Inc., 2288 Fulton St., #310, Berkeley, CA 94704-1449. 510-848-1841; Fax: 510-848-8531. (4)

Austin Children's Museum, 1501 W. 5th St., Austin, TX 78703. 512-472-2499; Fax: 512-472-2495. (14)

Austrian Cultural Institute, 11 E. 52nd St., New York, NY 10022-5390. 212-759-5165. (13)

Author Aid Associates, 340 E. 52nd St., New York, NY 10022. 212-PL8-4213. (8)

Auto-Graphics, Inc., 3201 Temple Ave., Pomona CA 91768. 714-595-7204, 800-776-6939. (2)

Autodesk, Inc., 11911 N. Creek Pkwy., Bothell, WA 98011. 206-487-2233, 800-228-3601; Fax: 206-485-0021. (2)

A/V Concepts Corp., 30 Montauk Blvd., Oakdale, NY 11769. 516-567-7227. (3)

AV Guide: The Learning Media Newsletter, Scranton Gillette Communications Inc., 380 E. Northwest Hwy, Des Plaines, IL 60016-2282. 708-298-6622; Fax: 708-390-0408. (10)

AV Systems, Inc., Box 60533, Santa Barbara, CA 93160. 805-569-1618. (2)

AVC Presentations Development & Delivery, PTN Publishing Corp, 445 Hollow Rd, Ste. 21, Melville, NY 11747-4722. 516-845-2700; Fax: 516-845-7109. (10)

Avery Institute of Afro-American History and Culture, 58 George St., Box 2262, Charleston, SC 29401. 803-792-5742. (13)

AVKO Educational Research Foundation, Inc., 3084 W. Willard Rd., Clio, MI 48420. 810-686-9283. (15)

Avon Books, 1350 Ave. of the Americas, New York, NY 10019. 212-261-6800, 800-238-0658; Fax: 212-261-6895. (1)

The B & R Samizdat Express, Box 161, West Roxbury, MA 02132. 617-469-2269. (1)

B5 Software Co., 1024 Bainbridge Place, Columbus, OH 43228. 614-276-2752. (2)

Babler State Park, River Hills Visitor Center, 800 Guy Park Dr., Chesterfield, MO 63005. 314-458-3813. (14)

Backyard Scientist, Box 16966, Irvine, CA 92713. 714-552-5351; Fax: 714-552-5351. (1)

Baha'i Publishing Trust, 415 Linden Ave. Wilmette, IL 60091. 708-251-1854, 800-999-9019; Fax: 708-251-3652. (1, 3)

Baker Book House, Box 6287, Grand Rapids, MI 49516-6287. 616-676-9185, 800-877-2665; Fax: 616-676-9573. (1)

Baker & Taylor, 5 Lake Pointe Plaza, Ste. 500, 2709 Water Ridge Pkwy., Charlotte, NC 28217. 704-357-3500, 800-775-1800; Fax: 704-329-8989. (4)

Baker & Taylor Software, 3850 Royal Ave., Simi Valley, CA 93063. 800-775-4100; Fax: 805-522-7300. (2)

Bala Books, 12520 Kirkham, Ct., #7, Poway, CA 92064. 619-679-9080. (1)

Ball-Stick-Bird Publications, Inc., Box 592, Stony Brook, NY 11790. 516-331-9164. (1)

Ballantine Publishing Group, 201 E. 50th St., New York, NY 10022. 212-751-2600, 800-726-0600; Fax: 212-572-870. (1)

Baltimore Children's Museum, 10440 Falls Rd., Brooklandville, MD 21022. 410-823-2551; Fax: 410-337-4914. (14)

Baltimore City Life Museums, 800 E. Lombard St., Baltimore, MD 21202. 410-396-3524; Fax: 410-396-1806. (14)

Banner Blue Software, Box 7865, Fremont, CA 94537. 510-794-6850; Fax: 510-794-9152. (2)

Bantam Doubleday Dell Books For Young Readers, 1540 Broadway, New York, NY 10036. 212-354-6500, 800-223-6834; Fax: 212-302-7985. (1)

Baobab Tree, 3736 Bee Caves Rd., Austin, TX 78746. 512-328-7636. (5)

Baptist Home Mission Board, 1350 Spring St. NW, Atlanta, GA 30367. 404-898-7000. (3)

Barbie Magazine, Welsh Publishing Group, Inc., 300 Madison Ave., New York, NY 10017. 212-687-0680. (9)

Barr Media, 12801 Schabarum Ave., Pasadena, CA 91706. 800-234-7878; Fax: 818-814-2672. (3)

Barron's Educational Series, 250 Wireless Blvd., Hauppauge, NY 11788. 516-434-3311, 800-645-3476; Fax: 516-434-3723. (1)

Baudville, 5380 52nd St., SE, Grand Rapids, MI 49508. 616-698-0888, 800-728-0880; Fax: 616-698-0554. (2)

William L. Bauhan, Publisher, Box 443, Old County Rd., Dublin, NH 03444. 603-563-8020. (1)

Bauman Rare Books, Hotel Lobby, 301 Park Ave., New York, NY 10022. 212-759-8300; Fax: 212-7598350. (6)

Bauman Rare Books, 1215 Locust St., Philadelphia, PA 19107. 215-546-6466; Fax: 215-546-9064. (6)

Bay Area Discovery Museum, 557 E. Fort Baker, Sausalito, CA 94965. 415-332-9646; Fax: 415-332-9671. (14)

Bear Audio Visual, Inc., 1602 W. Kings Hwy., San Antonio, TX 78201. 210-736-1714, 800-621-2327; Fax: 210-735-5331. (2)

Bearing Books, 219 Grant St., SE, Decatur, AL 35601. 205-340-1900. (5)

Bears For Books, Box 1158, Carpinteria, CA 93014. 805-569-2398; Fax: 805-969-4278. (1)

Peter Bedrick Books, Inc., 2112 Broadway, New York, NY 10023. 212-496-0751, 800-788-3123; Fax: 212-496-1158. (1)

Norman Beerger Productions, 3217-A50, S. Arville St., Las Vegas, NV 89102. 702-876-2328. (3)

Behrman House, Inc., 235 Wachtung Ave., West Orange, NJ 07052. 201-669-0447, 800-221-2755; Fax: 201-669-9769. (1)

Belarusan-American Association, Inc., National Headquarters, 166-34 Gothic Drive, Jamaica, NY 11432. (13)

Belarusan-American Women Association (BAWA), 146 Sussex Drive, Manhasset, NY 11030. 516-627-9195. (13)

Bellerophon Books, 36 Anacapa St, Santa Barbara, CA 93101. 805-965-7034, 800-253-9943; Fax: 805-965-8286. (1)

Benchmark Films, 569 North State Road, Briarcliff Manor, NY 10510. 800-438-5564. (3)

Robert Bentley, Inc., 100 Massachusetts Ave., Cambridge, MA 02138. 617-547-4170. 800-423-4595; Fax: 617-876-9235. (1)

Bergwall Productions, Inc., Box 2400, Chadds Ford, PA 19317. 800-645-3565; Fax: 215-388-0405. (3)

Berkeley Publishing Group, Div. of The Putnam Berkeley Group, Inc., 200 Madison Ave., New York, NY 10016. 212-951-8800, 800-223-0510. (1)

Berlet Films, 1646 W Kimmel Rd., Jackson, MI 49201. 517-784-6969. (3)

Meredith Bernstein, 2112 Broadway, #503A, New York, NY 10023. 212-799-1007. (8)

Bess Press, Box 37095, Honolulu, HI 96837. 808-845-8949; Fax: 808-847-6637. (1)

Bethany House Publishers, 11300 Hampshire Ave. S., Minneapolis, MN 55438. 612-829-2500, 800-328-6109; Fax: 612-829-2768. (1)

Channing L. Bete Company, 200 State Rd., S. Deerfield, MA 01373. (3)

BFA Educational Media, Div. of Phoenix Learning Group, 2349 Chaffee Dr., St. Louis, MO 63146. 314-569-0211. (3)

Bigfoot Publishing (GRT Corp.), Lofand Circle, Rockwall, TX 75087. 800-888-8044. (2)

Bilingual Educational Services, 2514 S. Grand Ave., Los Angeles, CA 90007. 213-749-6213, 800-448-6032; Fax: 213-749-1820. (1)

Bilingual Educational Services, 2514 S. Grand Ave., Los Angeles, CA 90007. 213-749-6213. (3)

The Bilingual Publications Company, 270 Lafayette St., Ste. 705, New York, NY 10012. 212-431-3500. (4)

Billy Budd Films, 235 E. 57th St., New York, NY 10022. 212-755-3968. (3)

Biology Bulletin Monthly, Curriculum Innovations Group, 60 Revere Dr., Northbrook, IL 60062-1563. 312-432-2700, 800-323-5471. (9)

Bisiar Music Publishing & Production, 134 Cherrywood Ln., Louisville, CO 80027. 303-673-0466. (3)

Black Forest Books And Toys, 115 Cherokee Rd., Charlotte, NC 28207. 704-332-4838. (5)

Blackbirch Press Inc., One Bradley Rd., Ste. 205, Woodbridge, CT 06525. 203-387-7525, 800-831-9183; Fax: 203-389-1596. (1)

Samuel R. Blate Associates, 10331 Watkins Mill Dr., Gaithersburg, MD 20879-2935. 301-840-2248. (3)

BLS Tutorsystems, 5153 W. Woodmill Dr., Ste. 18, Wilmington, DE 19808. 800-545-7766; Fax: 302-633-1619. (2)

Blue Marble, 1356 S. Fort Thomas, Fort Thomas, KY 41075. 606-781-0602. (5)

BMI Educational Services, 26 Hay Press Rd., Dayton, NJ 08810. 201-329-6991, 800-222-8100. (4)

Bo Peep Books, 1957 S. Wadsworth, Lakewood, CO 80227. 303-989-8127. (5)

Bob Jones University Press, 1700 Wade Hampton Blvd., Greenville, SC 29614-0060. 803-242-5100, 800-845-5731. (1)

Boca Children's Museum, 498 Crawford Blvd., Boca Raton, FL 33432. 407-368-6875. (14)

Bogas Productions, 751 Laurel St., Ste. 213, San Carlos, CA 94070. 415-592-5129; Fax: 415-592-5196. (2)

The Book & Tackle Shop, 29 Old Colony Rd., Chestnut Hill, MA 02167. 617-965-0459. (6)

Book Case Books, Box 60457, Pasadena, CA 91116-0457. 818-449-3443. (6)

The Book Den, 15 E. Anapamu St., Box 733, Santa Barbara, CA 93102. 805-962-3321; Fax: 805-965-2844. (6)

Book Kids, 55 Market St., Ipswich, MA 01938. 508-356-9624. (5)

Book Lady, 8144 Brentwood Dr., St. Louis, MO 63144. 314-631-6672. (5)

Book Mark, 5001 E. Speedway, Tucson, AZ 85712. 602-881-6350. (5)

Book Nook, 948 S. Stewart, Springfield, MO 65804. 417-882-2248. (5)

Book Rack, 316 W. Main, Blytheville, AR 72315. 501-763-3333. (5)

The Book Report, Linworth Publishing, Inc., 480 E. Wilson Bridge Rd., Ste. L, Worthington, OH 43085. 614-436-7107; Fax: 614-436-9490. (11)

Book Review Digest, The H. W. Wilson Co., 950 University Ave., Bronx, NY 10452. 212-588-8400, 800-367-6770; Fax: 718-590-1617. (11)

Book Shop, 908 Main, Boise, ID 83702. 208-342-2659. (5)

The Book Shop of Beverly Farms, 40 West St., Beverly Farms, MA 01915. 508-927-2122. (5)

Book Star, 912 Maplewood Ct., Andover, KS 67002. 316-733-0240. (5)

The Book Treasury, 1535 East Broadway, Box 20033, Long Beach, CA 90801. 213-435-7383. (6)

Book Vine For Children, 304 Lincoln, Fox River, IL 60021. 708-639-4220. (5)

Book Wagon, 2765 Yorkshire Rd., Pasadena, CA 91107. 818-578-0727. (5)

Book Wholesaler's Inc., 1847 Mercer Rd, Lexington, KY 40511. 606-231-9789, 800-888-4478; Fax: 800-888-6319. (4)

Book World, The Washington Post, 1150 15th St. NW, Washington, DC 20071. 202-334-6000; Fax: 202-334-5549. (11)

Bookazine Company, Inc., 75 Hook Rd., Bayonne, NJ 07002. 201-339-7777, 800-828-2430; Fax: 201-858-7574. (4)

Bookhouse, 10923 Prairie Bridge Rd., Omaha, NE 68144. 402-392-1931. (5)

Booklist, American Library Association, 50 E. Huron St., Chicago, IL 60611. 312-944-6780, 800-545-2433; Fax: 312-44-9374. (11)

Bookmine, 1015 Second St., Old Sacramento, CA 95814. 916-441-4609; Fax: 916-441-2019. (6)

Books and Bears, 137 W. Beaver, State College, PA 16801. 814-237-4454. (5)

Books and Company For Kids, 350 E. Stroop Rd., Dayton, OH 45429. 513-297-6357. (5)

Books for Children, Dept. of English & Office of Public Information, Clemson University, Clemson, SC 29631-1503. 803-656-5414. (11)

Books of Wonder, 439 North Beverly Dr., Beverly Hills, CA 90210. 310-247-8025; Fax: 310-247-9442. (6)

Books of Wonder, 132 Seventh Ave., New York, NY 10011. 212-989-3270; Fax: 212-989-1203. (5, 6)

Books on Tape, Box 7900, Newport Beach, CA 92658-7900. 800-541-5525. (3)

Booksmith Promotional Co., 100 Paterson Plank Rd., Jersey City, NJ 07307. 201-659-2768. (4)

The Bookstall, 570 Sutter St., San Francisco, CA 94102. 415-362-6353. (6)

Booktenders Children's Books, 62 W. State St., Doylestown, PA 18901. 215-348-7160. (5)

Georges Borchardt Inc., 136 E. 57th St., New York, NY 10022. 212-753-5785; Fax: 212-838-6518. (8)

Borland International, 1800 Green Hills Rd., Scotts Valley, CA 95066. 408-431-1000. 800-331-0877; Fax: 408-438-8696. (2)

Bound to Stay Bound Books, 1880 W. Morton Rd., Jacksonville, IL 62650. 800-637-6586. (4)

R. R. Bowker Company, 121 Chanlon Rd., New Providence, NJ 07974. 908-464-6800, 800-521-8110. (1, 2)

Boy Scouts of America, 1325 Wal—nut Hill Lane, Box 152079, Irving, TX 75015-2079. 214-580-2000. (15)

Boyds Mills Press, Subs. of Highlights for Children Inc., 910 Church St., Honesdale, PA 18431. 717-253-1164; Fax: 717-253-0179. (1)

Boys & Girls Camp Fire, 4601 Madison Ave., Kansas City, MO 64112-1278. 816-756-1950. (15)

Boys & Girls Clubs Of America, 771 First Ave., New York, NY 10017. 212-351-5900; Fax: 212-351-5972. (15)

Boys' Life, Boy Scouts of America, Box 152070, 1325 Walnut Hill Lane, Irving, TX 75015-2079. 214-659-2000. (9)

William K. Bradford Publishing Co., 310 School St., Acton, MA 01702. 508-263-6996, 800-421-2009; Fax: 508-263-9375. (2)

Braille Institute, 741 N. Vermont, Los Angeles, CA 90029. 213-633-1111, 800-BRAILLE. (15)

Braille Institute Press, 741 N. Vermont Ave., Los Angeles, CA 90029. 213-663-1111. (1)

Brazilian-American Cultural Institution, 4103 Connecticut Ave., NW, Washington, DC 20008. 202-362-8334. (13)

Breakaway, Focus on the Family, 8605 Explorer Dr., Colorado Springs, CO

80920. 719-531-5181, 800-232-6459; Fax: 719-531-3424. (9)

Brevard Museum, 2201 Michigan Ave., Cocoa, FL 32926. 407-632-1830; Fax: 407-631-7551. (14)

Brilliant Star, National Spiritual Assembly of the Baha'is of the United States, 536 Sheridan Rd., Wilmette, IL 60091. 708-869-9039. (9)

Brio, Focus on the Family , 8605 Explorer Dr., Colorado Springs, CO 80920. 719-531-5181, 800-232-6459; Fax: 719-531-3424. (9)

Broadman & Holman Publishers, Div. of Southern Baptist Convention, Sunday School Board, 127 Ninth Ave. N., Nashville, TN 37234. 615-251-2553, 800-251-3225 Fax: 615-251-3870. (1)

Lori Brock Children's Museum, 3803 Chester Ave., Bakersfield, CA 93301. 805-395-1201. (14)

Brodart Company, 500 Arch St., Williamsport, PA 17705. 800-233-8467. (2, 4)

Broderbund Software, Inc., 500 Redwood Blvd., Novato, CA 94948. 415-382-4400, 800-521-6263; Fax: 415-382-4419. (2)

Brooklyn Children's Museum, 145 Brooklyn Ave., Brooklyn, NY 11213. 718-735-4400. (14)

Brooklyn Museum of Art, Dept. of African, Oceanic and New World Art, 200 Eastern Pkwy., Brooklyn, NY 11238. 918-638-5000. (13)

Brooks/Cole Publishing Co., 511 Forest Lodge Rd., Pacific Grove, CA 93950. 408-373-0728, 800-354-9706; Fax: 408-375-6414. (2)

Curtis Brown Ltd., 10 Astor Place, New York, NY 10003. 212-473-5400. (8)

Brunner/Mazel, Inc., 19 Union Sq. W., New York, NY 10003-3382. 212-924-3344, 800-825-3089; Fax: 212-242-6339. (1)

Brystone Children's Books, 6101 Watauga Rd., Watauga, TX 76148. 817-485-8421. (5)

Budget Films, 4590 Santa Monica Blvd., Los Angeles, CA 90029. 213-660-0187. (3)

Bulletin Of The Center For Children's Books, University of Illinois Press,

1325 S. Oak St., Champaign, Ilinois 61820. 217-244-6856. (11)

Bullfrog Films, Box 149, Oley, PA 19547. 215-779-8226; Fax: 215-370-1978. (3)

Bureau Of Electronic Publishing, 141 New Rd., Parsippany, NJ 07054. 201-808-2700, 800-828-4766. (2)

Bureau of Indian Affairs, 18th and C Sts., NW, Washington, D.C. 20245-0001. 202-343-7445. (13)

Bureau of Indian Affairs Central California Agency, 1800 Tribute Rd., Sacramento, CA 95815. 916-978-4339. (13)

Bureau of Indian Affairs Sacramento Area Office, 2800 Cottage Way, Sacramento, CA 95825-1885. 916-978-4691. (13)

Burkwood Books, Box 172, Urbana, IL 61801. 217-344-1419. (6)

Harold M. Burstein & Company, 36 Riverside Dr., Waltham, MA 02154. 617-893-7974; Fax: 617-641-2918. (6)

Bytes Of Learning, SSI 908 Niagara Falls Blvd., North Tonawanda, NY 14120-2060. 416-495-9913, 800-465-6428; Fax: 416-495-9548. (2)

C and C Software, 5713 Kentford Circle, Wichita, KS 67220. 316-683-6056. (2)

Caere Corporation, 100 Cooper Ct., Los Gatos, CA 95030. 408-354-2743, 800-535-7226; Fax: 408-395-7000. (2)

Calico Inc. (Computer Assisted Library Information Co.), Box 6190, Chesterfield, MO 63017. 800-367-0416. (2)

California Curriculum & Instructional Resources Office, 560 J St., Ste. 290, Sacramento, CA 95814. 916-445-2731. (17)

California Language Laboratories, 10511 Castine Ave., Cupertino, CA 95014. 415-327-1112, 408-736-9477, 800-327-1147; Fax: 408-749-9682. (3)

California Library Association, c/o Mary Jo Levy, Palo Alto City Library, Downtown Branch, 270 Forest Ave., Palo Alto, CA 94301-2512. 415-329-2516. (16)

California Media And Library Educators Association, c/o Robert Skapura, Los Medanos College, 2700 E. Leland Dr., Pittsburg, CA 94565. 510-439-2181 Ext. 220; Fax: 510-427-6384. (16)

California Technology Project, 800-272-8743 (CA), 310-985-9631 (other states). (12)

California Weekly Explorer, California Weekly Explorer, Inc., 285 E. Main St., Ste. 3, Tustin, CA 92680. 714-730-5991. (9)

Cambridge Book Company, Sylvan Rd., Rte. 9W, Englewood Cliffs, NJ 07632. 201-592-2000, 800-221-4764. (1)

Cambridge Documentary Films Inc., Box 385, Cambridge, MA 02139. 617-354-3677; Fax: 617-492-7653. (3)

Campus Film Distributors Corp., 24 Depot Sq., Tuckahoe, NY 10707. 914-961-1900. (3)

Candlewick Press, 2067 Massachussets Ave., Cambridge, MA 02140. 617-661-3330; Fax: 617-661-0565. (1)

Canyon Cinema, 2325 Third St., Ste. 338, San Francisco, CA 94107. 415-626-2255. (3)

Capital Children's Museum, 800 Third St. NE, Washington, DC 20002. 202-543-8600. (14)

Capital Communications, (formerly AEE Entertainment), Box 70188, Nashville, TN 37207. 615-868-2040. (3)

Capstone Press Inc., 2440 Fernbrook Lane, Minneapolis, MN 55447. 612-551-0513; Fax: 612-551-0511. (1)

Career Publishing, Inc., 905 Allanson Rd., Mundelein, RI 60060. 312-949-0011. (3)

Career World, Weekly Reader Corporation, 3001 Cindel Dr., Delran, NJ 08370. 800-446-3355; Fax: 609-786-3360. (9)

Lewis Carroll Society of North America, 617 Rockford Rd., Silver Springs, MD 20902. 301-593-7077. (15)

Carolina Biological Supply Co., 2700 York Rd., Burlington, NC 27215. 919-584-0381. (3)

Carolrhoda Books, 241 First Ave. N., Minneapolis, MN 55401. 612-332-3345. (1)

Carousel Film & Video, 260 Fifth Ave., Ste. 405, New York, NY 10001. 212-683-1660. (3)

Mary Carvainis Agency, Inc., 235 West End Ave., New York, NY 10023. 212-580-1559; Fax: 212-877-3486. (8)

Caspr, Inc., 635 Vaqureos Ave., Sunnyvale, CA 94086. 800-852-2777. (2)

The Catalyst, Western Center for Microcomputers in Special Education, Inc., 1259 El Camino Real, Ste. 275, Menlo Park, CA 94025. 415-326-6997; 415-855-8064. (10)

Catch Our Rainbow, 3148 Pacific Coast Hwy., Torrance, CA 90505. 213-325-1081. (5)

Cathedral Films, Inc., Box 4029, Westlake Village, CA 91359. 800-338-3456. (3)

Catholic Library Association, 461 W. Lancaster Ave., Haverford, PA 19041. 215-649-5250; Fax: 215-896-1191. (15)

Catholic Library World, Catholic Library Association, 461 W. Lancaster Ave., Haverford, PA 19041. 215-649-5250. (11)

Cay-Bel Publishing Co., 272 Center St., Bangor, ME 04401. 207-941-2367. (1)

CBC Features, Children's Book Council, Inc, 568 Broadway, New York, NY 10012-3225. 212-966-1990. (10)

CD-Rom Inc., 603 Park Point Dr., Ste. 110, Golden, CO 80401. 800-821-5245; Fax: 303-526-7395. (2)

CD•Rom World, 11 Ferry Lane West, Westport, CT 06880. 203-226-6967; Fax: 203-454-5840. (10)

CE Software, 1801 Industrial Circle, Box 65580, West Des Moines, IA 50265. 515-221-1801, 800-523-7638; Fax: 515-221-1806. (2)

CEL Education Resources, 655 Third Ave., New York, NY 10017. 212-557-3400, 800-235-3339; Fax: 212-557-3440. (2, 3)

Center For Children And Technology, Bank Street College of Education, 610 W. 112th St., New York, NY 10025. 212-875-4560. (12)

Center for Cuban Studies, 124 W. 23rd St., New York, NY 10011. 212-242-0559. (13)

Center For Cultural Arts, 501 Broad St., Gadsden, AL 35901. 205-543-2787; Fax: 205-546-7435. (14)

Center For Early Adolescence, University of North Carolina at Chapel Hill, D-2 Carr Mill Town Center, Carrboro, NC 27510. 919-966-1148. (15)

Center for Japanese Studies, 223 Fulton St., Room 500, Berkeley, CA 94720. 412-642-3156. (13)

Center for Korean Studies, Institute of East Asian Studies, Univ. of California, 2223 Fulton St., Room 512, Berkeley, CA 94720. 415-642-5674. (13)

Center For New American Media, 524 Broadway, New York, NY 10012. 212-925-5665. (3)

Center for Southeast Asia Studies, 260 Stephens Hall, Univ. of California, Berkeley, Berkeley, CA 94720. 415-642-3608. (13)

Central Point Software, 15220 NW Greenbrier, Beaverton, OR 97006. 503-690-8090, 800-445-4208; Fax: 503-690-8083. (2)

Centre Communications, 1800 30th St. #207, Boulder, CO 80301. 303-444-1166. (3)

Chancery Software, 4170 Still Creek Dr., Ste. 450, Burnaby, BC, Canada V5C 6C6. 604-294-1233, 800-999-9931; Fax: 604-294-2225. (2)

Changing Hands Books, 414 Mill Ave., Tempe, AZ 85281. 602-966-4019. (5)

Character Education Institute, Dimension II Building, 8918 Tesoro, Ste. 220, San Antonio, TX 78217. (15)

Charill Publishers, 4468 San Francisco Ave., Box 150124, St. Louis, MO 10012. 212-491-3869. (1)

Chariot Family Publishing, Div. of David C. Cook Publishing Co., 20 Lincoln Ave., Elgin, IL 60120. 708-741-9558, 800-323-7543; Fax: 708-741-2444. (1)

Chariot Software Group, 3659 India St., San Diego, CA 92103. 619-298-0202, 800-242-7468; Fax: 800-800-4540. (2)

Charlesbridge Publishing, 85 Main St., Watertown, MA 02172. 617-926-0329, 800-225-3214; Fax: 617-926-5720. (1)

Charlotte's Corner, 2394 E. Stadium Blvd., Ann Arbor, MI 18104, 313-973-9512. (5)

Charlotte's Web, 2278 Union St., San Francisco, CA 94123, 415-441-4700. (5)

Chelsea House, Div. of Main Line Book Co., 300 Park Ave., New York, NY 10016. 212-677-4010; Fax: 212-683-4412. (1)

Chelsea House Publishers, 1974 Sproul Rd., Ste. 400, Broomall, PA 19008-0914. 215-353-5166; Fax: 215-359-1439. (3)

Cherokee National Historical Society (CNHS), Box 515, Tahlequah, OK 74465. 918-456-6007. (13)

Chesapeake Planetarium, Box 15204, Chesapeake, VA 23328. 804-547-0153 ext. 281. (14)

Cheshire Cat Book Store, 5512 Connecticut Ave., Washington DC 20015. 202-244-3956. (5)

Cheshire Cat Bookstore, 114 N. 3rd St., Clear Lake, IA 50428. 515-357-6302. (5)

Chicago Children's Museum, 465 E. Illinois St., 2nd Fl, Chicago, IL 60611. 312-527-1000; Fax: 312-527-9082. (14)

Chicano Studies Research Center, 3121 Campbell Hall, Univ. of California, Los Angeles, CA 90024. 213-825-2363. (13)

Child Dreams, 12242 1/2 Ventura, Studio City, CA 91604. 818-761-8508. (5)

Child Life, Children's Better Health Institute, 1100 Waterway Blvd., Box 567, Indianapolis, IN 46206. 317-636-8881; Fax: 317-684-8094. (9)

Child Welfare League Of America, 440 First St. NW, Ste. 310, Washington, DC 20001-2085. 202-638-2952. (1, 15)

Child's Play, 310 W. 47 St., Ste. 3-D, New York, NY 10036. 212-315-9623, 800-472-0099; Fax: 212-315-9613. (1)

Child's Play, 13 Mill Creek Rd., 440

Jefferson, NY 11777. 516-473-4630. (5)

The Children's Book Council, 568 Broadway, New York, NY 10012. 212-966-1900; Fax: 212-966-2073. (15)

The Children's Museum, Inc. in Dartmouth, 276 Gulf Rd., S. Dartmouth, MA 02748. 508-993-3361. (14)

Childen's Museum of the Arts, 72 Spring St., New York, NY 10012. 212-274-0986; Fax: 212-274-1776. (14)

The Children's Museum of Utah, 840 N. 300 W., Salt Lake City, UT 84103. 801-328-3383; Fax 801-328-3384. (14)

Childhood Education, Association for Childhood Education International, 11501 Georgia Ave., Ste. 312, Wheaton, MD 20902. 301-942-2443. (10)

Children & Animals, The Humane Society of the United States, Box 362, East Haddam, CT 06423. 203-434-8666. (10)

Children Naturally, 31727 Sheridan Dr., Birmingham, MI 48009. 313-642-7895. (5)

Children's Art Foundation, Box 83, Santa Cruz, CA 95063. 408-426-5557, 800-447-4569. (15)

Children's Book Barn, 8535 Reservoir Hill, Hammondsport, NY 14840. 607-569-2385. (5)

Children's Book Barn, 4570 S.W. Watson, Beaverton, OR 97005. 503-641-2276. (5)

Children's Book Cart, 6736 Brockton Ave., Riverside, CA 92506. 714-275-9860. (5)

Children's Book Cellar, 5 E. Concourse, Waterville, ME 04901. 207-872-4543. (5)

Children's Book Press, 6400 Hollis St., Ste. 4, Emeryville, CA 94608. 510-655-3395; Fax: 510-655-1978. (1)

Children's Book Review Index, Gale Research Company, 835 Penobscot Bldg, Detroit, MI 48226. 313-961-2242; Fax: 313-961-6083. (11)

Children's Book Shop, 237 Washington St., Brookline, MA 02146. 617-734-7323. (5)

Children's Book Shop, 5730 Union Mill Rd., Clifton, VA 22024. 703-818-7270. (5)

Children's Book Store, 604 Markham St., Toronto, Ontario M6G2L, Canada, 416-535-7011. (5)

Children's Book World, 10580 3/4 West Pico, Los Angeles, CA 90064. 213-559-2665. (5)

Children's Book World, 17 Haverford Station, Haverford, PA 19041. 215-642-6274. (5)

Children's Bookcase, Box 1947, Davis, CA 95617. 916-756-541. (5)

Children's Bookery, 1175 Smiley Ave., Cincinnati, OH 45240. 513-742-8822. (5)

Children's Bookhouse, Route 6 Box 500, Joplin, MO 64801. 417-624-7680. (5)

Children's Books & Co., 8130 C So. Lewis, Tulsa, OK 74137. 918-492-8825. (5)

Children's Books Review Service, 220 Berkeley Pl., No. 1 D, Brooklyn, NY 11217. 718-622-4036; Fax: 718-622-4036. (11)

Children's Bookseller, 7225 Wildridge Rd., Colorado Springs, CO 80908. 719-495-9256. (5)

Children's Bookshelf, 144 Roxbord Rd., Lawrenceville, NJ 08648. 609-530-1462. (5)

Children's Bookshop, 29791 Northwestern Hwy., Southfield, MI 48034. 313-356-2880. (5)

Children's Bookshop, 600 E. Meadow Grove, Appleton, WI 54915. 414-733-3397. (5)

Children's Bookshoppe, 1831 Westcliff Dr., Newport Beach, CA 92660. 714-675-1424. (5)

Children's Bookstore, 737 Deepdene Rd., Baltimore, MD 21210. 301-532-2000. (5)

Children's Braille Book Club, National Braille Press Inc., 88 St. Stephen St., Boston, MA 02115. 617-266-6160. (7)

Children's Corner, W. 814 Main Ave., Spokane, WA 99201. 509-624-4820. (5)

Children's Digest, Children's Better Health Institute, 1100 Waterway Blvd., Box 567, Indianapolis, IN 46202. 317-636-8881; Fax: 317-684-8094. (9)

Children's Discovery Museum, 265 Water St., Box 5056, Augusta, ME 04330. 207-622-2209. (14)

Children's Discovery Museum of San Jose, 180 Woz Way, San Jose, CA 95110-2780. 408-298-5437; Fax: 408-298-6826. (14)

Children's Discovery Museum of The Desert, 42-501 Rancho Mirage Ln., Rancho Mirage, CA 92270. 619-346-2900. (14)

Children's Hands-On Museum, 2213 University Blvd., Tuscaloosa, AL 35403. 205-349-4235. (14)

Children's Hour, 928 E. 900 South, Salt Lake City, UT 84105. 801-359-4150. (5)

Children's House - Children's World, Children's House, Inc., Box 111, Caldwell, NJ 07006. 201-239-3442. (10)

Children's Literature, Yale University Press, 302 Temple St., Box 92A, Yale Sta., New Haven, CT 06520. 203-432-0940. (10)

Children's Literature Association, Box 138, Battle Creek, MI 49016. 616-965-8180. (15)

Children's Literature in Education, Human Sciences Press, Inc., 233 Spring St., New York, NY 10013-1578. 212-620-8000; Fax: 212-463-0742. (10)

Children's Literature Review, Gale Research Co., 835 Penobscot Bldg., Detroit, MI 48226. 313-961-2242; Fax: 313-961-6083. (11)

Children's Mercantile Company, 1 Old Town Square, Ft. Collins, CO 80524. 303-484-9946. (5)

Children's Museum, 533 16th St., Bettendorf, IA 52722. 319-344-4106. (14)

Children's Museum, 10 Children's Way, Pittsburgh, PA 15212-5250. 412-322-5059; Fax: 412-322-4932. (14)

Children's Museum, 3037 SW Second, Portland, OR 97212. 503-823-2227. (14)

Children's Museum, 305 Harrison St., Seattle Ctr, Seattle, WA 98109-4645. 206-441-1768; Fax: 206-488-0910. (14)

Children's Museum, 500 S. 20th St., Omaha, NE 68102. 402-342-6164. (14)

Children's Museum at Holyoke, 444 Dwight St., Holyoke, MA 01040. 413-536-7048. (14)

Children's Museum at La Habra, 301 E. Euclid, La Habra, CA 90631. 310-905-9693. (14)

Children's Museum at Oak Ridge, 461 W. Outer, Oak Ridge, TN 37830. 615-482-1074. (14)

Children's Museum at Yunker Farm, 1201 28th Ave., N. Fargo, ND 58102. 701-232-6102. (14)

Children's Museum in Easton, 9 Sullivan Ave., North Easton, MA 02356. 508-230-3789. (14)

Children's Museum, Museum Wharf, 300 Congress St., Boston, MA 02210. 617-426-6500. (14)

Children's Museum of Arkansas, 1400 W. Markham, Ste. 200, Little Rock, AR 72201. 501-374-6655; Fax: 501-374-4746. (14)

Children's Museum of Colorado Springs, 750 Citadel Dr. E., #3044, Colorado Springs, CO 80909. 719-574-0077; Fax: 719-591-5519. (14)

Children's Museum of Denver, 2121 Children's Museum Dr., Denver, CO 80211-5221. 303-433-7444. (14)

Children's Museum of History, Natural History, & Science, 311 Main St., Utica, NY 13501. 315-724-6128 or 9129. (14)

Children's Museum of Houston, 1500 Binz, Houston, TX 77004-7112. 713-522-1138; Fax: 713-522-5747. (14)

Children's Museum of Indianapolis, 3000 N. Meridian, Indianapolis, IN 46208. 317-924-5431; Fax: 317-921-4019. (14)

Children's Museum of Kansas City, 4601 State Ave., Kansas City, KS 66102. 913-287-8888. (14)

Children's Museum of Lake Charles, 925 Enterprise Blvd., Lake Charles, LA 70601. 318-433-9420. (14)

Children's Museum of Maine, 142 Free St., Portland, ME 04101. 207-828-1234. (14)

Children's Museum of Manhattan, 212 W. 83rd St., New York, NY 10024. 212-721-1234. (14)

Children's Museum of Memphis, 2525 Central Ave., Memphis, TN 38104. 901-458-2678; Fax: 901-458-4033. (14)

Children's Museum of Portsmouth, 280 Marcy St., Portsmouth, NH 03801. 603-436-3853. (14)

Children's Museum of Rhode Island, 58 Walcott St., Pawtucket, RI 02860. 401-726-2591. (14)

Children's Museum of San Diego, 200 West Island Ave., San Diego, CA 92101. 619-233-8792; Fax: 619-233-8796. (14)

Children's Museum of Tampa, 7550 North Blvd., Tampa, FL 33604. 813-935-8441. (14)

Children's Museum of Washington, Inc., 4954 MacArthur Blvd., NW, Washington, DC 20007. 202-337-4954. (14)

Children's Museum, Operated by the Southern Oregon Historical Society, 206 N. 5th St., Jacksonville, OR 97501. 503-773-6536; Fax: 503-776-7994. (14)

Children's Museum, Primary Care Center, Box 231, Lee St. and Park Pl., Charlottesville, VA 22908. 804-924-1593. (14)

Children's Museum/Detroit Public Schools, 67 E. Kirby, Detroit, MI 48202. 313-494-1210; Fax: 313-873-3384. (14)

Children's Playmate, Children's Better Health Institute, 1100 Waterway Blvd., Box 567, Indianapolis, IN 46206. 317-636-8881, Fax: 317-684-8094. (9)

Children's Press, Subs. of Grolier Inc., 5440 N. Cumberland Ave., Chicago, IL 60656-1494. 312-693-0800, 800-821-1115; Fax: 312-693-0574. (1)

Children's Reading Round Table of Chicago, 2045 N. Seminary Ave., Chicago, IL 60631. 312-525-7257. (15)

Children's Television International, Inc, 8000 Forbes Pl., Ste. 201, Springfield, VA 22151. 800-284-4523; Fax: 703-321-8971. (3)

Children's Television Workshop, One Lincoln Plaza, New York, NY 10023. 212-595-3456. (15)

Childventure Museum And Shop, 3364 Susquehanna Rd., Dresher, PA 19025. 215-643-9906. (14)

Chinese American Civic Council (CACC), Box 166082, Chicago, IL 60616-6082. 312-225-0234. (13)

Chinese American Forum, 606 Brantford Ave., Silver Spring, MD 20904. 301-622-3053. (13)

A.M. Chisholm Museum/Duluth Children's Museum, 506 W. Michigan St., Duluth, MN 55802. 218-722-8563. (14)

Choo Choo Children's Books, 4615 Poplar, Memphis, TN 38117. 901-372-0128. (5)

Christian Schools International, Box 8709, 3350 E. Paris Ave. SE, Grand Rapids, MI 49518-8709. 616-957-1070, 800-635-8288; Fax: 616-957-5022. (1, 15)

The Christian Science Publishing Society, One Norway St., Boston, MA 02115. 617-450-2773, 800-288-7090; Fax: 617-450-2017. (1)

The Christophers, 12 E. 48th St., New York, NY 10017. 212-759-4050. (3)

Chronicle Books, 275 Fifth St., San Francisco, CA 94103. 415-777-7240, 800-722-6657; Fax: 415-777-8887. (1, 23)

Chronicle Guidance Publications Inc., 66 Aurora St., Box 1190, Moravia, NY 13118-1190. 315-497-0330, 800-622-7284; Fax: 315-497-3359. (1, 2, 3)

Church And Synagogue Library Association, Box 19357, Portland, OR 97280-0357. (15)

Churchill Media, 12210 Nebraska Ave., Los Angeles, CA 90025-3600. 800-334-7830; Fax: 310-207-1330. (3)

Cine-Pic Hawaii Corporation, 1847 Pacific Heights Rd., Honolulu, HI 96813. 808-533-2677. (3)

Cinema Concepts, Inc, 2461 Berline Trnpk, Newington, CT 06111, 203-667-1251. (3)

The Cinema Guild, Inc., 1697 Broadway, New York, NY 10019. 212-246-5522. (3)

Charles W. Clark Company, 170 Keyland Ct., Bohemia, NY 11716. 516-589-6643. (4)

Clarion Books, Div. of Houghton Mifflin Co., 215 Park Ave. S., New York, NY 10003. 212-420-5800, 800-225-3362; Fax: 212-420-5855. (1)

Claris Software, 5201 Patrick Henry Dr., Box 526, Santa Clara, CA 95054. 408-987-7000, 800-747-7483; Fax: 408-987-7563. (2)

Clarus Music Ltd., 340 Bellevue Ave., Yonkers, NY 10703. 914-591-7715. (3)

Classic Works, 13502 Whittier, Ste. H276, Whittier, CA 90605. 310-696-9331; Fax: 310-696-9331. (1)

Classical Calliope, The Muses' Magazine For Youth, Cobblestone Publishing, Inc, 20 Grove St., Peterborough, NH 03458. 603-924-7209. (9)

Clavier's Piano Explorer, Instrumentalist Co, 200 Northfield Rd., Northfield, IL 60093-3390. 708-446-5559. (9)

Cleveland Children's Museum, 10730 Euclid Ave., Cleveland, OH 44106-2200. 216-791-7114; Fax: 216-791-8838. (14)

Cliffs Notes Inc., Box 80728, Lincoln, NE 68501-0728. 402-477-6671, 800-228-4078; Fax: 402-423-9254. (1)

Clown Hall Of Fame & Research Center, 114 N. 3rd St., Delavan, WI 53115. 414-728-9075. (14)

Clubhouse, Focus on the Family , 8605 Explorer Dr., Colorado Springs, CO 80920. 719-531-5181, 800-232-6459; Fax: 719-531-3424. (9)

Clubhouse, Your Story Hour, Inc., 464 W. Ferry, Box 15, Berrien Springs, MI 49103. 616-471-9009; Fax: 616-471-4661. (9)

Cobb County Youth Museum, 649 Cheatham Hill Dr., Marietta, GA 30064. 404-427-2563. (14)

Cobblestone: The History Magazine For Young People, Cobblestone Publishing, Inc., 7 School St., Peterborough, NH 03458. 603-924-7209; Fax: 603-924-7380. (9)

Coda Music Technology, 6210 Bury Dr., Eden Prarie, MN 55346-1718. 800-843-2066; Fax: 612-937-9760. (2)

Hy Cohen Literary Agency, 111 W. 57th St., New York, NY 10019. 212-757-5237. (8)

Ruth Cohen Inc., Literary Agent, Box 7626, Menlo Park, CA 94025. 415-854-2054. (8)

Colgin Publishing, 7657 Farmington Rd., Manlius, NY 13104. 315-682-6081. (1)

Collage Children's Museum, 2065 30th St., Boulder, CO 80306. 303-440-0053. (14)

The College Board, 45 Columbus Ave., New York, NY 10023-6992. 212-713-8000. (3)

College Entrance Examination Board, 45 Columbus Ave., New York, NY 10023-6992. 212-713-8000; Fax: 212-713-8143. (1)

Colonial Williamsburg Foundation, Box 1776, Williamsburg, VA 23187. 804-229-1000. (1, 3)

Colorado Department of Education, 201 E. Colfax, Rm 309, Denver, CO 80203. 303-866-6730. (17)

Colorado Educational Media Association, c/o Su Eckhardt, Smoky Hill H.S. Media Center, 16100 East Smoky Hill Rd., Aurora, CO 80015. 303-693-1700 ext. 5590; Fax: 303-693-1700 ext. 5561. (16)

Colorado Library Association, c/o Margaret Owens, Jefferson County Public Library, 10200 W. 20th Avenue, Lakewood, CO 80215. 303-275-2216; Fax: 303-275-2225. (16)

Columbia Books, 13 N. 9th St., Columbia, MO 65201. 314-449-7417. (6)

Columbia Scholastic Press Association, Box 11, Central Mail Rx, Columbia University, New York, NY 10027. 212-854-9400; Fax: 212-854-9401. (15)

Columbia University Press, 562 W. 113th St., New York, NY 10025. 212-316-7100. (2)

Comex Systems, Inc, The Mill Cottage, Mendham, NJ 07945. 800-543-6959; Fax: 201-543-9644. (3)

Comic Magazine Association Of America, 355 Lexington Ave., 17th Fl., New York, NY 10017. 212-661-4261; Fax: 212-370-9047. (15)

Communication & Therapy Skill Builders, Inc., Box 42050, Tucson, AZ 85733. 602-323-7500, 800-866-4446; Fax: 602-325-0306. (1)

Communication For Change, Inc., (formerly Martha Stuart Communications, Inc.), 147 W. 22nd St., New York, NY 10011. 212-255-2718. (3)

Communication Skill Builders, Inc, 3830 E. Bellevue, Box 42050, Tucson, AZ 85733. 602-323-7500. (2, 3)

Communications Group West, 1640 Fifth St., Santa Monica, CA 90401. 310-451-2525. (3)

Community Council For The Arts Children's Museum, Box 3554, Kinston, NC 28502. 919-527-2517. (14)

Comp Ed, 18818 N. 99th Ave., Sun City, AZ 85373. 800-347-4242. (2)

Compact Disc Products, 272 Rte. 34, Aberdeen, NJ 07747. 908-290-0048. (2)

Compact Publishing, Box 40310, Washington, DC 20006. 202-244-4770. (2)

Compcare Publications, Div. of Comprehensive Care Corp., 3850 Annapolis Lane, Ste. 100, Minneapolis, MN 55447-5443. 612-559-4800, 800-328-3330; Fax: 612-559-2415. (1)

Comprehensive Health Education Foundation (CHEF), 22323 Pacific Hwy. S., Seattle, WA 98198. 206-824-2907; Fax: 206-824-3072. (1)

Compton's Newmedia, 2320 Camino Vida Roble, Carlsbad, CA 92009. 619-929-2500; Fax: 619-929-2690. (2)

Compu-Teach, 16541 Redwood Way, Redmond, WA 98052. 206-885-0517, 800-448-3224; Fax: 206-883-9169. (2)

Computer Book Review, 735 Ekekela Place, Honolulu, HI 96817. 808-595-7089. (11)

Computer Literature Index, Applied Computer Research, Inc., Box 82260, Phoenix, AZ 85071-2260. 800-234-2227. (10)

Computers & People, Berkeley Enterprises, 815 Washington St., Newtonville, MA 02160. 617-332-5453. (10)

Computing Teacher, International Society for Technology in Education, Univ. of Oregon, 1787 Agate St., Eugene, OR 97403-1923. 503-346-4414; Fax: 503-346-5890. (10)

Conduit, The University of Iowa, Oakdale Campus, Iowa City, IA 52242. 319-335-4100, 800-365-9774; Fax: 319-335-4077. (2)

Congress for Jewish Culture (CJC), 25 E. 21st St., New York, NY 10010. 212-505-8040. (13)

Connecticut Department of Education, Box 2219, Hartford, CT 06145. 203-566-5658. (17)

Connecticut Educational Media Association, c/o Carolyn Marcato, Fairfield High School, (H) 155 Catalpa Rd., Wilton, CT 06897. 203-255-8451; Fax: 203-284-1506. (16)

Connecticut Library Association, c/o Janet Vaill-Day, Woodbridge Town Library, 10 Newton Rd., Woodbridge, CT 06525. 203-389-3433; Fax: 203-389-3457. (16)

The Conover Company Ltd., Box 155, Omro, WI 54963. 800-933-1933. (2)

Consortium For School Networking (CoSN), Box 65193, Washington, DC 20035-5193. 202-466-6296. (12)

Consortium Of College & University Media Centers, Executive Office, CCUMC, Iowa State University, 121 Pearson Hall, Ames, IA 50011. 515-294-1811. (15)

Continental Book Company, 80-00 Cooper Ave, Glendale, NY 11385. 718-326-0560. (4)

Continental Press Inc., 520 E. Bainbridge St., Elizabethtown, PA 17022. 717-367-1836; 800-233-0759. (2)

Corel, Box 1252, Lake Grove, NY 11755. 516-689-3500, 800-245-7355; Fax: 516-689-3549. (2)

Corinthian Publications, Box 8279, Norfolk, VA 23503. 804-587-2671. (1)

Cornell University Media Services, Audio-Visual Resource Center, 8 Research Park, Ithaca, NY 14850. 607-255-2091. (3)

Coronet/MTI Film & Video, Distributors of Learning Corporation of America, 108 Wilmot Rd., Deerfield, IL 60015. 708-940-1260, 800-777-2400; Fax: 708-940-3646. (3)

Council For Children With Behavioral Disorders, Division of Council for Exceptional Children, 1920 Association Dr., Reston, VA 22091-1589. 703-620-3660 (voice/TDD); Fax: 703-264-9494. (15)

Council For Elementary Science International, University of Missouri, 212 Townsend Hall, Columbia, MO 65211. 317-274-6813. (15)

Council For Indian Education, Box 31215, Billings, MT 59107. 406-252-7451. (1, 15)

The Council of the Great City Schools, 1413 K St., NW, Ste. 400, Washington, DC 20005. 202-371-0163. (15)

Council On Interracial Books For Children, 1841 Broadway, Room 608, New York, NY 10023. 212-757-5339. (15)

Cover To Cover, 3337 N. High St., Columbus, OH 43202. 614-263-1624. (5)

Coyote Point Museum For Environmental Education, 1651 Coyote Point Dr., San Mateo, CA 94401, 415-342-7755. (14)

Crabtree Publishing Co., 350 Fifth Ave., Ste. 3308, New York, NY 10118. 212-496-5040; 800-387-7650. (1)

Crackerjacks, 7 Washington St., South Easton, MD 21601. 301-822-7716. (5)

Craighead Films, Box 3900, 6532 Switzer, Shawnee, KS 66203. 913-631-3040. (3)

Creative Child & Adult Quarterly, The, The National Association for Creative Children & Adults, 8080 Springvalley Dr., Cincinnati, OH 45236-1395. 513-631-1777. (10)

Creative Education Inc., Box 227, 123 S. Broad St., Mankato, MN 56001. 507-388-6273, 800-445-6209; Fax: 507-388-2746. (1)

Creative Kids, GCT, Inc., Box 6448, Mobile, AL 36660. 205-478-4700; Fax: 205-478-4755. (9)

Creative Kids, Prufrock Press, Box 8813, Waco, TX 76714-8813. 817-756-3337. (10)

Creative Kidstuff, 4313 Upton South, Minneapolis, MN 55410. 612-929-2431. (5)

Creative Multimedia Corporation (CMC), 514 NW 13th Ave., Ste. 400, Portland, OR 97209. 503-241-4351. (2)

Creative Press Works, Box 280556, Memphis, TN 38128. 901-382-8246. (1)

Creative Pursuits, 10433 Wilshire Blvd., Ste. 410, Los Angeles, CA 90024. 310-446-4111. (2)

Creativity For Kids, 1600 E. 23rd St., Cleveland, OH 44114. 216-589-4800. (5)

Cricket Magazine, Carus Corporation, 315 Fifth St., Box 300, Peru, IL 61354. 815-223-2520, 800-998-0868. (9)

Critical Thinking Press & Software, Box 448, Pacific Grove, CA 93950, 408-375-2455. 800-458-4849; Fax: 408-372-3230. (2)

Crocodile Pie, 866 S. Milwaukee Ave., Libertyville, IL 60048. 708-362-8766. (5)

Cross Educational Software, 504 E. Kentucky Ave., Ruston, LA 71270. 318-255-8921. (2)

Crossway Books, Div. of Good News Publishers, 1300 Crescent St., Wheaton, IL 60187. 708-682-4300, 800-323-3890; Fax: 708-682-4785. (1)

Crown Books For Young Readers, Affiliate of Random House, 201 E. 50th St., New York, NY 10022. 212-572-2600; Fax: 212-572-8700. (1)

Crusader, Calvinist Cadet Corps, 1333 Alger St., Box 7259, Grand Rapids, MI 49510. 616-241-5616; Fax: 616-241-5558. (9)

Cuisenaire Company Of America, 10 Bank Street, White Plains, NY 10602. 914-997-2600. (3)

Cultural Resources Inc., 30 Iroqouis Rd., Cranford, NJ 07016. 908-709-1574; Fax: 908-709-1590. (2)

Curious Kids' Museum, 415 Lake Blvd., St. Joseph, MI 49085. 616-983-2543; Fax: 616-983-3317. (14)

Current Events, Weekly Reader Corporation, 245 Long Hill Rd., Middletown, CT 06457. 800-446-3355; Fax: 609-786-3360. (9)

Current Health 1: A Beginning Guide To Health Education, Weekly Reader Corporation, 3001 Cindel Dr., Delran, NJ 08370. 800-446-3355; Fax: 609-786-3360. (9)

Current Science, Weekly Reader Corporation, 245 Long Hill Rd., Middleton, CT 06457. 800-466-3355; Fax: 609-786-3360. (9)

Curriculum Associates Inc., 5 Esquire Rd., North Billerica, MA 01862-2589. 617-667-8000. (2)

Curriculum Product News, (formerly Curriculum Product Review), Educational Media, Inc, 922 S. High Ridge Rd., Stamford, CT 06905. 203-322-1300; Fax: 203-328-9177. (11)

Richard Curtis Associates, Inc., 171 E. 74th St., Ste. 2, New York, NY 10021. 212-772-7363; Fax: 212-772-7393. (8)

Cygnus Software, 8002 E. Culver, Mesa, AZ 85207. 602-986-5938. (2)

Czech Heritage Foundation (CHF), Box 761, Cedar Rapids, IA 52406. 319-365-0868. (13)

D4 Film Studios, 749 Charles River St., Needham, MA 02192. 617-235-1119. (3)

Dana Productions, 6249 Babcock Ave., North Hollywood, CA 91606. 818-508-5331. (3)

Danish Sisterhood of America (DSA), 3429 Columbus Dr., Holiday, FL 34691-1027. (13)

Data Command Inc., Box 548, Kankakee, IL 60901. 815-933-7735, 800-528-7390. (2)

Data Trek, 5838 Edison Place, Carlsbad, CA 92008. 800-876-5484. (2)

Tom Davenport Films, Pearlstone, Delaplane, VA 22025. 703-592-3701; Fax: 703-592-3717. (3)

Ursula C. Davidson Books, 134 Linden Lane, San Rafael, CA 94901. 415-454-3939; Fax: 415-454-1087. (6)

Davidson & Assoc. Inc., 19840 Pioneer Ave., Box 2961, Torrance CA 90509. 310-793-0600, 800-545-7677; Fax: 310-793-0601. (2)

Davidson Films, 31 E St., Davis, CA 95616. 916-753-9604; Fax: 916-753-3719. (3)

Dawn Publications, 14618 Tyler Foote Rd., Nevada City, CA 95959. 916-292-3482, 800-545-7475; Fax: 916-292-4258. (1)

Day Care & Early Education, Human Sciences Press, Inc. (Sub. of Plenum Pub. Corp.), 233 Spring St., New York, NY 10013-157. 212-620-8000; Fax: 212-463-0742. (10)

Daybreak Star Press, Box 99100, Seattle, WA 98199. 206-285-4425. (1)

DCA Educational Products, Inc., 814 Kellers Church Rd., Box 338, Bedminster, PA 18910. 215-795-2841. (3)

DCM Instructional Systems, 80 Wilson Way, Westwood, MA 02090. 617-329-4300. (3)

Dec Computing, 5307 Lynnwood Dr., West Lafayette, IN 47906. 317-583-2230. (2)

Delaware Library Association, c/o Jonathan Jeffrey, University of Delaware, Hugh M. Morris Library, Reference Department, Newark, DE 19717-5267. 302-831-2432. (16)

Delaware State Department of Public Instruction Standards & Curriculum Branch, John G. Townsend Bldg., Box 1402, Dover, DE 19903. 303-739-3902. (17)

Delmar Publishers Inc., Subs. of International Thomson Publishing Inc., 3 Columbia Circle, Albany, NY 12203. 518-464-3500, 800-347-7707; Fax: 518-464-0316. (1)

Deltapoint, 2 Harris Ct., Ste. B-1, Monterey, CA 93940. 408-648-4000, 800-367-4334; Fax: 408-648-4025. (2)

Demco Inc., Box 7488, Madison, WI 53707. 800-356-1200; Fax: 800-245-1329. (4)

Demco Media, Box 14260, Madison, WI 53707. 800-448-8939; Fax: 800-828-0401. (4)

Deming Luna Mimbres Museum, 301 S. Silver St., Deming, NM 88030. 505-546-2382. (14)

Deneba Systems, 7400 SW 87th, Miami, FL 33173. 305-596-5644, 800-622-6827; Fax: 305-273-9069. (2)

Denoyer-Geppert Science Company, 5225 N. Ravenswood Ave., Chicago, IL 60640. 312-561-9200. (1)

Department of Education, Center for Occupation Education Experimentation and Demonstration Library 223 Broadway, Newark, NJ 07104. 201-648-2121; Fax: 201-648-3144. (17)

Depot Museum, 514 N. High St., Henderson, TX 75652. 903-657-4303. (14)

Joseph A. Dermont, Box 654, Onset, MA 02555. 508-295-4760. (6)

Design Science Inc., 4028 Broadway, Long Beach, CA 90803. 310-433-0685, 800-827-0685; Fax: 310-433-6969. (2)

Devware, 12520 Kirkham Ct., Ste. 1 Paway, CA 92064. 619-679-2826, 800-879-0759; Fax: 619-679-2887. (2)

Dharma Publishing, 2425 Hillside Ave., Berkeley, CA 94704. 510-548-5407, 800-873-4276; Fax: 510-548-2230. (1)

Dial Books For Young Readers, Div. of Penguin USA, 375 Hudson St., New York, NY 10014-3657. 212-366-2000. (1)

Anita Diamant, 310 Madison Ave., New York, NY 10017. 212-687-1122. (8)

Didatech Software, 4250 Dawson, Ste. 200, Burnaby, BC, Canada V5C 4B1. 604-299-4435, 800-665-0667; Fax: 604-299-2428. (2)

Digital Imaging Associates, 10153 York Rd., Ste. 107, Hunt Valley, MD 21030. 800-989-5353. (2)

Digital Vision, 270 Bridge St., Dedham, MA 02026. 617-329-5400, 800-346-0090; Fax: 617-329-6286. (2)

Dimension Films, 15007 Gault St., Van Nuys, CA 91405. 818-997-8065. (3)

Dimensions Of Early Childhood, Southern Early Children Association, Box 5403, Little Rock, AR 72215-5403. 501-663-2114. (10)

Direct Cinema Limited, Box 10003, Santa Monica, CA 90410-1003. 310-396-4774; Fax: 310-396-3233. (3)

Direction Sports, Inc., 600 Wilshire Blvd., Ste. 320, Los Angeles, CA 90017-3215. 213-627-9861. (15)

Discis Knowledge Research, Inc., 90 Sheppard Ave. E., 7th Fl., Toronto, Ontario, Canada M2N 3A1. 416-250-6537, 800-567-4321; Fax: 416-250-6540. (2)

Discovering Together, Standard Publishing Company, 8121 Hamilton Ave., Cincinnati, OH 45231. 513-931-4050. (9)

Discovery Center, 1944 N. Winery Ave., Fresno, CA 93703. 209-251-5533. (14)

Discovery Center, 711 N. Main St., Rockford, IL 61103. 815-963-6769; Fax: 815-965-0642. (14)

Discovery Center Of The Southern Tier, 60 Morgan Rd., Binghamton, NY 13903. 607-773-8661. (14)

Discovery Enterprises, 134 Middle St., Ste. 210, Lowell, MA 01852-1815. 508-459-1720, 800-729-1720; Fax: 508-937-5779. (1)

Discovery Museum, 51 Park St., Essex Junction, VT 05452. 802-878-8687. (14)

The Disccovery Museums, 177 Main St., Acton, MA 01720. 508-264-4201; Fax: 508-264-0210. (14)

Discovery Place, 1421 22nd St. S., Birmingham, AL 35205. 205-939-1177; Fax: 205-933-4111. (14)

Discovery Place, Inc., 301 N. Tryon St., Charlotte, NC 28202. 704-372-6261, 800-935-0553. (14)

Discovery Science Center Of Central Florida, 50 S. Magnolia Ave., Ocala, FL 32670. 904-620-2555. (14)

Disney Adventures, Walt Disney Publishing, Burbank Tower Bldg., 3800 W. Alameda Ave., BC100, Burbank,

CA 91505. 818-973-4333, 800-829-5146; Fax: 818-563-9344. (9)

Disney Book Publishing Inc., Div. of The Walt Disney Co. 114 Fifth Ave., New York, NY 10011. 212-633-4400; Fax: 212-633-4833. (1)

Walt Disney Computer Software, Inc., 500 S. Buena Vista St., Burbank, CA 91521. 800-271-9258. (2)

Walt Disney Records, 500 S. Buena Vista St., Burbank, CA 91521. 808-567-5327. (3)

Displays For Schools, Inc., 1825 NW 22nd Ter., Gainesville, FL 32605-3957. 904-373-2030. (1)

Distribution 16, 32 W. 40th St., Ste. 2L, New York, NY 10018. 212-730-0280. (3)

Distribution Video & Audio , 1060 Kapp Dr., Clearwater, FL 34625. 800-683-4147; Fax: 813-441-3069. (3)

District Of Columbia Library Association, c/o Trellis Wright, 8298 Quill Point Dr., Bowie, MD 20720. 202-707-2441; Fax: 202-707-8366. (16)

District of Columbia Public Schools, 1709 3rd St. NE, 4th Fl., Washington DC 20002. 202-576-8654. (17)

Carol Docheff Books, 1390 Reliez Valley, Lafayette, CA 94549. 415-935-9696. (5)

DOK Publishers, Div. of United Educational Services Inc., Box 1099, Buffalo, NY 14224. 716-668-7691, 800-458-7900; Fax: 716-668-7875. (1)

The Dolphin Log, The Cousteau Society, 8440 Santa Monica Blvd., Los Angeles, CA 90069. 312-656-4422. (9)

Don Bosco Multimedia, 475 North Ave., New Rochelle, NY 10802. 914-576-0122. (3)

Dorling Kindersley Inc., 232 Madison Ave., New York, NY 10016. 212-684-0404; Fax: 212-684-0111. (1)

Dorrance Publishing Co., Inc., 643 Smithfield St., Pittsburgh, PA 15222. 412-288-4543, 800-788-7654 (orders only). (1)

Dover Publications, 31 E. Second St., Mineola, NY 11501. 516-294-7000, 800-223-3130; Fax: 516-742-5049. (1)

Down East Books, Box 679, Camden, ME 04843. 207-594-9544, 800-766-1670; Fax: 207-594-7215. (1)

Down There Press, 938 Howard St., #101, San Francisco, CA 94103. 415-974-8985; Fax: 415-974-8989. (1)

Downtown Community Television Center (DCTV), 87 Lafayette St., New York, NY 10013. 212-966-4510. (3)

DQ University Library, Box 409, Davis, CA 95616. 916-758-0470. (13)

Dragon's Tale, 5138 Peach St., Erie, PA 16509. 814-868-9916. (5)

Drama Book Publishers, 260 Fifth Ave., New York, NY 10001. 212-725-5377; Fax: 212-725-8506. (1, 3)

Dramatists Play Service, 440 Park Ave. S., New York, NY 10016. 212-683-8960. (1)

Drew's Book Shop, Box 163, Santa Barbara, CA 93101. 805-682-3610. (6)

Dufour Editions, Chester Springs, PA 19425-0007. 215-458-5005; Fax: 215-458-7103. (1)

Dupage Children's Museum, 1777 S. Blanchard Rd., Wheaton, IL 60187. 708-260-9907; Fax: 708-690-5516. (14)

Dushoff Books, 3166 E. Camelback Rd., Phoenix, AZ 85016. 602-957-1176. (5)

Dutton Children's Books, Div. of Penguin USA, 375 Hudson St., New York, NY 10014. 212-336-2000. (1)

Dynacomp, Inc., 178 Phillip Rd., Webster, NY 14580. 716-265-4040. (2)

Dynix Scholar, 400 W. Dynix Dr., Provo, UT 84604-5650. 800-288-1145. (2)

EA*Kids, 1450 Fashion Blvd., San Mateo, CA 94404. 800-245-4525. (2)

Eakin Press, Div. of Sunbelt Media Inc., Drawer 90159, Austin, TX 78709-0159. 512-288-1771; Fax: 512-288-1813. (1)

Early Educator's Press, 70 Woodcrest Ave., Ithaca, NY 14850. 607-272-6223. (1)

Earthware Computer Services, 2386 Spring Blvd., Box 30039, Eugene, OR 97403. 503-344-3383. (2)

East Tennessee Discovery Center, 516 N. Beaman St., Box 6204, Knoxville, TN 37914-0204. 615-637-1192. (14)

Eastern Book Co, Box 4540, Portland, ME 04112-4540. 207-774-0331. (4)

Eastgate Systems, Box 1307, Cambridge, MA 02238. 617-924-9044, 800-562-1638; Fax: 617-924-9051. (2)

Ebook, Inc., 32970 Alvarado-Niles Rd., Ste. 704, Union City, CA 94587. 510-429-1331; Fax: 510-429-1331. (2)

Ebsco Publishing, Box 2250, Peabody, MA, 01960. 800-653-2726. (2)

Econo-Clad, 2101 N. Topeka Blvd., Topeka, KS 66608. 913-233-4252; Fax: 913-233-3129. (1)

Edcon, 30 Montauk Blvd., Oakdale, NY 11769. 516-567-7227. (2)

Eden Interactive, 1022 Natomi St., No. 2, San Francisco, CA 94103. 415-241-1450. (2)

Edmark Corporation, Box 3218, Redmond, WA 98073-3218. 206-556-8440, 800-426-0856; Fax: 206-556-8998. (2)

Education Digest, Prakken Publications, Box 8623, Ann Arbor, MI 48107. 313-769-1211; Fax: 313-769-8383. (10)

Education Leadership, Assn. for Supervision & Curriculum Development, 1250 N. Pitt St., Alexandria, VA 22314. 703-549-9110. (10)

Education, Project Innovation, 1362 Santa Cruz Ct, Chula Vista, CA 91910. 619-421-9377. (10)

Education Technology, Business Publishers Inc., 951 Pershing Dr., Silver Spring, MD 20910. 301-587-6300. (10)

Educational Activities Inc., 1937 Grand Ave., Baldwin, NY 11510. 516-223-4666, 800-645-6739; Fax: 516-623-9282. (2, 3)

Educational Design, Inc., 345 Hudson St., New York, NY 10014-4502. 212-255-7900. (3)

Educational Design Services Inc., Box 253, Wantagh, NY 11793. 516-221-0995, 718-539-4107. (8)

Educational Images, Box 3456, Westside Station, Elmira, NY 14905. 607-732-1090. (2, 3)

Educational Insights, 19560 S. Rancho Way, Dominguez Hills, CA 90220. 310-637-2131, 800-933-3277; Fax: 310-605-5048. (1)

Educational Media Association Of New Jersey, c/o Pam Chesky, Woodbridge Township School, (H) 135 Midwood Way, Colonia, NJ 07067. (16)

Educational Media Corp., Box 2311, Minneapolis, MN 55421. 612-781-0088. (2)

The Educational Products Information Exchange (EPIE Institute), 103-3 W. Montauk Hwy., Hampton Bays, NY 11946. 516-728-9100. (15)

Educational Research Service, 2000 Clarendon Blvd., Arlington, VA 22201. 703-243-2100. (15)

Educational Resources, 1550 Executive Dr., Elgin, IL 60123. 708-888-8300, 800-624-2926; Fax: 708-888-8499/8689. (2, 3)

Educational Services Press, 99 Bank St., Ste. 2F, New York, NY 10014, 212-924-7166. (1)

Educational Technology, Educational Technology Publications, Inc., 720 Palisade Ave., Englewood Cliffs, NJ 07632. 201-871-4007; Fax: 201-871-4009. (10)

Educational Technology/New Mexico AECT, a Roundtable of New Mexico Library Association, c/o Kathy Flanary, New Mexico Military Institute, 101 W. College Blvd., Roswell, NM 88201-5173. 505-624-8384; Fax: 505-624-8390. (16)

Educational Video Network, Inc., 1401 19 Street, Huntsville, TX 77340. 409-295-5767; Fax: 409-294-0233. (3)

Educators Progress Service, 214 Center St., Randolph, WI 53956. 414-326-3126; Fax: 414-326-3127. (1)

Educators Publishing Service, 75 Moulton St., Cambridge, MA 02138-11041. 617-547-6706, 800-225-5750; Fax: 617-547-0412. (1)

Educom K-12 Networking Project, 1112 16th St. NW, Ste. 600, Washington, DC 20036. 202-872-4200. (12)

Educorp, 7434 Trade St., San Diego, CA 92121-2410. 619-536-9999; 800-843-9497; Fax: 619-536-2345. (2)

Eduquest, 4111 Northside Pkwy., Atlanta, GA 30327. 800-426-4338. (2)

Edusoft, Box 2304, Berkeley, CA 94702. 510-548-2304, 800-338-7638; Fax: 510-548-0755. (2)

William B. Eerdmans Publishing Co., 255 Jefferson Ave. SE, Grand Rapids, MI 49503. 616-459-4591. 800-253-7521; Fax: 616-459-6540. (1)

Eight Cousins Children's Bookstore, 630 Main St., Falmouth, MA 02540. 508-548-5548. (5)

El Bireh Palestine Society of the U.S.A. (EBPSUSA), c/o Rafeek Farah, M.D., 2105 West Rd., Trenton, MI 48183. 313-675-7777. (13)

Electronic Arts, Box 7530, San Mateo, CA 94403. 415-571-7171. 800-245-4525; Fax: 415-513-7465. (2)

Electronic Bookshelf, 5276 S. Country Rd., Ste. 700, Frankfort, IN 46041. 317-324-2182, 800-327-7323; Fax: 317-324-2183. (2)

Electronic Courseware Systems Inc., 1210 Lancaster Dr., Champaign, IL 61821. 217-359-7099, 800-832-4965. (2)

Electronic Frontier Foundation (EFF), 666 Pennsylvania Ave. SE, Washington, DC 20003. 202-544-9237, Internet: EFF@EFF.ORG. (12)

The Elementary School Journal, Center for Research in Social Behavior, Univ. of Chicago Press Journals Division. 5720 S. Woodlawn Ave., Chicago, IL 60637. 312-753-3347; Fax: 312-753-0811. (10)

Ann Elmo Agency, 60 E. 42nd St., New York, NY 10165. 212-661-2880; Fax: 212-463-8718. (8)

EMA Software, Box 339, Los Altos, CA 94023. 415-969-4679. (2)

EMC Corp, 300 York Ave., St. Paul, MN 55101-4082. 612-771-1555, 800-328-1452; Fax: 612-771-5629. (1, 2)

EME Corporation, Box 2805, Danbury, CT 06813. 203-798-2050. (2, 3)

Emery-Pratt Co, 1966 W. Main St., Owosso, MI 48867-1372. 800-762-5683 (orders), 800-248-3887 (customer svc.); Fax: 800-523-6379. (4)

Enchanted Tale Bearer, 2100 Dixwell, Hamden, CT 06514. 203-287-8253. (5)

Enchanted World Doll Museum, 615 N. Main, Mitchell, SD 57301. 605-996-9896. (14)

Encyclopaedia Britannica Inc., 310 S. Michigan Ave., Chicago, IL 60604. 312-347-7400, 800-554-9862; Fax: 312-294-2136. (1)

Encyclopedia Britannica Educational Corp., 310 S. Michigan Ave., Chicago, IL 60604. 312-347-7947, 800-554-9862; Fax: 312-347-7966. (2, 3)

English Journal, National Council of Teachers of English, 111 W. Kenyon Rd, Urbana, IL 61801-1096. 217-328-3870; Fax: 217-328-9645. (10)

Enslow Publishes, Inc., Bloy St. & Ramsey Ave., Box 777, Hillside, NJ 07205. 908-964-4116; Fax: 908-687-3829. (1)

Entrekin Book Center, 446 Azalea Rd., Mobile, AL 36609. 205-660-0505. (5)

EPM Publications Inc., 1003 Turkey Run Rd., McLean, VA 22101. 703-356-5111, 800-289-2339; Fax: 703-442-0599. (1)

Equity & Excellence in Education, Greenwood Press, Inc., 88 Post Pd. W., Westport, CT 06881. 203-226-3571; Fax: 203-222-1502. (10)

Eric Clearinghouse On Information Resources (ERIC/IR), 303 Huntington Hall, Syracuse University, Syracuse, NY 1234-2340. 315-443-3640, Internet: ERIC@SUVM.ACS.SYR.EDU.. (12)

ETV Newsletter, Box 597, Ridgefield, CT 06877. 203-454-2618; Fax: 203-458-2618. (10)

Eureka Microskills III, Box 647, 241 26th St., Richmond, CA 94808-0647. 510-235-3883. (2)

M. Evans and Company, Inc., E. 49th St., New York, NY 10017-1502. 212-688-2810; Fax: 212-486-4544. (1)

Every Picture Tells, 836 North LaBrea, Los Angeles, CA 90038. 213-962-5420. (5)

The Exceptional Parent, Psy-Ed Corp., 1170 Commonwealth Ave., Boston, MA 02134-4646. 617-730-5800; Fax: 617-730-8742. (10)

Executive Educator, National School Boards Assn., 1680 Duke St., Alexandria, VA 22314. 703-838-6722; Fax: 703-683-7590. (10)

Exploration Station—A Children's Museum, 396 N. Kennedy Dr., Bradley, IL 60915. 815-935-5665. (14)

Exploratorium, 3601 Lyon St., San Francisco, CA 94123. 415-561-0360. (14)

Faber & Faber, Inc., 50 Cross St., Winchester, MA 01890. 617-721-1427, 800-666-2111; Fax: 617-729-2783. (1)

Faces (The Magazine about People), Cobblestone Publishing, 7 School St., Peterborough, NH 03458. 603-924-7209. (9)

Facts On File, Subs. of Infobase Holdings Inc., 460 Park Ave. S., New York, NY 10016. 212-683-2244, 800-322-8755; Fax: 212-213-4578. (1, 2)

Fairy Godmother, 319 7th St., SE, Washington, DC 20003. 202-547-5474. (5)

Faith & Life Press, 718 Main St., Box 347, Newton, KS 67114-0347. 316-283-5100. (1)

Falcon Software, Box 200, Wentworth, NH 03282. 603-764-5788; Fax: 603-764-9051. (2)

Family Communications, Inc., 4802 Fifth Ave., Pittsburgh, PA 15213. 412-687-2990. (3)

Family Films, 3558 S. Jefferson, St. Louis, MO 63118. 314-268-1105. (3)

W. J. Fantasy, 955 Connecticut, Bridgeport, CT 06607. 203-333-5212. (5)

Farrar, Straus & Giroux, 19 Union Sq. W., New York, NY 10003. 212-206-5366, 800-631-8571; Fax: 212-633-9385. (1)

Federation of Turkish-American Societies (FTAS), 821 United Nations Plaza, 2nd Fl., New York, NY 10017. 212-682-7688. (13)

Phillipp Feldheim Inc., 200 Airport Executive Park, Spring Valley, NY 10977. 914-356-2282, 800-237-7149; Fax: 914-425-1908. (1)

The Feminist Press at the City University of New York, 311 E. 94th St., New York, NY 10128. 212-360-5790; Fax: 212-348-1241. (1)

Festival Of Children's Books, 1809 Reisterstown, Baltimore, MD 21208. 410-486-7406. (5)

FFA New Horizons, National FFA Organization, Box 15130, 5631 Mount Vernon Memorial Hwy, Alexandria, VA 22309. 703-360-3600; Fax: 703-360-5524. (9)

Eugene Field House And Toy Museum, 634 S. Broadway, St. Louis, MO 63102. 314-421-4689. (14)

Filmic Archives, The Cinema Center, Botsford, CT 06404. 203-261-1920. (3)

Filmmakers' Cooperative, 175 Lexington Ave., New York, NY 10016. 212-889-3820. (3)

Films For The Humanities & Sciences, Box 2053, Princeton, NJ 08543. 609-275-1400, 800-257-5126; Fax: 609-275-3767. (2, 3)

Films Incorporated, 5547 N. Ravenswood, Chicago, IL 60640. 800-343-4312; Fax: 312-878-0416. (3)

Films Of India, Box 48303, Los Angeles, CA 90048. 213-383-9217. (3)

Finnish-American Historical Society of the West, Box 5522, Portland, OR 97208. 503-654-0448. (13)

Firefly Books Ltd, 250 Sparks Ave., Willowdale, ON M2H 2S4, Canada. 416-499-8412, 800-387-5080; Fax: 416-499-8313. (1)

First Folio, R.R. 1, Box 127A, Buchanan, TN 38222-9768. 901-644-9940. (6)

Florida Association for Media in Education, c/o Helen Tallman, Mast Academy, Dade County Schools, (H),7601 SW 94th Ave., Miami, FL 33173. 305-365-6278. (16)

Florida Educational Services Program, 251 Sliger Bldg., 2035 E. Dirac, Tallahassee, FL 32310. (17)

Florida Information Resource Network (FIRN), Florida Education Ctr., Rm. B 114, 325 W. Gaines St., Tallahassee, FL 32399. 904-487-0911. (12)

Florida Library Association, c/o Helen Moeller, Leon County Public Library, 200 W. Park Ave., Tallahassee, FL 32301. 904-487-2665. (16)

Focus International Inc., 1160 E. Jericho Tpke., Huntington, NY 11743. 516-549-5320; Fax: 516-549-2066. (3)

Focus Media, 485 S. Broadway, Ste. 12, Hicksville, NY 11801. 516-931-2500, 800-645-8989; Fax: 516-931-2575. (2)

Folklore Bromer Booksellers, 607 Boylston St., at Copley Square, Boston MA 02116. 617-247-2818; Fax: 617-247-2975. (6)

Follett Library Book Co., 4506 Northwest Hwy., Rtes. 14 & 31, Crystal Lake, IL 60014. 800-435-6170; Fax: 800-852-5488. (4)

Follett Software Company, 809 N. Front St., McHenry, IL 60050. 815-344-8700, 800-323-3397; Fax: 815-344-8774. (2)

Fordham Equipment & Publishing Co., 3308 Edson Ave., Bronx, NY 10469. 718-379-7300; Fax: 718-379-7300. (3)

Forest House, Box 738, Lake Forest, IL 60045-0738. 800-394-READ. (1)

Foundation For Library Reseach, 505 McNeill Ave., Point Pleasant, WV 25187. 304-675-4350, 304-343-6480. (2)

Four And Five, (Formerly 4 & 5 Story Paper), Standard Publishing Co., 8121 Hamilton Ave., Cincinnati, OH 45231. 513-931-4050; Fax: 513-931-0904. (9)

Four Walls Eight Windows, Box 548, Village Sta., New York, NY 10014. 212-206-8965; Fax: 212-206-8799. (1)

Fox Cities Children's Museum, 10 College Ave., Appleton, WI 54911. 414-734-3226; Fax: 414-734-0677. (14)

Frame Technology, 1010 Rincon Circle, San Jose, CA 95131. 800-843-7263. (2)

Fredmail Network, Box 243, Bonita, CA 91908. 615-475-4852. (12)

Free Spirit Publishing, Inc., 400 First Ave. N., Ste. 616, Minneapolis, MN 55401. 612-338-2068, 800-735-7323; Fax: 612-337-5050. (1)

W. H. Freeman and Co., 41 Madison Ave., 35th Fl., New York, NY 10010. 212-576-9400; Fax: 212-481-1891. (1)

Freesoft Company, 105 McKinley Rd., Beaver Falls, PA 15010. 412-846-2700; Fax: 412-847-4436. (2)

French & European Publishers, Inc., Exec. Off. & Natl. Dist. Ctr.: 115 Fifth Ave, New York, NY 10003. 212-673-7400. (4)

Friendlysoft, Inc., 3638 W. Pioneer Pkwy., Arlington, TX 76013. 817-277-9378. (2)

The Friend, The Church of Jesus Christ of Latter-Day Saints, 50 E. North Temple, Salt Lake City, UT 84150. 801-240-2947. (9)

Friends United Press, Subs. of Friends United Meeting, 101 Quaker Hill Dr., Richmond, IN 47374. 317-962-7573, 800-537-8838; Fax: 317-966-1293. (1, 3)

Friendship Press, Subs. of National Council of the Churches of Christ USA, 475 Riverside Dr., New York, NY 10115-0050. 212-870-2586; Fax: 212-870-2550. (1, 3)

Doris Frohnsdorff, Box 2306, Gaitherburg, MD 20886. 301-869-1256. (6)

Full Of The Dickens, 105 W. Water St., Sandusky, OH 44870. 419-626-6880. (5)

Fun Publishing Co., Box 2049, Scottsdale, AZ 85252. 602-946-2093. (1)

Future Problem Solving Program, 315 W. Huron, Ste. 140B, Ann Arbor, MI 48103-4203. 313-998-7377; Fax: 313-998-7663. (15)

G.R.C./S.W.L., 5383 Hollister Ave., Santa Barbara, CA 93111. 805-964-7724, 800-933-5383. (2)

Gale Research, 835 Penobscot Bldg., Detroit, MI 48226-4094. 313-961-2242, 800-877-GALE; Fax: 313-961-6083. (1, 2)

Gamco, 1411 E. Hwy. 350, Big Spring, TX 79720. 915-267-6327, 800-351-1404. (2)

Gamco Education Materials, Box 1911, Big Spring, TX 79721-1911. 915-267-6327, 800-351-1404; Fax: 915-267-7480. (3)

Garcia-Garst Booksellers, 2857 Geer Rd., #C, Turlock, CA 95380. 209-632-5054; Fax: 209-632-0805. (6)

Gareth Stevens Inc., 1555 N. River Center Dr., Ste. 201, Milwaukee, WI 53212. 414-225-0333, 800-341-3569; Fax: 414-225-0377. (1)

Jay Garon-Brooke Associates, 415 Central Park West, New York, NY 10025. 212-866-3654; Fax: 212-666-6016. (8)

Garrett Educational Corp., Box 1588, 130 E. 13th St., Ada, OK 74820. 405-332-6884, 800-654-9366; Fax: 405-332-1560. (1)

Gateway Productions, Inc., Box 55358, New Orleans, LA 70055. 504-482-3835, 800-837-4982; Fax: 504-833-4744. (3)

Gem Publications, 502 Second St., Hudson, WI 54016. 715-386-7113. (1)

Georgia Association For Instructional Technology, c/o Catherine Price, Valdosta State College, Dept. of Secondary Education, Valdosta, GA 31698. 912-333-5927; 912-333-7167. (16)

Georgia Department of Education, Atlanta, GA 30334-5040. 404-656-2418. (17)

Georgia Library Association, c/o Donna D. Mancini, Dekalb County Public Library, Administration, 215 Sycamore St., Decatur, GA 30030. 404-370-8450; Fax: 404-370-8469. (16)

Georgia Southern University Museum, Rosenwald Bldg., Georgia Southern University, Statesboro, GA 30460. 912-681-5444. (14)

German Society of Pennsylvania (GSP), 611 Spring Garden St., Philadelphia, PA 19123. 215-627-2332. (13)

Gessler Educational Software, 55 W. 13th St., New York, NY 10011. 212-627-0099, 800-456-5825; Fax: 212-627-5948. (1, 2, 4)

Gibbs-Smith, Publisher (formerly Peregrine Smith Books), Box 667, Layton, UT 84041. 801-544-9800. (1)

Gifted Child Quarterly, National Association for Gifted Children, 1155 Fifthteen St., NW, Ste. 1002. Washington, DC 20005-2706. 202-785-4268. (10)

Gifted Child Today, Prufrock Press, Box 8813, Waco, TX 76714-8813. 817-756-3337; Fax: 817-756-3339. (10)

The Gilbert House Children's Museum, 116 Marion St., NE, Salem, OR 97301. 503-371-3631. (14)

Ginger and Pickles Bookstore, 425 Second St., Lake Oswego, OR 97034, 503-636-5438. (5)

Girl Scouts of the USA, 420 Fifth Ave., New York, NY 10018-2702. 212-940-7500, 800-221-4715; Fax: 212-852-6511. (1, 15)

Girls, Inc., 30 E. 33rd St., New York, NY 10016. 212-689-3700. (15)

Glencoe Publishing Co., Div. of the Macmillan/McGraw-Hill School Publishing Co., 936 Eastwind Dr., Westerville, OH 43081. 614-890-1111, 800-848-1567; Fax: 614-899-4379. (1)

Glenn Books , 323 E. 55th St., Kansas City, MO 64113. 816-444-4447. (6)

Global Organization of People of Indian Origin, 60 Bradley Place, Stanford, CT 06905. 203-329-8010. (13)

David R. Godine, Inc., 300 Massachusetts Ave., Boston, MA 02115. 617-536-0761; Fax: 617-421-0934. (1)

Goethe House, 1014 Fifth Ave., New York, NY 10028. 212-439-8700. (13)

Golden Apple Press, Box 206, Mankato, MN 56002. 507-388-2601; Fax: 507-388-2746. (1)

Golden-Lee Book Distributors, 1000 Dean St., Brooklyn, NY 11238. 718-857-6333, 800-473-7475. (4)

GPN, (Great Plains National), Box 80669, Lincoln, NE 68501. 402-472-1785, 800-228-4630; Fax: 402-472-1785. (2, 3)

GPN Newsletter, Great Plains National Instructional TV Library, Box 80669, Lincoln, NE 68501-0669. 402-472-2007, 800-228-4630. (10)

Great Amazing Bookstore, 858 Marshall Ct., Palatine, IL 60074. 708-359-9258. (5)

Great Books Foundation, 35 W. Wacker Dr., Ste. 2300, Chicago, IL 60601-2298. 312-332-5870; 800-222-5870. (15)

Great Wave, 5353 Scotts Valley Dr., Scotts Valley, CA 95066. 408-438-1990, 800-456-5825; Fax: 408-438-7171. (2)

Greater Detroit and Windsor Japan-America Society, Ste. 1500, 150 West Jefferson, Detroit, MI 48226. 313-963-1988. (13)

Green Mountain Post Films, Box 229, Turners Falls, MA 01376. 413-863-4754; Fax: 413-863-8248. (3)

Greenhaven Press, Box 289009, San Diego, CA 92198-9009. 619-485-7424, 800-231-5163; Fax: 619-485-9542. (1)

Grolier Educational Corporation, Old Sherman Tpke., Danbury, CT 06816. 203-797-3500, 800-356-5590; Fax: 203-797-3838. (1, 2)

Grosset & Dunlap, 200 Madison Ave., New York, NY 10016. 212-951-8700; Fax: 212-532-3693. (1)

Group, Group Publishing, Inc., 2890 N. Monroe, Box 481, Loveland, CO 80539, 303-669-3836. (9)

Group Logic, Inc., 1408 N. Fillmore St., Arlington, VA 22201. 703-525-1555, 800-476-8781; Fax: 703-528-3296. (2)

Gryphon, 7220 Trade St., Ste. 120, San Diego, CA 92121. 619-536-8815, 800-795-0981; Fax: 619-536-8932. (2)

Gryphon House, Inc., Box 275, 3706 Otis St., Mt. Rainier, MD 20712. 301-779-6200. (4)

Guam Library Association, c/o Chih Wang, Dean; Learning Resources, University of Guam, Mangilao, GU 96923. 671-734-2482; Fax: 671-734-6882. (16)

Guidance Associates, Box 1000, Mt. Kisco, NY 10549. 914-661-4100; 800-431-1242. (3)

Guide, Review & Herald Publishing Assn., 55 W. Oak Ridge Dr., Hagerstown, MD 21740. 301-791-7000. (9)

Gumbs & Thomas, 142 W. 72nd St., Ste. 9, New York, NY 10023. 212-724-1110. (1)

G. K. Hall & Company, Box 159, Thorndike, ME 04986. 207-948-2962, 800-223-6121; Fax: 207-948-2863. (1)

Hall of Life Health Education Center, (Dept. of the Denver Museum of Natural History), City Park, 2001 Colorado Blvd., Denver, CO 80205. 303-329-5433; Fax: 303-331-6492. (14)

Hammond Inc., 515 Valley St., Maplewood, NJ 07040. 201-763-6000. (3)

Hands-On House, Children's Museum Of Lancaster, 2380 Kissel Hill Rd., Lancaster, PA 17601. 717-569-kids. (14)

Gerard Hamon, Inc., Box 758, 525 Fenimore Rd., Mamaroneck, NY 10543. 914-381-4649, 800-333-4971; Fax: 914-381-2607. (1, 4)

Happily Ever After, 2640 Griffith Park, Los Angeles, CA 90039. 213-668-1996. (5)

Happy Times, Concordia Publishing House, 3558 S. Jefferson Ave., St. Louis, MO 63118. 314-664-7000. (9)

Harbinger House, 1051 N. Columbus Blvd., #100, Tucson, AZ 85711 (ordering: Box 42948, Tucson, AZ 85733-2948). 602-326-9595, 800-759-9945; Fax: 602-326-8684. (1)

Harcourt Brace & Company, 525 B St., Ste. 1900, San Diego, CA 92101-4495. 619-669-6435, 800-543-1918 (orders); Fax: 619-699-6320. (1)

HarperCollins Children's Books, 10 E. 53rd St., New York, NY 10022. 212-207-7044, 800-242-7737; Fax: 212-207-7617. (1)

Don Harrington Discovery Center, 1200 Streit Dr., Amarillo, TX 79106, 806-355-9547; Fax: 806-355-5703. (14)

Cora Hartshorn Arboretum, 324 Forest Dr. S., Short Hills, NJ 07078. 201-376-3587. (14)

Hartley Courseware, Inc., 133 Bridge St., Dimondale, MI 48821. 517-646-6458, 800-247-1380; Fax: 517-646-8451. (2)

Haslam's Bookstore, 2025 Central Ave., St. Petersburg, FL 33713. 813-822-8616. (5)

Hawaii Children's Book World, 1132 Bishop St., Honolulu, HI 96813. 808-531-6245. (5)

Hawaii Children's Museum, 650 Iwilei Rd., Honolulu, HI 96817. 808-592-5437; Fax: 808-592-5433. (14)

Hawaii Library Association, c/o Jean Ehrhorn, 507 Koko Isle Circle, Honolulu, HI 96923. 671-734-2832; Fax: 671-734-6882. (16)

Hawkhill Associates, Inc., 125 E. Gilman St., Madison, WI 53703. 608-251-3934. (3)

John Hawkins & Associates, Inc., 71 W. 23rd St., New York, NY 10010. 212-807-7040; Fax: 212-807-9555. (8)

Hayes Microcomputer, 5923 Peachtree Industrial Blvd., Norcross, GA 30092. 404-840-9200. (2)

Hayward Shoreline Interpretive Center, 4901 Breakwater, Hayward. CA 94545, 510-881-6751. (14)

Health Adventure, 2 South Park Square, Asheville, NC 28801. 704-254-6373. (14)

Health Service Center For Educational Resources, University of Washington, T252 HSC, SB-56, Seattle, WA 98195, 206-685-1186; Fax: 206-543-8051. (3)

Heartsoft, Box 691381, Tulsa, OK 74167. 800-285-3475. (2)

D.C. Heath, School Division, 125 Spring St., Lexington, MA 02173.

617-860-1277, 800-235-3565; Fax: 617-860-1202. (1)

Heian International Inc., Box 1013, Union City, CA 94587. 510-471-8440; Fax: 510-471-5254. (1)

Heinemann Educational Books, Inc., (a division of Reed Publishing Inc.), 361 Hanover St., Portsmouth, NH 03801-3912. 603-431-7894, 800-541-2086. (1, 3)

Heinle & Heinle Publishers Inc., 20 Park Plaza, Boston, MA 02116-4507. 617-451-1940, 800-237-0053; Fax: 617-426-4379. (1)

Hendrick-Long Publishing Co., Box 25123, Dallas, TX 75225-1123. 214-358-4677; Fax: 214-352-4768. (1)

Henry Holt & Co., Inc., 115 W. 18th St., New York, NY 10011. 212-886-9200, 800-488-5233; Fax: 212-633-0748. (1)

Herald Press, Subs. of Mennonite Publishing House Inc., 616 Walnut Ave., Scottdale, PA 15683-1999. 412-887-8500, 800-245-7894; Fax: 412-887-3111. (1)

Hicklebee's, 1378 Lincoln Ave., San Jose, CA 95125. 408-292-8880. (5)

Hiddigeigei Books, 120 E. Sunset, DeKalb, IL 60115. 815-756-9908. (1)

High Technology Software Products, Inc., Box 60406, Oklahoma City, OK 73146. 405-848-0480. (2)

High/Scope Educational Research Foundation, 600 N. River St., Ypsilanti, MI 48198-2898. 318-485-2000. (15)

Highlights for Children, 2300 W. Fifth Ave., Columbus, OH 43216. 614-486-0631. (1)

Highlights for Children, Highlights for Children, Inc., Box 269, Columbus OH 43216-0269. 614-486-0631; Fax: 614-486-0762. (9)

Hillsdale Educational Publishers, Inc., 39 North St., Box 245, Hillsdale, MI 49242. 517-437-3179, 800-437-2268; Fax: 517-437-0190. (1)

Daniel Hirsch, Box 315, Hopewell Junction, NY 12533. 914-227-9631; Fax: 914-227-9632. (6)

Hispanic Books Distributors, Inc., 1665 W. Grant Rd., Tucson, AZ 85745. 602-882-9484; Fax: 602-882-7696. (1)

Historic Hermann Inc. Museum, Fourth & Schiller, Hermann, MO 65041. 314-486-2017 or 2781. (14)

Historic Richmond Town, 441 Clarke Ave., Staten Island, NY 10306. 718-351-1611; Fax: 718-351-6057. (14)

Hobbit Hall, 120 Bulloch Ave., Roswell, GA 30075. 404-587-0907. (5)

Hola Kumba Ya!, Box 50173, Philadelphia, PA 19132. 215-848-5118. (13)

Holiday House Inc., 425 Madison Ave., New York, NY 10017. 212-688-0085; Fax: 212-421-6134. (1)

Home Economics Education Association, Box 603, Gainesville, VA 22065. 703-349-4676. (15)

Home Education Magazine, Home Education Press, Box 1083, Tonasket, WA 98855. 509-486-1351. (10)

Home Office Computing, (formerly Family Computing), Scholastic, Inc., 730 Broadway, New York, NY 10003. 212-505-3000; 212-505-4223. (10)

Homer & Assocs., 1420 N. Beachwood Dr., Hollywood, CA 90028. 213-462-4710. (3)

The Horn Book Magazine, Horn Book, Inc., 11 Beacon St., Ste. 1000, Boston, MA 02108-3704. 617-227-1555. (11)

Houghton Mifflin Company, Children's Book Division, 222 Berkeley St., Boston, MA 02116-3764. 617-351-5000, 800-225-3362; Fax: 617-351-1111. (1)

Houghton Mifflin Co., School Division, 222 Berkeley St., Boston, MA 02116-3764. 617-351-5000; Fax: 617-252-3145. (2)

Houston Fire Museum, 2403 Milam St., Houston, TX 77006. 713-524-2526; Fax: 713-520-7566. (14)

HRM Software, 338 Commerce Dr., Fairfield, CT 06430. 203-335-0906, 800-232-2224; Fax: 203-336-2481. (2)

Hubbard Scientific Co., 1120 Halbleib Rd., Box 760, Chippewa Falls, WI 54729. 715-723-4427; Fax: 715-723-8021. (3)

Human Relations Media, Inc., 175 Tompkins Ave., Pleasantville, NY 10570. 914-769-6900. (3)

Humanics Publishing Group, 1482 Mecaslin St. NW, Box 7400, Atlanta, GA 30309. 404-874-2176, 800-874-8844; Fax: 404-874-1976. (1)

Humanities Software, Box 950, Hood River, OR 97031. 503-386-6737, 800-245-6737; Fax: 503-386-1410. (2)

Humpty Dumpty's Magazine, Children's Better Health Institute, 1100 Waterway Blvd., Box 567, Indianapolis, IN 46206. 317-636-8881, Fax: 317-684-8094. (9)

Hunter House Inc., Publishers, Box 2914, Alameda, CA 94501-0914. 510-865-5282; Fax: 510-865-4295. (1)

Hyperbole Studios, 1756 114th Ave., SE, Ste. 204, Bellevue, WA 98004, 206-451-7751. (2)

Hyperglot Foreign Language Software Co. (FLS CO.), Box 10746, Knoxville, TN 37939-0746. 615-558-8270, 800-726-5087; Fax: 615-588-6569. (2)

Hyperion Books For Children, Div. of the Walt Disney Co., 114 Fifth Ave., New York, NY 10011. 212-633-4400; Fax: 212-633-4833. (1)

I Love To Read, 12798 Rancho Pena, San Diego, CA 92129. 619-538-0118. (5)

Mariuccia Iaconi Book Imports, Inc., 1110 Mariposa, San Francisco, CA 94107. 415-255-8193. (4)

IBIS Software, 140 Second St., Ste. #603, San Francisco, CA 94105. 415-546-1917; Fax: 415-546-0361. (2)

IBM/National Education Association (NEA) School Renewal Network, NEA National Center for Innovation, 1201 16th St. NW, Washington, DC 20036. 202-822-7783. (12)

Idaho Association for Educational Communications And Technology, c/o David Peck, School District #25,

3115 Pole Line Rd., Pocatello, ID 83204. 208-235-3222; Fax: 208-235-3280. (16)

Idaho Library Association, c/o Karen Strege, 633 E. 25th Ave., Spokane, WA 99203. 509-455-6697. (16)

Idaho State Department of Education, Les B. Jordan Office Bldg., 650 W. State St., Boise, ID 83720. 208-334-3300. (17)

Ideal School Supply Company, 11000 S. Lavergne Ave., Oak Lawn, IL 60453. 708-425-0805. (3)

Ideals Publishing Corp., Box 140300, 565 Marriott Dr., Ste. 890, Nashville, TN 37414-0300. 615-885-8270, 800-558-4383; Fax: 615-885-9578. (1)

IEP, Rte. 671, Box 546, Fork Union, VA 23055. 804-842-2000. (2)

Illinois Association For Educational Communications And Technology, c/o Jim Bradford, Illinois State University, Instructional Technology Services, Normal, IL 61790-6370. 309-438-3694; Fax: 309-438-8788. (16)

Illinois Library Association, c/o Lee Logan, Illinois Valley Library System, 845-Brenkman Dr., Pekin IL 61554-1522. 309-353-4110. (16)

Illinois State Board of Education, Department of School Improvement & Services, 100 N. First St., Springfield, IL 62777-001. 217-782-2826. (17)

The Imaginarium, 725 W. 5th, Anchorage, AK 99501. 907-276-3179; Fax: 907-258-4306. (14)

Impact Publishers, Inc., Box 1094, San Luis Obispo, CA 93406. 805-543-5911; Fax: 805-461-0554. (1)

Imperial Fine Books, Inc., 790 Madison Ave., Rm. 200, New York, NY 10021. 212-861-6620. (6)

Imperial International Learning Corporation, 30 Montauk Blvd., Oakdale, NY 11769. 516-567-7227. (3)

Impressions Software, 7 Melrose Dr., Farmington, CT 06032. 203-676-9002. (2)

Independence Press, Div. Herald Publishing House, 3225 S. Noland Rd., Box 1770, Independence, MO 64055. 816-252-5010. (1)

Independent School, National Association of Independent Schools, 75 Federal St., Boston, MA 02110-1904. 617-451-2444. (10)

Indian House, Box 472, Taos, NM 87571. 505-776-2953. (3)

Indiana Department of Education, Rm. 229, State House, Indianapolis, IN 46204. 317-232-9127. (17)

Indiana Library Federation, c/o Diane Bever, 5150 N. Forest Ave., Forest, IN 46039-9547. 317-453-2000. (16)

Indiana University Instructional Support Services, Bloomington, IN 47405-5901. 812-855-2103; Fax: 812-855-8404. (3)

Individual Software Co., 5870 Stoneridge Dr., Pleasanton, CA 94588. 800-331-3313. (2)

Inet Corporation, 8450 Central Ave., Newark, CA 94560. 415-797-9600. (2)

Infobases International Inc., 1875 S. State St., Ste. 7-100, Orem, UT 84058-8037. 801-224-2223. (2)

Information Access, 362 Lakeside Dr., Foster City, CA 94404. 415-378-5249, 800-227-8431; Fax: 800-676-2345. (2)

Information Center on Children's Culture, 331 E. 38th St., New York, NY 10016. 212-686-5522. (13)

Ingram Book Company, One Ingram Blvd, LaVergn, IN 37086-1986. 615-793-5000, 800-937-8000 (orders); Fax: 615-793-5000. (4)

Inline Design, 308 Main St., Lakeville, CT 06039-1204. 203-435-4995, 800-453-7671; Fax: 203-435-1091. (2)

Innovative Data Design, 1820 Arnold Industrial Way, Concord, CA 94520-5311. 510-680-6818; Fax: 510-680-1165. (2)

Insight Books, Div. of Plenum Publishing Corp., 233 Spring St., New York, NY 10013-1578. 212-620-8000, 800-221-9369; Fax: 212-463-0742. (1)

Inspiration Software, 2920 SW Dolph Ct., Ste. 3, Portland, OR 97219. 503-245-9011; 800-877-4292; Fax: 503-246-4292. (2)

Institute for the Advancement of Philosophy for Children, Montclair State College, Upper Montclair, NJ 07043. 201-893-4277. (1)

Institute of Childhood Resources, 220 Montgomery St., #2811, San Francisco, CA 94104. 415-864-1169. (15)

Institute of Chinese Culture, 86 Riverside Drive, New York, NY 10024. 212-787-6969. (13)

Instructional Communications Technology, Inc./Taylor Associates, 10 Stepar Pl., Huntington Station, NY 11746. 516-549-3000, 800-225-5428; Fax: 516-549-3156. (2, 3)

Integrative Learning Systems, 140 N. Maryland Ave., Glendale, CA 91206. 818-243-2675. (3)

Intellimation, 130 Cremona Dr., Santa Barbara, CA 93117. 805-968-2291, 800-346-8355; Fax: 805-968-8899. (2)

Interface: The Computer Education Quarterly, Mitchell Publishing, Inc, 55 Penny Lane, Ste. 103, Watsonville, CA 95076. 408-724-0195. (10)

Interkom Software, Box 1147, Elk Grove Village, IL 60007. 312-472-0713. (2)

Interlink Publishing Group Inc., 99 Seventh Ave., Brooklyn, NY 11215. 718-797-4292; Fax: 718-855-7329. (1)

International Association Of School Librarianship, Box 1486, Kalamazoo, MI 49005. 616-343-5728. (15)

International Business Machines Corp., IBM United States, Old Orchard Rd., Armonk, NY 10504. 914-765-6548. (2)

International Deaf/Tek, Inc., Box 2431, Framingham, MA 01701-0404. 508-620-1777. (15)

International Federation of Children's Choirs, 120 S. 3rd St., Shallway Bldg., Connellsville, PA 15425. 412-628-8000. (15)

International Film Bureau Inc, 332 S. Michigan Ave., Chicago, IL 60604-4382. 312-427-4545, 800-432-2241; Fax: 312-427-4550. (3, 15)

International Gymnast Magazine, SundbySports, Inc., 225 Brooks, Box 2450, Oceanside, CA 92051. 619-722-0030. (9)

International Reading Association, 800 Barksdale Rd., Box 8139, Newark, DE 19711. 302-731-1600; Fax: 302-731-1057. (15)

International Romani Union, Manchaca, TX 78652-0822. (512) 282-1268. (13)

International Service Company, 333 Fourth Ave., Indialantic, FL 32903. Voice/Fax: 407-724-1443. (4)

International Society for Technology in Education (ISTE), 1787 Agate St., Eugene, OR 97403-1923. 503-346-4414; 800-336-5191 (orders); Fax: 503-346-5890. (15)

International Society for Technology in Education (ISTE), Special Interest Group For Telecommunications (SIG/TEL), 1787 Agate St., Eugene, OR 97403-1923. 503-346-4141, Internet: ISTE@UOREGON.EDU. (12)

Interracial Books for Children Bulletin, Council on Interracial Books for Children, 1841 Broadway, New York, NY 10023-7648. 212-757-5339. (10)

Intuit, Box 3014, Menlo Park, CA 94026. 415-592-3066. (2)

Iowa Department of Education, Grimes State Office Bldg., Des Moines, IA 50319-0146. 515-281-3707; Fax: 515-242-6025. (17)

Iowa Educational Media Association, c/o Lucille Lettow, University of Northern Iowa, (H) 1516 College St., Cedar Falls, IA 50613. 319-273-6167. (16)

Iowa Library Association, c/o Catherine Rod, Grinnell College, Burling Library, Grinnell, IA 50112. 515-269-3353; Fax: 515-269-4283. (16)

Island Press Publishing, 175 Bahia Via, Fort Myers Beach, FL 33931. 813-463-9482. (1)

Istituto Italiano Di Cultura (Italian Cultural Institute), 686 Park Ave., New York, NY 10021. 212-879-4242. (13)

Italian Cultural Institute, 1 Charlton Court, Ste. 102, San Francisco, CA 94123. 415-922-4178. (13)

Italian Cultural Institute, 500 N. Michigan Ave., Ste. 1850, Chicago, IL 60611. 312-822-9545. (13)

Italian Cultural Institute, 1601 Fuller St. NW, Washington, D.C. 20009. 202-328-5500. (13)

Jabberwocky, 113 W. Rich Ave., Deland, FL 32720. 904-738-3210. (5)

Jabberwocky, 2499 Lee Rd., Cleveland, OH 44118. 216-932-2419. (5)

Jack & Jill, Children's Better Health Institute, 1100 Waterway Blvd., Box 567, Indianapolis, IN 46206. 317-636-8881; Fax: 317-684-8094. (9)

Jacoby/Storm Productions, 22 Crescent Rd., Westport, CT 06880. 203-227-2220. (3)

Jalmar Press, 2675 Skypark Dr., Ste. 204, Torrance, CA 90505. 310-784-0016, 800-662-9662; Fax: 310-784-1379. (1)

January Productions, 210 Sixth Ave., Box 66, Hawthorne, NJ 07507. 201-423-4666, 800-451-7450; Fax: 201-423-5569. (1, 3)

Japan America Society of Alabama, Rm. 7N-0015, 600 N. 18th St., Birmingham, AL 35291-0015. 205-250-2077. (13)

Japan America Society of Chicago, Inc., 225 West Wacker Dr., Ste. 2250, Chicago, IL 60606. 312-263-3049. (13)

Japan America Society of Colorado, 707 Seventeenth St., Ste. 2300, Denver, CO 80202. 303-295-8862. (13)

Japan America Society of Georgia, 225 Peachtree St. N.E., South Tower, Ste. 710, Atlanta, GA 30303. 404-524-7399. (13)

Japan America Society of Kentucky, Box 333, Lexington, KY 40584. 606-231-7533. (13)

Japan America Society of New Hampshire, Box 1226, Portsmouth, NH 03802-1226. 603-433-1360. (13)

Japan America Society of Oregon, 221 N.W. Second Ave., Portland, OR 97209. 503-228-9411 Ext. 235, 236. (13)

Japan America Society of Pennsylvania, 500 Wood St., Ste. 1614, Pittsburgh, PA 15222. 412-281-4440. (13)

Japan America Society of Phoenix, 4635 E. Lake Shore Dr., Ste. 116, Tempe, AZ 85282. 602-893-0599. (13)

Japan America Society of St. Louis, Inc., 25 N. Brentwood Blvd., St. Louis, MO 63105. 314-726-6822. (13)

Japan America Society of Southern California, ARCO Plaza, Level C, 505 S. Flower St., Los Angeles, CA 90071. 213-627-6217. (13)

Japan America Society of the State of Washington, One Union Sq. Bldg., 600 University St., Ste. 2420, Seattle, WA 98101-3163. 206-623-7900. (13)

Japan America Society of Washington, Inc., (D.C.), Dacor-Bacon House Mews, 606 18th St. NW, Washington, DC 20006. 202-289-8290. (13)

Japan America Society of Wisconsin, Inc., The Wisconsin World Trade Center, 424 East Wisconsin Ave., Milwaukee, WI 53202-4406. 414-272-5160. (13)

Japan Foundation (JF), 152 W. 57th St., 39th Fl., New York, NY 10019. 212-489-0299. (13)

Japan Society , 333 E. 47th St., New York, NY 10017. 212-832-1155. (13)

Japan Society of Boston, Inc., 22 Batterymarch St., Boston, MA 02109. 617-451-0726. (13)

Japan Society of Northern California, 31 Geary St., San Francisco, CA 94104. 415-986-4383, 1-800-67JAPAN. (13)

Japan Society of South Florida, World Trade Center, 80 S.W. 8th St., Ste. 2809, Miami, FL 33130. 305-358-6006. (13)

Japan Virginia Society, 830 E. Main St., Ste. 304, Richmond, VA 23219. 804-783-0740. (13)

Japan-America Society of Central Florida, Inc., Box 23744, Tampa, FL 33623. 813-289-6283. (13)

Japan-America Society of Greater Cincinnati, 300 Carew Tower, 441 Vine St., Cincinnati, OH 45202-2812. 513-579-3114. (13)

Japan-America Society of Hawaii, Box 1412, Honolulu, HI 96806. 808-524-4450. (13)

Japan-America Society of Houston, 1360 Post Oak Blvd., Ste. 1760, Houston, TX 77056. 713-963-0121. (13)

Japan-America Society of Indiana, Inc., First Indiana Plaza, 135 N. Pennsylvania St., Ste. 1570, Indianapolis, IN 46204-2491. 317-635-0123. (13)

Japanese American Citizens League (JACL), 1765 Sutter St., San Francisco, CA 94115. 415-921-5225. (13)

Japanese American Library, Box 590598, San Francisco, CA 94159. 415-567-5006. (13)

Jewish Book Council of The Jewish Community Center Association Of North America, 15 E. 26th St., New York, NY 10010. 212-532-4949. (15)

Jewish Braille Institute Of America, Inc., 110 E. 30th St., New York, NY 10016. 212-889-2525; Fax: 212-689-3692. (1)

Jewish Publication Society, 1930 Chestnut St., Philadelphia, PA 19103. 215-564-5925, 800-234-3151; Fax: 215-561-6640. (1, 7, 15)

The John Dewey Society for the Study of Education and Culture, c/o Dr. Robert C. Morris, School of Education, 1400 E. Hanna Ave., Indianapolis, IN 46227. 317-788-3286. (15)

Journal of Computers in Mathematics & Science Teaching, Assoc. for the Advancement of Computing in Education, Box 2966, Charlottesville, VA 22902-2966, 804-973-3987. (10)

Journal of Educational Technology Systems, Society for Applied Learning Technology, Baywood Publishing, Inc, 26 Austin Ave., Box 337, Amityville, NY 11701. 516-691-1270; Fax: 516-691-1770. (10)

Journal of Reading Behavior, National Reading Conference Inc., 11 E. Hubbard, Ste. 200, Chicago, IL 60611. 312-329-2512. (10)

Journal of Reading, International Reading Assn., 800 Barksdale Rd., Box 8139, Newark, DE 19714-8139. 302-731-1600; Fax: 302-731-1057. (10)

Journal of Secondary Gifted Education, Prufrock Press, Box 8813, Waco, TX 76714-8813. 817-756-3337; Fax: 817-756-3339. (10)

Journal of Visual Impairment & Blindness, American Foundation for the Blind, 15 W. 16th St., New York, NY 10011. Fax: 212-620-2105. (10)

Journal of Youth Services in Libraries, Assn. for Library Service to Children & Young Adult Library Services Association, American Library Association, 50 E. Huron St., Chicago, IL 60611-2795. 312-944-6780, 800-545-2433; Fax: 312-440-7374. (10)

Judaica Press, 123 Ditmas Ave., Brooklyn, NY 11218. 718-972-6200; Fax: 718-972-6204. (1)

Judi's Books, 120 Main Ave., North Twin Falls, ID 83301. 208-734-4343. (5)

Judy/Instructo, Div. of Paramount Publishing, Elementary Division, 4424 W. 78th St., Bloomington, MN 55435. 800-525-9907; Fax: 612-832-9033. (1)

Jump Cut (A Review of Contemporary Media), Jump Cut Associates, Box 865, Berkeley, CA 94701. 510-658-4482. (10)

Junior Arts Center, Barnsdall Art Park, 4814 Hollywood Blvd., Los Angeles, CA 90027. 213-485-4474; Fax: 213-485-8396. (14)

Junior Editions, 2049 Columbia Mall, Columbia, MD 21044. 301-730-2665. (5)

The Junior Museum, 282 Fifth Ave., Troy, NY 12182. 518-235-2120. (14)

Junior Museum Of Bay County, 1731 Jenks Ave., Panama City, FL 32405. 904-769-6128. (14)

Junior Scholastic, Scholastic Inc., 730 Broadway, 9th Fl., New York, NY 10003. 212-505-3000; Fax: 212-505-3653. (9)

Junior Trails, Gospel Publishing House, 1445 Boonville Ave., Springfield, MO 65802. 417-862-2781. (9)

Just Us Books, 301 Main St., Ste. 22-24, Orange, NJ 07050. 201-672-7701; Fax: 201-677-7570. (1)

K-12 Micromedia, 6 Arrow Rd., Ramsey, NJ 07446. 201-825-8888. (2)

K12Net, 1151 SW Vermont St., Portland, OR 92719. 503-280-5280. (12)

Kaleidoscope, #132, Box 414580, Kansas City, MO 64141. 816-274-8300; Fax: 816-274-3148. (14)

Kalimat Press, 1600 Sawtelle Blvd., Ste. 34, Los Angeles, CA 90025-3114. 213-479-5668. (1)

Kalmbach Publishing Company, 21027 Crossroads Circle, Box 1612, Waukesha, WI 53187. 414-796-8776, 800-558-1544; Fax: 414-796-0126. (1)

Kane/Miller Book Publishers, Box 529, Brooklyn, NY 11231-0005. 718-624-5120; Fax: 718-858-5452. (1)

Kansas Association for Educational Communications and Technology, c/o Susanne Bradley, Concordia Jr.-Sr. High School, 436 W. 10th, Concordia, KS 66901. 913-243-2453. (16)

Kansas Library Association, c/o Virginia Prither, Ellinwood School & Community Library, 210 N. Shiller, Ellinwood, KS 67526-1651. 316-564-2306. (16)

Kansas State Board of Education, 120 Southeast 10th Ave., Topeka, KS 66612-1182. 913-296-2144. (17)

Kar-Ben Copies Inc., 6800 Tildenwood Lane, Rockville, MD 20852. 301-984-8733, 800-452-7236 (800-4KARBEN); Fax: 301-881-9195. (1, 3)

Karshner Memorial Museum, 309 Fourth St. NE, Puyallup, WA 98372, 206-841-8748. (14)

Kaw Valley Films, Inc., Box 3900, Shawnee, KS 66203. 913-631-3040. (3)

Keeping Posted with NCSY, National Conference of Synagogue Youth, 333 Seventh Ave., 19th Fl., New York, NY 10001-5004. 212-244-2011; Fax: 212-268-6819. (9)

Kendall Green Publications, Div. of Gallaudet University Press, 800 Florida Ave. NE, Washington, DC 20002. 202-651-5488, 800-451-1073; Fax: 202-651-5489. (1)

Kent State University, Audio Visual Services, Kent, OH 44242. 216-672-3456. (3)

Kentucky Association for Communcations And Technology, c/o Fred. C. Kolloff, Eastern Kentucky University, 102 Perkins Bldg., Richmond, KY 40475-3127. 606-622-2474; Fax: 606-622-6276. (16)

Kentucky Department of Education, 500 Mero St., Frankfort, KY 40601. 502-564-7168; Fax: 502-564-6470. (17)

Kentucky Library Association, c/o June Martin, Eastern Grant Crabbe Library; Richmond, KY 40475-3121. 606-622-6176; Fax: 606-622-1174. (16)

Key Book Service, Inc., Box 1434, SMS, Fairfield, CT 06430. 203-374-4936. (4)

Key Curriculum Press, Box 2304, Berkeley, CA 94702. 510-548-2304; 800-338-7638; Fax: 510-548-0755. (2)

Kid City, (formerly The Electric Company Magazine), Children's Television Workshop, One Lincoln Plaza, New York, NY 10023. 212-595-3456. (9)

Kid Stuff, 123 Greene St., Mariette, OH 45750. 614-374-3114. (5)

Virginia Kidd, Box 278, Milford, PA 18337. 717-296-6205; Fax: 717-296-7266. (8)

Kidlit, 616 E. Berger St., Emmaus, PA 18049. 215-967-3916. (5)

Kidlit, 865 Duchess Dr., Yardley, PA 19067. 215-321-0688. (5)

Kids Can Press Ltd., 29 Birch Ave., Toronto, Ontario, Canada M4V 1E2. 416-534-6389, 800-265-0884; Fax: 416-960-5437. (1)

Kids' Center, 1725 N. Swan Rd., Tucson, AZ 85732. 602-322-5437. (5)

Kids Discover, Mark Levine Publishers, 170 Fifth Ave., New York, NY 10010. 212-242-5133; Fax: 212-242-5628. (9)

Kids Ink, 5619 N. Illinois, Indianapolis, IN 46208. 317-255-2598. (5)

Kids Like Me, 225 Emerson St., NW, Washington DC 20011. 202-882-2415. (5)

Kids' Lore, 603B College Rd., Greensboro, NC 27410. 919-855-5121. (5)

The Kids on the Block, Inc., 9385 C. Gerwig Lane, Columbus, MD 21046. 410-290-9095, 800-368-KIDS. (3, 15)

Kids' Shelf, 521 S. Main, Mt. Vernon, OH 43050. 614-397-5586. (5)

Kidsense, 11 E. 48 St., Minneapolis, MN 55417. 612-822-0623. (5)

Kidspace Museum, 390 S. El Molino Ave., Pasadena, CA 91101. 818-449-9144. (14)

Kimbo Educational, 10 N. Third Ave., Box 477, Long Branch, NJ 07740. 908-229-4949. (3)

Kind News, (Kids In Nature's Defense), Box 362, East Haddam, CT 06423-0362. 203-434-8666. (9)

Kingman Museum Of Natural History, W. Michigan Ave. & 20th St., Battle Creek, MI 49017. 616-965-5117. (14)

Kirkus Reviews, The Kirkus Service, 200 Park Ave. S., New York, NY 10003. 212-777-4554. (11)

Kirkwood Community College, Box 2068, Cedar Rapids, IA 52406. 319-398-5660; Fax: 319-398-5492. (3)

Bertha Klausner International Literary Agency, Inc., 71 Park Ave., New York, NY 10016. 212-MU5-2642; Fax: 212-532-8638. (8)

Gail Klemm Books, Box 518, Apple Valley, CA 92307. 619-242-5921. (6)

Kliatt, (formerly Young Adult Paperback Book Guide), Kliatt Paperback Book Guide, 33 Bay State Rd., Wellesley, MA 02181-3244. 617-237-7577. (11)

Alfred A. Knopf Books for Young Readers, 210 E. 50th St., New York, NY 10027. 212-572-2600, 800-638-6460; Fax: 212-572-8700. (1)

Know Your World Extra!, Weekly Reader Corporation, 245 Long Hill Rd., Middleton, CT 06457. 800-446-3355; Fax: 609-786-3360. (9)

Knowledge Adventure Inc., 4502 Dyer St., La Crescenta, CA 91214. 818-542-4200, 800-542-4240. (2)

Knowledge Revolution, 15 Brush Pl., San Francisco, CA 94103. 415-553-8153, 800-766-6615; Fax: 415-553-8012. (2)

Knowledge Unlimited, Box 52, Madison, WI 53701. 608-836-6660; Fax: 608-831-1570. (3)

Koala Acquisitions Inc., 16055 Caputo Dr., Unit H, Morgan Hill, CA 95037. 408-776-8181; Fax: 408-776-8187. (2)

The Kobrin Letter, 732 Greer Rd., Palo Alto, CA 94303. 415-856-6658. (11)

Koen Book Distributors, 10 Twosome Dr., Box 600, Moorestown, NJ 08057. 609-235-444, 800-257-8481. (4)

Kohl Children's Museum, 165 Green Bay Rd., Wilmette, IL 60091. 708-256-6056; Fax: 708-256-2921. (14)

Korean Cultural Service, 5505 Wilshire Blvd., Los Angeles, CA 90036. 213-936-7141. (13)

Barbara S. Kouts, Box 558, Bellport, NY 11713. 516-286-1278; Fax: 516-286-1538. (8)

Kurdish Heritage Foundation of America, 345 Park Pl., Brooklyn, NY 11238. 718-783-7930. (13)

Laclede Communication Services, Inc, 2675 Scott Ave., St Louis, MO 63103-3047. 314-535-3999. (3)

Landers Film Reviews, Lander Associates, Box 69760, Los Angeles, CA 90069. 213-657-1686. (11)

Landmark Media Inc, 3450 Slade Run Dr., Falls Church, VA 22042. 800-342-4336; Fax: 703-536-9540. (3)

Language Arts, National Council of Teachers of English, 1111 Kenyon Rd, Urbana, IL 61801-1096. 217-328-3870; Fax: 217-328-9645. (10)

Lantern Press, 354 Hussey Rd., Mt. Vernon, NY 10552. 212-838-7821. (1)

Laotian Cultural and Research Center, 1413 Meriday Ln., Santa Ana, CA 92706. 714-541-4533. (13)

Laredo Publishing Co., 22930 Lockness Ave., Torrance, CA 90501. 310-517-1890; Fax: 310-517-1892. (1)

Larksdale, Box 70456, Houston, TX 77270-0456. 713-461-7200; Fax: 713-973-0511 (orders: Box 801222, Houston, TX 77280. 800-666-2332). (1)

Las Vegas Natural History Museum, 900 Las Vegas Blvd., N, Las Vegas, NV 89101. 702-384-DINO; Fax: 702-384-5343. (14)

Laser Learning Technologies, 120 Lakeside Ave., Ste. 240, Seattle, WA 98122-3505. (2)

Latin American Studies Association (LASA), William Pitt Union, 9th Fl., Univ. of Pittsburgh, Pittsburgh, PA 15260. 412-648-7929. (13)

Laureate Learning Systems, Inc., 110 Eastspring St., Winooski, VT 05404. 802-655-4755, 800-562-6801; Fax: 802-655-4757. (2)

Lawrence Productions, Inc., 1800 S. 35th St., Galesburg, MI 49053-9687. 616-665-7075, 800-421-4157; Fax: 616-665-7060. (2)

Kathleen And Michael Lazare, Box 117, Sherman, CT 06784. 203-354-4181; Fax: 203-350-1761. (6)

LCSI (Logo Computer Systems, Inc.), Box 162, Highgate Springs, VT 05460. 514-331-7090, 800-321-5646; Fax: 514-331-1380. (2)

Leadership Publishers, Box 8358, Des Moines, IA 50301-8358. 515-278-4765; Fax: 515-270-8303. (1)

Learn Me Books, 175 Ash St., St. Paul, MN 55126. 612-490-1805. (5)

Learnco, Inc., Box L, Exeter, NH 03833. 603-778-0813, 800-542-0026. (2)

Learning Arts, Box 179, Wichita, KS 67201. 316-636-9274. (2)

The Learning Company, 6493 Kaiser Dr., Fremont, CA 94555. 415-792-2101, 800-852-2255; Fax: 510-792-9628. (2)

The Learning Cube (Educational Software Collection), 3 Pine Ridge Way, Mill Valley, CA 94941. 800-733-6733. (2)

Learning Disabilities Association of America, 4156 Library Rd., Pittsburgh, PA 15234. 412-341-1515. (15)

Learning Disability Quarterly, Council for Learning Disabilities, Box 40303, Overland Park, KS 66204. 913-492-8755. (10)

Learning Magazine, Springhouse Corp, 1111 Bethlehem Pike, Box 908, Springhouse, PA 19477-0908. 215-646-8700. (10)

Learning Research Inc, 420 NW 5th St., Evansville, IN 47708. 812-426-6377; Fax: 812-421-3270. (3)

Learning Team, 10 Long Pond Rd., Armonk, NY 10504-0217. 914-273-2226, 800-793-TEAM(8326), Fax: 914-273-2227. (2)

Learning Well, 2200 Marcus Ave., New Hyde Park, NY 11040-1042. 516-621-1540. (3)

Lectorum Publications, Inc., 127 W. 14th St., New York, NY 10011. 212-929-2833, 800-345-5946; Fax: 212-727-3035. (1)

Lee & Low Books Inc., 228 E. 45th St., New York, NY 10017. 212-867-6155; Fax: 212-338-9059. (1)

Legacy Software, 8521 Reseda Blvd., Northridge, CA 91324. 818-885-5773, 800-532-7692; Fax: 818-885-5779. (2)

Lego, 550 Taylor Rd., Enfield, CT 06082. 203-749-2291. 800-527-8339; Fax: 203-763-2466. (2)

Hal Leonard Publishing Corp., 777 W. Bluemound Rd., Box 13819, Milwaukee, WI 53213. 414-774-3630, 800-524-4425; Fax: 414-774-3259. (1, 3)

Lerner Publications Company, 241 First Ave. N., Minneapolis, MN 55401. 612-332-3344, 800-328-4929; Fax: 612-332-7615. (1)

Lexington Children's Museum, 401 W. Main St., Lexington, KY 40507. 606-258-3253; Fax: 606-258-3255. (14)

Libraries Unlimited, Box 6633, Englewood, CO 80155-6633. 303-770-1220, 800-237-6124. (1, 2)

Library Corporation, Research Park, Inwood, WV 25428. 304-229-0100. (2)

Library Journal, Cahners/R. R. Bowker Magazine Group, 249 W. 17 St., New York, NY 10011. 212-645-0067, 800-669-1002; Fax: 212-468-6734. (11)

Library Literature, The H. W. Wilson Co., 950 University Ave., Bronx, NY 10452. 212-588-8400, 800-367-6770; Fax: 718-590-1617. (11)

Libros Sin Fronteras, Box 2085, Olympia, WA 98507-2085. 206-357-4332. (1)

Lied Discovery Museum, 833 Las Vegas Blvd., N. Las Vegas, NV 89101. 702-382-3445; Fax: 702-382-0592. (14)

Liguori Publications, One Liguori Dr., Liguori, MO 63057-9999. 314-464-2500, 800-325-9521; Fax: 314-464-8449. (1)

Lincoln Children's Museum, 121 S. 13th St., Lincoln Sq., Lincoln, NE 68506. 402-477-0128. (14)

Hannah Lindahl Children's Museum, 1402 S. Main St., Mishawaka, IN 46544. 219-258-3056. (14)

Linden Tree Children's Books, 170 State St., Los Altos, CA 94022. 415-949-3390. (5)

The Lindsey Museum, 1931 First Ave., Walnut Creek, CA 94596. 510-935-1978. (14)

Lingo Fun, Inc., Box 486, Westerville, OH 43081. 614-882-8258. 800-745-8258; Fax: 614-882-2390. (2)

Linworth Publishing Inc., 480 E. Wilson Bridge Rd., Ste. L, Worthington, OH 43085-9918. 800-786-5017; Fax: 614-436-490. (1)

Lion Books, Div. of Sayre Publishing, 210 Nelson Rd., Ste. B, Scarsdale, NY 10583. 914-725-3572; Fax: 914-723-7012. (1)

Listen, Health Connection, 552 W. Oakridge Dr., Hagerstown, MD 21740. 800-777-9098. (9)

Little Book House, Stuyvesant Plaza, Albany, NY 12203. 518-489-4761. (5)

Little Book Room, 561 Adams St., Milton, MA 02186. 617-696-0044. (5)

Little, Brown & Company, 34 Beacon St., Boston, MA 02108-1493. 617-227-0730, 800-343-9204; Fax: 617-227-4633. (1)

Little Dickens Bookshop, 126 S. Main, Mt. Pleasant, MI 48858. 517-773-1074. (5)

The Little Red Filmhouse, Box 691083, Los Angeles, CA 90069. 213-855-0241. (3)

Little Red Schoolhouse, 73 S. Professor St., Oberlin, OH 44074. 216-774-1700. (14)

Live Oak Media, Box 652, Pine Plains, NY 12567. 518-398-1010; Fax: 518-398-1070. (3)

Living Arts And Science Center, 362 N. Martin Luther King Blvd., Lexington, KY 40508. 606-252-5222. (14)

Living Soft, Box 970, Janesville, CA 96114-0970. 916-253-2700, 800-626-1262; Fax: 916-253-2703. (2)

Tee Loftin Publisher, Inc., 685 Gonzales Rd., Santa Fe, NM 87501-6190. 505-989-1931. (1)

Log Cabin Children's Museum, 1638 Crescent Dr., Kingsport, TN 37064. 615-246-6635. (14)

Logo Exchange, International Society for Technology in Education, Special Interest Group for Logo-Using, 1787 Agate St, Eugene, OR 97403-1923. 503-346-4414; Fax: 503-346-5890. (10)

Lollipop Power Books, Carolina Wren Press, 120 Morris St., Durham, NC 27701. 919-560-2738. (1)

Long Beach Children's Museum, 445 Long Beach Blvd., #60, Long Beach, CA 90802. 310-495-1653; Fax: 310-495-2188. (14)

Long Filmslide Service, 7505 Fairmount, El Cerrito, CA 94530. 510-524-2744. (3)

Los Angeles Children's Museum, 310 N. Main St., Los Angeles, CA 90012. 213-687-8801. (14)

Los Angeles Times Book Review, Los Angeles Times, Inc., Times Mirror Sq., Los Angeles, CA 90053. 213-237-7777. (11)

Lothrop, Lee & Shepard Books, Div. of William Morrow, 1350 Ave. of the

Americas, New York, NY 10019.
212-261-6793, 800-843-9389; Fax:
212-261-6689. (1)

Lotus Development Corp., 55 Cambridge Pkwy., Cambridge, MA
02142. 617-577-8500, 800-343-
5414; Fax: 617-693-3899. (2)

Louisiana Arts and Science Center,
100 S. River Rd., Baton Rouge, LA
70802. 504-344-5272; Fax:
504-344-9477. (14)

Louisiana Association for Educational
Communications and Technology,
c/o Gail G. Griffin, A.C. Steere
Elementary, 4009 Youree Dr.,
Shreveport, LA 71105. 318-865-
5675; Fax: 318-631-5241. (16)

Louisiana Children's Museum, 428
Julia St., New Orleans, LA 70130.
504-586-0725; Fax: 504-529-3666.
(14)

Louisiana Department of Education,
Box 94064, Baton Rouge, LA
70804-9064. 504-342-3464. (17)

Louisiana Library Association, c/o Dr.
Walter Wicker, 5027 Stow Creek,
Ruston, LA 71270. 318-257-2577.
(16)

Louisville Visual Art Association, 3005
Upper Rd., Louisville, KY 40207.
502-896-2146. (14)

Loyola University Press, 3441 N. Ashland Ave., Chicago, IL 60657. 312-
281-1818, 800-621-1008; Fax:
312-281-0555. (1)

Lucent Books, Affil. of Greenhaven
Press, Inc., Box 289009, San Diego,
CA 92198-9009. 619-485-7424, 800-
231-5163; Fax: 619-485-9542. (1)

Lucerne Media, 37 Ground Pine Rd.,
Morris Plains, NJ 07950. 201-538-
1401, 800-341-2293; Fax: 201-538
-0855. (3)

Luso-American Education Foundation
(LAEF), Box 1768, Oakland, CA
94604. 415-452-4465. (13)

Lutz Children's Museum, 247 S. Main
St., Manchester, CT 06040.
203-643-0949. (14)

Lyceum Productions, Box 1295, La
Puente, CA 91749. 310-968-6424.
(3)

Lyrical Ballad Bookstore, 7 Philadelphia
St., Saratoga Springs, NY 12866.
518-584-8779. (6)

Macmillian New Media (Maxwell Electronic Publishing), 124 Mt. Auburn
St., Ste. 320, Cambridge. MA 02138.
617-661-2955. (2)

Macromedia, Inc., 600 Townsend, Ste.
310W, San Francisco, CA 94103.
800-828-6067; Fax: 410-244-2876.
(2)

Mage Publishers Inc., 1032 29 St.,
NW, Washington, DC 20007. 202-
342-1642, 800-962-0922; Fax:
202-342-9269. (1)

Magic Door, 4112-112 Pleasant Vale,
Raleigh, NC 27612. 919-783-6177.
(5)

Magic Dragon, 1339 South Mooney,
Visalia, CA 93277. 209-733-3126.
(5)

The Magic House, St. Louis Children's
Museum, 516 S. Kirkwood Rd., St.
Louis, MO 63122. 314-822-8900;
Fax: 314-822-8930. (14)

Magic Quest, 125 University Ave., Palo
Alto, CA 94301. 415-321-5838,
800-321-8925; Fax: 415-321-8560.
(2)

Magic Tree Bookstore, 141 N. Oak
Park Ave., Oak Park, IL 60301.
708-848-0770. (5)

Magna Systems, Inc., West Countyline
95, Barrington, IL 60010.
312-382-6477. (3)

Main Street Kids Book Company,
10217 Main St., Bellevue, WA
98004. 206-455-8814. (5)

Maine Educational Media Association,
c/o David W. Anderson, Thomton
Academy, 438 Main St., Saco, ME
03909. 207-363-3621. (16)

Maine Library Association, c/o Valerie
Osborne, Old Town Public Library,
64 Middle Street, Old Town, ME
04468. 207-827-3972. (16)

Maine State Library, State House Station, #64, Maine State Library, Augusta, ME 04333. 207-287-5620.
(17)

Malibu Films, Box 428, Malibu, CA
90265. 310-456-2859. (3)

Manhattan Graphic Corp., 250 E.
Hartsdale Ave., Hartsdale, NY
10530. 916-725-2048. 800-
572-6533; Fax: 916-725-2450.
(2)

Marine Life Center Of Juno Beach,
1200 U.S. Hwy. 1, Loggerhead Park,
Juno Beach, FL 33408. 407-627-
8280. (14)

Betty Marks Literary Agency, 176 E.
77th St., New York, NY 10021.
212-535-8388. (8)

Maroten & Co., 1500 16th St., #100,
San Francisco, CA 94103-5112.
415-863-6100. (3)

Marshall Cavendish Corp., Member of
Times Mirror Group, 2415 Jerusalem
Ave., North Bellmore, NY 11710.
516-826-4200; Fax: 516-785-8133.
(1)

Marshfilm, Box 8082, Shawnee Mission, KS 66208. 816-523-1059.
(3)

Marshware, (Division of Marshfilm Enterprises, Inc.), Box 8082, Shawnee
Mission, KS 66208. 816-523-1059,
800-821-3303 (not MO, HI, AK); Fax:
816-333-7421. (2)

Maryka Books For Kids, 7536 Forsyth,
Clayton, MO 63105. 314-862-6709.
(5)

Maryland Department of Education,
200 W. Baltimore St., Baltimore,
MD 21201-2595. 410-333-2125.
(17)

Maryland Educational Mediaorganiza-
tion c/o Fred Thomas, Cecil Co.
Public Schools, 201 Booth St., Elkton, MD 21921. 410-996-5400.
(16)

Maryland Historical Press, 9205 Tuckerman St., Lanham, MD 20706.
301-577-5308. (1)

Maryland Library Association, c/o
Joyce Demmitt, Information Services, Howard County Library, 10375
Little Patuxent Pkwy., Columbia, MD
21044. 410-313-7800. (16)

Massachusetts Department of Education, 1385 Hancock St., Quincy, MA
02169. (17)

Massachusetts Library Association, c/o
Ellen Rainville, J.V. Fletcher Library,
50 Main St., Westford, MA 01886.
508-692-5557. (16)

Massachusetts School Library Media
Association, c/o Rolf Erikson, Minuteman Regional Voc. Tech., 758 Marrett Rd., Lexington, MA 02173.
617-61-6500 Ext. 263; Fax:
617-862-6010. (16)

Math & Computer Education Project, Lawrence Hall of Science, University of California, Berkeley, CA 94720. 415-642-3167. (2)

Math/Science Network, Preservation Park, 678 13th St., Ste. 100, Oakland, CA 94612. 510-893-6284. (15)

Mathegraphics Software, 61 Cedar Rd., E. Northport, NY 11731. 516-368-3781. (2)

Mathematics Teacher, National Council of Teachers of Mathematics, 1906 Association Dr, Reston, VA 22091. 703-620-9840; Fax: 703-476-2970. (10)

Mathsoft, Inc., 201 Broadway, Cambridge, MA 02139-1901. 617-577-1017, 800-628-4223; Fax: 617-577-8829. (2)

Maui Children's Toys And Books, Box 1869, Makawau, HI 96768. 808-527-2765. (5)

Maveric Software, 9801 Dupont Ave. S., Bloomington, MN 55431. 612-881-3738. (2)

Maxis, 2 Theatre Sq., Ste. 230, Orinda, CA 94563. 510-254-9700, 800-336-2947; Fax: 510-253-3736. (2)

McCurdy Historical Doll Museum, 246 N. 100 East, Provo, UT 84601. 801-377-9935. (14)

McDougal, Littel & Co., Box 1667, Evanston, IL 60204. 708-869-2300; Fax: 708-869-0841. (1)

McFarland & Co., Inc., Publishers, Box 611, Jefferson, NC 28640. 910-246-4460; Fax: 910-246-5018. (1)

Peter J. McGovern Little League Baseball Museum, Rte. 15 S., Williamsport, PA 17701. 717-326-3607. (14)

McGraw-Hill Inc., Blue Ridge Summit, PA 17294-0850. 717-794-2191; Fax: 800-932-0183. (2)

McIntosh & Otis Inc, 310 Madison Ave., New York, NY 10017. 212-687-7400; Fax: 212-687-6894. (8)

MECC (Minnesota Educational Computing Corp.), 6160 N. Summit Dr., Minneapolis, MN 55430. 612-569-1500, 800-685-6322; Fax: 612-569-1551. (2)

B.L. Means Rare Books, 17849 SE 105 Ave., Summerfield, FL 32691. 904-245-9054. (6)

Media Alive, 766 San Aleso Ave., Sunnyvale, CA 94086. 408-752-8500. (2)

Media & Methods, American Society for Educators, 1429 Walnut St., Philadelphia, PA 19102. 215-563-3501; Fax: 215-563-1588. (10)

Media Flex, Box 1107, Champlain, NY 12919. 518-298-2970. (2)

The Media Guild, 11722 Sorrento Valley Rd. E., San Diego, CA 92121. 619-755-9191; Fax: 619-755-4931. (3)

Media Loft, Inc., 10720 40 Ave. N., Minneapolis, MN 55441. 612-375-1086, 800-532-8457. (3)

Media Materials, 111 Kane St., Baltimore, MD 21224. 800-638-6470. (1, 3)

Media Review Digest, Pierian Press, Box 1808, Ann Arbor, MI 48106. 313-434-5530; Fax: 313-434-6409. (11)

Media Review, Education Funding Research Council, 1611 N. Kent St., Ste. 508, Arlington, VA 22209. 703-528-1000. (11)

Media Vision, 47300 Bayside Pkwy., Fremont, CA 94538. 510-770-8600, 800-684-6699; Fax: 510-440-8837. (2)

Melton Book Company, Box 140990, Nashville, TN 37214-0990. 615-228-3204, 800-441-0511. (4)

Scott Meredith Literary Agency, 845 Third Ave., New York, NY 10022-6687. 212-245-5500. (8)

Meridian Educational Corporation, 236 E. Front St., Bloomington, IL 61701. 309-827-5455; Fax: 309-829-8621. (3)

Merit Audio Visual, Box 392, New York, NY 10024. 800-753-6488. (2)

Merit/NSF Information Services, Merit Network, Inc., 2901 Hubbard, Pod G, Ann Arbor, MI 48105-2016. 800-66-MERIT, 313-936-3000, Internet: NSFNET-INFO@MERIT.EDU. (12)

Meriwether Publishing Inc., 885 Elkton Dr., Colorado Springs, CO 80907.

719-594-4422, 800-93PLAYS; Fax: 719-594-9916. (1, 3)

Mary Merritt Doll Museum, Rte. 2, Douglassville, PA 19518. 215-385-3809. (14)

Merlyn's Pen, Merlyn's Pen, Inc., Dept. UPD, Box 1058, East Greenwich, RI 02818. 401-885-5175; Fax: 401-885-5222. (9)

Metier, 1951 Davina St., Henderson, NV 89014. 702-897-6795. (2)

Metropolitan Museum Of Art, 1000 Fifth Ave., New York, NY 10028-0198. 212-570-3961; Fax: 212-570-3972. (14)

Mews Books Ltd, 20 Bluewater Hill, Westport, CT 06880. 203-227-1836. (8)

Mexican American Studies and Research Center, Modern Language Bldg., Univ. of Arizona, Tucson, AZ 85721. (13)

Miami Youth Museum, 5701 Sunset Dr., Miami, FL 33143. 305-661-3046; Fax: 305-669-0917. (14)

Michigan Association for Media in Education, c/o Victoria DeFields, Bridgman Public Schools, 9964 Gast Rd., Bridgman, MI 49106. 616-466-0229; Fax: 616-460-0229. (16)

Michigan Department of Education, Library Media & Telecommunications, Box 30008, Lansing, MI 48909. 517-373-1806. (17)

Michigan Library Association, Sandra Scherba, Cromaine Library; 3688 N. Hartland Rd., Hartland, MI 48353-0950. 313-632-5200; Fax: 313-632-5279. (16)

Micro Learningware, Hwy. 169 S., Amboy, MN 56010-9762. 507-674-3705. (2)

Microcomputer Index, Learned Information Inc, 143 Old Marlton Pike, Medford, NJ 08055. 609-654-6266; Fax: 609-654-4309. (10)

Microed Inc., Box 24750, Edwina, MN 55424. 612-929-2242. (2)

Micrograms, 1404 N. Main, Rockford, IL 61103. 815-965-2464, 800-338-4726. (2)

Microphys, 12 Bridal Way, Sparta, NJ 07871. 800-832-6591. (2)

Microsoft, One Microsoft Way, Redmond, WA 98052-6399. 206-882-8080, 800-426-9400; Fax: 206-936-7329. (2)

The Middle Atlantic Press Inc., 848 Church St., Wilmington, DE 19899. 302-654-4107; 302-455-9382. (1)

Middle School Journal, National Middle School Assn., 4807 Evanswood Dr., Columbus, OH 43229-6292. 614-848-8211; Fax: 614-848-4301. (10)

Midwest Software, 22500 Orchard Lake Rd. #1, Farmington, MI 48024. 313-477-0897, 800-422-0095. (2)

Milkweed Editions, 430 First Ave. N., Ste. 400, Minneapolis, MN 55401. 612-332-3192; Fax: 612-332-6428. (1)

Millbrook Press, 2 Old New Milford Rd., Brookfield, CT 06804. 203-740-2220, 800-462-4703; Fax: 203-740-2526. (1)

Miller Books, 2908 W. Valley Blvd., Alhambra, CA 91803. 818-284-7607. (1)

Milligan News Company, 150 N. Autumn St., San Jose, CA 95110. 408-286-7604, 800-873-2387; Fax: 408-298-0235. (4)

Milliken Publishing Co., 1100 Research Blvd., St. Louis, MO 63132-0579. 314-991-4220, 800-643-0008; Fax: 800-538-1319. (2)

Mindplay, 3130 N. Dodge Blvd., Tucson, AZ 85716. 602-322-6365, 800-221-7911; Fax: 602-322-0363. (2)

Mindscape Educational, 1345 Diversey Pkwy., Chicago, IL 60614-1299. 312-525-1500, 800-829-1900; Fax: 312-525-9474. (2)

Minnesota Children's Museum, 1217 Bandana Blvd., N, St. Paul, MN 55108. 612-644-5305; Fax: 612-644-4708. (14)

Minnesota Department of Education, 550 Cedar St., St. Paul, MN 55101. 612-296-1570. (17)

Minnesota Educational Media Organization, c/o Jim Marshall, Minnesota Center for Arts Education, 205 Birnanwood Dr., Bumsville, MN 55337. 612-591-4742; Fax: 612-591-4747. (16)

Minnesota Library Association, c/o Mark Ranum, East Central Regional Library, 244 S. Birch, Cambridge, MN 55008-1521. 612-689-1901; 612-689-9605. (16)

Mississippi Department of Education, Educational Media Service, Box 771, Ste. 604, Jackson, MS 39205. 601-359-3778. (17)

Mississippi Educational Communications And Technology Roundtable, c/o Becky Dailey, Thomas St. School, 901 S. Thomas, Tupelo, MS 38801. 601-841-8602; Fax: 601-841-8887. (16)

Mississippi Library Association, c/o Charline Longino, Biloxi Library, Harrison County Library System, 139 Laheuse St., Biloxi, MS 39530. 601-374-0330. (16)

Missouri Association For Educational Communications And Technology, c/o Hal Gardner, Missouri School Service Center, (H) 318 Grover, Warrensburg, MO 64093. (16)

Missouri Department of Elementary & Secondary Education, Box 480, Jefferson City, MO 65101. 314-751-4445. (17)

Missouri Library Association, c/o Beth Eckles, Wolfner Library, Missouri State Library, 600 W. Maine, Jefferson City, MO 65101. 314-751-8720, (16).

Misty City Software, 11866 Slater Ave. NE, Kirkland, WA 98034. 206-820-5559, 800-795-0049; Fax: 206-820-4298. (2)

MMI Corporation, 2950 Wyman Pkwy., Box 19907, Baltimore, MD 21211. 410-866-1222; Fax: 410-366-6311. (2, 3)

Modan/Adama Books, Box 1202, Bellmore, NY 11710-0485. 516-679-1380. (1)

Modern Curriculum Press, Imprint of Paramount Publishing, Elementary Division, 13900 Prospect Rd., Cleveland, OH 44136. 216-238-2222. (1)

Arthur Mokin Productions, Inc., Box 1866, Santa Rosa, CA 95402-1866. 707-542-4868. (3)

Monmouth Museum, Newman Springs Rd., Lincroft, NJ 07738. 908-747-2266. (14)

Monroe Books, Mission Village, 359 E. Shaw Ave., Suite 102, Fresno, CA 93710-7609. 209-224-7000. (6)

Montana Council For Indian Education, 517 Rimrock Rd., Box 31215, Billings, MT 59107. (1)

Montana Library Association, c/o Steve Cottrell, Bozeman Public Library, 220 E. Lamme, Bozeman, MT 59715. 406-586-4788; Fax: 406-587-7785. (16)

Montessori Life, (formerly Constructive Triangle), 17583 Oak St., Fountain Valley, CA 92708. 714-968-0107; Fax: 714-964-0800. (10)

Moody Institute Of Science, 820 N. La Salle, Chicago, IL 60610-3284. 312-329-2190; Fax: 312-329-4350. (3)

Mook & Blanchard, Box 1295, La Puente, CA 91749. 818-968-6424, 800-875-9911. (4)

Morning Glory Press, 6595 San Haroldo Way, Buena Park, CA 90620-3748. 714-828-1998; Fax: 714-828-2049. (1)

Morrow Junior Books, Div. of William Morrow & Co., 1350 Ave. of the Americas, New York, NY 10019. 212-261-6793, 800-843-9389; Fax: 212-261-6689. (1)

Mrs. Liz's Children's Bookshop, 84 West St., Chagrin Falls, OH 44022. 216-423-0121. (5)

John Muir Publications, Box 613, Santa Fe, NM 87504. 505-982-4078, 800-888-7504; Fax: 505-988-1680. (1)

Mulisog Corporation, 26 W. Mission, #6, Santa Barbara, CA 93101. 805-966-3187. (3)

Muller Media, Inc., 23 E. 39th St., New York, NY 10016. 212-683-8220. (3)

Multimedia Product Development, Inc., 410 S. Michigan Ave., Chicago, IL 60605. 312-922-3063. (8)

Multimedia Publishers Group, 60 Cutter Mill Rd., Ste. 502, Great Neck, NY 11021. 516-482-0088; Fax: 516-773-0990. (2)

MultiMedia Schools, Online Inc., 462 Danbury Rd., Wilton, CT 06897-2126. 1-800-248-8466, 203-761-1466; Fax: 203-761-1444. (9)

Munchkin Bookery, 1318 Lufkin Mall, Lufkin, TX 75901. 409-637-1156. (5)

Muncie Children's Museum, 306 S. Walnut, Muncie, IN 47305. 317-286-1660; Fax: 317-286-1662. (14)

Museum of the American Indian, Broadway at 155th St., New York, NY 10032. 212-283-2420. (13)

Museum Of The Southwest, 1705 W. Missouri Ave., Midland, TX 79701-6516. 915-689-2882; Fax: 915-570-7077. (14)

Museums Of Abilene, 102 Cypress, Abilene, TX 79601. 915-673-4587. (14)

MVP, 9424 Eton Ave., #C, Chatsworth, CA 91311. 800-637-3555; Fax: 818-709-7846. (3)

My Friend: A Magazine For Boys & Girls, Daughters of St. Paul, 50 St. Paul's Ave., Boston, MA 02130. 617-522-8911; Fax: 617-524-8025. (9)

Jean V. Naggar Literacy Agency, 216 E. 75th St., New York, NY 10021. 212-794-1084. (8)

Narnia Books, 2927 W. Cary St., Richmond, VA 23221. 804-353-5675. (5)

Nashua Center For The Arts, 14 Court St., Nashua, NH 03060. 603-673-4475; Fax: 603-882-7705. (14)

Nassau Kids Books, 7952 Jericho Tpke., Woodbury, NY 11797. 516-921-9255. (5)

National Archives and Records Administration, Eighth and Pennsylvania Ave., NW, Washington, D.C. 10408. 202-523-3236. (13)

National Art Education Association, 1916 Association Dr., Reston, VA 22091-1590. 703-860-8000; Fax: 703-860-2960. (15)

National Asian American Telecommunications Association (NAATA), 346 Ninth St., Second Fl., San Francisco, CA 94103. 415-863-0814. (13)

National Association For Bilingual Education, Union Center Plaza, 810 1st St. NE, 3rd Fl., Washington, DC 20002. 202-898-1829, Fax: 202-789-2866. (15)

National Association For Creative Children & Adults, 8080 Springvalley Dr., Cincinnati, OH 45236-1395. 513-631-1777. (15)

National Association For Gifted Children, 1155 15th St. NW, #1002, Washington, DC 20005-2706. 202-785-4268. (15)

National Association for the Advancement of Colored People (NAACP), 4805 Mt. Hope Dr., Baltimore, MD 21215. 301-358-8900. (13)

National Association for the Education of Young Children, 1509 16th St., NW, Washington, DC 20036-1426. 202-232-8777, 800-424-2460. (15)

National Association for the Preservation and Perpetuation of Storytelling, Box 309, Jonesborough, TN 37659. 615-753-2171. (15)

National Association for the Visually Handicapped, 22 W. 21st St., New York, NY 10010. 212-889-3141. (15)

National Association of Black Storytellers, Box 27456, Philadelphia, PA 19118. 215-844-8463. (13)

National Association of Dramatic & Speech Arts, 208 Cherokee Dr., Blacksburg, VA 24060. 703-231-5805. (15)

National Association of Elementary School Principals, 1615 Duke St., Alexandria, VA 22314-3483. 703-684-3345. (15)

National Association of the Deaf, 814 Thayer Ave., Silver Spring, MD 20910. 301-587-1788. (15)

National Black Child Development Institute, 1023 15th St. NW, Ste. 600, Washington, DC 20005. 202-387-1281; Fax: 202-234-1738. (15)

National Book Company, Box 8795, Portland, OR 97207-8795. 503-228-6345. (2, 3)

National Braille Association, Inc., 3 Townline Circle, Rochester, NY 14623-2513. 716-427-8260; Fax: 716-427-0263. (15)

National Braille Press Inc., 88 St. Stephen St., Boston, MA 02115. 617-266-6160; Fax: 617-437-0456. (1)

National Captioning Institute, 5203 Leesburg Pike, Falls Church, VA 22041. 703-998-2400, 800-533-9673 (voice), 800-321-8337 (TDD). (15)

National Center For Health Education, 72 Spring St., Ste. 208, New York, NY 10012. 212-334-9470; Fax: 212-334-9845. (15)

National Committee For Prevention Of Child Abuse (NCPCA), 332 S. Michigan Ave., Ste. 1600, Chicago, IL 60604-4357. 312-663-3520. (15)

National Council For Geographic Education (NCGE), Indiana University of Pennsylvania, 16A Leonard Hall, Indiana, PA 15705. 412-357-6290; Fax: 412-357-7708. (15)

National Council For Languages and International Studies (NCLIS), 300 I St., NE, Ste. 211, Washington, DC 20002. 202-546-7855. (13)

National Council Of Teachers Of English, 1111 W. Kenyon Rd., Urbana, IL 61801-1096. 217-328-3870, 800-369-6283; Fax: 217-328-9645. (1, 15)

National Council Of Teachers Of Mathematics, 1906 Association Dr., Reston, VA 22091-1593. 703-620-9840; Fax: 703-476-7560. (15)

National Education Association, 1201 16th St., NW, Washington, DC 20036. 202-833-4000. (15)

National Federation of Indian American Associations, Box 462, Wakefield Station, Bronx, NY 10466. 203-329-8010. (13)

National Film Board of Canada, 1251 Ave. of the Americas, 16th Fl., New York, NY 10020. 212-596-1770; Fax: 212-596-1779. (3)

National Gallery of Art Extension Programs, 6th St. & Constitution Ave. NW, Washington, DC 20565. 202-842-6273,6263. (3)

National Geographic Kids Network, National Geographic Society, Educational Services, Washington, DC 20036. 800-368-2728. (12)

National Geographic Society, 1145 17th St. NW, Washington, DC 20036. 202-857-7000, 800-638-4077; Fax: 202-775-6141. (1, 3)

National Geographic Society Educational Services, Box 98018, Washington DC 20090-8018. 202-828-6605, 800-368-2728; Fax: 301-921-1575. (2)

National Geographic World, National Geographic Society, 17 & M Sts., NW, Washington, DC 20036. 202-857-7000, 800-638-4077. (9)

National Indian Youth Council, 318 Elm St., SE, Albuquerque, NM 87102. 505-247-2251. (15)

National Information Center For Educational Media, Box 40130, Albuquerque, NM 87196. 505-265-3591. (15)

National Italian American Foundation (NIAF), 666 11th St. NW, Ste. 800, Washington, DC 20001. 202-638-0220. (13)

National Middle School Association, 4807 Evanswood Dr., Columbus, OH 43229-6292. 614-8484-8211; Fax: 614-848-4301. (15)

National Native American Cooperative, Box 5000, San Carlos, AZ 85550-0301. 602-230-3399. (13)

National Organization of Italian-American Women, 445 W. 59th St., Rm. 1248, New York, NY 10019. 212-237-8574. (13)

National School Orchestra Association, 345 Maxwell Dr., Pittsburgh, PA 15236-2067. 412-882-6996; Fax: 614-848-4301. (15)

National Science Foundation's Network Service Center (NNSC), 10 Moulton St., Cambridge, MA 02138. 617-873-3400, Internet: NNSC@NNSC.NSF.NET. (12)

National Science Supervisors Association, 82 Deepwood Dr., East Hartford, CT 06118-2411. (15)

National Science Teachers Association (NSTA), 1742 Connecticut Ave., NW, Washington, DC 20009-1171. 202-328-5800. (15)

National Story League, c/o Virginia Dare Shope, 1342 4th Ave., Juniata, Altoona, PA 16601. 814-942-3449. (15)

National Teaching Aids, 1845 Highland Ave., New Hyde Park, NY 11040. 516-326-2555. (3)

National Telemedia Council (NTC), 120 E. Wilson St., Madison, WI 53703. 608-257-7712; Fax: 608-257-7714. (15)

National Textbook Company, 4255 W. Touhy Ave., Lincolnwood, IL 60646. 708-679-5500, 800-323-4900; Fax: 708-679-2494. (1, 2, 3)

National/State Leadership Training Institute On The Gifted/Talented, Hilton Center, 900 Wilshire Bldg., Ste. 1142, Los Angeles, CA 90017-3311. 213-489-7470. (15)

Native American Newspapers Collection, 815 State St., Madison, WI 53706. 608-262-9584. (13)

Native American Public Broadcasting Consortium, Box 8311, Lincoln, NE 68501. 402-472-3522. (13, 15)

Native American Research Information Service, American Indian Institute, 555 Constitution Ave., Norman, OK 73037. 405-325-1711. (13)

Natural Science Center Of Greensboro, 4301 Lawndale Dr., Greensboro, NC 27455. 910-288-3769; Fax: 910-288-0545. (14)

The Nature Museum, 1658 Sterling Rd., Charlotte, NC 28204. 704-337-2665; Fax: 704-337-2670. (14)

Neal-Schuman Publishers, 100 Varick St., New York, NY 10013. 212-925-8650; Fax: 212-219-8916. (1)

Nebraska Department of Education, 301 Centennial Mall S., Lincoln, NE 68509-4987. 402-471-2295. (17)

Nebraska Educational Media Association, c/o Phyllis Brunken, Education Service Unit (ESU) #7, 2657 44th Ave., Colombus, NE 68601. 402-564-5753; Fax: 402-563-1121. (16)

Nebraska Library Association, c/o Rod Wagner, Nebraska Library Commission, 1200 N. St., Ste. 120, Lincoln, NE 63508-2006. 800-307-2665; Fax: 404-471-2083. (16)

Netherland-America Foundation, 54 W. 39th St., New York, NY 10018. 212-767-1616. (13)

Nevada Department of Education, Education Branch 400 W. King, Capital Complex, Carson City, NV 89710. 702-687-5160. (17)

Nevada Library Association, c/o Gary Avent, Elko County Public Library, 720 Court St., Elko, NV 89801. 702-738-3066; Fax: 702-738-8262. (16)

Never Never Land, 134 Front St., Wheaton, IL 60187. 708-690-7909. (5)

Neverending Tales, 6147 P.M. 1960 West, Houston, TX 77069. 712-586-7345. (5)

The New Advocate, Christopher-Gordon Publishers, Inc., 480 Washington St., Norwood, MA 02062. 617-762-5577. (10)

New Britain Youth Museum, 30 High St., New Britain, CT 06051. 203-225-3020. (14)

New Day Press, Karamu House, 2355 E. 89th St., Cleveland, OH 44106. 216-795-7070. (1)

New Dimension Films, 85803 Lorane Hwy., Eugene, OR 97405. 503-484-7125. (3)

New England Press, Inc., Box 575, Shelburne, VT 05482. 802-863-2520; Fax: 802-863-1510. (1)

New Expression, Youth Communication/Chicago Center, 70 E. Lake St., Ste. 815, Chicago, IL 60601-5907. 312-663-0543. (9)

New Hampshire Department of Education, 101 Pleasant St., Concord, NH 03301. 603-271-2632. (17)

New Hampshire Educational Media Association, c/o Deirdre Angwin, McKelvie Middle School, 108 Liberty Hill Rd., Bedford, NH 03110. 603-472-3729. (16)

New Hampshire Library Association, c/o Randy Brough, Franklin Public Library, 310 Central St., Franklin, NH 03235. 603-934-2911. (16)

New Jersey Library Association, c/o Mary Lou Abrams, Paramus Public Library, E 116 Century Rd., Paramus, NJ 07652. 201-599-1302. (16)

New Media Source, 3830 Valley Centre Dr., Box 2153, San Diego, CA 92130-9834. 800-344-2621; Fax: 619-438-2330. (2)

New Mexico Department of Education, Education Bldg., Santa Fe, NM 87501-2786. 505-827-6504. (17)

New Mexico Library Association, c/o Barbara Billey, San Juan College Library, 4601 College Ave., Farmington, NM 87402. 505-599-0256; Fax: 505-599-0385. (16)

New Readers Press, Div. of Laubach Literacy International, 1320 Jamesville Ave., Box 131, Syracuse, NY 13210. 315-422-9121, 800-448-8878; Fax: 315-422-6369. (1)

New Seed Press, Box 9488, Berkeley, CA 94709-0488. 510-540-7576. (1)

New York Library Association, c/o Sandra Miranda, White Plains Public Library, 100 Marine Ave., White Plains, NY 10601. 914-422-1406. (16)

The New York Public Library, Office of Children's Services, 454 Fifth Ave., New York, NY 10016-0122. 212-340-0903; Fax: 212-340-3988. (1)

New York State Education and Research Network (NYSERNet), 111 College Place, Syracuse, NY 1324 4100. 315-443-4120, Internet: INFO@NYSERNET.ORG. (12)

New York State Education Department, Bureau of School Library Media Programs, Rm. 676 EBA, Albany, NY 12234. 518-474-2468. (17)

New York Times Book Review, New York Times Co, 229 W. 43rd St., New York, NY 10036. 212-556-1234, 800-631-2580. (11)

NewMedia Magazine, HyperMedia Publications, Inc., 901 Mariner's Island Blvd., Ste. 365, San Mateo, CA 94404. 415-573-5170; Fax: 415-573-5131. (10)

Newsbank, 58 Pine St., New Canaan, CT 06840-5416. 800-762-8182. (2)

Newsweek Educational, Box 414, Livingston, NJ 07039. 201-316-2000, 800-526-2595; Fax: 201-316-2370. (2)

Nimco, Box 9, 117 Hwy. 815, Calhoun, KY 42327-0009. 800-962-6662; Fax: 502-273-5844. (2, 3)

The Norma-Lewis Agency, 521 Fifth Ave., New York, NY 10175. 212-751-4955. (8)

North Carolina Association for Educational Communications and Technology, c/o Libby Gray, McClintock Junior High School, (H) 6900 Ronda Ave., Charlotte, NC 28211. 704-343-6425; Fax: 704-343-6509. (16)

North Carolina Department of Public Instruction, 301 N. Wilmington St.,

Education Bldg., Raleigh, NC 27201-2825. 919-715-1530. (17)

North Carolina Library Association, c/o David Ferguson, Forsyth County Public Library, 660 W. Fifth St., Winston-Salem, NC 27101-2705. 919-727-2556; Fax: 919-727-2549. (16)

North Dakota Department of Public Instruction, 600 E. Boulevard Ave., Bismarck, ND 58505-0440. 701-224-2295, Fax: 701-224-4770. (17)

North Dakota Library Association, c/o Sharon Evensen, UND-Lake Region, 1800 N. College Dr., Devil's Lake, ND 58301. 701-662-2220. (16)

North-South Books, Affil. of Nord-Sud Verlag AG, 1133 Broadway, Ste. 1016, New York, NY 10010. 212-463-9736, 800-282-8257; Fax: 212-633-1004. (1)

Northeast Literary Agency, 69 Broadway, Concord, NH 03301. 603-225-9162. (8)

Northern Illinois University, University Libraries Film Library, De Kalb, IL 60115. 805-753-1000. (3)

Northland Publishing Co., Box 1389, Flagstaff, AZ 86002. 602-774-5251, 800-346-3257; Fax: 602-774-0592. (1)

Jeffrey Norton Publishers Inc./Audio-Forum, The Language Source on the Green, 96 Broad St., Guilford, CT 06437-2635. 203-453-9794; Fax: 203-453-9774. (3)

Northwest Regional Educational Laboratory (NWREL), 101 Southwest Main St., Ste. 500, Portland, OR 97204. 503-275-9500. (12)

Edward D. Nudelman, Fine and Rare Books, Box 20704 Broadway Station, Seattle, WA 98102. 206-367-4644. (6)

Nystrom, Div. of Herff Jones, Inc., 3333 N. Elston Ave., Chicago, IL 60618. 312-463-1144; Fax: 312-463-0515. (3)

OCLC/Forest Press, 6565 Frantz Rd., Dublin, OH 43017-3395. 800-848-5878, ext. 6237; Fax: 614-764-6096. (2)

Oddo Publishing, Storybook Acres, Box 68, Fayetteville, GA 30214. 404-461-7627. (1)

Odyssey, Kalmbach Publishing Co, 1027 N. Seventh St., Milwaukee, WI 53233. 414-272-2060. (9)

Office of Public Instruction, Rm. 106, State Capitol, Helena, MT 59620. 406-444-2979. (17)

Ohio Department of Education, 65 S. Front St., Rm. 611, Columbus, OH 43266-0308. 614-466-9272. (17)

Ohio Educational Library Media Association, c/o Lynda Sadowski, Mentor High School, 6477 Center St., Mentor, OH 44060. 216-974-5348. (16)

Ohio Library Council, c/o Morton Thomas, 1582 Mohican Rd., Stow, OH 44224. 216-688-3106. (16)

Oklahoma Library Association, c/o Robert Swisher, University of Oklahoma; School of Lib & Info Studies; 401 W. Brooks, Norman, OK 73019. 405-325-3921. (16)

Oklahoma Library Media/ITV, 2500 N. Lincoln Blvd., Rm. 215, Oklahoma City, OK 73105-4599. 405-521-2956. (17)

Olomeinu-Our World, Torah Umesorah, National Society for Hebrew Day Schools, 5723 Eighteenth Ave., Brooklyn, NY 11204. 718-259-1223; Fax: 718-259-1795. (9)

Olympic Media Information, Box 190, West Park, NY 12493. 201-963-1600. (15)

On The Line, Mennonite Publishing House, 616 Walnut Ave., Scottdale, PA 15683. 412-887-8500. (9)

Once Upon A Lap, 215 Forbush Mountain Dr., Chapel Hill, NC 27514. 919-932-3300. (5)

Once Upon A Mind, 4825 Farthing Dr., Colorado Springs, CO 80906. 719-540-9017. (5)

Once Upon A Time, 2284 Honolulu Ave., Montrose, CA 91020. 818-248-9668. (5)

Once Upon A Time, 3220 Johnston St., Lafayette, LA 70503. 318-981-2255. (5)

Once Upon A Time, 77 Quaker Ridge Rd., New Rochelle, NY 10804. 914-632-2665. (5)

Once Upon A Time, 3795 East North, Greenville, SC 29615. 803-292-2132. (5)

Once Upon A Time, 7 Green St., Vergennes, VT 05491. 802-658-3659. (5)

Online Computer Systems, 20251 Century Blvd., Germantown, MD 20874. 800-922-9204; Fax: 301-428-2093. (2)

Open Door Bookstore Ltd., 128 Jay St., Schenectady, NY 12305. 318-346-2719. (5)

Optical Data, 30 Technology Dr., Warren, NJ 07059. 908-668-1322, 800-524-2481. (2)

Orbis Books, Div. of Maryknoll Fathers & Brothers, Box 308 (Walsh Bldg), Maryknoll, NY 10545. 914-941-7590, 800-258-5835; Fax: 914-941-7005. (1)

Orchard Books, Subs. of Grolier Inc., 95 Madison Ave., New York, NY 10016. 212-951-2600, 800-433-3411; Fax: 212-213-6435. (1)

Orchard House, Louisa May Alcott Memorial Association, Box 343, Concord, MA 01742-0343. 508-369-4118. (15)

Oregon Department of Education, Instructional Technology Unit, 700 Pringle Pkwy., SE, Salem, OR 97310-0290. 503-378-4974. (17)

Oregon Educational Media Associaiton, c/o Dr. Richard Forcier, Western Oregon State College, (H) 25335 SW Neill Rd., Sherwood, OR 97140. 503-838-8441, 503-838-8474. (16)

Oregon Library Association, c/o Ann Billeter, Jackson County Library System, 413 W. Main, Medford, OR 97501-2730. 503-776-7285; Fax: 503-776-7290. (16)

The Oryx Press, 4041 N. Central Ave., Ste. 700, Phoenix, AZ 85012-3397. 602-265-2651, 800-279-6799; Fax: 800-279-4663. (1)

Our Little Friend, (Seventh Day Adventist Assn.), Pacific Press Publishing, 1350 Kings Rd., Nampa, ID 83651. 208-465-2500; Fax: 208-465-2531. (9)

Outdoor Empire Publishing, Inc., 511 Eastlake Ave., Seattle, WA 98109. 206-624-3845; Fax: 206-340-9816. (1)

Over The Rainbow, 440 River Rd., Ste."E", Corona, CA 91720. 714-736-7707. (5)

Over The Rainbow, 421 Lincoln Center, Stockton, CA 95207. 209-473-0220. (5)

The Overlook Press, 149 Wooster St., 4th Fl., New York, NY 10012. 212-477-7162; Fax: 212-477-7525. (1)

Richard C. Owen Publishers, Inc., Box 585, Katonah, NY 10536. 914-232-3903. 800-336-5588; Fax: 914-232-3977. (1)

Owl And The Pussycat, 316 S. Ashland, Lexington, KY 40502. 606-266-7121. (5)

Oxford University Press, 200 Madison Ave., New York, NY 10016. 212-679-7300. (3)

Oxford University Press, Children's Books Department, 200 Madison Ave., New York, NY 10016. 212-679-7300, ext. 7130, 800-451-7556; Fax: 212-725-2972. (1)

Oz Books, 125 Main St., Southwest, ME 04679. 207-244-9077. (5).

Pacific Books Publishers, Box 558, Palo Alto, CA 94302-0558. 415-965-1980; Fax: 415-965-0776. (1)

Pacific Cascade Records, Sub. of Joan Lowe Enterprises, 47534 McKenzie Hwy, Vida, OR 97488. 503-896-3290. (3)

Pacific North West Library Association, c/o Audrey Kolb, 2471 NW Williams Loop, Redmond, OR 97756. (16)

Pages For Young Ages, 47 S. Monroe, Monroe, MI 48161. 313-457-0420. (5)

Pages Read Aloud Book Club, Pages School Book Fairs, 801 94th Ave. N., St. Petersburg, FL 33702. 813-578-7600. (7)

Pages/Books For Children, 18399 Ventura Blvd., Tarzana, CA 91356. 818-342-6657. (5)

Papa Bear's Books, 4401 S. Elm St., Tempe, AZ 85282. 602-838-9370. (5)

Parent Child Press, Box 675, Hollidaysburg, PA 16648-0675. 814-696-7512; Fax: 814-696-7510. (1)

Parent Cooperative Preschools International, c/o Kathy Mensel, Box 90410, Indianapolis, IN 46290. 317-849-0992. (15)

Parenting Press, Inc., Box 75267, Seattle, WA 98125. 206-364-2900, 800-992-6657; Fax: 206-364-0702. (1)

Parents' Choice, Parents' Choice Foundation, Box 185, Waban, MA 02168. 617-965-5913. (11)

Parkwest Publications, Inc., 452 Communipaw Ave., Jersey City, NJ 07304. 201-432-3257; Fax: 201-432-3257. (1)

Paulist Productions, Box 1057, Pacific Palisades, CA 90272. 310-454-0688; Fax: 310-459-6549. (3)

PBS Learning Link, PBS Online, 1320 Braddock Pl., Alexandria, VA 22314. 703-739-8464. (12)

PBS Video, Dept. of Public Broadcasting Service, 1320 Braddock Pl., Alexandria, VA 22314-1698. 703-739-5380, 800-424-7963 (information), 800-344-3337 (orders); Fax: 703-739-5269. (3)

Peaceable Kingdom, 1051 Folger Ave., Berkeley, CA 94710. 800-444-7778. (5)

Peachtree Publishers Ltd., 494 Armour Circle NE, Atlanta, GA 30324-4088. 404-876-8761, 800-241-0113; Fax: 404-875-2578. (1)

Pebble Beach Press, Ltd., Box 1171, Pebble Beach, CA 93953. 408-372-5559; Fax: 408-375-4525. (1)

Ray Peekner Literary Agency, Inc., Box 3308, Bethlehem, PA 18107. 215-974-9154; Fax: 315-974-8228. (8)

Pelican Publishing Company, Box 3110, Gretna, LA 70054. 504-368-1175, 800-843-1724; Fax: 504-368-1195. (1)

A.W. Peller & Assoc., 249 Goffle Rd., Hawthorne, NJ 07507. 201-423-4666. (3)

Penguin USA, 375 Hudson St., New York, NY 10014-3657. 212-366-2000, 800-331-4624. (1)

Pennsylvania Association for Educational Communications & Technology, c/o Kyle Peck, Penn State University, 270 Chambers Bldg., University Park, PA 16802. 814-863-4316; Fax: 814-863-7602. (16)

Pennsylvania Department of Education, 333 Market St., Box 911, Harrisburg, PA 17126-0333. 717-787-6704. (17)

Pennsylvania Library Association, c/o Kathy Kennedy, Monroeville Public Library, 2615 Mosside Blvd., Monroeville, PA 15146. 412-372-0500. (16)

Pennsylvania State University, Audio Visual Services, Special Services Bldg., 1127 Fox Hill Rd., University Park, PA 16803-1824. 814-865-6314, 800-826-0132; Fax: 814-863-2574. (3)

Peter Pan Industries, 88 St. Francis St., Newark, NJ 07105. 201-344-4214. (1)

Petunia's Place, 2017 W. Bullard, Fresno, CA 93711. 209-438-1561. (5)

Pfeifer-Hamilton, Whole Person Associates Inc., 210 W. Michigan St., Duluth, MN 55802-1908. 218-727-0500, 800-247-6789; Fax: 218-727-0505. (1)

Phi Delta Kappan, PDK, Inc., Box 789, Bloomington, IN 47402-0789. 812-339-1156; Fax: 812-339-0018. (10)

Philippine Resource Center, Box 40090, 2288 Fulton, #103, Berkeley, CA 94704. 415-548-2546. (13)

S.G. Phillips Inc., 83 Chatham, NY 12037. 518-392-3068. (1)

Phoenix Films, A Div. of Phoenix Learning Group, 2349 Chaffe Drive, St. Louis, MO 63146. 314-569-0211; Fax: 314-569-2834. (3)

Picture Book Studio, 10 Central St., Saxonville, MA 011701. 508-788-0911; Fax: 508-788-0919 (ordering: 200 Old Tappan Rd., Old Tappan, NJ 07675, 800-223-2336). (1)

Pineapple Press, Inc., Drawer 16008, Southside Sta., Sarasota, FL 34239. 813-952-1085. (1)

Pinocchio Bookstore, 826 S. Aiken Ave., Pittsburgh, PA 15232. 412-621-1323. (5)

Pinocchio's Books & Toys, 322 High St., Morgantown, WV 26505. 304-296-2332. (5)

Pioneer, Brotherhood Commission, Southern Baptist Convention, 1548 Poplar Ave., Memphis, TN 38104. 800-727-6466. (9)

Pioneer Farm Museum and Ohop Village, 7716 Ohop Valley Rd., Eatonville, WA 98328. 206-832-6300. (14)

PJD Learning Materials, 5080 Timberway Trail, Clarkston, MI 48346. 313-620-2736. (1)

Planetary Publications (formerly Univ. of the Trees Press), Box 66, Boulder Creek, CA 95006. 408-338-2161. (1)

Players Press, Inc., Box 1132, Studio City, CA 91604. 818-789-4980. (1)

Playmore Inc., Publishers, 200 Fifth Ave., New York, NY 10010. 212-924-7447; Fax: 212-463-7719. (1)

Plays, Inc., 120 Boylston St., Boston, MA 02116-4615. 617-423-3157. (1)

Plays (The Drama Magazine for Young People), Plays, Inc., 120 Boylston St., Boston, MA 02116-4615. 617-423-3157. (9)

Pleasant Company Publicatons, Inc., 8400 Fairway Pl., Middleton, WI 53562. 608-836-4848, 800-233-0264; Fax: 608-836-1999. (1)

Please Touch Museum, 210 N. 21st St., Philadelphia, PA 19103. 215-963-0667. (14)

Pocket Books, Subs. of Simon & Schuster, 1230 Ave. of the Americas, New York, NY 10020. 212-698-7000. (1)

Pockets, The Upper Room, 1908 Grand, Box 189, Nashville, TN 37202. 615-340-7333; Fax: 615-340-7006. (9)

Point of View Productions, 2477 Folsom St., San Francisco, CA 94110. 415-821-0435; Fax: 415-931-0948. (3)

POLART, 5973 Cattlemen Lane, Sarasota, FL 34232. 813-378-9393. (3, 13)

Polish Institute of Arts and Sciences of America, 208 E. 30th St., New York, NY 10016. 212-686-4164. (13)

Polish Museum of America (PMA), 984 N. Milwaukee Ave., Chicago, IL 60622. 312-384-3352. (13)

Pooh Corner, 1843 Monroe St., Madison, WI 53711. 608-256-0558. (5)

Pooh's Corner, 1830 Breton Rd., SE, Grand Rapids, MI 49506. 616-942-9887. (5)

Poppets, 3124 Elliot Ave., Seattle, WA 98121. 206-285-3107. (5)

Popular Culture Library, Bowling Green State Univ., Bowling Green, OH 43403-0600. 419-372-2450. (13)

Porter Sargent Publishers, 11 Beacon St., Boston, MA 02108. 617-523-1670; Fax: 617-523-1021. (1)

Portsmouth Children's Museum, 420 High St., Portsmouth, VA 23704. 804-393-8393. (14)

Portuguese Continental Union of the United States of America (PCU), 899 Boylston St., Boston, MA 02115. 617-536-2916. (13)

Prakken Publications, Box 8623, Ann Arbor, MI 48107-8623. 313-769-1211, 800-530-9673; Fax: 313-769-8383. (1)

Prebound Children's Books, (Formerly Associated Libraries), 229-33 N. 63 St., Philadelphia, PA 19139. 800-222-4994; Fax: 215-476-3207. (4)

Primary Treasure, (Seventh Day Adventist Assn), Pacific Press Publishing, 1350 Kings Rd., Nampa, ID 83651. 208-465-2500; Fax: 208-465-2531. (9)

Printed Page, 1219 Pearl St., Boulder, CO 80302. 303-443-8450. (5)

Project ASIA (Asian Shared Information and Access), 2225 W. Commonwealth Ave., Ste. 315, Alhambra, CA 91803. 818-284-7744. (13)

Psychology in the Schools, Clinical Psychology Publishing Company, 4 Conant Sq., Brandon, VT 05733. 802-247-6871; Fax: 802-247-6853. (10)

Publishers' Graphics, Inc., 251 Greenwood Ave., Bethel, CT 06801. 203-797-8188. (8)

Publishers Media, 5507 Morella Ave, North Hollywood, CA 91607. 818-980-2666. (4)

Publishers Weekly, R. R. Bowker Co., 249 W. 17 St., New York, NY 10011. 212-645-0067, 800-842-1669; Fax: 212-242-7216. (11)

Pumpkin Patch, 302 Main St., Ames, IA 50010. 515-292-5293. (5)

Puppeteers of America, Five Cricklewood Path, Pasadena, CA 91107. 818-797-5748. (15)

Puppetry Journal, Puppeteers of America, 8005 Swallow Dr., Macedonia, OH 44056. 314-825-2526.(10)

Purple Crayon, 7515 Huntsman Blvd., Springfield, VA 22153. 703-455-6100. (5)

Puss'n Books, Inc., 15788 Redmond Way, Redmond, WA 98052. 206-885-6828. (5)

Pussywillow Publishing House, Box 1806, Gilbert, AZ 85234. 602-892-1316. (1)

The Putnam Berkeley Group Inc., 200 Madison Ave., New York, NY 10016. 212-951-8400, 800-631-8671; Fax: 212-532-3693. (1)

Pyramid Film & Video, Box 1048, Santa Monica, CA 90406. 310-828-7577; Fax: 310-453-9083. (3)

Quiet Valley Living Historical Farm, 1000 Turkey Hill Rd., Stroudsburg, PA 18360. 717-992-6161. (14)

R-A-D-A-R, Standard Publishing Company, 8121 Hamilton Ave., Cincinnati, OH 45231. 513-931-4050. (9)

Edward T. Rabbitt & Co., 7029 Three Chopt Rd., Richmond, VA 23226. 804-288-2665. (5)

Rabbit Hill Children's Bookstore, 1235 Broadway, Hewlett, NY 11557. 516-295-3216. (5)

Antonio Raimo, Fine Books, 401 Chestnut St., Columbia, PA 17512. 717-684-4111, 717-684-9411; Fax: 717-684-3151. (6)

Rainbow Books and Learning Center, C5 Cullen Mall, Corpus Christi, TX 78412. 512-992-0590. (5)

Rainbow Educational Video, Inc., 170 Keyland Ct., Bohemia, NY 11716. 516-589-6643, 800-331-4047; Fax: 516-589-6131. (3)

Ramic Productions, Inc., Box 9518, Newport Beach, CA 92658. 714-640-9115. (3)

Josephine Randall Junior Museum, 199 Museum Way, San Francisco, CA 94114. 415-554-9600. (14)

Random House, 201 E. 50th St., New York, NY 10022. 212-572-2600; Fax: 212-572-8700. (1)

Random House & Bullseye Books for Young Readers, 201 E. 50th St.,

New York, NY 10022. 212-572-2600; Fax: 212-572-8700. (3)

Ranger Rick, The National Wildlife Federation, 1400 16th St., NW, Washington, DC 20036-2266. 202-797-6800, 800-432-6564; Fax: 703-442-7332. (9)

Read, America!, The Place in the Woods, 3900 Glenwood Ave., Golden Valley, MN 55422-5302. 612-374-2120; Fax: 612-593-5593. (10)

Read Magazine, Weekly Reader Corporation, 245 Long Hill Rd., Middleton, CT 06457. 800-446-3355; Fax: 609-786-3360. (9)

Reader's Clubhouse, 18326 Susan Pl., Cerritos, CA 90701. 213-865-2788. (5)

Reading Express, 3880 Fairway Dr., Florissant, MO 63033. 314-839-0155. (5)

Reading Improvement, Project Innovation of Mobile, Box 8508, Spring Hills Sta., Mobile, AL 36608. 205-343-7802. (10)

Reading Reform Foundation, Box 98785, Tacoma, WA 98498-0785. 206-588-3436. (15)

Reading Rhinoceros, 24000 Alicia Pkwy., Mission Viejo, CA 92691. 714-588-0898. (5)

The Reading Teacher, International Reading Association, Box 8139, 800 Barksdale Rd., Newark, DE 19714-8139. 302-731-1600; Fax: 301-731-1057. (10)

Red Balloon Bookshop, 891 Grand Ave., St. Paul, MN 55105. 612-224-8320. (5)

Redbird Press Inc., Box 11441, Memphis, TN 38111. 901-323-2233. (1)

REFORMA (National Association to Promote Library Services to the Spanish Speaking), c/o American Library Association, Office of Library Outreach Services, 50 E. Huron St., Chicago, IL 60611. 800-545-2433. (13)

Regent Book Company, 101A Rte. 46, Saddle Brook, NJ 07662. 201-368-2208, 800-999-9554; Fax: 201-368-9770. (4)

Jo Ann Reisler, Ltd., 360 Glyndon St., NE, Vienna, VA 22180. 703-938-2967, 703-938-2237; Fax: 703-938-9057. (6)

Nancy Renfro Studios, Box 164226, Austin, TX 78716. 512-327-9588, 800-933-5512. (1)

Resco P/R Graphics & A/V Productions, 99 Draper Ave., Meriden, CT 06450. 203-238-9633. (3)

Review & Herald Publishing Association, 55 W. Oak Ridge Dr., Hagerstown, MD 21740. 301-791-7000, 800-234-7630; Fax: 301-791-7012. (1)

Rhode Island Educational Media Association, c/o Susan Bryan, Warwick Veterans High School, 2401 West Shore Rd., Warwick, RI 02886. 401-737-3300 Ext. 5329. (16)

Rhode Island Library Association, c/o James Giles, Cranston Public Library, 140 Socanossett Cross Rd., Cranston, RI 02920. 401-943-9080; Fax: 401-943-5079. (16)

Rhode Island State Department of Education, 22 Hays St., Providence, RI 02908. 401-277-2617. (17)

Rhythms Productions/Tom Thumb Music, Box 34485, Los Angeles, CA 90034-0485. 310-836-4678. (3)

Richmond Children's Museum, 740 Navy Hill Dr., Richmond, VA 23219. 804-788-4949. (14)

John R. Riina, 5905 Meadowood Rd., Baltimore, MD 21212. 301-433-2305. (8)

Rizzoli International Publications, 300 Park Ave. S., New York, NY 10010. 212-387-3400, 800-462-2387; Fax: 212-387-3535. (1)

Roberts Rinehart, 121 Second Ave., Niwot, CO 80544-0666. 303-652-2921, 800-352-1985; Fax: 303-652-3923. (1)

Rock Creek Nature Center, 5200 Glover Rd., NW, Washington, DC 20015. 202-426-6829. (14)

Rocky Mountain Children's Museum, 1610 Gay St., Rocky Mount, NC 27804. 919-972-1168. (14)

Rodale Press, Book Division, 33 E. Minor St., Emmaus, PA 18098. 215-967-5171, 800-441-7761; Fax: 215-967-3044. (1)

Rootabaga Bookery, 6717 Snider Pl,, Dallas, TX 75205. 214-361-8581. (5)

The Rosen Publishing Group, 29 E. 21st St., New York, NY 10010. 212-777-3017, 800-237-9932; Fax: 212-777-0277. (1)

Rourke Publishing Group, Box 3328, Vero Beach, FL 32964. 407-465-4575; Fax: 407-465-3132. (1)

Running Press Book Publishers, 125 S. 22nd St., Philadelphia, PA 19103. 215-567-5080, 800-345-5359; Fax: 212-568-2919. (1)

Russell & Volkening, 50 W. 29th St., New York, NY 10001. 212-684-6050; Fax: 212-889-3026. (8)

Rykken and Scull, 1031 Trillium Lane, Mill Valley, CA 9494. 415-381-5701. (6)

Rymer Books, 22249 E. Tollhouse Rd., Clovis, CA 93611-9761. 209-298-8845. (1)

SALALM (Seminar on the Acquisition of Latin American Library Materials), Secretariat, Memorial Library, Univeristy of Wisconsin, Madison, WI 53706. 608-262-3240. (13)

San Francisco Chronicle Review, San Francisco Chronicle, 901 Mission St., San Francisco, CA 94119. 415-777-7042. (11)

San Francisco Studies Center, 1095 Market St., Ste. 602, San Francisco, CA 94103. 415-626-1650. (1)

San Marino Book and Toy Shoppe, 2475 Huntington Dr., San Marino, CA 91108. 818-795-5301. (5)

Sandlapper Publishing, Inc., Box 730, Orangeburg, SC 29116. 803-531-1658; Fax: 803-534-5223. (1)

Santa Fe Children's Museum, 1050 Old Pecos Trail, Santa Fe, NM 87501. 505-989-8359. (14)

Santillana Publishing Co., 901 W. Walnut St., Compton, CA 90220. 310-763-0455, 800-245-8584; Fax: 310-763-4440. (1)

Scarecrow Press, Sub. of Grolier, Box 4167, 52 Liberty St., Metuchen, NJ 08840. 908-548-8600, 800-537-7107; Fax: 908-548-5767. (1)

Justin G. Schiller, Ltd., Place des Antiquaires, 125 E. 57th St., Gallery 48, New York, NY 10022. 212-832-8231, 212-751-5450; Fax: 212-688-1139. (6)·

Schocken Books, Div. of Random House Inc., 201 E. 50th St., New York, NY 10022. 212-572-2559, 800-638-6460; Fax: 212-572-6030. (1)

Scholastic Action, Scholastic Inc., 730 Broadway, New York, NY 10003-9538. 212-505-3000; Fax: 212-505-3653. (9)

Scholastic Art, (formerly Art & Man), Scholastic Inc., 730 Broadway, New York, NY 10003-9538. 212-505-3000; Fax: 212-505-3653, 800-631-1586. (9)

Scholastic Choices, 730 Broadway, New York, NY 10003-9538. 212-505-3105; Fax: 212-505-3653. (9)

Scholastic Coach, Scholastic Inc., 730 Broadway, New York, NY 10003. 212-505-3000. (10)

Scholastic Inc., 555 Broadway, New York, NY 10012. 212-505-3000, 800-392-2179; Fax: 212-505-3377. (1, 7)

Scholastic Let's Find Out, Scholastic Inc., 730 Broadway, New York, NY 10003. 212-505-3000. (9)

Scholastic Math, Scholastic Inc., 730 Broadway, New York, NY 10003. 212-505-3000; Fax: 212-505-3653. (9)

Scholastic News, Scholastic Inc., 730 Broadway, New York, NY 10003. 212-505-3000; Fax: 212-505-3653. (9)

Scholastic Science World, Scholastic Inc., 730 Broadway, New York, NY 10003. 212-505-3000. (9)

Scholastic Scope, Scholastic Inc., 730 Broadway, New York, NY 10003. 212-505-3117. (9)

Scholastic Update, (Inc. Scholastic Search), Scholastic Inc., 730 Broadway, New York, NY 10003. 212-505-3064. (9)

School Library Journal, A Cahners/R.R. Bowker Publication, 249 W. 17th St., New York, NY 10011. 212-463-6759, 800-669-1002; Fax: 212-463-6734. (11)

School Library Media Activities Monthly, LMS Associates, 17 E. Henrietta St., Baltimore MD 21230. 410-685-8621. (10)

School Library Media Quarterly, American Association of School Librarians, 50 E. Huron St., Chicago, IL 60611-2795. 312-944-6780, 800-545-2433; Fax: 312-440-9374. (10)

School Science And Mathematics, School Science & Math Assn, Inc., Memorial Gym 300 B, Virginia Tech. C & I, Blacksburg, VA 24061. 703-231-5558; Fax: 703-231-3717. (10)

School Science & Mathematics Association, Bloomsburg University, 400 E. Second St., Bloomsburg, PA 17815-1301. 717-389-4915; Fax: 717-389-3894. (15)

Schoolmasters/Champions on Film & Video, 745 State Circle, Box 1941, Ann Arbor, MI 48106. 313-761-5175. (3)

Harry Schwartz Children's Books, 17147-A West, Brookfield, WI 53005. 414-786-7565. (5)

Schroder Music Company, 1450 Sixth St., Berkeley, CA 94710. 415-524-5804. (1, 3)

Sci-Tech Center of Northern New York, 154 Stone St., Watertown, NY 13601. 315-788-1340. (14)

Science Activities, Heldref Publications, 1319 Eighteenth St., NW, Washington, DC 20036-1802. 202-296-6267; Fax: 202-296-5149. (10)

Science & Children, National Science Teachers Association, 1742 Connecticut Ave, NW, Washington, DC 20009. 202-328-5800. (10)

Science Books & Films, American Association for the Advancement of Science, AAAS Science Books & Films, 1333 H St., NW, Washington, DC 20005. 202-326-6454. (11)

Science Center of Connecticut, 950 Trout Brook Dr., West Hartford, CT 06119. 203-231-2824. (14)

Science Kit, 777 E. Park Dr., Tonawanda, NY 14150. 716-874-6020. (3)

Science Station, 427 First St., SE, Cedar Rapids, IA 54201. 319-366-0968. (14)

The Science Teacher, National Science Teachers Association, 1742 Connecticut Ave., NW, Washington, DC 20009. 202-328-5800. (10)

Scienceland, Scienceland Inc., 501 Fifth Ave., New York, NY 10017. 212-490-2180; Fax: 212-490-2187. (9)

Scotia-Glenville Children's Museum, 102 N. Ballston Ave., Scotia, NY 12302. 518-346-1764. (14)

Scott, Foresman & Co., 900 E. Lake Ave., Glenview, IL 60025. 708-729-3000, 800-782-2665; Fax: 708-486-3968. (1)

Scott Resources, Box 2121, Fort Collins, CO 80522. 303-484-7445. (3)

Scottish Historic and Research Society of Delaware Valley (SHRSDV), 102 St. Paul's Rd., Ardmore, PA 19003. 215-649-4144. (13)

Seal Press, 3131 Western Ave., Ste. 410, Seattle, WA 98121-1028. 206-283-7844; Fax: 206-285-9410. (1)

Secret Garden, 204 N. Victory Blvd., Burbank, CA 91502. 818-846-8038. (5)

Secret Garden, 5309 Oakland Rd., Chevy Chase, MD 20815. 301-652-6918. (5)

Secret Garden, 7900 E. Greenlake Dr., Seattle, WA 98103. 206-522-8207. (5)

Seedling Series: Short Story International, International Cultural Exchange, 6 Sheffield Rd., Great Neck, NY 11021. 516-466-4166. (9)

Sendit, Box 5164, NDSU Computer Center, Fargo, ND 58105. 701-237-8109. (12)

Sesame Street Magazine, Children's Television Workshop, One Lincoln Plaza, New York, NY 10023. 212-595-3456, 800-678-0613. (9)

Seventeen, K-111 Magazines, 200 Madison Ave., New York, NY 10016. 212-447-4700, 800-628-7300; Fax: 215-688-3285. (9)

Shenanigans, 2146 Barracks Rd., Charlottesville, VA 22903. 804-295-4797. (5)

The Shoe String Press, Inc., 925 Sherman Ave., Hamden, CT 06514. 203-248-6307; Fax: 203-230-9275. (1)

Shofar, 43 Northcote Dr., Melville, NY 11747. 516-643-4598. (9)

Shorewood Fine Art Reproductions, 27 Glen Rd., Sandy Hook, CT 06482. 203-426-8100; Fax: 203-426-0867. (3)

Show-Book Week, Chicago Sun-Times, 401 N. Wabash Ave., Chicago, IL 60611. 312-321-3000. (11)

Sierra Club Books For Children, 100 Bush St., San Francisco, CA 94101. 415-291-1619; Fax: 415-291-1602. (1)

Simon & Schuster Books For Young Readers, Simon & Schuster, Inc., 866 Third Ave., New York, NY 10022. 212-702-2000, 800-223-2336. (1)

Simulation Training Systems, Box 910, Delmar, CA 92014. 619-755-0272; Fax: 619-792-9743. (3)

Sing Out!, Sing Out Corporation, Box 5253, Bethlehem, PA 18015-5253. 212-865-5366; Fax: 215-865-5129. (9)

Evelyn Singer Literary Agency, Box 594, White Plains, NY 10602. 914-949-1147; 914-631-5160. (8)

Singer Media Corp., Seaview Business Park, 1030 Calle Cordillera, Unit 106, San Clemente, CA 92673. 714-498-7227; Fax: 714-498-2162. (8)

Sino Broadcasting, 137 Waverly Pl., San Francisco, CA 94108. 415-433-3340. (13)

Sino-American Amity Fund (SAAF), 86 Riverside Dr., New York, NY 10024. 212-787-6969. (13)

Sister Vision Press, Box 217, Station E, Toronto, Ontario, M6H 4E2 Canada. 416-532-2184. (1)

Sisters' Choice Press, 1450 Sixth St., Berkeley, CA 94710. 510-524-5804. (3)

16 Magazine, Sterling-MacFadden Partnership, 233 Park Ave. S., New York, NY 10003-1606. 212-979-4800. (9)

Smithmark Publishers Inc., 16 E. 32nd St., New York, NY 10016. 212-532-6600, 800-645-9990; Fax: 212-683-5768. (1)

S.N.A.P. Production Services, 18653 Ventura, Tarzana, CA 91356. 818-343-0283. (3)

Social Education, National Council for the Social Studies, 3501 Newark St., NW, Washington, DC 20016. 202-966-7840. (10)

Social Studies School Service, 10200 Jefferson Blvd., Culver City, CA 90232-0802. 310-839-2436, 800-421-4246; Fax: 310-839-2249. (3)

Society for French American Cultural Services and Educational Aid, 972 Fifth Ave., New York, NY 10021. 212-439-1439, 800-937-3624. (13)

Society for German-American Studies, c/o Dr. Don Heinrich Tolzmann, Central Library, M.L. 33, Univ. of Cincinnati, Cincinnati, OH 45221. 513-556-1859. (13)

Society For Visual Education, 1345 Diversey Pkwy., Chicago, IL 60614. 312-525-1500. (3)

Society Of Children's Book Writers and Illustrators, 22736 Vanowen St., West Hills, CA 91306. (15)

Sons of Norway, 1455 West Lake St., Minneapolis, MN 55408. 612-827-3611. (13)

South Carolina Library Association, c/o Mary L. Smalls, 7313 State University, Orangeburg, SC 29117. 803-536-8825; Fax: 803-536-8902. (16)

South Carolina State Department of Education, 801 Rutledge Bldg., 1429 Senate St., Columbia, SC 29201. (17)

South Dakota Association For Communciations And Technology, c/o Mary Schwartz, Redfield School District, Box 560, Redfield, SD 57469-0560. 605-472-0560; Fax: 605-472-2316. (16)

South Dakota Library Association, c/o Elvita Landau, Brookings Public Library, 515 3rd St., Brookings, SD 57006. (16)

South Dakota State Library, 800 Governors Dr., Pierre, SD 57501-2294. 605-773-3131; Fax: 605-773-4950. (17)

South Florida Science Museum, 4801 Dreher Trail N., West Palm Beach, FL 33405. 407-832-1988; Fax: 407-833-0551. (14)

Southeastern Regional Vision for Education (SERVE), 41 Marietta St., NW, Ste. 1000, Atlanta, GA 30303. 800-659-3204. (12)

Southern Association of Colleges and Schools, 1866 Southern Lane, Decatur, GA 30033. 404-789-4500; Fax: 404-329-6598. (15)

Southern Association on Children under Six, Box 6130, Little Rock, AR 72215-6130. 501-663-0353. (15)

SpecialNet, GTE Education Services, GTE Place, W. Airfield Dr., Box 619810, Dallas/Fort Worth Airport, TX 75261-9810. 800-927-3000. (12)

Spoken Arts Inc., 801 94th Ave. N., St. Petersburg, FL 33702. 813-578-7600; Fax: 813-578-3101. (3)

Spoken Language Services, Box 783, Ithaca, NY 14851-0783. 607-257-0500. (1)

SRA School Division, Macmillan/ McGraw-Hill School Publishing Co., 250 Old Wilson Bridge Rd., Ste. 310, Worthington, OH 43095. 614-438-6600. (3)

St. David's Society of the State of New York (SDS), 71 W. 23rd St., New York, NY 10010. 212-924-8415, 212-924-3945. (13)

St. Paul Books & Media, Div. of Daughters of St. Paul, 50 St. Paul's Ave., Boston, MA 02130. 617-522-8911. 800-876-4463; Fax: 617-541-9805. (1, 3)

Standard Educational Corporation, 200 W. Madison St., #300, Chicago, IL 60606. 312-346-7440; Fax: 312-580-7215. (1)

Standard Publishing Company, 8121 Hamilton Ave., Cincinnati, OH 45231. 513-931-4050, 800-543-1301; Fax: 513-931-0904. (1)

Stanton Films, 2417 Artesia Blvd., Redondo Beach, CA 90278. 310-542-6573. (3)

State of Alaska Department of Education, Div. of State Libraries, 344 W. 3rd Ave., Ste. 125, Anchorage, AK 99501. 907-269-6568. (17)

State of Hawaii, Department of Education, 2530 10th Ave., Rm. A-20, Honolulu, HI 96816. (17)

State University of New York at Buffalo, Media Library, 24 Capen Hall, Buffalo, NY 14260-1651. 716-645-2802. (3)

Staten Island Children's Museum, 1000 Richmond Terrace, Staten Island, NY 10301. 718-273-2060; Fax: 718-273-2836. (14)

Steck-Vaughn Company, Box 26015, Austin, TX 78755. 512-795-3222, 800-531-5015; Fax: 512-795-3229. (1)

Stemmer House Publishers, 2627 Caves Rd., Owings Mills, MD 21117. 410-363-3690; Fax: 410-363-8459. (1, 3)

Sterling Publishing Co., 387 Park Ave. S., New York, NY 10016-8810. 212-532-7160, 800-367-9692; Fax: 212-213-2495. (1)

Stewart, Tabori & Chang, Subs. of Brant Publications Inc., 575 Broadway, New York, NY 10012. 212-941-2929, 800-722-7202; Fax: 212-941-2982. (1)

Stickers & Stuff Magazine, Ira Friedman Inc., Ten Columbus Circle, Ste. 1300, New York, NY 10019. 212-541-7300. (9)

Stillpoint Publishing, Div. of Stillpoint International, Inc., Box 640, Walpole, NH 03608. 603-756-9281, 800-847-4014. (3)

Stone Soup, The Magazine by Children, Children's Art Foundation, Box 83, Santa Cruz, CA 95063. 408-426-5557; Fax: 408-426-1161. (9)

Stories'n Stuff, 1345 Creston Park, Janesville, WI 53545. 608-752-7202. (5)

Story Friends, Mennonite Publishing House, 616 Walnut Ave., Scottdale, PA 15683. 412-887-8500; Fax: 412-887-3111. (9)

Story House Corporation, Bindery Lane, Charlotteville, NY 12036. 607-397-8725. (4)

Story Shop, 10900 Menaul Blvd., Albuquerque, NM 87112. 505-291-0711. (5)

Storybook Palace, 9538 Old Keene Mill, Burke, VA 22015. 703-644-2300. (5)

Storybook Station, 7101 N.E. Expwy., Oklahoma City, OK 73132. 405-720-2665. (5)

Storybooks, 1356 S. Gilbert #13, Mesa, AZ 85204. 602-926-7323. (5)

Straight Talk for Young Teens, Standard Publishing Company, 8121 Hamilton Ave., Cincinnati, OH 45231. 513-931-4050. (9)

Student Series: Short Story International, International Cultural Exchange, 6 Sheffield Rd., Great Neck, NY 11021. 516-466-4166. (9)

Gunther Stuhlmann Author's Representative, Box 276, Becket, MA 01223. 412-623-5170. (8)

Success Publishing, Div. of Success Group, 812 Bayonne Dr., Box 30965, Palm Beach Gardens, FL 33420. 407-626-4643, 800-330-4643; Fax: 407-775-1693. (1)

Sullivan Associates, Imprint of Good Morning Teacher! Publishing Co., 819 Mitten Rd., #37, Burlingame, CA 94010. 415-697-6657. (1)

Sulphur Creek Nature Center, 1801 D. St., Hayward, CA 94541. 510-881-6747. (14)

Summy-Birchard Inc., Div. of Warner/ Chappell Inc., 265 Secaucus Rd., Secaucus, NJ 07096-2037. 201-348-0700; Fax: 201-348-1782. (1)

The Sun Group, 1133 Broadway, New York, NY 10010. 212-255-2718. (3)

Sundance Publishers & Distributors Inc., Newtown Rd, Littleton, MA 01460. 508-486-9201. (4)

Sunnybooks for Kids, 4233 South Buckley Rd., Aurora, CO 80013. 303-690-9590. (5)

Sunrise Museum/Sunrise Science Hall, 746 Myrtle Rd., Charleston, WV 25314. 304-344-8035. (14)

Sunstone Press, 239 Johnson St., Box 2321, Sante Fe, NM 87504-2321. 505-988-4418; Fax: 505-988-1025. (1)

Surprises, (formerly Surprises, Activities for Kids & Parents), Homestyles Publishing & Marketing Co., 275 Market St., Ste. 521, Minneapolis, MN 55405-5570. 612-937-0909. (9)

Swank Motion Pictures, 201 S. Jefferson, St. Louis, MO 63166. 314-534-6300. (3)

Swedish Council of America, 2600 Park Ave., Minneapolis, MN 55407. 612-871-0593. (13)

Swimming World & Junior Swimmer, Sports Publications, Inc., Box 45497, Los Angeles, CA 90045. 213-674-2120; Fax: 213-674-0238. (9)

Syracuse University Press, 1600 Jamesville Ave., Syracuse, NY 13244-5160. 315-423-2596, 800-365-8929; Fax: 315-443-5536. (1)

Tallahassee Museum of History and Natural Science, 3945 Museum Dr., Tallahassee, FL 32304. 904-575-8684. (14)

Taplinger Publishing Company, Box 1324, New York, NY 10185. 201-432-3257. (1)

Tapori, New Inc. / Fourth World Movement, 7600 Willow Hill Dr., Landover, MD 20785-4658. 301-336-9489; Fax: 301-336-0092. (9)

Chip Taylor Communications, 15 Spollett Dr., Derry, NH 03038. 603-434-9262; Fax: 603-434-9262. (3)

Teachers & Writers Collaborative, 5 Union Sq. W., New York, NY 10003-3306. 212-691-6590; Fax: 212-675-0171. (1, 15)

Teachers College Press, Teachers College, Columbia University, 1234 Amsterdam Ave., New York, NY 10027. 212-678-3929; Fax: 212-678-4149. (1)

Teaching & Computers, Scholastic, Inc., 730 Broadway, New York, NY 10003-9538. 212-505-3000. (10)

Teaching Exceptional Children, Council for Exceptional Children, 1920 Association Dr, Reston, VA 22091. 703-620-3660; Fax: 703-264-9494. (10)

Teaching K-8, Early Years, Inc., 40 Richards Ave, Norwalk, CT 06854-2309. 203-855-2650; Fax: 203-855-2656. (10)

Teague's Books for Children, 1801 Hilltop Lane, Arlington, TX 76013. 817-275-4213. (5)

Technical Education Research Centers (TERC), 2067 Massachusetts Ave., Cambridge, MA 02140. 617-547-0430. (12)

Technology & Learning, Peter Li, Inc., 330 Progress Road, Dayton, OH 45449. 415-457-4333. (10)

Technology Education for Children Council (TECC), 1914 Association Dr., Reston, VA 22091-1502. 703-860-2100. (15)

Technology Student Association, (formerly American Industrial Arts Student Association), 1914 Association Dr., Reston, VA 22091. 703-860-9000. (15)

Techtrends, Association for Educational Communications & Technology, 1025 Vermont Ave., NW, Ste. 820, Washington DC 20005-3516. 202-347-7834; Fax: 202-347-7839. (10)

Teens Today, Nazarene Publishing House, Word Action, 6401 The Paseo, Kansas City, MO 64131. 816-333-7000. (9)

Television Associates, Inc., 2410 Charleston Rd., Mt. View, CA 94043. 415-967-6040. (3)

Ten Eyck Books, Box 84, Southboro, MA 01772. 508-481-3517. (6)

Ten Speed Press, Box 7123, Berkeley, CA 94707. 510-559-1632, 800-841-BOOK; Fax: 510-559-1637. (1)

Tennessee Department of Education, 7th Fl., Gateway Plaza, 710 James Robertson Pkwy., Nashville, TN 37243-0381. 615-532-1242, 800-538-1497; Fax: 615-741-6236. (17)

Tennessee Library Association, c/o Carolyn Daniel, McGavock High School Library, 3150 McGavock Pike, Nashville, TN 37214. 615-885-8881. (16)

Texas Association For Educational Technology, c/o Doug Rogers, Center for Educational Technology, Baylor University College of Education, Box 97314, Waco, TX 76798-7314. 817-755-3111; Fax: 817-755-3265. (16)

Texas Education Network (TENET), Texas Education Agency, 1701 N. Congress Ave., Austin, TX 78701. 512-463-9091. (12, 17)

Texas Historian, Texas State Historical Assn., Sid Richardson Hall/2-306, University Station, Austin, TX 78712. 512-471-1525. (9)

Texas Library Association, c/o Ruth Dahlstrom, Goliad Independent School Dist., Box 830, Goliad, TX 77963. 512-645-3257. (16)

Thames Book Company, Inc., 34 Truman St., New London, CT 06320. 203-444-2400. (4)

T.H.E. Journal (Technological Horizons In Education), 150 El Camino Real, Tustin, CA 92680-3670. 714-730-4011; Fax: 714-730-3739. (10)

Theytus Books, Ltd., Box 20040, Penticton, B.C., Canada V2A 8K3. 604-493-7181. (1)

Third World Press, Box 730, Chicago, IL 60619. 312-651-0700; Fax: 312-651-7286. (1)

Charles C. Thomas, 2600 First St., Springfield, IL 62794-9265. 217-789-8980, 800-258-8980; Fax: 217-789-9130. (1)

Thomasson-Grant Publishers, One Morton Dr., 5th Fl., Charlottesville, VA 22903-6806. 804-977-1780, 800-999-1780; Fax: 804-977-1696. (1)

Thomson Learning, 115 Fifth Ave., New York, NY 10003. 212-979-2210, 800-880-4253; Fax: 212-979-2819. (1)

Thor Publishing Company, Box 1782, Ventura, CA 93002. 805-648-4560; Fax: 805-653-6359. (1)

Thorn Books And Bindery, 624 Moorpark Ave., Box 1244, Moorpark, CA 93020. 805-529-7610. (6)

Thorndike Press, Box 159, Thorndike, ME 04986. 207-948-2962, 800-223-6121; Fax: 207-948-2863. (1)

Thornton W. Burgess Museum, 4 Water St., Sandwich, MA 02563. 508-888-4668. (14)

3-2-1 Contact, Children's Television Workshop, One Lincoln Plaza, New York, NY 10023. 212-595-3456. (9)

Through A Child's Eyes, 10519 Chaney, Downey, CA 90241. 310-862-0415. (5)

Ticknor & Fields, Subs. of Houghton Mifflin, 215 Park Ave. S., New York, NY 10003. 212-420-5800; Fax: 212-420-5850. (1)

Tiger Tales, 420 5th Ave. S., Edmonds, WA 98020. 206-775-7405. (5)

Timed Exposures, 79 Raymond Ave., Poughkeepsie, NY 12601. 914-485-8489. (3)

Tiny Tales Children's Book Store, 2048 Newbridge Rd., Bellmore, NY 11710. 516-783-9539. (5)

Titles, Inc., 1931 Sheridan Rd., Highland Park, IL 60035. 708-432-3690; Fax: 708-945-4644. (6)

Toad Hall, 1206 W. 38th St., Austin, TX 78705. 512-323-2665. (5)

Toad Hall Bookstore, 51 Main St., Rockport, MA 01966. 508-546-7323. (5)

Tor Books, Subs. of Tom Doherty Associates; Affil. of St. Martin's Press, 175 Fifth Ave., 14th Fl., New York, NY 10010. 212-388-0100, 800-221-7945; Fax: 212-388-0191. (1)

Touch, Calvinettes, Box 7244, Grand Rapids, MI 49510-7244. 616-241-5616. (9)

Toy Manufacturers of America, Inc., 200 Fifth Ave., Ste. 740, New York, NY 10010. 212-675-1141. (15)

Toy School, 5517 Chamblee, Dunwoody, GA 30338. 404-393-272. (5)

Toy Train Museum, 300 Paradise Lane, Strasburg, PA 17579. 717-687-8976. (14)

TQ (Teen Quest), The Good News Broadcasting Association, Box 82808, Lincoln, NE 68501. 402-474-4567. (9)

Trafalgar Square Publishing, Box 257, North Pomfret, VT 05053. 802-457-1911; Fax: 802-457-1913. (1)

Transatlantic Arts, Inc., Box 6086, Albuquerque, NM 87197. 505-898-2289. (1)

Treasures from the Castle, 1720 N. Livernois, Rochester, MI 48306. 313-651-7317. (6)

Tree House Children's Books, 2804 W. Division St., St. Cloud, MN 56301. 612-255-1776. (5)

Treehaus Communications, Inc, 906 W. Loveland Ave., Loveland, OH 45140. 513-683-5716. (3)

Tribune Books, Chicago Tribune, 435 N. Michigan Ave., Chicago, IL 60611. 312-222-3232. (11)

Trillium Press, Box 209, Monroe, NY 10950. 914-726-4444; Fax: 914-726-3824. (1, 3)

Troll Associates, 100 Corporate Dr., Mahwah, NJ 07430. 201-529-4000, 800-526-5289; Fax: 201-529-9347. (1)

Troll Book Club, 2 Lethbridge Plaza, Mahwah. NJ 07430. 800-541-1097, Fax: 201-529-8382. (7)

Trumpet Club, Sub. of Bantam, Doubleday, Dell Publishing Co, Inc., Box 604, Holmes, PA 19043. 800-826-0110. (7)

Tucson Children's Museum, 200 S. 6th Ave., Tucson, AZ 85702. 602-792-9985; Fax: 602-792-0639. (14)

Tundra Books, Box 1030, Plattsburgh, NY 12901. 514-932-5434; Fax: 514-484-2152. (1)

Turner Multimedia, 10 N. Main St., Yardley, PA 19067-1422. 800-742-1096; Fax: 215-493-5320. (3)

Turtle, Children's Better Health Institute, 1100 Waterway Blvd., Box 567, Indianapolis, IN 46206. 317-636-8881; Fax: 317-684-8094. (9)

Charles E. Tuttle Company, 28 Main St., Rutland, VT 05701. 802-773-8930, 802-773-8229, 800-525-2778; Fax: 802-773-6993. (1)

Mark Twain Boyhood Home & Museum, 208 Hill St., Hannibal, MO 63401. 314-221-9010. (14)

Twayne Publishers, 866 Third Ave., New York, NY 10022. 212-702-2000; Fax: 212-605-9375. (1)

Twenty-First Century Books, Div. of Henry Holt, Inc., 115 W. 18th St., New York, NY 10011. 212-886-9200, 800-488-5233; Fax: 212-633-0748. (1)

Tyndale House Publishers, 336 Gundersen Dr., Wheaton, IL 60187. 708-668-8300, 800-323-9400; Fax: 708-668-9092. (1)

UAHC Press, Div. of Union of American Hebrew Congregations, 838 Fifth Ave., New York, NY 10021-7046. 212-249-0100; Fax: 212-734-2857. (1, 3)

U.S. Committee For United Nations Children's Fund, 333 E. 38th St., New York, NY 10036. 212-686-5522. (15)

U.S. Government Printing Office, Superintendent of Documents, Washington, DC 20402. 202-783-3238. (1)

U.S. Section of International Board on Books for Young People, Box 8139, 800 Barksdale Rd., Newark, DE 19714. (15)

Uncle Remus Museum, 214 Oak St., Eatonton, GA 31024. 706-485-6856. (14)

United Learning, 6633 W. Howard St., Niles, IL 60714. 312-647-0600, 800-424-0362. (3)

United Methodist Communications, 810 12th Ave., S., Nashville, TN 37203. 615-742-5400. (3)

United States Committee for UNICEF, 333 E. 38th St., New York, NY 10016. 212-686-5522. (1)

United Synagogue of Conservative Judaism, Commission on Jewish Education, 155 Fifth Ave., New York, NY 10010-6802. (15)

University Book Service, 2219 Westbrooke Dr, Columbus, OH 43228-9605. 800-634-4272. (4)

University of California, Extension Media Center, 2176 Shattuck Ave., Berkeley, CA 94704. 510-642-0460. (3)

University of Minnesota, University Film & Video, 1313 Fifth St., SE, Suite 108, Minneapolis, MN 55414. 612-627-4270. (3)

University Of Oklahoma Press, 1005 Asp, Norman, OK 73019-0445. 405-325-5111, 800-627-7377; Fax: 405-325-4000. (1)

University of South Florida Film/Video Distribution, Div. of Learning Technologies, 4202 Fowler Ave., Tampa, FL 33620. 813-974-2874. (3)

The University of Texas Institute of Texan Cultures at San Antonio, Box 1226, San Antonio, TX 78294-1226. 210-558-2300, 800-776-7651 (orders). (3)

University of Texas Press, Box 7819, Austin, TX 78713-7819. 512-471-7233; Fax: 512-320-0668. (1)

University of Washington Press, Box 50096, Seattle, WA 98145. 206-543-4050. (3)

Urasenke Tea Ceremony Society (UCTS), 153 E. 69th St., New York, NY 10021. 212-988-6161. (13)

US Committee For UNICEF, 331 E. 38 St., New York, NY 10017. 212-686-5522. (3)

U*S* Kids, Children's Better Health Institute, 1100 Waterway Blvd., Box 567, Indianapolis, IN 46206. 317-636-8881, Fax: 317-684-8094. (9)

Utah Educational Library Media Association, c/o David Walton, Instructional Technology, Alpine School District, 50 North Center, American Fork, UT 84003. 801-756-8400; Fax: 801-756-8404. (16)

Utah Library Association, c/o Pete J. Giacoma, 365 Emery, Salt Lake City, UT 84104. 801-451-2322. (16)

Utah State Office of Education, Curriculum Division 250 E. 500 South St., Salt Lake City, UT 84111. 801-538-7774. (17)

Utah State University Press, Logan, UT 84322-7800. 801-750-1362; Fax: 801-750-1541. (1)

Valiant International Multi-Media Corp, 195 Bonhomme St., Hackensack, NJ 07602. 201-487-6340, 800-631-0867; Fax: 201-487-1930. (3)

Van Nostrand Reinhold Company, 115 Fifth Ave., New York, NY 10003. 212-254-3232; Fax: 212-254-9499. (1)

Vedanta Press, Vedanta Society of Southern California, 1946 Vedanta Pl., Hollywood, CA 90068. 213-465-7114; Fax: 213-465-9568. (1)

Vedo Films, 85 Longview Rd., Port Washington, NY 11050. 516-883-2825; Fax: 516-883-7460. (3)

Vermont Department of Education, 120 State St., Montpelier, VT 05620. 802-828-3111. (17)

Vermont Educational Media Association, c/o Karen Hennig, Craftsbury Academy, R.R. 1, Box 94, Craftsbury Common, VT 05827. 802-586-7706. (16)

Vermont Library Association, c/o Nancy Wilson, Lawrence Public Library, 40 North St., Briston, VT 05443. 802-453-2366. (16)

Victorian Doll Museum, 4332 Buffalo Rd., North Chili, NY 14514. 716-247-0130. (14)

Video Aided Instruction, Inc., 182 Village Rd., Roslyn Heights, NY 11577. 516-621-6176. (3)

Video Knowledge, Inc., 29 Bramble Lane, Melville, NY 11747. 516-367-4250; Fax: 516-367-1006. (3)

Vietnamese American Social and Cultural Council and the Vietnamese American Good Neighborhood Committee, 1115 E. Santa Clara St., San Jose, CA 95116. 408-971-8281. (13)

Viking Children's Books, Div. of Penguin USA, 375 Hudson St., New York, NY 10014. 212-366-10014. (1)

Vineyard Video Productions, Box 370, West Tisbury, MA 02575. 508-693-3584. (3)

Virginia Department of Education, Box 2120, Richmond, VA 23216-2120. 804-225-2539; Fax: 804-736-1703. (17)

Virginia Discovery Museum, Box 1128, Charlottesville, VA 22902. 804-977-1025. (14)

Virginia Educational Media Association, c/o Vickie Pearce, Norfolk Public Schools, (H) 1077 Lord Dunmore Dr., Virginia Beach, VA 23464. 804-441-1916; 804-441-2430. (16)

Virginia Library Association, c/o Linda Farynk, Ratford University, McConnell Library, Ratford, VA 24142. 703-831-5471. (16)

Virginia Living Museum, 524 J. Clyde Morris Blvd., Newport News, VA 23601. 804-595-1900. (14)

Virginia's Pen, Virginia Dept. of Education, 101 N. 14th St., 22nd, Richmond, VA 23219. Internet: HCATHERN@VDOE386.VAK12ED.EDU. (12)

Visual Communications, Southern California Asian American Studies Central, Inc., 263 S. Los Angeles St., Rm. 307, Los Angeles, CA 90012. 213-680-4462. (13)

Visual Education Association, 581 W. Leffel Lane, Box 1666, Springfield, OH 45501. 513-864-2891 (AK, HI), 800-543-5947 (U.S.), 800-243-7070 (OH). (3)

Volcano Press, Box 270, Volcano, CA 95689. 209-296-3445; Fax: 209-296-4515. (1)

VOYA (Voice Of Youth Advocates), Scarecrow Press, Box 4167, Metuchen, NJ 08840. 201-548-8600, 800-537-7107; Fax: 908-548-5767. (11)

VSE Publisher, 212 S. Dexter St., Denver, CO 80222-1055. 303-322-7450. (1)

Bill Wadsworth Productions, 1913 W. 37th St., Austin, TX 78731. 512-452-4243. (3)

J. Weston Walch, 321 Valley St., Portland, ME 04104. 207-772-2846, 800-341-6094. (1, 3)

Walker & Co., 435 Hudson St., New York, NY 10014. 212-727-8300, 800-AT-WALKER. (1)

Ward Hill Press, Box 04-0424, Staten Island, NY 10301-0424. 718-816-9449. (1)

Warner Books, Subs. of Time, Inc., 1271 Ave. of the Americas, New York, NY 10020. 212-522-7200; Fax: 212-522-7991. (1)

Warner Educational Productions, Box 8791, Fountain Valley, CA 92708. 714-968-3776, 800-394-2905. (3)

Washington Library Association, c/o Sharon Hammer, Fort Vancouver Regional Library, 1007 E. Mill Plain Blvd., Vancouver, WA 98603-3504. 206-695-1561.; Fax: 206-693-2681. (16)

Washington Library Media Association, c/o Susan Baker, Bremerton School District, (H) 304 White Pine Dr., Bremerton, WA 98310. 206-478-0753 Ext. 3232; Fax: 206-478-5061. (16)

Washington State Superintendent of Public Instruction, Old Capital Bldg., Olympia, WA 98504. 206-753-6723. (17)

Waterfront Books, 85 Crescent Rd., Burlington, VT 05401-3326. 802-658-7477, 800-639-6063. (1)

Watson-Guptill Publications, 1515 Broadway, New York, NY 10036. 212-764-7300, 800-451-1741; Fax: 212-536-5359. (1)

Weekly Bible Reader, Standard Publishing Company, 8121 Hamilton Ave., Cincinnati, OH 45231. 513-931-4050; Fax: 513-931-0904. (9)

Weekly Reader Children's Book Club, New Field Publications, Inc., 2 Corporate Dr., Shelton, CT 06484-0857, 203-944-2400. (7)

Weekly Reader, Weekly Reader Corporation, 245 Long Hill Rd., Middleton, CT 06457. 800-466-3355; Fax: 609-786-3360. (9)

Welsh Library, c/o The Welsh Guild, Arch Street Presbyterian Church, 1724 Arch St., Philadelphia, PA 19103. (13)

Wentworth & Leggett Rare Books, 905 W. Main St., Brightleaf Square, Durham, NC 27701. 919-688-5311, 919-941-1938. (6)

West Virginia Dept. of Education, Bldg. 6, Rm. 346, 1900 Kanawha Blvd., E., Charleston, WV 25305-0330. 304-558-7880; Fax: 304-558-2584. (17)

West Virginia Educational Media Association, c/o Lynne Curran, Doddridge County Middle School, (H) 408 1/2 Pennsylvania Ave., Nutter Fort, WV 26301. 304-873-2390; Fax: 304-873-2541. (16)

West Virginia Library Association, c/o Dr. Charles Julian, National Tech Transfer Center, Div. of Education & Training, Wheeling Jesuit College, 1108 W. Washington Ave., Wheeling, WV 26003. 304-243-2595. (16)

Western Instructional Television, 1438 N. Gower St., Los Angeles, CA 90028. 213-466-8601. (3)

Western Publishing Co., Inc., 850 Third Ave., 15th Fl., New York, NY 10022. 212-753-8500; Fax: 212-371-1091. (1)

Westminster Press/John Knox Press, 100 Witherspoon St., Louisville, KY 40202-1396. 502-569-5043, 800-523-1631; Fax: 502-569-5018. (1)

Weston Woods Studios, Weston, CT 06883. 203-226-3355. (3)

WFFN Proof Learning Games Associates, 1490-JJ South Blvd., Ann Arbor, MI 48104-4699. 313-665-2269. (3)

Whale of A Tale, 4187 Campus Dr., Irvine, CA 92715. 714-854-828. (5)

Barbara Wilk Productions, 29 Surf Rd., Westport, CT 06880. 203-226-7669. (3)

Whippersnappers, 207 S. 2nd St., Laramie, WY 82070. 307-721-8853. (5)

Whispering Coyote Press, 480 Newbury St., Ste. 104, Danvers, MA 01923. 508-281-4995; Fax: 508-777-6148. (1)

White Rabbit, 70 Main St., Pine Bush, NY 12566. 914-744-6414. (5)

White Rabbit, Children's Books, 7755 Girard Ave., La Jolla, CA 92037. 619-454-3518. (5)

Albert Whitman & Company, 6340 Oakton St., Morton Grove, IL 60053. 708-581-0033, 800-255-7675; Fax: 708-581-0039. (1)

George Whittell Memorial Press, 3722 South Ave., Youngstown, OH 44502. 216-788-1064. (1)

Whizkids Books and Toys, 1737 E. Prince, Tucson, AZ 85719. 602-795-3729. (5)

Wild About Books, 12110 Business Blvd., Eagle River, AR 99577. 907-694-7323. (5)

Wild Rumpus, 2720 W. 43 St., Minneapolis, MN 55410. 612-920-5005. (5)

Wildlife Conservation, New York Zoological Society, Zoological Park, Bronx, NY 10460. 718-220-5121; Fax: 718-584-2625. (9)

Laura Ingalls Wilder Home and Museum, Rte. 1, Box 24, Mansfield, MO 65704. 417-924-3626. (14)

John Wiley & Sons, 605 Third Ave., New York, NY 10158-0012. 212-850-6000, 800-CALL-WILEY; Fax: 212-850-6799. (1)

Wilson Library Bulletin, The H. W. Wilson Company, 950 University Ave., Bronx, NY 10452. 212-588-8400, 800-367-6770; Fax: 718-590-1617. (11)

Windswept House Publishers, Mount Desert, ME 04660-0159. 207-244-7149; Fax: 207-244-3369. (1)

Winston-Derek Publishers, 1722 West End Ave., Nashville, TN 37203. 615-321-0535, 800-826-1888; Fax: 615-329-4824. (1)

Wisconsin Children's Center/Madison Children's Museum, 100 State St., Madison, WI 53703. 608-256-6445; Fax: 608-256-3226. (14)

Wisconsin Department of Public Instruction, 125 S. Webster St., Box 7841, Madison, WI 53707. 608-266-1924. (17)

Wisconsin Educational Media Association, c/o Terri Iverson, CESA #3, 1835 Ridgeview Acres, Platteville, WI 53818. 608-822-3276; Fax: 608-263-2046. (16)

Wisconsin Foundation, 2564 Branch St., Middleton, WI 53562. 608-831-6313; Fax: 608-831-2960. (3)

Wisconsin Library Association, c/o Venora McKinney,, Milwaukee Public Library, 814 W. Wisconsin Ave., Milwaukee, WI 53233-2385. 414-286-3025. (16)

With, Faith & Life Press, Box 347, Newton, KS 67114. 316-283-5100. (9)

Wolf's Head Books, 48 San Marco Avenue, Box 3705, St. Augustine, FL 32085-3705. 904-824-9357. (6)

Women Make Movies, 462 Broadway, Ste. 500, New York, NY 10012. 212-925-0606; Fax: 212-925-2052. (3)

Women's Action Alliance, Sex Equity In Education Program, 370 Lexington Ave., New York, NY 10017. 212-532-8230. (1)

Women's National Book Association, 160 Fifth Ave., Rm. 604, New York, NY 10010, 212-675-7805. (15)

Wonder Time, Nazarene Publishing House, Word Action, 6401 The Paseo, Kansas City, MO 64131. 816-333-7000. (9)

Wonder Works, A Children's Museum, 419 E. Second, The Dalles, OR 97058. 503-296-2444. (14)

Wonderscope Children's Museum, 16000 W. 65th St., Shawnee Mission, KS 66217. 913-268-8130; Fax: 913-268-4608. (14)

Word Inc., Div. of Thomas Nelson Publishing, 5221 N. O'Connor Blvd., Ste. 1000, Irving, TX 75039. 214-556-1900, 800-933-9673; Fax: 214-401-2344. (1)

Wordware Publishing, Inc., 1506 Capital Ave., Plano, TX 75074. 214-423-0090, 800-229-4949; Fax: 214-881-9147. (1)

Workman Publishing, 708 Broadway, New York, NY 10003. 212-254-5900, 800-722-7202; Fax: 212-254-8098. (1)

World Around Songs, 5790 Hwy. 80 S., Burnsville, NC 28714. 704-675-5343. (13)

World Around Songs, Inc., 20 Colberts Creek Rd., Burnsville, NC 28714, 704-675-5343. (15)

World Book, Inc., Subs. of The Scott Fetzer Co., 525 W. Monroe, Chicago, IL 60661. 312-258-3700, 800-621-8202; Fax: 312-258-3950. (1)

World Education Fellowship, U.S. Section, c/o Dr. Mildred Haipt, College of New Rochelle, 29 Castle Pl., New Rochelle, NY 10805. 914-654-5578. (15)

World News Map of the Week, Weekly Reader Corporation, 3001 Cindel Drive, Delran, NJ 08370. 800-446-3355; Fax: 609-786-3360. (9)

Writer's Digest Books, Div. of F & W Publications, 1507 Dana Ave., Cincinnati, OH 45207. 513-531-2222, 800-289-0963; Fax: 513-531-4744. (1)

Writers & Readers Publishing Inc., Box 461, Village Sta., New York, NY 10014. 212-982-3158; Fax: 212-777-4924. (1)

Writers House, 21 W. 26th St., New York, NY 10010. 212-685-2400. (8)

Writing!, Weekly Reader Corporation, 3001 Cindel Dr., Delran, NJ 08370. 800-446-3355; Fax: 609-786-3360. (9)

Wyoming Children's Museum & Nature Center, 710 Garfield St., Laramie, WY 82070. 307-745-6332. (14)

Wyoming Department of Education, Hathaway Bldg., Cheyenne, WY 82002. 307-777-5883. (17)

Wyoming Educational Media Association, c/o Douglas Hinkle, Wheatland High School, 13th & Oak Sts., Wheatland, WY 82201. 307-322-2075; Fax: 307-322-2084. (16)

Wyoming Library Association, c/o Kathy Carlson, Wyoming State Law Library; Supreme Court Bldg., Cheyenne, WY 82002. 307-777-7509. (16)

X-S Books, Inc., 95 Mayhill St., Saddlebrook, NJ 07662. 201-712-9266. (4)

Yaba Framework, (formerly YABA World), Young American Bowling Alliance, 5301 S. 76th St., Greendale, WI 53129. 414-421-4700; Fax: 414-421-5301. (9)

Yankee Book Peddler Inc., 999 Maple St., Contoocook, NH 03229-3374. 603-746-3102, 800-258-3774; Fax: 603-746-5628. (4)

Yellow Ball Workshop, 62 Tarbell Ave., Lexington, MA 02173. 617-862-4283. (3)

Young Adult Library Services Association, Div. of the American Library Association, 50 E. Huron St., Chicago, IL 60611. 312-280-4390. (15)

Young Ages, Box 867656, Plano, TX 75086. 214-867-7021. (5)

Young at Art Children's Museum, A Unique Children's Museum, 801 S. University Dr., Plantation, FL 33324. 305-424-0085. (14)

Young Audiences, 115 E. 92nd St., New York, NY 10128. 212-831-8110. (15)

Young Discovery, 217 Main St., Ossining, NY 10562. 914-945-0600. (5)

Young Men's Christian Association, 101 N. Wacker Dr., Chicago, IL 60606. 312-977-0031. (15)

Young Readers, 21611 Center Ridge, Rocky River, OH 44116. 216-333-7828. (5)

Young Rider, Hunters Hill Press, Box 725, Williamsburg, VA 23187-0725. 804-229-6294. (9)

Your Heritage House, 110 E. Ferry Ave., Detroit, MI 48202. 313-871-1667. (14)

Youth Museum of Southern West Virginia, Box 1815, Beckley, WV 25802-1815. 304-252-3730. (14)

Youth Science Institute, Alum Rock Discovery Center, 16260 Alum Rock Ave., San Jose, CA 95127. 408-258-4322. (14)

Youth Science Institute, Sanborn Discovery Center, 16055 Sanborn Rd., Sanborn-Skyline Park, Saratoga, CA 95070. 408-867-6940. (14)

Rose Zell Books, 136 Ilehamwood, DeKalb, IL 60115. 815-756-2801. (5)

O to 5 Books, 615 76th St., Brooklyn, NY 11209. 718-748-5770. (5)

Zillions, (formerly Penny Power), Consumers Union, 101 Truman Ave., Yonkers, NY 10763-1057. 914-378-2000. (9)

Zink Entertainment, 245 W. 19th St., New York, NY 10011. 212-929-2949. (3)

Zipporah Films, One Richdale Ave., Unit #4, Cambridge, MA 02140. 617-576-3603. (3)

Zondervan Publishing House, Subs. of HarperCollins Publishers, 5300 Patterson Ave., SE, Grand Rapids, MI 49530. 616-698-6900, 800-727-3480; Fax: 616-698-3439. (1)